Gerhard H. Wächter
The Capitalist Economy and its Prosthetics

Edition transcript | Volume 13

Gerhard H. Wächter, born in 1955, is a business lawyer in Berlin, specializing in M&A and M&A-Litigation, and a law professor at Leipzig University. He did his doctorate on the theory and history of criminal law with Klaus Lüderssen at Frankfurt's Goethe University, and studied with Niklas Luhmann at Bielefeld University and Stanley Diamond at the New School for Social Research in New York, before he worked with an international law firm, the German Treuhandanstalt and ultimately founded his own law firm in 1992.

Gerhard H. Wächter

The Capitalist Economy and its Prosthetics

Necessity, Evolution and Dilemmas of a Brotherhood

[transcript]

Bibliographic information published by the Deutsche Nationalbibliothek

The Deutsche Nationalbibliothek lists this publication in the Deutsche Nationalbib-liografie; detailed bibliographic data are available in the Internet at https://dnb.dnb.de/

First published in 2024 by transcript Verlag, Bielefeld
© Gerhard H. Wächter

Cover layout: Kordula Röckenhaus, Bielefeld
Editor: Sean O'Dubhghaill
Printed by: Majuskel Medienproduktion GmbH, Wetzlar
https://doi.org/10.14361/9783839472781
Print-ISBN: 978-3-8376-7278-7
PDF-ISBN: 978-3-8394-7278-1
EPUB-ISBN: 978-3-7328-7278-7
ISSN of series: 2626-580X
eISSN of series: 2702-9077

In memory of Gertrud Wächter and Hermann Wächter

Contents

Part III:
The deficiency of employment-generating spending in modern capitalism

Part IV: The prosthetics of modern capitalism and their dilemmas

Appendix

"Ehemals sah man mit ehrlicher Vornehmheit auf die Menschen herab, die mit Geld Handel treiben, wenn man sie auch nötig hatte; man gestand sich ein, daß jede Gesellschaft ihre Eingeweide haben müsse. Jetzt sind sie die herrschende Macht in der Seele der modernen Menschheit, als der begehrlichste Teil derselben" (*Friedrich Nietzsche*, Richard Wagner in Bayreuth, Abschnitt 6, 1876)

***

"In the "entrepreneur economy" with, "on the one hand, of a number of firms or entrepreneurs possessing a capital equipment and a command over resources in the shape of money, and, on the other hand, a number of workers seeking to be employed.... the starting up of productive processes largely depends on a class of entrepreneurs who hire the factors of production for money and look for their recoupment from selling the output for money... A process of production will not be started up, unless the money proceeds expected from the sale of the output are at least equal to de money costs which could be avoided by not starting up to process... The firm... has no object in the world except to end up with more money than it has started with. That is the essential characteristics of an entrepreneurial economy." (*John Maynard Keynes*, Collected Writings XXIX, page 63, 77, 78, 89 et seq.).

***

The first economic experience of the author came when he was nine years old. The son of his grandparents' landlord, Armin, who lived one floor above, had a new gadget; namely, an old electric slot machine. The machine was exceptional in as much as it was – perhaps it was a relic from a more philanthropic age – programmed *to let you win*. This made Armin, who was already a very nice person in his own right, even more well-liked amongst his peer boys. The building's other kids, the author included, would visit him, more than they had ever visited him before, and never forget to bring some coins. He allowed them to play with his machine, and they would happily return with the pockets full of "Groschen". Armin's father, Herr Jung, initially appeared to be glad about his son's increased popularity and silently refilled the machine for some time. Of course, the day came when the fun was over. If the winners take their winnings home, somebody must refill the ante...

Foreword

A deep-level and long-term understanding of capitalist society

The author decided to undertake the effort, which he now hands over to the public, in the aftermath of the world financial crisis – to understand what had happened then. He had seen himself as a Marxist in his youth, from around 1971 to 1981, but then found that systems theory (in particular of *Niklas Luhmann*) had higher explanatory potential. The writing of *Peter Drucker* also impressed him greatly. It took away some of his aesthetic aversion against money making and convinced him that business was a good place for creativity and thinking. Thus, the author, who was about to complete his legal education, made a turn and became a business lawyer, primarily in M&A, rather than, as originally intended, a criminal lawyer. As business lawyer, he was basically as neoliberal as most of his colleagues, if probably with somewhat more ongoing theoretical reading; of course, there was little time for that aside the daily work. He saw the EU as an instrument of peace, in particular to lastingly settle the scores between France and Germany, which pleased the author who was born just a few kilometers from the French border in the Saar region especially. He lived with this view throughout most of his professional life: Capitalism, in this period, appeared to him as certainly aggravating prior inequalities but without deeper flaw. Ultimately, the financial crisis of 2008 shook him up: If the substance of capitalism was competition in markets that moved from irritations to new equilibriums, how could such an unhealthy long-term ossification that unloaded in the crisis at all have been built up? The author was very impressed with the reaction of politics to the crisis, too. The nineties had been times of an apparent historic triumph of liberal and neoliberal thinking in economics. Why did politics then not stick to liberal "Laisser-Faire" and let the markets do the job after the crisis and clear things up but quickly – after a moment of "Laisser Faire" only, (when they allowed Lehmann Brothers to go down its natural paths) – declared state emergencies all over and began to apply extreme anti-liberal anti-market-policies on a world-wide scale? Politics – no other explanation was possible – had much less trust in self-regulation of capitalism than the author at the time. Did they know or fear something the author did not see?

When the author began to collect questions and ideas for this book and made his first sketches in 2011, he nevertheless still believed that the project would remain a purely economic endeavor, "macro-economic" rather than "political-economical". That only changed after he had finished the historical part on antiquity and conceived of what he would be calling "deficient producive spending" in Part III. By then he had learned to understand that prosthetics and, hence, politics, ought always to have an important place in capitalism; capitalism did have a flaw, which was *deficient employment-generating spending*. It was incomplete and it needed prosthetics as a form of politics to deal with this flaw. But that was not the end. Around 2019, when the author had also worked his way through the echelon of methods of funding prosthetics, in what is now Part IV, because he could not believe that the method of money creation, which had come to crown the funding of prosthetics, would work forever, all of a sudden the *fear of future wars began to creep into the book*. This resulted from the insight that even if money creation was exhausted, the necessity of prosthetics would stay. The echelon of prosthetics or of their funding, respectively, now appeared not as an echelon but rather as a Nietzschean wheel of eternal recurrence, with war, accordingly, to reappear in the future. History, unfortunately, was faster than the completion and publishing of this book.

Three basic concepts are used in this book; the first is the profit motive as the fundamental economic driver and the economic essence of capitalism; it is commonly referred to as M–C–M'.[1] This motive leads, out of itself, to a *deficiency of employment-generating spending* or of producive[2] spending. This syndrome, antinomy, contradiction, etc. lies at the heart of everything; it is purely economic in nature but has crucial social consequences. The second concept is prosthetics, now a social, in fact, mainly political, brotherly complementary correction mechanism, which is executed by the state. Prosthetics try to moderate the problems that capitalist societies have with the deficient producive spending. They mitigate the destiny of the victims of the ancient and modern social drama. But prosthetics are, unfortunately, unthinkable without their dilemmas; the dilemmas of prosthetics are the third concept, which the book uses. These three central concepts capture three moments, which, through their evolution and interplay, largely determine the history of capitalist societies – in the long

---

1   "Money – commodities – more money'", abbreviated as or M–C–M'. See "Conventions" and page 81 et seq.

2   We have made up the word "producive", as opposed to "productive", as a short label for "employment-generating" or "inducive to employment and production". (We might even have used the made-up word "employcive"). Whether spending or revenues are "producive" or "employment-generating" looks at whether they lead to certain *inputs* in economic processes, namely labor-inputs, while "productive" looks at the output of processes, namely whether a new good or service is created. Typically, productive processes are also producive. But sometimes they are not. E.g., if bottles with money are buried and excavated, or if soldiers are employed to destroy a city, this is producive but not productive.

run at their deepest level–: capitalism's flaw of deficient employment-generating (or producive) spending, states' corrective reaction to this flaw with prosthetics, and the dilemmas of the applied prosthetics. They allow to re-frame our view of the past and present of capitalism.

As to style, the author aims at providing as realistic an account of the economy as, e.g., Han Fei, Thucydides, Machiavelli, Pufendorf, Hobbes, Clausewitz, Marx, Nietzsche, Theodor Mommsen, Carl Schmitt, Lenin, Paul Kennedy and Henry Kissinger or Niklas Luhmann have provided, as the case may be, on history, the state, geopolitics, society or war (notwithstanding their obvious differences).

Capitalism, today, is as vigorous, creative, and dynamic as ever before; yet, by the same token, it always was and still is also an ailing patient. In fact, it has very recently been moved from a regular day ward to intensive care. We witness protectionist state interventions, huge fiscal state subventions, and, over two decades permanent, massive horror-monetary policies (such as "ultra-unconventional" quasi-zero-interest-rates and massive asset holding of central banks), which the leading ideologists of capitalism would themselves have considered unbelievable just fifteen years ago.[3] The massive central bank asset purchases are ultimately financed by state fiat money creation. Occasionally, we see measures, which are directly borrowed from socialist revolutionaries, such as bank nationalizations after the crisis of 2008, yet they are implemented in order to save capitalism. Nevertheless, economic liberalism still occupies center stage in pro-capitalist arguments. A patient, capitalism, if permanently attached to dozens of hoses, tubes, pumps, cables, electric engines, and suction-mechanisms, yet still quite powerful, continues to chant the song of economic "liberty" and non-intervention.

The theoretical approach of this book and mainstreams' economics

It may be useful to relate this book's theoretical approach to the prevailing teachings of mainstreams economics[4] of the day. First, if anatomists could carve open

---

3   See *Roitzsch/Wächter*, ZIP 2008, 2301 et seq.; *Roitzsch/Wächter*, DZWIR 2009, 1 et seq,

4   We use the expression "mainstreams economics", which in our view encompasses neoclassical economics and the neoclassical synthesis, in the plural to counteract the misunderstanding that there is only one single main stream of economic reasoning, which quasi-officially reflects, supervises, defends and represents capitalism. Capitalism, contrary to Catholicism and a socialist state managed economy, neither needs a single commando post to rule it nor a single orthodox theory. Rather, an eclectic landscape, in fact, increases the flexibility of changing policy interference. By the way, theories with a cathedral-like doctrinal design have anyhow become endangered species. Hegemony is today no longer achieved by conceiving and purifying a doctrine and propagating and defending it intellectually but by influencing swarms never to unite on an undesired course.

the economy like a human body in a dissection room, then they would find a purée of fast-moving communications, money and commodities between billions of emitters and recipients, but no substrate of pre-arranged moving parts in an order with predetermined operations;[5] there is nothing like hearts, lungs, livers, or connections like an aorta and nerves, like a clockwork or like a connected gasoline tank, a carburetor, cylinders, pistons, a crankshaft, wheels etc. The distinguishable, visible realities – wealth owners, businesses, workers, canals, trade routes, naval connections, pipelines, antennas, satellites, cables, production, the internet or money transfer systems – have no meaningful overall structure or connections. Therefore, the attempt to view "the economy" as a system comprised of stations with a spatial organization is doomed to fail. Rather, as *Dirk Baecker*, a pupil of the well-known German systems theorist *Niklas Luhmann*, puts it, the economic system consists of elementary events in time; they "are the system, which reproduce it and through whose reproduction they reproduce themselves...".[6] Accordingly, the economy is comparable to an epidemic, a neurosis, a psychosis, a weather system or even an explosion. This exposes economic theory to the daunting task to categorize highly ephemeral events into elements and to analyze systemic connections between such elements.

Second, economic theory that tries to attack the task is hampered by two experiences in the recent history of economics. A great historic passage of arms occurred between Marxism/Socialism/Communism. It ended with the loss of the Marxist side politically, and in a rigidified and dogmatized aggressive schism intellectually. Both sides were wrong in essential regards, but the fact of their enmity helps them to entrench and to both survive. The fallacies of Marxism save mainstreams economics (certainly in the eyes of mainstreams economists) and the fallacies of mainstreams economics save Marxism (certainly in the eyes of left-wing audiences). The veterans of an exhausted battle collude to block progress. A lesser passage of arms resulted from the challenges posed by Keynes. The outcome was more amicable, but it was not more favorable to theoretical progress as it drove economics into intellectual eclecticism. Therefore, today's general landscape of economic theory is false doctrinarism with eclecticism superimposed; it could not be worse. Concepts, which rule in pro-capitalist mainstreams economics, such as competition or price levels, are macroeconomically almost irrelevant. This fate is shared by leading anti-capitalist concepts. Like inequality is not the crucial moment in society, history is not the history of class battles. Marxian "exploitation" is even more misleading than the focus on inequality. Exploitation does – quite simply – not exist.

---

5   Marx, when he famously stated in the first sentence of *Capital* volume I that the capitalist mode of production "presents itself" as an "immense accumulation of commodities"; pointed to very much the same problem.

6   *Baecker* (2008) page 34, translated by the author.

Third, economic academia has invented methodological instruments that all but guarantee that economics remains in this sad state. On the side of mainstreams economics, mathematization structurally disenables historic and sociological thinking, which would be required for a jump ahead. But history cannot deliver quantitative data, which the mathematized reasoning of today's economics can only digest.[7] Furthermore, mainstream economic academia has a preference for "papers" that have a certain size and style of argument; this also blocks attempts of self-liberation from the outset because the format of "papers" educates economists to restrict themselves to low-caliber amendments.

Fourth, we need to distance ourselves from Marshallian supply and demand graphs, by which many mainstreams' economists are mesmerized. While there is, of course, "Walrasian tâtonnement", it only illustrates how individual prices for commodities are affected by competition. What, yet, macroeconomically matters are *not* ups and downs of such prices or price levels, but whether elementary economic events in the form of C–M–C' and M–C–M'-circuits can close in such a volume as to provide firms with the revenues to keep them going and property less workers to subsist. For that, we need *interrelations between price levels* for meaningfully selected commodities, in particular for labor, equipment, and inventories, final produce and means of subsistence. Hence, we would at least need a series of interrelated graphs, which show the feasibility of system-building in in the sense of C–M–C' and M–C–M'.[8]

Fifth, methodologically, as already hinted at, we use concepts of modern systems theory. To repeat, there is an ongoing autopoietic building of the economic system through elementary events, which emerge over time, which are the system, reproduce it and through whose reproduction they reproduce themselves.[9] Ongoing system-building is, accordingly, far from assured, but instead a problem. Theoretical analysis of capitalism, then, must look out for the conditions that must exist for system-building to continue, for the preconditions of ongoing successful economic system-building. This allows us to re-conceive of a great deal of economic problems from being problems *within* the system (the system works, but it ought to work *better*) to issues of there being "too little system" (the system's diameter or activity being deficient). "More" economic system may, e.g., be more employment contracts, more

---

7   "Traditional economics were not developed because anyone thought they were a good description of real human behavior; *they were adopted to make the math work in the equilibrium framework.*" (*Beinhocker* (2007) page 118).

8   The common supply and demand curves do not offer insights about *why* they are shaped in the way they are. What are the offered prices for labor derived from? From the costs of workers' subsistence? Are firm's supply prices for products derived from their productions costs plus a profit margin? What "rigidities" are there? Accordingly, the curves do not explain why they don't cross and deals are not concluded, i.e., in times or areas of unemployment.

9   See again *Baecker* (2008) page 34.

contracts between firms and suppliers (e.g., following new inventions and technological breakthroughs), and more purchases of consumptive goods that enable circuit closure.

Ongoing system-building depends upon interconnectivity in time over several generations. Earlier generations cause, and enable later generations of economic events (by rendering commodities and money available) and *expected* events of future generations of economic events *motivate and induce* system-building the present middle generation. The generations overlap; each generation of events is a middle generation to future generations. Successful system-building propagates in many lines into many directions, like – to return to the already given example – an epidemy or explosion. But one can also compare economic system building to melodies, where prior tones, their relationship, their rhythm, beat, meter, scale etc. determine whether and how the melody can go. Or take a Vienna Waltz, in which a pair of dancers' prior movements (the positions, through which they pass, and their ongoing movements, when they arrive there) as well as their idea of how they will continue, determines how the dance will unfold . A false tune in a melody or a dancer being "on the wrong foot" at a certain moment will interrupt system-building. Other examples include "pass systems" in team sports, e.g., soccer. Situations such as these emerge if players without the ball can move into a position and when the passing players see them and are able to deliver the ball at the right moment. Predator-prey-systems survive and propagate on condition that predators can find and kill enough prey for them to survive (without killing too much of it wherein they would extinguish the prerequisites of the predators' survival).

Economic system-building is by no means a homogenous or a steady flow (at the same speed of the same material), but is a discrete, discontinuous activity which comes in eruptive and stuttering pushes, in a certain one-two-rhythm. What "runs" through society, if it does, and "builds economy", if it does, is a structured, self-conditional, self-determining (self-hindering, self-enabling, self-observing) process, which is as well past-related as future-related. It is "on" if certain material and motives are there, certain filters and portals are on (and others are off), each at the right moment.

We connect the systems theoretical concept of elementary economic events with the proposition that system-building in profit economies operates, especially, via the *integration of economic events into two particular types of sequential two-leg-patterns*. These two-step combinations, which are always two exchanges, are C–M–C' (a sale of a commodity to obtain money and to purchase another commodity to use it as value-in-use) and M–C–M' (a purchase of commodities, including labor, to sell the un-processed or processed commodities at a higher price). Mankind have been well aware of the distinction between these two circuits, with their two legs, for millennia; this awareness often surfaced as the worries of spiritual leaders, religious men and philosophers, about production being abused for money-making. And it was, of course, also present, at least intuitively in the consciousness of merchants since antiquity.[10]

The operation of the two types of circuits is the only form in which economic system-building is possible and they are interdependent. The expectation of the closure of a C–M–C'-circuit by its M–C'-leg induces firms to trigger investive M–C–M'-circuits, the M–C-leg of which will enable the closure of other investive M–C–M'-circuits. Because this is so, the *expected* new investive M–C–M'-circuits will also induce other new investive M–C–M'-circuits. Finding and telling the narrative of capitalism, therefore, requires *looking out* for when and how C–M–C'-circuits and M–C–M'-circuits can close. Economic system-building, to repeat, is as much causal as teleological; causality and finality work together.

Sixth, we must do away with the idea that the economy has an inner "original purpose" or a "function" for society (e.g., the procurement of goods or of scarce goods) with such assumed function intrinsically controlling the economy. The economic system has no steering mechanisms, which seek to ascertain such goal-attainment. Discussions about "the" economy's purpose or function are, thus, empty, magical, mystical and romantic at best, putting a veil over the quest for profit as the economy's major, dictatorial system-builder, which, in addition, only operates at the level of individual wealth owners. We can approach the same issue from another side: Even if triggered C–M–C'-circuits or M–C–M'-circuits do close, including productive, employment-generating circuits, there is no built-in assurance that *enough* of them will be triggered and close given the number of non-owners, property less workers, whose subsistence depends on employment. Only Quesnay's holistic "royaume agricole" allowed that all members of his classes could live from the "dépenses" of the other classes – but that is not the reality.

Seventh, while we reject an original purpose of the economic system in the sense of the existence of an *economic* steering mechanism, which compares economic output with social requirements and takes correcting action, we, of course, do observe that *society and politics* take a lot of corrective actions if the economy does not deliver what they expect. In fact, these correction mechanisms will shift into the center of this book; this is what prosthetics is all about. In other words, the economy is "neutral" to society (it is only guided by profit and does not care about the society), but the society is *not* "neutral" to the economy. If individual humans react to economic outcomes with hunger, homelessness, suffering, depravation, illness, etc., then society and politics *will* react, society spontaneously with anomy, banditry, unrest, etc., and politics, more organized and purposeful, with rebellion, political entrepreneurship, military entrepreneurship,[11] warlordship, revolutions – or prosthetics.

---

10 A well-known merchant's reference to M–C–M' is "Buy cheap and sell dear!".
11 The term "military entrepreneur" is used by *Smith*, Introduction: The Sung dynasty and its precursors, 907–1279, page 5.

Marx and other predecessors, truisms, banalities, centaurs and pans in economics

Authors like Sismondi, Malthus, Marx, Luxemburg, Keynes, Kalecki, and Minsky have in part pursued a perspective similar to the one here adopted. Marx, the list's most monumental figure, requires a separate introduction. He was a man of broad knowledge, had a deep understanding of society and history, and was a strong critical independent thinker. Based on his acquaintance with Hegel, as well as with materialist theory of history, he was better equipped to generate early "systems-theoretical" and "evolution-theoretical" insights than most of his generation-mates. His use of Hegelian dialectics to pursue "contradictions" in the economic system was breathtaking and leaned towards a theory of system-building in the economy over time. He also correctly pointed at profit as the driving mechanism from which the contradictions of capitalism would ensue (such as M–C–M', which we have, of course, adopted from Marx). Yet, he was also utterly wrong in what he elevated to his most important economic dogma, i.e., in his *fallacious labor-theory of value* and his concomitant *exploitation theory*. He, in fact, probably adapted Ricardo's labor-theory of value *because* he wanted to evolve his exploitation theory out of it. His doing greatly damaged the advance of economic theory. It is true that *everybody* in a profit economy or in a capitalist economy tries to "exploit" everybody else as a means for their purposes. It is also true that firms, entrepreneurs, or capitalists "exploit" the fact that workers are without the means of production and have no alternative to seeking employment by firms. However, Marx wanted to use the term "exploitation" in a narrower, more specific and, as he believed, deeper economic sense. Only labor value created by employed workers could create surplus value and profit, and exploitation consisted in an appropriation of that surplus value. This was exactly wrong, yet after Marx had reached his historic status (it should be borne in mind that from 1919 to 1990 he was the most important ideological founding father of the largest country in the world, the USSR, and since 1949 to today he has retained this position in the world's most populous country, China), his theory became so entangled in political necessities that it became quasi-impossible for critics of capitalism to correct this central doctrine. Doing so would have constituted high treason at in the eyes of the workers' movement, and possibly in the eyes of revolutionary states as well. We are free of this concern. Accordingly, we dare to connect to a time of the economic history *before the theory of labor value and exploitation had been invented*, to Sismondi and Malthus in particular. Furthermore, we also find that Marx' "general formula of capitalism", which is M–C–M', can operate very well without a theory of labor theory and of exploitation. We hope that we can use Sismondi, Malthus and Marx' "general formula of capitalism" to work out extremely valuable and powerful insights further down in the book.

Our re-narration of capitalism will build upon a great deal of content that has been known for a long time. It even sometimes approaches the status of truisms, banalities, or tautologies. This applies already to M–C–M', which, as we already stated, was known to and often consoled by spiritual and religious leaders and philosophers for millennia and of which merchants must also have always been aware. Hyman Minsky correctly analyzed the lack of payment capability as depressing capitalist investment, production, and employment; but this insight too, goes hardly beyond what every schoolgirl knows (you run into problems if you do not pay your debt when due). Keynes correctly saw investment alternatives competing in the minds of entrepreneurs. Yet, is it not obvious that entrepreneurs, capitalists or firms will seek to maximize their profit? In other words, the elementary building blocks, which have to appear in economics seem to be quite simple and easily accessible. If economics is, nevertheless in a deplorable state, then that may result from them not being put into the proper order as well as from attaching all sorts of false add-ons and outgrows to them. The world of economic concepts, we believe, resembles a fairy tale world of centaurs, minotaurs, and pans and a lot of our reasoning has to go into telling the sound parts from bad parts, where to make cuts, and how to recombine both the existing heads and bodies of such creatures.

Productive and sterile economy

In Part I of this book, we introduce to the elementary economics of profit economies and establish fundamental economic terms and doctrines. In specific, we observe the conditions under which the masses of non-owners might find employment and subsistence in modern capitalism. In order to do so, we indeed coin this book's central terms from the perspective of political intervention. Like a physician imposes terms upon human biology so as to best detect illness and steer therapy, we impose our terms upon the economy to best capture what matters for society in the economy, and what best guides its political interventions. Since antiquity, states have regarded profit economies as powerful, but also as half-finished and incomeplete and considered and applied prosthetics; we follow them in their observation and elevate distinctions, they already used implicitly, to explicitness and higher clarity. We will, particularly, use a distinction, which has long silently guided prosthetics from the background: the distinction between the productive and the sterile economy. In the tradition of Quesnay, we, thereby, split up the economy into two *abstract* and *purified economies*: a productive economy with employment-generating or producive spending and with employment and subsistence-effect for the non-owners and in a sterile economy, or a wealth economy, without employment effect.[12] In other words: One economy contributes everything to the subsistence of property-less workers; the other, the sterile economy, contributes nothing. Yet unlike in humans, where the "red" blood with oxygen and the "blue" blood without oxygen each have clearly distinguishable circulation channels (heart chambers, arteries, and veins), through which they travel separately, the productive and sterile economy are not physically apart. Nevertheless, for the sake of clarity, it makes sense to use the abstract idea of a *pure and wholly employment-free and sterile* wealth economy and of an equally *pure productive only-employment economy*, which are both regarded as after "carve-outs" of what does not belong there. E.g.: While selling a house, in contrary to building one, does not lead to massive employment-generating or producive spending on construction workers etc., it still involves a certain amount of spending on legal, notarial, clerical activities, which is employment-generating, etc. We, thus, arrive at the pure idea of a distinct productive and sterile economy only after such corrections or carve-outs. But this will not affect the principle: It is much better to use terms and concepts, which have explanatory power but difficult borderlines, than terms and concepts with clean borderlines but with fuzzy content and little explanatory power.[13]

If we lay the distinction between the productive economy and the sterile wealth economy *crosswise* over the customary distinction of "consumptive" vs "investive", this gives us Matrix I.

---

12   We shall, of course, acquit Quesnay's *classe stérile*, artisans, trade, manufacturing and factory owners, hence, capitalists and the free professions, of being "sterile". We shift the blame to Quesnay's *classe de propriétaires*, about whom Quesnay says himself "ils sont utiles à l'état que par leur consommation." (*Cartelier* (2008) page 36).

13   Of course, there is a need for lawyers, notaries, secretaries, clerks, traders, tax advisors, IT-people, taxi-drivers, cooks and waiters, security services and often even for construction firms to erect high rise buildings, which serve the wealth economy and which involve producive spending. Yet, the dollar-trillions shaffled around and dollar-billions earned in the wealth economy, e.g., derivatives, sovereign bonds, forex, the stock markets, M&A-deals, or private equity, generate by far less employment than the productive economy. There are, in fact, also sterile components in house and factory-construction etc., e.g., interest payments. Details must be postponed to the main part. See on page 123.

Figure 1: Matrix I – Consumptive vs investive and producive vs sterile spending

	consumptive	investive
sterile	sterile consumptive	sterile investive
producive	producive consumptive	producive investive

It tells us that *only what happens in the lower part* matters for employment, and it also tells us that it does not matter for employment whether an action is "consumptive" or "investive". The two lower boxes decide upon the social "master drama of modernity", on the subsistence of property-less workers, mass prosperity or suffering, anomy, banditry, upheaval and revolution, and often on civil and external wars. Conversely, the distinction between investive or consumptive spending does not matter greatly for macroeconomics. The distinction between employment-generating or producive and sterile spending does.

Deficient producive spending

In Part II we revisit the ancient master drama, i.e., whether the predecessors of today's property-less workers in antiquity could hold onto their land. They could obviously not –and this in the departure point of to the modern master drama. Non-owners need employment to subsist. Will modern capitalism generate the needed employment? Part III attacks the question as an analysis of the preconditions of circuit closure in the productive economy, assuming that capitalism is left to operate according to its own logic, "stand alone", so to speak. The closure of M–C–M'-circuits then depends on either the consumption of wealth owners or workers or on investments by productive wealth owners, which expect a profit from it. Circuits, which are not expected to close (and are not satisfying the profit-criterion), are not initiated and omitted circuits cannot generate employment. This analysis will debunk an essential intrinsic dynamic of capitalism: deficient producive spending. The problem lies not in the consumption of workers. To the extent they were employed, they will reliably largely (not wholly) return their salaries to productive capitalists for subsistence goods as employment-generating spending; they cannot do otherwise. The problem also does not lie in the consumption of wealth owners; they are phenomenally good consumers, yet, their consumption is by far insufficient due to their limited number and due to the limits of what humans can reasonably consume. *The problem mostly lies with M–C–M'-players* who will only make purchases (thereby closing the circuits of earlier investors) if they expect to resell their purchases – often after processing them – for a profit. Only players who seek profit in the future enable earlier players to realize their profits; earlier player generations succeed only because subsequent generations seek out profit too. The expectation of there being enough "sucking behavior" in the future, ignites present sucking-in of labor and other commodities, i.e., employment. The power behind the present flow of money is the expected later flow; the sacrifice of money later triggers the previous sacrifice. "...in other words," writes *Kalecki*, "the capitalists must spend immediately all their additional profits on consumption and investment".[14] Already the *suspicion* only that future generations of firms may not sufficiently do this, creeps backwards into other firms present investive employment-generating spending and depresses economic activity here and now. Here comes the bitterly dull point to which the term "wealth economy" draws attention: Even what firms intrinsically love to do most – hunting for profit – will turn them away from what they have to do to enable other firms to realize and expect profit in the productive economy: They are seduced to migrate into the wealth economy to find an easier game. We are, thus, not only in a state of circular conditionality[15] and uncertainty, where things can easily go wrong, but the ruling dynamics of capitalism are, in fact, tilted *against* an outcome that is macroeconomically desired by the political system. There is a solid systematic cause for "secular stagnation", "savings glut" or "investment dearth" *at the deep level of the elementary heartbeat of capitalism* already.

Accordingly, if there was (as there was) significant growth in the productive economy and improvement of living standards in many countries over significant periods of the past or even, very recently, in China or India etc., it was not because capitalism *per se* runs in an integrated manner, but that growth was due to a *series* of (either accidental or premeditated) *favorable circumstances*, which smoothed out and remedied the innate deficiencies of capitalism at these times.

Prosthetics, their evolution and dilemmas

Part IV investigates how states deal with this systemic deficient employment-generating spending and progresses to prosthetics. States either somehow try to help to procure surplus value for firms, i.e., the money to finance their profits or they simply and directly pour social transfer payments into workers pockets. Such prosthetics may be financed by violent wealth procurement or protectionism (to the detriment of other economies abroad), by taxation and by other forms of expropriation

---

14   *Kalecki* (1971) page 27.
15   Quesnay had this circular situation in mind when he spoke of his tableau as "l'ordre de la distribution des dépenses et de la *reproduction du revenue par la dépense même du revenue*". (*Quesnay*, Philosophie rurale, in : Cartelier (2008) page 190, italics added).

(now mainly to the domestic wealth owners' detriment). States also use redistributive debt or money creation as a means to finance prosthetics. All means lead into dilemmas. The volume of prosthetic value-in-exchange that violent wealth procurement or protectionism could mobilize in minor "classical" hinterland-countries is, at least today, a drop in the ocean of the prosthetics required. Furthermore, renewed protectionism (or even outright violent wealth procurement) needs to establish and uphold a metropolis-vs-hinterland-difference, which will require military, political and ideological domination. Chinese cannon boats, if even they wanted it as a revanche, have no chance to ascend the river Thames to enforce the British buying of Chinese Opium or telecommunication equipment... China, too, will never allow the British to once again patrol along the "Bund" in Shanghai for such purposes. Any such attempt in (in whatever direction) would likely trigger World War III. If states push towards higher taxation and other forms of expropriation of their domestic wealth owners, this will not only quickly hit economic limits, but wealth owners will stand up against it. The political system, well aware of these limits, has reacted with debt-financing prosthetics. If wealth owners do not buy the products of the productive economy, so as to enable sufficient profit and employment, and cannot be taxed in the amounts required to buy them, then they should at least – voluntarily – grant loans. This strategy worked well for a while, but the highly developed capitalist economies have now reached the twilight of this period. Wealth owners are only interested in holding "good", profitable debt, i.e., on which sufficient interest is paid and which is normally repaid. If the available sovereign or private debt gets too "subprime", they turn away. Debt cancellations, as recommended in the Book of Deuteronomy to take place every seven years or as executed by Solon's reforms, might be an option. They can improve the solvency of those released from their debt and prepare the ground for them to take out new debt.[16] Yet, this option only exists if the debt is held by public institutions, not if it is held by private wealth owners. This explains the crisis of debt financing of prosthetics in the last decades and explains the most recent financial invention: Central banks have transmuted their longstanding two-directional "open market operations" in straight forward debt purchase programs, thereby allowing wealth owners to dispose of uncomfortable excess debt. This came up as an emergency-strategy in the years following 2008, but has since become standard everyday practice. Central bank "asset purchases" have financed the recovery from the 2008 crisis, the anti-Corona policies and are, of course, also financing the Western costs of the Ukrainian war. A circus of debt financing of prosthetics, debt build-up by wealth owners, and debt recycling to central banks is rolling with an increasing percentage remaining stuck with the central banks. The problem with this is not that this practice brushes aside orthodox credence of economics,

---

16   E.g., US-President Biden has been promoting a campaign aimed at the cancellation of private educational debt in the US in 2021.

e.g., of von Mises, Hayek, and of the German "Ordnungspolitik"; the globalized capitalist ecstasy is since long comfortably united with general massive state interference and abjuration of all beloved old-liberal dogmas. The problem is also not that central banks might run out of money to buy debt (in fiat money regimes they can technically create fiat money without limits), but is rather that at some stage the funding of prosthetics via expansive debt combined with state fiat money creation will also hit intrinsic limits (which we shall pursue later further).

Money creation vs no money creation, fiat money vs commodity money

To study the financing of prosthetics, the book sharpens a distinction between two other distinctions, which is often blurred. The first distinction between *fiat money* versus *commodity money* (gold and silver and "credit money", which grants a legal claim against banks for the delivery of gold or silver) must be distinguished from the distinction between *existing money* and *new money*, i.e., between no money creation and money creation. Laying the two distinctions crosswise over one another yields Matrix II.

Figure 2: Matrix II – No money creation vs money creation and commodity and merchant or private bank credit money vs state fiat money

	No money creation	**money creation**
Commodity and merchant or private bank credit money	No new commodity or credit money issued	New commodity money issued (e.g. new gold or silver embossed) New bank credit money (bank notes, bank token coins, bank deposits) issued beyond reserves held
Fiat money	At issuance of fiat money commodity and/or credit money is withdrawn in the same amount	At issuance of fiat money commodity and credit money is withdrawn in a lesser amount

This matrix makes it clear, first, that money creation, which is a version of value-in-exchange-creation, already existed in the world of commodity money (e.g., by finding and mining gold, by issuing merchants' notes and drafts, or by bank credit money creation), long before state fiat money emerged, even if it was a more cumbersome or unreliable instrument at that time. Second, the matrix allows a fresh look at the advantages of fiat money. The conventional story is that fiat money is great because it is practical by freeing us from shuffling heavy gold or silver around in transactions. But the property, which has made fiat money the "money of choice" of modern capitalist states, may more simply consist in its *tremendously increased quasi-unlimited potential of money creation*. Fiat money allows states to create value-in-exchange (for warfare and prosthetics) ex nihilo and, therefore, makes weak states into strong states and strong states into great empires – as long as the newly created state fiat money is accepted. Much like how sovereignty enables states to make new laws and other political decisions, thereby displacing families as natural-born leaders of society and tradition, so too does state fiat money displace the spontaneous natural-born money creation by finding and mining gold and through modest commercial and bank credit money creation. While M–C–M' represents capitalism's dynamism as a strict logic with an inner antinomy, money creation through fiat money represents a utopian moment, a miraculous cure-all state-strategy, even potentially stronger more than taxation, expropriation and sovereign debt – but it too is on the way to its exhaustion.

Novelty in this book

This book will, of course, begin by examining how doctrines (terms and their relations) in theoretical systems, which existed before it was written, reflected the economy. It will focus on the question whether and when capitalist circuits generate employment, in particular for non-owners, via producive, employment-generating spending. This provides a defined, single perspective for its voyage. It then selects certain pre-existing distinctions, such as consumption and investment, or owners and non-owners, contract and violence etc., which it partially further evolves and adjusts to its explanatory needs, e.g., fiat money vs commodity money and money creation. It also rejects certain other prominent terms and does not use them at all. The book also adds a few distinctions, mainly the one between the productive economy and the sterile wealth economy and producive, employment-generating spending and sterile spending, which are not common. The novelty of this book lies primarily in composing the selected distinctions into an integrated explanation of the fundamental forces, antinomies, dynamics and dilemmas in capitalism in a certain elaboration and conciseness.

Credentials

This book deals more with social philosophy, state theory, political theory, and history than most other economics books. Even though references do not appear

on every page or if some authors do not appear at all in the book, I will nevertheless begin by paying tribute authors that were very important to writing it:
Thucydides (454–399 BC), Han Fei (~280-233 BC), Niccolò Machiavelli (1468–1527),
Thomas Hobbes (1588–1679), Samuel Pufendorf (1633~1694 BC), Carl Phillip Gottlieb von Clausewitz (1780–1831), and Friedrich Nietzsche (1844–1900). The book
also uses sociological reasoning and economic history. In so far it is indebted to
Niklas Luhmann, a systems-theoretician and sociologist, with whom I studied
at Bielefeld University in 1981 and 1982. Other relevant social scientists include
Werner Sombart (1863–1941), Max(imilian) Carl Emil Weber (1864–1920), Jürgen
Kuczynski (1904–1997), Karl Paul Polanyi (1886–1946), Stanley Diamond (1922–1991),
with whom I studied Social Anthropology at the New School in New York in 1984,
and David Graeber (1961–2020). Concerning the theory of modern Western mass
democracies, I owe a lot to both Peter Furth (1930–2019), a social philosophy professor at the Berlin Free University, whose private reading circle I had the pleasure
of attending for over 15 years. Peter Furth also introduced me to Panajotis Kondylis
(1943–1998), a Greek social philosopher.[17]

My own experience, as a business lawyer in M&A transactions and post-M&A-
disputes for almost 40 years, including exciting years inside and for the German
state agency privatizing East-German former "people-owned businesses" (Treuhandanstalt) in the early nineties, and the reflective experience of extensive teaching
and writing on M&A (e.g., "M&A-Litigation", 1000 pages, 4th ed. 2022) helped me to
gain a business perspective on economics. My trial advocacy in post M&A litigation
and arbitration, up to today, has also proven helpful in an unexpected way. Studying
the facts in order to develop a script that comes as close as possible to the real story
(to win a case before judges or arbitrators who are assumed to both intelligent and
honest) is not so different from trying to find the true story in social sciences and
economics. What can be surgically removed or argumentatively smashed in a court
case is probably wrong and should not survive in scientific discourse either.

Still, most of the work for this book, most certainly, went into reading
economists and thinking about them. The author is indebted in the first rank
to Francois Quesnay (1694–1744), Anne Robert Jacques Turgot (1727–1781), Jean-
Charles-Léonard Simonde de Sismondi (173–1842), Thomas Robert Malthus
(1766–1834), Karl Marx (1818–1883), Lord John Maynard Keynes (1883–1946), Ludwig Heinrich Edler von Mises (1882–1973), Michal Kalecki (1899–1970), and Hy-

---

17   We do not like the term "interdisciplinarity" as it is reminiscent of meetings in which diplo-
mats negotiate deals by mutually respecting their field's autonomy. Truth-searching-think-
ing, however, must disregard borderlines and encourage to take the risk of crossing bound-
aries into the territories of other "disciplines". Theoretical work, thus, ought to be "trans-
disciplinary", "non-disciplinary", "proto-disciplinary", "meta-disciplinary", "post-disciplinary"
or "cross-disciplinary. A similar argument is made in *Beinhocker* (2006) page 11.

man Philip Minsky (1919–1996). Other important authors include Adam Smith (1723–1790), Rudolf Hilferding (1877–1941), Rosa Luxemburg (1871–1919) and Josef Alois Schumpeter (1883–1950). As for more recent writers, Georg Soros (1930-), Steve Keen (1953-), Richard Koo (1954-), Adair Turner, Baron of Ecchinswell (1955-), Perry Mehrling (1959-) and Martin Wolf (1946-) were particularly stimulating reading experiences.

The book, which preoccupied the author for more than ten years, was written for pleasure, with pleasure, and some humor, and it will hopefully be read a similar spirit. Relaxing phases alternate with phases of more serious work. Occasional smiling is not prohibited. Eventually, a feeling of achievement will hopefully be reached, as though you have poked your head above the clouds after a long climb; if dizziness is the result of the venture, then so be it. This book's aim is to improve abstract understanding. Whether the insights acquired can be used for state policies, central bank policies, party policies (revolution, reform, and counter-revolution), or macro-speculation is beyond the author's current interest. Still: "...wie du da redest, wühlt sich mir das Innre um und gräßlich fliegt im Hirn das Denken." (Sophokles, König Oedipus, translation from Greek into German by Hugo von Hofmannsthal).

The author can be reached at *waechter@waechterlaw.de.* He may post amendments, reactions, corrections, etc. concerning the book at the website of his law firm at http://www.waechterlaw.de.

Berlin and Chamonix Mont Blanc, March 2024

Part I:
Introduction to elementary economics
of profit economies

Part I is a systematic introduction to profit economies. It sets out elementary terms or notions, such as value-in-use, value-in-exchange, trade systems, money, wealth procurement by violence, wealth procurement by exchange, profit economy, and capitalism. It explains the important distinction between the productive economy with employment-generating (investive and consumptive) spending, the wealth economy with sterile (consumptive and investive) spending, and deals with some subsequent notional issues. The concept of M–C–M'-circuits is also presented.[1] Initially, we consider praeter-economic goods or wealth procurement by violence.

---

1   The book has a small apparatus with conventions and explanations, see on page 509 et seq.

Chapter I. Praeter-Economics: Wealth procurement by violence

Men are dependent upon their environment with regard to oxygen, water, and nutrition. They take oxygen and water as unanimated inputs from the air, rivers, lakes, or wells and nutrition by tearing plants from the ground or by killing animals as positive inputs for their bodies. Furthermore, their conditions demand to protect themselves against certain damaging influences, such as cold, rain, wind etc., e.g., with housing. This dependency of men from its environment cannot be stressed enough. Human needs dictate what men have to do and they have the greatest impact in their motivational system. These needs work by inducing humans to try to procure what they physically need in the first place, but also to avoid such objects being taken away from them again, e.g., as taxes, tribute payments, or other expropriations. Humans also depend on nature insofar as they suffer greatly from physical damage done to their bodies, through injuries, or from restrictions of their freedom of movement, e.g., by being imprisoned. Narrative desires of humans are also of great impact in their motivational systems.

At some stage of science and technology, in the neolithic, humans organized their nutrition in farming, agriculture, forced domestication, breeding, and the pasturage of animals. Men basically knew that they were part of the same species as other men, but this awareness never prevented them from taking away from other men which they had previously procured from nature. They generally discovered that it was possible to apply the idea of farming and domesticating to other humans too, and, for instance, to farm slaves in plantations in Sicily or, much later, in the South of the US and Spanish and French colonies, or to subjugate tribes and countries in order to draw tributes from them. This enabled them to also appropriate what other men could appropriate from nature in the future, not only on an ad hoc basis but in a lasting and systematic manner. If they felt the need to justify this, as they occasionally did, they found good reasons in the differences of physical appearance (race), the respective degree of civilization (barbarians), in religious or other beliefs, or in terms of a form of political organization.

The economic system comprises emergent operations based on the attribution of emergent qualities, such as ascribing property to both things around humans and humans themselves. The acceptance of property within a state is normally connected to the monopoly of state power and to the law, which keeps citizens from robbing and subjugating each other domestically. Quitting robbing and subjugation between tribes and states is a different episode. It is normally connected to a balance of military or political power or the international community reaching a certain level of civilization (acting for the time as if they were all operating within one state). Wealth procurement by violence takes place outside of what we shall get to know as the economic system, and it is not the subject of economics. However, we cannot deny that pre-economic and praeter-economic wealth procurement, the dark way of wealth procurement, from the ancient profit economies in Greece, Rome, and China through to colonialism and imperialism, always was *the grand alternative* to wealth procurement by exchange and was even the preferred method in many regards. In fact, simply taking riches away from their neighbors by force and threats, or getting them to work at no or at an unfair remuneration, was *the more plausible thing to do* in the eyes of the world's elites and upper classes for most of history. It came a good deal before commerce. Here we also meet a strong reason why we should not fall too deeply in love with the lower classes: After they lost their economic and social battles, and their land was bequeathed to their domestic upper classes, they were just too willing to ally with their conquerors and to jointly with them turn around to rob their neighbors. Violent wealth procurement was, thus, from Roman legions to the Nazis, typically a semi-socialist camaraderie, which the upper and lower classes joined in on. Warring, robbing, and subjugation were always partially meant to appease the participating lower classes and was quite successful in this regard, at least for a time. Humanity deserves no better than having to remember this past. We cannot even be sure that procuring wealth or profits by violence is a closed chapter of human history. The prevailing of democracy in most of the world's important advanced countries is certainly *no* sufficient reason here. Think of ancient Athens: While it was celebrated for its early democracy, the ekklesia (people's assembly) on the Pnyx was always as quick as any tyrant (if not quicker) in its demanding and applauding acts of aggressive warfare and economic violence against neighbors.

Marxist and some radical anthropologists, e.g., *Stanley Diamond*, argue that humans robbing and subjugating other humans was not a feature of the earliest times of primitive society,[1] but only arose with civilization, proto-states[2] and the state. We can leave this issue open – we at least know quite reliably from art, archaeological findings, e.g., of the Shang and Ch'ou dynasties or of Minoan and Mycenae Greece, and historic writers that warfare was *by those times* a fully legitimate means (more exciting than prodcution) by which to procure riches. During higher education, most

---

1   See *Kuczynski* (1951, pages 17, 20 and 33 et seqs.), who distinguishes between savagery (Wildheit) and barbarism (Barbarei).

2   *Diamond* (1971) pages 42–72.

German college students in their middle teens, at the so-called Gymnasiums, used to read *Gaius Julius Caesar's* book *De bello Gallico* (in Latin). The general picture it conveyed was that there were different tribes in and around today's France (Caesar also made trips to *Britannia* across the channel and *Germania* across the Rhine) that had different cultures and traditions, some likeable, others less so (by reason of human sacrifice in some tribes). As Caesar attacked them, they passionately defended their "liberty" against having to pay tribute or to render services to the Romans. Some charismatic leaders would emerge, stir up uproar, form an alliance with other tribes, and would organize their fight jointly. There are passages in Caesar's *De bello Gallico*, in which this all sounds very much like a harbinger of national liberation fights or of anti-colonial fights witnessed two thousand years later. However, the French tribes' desire to remain free, as in later national liberation fights, was only half the story. "Liberty", as it was understood both then and thereafter, almost always had the remarkable dialectical property that once a tribe or country had liberated itself, *it would go on the offense and try to do unto others that which had been done to itself previously.* Liberation from an oppressor would not lead to a stable, oppression-free symmetrical structure, but would only turn things upside down. Its ultimate idea was to become the new *dominus* over the former subjugator. A certain honesty prevailed. The new oppressors would often understand the loser's hatred and the legitimacy of its future rebellions and their fight for *their* liberty. The French tribes who fought Caesar never got that far, but the Spanish *Reconquista* was the beginning of the Spanish *Conquista*. The best way to be free was to become the master of somebody else.

In antiquity, thus, and for a long time thereafter, robbing and conquest were the *primary, preferred, and most noble means by which to generate wealth.* "In heroic societies", David Graeber writes, "the role of violence is not hidden – it's glorified".[3] The sons of noble gentries were educated in fighting since childhood; their juvenile desires were directed towards both hunting and warfare. They were trained in fencing with wooden sticks and horse riding, and prided themselves on their fine bronze, iron, or steel weapons and helmets that they had received as birthday gifts. Weaponry is amongst the exhibits most commonly displayed in the world's archaeological and historical museums, often crafted for representative purpose much more than for actual warfare. There was also no doubt that robbing humans and enslaving them was absolutely honorable – "In the Iliad", to hear from *David Graeber* again, "Achilles sees nothing shameful in his relation with his slave-girl Briseis, whose husband and brothers he killed".[4] On the contrary, the alternatives –work on fields or the not particularly relevant handicrafts and peaceful trades – were mostly despised. Women,

---

3   *Graeber* (2011) page 209.
4   *Graeber* (2011) page 209. Agamemnon, by the way, killed the husband of his first wife (Clytemnestra) and she would, as is well known, take bitter revenge after his return from Troy.

as the great military historian *Martin van Creveld* has said, may not like war, but they loved warriors (this was as true then as it is today).[5] The most glamorous careers for sons of a robber-state's elite were connected to finding new victims for robberies; they were "start-up" or "new economy"-ventures" in violent wealth procurement. The more bureaucratic or corporate careers of the time[6] involved crushing rebellions and leading punishment campaigns, or, at the very least, overseeing and administrating tribute payments; in this job, if you diverted some more into your own pockets than officially confessed, that was often accepted as well.

Marx, like others before him, distinguished a part of the produce, which was required to reproduce the immediate producers, and a surplus part that could be taken away without killing or severely hurting them. This idea could, first, be applied at an individual level. It meant that a good hunter, fisher, or gatherer would create more than he needed to individually sustain himself. Weaker members of the community, children, pregnant women, the elderly, the ill, and the incapacitated, would then be forgotten. However, this concept also makes sense if applied to the social level and involves asking whether a tribe's actively working population or community, after supporting their weaker members, still had an *excess* or *surplus produce* left over. If so, this surplus could be used in different ways: It could be destroyed, allowed to rot, sacrificed to gods, consumed in orgies, or put in storehouses as reserves. Alternatively, this surplus produce could also be appropriated by a domestic ruling elite or class, which, became the most commonly favored historic response. Finally, the surplus could be appropriated by a foreign might in the place of a domestic ruling class. In Marx, the implication was that only such progress of productive forces, which had enabled surplus generation, would enable others to appropriate riches or the work of others in exploitation and on a *regular basis* (and without killing the producers). That was a fine idea in principle. However, who was going to make sure that the oppressors observe the fine line between necessary produce and surplus produce and *not* to kill but to only exploit their victims on a "sustainable" basis?

---

5   The idea is clear in *van Creveld* (2001) page 38. I did not find the quote that I remember. Perhaps van Creveld made the comment only orally in a speech at a conference in Heidelberg in 2008 on the work of Panajotis Kondylis, which I attended.

6   Sombart observes "Der Raubhandel ist der Zwillingsbruder des Raubes. Er besteht darin, daß (meistens berufsmäßig) Waren verkauft werden, die von den Verkäufern weder produziert noch gekauft, sondern durch Gewalt erworben worden sind." (1902, volume 1, page 163). According to Sombart, the "natural man" even prefers this, "... dass der Erwerb der als Verkaufsobjekt dienenden Waren nicht auf dem Wege eines freihändigen Kaufs zu erfolgen habe, sondern thunlichst durch entgeltlose oder entgeltniedrige Wegnahme der Waren. Ebenso wie aller Kolonialhandel noch heute zum großen Teil einseitiger Handel geblieben ist, d. h. Verkauf von Erzeugnissen anderer, die man auf dem Wege der Ausplünderung diesen abgenommen hat." (1902, volume 1, page 164).

Nevertheless, if there is surplus production, then this certainly makes for a better and possibly more long-lasting series of robberies and for better subjugation. A great step forward was discovered in the Neolithic Age. Its settlements, farming, and breeding (which substituted hunting and gathering) and which is normally dated between 10,000 and 8,000 BC, pushed productive forces, thereby allowing for a more sizable surplus and, thus, enabled robber-oppressors to build surplus-appropriation systems and empires on this basis. The late Neolithic Age roughly coincided with proto-state and state formation and most or all proto states or states started to attack and rob their neighbors systematically at this time.

The violent procurement of goods, even if it takes place outside of what we consider the "economy", can still be analyzed with the business-tools of profit-and-loss-accounting. The "asset" of a subjugated tribe or country has initial acquisition costs, which come in both money and in kind (sacrificed human lives and body-parts) be it from the ruling nobility or from lower classes and even from unfree humans. Furthermore, after the original acquisition of the asset, after victory, there are multiple ongoing operational costs of running the asset and collecting the revenues. The production of things by subjugated populations and carrying the produce to a hundred or thousand miles away homeland is a burdensome task. Unfortunately, if oppressed populations have to work for an oppressor, they are not really very good workers. The motivation of the workers to toil for a foreign upper class is even lower than it was when the produce was for the domestic upper classes and plantations slaves, e.g., in Roman-era Sicily, French Guadeloupe or in the US' south, can only be given primitive tools – as better tools would be mistreated and destroyed. The workers also need overseers, other cost-inducing surveillance personnel, and a good deal of policing – a military must remain on standby in the case of upheavals. Furthermore, the distance from the subjugator's population to the homeland requires transportation and communications lines, e.g., roads and ports, which have to be constructed, maintained and defended. Of course, somebody also has to physically carry out the transportation, preferably the oppressed themselves, which they will only do as reluctantly as anything else (and will require further overseers, policing and military reserves on these lines of communication). All this has to take place in an overall disadvantageous medium of hatred, resistance, sabotage, and occasional violent rebellion. Thus, for any material gain in terms of wealth to arrive happily in Rome, a manifold of this gain may have had to be produced in Sicily, with only a small net operating profit outweighing the asset's original "acquisition costs" and allowing for a positive internal rate of return. So far, our "business-look" on how capital has to operate in the realm of violent wealth procurement has still ignored the most important cost-block of modern venture capital, the costs of the 90 % of the ventures that fail altogether and never make any money: Military campaigns to acquire the asset of control over a subjugated population may and will occasionally be lost. The cost of these ventures with a pure negative return must obviously be set off against the profits from more successful ones.

All this sounds very discouraging for the considered ventures of violent wealth procurement. But if this so, then why did the states of antiquity and beyond so frequently engage in such ventures? The suspicion arises that apart from the upper classes being desirous of occasionally profiting from violent wealth procurement, and apart from those upper-class members who were running the show expecting particular high profits, the ventures served as an "employment policy" for the lower classes from the very outset. In fact, every grain of wheat, which was extracted from the oppressed populations, and which did not make its way to the storehouses of the Roman nobility at the Tiber, fed the hundred thousand of Roman legionaries, administrators, coachmen, sailors etc. who were part of the gigantic project apparatus. Ventures in violent wealth procurement, in other words, were solid and large-scale means to externalize the costs of prosthetics for lower classes. In addition, states, of course, had to consider that if they did not throw such ventures against their neighbors, their neighbors might throw them against themselves. After this examination of violent wealth procurement as a praeter-economic way by which to procure wealth, which always remains an alternative option, we will now move on to the economic method itself.

Chapter II. Value, money and the economic system

Section 1. Value and value attribution

Goods are initially procured – gathered, hunted, fished, farmed and pastured – without the intermediation of exchange. In primitive societies, i.e., without an economic system, goods have value-in-use, but they have no value-in-exchange. Even if goods are forwarded or shared between tribe members, they are not "exchanged" in the sense proper. This is different in an exchange or barter economy, where we must distinguish between a flow of goods and services[1] travelling in one and a flow of other goods and services travelling in the other direction as a *quid pro quo*. Values-in-use have an infinite number of shapes, which matter for users' value-in-use-considerations. In an exchange economy, commodities' value-in-exchange means their power to be exchanged against other values-in-use or against more or less money. As soon as money emerges, everything is valued in money; as money is one-dimensional, a mere number in the respective money currency, be it a quantity of oxen, of pounds of grains, of gold or of Euro, says everything.

Many great economists have awarded an eminent place to the theory of value. Adam Smith did so in Book I of the *Wealth of Nations* and David Ricardo did likewise in chapter I of his *Principles*. Marx did the same thing in *Capital* and even shifted the theory of value and surplus value into the absolute center of his economics (and derived his disastrous theory of exploitation therefrom). The "marginalist revolution" largely consisted of amending the theory of value-in-exchange by adding a new aspect of utility (utility of the last unit). Other authors, however, e.g., Silvio Gesell or Max Weber,[2] regarded the notion of value as redundant and suggested working with prices only. We side with the first group of aforementioned authors and also find that the notion of value-in-exchange is basic to a conceptualization of the economy. Value-in-exchange is the stuff of which wealth consists. It also already exists even if,

---

1   We will often refer to "goods" if the emphasis is on value-in-use and to "commodities" if it is on value-in-exchange. Both terms also include services.

2   *Gesell* (1916) chapter 3.3; *Weber* (1980) page 31.

as we shall see, it is ascribed by third persons, before the price is paid. Value motivates purchases, makes prices, moves the economy's wheels even prior to payment. The expected ascribed value (M' in M'-M is always the expected value) kickstarts capitalist circuits in both the productive and the sterile economies. The economic and social effect of expected future value at t1 are not wiped out by the disappointing finding that no value-in-exchange, or perhaps less value-in-exchange than expected, remains when the return on the investment arrives at t2. Even after a transaction, the value remains important, e.g., for pledges, for bookkeeping purposes, or in the case of a resale.

Value-in-use depends on future utilities. Utilities ascribed in the future will make values-in-use and values-in-exchange and will lead to future prices. This expectation works its way backwards into the present and makes present values-in-exchange and prices. In values the difference between the presence and the future, thereby losing its relevance to some extent. Future values-in-use, future values-in-exchange and future prices are as uncertain as the future in general. Therefore, as Richard Cantillon has stated, an entrepreneur buys at a "prix certain" in order to sell at a "prix uncertain".[3] A commodity owner can try to assess his commodity's future value-in-exchange by imagining future utilities (and market conditions), but prices may deviate from values-in-exchange – thanks to misjudgment, state price fixing, etc.[4]

If theories of value care about the potential of commodities to exchange against a certain amount of money, then they have different options about what degree of certainty they require for the exchange to take place. In an extreme version, they may identify value with the amount actually being paid as price. In this case, the payment of a price is not only the ultimate test for value ascription, but is identical with there being value and value-in-exchange; prices collapse into a theory of demand, of *débit*, of *Absatz* or *"off-sale"*.[5] We will not go so far and will instead consider value-in-ex-

---

3   See *Murphy* (2016) volume I, page 21.

4   Value and price have an interesting relationship. Value-in-exchange is very meaningful long-term, if only as the *prognosis* of a price, which may be realized because of a *later* value-in-exchange *attribution*. If you have a great product, then you have value before you have sold it for a price. (In this regard Marx was quite right to point to the increased value-in-exchange already existing in C'). Price is a much more practical and reliable thing, but it is only meaningful in the single moment of exchange and only if it is paid. Thereafter, it has already become a *past price* and past prices do not matter. The buyer now has the object and the object, again, has merely a value-in-exchange as a likely future price. Even if the price is the moment of truth for value, it makes sense to maintain the distinction for several reasons. E.g., imagine that the state was to fix prices. If the price is above the value-in-exchange, then nobody will buy it voluntarily; if the price is fixed underneath, it will sell easily (see also page 39).

5   See footnote 24 on page 207.

change as independent of a sale at this value-in-exchange (as a price) actually taking place. E.g., a bank may calculate somebody's net worth in order to hand out a loan. Value-in-exchange exists here as a relevant "fait économique" even if the amount assessed is never realized thereafter.

Value-in-use-attribution

Value-in-exchange ought to be developed from value-in-use. Values-in-use are attributed to things or services based on five aspects. They depend first on the thing or service; second, on the user and the uses; third on the availability of identical or substitute things or services; fourth, they depend on systems that emerge between values-in-use (or humans with regard to them) more generally; and fifth, they depend on the state.

Use-relatedness of objects

Things and services have properties. The properties have utilities for some purpose. Values-in-use are good *for* something from the outset and are, hence, *relational*. This something might involve storing fluids or cutting meat. While it may be possible to cut the skin of a deer on the sharp-edged rim of a pot, knives normally have higher levels of utility for cutting – as can be seen in the pottery and knives-section of the world's many archeological museums. Services, which prepare a field for wheat cultivation, are different from other services directed towards rice cultivation – as are the prepared fields and the crop. Bronze used to make a knife is different from the bronze used for jewelry. If I have an ox, a horse, or a cow, then what race they are matters as does whether they are young, healthy, strong, and well trained or not. The value-in-use of an ox also depends on the soil type I have.

If the objects change or the purposes of men change, then the utilities will change as well; the specific uses that I can make of an object or service result from the "fit" between the object and these uses. In stationary primitive (or tribal, segmented etc.) societies, only a few products existed; if the soils in a given region were similar, then only a *few utilities* for oxen and other tools actually existed. No relevant changes took place over many centuries, usually, given the then low speed of evolution. This began to differ in stratified societies[6] when advances in science and technology led to the refinement of objects and utilities. Most utilities continued to refer to basic needs or social status.[7] An explosion-like differentiation, complexifi-

---

6   We borrow the differentiation between segmented, stratified, and functional differentiation from *Talcott Parsons* and *Niklas Luhmann*.

7   An example of this can be observed in the way in which Champa-rice, which can be reaped only 60 days after seed, was introduced from Vietnam into China during the Sung dynasty. See *McDermott/Yoshinobu*, Economic change in China, 960–1279, page 394.

cation, and a new interdependence set in only when functional differentiation and the division of labor arrived. Every specialized functional subsystem now developed its own utilities and demanded much greater adjustment from the objects that it could use. Men also had to relate to several functional subsystems and value-in-use accrued to a greater number of objects. For example, handicraft production of final goods demanded better raw materials from primary production and scientific or technological knowledge allowed and facilitated better tool engineering (which in turn demanded better materials). New lines of communications created awareness of substitute or complementary products elsewhere and alternative inputs for their production in general more rapidly. Such inputs were available faster, via newly opened trade and transport routes from farther away. The same applies to parts and complementary products. The opening up of such routes was initiated upon the discovery of such potential uses.

Subject-relatedness and the systemic character of values-in-use

Even from their first breaths, and even in the most remote periods of time, men have been biased. Man, the subject, brings needs and purposes with it; only an understanding of the interplay of these, and how they relate to the world, will allow us to discover utilities or disutility. The utility of a thing or a service depends not only on the use but also on the *user*; it also depends on other objects and practices that can be found in the environment. The same thing may have different utilities for different men. If I have shelter and a warm bed for the night, then an available similar bed has less value-in-use for me. The fourth, fifth, and sixth things normally have generally less utility for me than the first thing (and the second or third, which may serve as reserves). The value-in-use of an additional, seventh ox may be negligible if my land is small. Its value-in-use also depends on whether I have substitutes, such as horses, slaves,[8] or tractors. High concept users, technologically or with regards to markets, can ascribe higher utilities to things than low concept users. If there are uses for rare earths or for a movie star in an advertising campaign for coffee, this is because a particular scientific and technological stage has been reached or a certain cultural environment with certain available marketing tools has arisen. If we combine the object- and use-relatedness, as presented in the previous section, and the subject-relatedness,[9] as presented in the present section, then we might even speak

---

8   On the advantages of using free labor, rather than slave labor, See *Weber* (1980) page 40 and 94 et seq.

9   Talking about value-in-use in terms of "*subject-relatedness of value*" means that every patient needs medicine that is correct for his specific illness and condition, that a hand injury causes more financial damage to a professional piano player than to a high school kid etc. This "subject-relatedness", though, has little to do with people seeing things too rosy, too grey, discretionarily or with error. Sound subject-relatedness of value ≠ subjective fallacy.

of a *systemic character of values-in-use*. Hundreds of millions of cables lose their values-in-use if large electronic firms change the types of their plug connections.

The state and time horizons for values-in-use

Quite obviously, values-in-use have time horizons. As grain rots, old grain has less value-in-use than new grain.[10] Everybody (robber individuals, war lords, gangs of bandits, social revolutionary movements, or even your neighbor) may rob from you at the next street corner whatever you obtained at the street corner before it, at least in a situation of anomy or civil war and if there is no law and no state with an effective monopoly on physical violence. Your house, your cattle, your harvest, and your land may be subject to requisition, whereby they lose much of their utility and of their value-in-use for you. This is because the *expected time span* of their use or utility goes down; it becomes uncertain but will very likely be much shorter than the time until its natural decay. If you are calculating advantages from the use of these objects, you will not know whether you can keep them for five days, five months, or five years. In fact, you will be aware that the more useful the object is for you, the more likely it will be that somebody will try to take it away from you. In anomy, thus, the time span you can keep it, depends on your proficiency at hiding or to defending it (either with your personal force and weapons, with your private army or at least thanks to a warlord who is friendly to you and who will hopefully continue to control the area and remain strong, friendly, and loyal to you). Unfortunately, there will be, in such circumstances, little motivation for you to engage in activities that require a lot of time and continuous effort to bring about results. Kill your cow, if you can, and distribute it amongst your family and friends and eat it up quickly because there is probably no point in raising cattle or sowing seed[11] or even filling storehouses with grains or smoked meat (unless, again, you have a strong army or warlord to protect you). Get weapons for yourself, if you can, to defend you (even if the weapons themselves might attract others to take them away from you). Production goes down dramatically in these Hobbesian situations of *bellum omnium contra omnes* where *homo hominem lupus*[12] (of which there were many throughout history and which should still be regarded as a point of departure for modern social sciences). Fields lie fallow, fences fall, irrigation systems decay, the number of cattle and horses shrink,

---

10 Therefore, it has also less value-in-exchange. See *Golas*, The Sung fiscal administration, p. 205, with regard to grain in granaries, which has to be replaced after some time being worth less than the amount need to pay for new grain ... at times of the Sung dynasty.

11 The increase of the planting of olive trees under Peisistratus is seen as an indicator of confidence in future prosperity. (*Burn* (1990) page 124).

12 Some say that Hobbes' metaphor missed the point, as wolves are not nearly as bad as humans.

deer is hunted, and fish are fished to extinction, trade collapses, bridges and roads degenerate.

All this was well understood already by the Chinese legalist state theorists of the 3rd century BC, e.g., *Han Fei*, and many centuries later by European natural law thinkers such as *Hobbes, Pufendorf*, and may others. Pacification is required and it is in the general interest that any *one* of the combatants (which may all be very horrible people) actually win. The victory of *any* warlord (or even of a bandit gang[13]) is, at the very least, much better than a continued state of war or of civil war. A certain softening of the state power is, in fact, very likely to occur not very long after victory (perhaps after one more proscriptive drive to preventively eliminate assumed remaining challengers). Despots learn that states must be run in a different way than the way in which they were conquered and that they need to find consensus, acceptance, and legitimacy (even if with a healthy dose of fear in the background). Ideologies or religions, which new regimes will promote, e.g., Confucius in Han China, Buddhism in T'ang China or Christianity in Christian Rome, will educate their promoter-despots themselves. If not, the despots' daughters and sons (sometimes even their wives, although this is less likely) may educate and moderate their fathers. Laws are drafted, judicial interpretations are finetuned, administrations develop routines, regularity and foreseeability evolves... Even the worst despots, if their regime only acquires a certain stability, thus, will likely soon bring some sense of security and raise values-in-use as people can enjoy uses from objects over longer terms. Agriculture resumes, the number of cattle and of horses recovers, bridges and roads are repaired, and trade quickly reaches and overshoots prior peaks. The governance of an undisputed monopoly state power – *status civilis* – endows goods with surplus value-in-use without any physical feature of these objects having been changed. We may even speak of a *state theory of value-in-use*, which explains the increase of the present value of things, due to the anticipated enjoyment of "future values-in-use"[14] over longer periods. "Etatism" sometimes works.

Value-in-exchange-attribution

We meet the features encountered in values-in-use at the level of values-in-exchange once again. Value-in-exchange is also object-related, subject-related, and both subjective and systemic. And it also depends on the state. Some aspects of this relationship still deserve a special emphasis.

---

13   E.g., *Chu Yüan-chang* (1328–1367), borne in a household of destitute farmers became a leader of the Red Turbans' rebellion against the Mongol Yüan dynasty and, under the name of *Hung wu*, later the founder of the Ming dynasty (1368–1644). See *Mote*, The rise of the Ming dynasty, page 44 et seqs.

14   As we know from business valuation, uncertainty and risk increase discount rates.

The state, owner power, and value-in-exchange

Once a monopoly of physical force of the state and the law are established, you cannot normally, as we have seen, take something away from somebody *without his consent*; this has tremendous structural and social benevolent consequences on the pacified territory. It not only greatly increases values-in-use, but also helps an exchange economy to take off, to develop, and to stabilize as a distinct and largely independent social system.

Make no mistake, though, the suppression of prior forms of violent and physical power and of tradition and myth only enables a regime of a different and new form of social power, of owner power. The basis of the new regime is the decision of owners to allow or forbid specific uses of their property. Pacification plus owner power is the *conditio sine qua non* of exchange and of the arrival of values-in-exchanges. Value-in-exchange accrues to goods – based on their value-in-use – because prospective users cannot access them except for by buying the owner's consent by paying. Other would-be-users will have to *lure* me with something they offer in exchange, but only if I am free to do what pleases me. Now society begins to think and talk about values-in-exchange and can move towards it as its main principle of distribution of goods.[15] As owner's power results from the power to exclude the non-haves from using objects owned by the haves,[16] it, of course, works best for those who already have considerable possessions, notably for large landowners, and less for small farmers and slaves. It will also become the basis for city landlords' power over those who seek shelter, and, in a famine, of merchants (who have filled granaries) over those who are hungry.

In a way, thus, all pricing is "power-based" and all prices are "monopoly prices" and "rent-seeking" from the very beginning. This monopoly power of owners is only mitigated by competition from other owners,[17] and if that competition ends for some reason, then the original pure owner power becomes visible once again as monopoly power. Therefore, owners react to competition by setting up coalitions, cartels, and alliances, etc. to reduce its detrimental effects on their collective power

---

15   Quesnay sees this so clearly that he puts it in capital letters: "LA SÛRETÉ DE LA PROPRIÉTÉ EST LE FONDEMENT ESSENTIELL DE L'ORDE ÉCONOMIQUE DE LA SOCIIÉTÉ." *Quesnay* in Cartelier (2008) page 238. See also *Macpherson* (1962).

16   See, e.g., Sect. 903 of the German Civil Code: "The owner of a thing may, to the extent that a statute or third-party rights do not conflict with this, deal with the thing at his discretion and exclude others from every influence."

17   There is an interesting evolution in the views on competition in the history of economic thought. Quesnay derives competition as a cheap substitute for *policing*, which forces the merchants to fulfil their role in his royaume agricole. "Qu'on maintienne l'entière liberté du commerce; car la police du commerce extérieur et intérieure la plus sure, la plus exacte et la plus profitable à la nation et à l'état consiste dans la pleine liberté de la concurrence." (*Quesnay*, Cartellier (2008) page 244).

(organizing cooperation between owners instead of letting the prisoner dilemma damage them). At the next level, states pass antitrust and anticartel laws to mitigate owners' power.

The non-owners (without significant land, other means of production, etc.) also live in a general "ownerhood"-structure, in a world of possessive individualism. As such, they are at least not slaves and are not bound to some plot of land, but are instead in control of their body and of their brains and, hence, of their labor power. They can, thereby, exercise supplier power in the labor market and, at least to the extent that they have earned salaries, also enjoy some power as demanders in consumption goods markets. The liberty of owners of all sorts to decide on what they own is the very basis of market discipline and for the value-in-exchange of a commodity becoming relevant in both profit economies and in capitalism more generally. As soon as both sides march into markets, they know, before their first encounter, that they will be subjected to the power resulting from the owners' power of other owners which is guaranteed by the state and by the law.

Theory of value and theory of "deal-making" and pricing

Many authors have propagated the view that equal values exchange against each other, in principle at least, which implies that the paid price is also, at least in principle, the commodity's value-in-exchange. Marx, being one of these authors, made this proposition a corner stone of his economics and called it the "brazen law of value" (ehernes Wertgesetz). Many practical people are to be blamed for making the same mistake. E.g., jurists typically assume that in transactions, e.g., in M&A-transactions, the price paid corresponds to the business-value. They, therefore, refer to the relationship between the price and the transferred business as "equivalence" and, if they find that, e.g., due to a deception or a breach of warranty, the price has to be adjusted, then they speak of the "adjustment" of the "equivalence". However, the theorem of an exchange of equal values, whether of Marxian or whatever origin, is meaningless and fallacious.

We can already see intuitively that something is wrong with the idea: First, why would businesses be so desirous to dispose of their produce if they were as wealthy before (with their produce) as afterwards (with the sales proceeds)? Moreover, why would sellers, if a buyer wants to return a commodity, normally refuse to repay the price received? Second, if bookkeeping conventions try to give a fair and true view of a business's financial position, why do they not already allow for capitalization if the production of a commodity is only completed? Why only after the commodities have been sold and delivered? Third, how come manufacturers give away commodities to intermediary traders for 70 % of the resale price, or even less? Fourth, and finally, when a bank assesses a person's credit worthiness, would it not normally – as an expert in value – prefer to see that person holding an amount in cash rather than owning furniture just purchased for that same amount?

We can distinguish between a *theory of value* and a *theory of deal-making* and we can combine it with another distinction, which comes from mathematics, between *mono*mial *theories* and *poly*nomial (*bi*nomial) *theories*. There are monomial theories of seller's value, buyer's value, and bystander's value, which follow a single mono-logic, and there is a polynomial (here binomial) theory of when a deal is struck, which is also a theory of pricing.

(Monomial) theory of value: Seller's value, buyer's value and bystander's value

The proposition that "commodities exchange at *their* values" is irreconcilable with the *value's subject-relatedness*. Different valuation subjects have different utilities, concepts, and synergies and they, therefore, also have different subject-related values-in-use and values-in-exchange. Accordingly, there is simply *no* such thing as the *"one and only value-in-exchange"* of a commodity, of a business, or of anything; there are always two at least, normally many more.

The *value-in-exchange attributed by the buyer* comes from utility – but that means what, exactly? Assuming a *single commodity* is an investment good (to allow quantification in money units), such as equipment or inventories, he will look at his present financial state without the commodity and at a (by that time still fictive) financial state with the commodity; he will do so by setting up two business plans and by calculating present values. If the present value of his business with the commodity is sufficiently higher than the costs of the commodity (considering alternative investments), then he will try to buy. If we look at the other side of the trade, we might ask: Where does the value-in-exchange attributed by the seller, come from? It does not come from his costs of production plus the added profit margin. It is true that the seller hopes to recover his costs and to make a profit (and will only continue producing under this assumption), but if a seller hopes to sell for a certain amount, he does not attribute value-in-exchange to a commodity; only non-owners of the commodity in question with the needed financial means and the will to sacrifice them can do this. Still, the commodity may retain some other value-in-exchange, but how much? The general answer is: If the seller can use the commodity to generate a surplus by holding onto it, e.g., if he can use a horse on his fields or if a builder can rent out a house that he has built for sale, then the seller's value-in-exchange will at least be the present value of his surpluses from the use of the horse or from the leasing out of the house. If the commodity, if it is kept in the seller's property, does not generate such a surplus, e.g., a car in a car manufacturer's storehouse, then the seller's value will only be the present value of the highest sales prices that he can expect (adjusted by costs of storage, marketing, etc.).

If the purchase or sale of a business is considered as a whole (in M&A), then the approaches taken by sellers and purchasers will not be different. The purchaser will plan the surpluses of the purchased business, on the basis of his specific concepts, synergies, and dis-synergies and will compare its present value to his specific alternative investment opportunities. The seller of a business will compare the purchase price that he will receive to the present value of the surpluses if he continues to run the business "stand alone". We may call this valuation *cardinal*.

If a consumer values a meal, a piece of furniture, a vacation, or another consumption good, then the value-in-use or utility for him is too fuzzy to be expressed in a cardinal number (as x or y Euros). The consumer will, guided by his budget limitations and, after having taken other goods into consideration for which he has esoteric demand, normally only be able to attribute an *ordinal* number (as a rank of preference) thereto. From there, the consumer enters into a price negotiation with the seller.

All of this is also valid if we eliminate "bad subjectivity", error, misunderstanding, discretionary assumptions, or problems of anticipation. Even in a world of (fictive) perfect foresight, where "bad subjectivity" does not exist, attributed values-in-use and values-in-exchange are, thus, always "subject-related" because of different concepts, synergies, and dyssynergies (which all reflect subjects' different properties).[18] If we embrace the view that all value is subject-related, then it becomes clear that the statement "commodities exchange at their value" is meaningless, given that it does not tell us whether they exchange at the seller's value, at the buyer's value, or at the value of other competing or prospective buyers, such as the value attributed by bystanders.[19]

(Binomial) theory of deal-making and pricing

Assume men and women consider pairing up. It is clear that men have criteria and that women have (other) criteria. The result – a pair coming together – is only brought about if she meets his criteria and if he meets hers and if both have no better alternatives. Two sets of criteria, logics, or algorithms, a specific male and a female set, must coincide in order to yield a result. Interestingly, the success of paring-up can be described from each perspective in a monomial way (forgetting about the criteria of the other side). He may think "she is the wonderful and wealthy Rubenesque-lady that I have always dreamt of" – and may believe that this alone is the reason why they got together. Or she might think "he is the beautiful and slender intellectual I have always admired from French movies" – and may believe that that explains everything. Insofar, if the match-up works, monomial theories seem to

---

18   This speaks to the benefits of avoiding the expression "subjective theory of value" in favor of "subject-related theory of value". See: *Wächter/Wollny* (2018) page 80 et seqs.

19   The term "subjectivity of value" already implies this. With there being more than one subject, objects of exchanges should have *different* values. Yet, *Turgot* also saw that the commodity received must have a higher value for the purchaser than the commodity given away by the seller. See *Faccarello* (2016) page 79. *Menger*, too, saw the inequality of the value for the two parties (*Hoffmann* (1964) page 137). On the effects of this on damages in post M&A-disputes, see *Wächter* (2022), pages 552 and 587 et seq.

work as well. But that is a self-deception. Assume she loves body-builders – the slender intellectual will get nowhere. Thus, to truly function, a "theory of closure" or of "deal-making" or a "theory of pricing" must be binomial. The seller's *and* the buyer's algorithms, which are different, must allow an overlap-range of attributed subject-related values coming from two different points of departure.

As such, *mono*mial theories of deal-making quite simply do not work and the proposition that "commodities exchange at their values" must be substituted by the proposition that the buyer's value must be above the seller's value in order for a deal to be concluded. Only then will it be possible to agree on a price above the seller's and below or equal with the buyer's value-in-exchange; this enables both sides to increase their wealth and makes economic sense. The exchange is useless even if the buyer's value-in-exchange is only equal to the sellers' value; both parties only avoid worsening their situation, but nobody improves on this basis. Things travel to where they are valued most highly. This leads us to the observation that exchanges normally transport goods and services "uphill", from owners with less utility to owners with higher utility and investment goods are transported from low concept and low synergy sellers to high concept and high synergy buyers.

As we have seen, the fallacy of monomial theories of deal-making or of the "commodities exchange at their values"-proposal is often hidden. *If* a deal is concluded – in this case, there is an overlap of the price ranges by definition –, the agreed upon price can *always* be explained in two monomial ways from both perspectives. A monomial theory of deal-making can also explain why a deal failed very well. It can always argue that the buyer was not offering "the" value of the commodity (meaning the seller's value) or that the seller was asking more than "the" value (now meaning the buyer's value). However, monomial approaches continue to miss out on the fact that a price or an agreed valuation always depends on two different logics and two different valuations, which may or may not enable an overlap.

Nominalism and reflexivity in the theory of value-in-exchange

It is generally more realistic to be a "nominalist" than a "realist" within the meaning of the medieval debate between nominalists and realists. Value-in-exchange, as it is understood by believers in the labor theory of value, i.e., by Ricardo, Marx and his followers, is also in the grip of reifying "realistic" thinking. Value-in-exchange becomes a stuff, a mass or weight, an abstract substance or an abstract "real" property of objects. Although Marx elsewhere strongly, advocates capital as a *relationship*, he here flips into reification, and, via Hegel, even comes close to Plato. Let us phrase the issue in terms of the central question of medieval philosophy: Is value-in-exchange *ante rem* or *in rem*, as the realists, e.g., Plato and Aristotle, thought? Or is it *post rem*, *as the nominalists, e.g.*, Roscelin, Abaelard, Wilhelm von Ockham, and the Salamanca school thought? The correct answer must be that value-in-exchange is attributed *post rem*, much like how attraction of "mass" depends on other mass and love lies in the eyes and desires of others.

Value-in-exchange is also *reflective ab initio*. Value is not attributed by solipsistic units, which only observe and attribute value to things in parallel: Rather, everybody is also observing how the thing is observed and valued by others. One must observe the observations of others to fully "see the value". In a constructionist or systems theoretical expression, there is observation of observers, observation of the second or third degree. This leads to a feature of values-in-exchange which is as important as it is irritating: If only one agent values a single good, service, or business more highly than the subjective values-in-exchange of any number or other valuation subjects, then the *value-in-exchange of this object rises for everybody*. A price, which will realistically be paid in the market, feeds back at the level of values and moves up the value more generally. One might say that only the price, at which the commodity can be sold, moves up, but that underrates what actually happens. The readiness to pay a top price by the "top value attributor" (which goes along with the money and the will to sacrifice it) creates a new utility for everybody: buying the object and selling it to the top value attributor.[20] It is irrelevant for this effect to materialize, whether the top valuation is economically sound or erroneous. Even frivolous value attributions move the market, if they readiness to pay the top price is only serious, sufficiently lasting, and is accompanied by the purchase power required.

Hence: an erroneous, irrational, or outright absurd valuation, as long as it only materializes in a price offer, changes the world for everybody and justifies the same valuation by all secondary valuers whose secondary valuations will now be correct, rational, and responsible! It is like magic and a wrong valuation by one valuation subject (and consequential market behavior) renders the same valuation by all other valuation subjects correct! We can observe this in bubbles, e.g., in bullish real estate, bonds, or M&A markets. Real estate agents and investment bankers will tell buyers that they are lucky if they can still buy at 110 % of the price of last month and as they all continue to tell this story, it will vindicate itself and will propel the market higher. We have self-fulfillment and wrong statements render themselves correct. The mechanism has already been illuminated by Keynes when he compares the stock market

---

20   Three comments: First, there is obviously no certainty that the top valuer will stick to his valuation forever. Appreciation may end, utilities may change, or the purchasing power, which must join in, may be spent elsewhere or lost. Second, the margin by which the value attributed by the top valuer exceeds the new value will normally not be equal to the net procceds from a hypothetical sale thereto. Costs of sale and opportunity costs must be deducted and the top valuer may succeed in paying less than his top value etc. Third, as we have said, even if we favor using the notion "value-in-exchange" apart from price or expected price, "value-in-exchange" always remains dependent on future behavior – will they pay? – of third agents and, thus, also remains a prognosis. Disappointments, lucky surprises and radical uncertainty are ubiqutous, and economic theory must capture them.

to a particular kind of beauty contest: Not the most beautiful person is to be picked in this contest, but instead the person whom the majority of the jurors believe the majority of the jurors will pick. Keynes correctly speaks here of "the third degree, where we devote our intelligence to anticipating what average opinion expects the average opinion to be" being reached.[21] Systems theorists,[22] *Heinz von Foerster, Niklas Luhmann*, and *Dirk Baecker* for instance, are also working with second level and third level observations. If systems observe themselves, then there is second level-observation; if they observe self-observing systems, there is a third level-observation.[23] There is always third level-observation at work in the economic system: third observers observe observers observe. "Man kann anhand von Preisen... beobachten wie andere den Markt beobachten."[24] Valuation, as such, is intrinsically an observation of observers, i.e., observation of the second or third order. In "situations with thinking participants", according to *George Soros*, in what he calls his "theory of reflexivity", "the participants' view of the world is always partial and distorted. That is the principle of fallibility. The other is that these distorted views influence the situation to which they relate because false views lead to inappropriate actions. That is the principle of reflexivity".[25] Provided that we believe him, Soros owes much of his financial success to this theory.[26] The point is not solely that a deception is effective (that is often so, but deceptions still do not influence what they observe). The point is that deceptions stop being wrong and instead become true, indistinguishable from other truths, because they change what they observe. Bubbles are not systems of deception, but they do create true value which is as good as value can be as long as the

---

21   *Keynes* (1936) page 156.

22   For an introduction to systems theory see *Luhmann* (2011).

23   *Luhmann* (1984) page 25 and 593 et seqs.

24   "Via prices... one can observe how others observe the market", translation by the author, quoted from *Luhmann* (1988) page 18. This is already, as in Keynes' metaphor, "third level", given that prices already reflect observations. See also *Luhmann* (2002) page 136 and *Baecker* (2008 and 1988). Luhmann and Baecker see prices as the way of operation of the "internal autopoiesis of the system" and "values" as "representing the social relevance of economic occurrences" (*Luhmann* (1988) page 55). Hence, values belong to the non-economic parts of the social system. We differ in this point.

25   *Soros* (2010) page 10 and (2003). See also *Luhmann* (1974) page 92 et seq.; (2006) page 85 et seq.

26   Soros explains how he operates: "According to my theory of initially self-reinforcing but eventually self-defeating trends, the trend is your friend most of the way; trend followers only get hurt at inflection points.... Most of the time I am a trend follower, but all the time I am aware that I am a member of a herd and I am on the lookout for inflection points...This line of reasoning leads me to look out for the flaw in every investment thesis. My sense of insecurity is satisfied if I know what the flaw is....I know what is wrong while the market does not. I am ahead of the curve, watch out for tell-tale signs that a trend may be exhausted. Then I disengage from the herd..." (*Soros* (1995) page 12).

bubble lasts (just as thunderstorms lift up air). Value is homogenous, as long as it is there; as long as it remains there, it is not possible to distinguish reflexivity-driven value from other value. Everything is based on reflexivity – observing the observations of suppliers, of customers, and of competitors – and what may first be based on an error of judgement may vindicate itself and become a reality first for others and then even for the original inventor of the error; in that case, the error is no longer an error, in fact, it is indistinguishable from truth. Something was created that was originally false but which then became true, even for the creator. This effect is not reserved for lofty stock, bonds, FOREX, and derivatives markets but may, in principle, apply to all value-in-exchange, including even money.[27]

Attribution of value-in-exchange and "esoteric", "effectual", and "effective" demand

We have already touched several times on the fact that for demand to be economically relevant, it needs to be accompanied by purchasing power and the will to make the financial sacrifice of the payment. When *Adam Smith* referred to *"effectual"* demand, he meant exactly this, demand in the sense of a need or desire for something which was combined with both the purchasing power and the will to pay.[28] The name-giving "effect" of this "effectual demand" was, thus, *making the final purchase* in the second leg of M–**C**–**M'**, the money M' flowing to the firm for the commodity C. Accordingly, "effectual demand", points to the final goal of capitalist firms, whereby the initial investment is vindicated and the outlays are recovered with a profit. If there are either no means or no will to make the payment, including instances in which other expenditures take priority, then there is only *"esoteric"* demand (e.g., the hungry, the homeless, or the sick can have esoteric demands for food, shelter, or medical treatment, even if they cannot pay for them).

If people have money, then it is still a serious *sacrifice to part with it* in order to obtain a valued good. This is so because money represents the capability to make payments and, hence, to make purchases in the future. There is less left for future purchases after each payment, and he who pays increases his inability to be able to pay for desired goods in the future. Transferring money not only means transferring "payment capability" in one direction, it also means transferring "payment-

---

27   *Luhmann* greatly stresses the power of theories of reflexivity to feed back on the observed system; "Reflexionstheorie" has to "vor allem auf die durch die selbst mitbewirkten Zustandsänderungen (zu) reagieren..." (*Luhmann* (1988) page 81).

28   The term "effectual demand" was used by *Smith* (1776) Book I Chap. 7, to distinguish mere "physical demand" from demand with purchasing power. *Mill* refered to earlier writers having "... defined demand as "the wish to possess, combined with the power of purchasing" and continued "(to) distinguish demand in this technical sense, from the demand which is synonymous with desire, they call the former effectual demand." (*Mill* (1848) Book III, Chap. II., § 3.)

incapability" in the other.[29] In order to properly understand the economy, Niklas Luhmann argues, it may be more helpful to think of a flow "payment capability" in one direction and of "payment incapability" in the other, rather than thinking of a flow of goods in one and a flow of money in the other direction.[30] This view renders the function of the money code, which is to organize legitimacy for the distribution of scarce goods socially manageable, more palpable: Money solves the social problem of dealing with scarcity of goods by making legitimate access to scarce goods dependent upon payment of scarce money.[31]

If Keynes used the term "*effective*" demand, we believe, he, at least in many instances, meant something else than Smith's term of "effectual" demand.[32] He means demand, which already becomes "effective" at an *earlier stage* by the entrepreneur *making* (not receiving) money payments. This type of demand's name-giving effect is to initially *induce an entrepreneur to make investments* and to start a new circuit. If we apply Marx's M–C–M'-notation, the effect of Keynes' "effective demand" is already the *pay-out* of the amount M by the entrepreneurs that allows the circuit to be *started*. The first leg of **M–C**–M', the purchasing of equipment, inventories, and labor, is "effected", not only the later reception of the amount M' to conclude the circuit (by C–M').

Most importantly, "effective demand" remains "effective" in this regard even if the underlying expectation that there will later be "effectual demand" for the produce proves erroneous and if the investment is not vindicated. For macroeconomics or political economy,[33] thus, Keynes' "effective" demand is more important than Smith's

---

29   *Luhmann* (1998) page 134 f.; *Baecker* (2006) page 63. *Sismondi* (1827) page 379, 318 also uses the French word "sacrifice".

30   *Luhmann* (1998) page 136.

31   *Luhmann* (1998) page 252. To enable this, the money code, although it remains "communication" – the general mode of operation of social systems – acquires a particular property. While other communication only *share meaning* (the emitter does not give away what he shares), communication in the economic system becomes a *transfer*. The payor loses what the payee receives (page 247).

32   "... the effective demand is simply the aggregate income (or proceeds) which the entrepreneurs expect to receive..." (*Keynes* (1936) page 55). Or: "The actually realized results of the production and the sale of output will only be relevant to employment in so far as they cause a modification of subsequent expectations" (see Keynes (1936) pages 55, 47 and 25). Even if Keynes had meant the same thing as Smith, our distinction between "effectual" and "effective" remains helpful.

33   The traditional term "political economy" (with no named opposite; e.g., "economic economy", "physical economy" etc.) pointed to that part of the economy which was politically relevant. An understanding of political economy served princes, kings, and emperors to bring about growth and prosperity, to win wars and to avoid rebellions. The term macroeconomics (with microeconomics as its opposite) gives up "politics" as a criterion and implies a more neutral "small"/"big"-or "outer"/"inner" difference.

"effectual" demand because only Keynes' "effective" demand triggers circuits. The amounts paid out, as parts of effective demand to other firms for equipment and inventories and as salaries, are employment-generating spending; they refill the reservoirs which feed the worker's effectual demand in the future. Effective demand – set loose by the anticipation of future effectual demand – is key to greasing the economy's wheels. Whether there will be "effectual demand" allowing profits matters mainly for the generation of investing capitalists later; whether there is effective demand matters immediately for workers, other firms and everybody.

Merchant heroes and trade systems

The systemic character of values-in-use entails the possibility to jointly create higher values-in-use through cooperation. Millions of short-, medium-, and long-term, local, national, or supra-national trade chains, trade systems, or trade networks (we use trade systems) have come into being and disappeared throughout the course of economic history, like species throughout natural history. It is their destiny to always be in the process of being discovered, growing, fighting for survival, shrinking, or decaying – depending on whether the products of their cooperation are valued sufficiently. War heroes often come first. Those who conquer foreign territories, e.g., Ephialtes and Pericles for Athens, Alexander the Great for Macedonia, Scipio Africanus and Caesar for Rome, Charles V for Spain, William the Conqueror or Henry V for Great Britain, Louis XIV and Napoléon for France, Fredric the Great and Bismarck for Germany, thereby also lay the foundations for new trade systems; these systems naturally mostly favor the firms from the conqueror's country. The war heroes are often merchant heroes too; otherwise, merchant heroes follow soon afterwards, as the Venetian, Spanish, Dutch, or English merchants followed their fleets and military. Alternatively, there was a mix of adventure, private warfare, and commercial ingenuity from the outset, which is nicely captured in the term "merchant adventurers".[34] Merchant heroes were also occasionally scientists or technicians, who built trade systems around new technologies, or social innovators, great marketeers or salesmen who built them around new products or services or new ways to distribute them (without warfare), the Fugger, the Hanse merchants, James Watt, Thomas Edison, Gottlieb Daimler, Henry Ford, Bill Gates, Steve Jobs, Jeff Bezos, and Mark Zuckerberg.

The crucial breakthrough sometimes came from venturing into oceans that nobody had crossed before and from discovering new continents, as Columbus had, from opening new routes of travel and commerce for goods and men on land and water, such as the silk road, the trading places of Hanseatic League, the traffic to the Americas, the Magellan Street, or the sailing route around the Cape of Good Hope.

---

34   See *Graeber* (2011) page 293 et seq.

Merchant heroes were also builders of Canals, such as of the "Great Canal" connecting the southern rice patties of China to the northern capitals for centuries, or the Panama- or Suez-Canal. Merchant heroes also introduced new methods for men and goods to travel, by boat, ship, railway, car, truck, airplane, drones, spacecraft, etc.

Once trade systems were established, e.g., a logistic infrastructure to carry great loads through a desert by a sufficient number of camels, less adventurous people followed to stabilize, administer, and optimize them, like sons of the Roman nobility or of the British gentry in their respective Empires. They attracted and directed flows of goods and capital and educated and disciplined the traders, political powers, and workers along their routes to provide their services and to accept appropriate remuneration. New trade systems always encounter opposition from those involved in old trade systems, with the latter often representing the wealthy and powerful of their times who were supported by states, ideologists, and priests. A battle between trade systems lay behind many bloody wars. If new trade systems win, as they mostly do, at least after some time, their profiteers, of course, turn conservative and now it is up to them to seek the support of states, ideologists, and priests to petrify the situation.

Trade systems follow the principles of value-in-use and value-in-exchange generation and are relational, systemic, and synergetic. The trade system dies, beginning at the end product, if the utility disappears, which is served by the end product. Not only is, then, the end product itself cleared from the shelves of the retail dealers and from the storehouses of the wholesalers, but the raw materials and semi-finished and spare parts also lose their utility. As the production of the input grinds to a halt, no one requires the old services of the different intermediaries, agents and brokers, banks, consultants, lawyers, translators any more. A breakdown of a trade system may also start from the early chain links. If mines of a raw material are exhausted, e.g., the silver mines of ancient Athens in Laurium or the Spanish silver mines in Potosi in Bolivia,[35] then security people, policemen, bartenders, cooks, shopkeepers, and prostitutes in Laurium and Potosi can go home and many jobs on the road to Athens and in the ports and cities of Havana, Seville, or Cadiz will be lost. The chain may also break in the middle: If *Lin Zexu*, a Chinese official, succeeded in enforcing the prohibition on the English to import opium into China in 1839,[36] the English Triangle trade (luxury goods from the UK to India, Opium from

---

35   Between 1556 and 1783, writes *Ferguson* (2008) page 24, the Spaniards carried 45,000 tons of pure silver from Potosi to Seville, leading to the value of the metal dramatically declining and to the "price revolution" of 1540–1640 in Europe. According to *Beck/Bacher/Hermann* (2017) page 46, 17 million kilograms of silver and 181,000 kilogram of gold were carried to Spain from Peru and Mexico.

36   *Ferguson* (2008) page 290. It is noteworthy that the British historian *Ferguson* also refers to the British Empire as "...history's most successful narco-state" (page 291). If Lin Zexu, the

India to China, tea from China to the UK) would have been severely damaged, not just with regard to opium in storehouses in Calcutta, but also with regard to tea in storehouses in Shanghai and luxury goods in storehouses in Liverpool. Wars and natural catastrophes can interrupt trade systems at any link. They may destroy production facilities, render raw materials inaccessible, drive away or kill labor, disconnect logistic transportation lines, or block activities through a pandemic.[37] Parts of former unified supply systems, if interrupted and much like a worm cut into half, seek to survive separately. The lower part, which is closer to raw materials and basic inputs, will attempt to develop alternative products in order to sell them to wholesalers; this part and the upper part will study sales markets and look for suppliers of more promising goods. However, if the upper part of the lower, cut-off, part does not find new customers quickly, then it will lose its lower end. If the lower part of the upper cut-off part does not find new suppliers quickly, then its upper part will also disconnect. While the parts of the "worm" fight for survival, of course, the market for the end-users may be taken over by substitute products from completely new trade systems.

The pacegeneticity and bellogeneticity of trade systems

Domestic, regional, and international trade systems may favor and induce both peace or war – but it is difficult to anticipate if they will turn *pacegenetic* or *bellogenetic* in the individual case. Malthus spelled out this paradox. On the one hand, easily accessible sales markets and many other supplier firms may be great for each other: "It is... a ...general rule in political economy, that the wealth of a particular nation is increased by the increasing wealth and prosperity of surrounding states ...". However, Malthus qualifies in the same sentence, that this is only valid "...*if these states are not successful competitors in those branches of trade in which the particular nation had excelled.*"[38] Hence, the increasing wealth must lead to increased "demand for its products, and call forth more effectively its resources." "But", Malthus goes on to remark, "if this rule [meaning the positive effect of wealthy surrounding states] be repeatedly insisted upon without noticing the above most important limitation, how is the student in political economy to account for some of the most prominent and best attested facts in the history of commerce. How is he to account for the

---

leader of the Chinese "war on Opium", had Opium thrown into the sea, the Cantonese variant was not quite as successful as its "Boston" predecessor. Rather, the English won, reinstalled the freedom for their trade and annexed Hong Kong.

37   Today's capitalism, driven by highly leveraged financing and low costs of communication and transport, has an aggressive bias for huge interdependent "un-robust" trade systems in space (many partial inputs) and time ("just-in-time-delivery"). Since the Corona crisis many business leaders now praise stable supply structures, but they will soon resume the hunt for cost savings through riskier supply chains.

38   Italics added.

rapid failure of the resources of Venice under the increasing wealth of Portugal and the rest of Europe, after the discovery of a passage to India by the Cape of Good Hope,[39] the stagnation of the industry of Holland, when the surrounding nations grew sufficiently rich to undertake their own carrying trades, the increasing trade and wealth of Great Britain, during the war of the French Revolution, under the diminishing trade and increasing poverty of the greatest part of Europe, and the comparative distress of America, when other states were enabled to participate in those trades, which as a neutral she had carried on during a great part of the late war with such signal success."[40] In other words, large markets with easy access, many firms, and rich neighbors are *not always* good for businesses in the surroundings, but may also kill them. Whether accumulations of other firms are *benevolent* or *malicious* for their fellow firms depends on the roles these other firms (and their mother countries) play in trade systems and upon whether they nurture trade systems with cheap inputs (in a complementary way) or as rich voluminous demanders of the end product – which is both benevolent and yields love and peace –, or whether they compete for cheap supplies and demand for the end product – which yields dislike, hatred, and may mean war. Profit economies and capitalism are, in other words, pacegenetic and bellogenetic *depending on the circumstances* and, at the same time, may *be pacegenetic or bellogenetic in different directions*. Explanation for all this can already be found in trade systems. Much warfare in capitalism may already be conditioned as deep as at the level of the theory of value.[41]

Our elementary economics of profit economies will now move on to examining the issues of money and of money creation.

---

39 Doing away with the century old Asian Spice Road, see *Ferguson* (2008) page 128.

40 *Malthus* (1836) page 13.

41 As *Polanyi* (1944) puts it: "In the past the organization of trade had been military and warlike; it was an adjunct of the pirates, the rover, the armed caravan, the hunter and trapper, the sword-bearing merchant, the armed burgesses of the town, the adventurers and explorers, the planters and conquistadores, the man-hunters and slave-traders, the colonial armies and chartered companies" (quote from page 16). Only the 19th century shows "a decisive turn in favor of measures to safeguard the economic system in times of war" (page 16). He connects this to haute finance, that functioned as "The main link between the political and the economic organization of the world" (page 10). "They [the Rothschilds] were anything but pacifists; they had made their fortune in the financing of wars; they were impervious to moral consideration; they had no objection against any number of minor, short or localized war. But their business interest would be impaired if a general war between the Great Powers should interfere with the monetary foundations of the system". (p. 11).

Section 2. Money and money creation

Most economists, philosophers, sociologists, historians see the crucial thing in
money in its being a practical intelligent technical improvement over barter and
in state fiat money in its being a similar improvement over commodity money
(gold and silver). In addition, they are interested in theoretically understanding the
"phylogenetic" origin of money and of state fiat money, as a social invention, a technique, a structure, an institution, or as a code or as a media of communication as
a more academic issue. These are all, indeed, interesting and important questions.
However, the crucial thing about money, for a theory of capitalism, which includes
its prosthetics, is neither the general origination of money nor the technical advantages, which money and state fiat money carry. It rather is that in an *existing*
world of money, you may be able to create more of this scarce and powerful stuff,
already via merchant credit money creation, much more via private bank credit
money creation and limitlessly more via state fiat money creation. In particular,
state fiat money gives a power to the states, which is often more valuable than all
its policemen and soldiers. It is also the single method of the state to procure value
without having to take something away from somebody else and using force. In
other words, it makes a lot of sense to look at money backwards from what it can do
today

If we take this into account, then the insight may strike us that the rather recent ultimate historic transition from commodity money, gold and silver, to state
fiat money in 1971 (paper, token coins and account entries with no right of conversion into commodity money) may not have been due to the greater elegance, prac-
ticability, and cost efficiency, etc. of state fiat money over commodity money, but
primarily to state fiat money radically easing money creation, to an extent, which
was far beyond alchemist hopes.

Yes, money creation also existed prior to state fiat money, but how clumsy it was
to find gold or silver and to mine it (or to rob it)! In fact, even money creation by
merchants and private fractional reserves banks, as we shall see later, while much
more powerful than finding and mining or robbing gold and silver, turns out only to
be an intermediate stage on the way to state fiat money and to state alchemy at an
industrial scale.

Money

Many "left-wing" economists – Sismondi, Marx, Keynes, Kalecki, Minsky – occupy
prominent places in this book. However, regarding insights into money, money creation, and fiat money this book owes more to the other side of the spectrum. Marx
made a few interesting and critical remarks about money creation in the third volume of *Capital*, but even he presented himself as more amused by just another of

capitalism's absurd features, rather than trying to systematically work out the issue. Keynes, obviously, deals more with money, but mainly with bank credit money creation and this did not have a great effect on his *General Theory*. More recently, radical social anthropology, e.g., *David Graeber*, and so-called *modern monetary theory*, which may be regarded as "left-wing", have also expressed certain insights. However, the greatest contribution to a critical analysis of monetary phenomena still comes from the "Austrian Economists", and from their conservative branch in particular. As radical liberals and political supporters of conservative middle-classes, this branch of the "Austrians" abhorred socialist, semi-socialist, and national-socialist state interference, particularly in monetary matters, and fought to defend "pure capitalism". For this purpose, they liked sharp terms and notions. Their work is, thus, a good starting point for monetary analysis. For this book *Ludwig von Mises'* critical theoretical analysis of monetary issues and money creation through credit money and fiat money is particularly important. Certain amendments will, however, also be necessary.[42]

Indirect exchange, media of exchange, and the origin of commodity money

After exchange and value-in-exchange appear in history, there is normally no lengthy period of barter before money appears too. Money allows you not to wait until, by chance, somebody shows up at your place, at the right time, who needs what you have and *also* offers what you desire. Money, rather, renders it sufficient that somebody wants what you offer, here and now, and somebody else, later and even elsewhere, has and offers what you want; credit allows us to even turn the sequence

---

42   The name "Austrian Economists" may have originally been invented to ridicule thinkers coming from a country better known for alps, opera, and Mozart kugels than for economic theory, but the name later grew into an expression of respect for notional sharpness and intellectual consistency. The political and theoretical orientation of the "Austrians" is, yet, far from homogenous. *Carl Menger*, alongside Jevons and Walras, invented the subjective theory of value and marginalism, *Eugen von Böhm-Bawerk* authored strong early criticism of Marx's labor theory of value– Karl Marx and the close of his system, 1898 –, which should already have buried it. *Josef Schumpeter's* work contributed to a better understanding of entrepreneurship, and its financing, and provided deep insights into the history of economic theory. He was also an important theoretician of democracy (Capitalism, Socialism and Democracy, 1942). Moreover, Schumpeter was a colorful person who allegedly took Vienna prostitutes to the Vienna Opera in convertibles to make a point and challenged the director of the Vienna library to a duel because of the early closure of its reading room (well done!). *Friedrich von Hayek* was less picturesque than Schumpeter. Yet, he delivered a fierce and important critique of state interference and saw money creation, fiat money, and inflation as milestones on "the road to serfdom". While the conservative branch of the Austrians was not quite as insightful about the limits of capitalism, it was, indeed, very insightful in almost everything else. In this book, we mainly refer to the powerful monetary theories of *Ludwig von Mises*.

around.[43] Money splits up barter into two transactions, a sale and a purchase, and shifts itself in between as a *media of exchange* that connects these two transactions. Von Mises called the separation of sale and purchase "indirect exchange".[44] Indirect exchange renders the economy much more effective and greatly contributes to the propagation of the economic system. These practical advantages, which money conveys, cannot be denied and they are rightly used to explain the money's rapid historic success as an institution. While we do not deny their relevance, we might add that M–C–M'-players have a particular interest in the dissemination of the use of money.[45]

Marx, of course, tried to use his theory of labor value to explain how the value-in-exchange arrived in commodity money and to derive a dialectic explanation of money therefrom. However, he only carried the mystification, which is immanent in his labor theory of value, one step further – into money. Recent radical social anthro-pologists and so-called modern monetary theorists tend to attack the view of money as essentially a valuable *thing* and try instead to explain it as a *debt-relationship*. We do not agree, as will be explained below. In credit money (bank deposits, bank notes, bank token coins of non-precious metals, or claims against states/central banks to convert state notes or entries on state accounts into gold or silver) money may, in-deed, appear as debt, but money's decisive general property, on the contrary, lies in its capacity to *fulfill* claims, do away with debt, and absolve from it.

Von Mises places interest in the question of what kind of commodity will be se-lected as a medium of exchange. If I want to exchange something in a system of barter, I will observe that there are commodities that are "more sought" in the mar-ket by more counterparties. I shall seek to obtain these more sought out and more marketable commodities in order to make the exchanges, which will get me what I want quickly. I shall, thus, attempt to "move up on the ladder" to the more desired or more "liquid" commodities. In *von Mises*, this ultimately leads to the *general selection* of one or several commodities as preferred media of exchange which, thereby, be-come "*commodity money*". "A medium of exchange is acquired neither for the purpose of its consumption nor for the employment in productive activities but with the in-tention of exchanging it at a later date..."[46]. The best suited media of exchange are those that have widely sought-after values-in-use, can easily be split into parts, are endurable, and have high value-in-exchange to weight ratios. Commodities, which

43   Money is generally seen as freeing exchange on the spatial, time, and personal levels, (e.g., *Felderer/ Homburg* (2003) page 78.

44   E.g. *von Mises* (1949) page 327.

45   See page 86. The advantages mentioned are often used to explain fiat money. That is a mis-take. Fiat money does not convey significant transactional advantages over credit money, which represents a claim for gold or silver.

46   *von Mises* (1949) page 401 and 405 et seq.

were highly fit for the monetary function were, thus, platinum, diamonds, grains, or gold and silver. Yet, from here on, we shall develop the argument in terms of gold and silver alone.

Commodity money, credit money, and fiat money

When von Mises wrote *The Theory of Money and Credit* (2nd edition of 1924), monetary theory still largely labored the distinction between "metallic money" and "paper money". Von Mises, quite rightly, discarded this distinction as superficial, misleading, and obsolete. The term "metallic money" encompassed money out of gold or silver, metallic coins with value-in-exchange outside of their monetary use, hence commodity money, as well as money out of non-precious metals, metallic "token money", which had no value-in-exchange outside of its monetary use; in other words, the term "metallic money" confused commodity money and state fiat money. "Paper money", on the other hand, included banknotes, which represented *legal claims* for the delivery of gold or silver against a bank or the state,[47] hence credit money, which is essentially as good as commodity money, (unless the debtor becomes illiquid), and fiat money, which involved no legally enforceable claim against the issuer for conversion. Thus, both sides of the distinction between "metallic money" and "paper money" confused apples and pies and hid the essential economic difference. Furthermore, the distinction wholly ignored the appearance of "deposit money" or "book money", consisting of credits on bank accounts[48] – a modern monetary phenomenon of the utmost importance.

Substantial insights into money, and in money creation in particular, require better distinctions than between "paper" or "metallic". *Von Mises* writes: "The economic theory of money is generally expressed in a terminology that is not economic but juristic. This terminology has been built up by writers, statesmen, merchants, judges, and others whose chief interests have been in the legal characteristics of the different kinds of money and their substitutes." However, he proceeds by saying that "...for purposes of economic investigation" this categorization "is practically valueless".[49] Von Mises then introduces a new terminology, one independent of legal or commercial distinctions, which serves the purpose of economic theory much better. He proposes three main monetary categories: *commodity money, fiat money, and credit money*: "We may give the name of commodity money to that sort of money that is at

---

47   Even "money certificates" or "money substitutes", which von Mises defines as fully and immediately liquid and as valuable as commodity money, see *von Mises* (2013) page 52.

48   "...for banknotes... and cash deposits differ only in mere externals, important perhaps from the business and legal points of view, but quite insignificant from the point of view of economics" (*von Mises* (2013) page 53). From a legal point of view, a credit entry on a deposit account represents a claim similar to a claim for repayment of a loan; yet economically it is already money in the form of "credit money".

49   *von Mises* (2013) page 59.

the same time a commercial commodity; and that of fiat money to money that comprises things with a special legal qualification. A third category may be called credit money, this being that sort of money which constitutes a claim against any physical or legal person. But these claims (which constitute credit money) must not be both payable on demand and absolutely secure; if they were, there could be no difference between their value and that of the sum of money to which they referred...".[50]

Von Mises' most fundamental distinction is between commodity money and fiat money. In *commodity money*, the money-thing itself is a commodity with value-in-exchange outside of its monetary use (e.g., oxen, grains, skins, silks, etc., cupper,[51] even iron, or, later, mainly gold or silver), while the money-thing has no value-in-exchange outside of its monetary use in fiat money.[52]

Commodity money, thus, has the "down-side protection" that even if it is demonetized, its holder still owns gold or silver with a market-value. If commodity money is ever artificially pushed underneath the value-in-exchange of its precious

---

50   *von Mises* (2013) page 61. In this statement, von Mises emphasizes the difference between commodity money and credit money in terms of the security and the speed at which the holder can access the underlying commodity. While this point is well made, for the purposes of our argument, the commonality between commodity money and credit money is more important. Commodity money "consists" physically of a commodity with value-in-exchange outside of its monetary function; credit money, while it consists only of paper, token coins, or bookkeeping credits, *also at least conveys a legal claim for the delivery of commodity money*. Commodity money carries the value-in-exchange "piggy back" and cannot even physically be separated from it, credit money. e.g., a bank note, only carries a legal claim for the value-in-exchange "piggy back". Fiat money carries nothing "piggy back".

51   Cupper was mainly used in China from the Ch'in to the Ch'ing dynasty over two thousand years of monetary history. Cupper money was commodity money, as far as its nominal value-in exchange did not exceed the market value of the cupper content. E.g., bronze, which is mostly made out of cupper, was an important export commodity in the Sung dynasty, just behind silk, tea and porcelain (*Golas*, The Sung fiscal administration, page 208). To the extent, the nominal value of cupper coins was above the value.in-exchange of the minted cupper, it was fiat money.

52   It should be noted that the "fiat" in fiat money does not suggest that its opposite, commodity money, may not be "man-made" or produced – of course, the typical commodity-money-things, gold or silver, are extracted from mines and often embossed and insofar man-made. Furthermore, the money-thing of commodity money possessing value-in-exchange prior to its monetary use does not mean that this value-in-exchange is "inherent", "intrinsic", "innate", "in rem", or God-given in the commodity-money-thing. *No value-in-exchange in human society is ever "in rem", but all value-in-exchange is attributed or ascribed.* Hence, commodity money does not force us to fall back on reifying thinking. In particular, economists who see themselves in the tradition of Austrian economists, should not fall victim to this fallacy. Many Austrian thinkers were heroes of subjectivist and constructionist reasoning; think of *Menger*, as the co-inventor of the subjective theory of value, of *Mach, Wittgenstein, Freud, Gödel* and of *Heinz von Foerster*.

metal content, then its holder can demonetize it and sell it as the precious metal it-self (disregarding its embossment). Fiat money has no such downside protection. Conversely, commodity money may acquire an *additional layer value-in-exchange* be-cause of their additional monetary utility. This layer can surface as an initial *seignorage* (as an excess of nominal value over and above the value of the precious metal) or through a later *debasement* of the precious metal content underneath the nominal value, both enabling a gain for the issuer. Von Mises points to this fact,[53] but does not delve into the issue further. The layer possesses all properties of *fiat money* and should be considered as a *fiat money-layer in commodity money*, given that this add-on-layer originates with monetization of a commodity and disappears again with its de-monetization. As fiat money creation in such add-on-layers is always quite lim-ited in volume, e.g., as the embossing state normally only collects a small seignorage, such add-on-layers only gained a limited relevance to fund of prosthetics. Still, the observation is important for theoretical reasons.

Credit money, as we have already observed, includes bank notes, tokens coins, or credit entries on deposit accounts, *if* they convey a claim for conversion into commodity money.[54] The legal claim for conversion is independent of the respective credit money's monetary use and survives it; accordingly, if the credit money has been demonetized, the creditor still holds a claim against the issuer, e.g., the bank, for commodity money. Obviously, if the debtor also becomes illiquid or the legal system collapses too, then credit money may get as bad as fiat money – but other-wise credit money is superior. Accordingly, *credit money also provides some downwards protection*, like commodity money and unlike fiat money, but only in the amount of the value-in-exchange of the claim for commodity money. As it is normally better to own a thing than a claim for that thing, this conversion-claim is normally less valuable than its ultimate goal: commodity money itself; the creditor carries the risk of insolvency of the issuer, the "address risk"; he has a "default concern". On the other hand, in exceptional circumstances, as the claim is directed towards standard quality and a standard weight of gold or silver, if the bank remains solvent, the claim may even be somewhat "better" than specific commodity money (1) as coins of commodity money are exposed to risks of wear and tear, debasement or fraud

---

53   *von Mises* (1949) page 408.
54   "Credit money" might, thus, also be called "claim money". We repeat that *von Mises* restricts the term credit money to such claims that are *not* perfectly and absolutely secure and imme-diately due and, thus, *no* "money certificates" or "money substitutes" and that, hence, they are not as good as commodity money. See *von Mises* (1949) page 432 et seq. In this book, we use the term *credit money* for all money whose value-in-exchange comes from the con-veyance of a legal claim, irrespective of whether reserves are held or where the claim is fully valuable.

or (2) if you live under circumstances in which you are in danger of losing your commodity money, e.g., in case of a shipwreck, or of being robbed.[55]

The question of reserve holding (full or fractional reserves) must be seen as a separate matter. It concerns a special banking issue; it is comparable to an airline allowing a special flight to be overbooked or not allowing it. It must be well distinguished from the issue of the general solvency of the bank or of the airline. Even if a flight is overbooked, and a passenger misses their flight, they will receive their fare back from the airline – as long as it is solvent. If the airline is insolvent, then he misses the flight and loses the fare paid. Equally, a fractional reserve bank may be solvent, or a full reserves bank, like an airline who does no overbooking, can become insolvent.[56] We have a first hint here concerning an important distinction, to which we will return later.

Fiat money, von Mises' third main category,[57] is at the other extreme end of the spectrum. The money-thing in a fiat money regime neither has value-in-exchange outside of its monetary use, nor does it convey a claim for a commodity with such value-in-exchange. It is still the best and most convenient money one can have as long as the fiat money remains monetized. Fiat money is normally state fiat money; it can, as a rule, only come into being alongside the introduction of a general fiat money regime by a state.[58] Three strategies are typically applied to support fiat

---

55   This was so in the early years of the *Amsterdam Wisselbank*, when its credit money was allegedly often preferred over commodity money as the money holders were relieved of checking coins for wear and tear and were less exposed to robbery or theft.

56   Note that even a bank that holds 100 % reserves for deposits, bank notes and token coins issued, it is not protected against insolvency. The statement that a bank holds 100 % reserves for issued bank credit money only looks at the relation between *certain assets* on the asset side (gold or silver holdings) and *certain liabilities* on the liability side (conversion liabilities for bank credit money), yet the bank's solvency depends on more.

57   Monetary theory uses the distinction of *exogenous* and *endogenous* money. If a system of commodity money exists, then the gold and silver or other precious metal money is said to have been determined exogenously. Likewise, if fiat money exists, then the money issued by the central bank is said to have been determined exogenously. On the other hand, if banks create money by granting circulation credit out of fiduciary media of exchange, then the money supply is said to have been expanded endogenously. From our perspective, money creation by the state or by the central bank and money creation by private banks are functionally very similar. That being said, it is true that state fiat money creation is much more powerful than private bank credit money creation.

58   The transition to state fiat money is probably easier than is often believed. There is no necessity to first build up a general consensus or significant trust in the society at large. People will initially only need to hold onto a small portion of their wealth in fiat money, so small that this is almost riskless. Trying out fiat money with such riskless amounts will greatly strengthen it everywhere. A few years ago, the National Museum of India in New Delhi exhibited *shells*, which were allegedly used as money in the very early strong local city-community of Harappa, which was a part of the Indus Valley Culture (IVC; 2600–1900 BC). Given

money regimes, (1) states *accept fiat money to pay state taxes*; this is the most important strategy; it adds a Chartalist moment to von Mises' theory, (2) to make fiat money *legal tender*, thereby forcing private citizens to accept it as payment for private debt instead of gold or silver (even if it may sometimes be difficult to enforce), and (3) to *suppress gold and silver (or other commodities, e.g. cupper, iron and silk) as commodity money* as an alternative medium of exchange, e.g., by trying to absorb it by the state or the central bank, and illegalizing its monetary use and private gold and silver possession etc.

The value of state fiat money and the reasons for its acceptance

State taxes, legal tender, and fiat money

We shall begin our account of "the value of state fiat money" and the reasons for its acceptance with a historical argument, which departs from a case made by *David Graeber*. He proposed a theory of how small unit money coins originated in direct connection with warfare by mass armies, a "*mass-army-theory of money-coins*", which introduces into the issue very well. The need for humans to eat, drink, and for some fun does not go away during warfare, of course. In very simple and local conditions, it is taken care of by warriors carrying subsidies for a few days with them (and then going home to re-fill their supplies). Later, tribes or states establish lines of communications and transport supplies to their armies' camps. In historic mass migrations, when whole tribes moved slowly to distant target locations over decades, the fighters were supported by their villages, which followed their moves. In all of these cases, the supporters at the "home front" were rewarded by the outcome of the war – by receiving a share of the loot or by not losing their women, children, property, and life. Of course, warriors also always sought to source supplies in the theaters of war, plants from the field, hunted game, pastured cattle and, occasionally, robbed valuables; in smaller early ventures they appear to have done so mainly by force, without paying for local supplies.

The old-fashioned way of supply had to be adjusted as settlements and armies grew in size (to mass armies, e.g., enabled by the use of iron instead of bronze), as distances became larger, and as campaigns grew longer, e.g., for the armies of the Chinese Warring States period, for the Greek armies of the Persian and the Peloponnesian war, the armies of Alexander the Great, and for the Roman legions. Huger volumes of supplies had to be secured now in more distant and hostile environments.

---

the obvious convenience of using them and, e.g., assuming a lack of gold and silver, today's museum-visitor can easily imagine that they would have willingly accepted the mussels for small transactions as well, the acceptance of which would have helped to trigger a positive trust-spiral. (Yet, some historians also argue that the shells were mostly used for badges and ornament.)

Of course, that could still be done by force (and often was). However, if armies or soldiers could pay, such sources would flow more abundantly. In addition, supplies from home also took the form of a convoy of merchants following armies who sold their goods for money to the troupes and an increasing number of soldiers became mercenaries, who no longer fought for their home villages, tribes, or states – but for the pay. That money had to be in small and robust units, hence in coins, in order to pay the soldiers of the new mass armies.

Commodity money (gold and silver) was, of course, the money that was most easily accepted in the field. It would maintain its value even if it was issued by an enemy state and after this state was defeated, notwithstanding the coins carrying embossment or stamps of it. Athens was, thus, enormously lucky to discover a new rich streak of silver in its mines in Laurium (preceding the second Persian war) just as the Spaniards and Portuguese were to find and be able to (have the local population) mine tons of gold and silver in the Americas. Alexander the Great was equally lucky to even capture the Persian state treasure after the fall of Persepolis and some Persian mines[59] in 330 BC: Alexander is said to have paid out half a ton of silver to the 12,000 men in his army each day.[60]

However, Graeber's approach also allows us to explain war financing by fiat money. Taxation is crucial in this context: If states levy taxes and accept their own state fiat money to discharge tax obligations, then they thereby attribute value to the fiat money they issue, – even if the state fiat money would otherwise not be accepted as a general medium of exchange. In other words: The states give fiat money, e.g., coins, to soldiers, they give them to merchants and peasants for their supplies and cheap thrills, and the recipients can use them to pay taxes to the state. State fiat money coins not only work for those who directly receive them as "free passes" against taxation, but for anybody who is taxable. In this way, they become tradable. If the merchants and peasants who collect them are not taxable by the issuing states, then the coins flow to somebody who is (likely at a discount). Military suppliers of the state paid with coins (or notes) can also make good use of them, they can keep their gold or silver and still avoid tax execution, expropriation, prison etc. by using the fiat money.[61] The point is not that the tax-collecting state would be very eager to pocket its own fiat money chips again (it can create them anew at discretion anyway), but that taxable subjects, who do not want to spend their superior gold or silver, can use the state fiat money instead. The mechanism would even work, if states would, instead of collecting taxes in fiat money, force tax-"payers" to *burn* or otherwise destroy the amount of state fiat money, which was assessed as taxes

59   Graeber (2011) page 229.
60   Graeber (2011) page 229.
61   Graeber (2011) page 49 et seq.

against the respective individuals in a supervised manner– and then coin or print new money.

The mechanism, hence, must be understood as working backwards. The state first enshrines laws to pay taxes in commodity money (or fiat money) and, second, accepts fiat money as tax payments in order to give value to state fiat money.

This general idea was already developed by *Georg Friedrich Knapp*. Fiat money had value and was accepted for a *very solid and earthly reason*: It is a reliable means against state violence in a circuit set up by states and consisting of state fiat money spending and state fiat money tax collection. Fiat money, in other words, derives its value from the state's sovereignty and from state violence, and from the state's ability to levy taxes, fees, and other contributions specifically.[62]

Certain quantitative limitations apply: They can be best understood in situations, in which – like in Graeber's case of mass armies – lasting and stable stateship is not secured. First, state fiat money will work only with a view to the period ahead, in which the issuing state is expected to remain sufficiently strong to collect taxes. Second, the accepted volume of fiat money will be limited by the expected volume of the taxes (or other state contributions), which are likely collected in that period. "Excess-fiat money", fiat money beyond the volume, which can foreseeably be spent on taxes in the expected period of remaining strength of the issuing state, may, thus, only reluctantly be accepted; e.g., military suppliers may ask their deliveries to be partially paid in commodity money. In view of this mechanism, states can, absurdly enough, raise the volumes of useful state fiat money *by* increasing taxes, as this will open up new possibilities to make good use of it. While this reasoning shows limits concerning the propagation of state fiat money in situations of unstable stateship, it also implies that fiat money automatically acquires strength with an increasing ratio of taxation or the state quota to GDP and with increasing political stability of the state. The more Leviathan evolves into a Behemoth, a "social state", and the more undisputed it becomes, the stronger its fiat money.

States also attribute value to fiat money by forcing private creditors to accept fiat money as payment for private debt. Hence, states side with debtors and force creditors to accept payments in dubitable fiat money instead of in better commodity money. Thereby, fiat money becomes "legal tender". Rendering fiat money legal tender is, though, not nearly as effective in supporting fiat money as allowing taxes to be paid in fiat money. If the value of fiat money becomes dubitable, then creditors will simply only enter into exchange contracts if payment in "commodity money" is agreed or if other goods are bartered. "Legal tender" as a support-mechanism for state fiat money, thus, often weakens if it would be most needed.

---

62   See *Knapp* (1905) and *Polanyi* (1944) page 205: "The state… was in fact the guarantor of the value of token money, which it accepted in payment for taxes".

If a fiat money currency is demonetized, states may still accept it to settle taxes or, which has the same effect, exchange the old fiat money into a new state fiat money, such as when the German Mark was introduced in the former German Democratic Republic or when the Euro substituted the old currencies of the Euro-zone-countries. In more dramatic circumstances of demonetization – in the French Revolution, after the Russian Revolution, after the German hyperinflation of 1923, etc. –, states will, yet, typically not exchange the old currency into the new currency (at least at a reasonable rate) and will also no longer accept it for tax payments.[63] In this case, "demonetization" not only puts an end to the use of the fiat money currency as money in the markets and discontinues its status as legal tender, but it also abolishes its power as "free pass" against taxes. Leviathan, master of the law, as it created a kernel of value in fiat money at its introduction, destroys that kernel again and makes the fiat money completely worthless.

We conclude this section with a formal observation: Credit money (e.g., paper bank notes, non-precious token coins, and credit entries on deposit accounts) have a *legal claim* attached thereto. What underlies the value of state fiat money is different – in a way, it is the opposite. State fiat money only possesses the capacity to *fulfill* tax (and other state) claims. Fiat money is, thus, like a *set-off-potential*, a *counter-claim*, a *tax credit* (a credit usable against future state taxes, state fees, and state contributions), a *tax exemption*, or a *tax privilege*. If state fiat money has been made legal tender, this, in a way, also allows you to raise an objection against private creditors of yours who asks for commodity money; you can send them home with mere state fiat money. Fiat money is, in other words, only good for defense. Its value can only be realized if you are a debtor already. If you rend a visit to Leviathan and tell him: "See I have this amount of your fiat money, please give me gold for it, or a house, or food...", Leviathan might shake his head. "But", he might add "... wait until I tax you, which I certainly will, – then I will have to take it and you can get rid of your fiat money!"

Additional comments on state fiat money

A few comments on state fiat money may be added. The first is that a reflective mechanism doubles up on the power of the hard kernel of value of fiat money derived from its power to discharge taxes and of its being legal tender in stable, normal situations. In such situations, everybody expects everybody else to accept fiat money and expect fiat money to be accepted in the medium term at least. Therefore, people will not worry and calculate volumes of tax volumes, execution power of the state, etc. but will simply *trust* that the fiat money will be accepted in at least the near future. We

---

63   The German middle classes, which were by the hyperinflation of 1923 would have loved to be allowed to continuously use their pre-inflation "Mark"-notes to pay their taxes.

are, thus, again, in the arena of self-fulfilling prophecy or reflexive witchcraft of society. We have already pointed to the astonishing fact that observations, that can be straightforwardly incorrect at the beginning, if observed by others, have the miraculous capacity, to not only practically justify themselves because everybody shares the error, but to render themselves right and true and dissolve the "errorness" of the idea at a second level. Because this works even in favor of initially clearly false observations, it will work even more powerfully for observations which already initially have a kernel of truth, such as the state's acceptance of fiat money for tax payments.

Second, we see that state fiat money is not based on some kind of implicit "social contract", whereby the members of society agree to give up their archaic obsession with bulky commodity money or credit money and progress to a modern, more civilized, more enlightened, and more efficient type of money. The ascent of fiat money is also not due to society's collective insight that money does not need to possess an "intrinsic value" to fulfill its function". This "modernization" or "rationalization"-theory of fiat money misses the fact that the weakening of the value of money, which comes along with fiat money, does not go as far as it assumes. It fails to see the surviving, strong "materialistic" moment in fiat money, which is as strong as the modern state.

Third, there is both some justification as well as a possibility to tumble into fallacy when using semiotics to analyze monetary phenomena. Von Mises' original German word for fiat money was "Zeichengeld", literally translated as "sign-money",[64] which at least carries a trace of semiotics. And in fact, the question is legitimate: Should one not look at state fiat money as a *sign*, whose *signifier* would represent commodity money as its denotation or as the signified (albeit, admittedly, without conveying a claim for its delivery)? This signifier-signified-model could elegantly explain why, if the gold or silver content in coins is lower than the nominal value (because of seignorage or debasement), the coins may still keep their value-in-exchange. The reasoning could go: The value-in-exchange of the substance of the coin, realizable outside of its monetary function, goes down; however, this loss is compensated for by a semiosis simultaneously raising the signified value, so that the total of the hybrid value of the coin (a mix of the market value of the gold or silver substance and of the value communicated by the semiosis) remains the same.[65] As nice

---

64   Here a translation freed a term of a misunderstanding that the original term nurtured. This book would not have used the term "Zeichengeld" as prominently as it uses "fiat money".

65   If an originally 100 % gold-coin is successively debased by 100 %, but retains its nominal value, then this could, accordingly, be explained as 100 % of the market value of the gold in the former commodity money or "currant money" having been substituted by "semiotic value". This could operate on a gliding scale, with a nominal value of money always being backed by a mix of commodity value content and "semiotic" value content.

as it sounds, this semiotic approach is fallacious for two reasons. (1) It silently pre-supposes that "money proper" ought to be gold or silver with an "intrinsic" value and concludes, from that presupposition, that if state fiat money is used, then it ought to at least denote "money proper". We cannot agree with this. (2) It ignores the true "materialistic" power of state fiat money, providing a "free pass" against taxation. (3) It cannot explain why people would accept money, which admittedly *only* signifies something with value proper without actually also conveying a legal claim for it. Any debtor can produce a piece of paper that "signifies" the payment he owes, but his creditors will certainly not accept this as payment. People know that fiat money has no value-in-exchange outside of its monetary use, but they accept it nevertheless. They accept fiat money not because it signifies anything, but because they can settle tax debt and acquire the trust to also continuously be able to settle other debt with it. A semiotic theory of fiat money misses that point.

Money creation

Creation of commodity money, credit money and fiat money

We have already put a great deal of emphasis on the relationship between fiat money and money creation. It is important to understand that money creation also existed in the world of commodity money already. Not only would the Greek mine commod-ity money at Laurium, and the Spanish mine silver at Potosi, both leading to money creation, but banks could also create money in a commodity money regime, via frac-tional reserve banking, by issuing credit money beyond their reserves in commodity money. *In all these cases money was created without the involvement of state fiat money.* Fur-thermore, if fiat money is issued, then this may happen without money creation (the creation of additional money), if the issuing state simultaneously withdraws a cor-responding amount of gold or silver from circulation, e.g., to put it into reserves. If a state issues a higher amount of fiat money than the nominal value of the gold or silver that it puts into reserves, then it only creates money in the excess of the fiat money issued over the gold or silver dispatched to the vaults.[66] If a state issues fiat money beyond the reserves held, then the excess of the fiat money emitted is money creation. It is comparable to the open or hidden seignorage added by a state when it issues embossed commodity money coins; the added seignorage-layer is fiat money.[67]

---

66   Reference is made to Matrix II on page 26.

67   Commodity money can, theoretically, also function as credit money and can have a fiat money component: Assume a state issues an embossed 50-gram gold coin (with a nice por-trait on it, of course) and which, for some reason, conveys a claim for an additional 100-gram's worth of gold, but is given a nominal value, accepted by the markets, of 250-gram of gold. This coin, then, is commodity money with its real gold component, credit money with its claim component and fiat money with the excess.

Commodity money is a very unsuitable tool for money creation because it must carry its commodity, gold or silver piggyback – otherwise it is not commodity money. Accordingly, one has to "get physical", go out and find,[68] mine, rob, or otherwise procure gold or silver, at the least by giving other commodities away for it, and transport it to where it will be used as money in order to create new commodity money. The same is true even if a less precious metal, cupper, is used, as the Chinese did from the Ch'in to well into the Ch'ing dynasty. Over two thousand years, they minted small round coins with a square whole in the middle which allowed assemble standardized numbers of the coins to so-called "strings" to overcome the comparatively little commodity value of cupper, e.g., of 1000 coins; off course seignorage was often added and the nominal value of the coins or strings was mostly much higher than the market value of the cupper. Still, there were times, when the desired growth of the monetary base was impeded by the lack of cupper.[69] Credit money, with full reserve holding in commodity money, only somewhat loosens the closeness and directness of the "piggyback"-relationship to gold or silver – but it does little more than that. Yes, gold and silver no longer have to be carried around with the money, but the bars must still sit, if idly, in a vault. It does not matter, then, whether they have a ribbon around their neck, relating them to specific credit money bank notes, token coins, or credit entries on customer deposits, or if they only have a certain value-relation to the issued notes in the aggregate, e.g., full reserve banking. Money can still not be created without procuring new gold or silver. Indeed, even if states issue fiat money and want to back it, although it does not convey a claim for conversion, with gold or silver in the amount of its nominal value, as they sometimes do, they still need new gold or silver.[70] Reserve holding in commodity money, thus, keeps money creation as impractical as it always was. We can now see that the ease of money creation is not a matter of whether the gold or silver is carried around piggyback or stored in vaults, but is instead solely a matter of whether there have to be gold or silver reserves at all. Money creation by credit money or fiat money are both equally easy, provided that they are not backed by reserves. Banks just print bank notes, emboss token coins, and book deposit entries against which they do not hold commodity money. Alternatively, states issue credit money (with a conversion claim) or straightforward state fiat money (without a conversion claim) in precisely this way.[71]

---

68   See on page 66 on how Pallas Athene helped the Athenians in their war against the Persians.

69   See, e.g., on the Sung: *Golas*, The Sung fiscal administration, p. 207 et seq.

70   Germany used to back its fiat money with reserves at a third of the fiat money issued before World War I.

71   To repeat: Fiat money being covered by reserves does not mean that it involves a legal claim for conversion into commodity money; it only means that the state has put the same amount of commodity money in a vault. Credit money always involves a claim for conversion into commodity money, whether reserves are kept or not.

Money creation and reserve holding vs credit money and solvency

Our later analysis, on prosthetic spending financed by money creation, will help us to better understand and to disentangle two other monetary issues. The question of whether newly created credit money issued by private banks is fully, fractionally, or not all covered by reserves (reserves holding) must be kept separate from the question of whether and under what condition such credit money may lose its value and banks may default on it. These questions are *not* the same.

Money creation and reserve holding

The easiest way to think of the issue is to imagine credit money creation in a commodity money regime and to consider the relationship between credit money issued and commodity money reserves. As seen, it depends solely on the commodity money reserve holding whether or not there is money creation; if 100 % commodity money reserves are held in reserves for newly issued bank notes or entries on deposit accounts, then there is no money creation; if 50 % commodity money reserves are held, half the amount of newly issued credit money is newly created; if 0 % reserves are held, the full amount of newly issued credit money is money creation. However, the reserves percentage also decides upon money creation if existing credit money, e.g., issued by another bank, or even fiat money is kept in reserve. Amounts put into reserves, and "blocked" there, reduce the aggregate volume of the money that is in circulation. They, thus, are to be "netted" against newly created money. Reserve holding (of all types of money) compared to newly issued money (also of all types, today mostly credit money and state fiat money) decide upon the volume of money creation. This is the most important issue macroeconomically.

Credit money and solvency

The second issue – credit money and solvency –, which is easily confused with the first issue, is of a lesser caliber macroeconomically, but still of great bearing for the credit money holders. If a private bank issues credit money in a commodity money regime, like with any other debt that it has, it may or may not be able to honor the obligations arising therefrom. Accordingly, it may not be able to convert the credit money in commodity money on demand (or at least in credit money of other issuers). The issue does not disappear in a state fiat money regime. In a fiat money regime, the bank that issues credit money may also be able or unable to exchange the credit money issued into state, e.g., state bank notes (or at least credit money from other issuing banks). Its credit money holders will suffer a loss in the event that it defaults. Now, this possibility is, in fact, ultimately independent of whether the bank carries full reserves, fractional reserves, or no reserves at all. A debtor's solvency depends on the debtor's balance sheet *as a whole*, i.e., on what aggregate assets are opposed to what aggregate liabilities, and *not* on the relationship of a *special part of its debt* to a *special part of its assets*. It is certainly nice to know that a bank held a

100 % coverage in gold or silver,[72] when it issued credit money, but that is no guarantee that it will always be able to honor the whole of its debt or even the whole of its debt resulting from issuing credit money. A full reserves bank can also go bust if it loses too much money elsewhere – without any customer asking for conversion of his bank credit money into gold or silver. Conversely, a fractional or no reserves bank, whose customers have invested the loans received wisely and who can meet their repayment obligations (and who itself runs its own operations carefully), may prosper. Accordingly, if a state instructs banks to hold a certain fraction of their credit money issued as reserves, this is *primarily directed towards monetary politics*. In addition, at best, it may have an intermediate favorable, yet unreliable, effect on the bank's solvency.

For central banks or states It is much easier to save fractional reserves banks in state fiat money regimes than in commodity money regimes. If depositors demand conversion of their credit money into gold or silver in a commodity money regime, then the uncommitted gold and silver even in the vaults of the central bank, may be too scarce to satisfy all demands. In a state fiat money regime, this restriction no longer exists. The central bank can never run short of state fiat money a base money. It can either loan fiat money to the troubled bank as a "lender of last resort" in the sense meant by *Walter Bagehot* or it can buy the bad assets from the troubled bank as "dealer of last resort" in the sense meant by *Perry Mehrling* [73] and, thereby, can bail out the troubled bank. Bailouts have become an issue of will only, rather than of limited firepower.

The possible default of debtors must, of course, be distinguished from the other issue of whether a certain type of money can default as such. We have already observed that commodity money cannot possibly default (as it carries its downside

---

72 While the *Amsterdam Wisselbank* is said to initially have been a full reserves bank, the *Stockholm's Banco*, which opened in 1657, is said to have been a fractional reserve bank from the very beginning, see *Ferguson* (2008) page 50.

73 See *Mehrling* (2011) page 132 et seq. Mehrling describes how central banks, the Fed in particular, transformed from classic "lenders of last resort" in *Bagehot's* sense to "dealers of last resort" and how the institutions and practices (primary dealers, repo-market) adjusted in this context. Instead of making loans to cover private banks' losses or liquidity problems, the central bank would simply buy the assets. Liquidity then becomes a question of "shiftability" to the central bank (page 35), which has the tendency to eliminate the distinction between liquidity and solvency as such (page 44). Mehrling comes close to stating that the willingness and capability of private dealers to purchase assets may, at some stage, become exhausted. "The point is that, in a really severe crisis market liquidity is no longer a matter of the funding liquidity of private dealers, but rather of shiftability to the Fed. If an asset is not shiftable to the Fed, it may not be shiftable at all..." (page 106). However, Mehrling does go so far as to make the point that the willingness of private wealth owners to absorb both private and sovereign debt could, as such, reach its limits and that then central banks ought to become the main "holder of last resort".

protection piggyback), but that credit money, whether it holds reserves or not, can default. Fiat money cannot default as such, given that from the very beginning it does not claim to convey any claim against a debtor (who does not exist). It may, however, lose its value if it is no longer accepted in the markets following inflation, hyperinflation, demonetization, or currency reform. Matrix II of the Foreword (on page 26) is now further evolved by showing these cases in Matrix III.

Figure 3: Matrix III – Reserves and money creation vs default concern

	Commodity money	**fiat money**	**Credit money based on commodity money**	**Credit money based on fiat money**
Reserves and money creation	reserves carried piggyback no money creation without new gold or silver	money creation if no commodity money reserves are held for newly issued fiat money	money creation if no commodity money reserves are held for newly issued credit money	money creation if no fiat money reserves held for newly issued credit money
Default concern	no default risk, default risk protection carried piggyback	no conversion claim no protection of fiat money holder in inflation or demonetization	value-in-exchange of claim for commodity money mainly depending on solvency of issuer of credit money	value-in-exchange of claim for fiat money depending on solvency of issuer of credit money and value of fiat money

Where the new money goes: Money creation and the geopolitical rivalry of states

If people participate in a gold rush, alchemist experiments to produce gold, or criminals engage in counterfeiting schemes, they are driven by the expectation that the gold, silver, or counterfeit money that they may get out of this venture will be *theirs*. The ultimate motive for money creation lies, thus, where "normal people on the streets" will suspect it – money is created to spend it in favor of its recipients. Private banks, too, use newly created credit money to enrich themselves via the interest they earn on it or via other profits from investing it. And states, finally, also go after the gain they realize through the spending it enables, be it in armament build-up, infra-structure development or financing social transfers. Money creation is not like adding water to the oceans because of smelting ice at the North

Pole or South Pole, but the new monetary wealth *immediately accrues to some specific owner*. Still, macroeconomically, money creation is a means to extend processes of economic systems building through time and beyond presently covered spaces – to enable exchanges (additional elementary economic events) which would not have taken place without it.

Most economists, it they think about money creation, do not sufficiently consider the *point of entry of* the additional money; they rather only look at the overall quantity of money raised. Often, they move from here to deduct a general rise of the price level based on the quantity-theory-of- money. Insofar, they consider the inside of the economic body as quasi "structure-less", like a basin with water, in which only the total swapping quantity matters, or, to give another example, they make no difference about whether blood is being injected into the belly or veins of a human being or if food is placed into a human being's stomach or rectum.[74] However, money, which, resulting in an increase of the money volume, is sitting idle in accounts of a sterile wealth owner, does not do a thing. Only new money that buys additional produce in the productive economy has a macroeconomically stimulating effect or, if supplies cannot be increased, competes with for the same goods (which may lead to inflation regarding these products and regarding the inputs going into them). The rise's size depends on the specific situation. Reserves of stored products or assets, fast additional supplies for additional demand, reserves in production capacities, or existing or upcoming rigidities influence the prices, as do the strategies of suppliers and demanders, cartels, or by the state's anti-cartel-policies.

The main historic use for state money creation was for the military and warfare. This particular use subsumes states' money creation to a *law of escalation*. Strategic and military contests, e.g., those, which the planet has seen since 1500 AD, are contests without an umpire, and, thus, without anybody having the power to limit the efforts of the contestants, the money invested, the means applied, the places where wars are fought, and their duration. Accordingly, if any side escalates, which it can at its discretion, the other side is forced to follow suit or to be defeated. No strategic situation is stable as long as another side can grab an advantage by escalation. Oftentimes, it may be enough to only show your readiness to escalate to avoid further escalation, but already this will require significant build-up of armament; which will already put great pressure on financing. Sometimes, of course, you have to show your cards. Clausewitz's thinking centers on how the law of escalation may drive war to an "absolute war" while other moments have a moderating effect.[75] War, though, is the master of everything, and ultimately, its escalating logic feeds back on prewar military and politics. Thereby it also becomes to dominate economic state polices, fiscal and monetary, including money creation. This, then, drives state lead-

74   See already *von Mises* (2013) page 139; *von Mises* (1949) page 447.
75   See *von Clausewitz* (1980) Chapter I.

ers not only beyond international and military politics, which they might have preferred as otherwise conservative family fathers, businessmen, or bankers, but also beyond economic policies, which they would normally have pursued as sound. In other words, imperial competition and the search to dominate others rather than to be dominated by them triggers a military logic of escalation, and as long as this logic prevails, financially "stretching to the utmost" and "over-stretching" in indebtedness and money creation becomes rational and responsible (one might think). In fact, the decisive advantage may come from not only spending the financial resources you have, but from spending resources *you do not have*, including by taking on debt and by money creation[76] The law of escalation, accordingly, renders necessary what is normally irresponsible and unreasonable. It makes the unreasonable reasonable and the reasonable unreasonable. In summary, we find that not only microeconomic motives of private banks to the raise the volume of loans they can hand out or of firms to use such loans, but probably mainly geostrategic and military motives of states pushed money creation in the past and may continue to push it in the future, far beyond what common wisdom would consider responsible.

Section 3. The economic system

With *Max Weber*, we do not consider goods procurement by violence to be part of the economic system.[77] Strictly speaking, thus, an expression like "violence economics" or "robber economies" would be incorrect. If, in the environment of an economic

---

76   The law of escalation also operates by raising the readiness to take on sovereign debt. However, as long as debt remains redistributive (without money creation), its redistributive character (somebody must be willing to depart with the limited scarce money and it must be repaid), sets strict limits on the possibilities of escalation. These limits can be pushed, e.g., if an externally strong state can debt-finance war efforts with existing wealth of foreign countries, but only the combination of debt and money creation can wholly unleash the law of escalation. The distinction between redistributive debt (without money creation) and expansive debt (with money creation, e.g., fractional reserves credit money creation or fiat money creation) will be further developed below on page 399 et seq. and page 407 et seq.

77   Max Weber writes: "'Wirtschaftlich orientiert' soll ein Handeln insoweit heißen als in seinem gemeinten Sinne nach an der Fürsorge für einen Begehr nach Nutzleistungen orientiert ist. ‚Wirtschaftlich' soll eine friedliche Ausübung von Verfügungsmach heißen..." (*Weber* (1980) page 31). "'Wirtschaftlich orientiertes Handeln' (verwendet) die die aktuelle Gewaltsamkeit als Mittel" (loc. cit. page 31). "Wirtschaftlich orientiert kann jede Art von Handeln, auch gewaltsames (z.B. kriegerisches) Handeln sein (Raubkriege, Handelskriege). Das Pragma der Gewaltsamkeit ist (aber) dem Geist des Wirtschaftens – im üblichen Wortsinn – sehr stark entgegengesetzt. Die unmittelbare aktuelle gewaltsame Fortnahme von Gütern und die unmittelbare aktuelle Erzwingung eines fremden Verhaltens durch Kampf soll also nicht Wirtschaften heißen." (loc. cit. page 32).

system, goods are procured by violence, which happens regularly, then the acting humans glide off into a praeter-economic method. That understood, we will remind the reader that state violence in the form of abstract protection of the power of property, is still a crucial pre-condition of an otherwise violence-free economy. The ownership of objects and the performance of contractual obligations being enforced by the law, by state violence in the last instance, is the basis for the freedom of owners in markets and for the use of economic owner power. A positive definition of the economic system should use the criterion of *exchange*. We conceive of exchange in this context as mainly earmarked upon the formal moment of a certain freedom of choice and consent and, thus, in terms of the need to give away a remuneration in order to obtain something.

Our perspective is close to the views held by systems theoretical sociology of the economy, mainly as conceived by the German sociologist *Niklas Luhmann* (1927–1998).[78] After his death, Luhmann's views on the economic system were developed and enriched by *Dirk Baecker*. Systems theoretical sociology views society as consisting only of communications: "Communications are the elementary events and elementary operations of social systems".[79] Communicative events occur *in time*. Accordingly, as we already stated, the society (and the economy as a social subsystem) should not be regarded so much as a spatial structure, but a "temporalization of the notion of elements to elementary events"[80] should take place. "Events appear and disappear – if no new events are found, the autopoiesis of the system comes to a stillstand, and with it the system. The border of the system is set by nothing else but by the elementary events themselves...; to the extent they occur, they distinguish the system from everything, which it is not."[81]

---

78   Niklas Luhmann's work, in its turn, was based on the sociology of *Talcott Parsons*, on second order cybernetics (theory of observing systems, observers of observers), connected to e.g., *Heinz von Foerster*, the theory of recursive and autopoietic systems of *Humberto Maturana*, and on *Francisco Javier Varela García* and on *George Spencer Brown*'s theory and logic of distinction. As mentioned in the Foreword, the author who studied with Prof. Luhmann in Bielefeld in the early eighties, owes to him a recommendation for a grant to the New School for Social Research to New York in 1984 to study legal anthropology with *Stanley Diamond*.

79   The quote is from *Baecker* (2008), page 41, translated by the author.

80   On the radical "temporalization of the notion of elements" in modern systems theory in general, see *Luhmann* (1984) page 28, 387 et seq. On the economic system "as consisting of temporalized elements, which cannot, as elements, have duration", see *Luhmann* (1988) page 20. Quotation from *Baecker* (2008) page 34, translated by the author.

81   *Baecker* (2008), page 34, translated by the author. Again, this may tell us that what economists often see as problems *within* the economic system might better be conceived as the economic system coming to a temporary *halt*. Unemployment of labor or capital may be understood as the economic system not reaching out far enough – there are not enough dancers at the dancefloor for the present dance...

Society's subsystems all consist of communications and develop and differentiate from each other through the use of generalized symbolic media of communication. They each allow for a specific distinction that becomes the *code* through which the subsystem operates. The economy uses money as its generalized symbolic media of communication and the code of payment or no payment.[82] "The social function of the economy is the communication of scarcity".[83] "Operation scarcity"[84] takes always place "if somebody, (1) visibly for others, catches hold of things, services or relations, (2) thereby increases the stock of these things, services or relations for himself and diminishes it for others and (3) finds a form of consent for his behavior, which modestly only observes... and does not try to prevent this catching hold through the use of violence, moral prohibitions, requirements of the law, threatening with political power, seduction, educational admonitions or scientific evidence".[85] "Operation scarcity" finds social consent through a "scarcity communication",[86] as a payment, which is further specified by the money amount, and which one person pays in order to "catch hold" of a scarce object.

It is also important that the economy is an *autopoietic* system. "An autopoietic system is a system, which reproduces itself through reproduction of the elements, of which it consists, through the elements, of which it consists"[87] *Baecker* adds: "The system consists of the elements, which reproduce it. The elements are the system, which reproduce it and through whose reproduction they reproduce themselves."[88]

The reader may have noted that this book uses "exchanges", distinguishing a moment in the economy, while *Luhmann/Baecker* use payments. There are further differ-

---

82   The political system operates through the distinction between power and no power; the legal system through the distinction between lawful and unlawful; the scientific system through the distinction between true and untrue; interaction systems through the distinction between love and no love, etc.

83   *Baecker* (2006) page 12, translated by the author.

84   As almost everything is scarce, the notion "scarcity", which is often used to define the economy, is near to tautological. Overproduced cars are scarce, water, heat, cold and fresh air may be scarce and even God could be made scarce by selling indulgences. While the point is right in principle, it becomes misleading if overemphasized. The essence is: If one private individual owns something, which at all matters as it is wanted by another private individual, that object is scarce.

85   *Baecker* (2006) page 12, translated by the author. See also page 76 on Max Weber.

86   *Baecker* (2006) page 72, translated by the author.

87   *Baecker* (2008) page 33, translated by the author. The German original reads: "Ein autopoietisches System ist ein System, das sich mittels der Reproduktion der Elemente, aus denen es besteht, durch die Elemente, aus denen es besteht, reproduziert." See *Luhmann* (1988) page 17, 43 et seq., 52.

88   *Baecker* (2008) page 34, translated by the author. The German original reads: "Das System besteht aus den Elementen, die es reproduzieren. Die Elemente sind das System, das sie reproduzieren, und durch dessen Reproduktion sie sich selbst reproduzieren."

ences, but these differences have no relevant consequences for the macroeconomics dealt with in this book and may remain unresolved. It suffices to know that violent wealth procurement, examined previously, is certainly *not* part of the economic system and that the economic system consists of elementary economic events in time, which at least include exchanges.

Chapter III. Wealth procurement by exchange

In this chapter, we will turn our attention to how wealth procurement operates if profits are made by exchange, i.e., within the economic system. This type is not utterly violence free, but the role of violence in the economy is reduced, as we saw, to enforcing contracts, which persons have freely concluded (pacta sunt servanda).

Section 1. Consumptive and investive spending: C–M–C' and M–C–M'

Two types of circuits

"Out-legs" and "in-legs" of circuits
As we saw, systems theoretical sociology, when applied to economics, developed the concept of elementary economic events in time. The most important elementary economic events in time are exchanges (do-ut-des, quid-pro-quo). In money economies, they organize themselves in *sequences of two exchanges*, which only together, and only after completion of the second exchange, bring about the intended meaningful result, i.e., closure of a circuit. Exchanges thus integrate systemic wholes of two steps, drives or circuits, with an "out-leg" or an "in-leg" or a "first leg" and a "second leg".

Two types of circuits: C–M–C' and M–C–M'-circuits
The existence of the two-leg-circuits and the resulting the two phase-rhythm was known about since long ago, as we already said: M–C–M' was present as the implicit algorithm on which merchants acted for millennia and as an outspoken and explicit regret of mythical and religious men, reformers, philosophers,[1] artists, social critics,

---

1   See *Aristotle*, Politics, I IX. In essence, he puts forward the distinction between C–M–C' and M–C–M' as follows: "One kind of acquisition ... is a part of the household art... that art must procure to be forthcoming a supply of those goods..., which are necessary for life and useful for the community of city or household. ... the amount of such property sufficient in itself for a good life is not unlimited... But there is another kind of acquisition that is specially called wealth-getting, and ... and to this kind ... there is thought to be no limit to riches and

and statesmen who lamented that production was being "abused" for profit-making. Finally, it also already existed in economists' analytical observations on the precondition of capitalist production and circuit closure prior to Marx's time.[2] How-

property. [1257a] [1] ... One of them is natural, the other is not natural .... with every article of property there is a double way of using it; both uses are related to the article itself, but not related to it in the same manner—one is peculiar to the thing and the other is not peculiar to it. Take for example a shoe—there is its wear as a shoe and there is its use as an article of exchange .... And the same also holds good about the other articles of property; for all of them have an art of exchange related to them, which began in the first instance from the natural order of things, because men had more than enough of some things and less than enough of others. This consideration also shows that the art of trade is not by nature a part of the art of wealth-getting; for the practice of barter was necessary only so far as to satisfy men's own needs. ... Exchange on these lines therefore is not contrary to nature, nor is it any branch of the art of wealth-getting, for it existed for the replenishment of natural self-sufficiency; yet out of it the art of business in due course arose... So, when currency had been now invented as an outcome of the necessary interchange of goods, there came into existence the other form of wealth-getting, trade. ... natural wealth-getting belongs to household management, whereas the other kind belongs to trade, producing goods not in every way but only by the method of exchanging goods. It is this art of wealth-getting that is thought to be concerned with money, for money is the first principle and limit of commerce. And these riches, that are derived from this art of wealth-getting, are truly unlimited; ... so also this wealth-getting has no limit in respect of its end, and its end is riches and the acquisition of goods in the commercial sense. But the household branch of wealth-getting has a limit.... Hence from this point of view it appears necessary that there should be a limit to all riches, yet in actual fact we observe that the opposite takes place; for all men engaged in wealth-getting try to increase their money to an unlimited amount." (English translation http://www.perseus.tufts.edu). In fact, history is rich with almost identical insights of other most famous thinkers, which will occasionally surface in this book. Disdain for primacy of money accumulation is also expressed in the statement of Nietzsche quoted in the opening pages of this book. See generally on the issue: *Polanyi* (1944) page 56.

2   "...Revendre avec profit est produire" (*Quesnay*, Sur les travaux des artisans. Second dialogue, page 373). *Quesnay* spoke of produce needing a "valeur vénale", a "sales value" in excess of the production costs. "It is... not ... the productions of the territory of a kingdom, which form the revenues of the nation; it is ... necessary that these productions have a sales value, which exceeds the prices of the costs of the exploitation of the cultivation" (*Quesnay*, page 158). *Smith* is also explicit about the expectation of profit being the sole motive for investment and production in capitalism. "The consideration of his own private profit is the sole motive which determines the owner of any capital to employ it either in agriculture, in manufactures, or in some particular branch of the wholesale or retail trade." (Wealth of Nations, Book II, Chapter III, page 335.). *Malthus* held the same view: "No fresh hands can be employed in any sort of industry merely in consequence of the demand for its produce occasioned by the persons employed. No farmer will take the trouble of superintending the labour of ten additional men merely because his whole produce will then sell in the market at an advanced price just equal to what he had paid his additional labourers." (*Malthus* (1820) chapter 7 section 2, page 348.). Malthus also wrote: "But where wealth and value are perhaps the most nearly connected, is in the necessity of the latter to the production of the former. ... no consider-

ever, Marx made, at least at first, more out of it (just as Heidegger made more out of "Sorge") and elevated it to a central piece of economic thinking. He could not have emphasized its importance more than by calling it *"the general formula of capital"* and he came up with a specific notation, which we have already used and which is used throughout this book. While

Commodity – money – (other) commodity (or **C–M–C'**)

represents an "out-leg" into money and an "in-leg" into a good,

money – commodity – (more) money (or **M–C–M'**),[3]

which is the more famous one, represents an investment or profit driven circuit. Its emergence marks the birth of profit economies and capitalism. Profit economies or capitalism means: M–C–M'-players working their way, in M–C–M'-drives, through a complementary environment of C–M–C'-players. Profit economies and capitalism are, insofar, guest systems in the economic system at large, which is the host-system.

In other words, circuits with "in-legs" and "out-legs" split up into two types of combinations of elementary economic events: C–M–C' and M–C–M'-circuits. [4] The motive behind a C–M–C'-circuit is the *consumption* of C', of a needed or desired good; the motive for initiating such circuits arises from nature, society, politics or culture etc. Whether the completion of such a circuit achieves the intended purpose, is normally rather reliably foreseeable; if I can exchange my honey against money, I can buy chicken for my Sunday dish. Or: If I am employed in a factory, I can buy my Sunday dish with my salary. The motive behind an M–C–M'-circuit is investment or *profit*. Whether profit can be achieved is more conditional. The motive depends on the investor's *expectation* of a future spending M' by somebody else. This M', which I need to close my circuit, will either arise from other players' C–M–C'-circuits – it will then be their consumptive M–C'-leg – or from other players' M–C–M'-circuits

---

able quantity of wealth can be obtained ... unless the value which an individual or the society places on the object, when obtained, fully compensates the sacrifice which has been made to obtain it, such wealth will not be produced in future." (*Malthus* (1836) volume II, page 263 and editorial comments page 447.) *Minsky* rephrased the same idea 144 years later as follows "For a capitalist system to function well, *prices must carry profits*". Minsky (1986) page 158, emphasis in the original. Therefore: "A capitalist economy only works well as an investing economy, for investment creates profits." (*Minsky* (1966) page 104).

3   *Marx*, Capital, volume I chapter 4.

4   The legs C–M and M–C' (in M–C–M') or M–C and C–M' (in M–C–M'), which are each elementary economic events, exist, as we shall see, in both the wealth economy and in the productive economy.

– it will then be their investive M–C-leg. Whether the completion of such a circuit achieves the intended purpose, is normally less reliably foreseeable. I depends not on my prospective counter-parties having a want for money, which they always have, but on their having sufficiently budgeted money for what I offer.

Marx' "under-use" of the distinction between C–M–C' and M–C–M'-circuits

Unfortunately, as Marx's ambition was not mainly to analyze an economy based on profit-making, but to debunk exploitation as the essence of profit-making, he used M–C–M' only as his theoretical "door-opener". Even if he touched upon M–C–M' in his reflection on the "realization of profit",[5] he did not attempt to evolve it into a proper theory of macroeconomic circuit closure. Insofar, he did not exhaust its potential but moved "forward" to the fallacious attempt to "improve" upon Ricardo's theory of labor value in Marx's theory of exploitation. Labor power, according to Marx, could exchange its value (which was its objective labor value), but it could nevertheless be exploited (in a novel and specifically Marxian sense): The labor-power purchased by the capitalist would generate more labor value than it was worth itself in the form of the output-commodities, which would belong to the capitalist. Marx's theory of labor value and exploitation, thus, aimed to explain why and how the gain of value between M' and M (M'-M) was possible. And it was most important for him that this – the origination of surplus value – occurred already in production and through labor. This labor-value and exploitation-theory, even if Marx and most of his followers considered it to be his greatest achievement and a holy cow of Marxism, was a trap, however. It followed Newtonian and Hegelian preferences and was, ultimately, not only false but also reifying. It was, however, very successful as an ideological and a propaganda tool for communist and socialist parties – even Christian philanthropists loved it. Therefore, probably, it was upheld in left wing circuits and parties ever since. This book, though, believes that M–C–M', possesses enormous analytical power, but on condition that it is examined *without* Marx's theory of labor value and exploitation.

C–M–C'

As we have observed, the economy emerged as a separate social sub-system alongside the emergence of proto-states or states during roughly the Neolithic or late Neolithic eras. This new system inserted itself between nature and men's biological and

---

5   By "realization of profit" Marx meant the formal transformation of the profit C'-C already "sticking" in the produce C' into M', hence into money form (in M–C...C'–M'). The term "realization" implies that the profit is already there before the commodity has been sold. At his most "deep-structural" level, Marx, accordingly, at first ignores the problem of finding a buyer for the output.

social reproduction.[6] Its modus operandi and main means of propagation was exchange; money followed almost instantly thereafter. Exchange and money were infectious, given that they were advantageous for everybody – but only after overcoming the resistance of traditional life-styles of course.

Exchange and money opened access to goods and services – grains, animals, or labor, and positional goods –, which humans could not have obtained previously, and the interest to possess these more and better values-in-use made almost everybody into a partisan of the innovations. Money eased transactions greatly. Marx looked at this economy, at first, from the view of consumer-interest, which led to C–C' or C–M–C'.[7] People start with one commodity, which is their property. That may be their naked capacity to work, their labor power, or if they also own means of production, e.g., land, something they produced with them, e.g., grains, honey, or wine. They can exchange it against a second commodity, which they need or desire (barter) or they can start with the same commodity again, exchange it against money as a first, intermediate step, and then exchange it, in the second, ultimate step, with the needed or desired commodity. This motion consists of two exchanges and involves *three states*: an *initial state, a transitory interim state, and a final state*, which closes the circuit; it is both consumption-driven and value-in-use-driven.

If the majority of the population still owned land and were "self-employed" small producers, the classical example for such exchanges were Neolithic societies' peasants bartering or selling parts of their harvest to obtain clothing, tools, or services at nearby town markets. Later, the classical example became simpler; workers would trade their labor against goods or sold it for money to obtain a means of subsistence. The old social imperative had been: "Procure from nature what you need to survive" (or rob it or subjugate people to make it for you), the new social imperative became: "Get yourself something that you can exchange against what you need to survive". For landless people, this soon became identical with: "Find a buyer for your labor". More generally speaking, the imperative was: "Get yourself value-in-exchange!". Thus, many anonymous Alter – with their often-unknown interests, opinions, tastes, acts of valuation, and with what they were willing and able to produce – became crucial for Ego's survival. If you could procure what Alter needed, and if Alter could procure what you needed, then you would survive; if you could procure a lot thereof, and Alter could procure a lot thereof, then you would have a prodigious

---

6   Once again, we use the notion "economy" not to mean the physical provision or procurement of the means of subsistence or conveniences of life, which must take place as soon as humans exist, but only for a *special way* to organize this, though a system of exchange and payments, and not by collective gathering, hunting, farming, pasturing, handywork-production, and also not by robbing or violent wealth procurement.

7   *Marx*, Capital, volume I, chapter 4.

live and you might even get rich in the process. If you could not, or if Alter could not (and you could not regress to autarch production), then you would fall into ruin.

A general mutual cross-wise economic interdependency emerged already at the level of C–M–C' and prior to M–C–M'. An Ego depends on an Alter and an Alter depends upon an Ego. Ego cannot not obtain from Alter that which Alter does not produce, and Alter cannot obtain from Ego that which Ego does not produce. Moreover, this interdependency does not only operate if Ego and Alter meet on markets, – sitting, e.g., behind a mountain of grains or the cackle of a few dozen of chickens –, but already Ego's and Alter's decisions to produce what they produce and their means to produce are affected by interdependency. Ego's expectation to be able to trade its grains against chickens (with or without money-intermediation) may induce it to produce more grains in order to satisfy the growing chicken-hunger of its family, etc. In fact, it may also enable it to produce more grains – the family is better nourished thanks to the chicken-component on the menu. We already have here, *in nuce* and un-developed, what will lead Malthus to speak of a macroeconomic "union between production and distribution", what *Quesnay* will try to evolve into a *tableau économique*, what Ricardo will fallaciously conceive of as Ricardo's Law of Say, and what Marx's will try to analyze in his reproduction schemes. The issue becomes bigger and takes on a different shape as soon as M–C–M' arrives on the scene.

M–C–M' (M–C...C'–M')

M–C–M' (M–C...C'–M') in general

C–M–C' has a built-in evolutionary option. This option is soon discovered and is brought to operation by the brightest, fittest, and most endeavouring, whom we sometimes call "merchant heroes". The advantages conveyed by this option are an even stronger pro-money-economy-stimulus than the value-in-use related stimuli, which we already saw at work in C–M–C'. Exchanges and money are good for everybody, *but they are particularly good for those who want to become wealthy as M–C–M'-players*; money *plus* M–C–M' is the turbo-mechanism to become rich. The condition of the possibility to play C–M–C' or M–C–M' is, as we have already seen, private property. Both classes of players must be free to decide what to do with the commodities or money that they own.[8] This also applies to labor power.[9]

---

8   *Heinsohn/Steiger* (2009) page 462 et seq. also place great emphasis on property and the legal power of owners.

9   Noteworthily, while labor power must be owned by *somebody*, the owner does not have to be the person who is its natural bearer. If private ownership of humans exists, the owner is different from the natural bearer of the labor power. M–C–M' also works if laborers are purchased like seed or cattle.

To realize the M–C–M'-option, one has to only approach C–M–C' with a different punctuation and look at M not as an intermediary transitory stage in the middle of a drive, but as its starting point. One also has to extend the drive by adding a new final stage, which is not the satisfaction of consumption needs or desires, but the collection a money amount M', which is higher than the initial M-pay-out. The motive for the player to move through these mutations, too; it is no longer value-in-use-driven but value-in-exchange-driven. Exchange is an open, generous, and neutral form that allows counterparties' full discretion concerning their motives and integrates profit and consumption interests harmoniously in one transaction. Moves of innocent and naïve value-in-use-driven C–M–C'-players who are pursuing their consumption motives – they may be hungry, in need of clothing or shelter, or just seeking pleasures or positional goods – are welcome to cohabit with complementary, albeit fundamentally different moves, value-in-exchange-driven moves made by M–C–M'-players.[10] Within an individual transaction C–M–C' is also like a symbiotic host to M–C–M'. What is the first consumption-driven leg in a consumptive **C–M**–C'-circuit for one party (peasants sell grains to a town merchant with to purpose to later buy medical services) may be the first profit-driven leg of a firm's **M–C**–M'-circuit (town merchant buys grains to resell them). The merchant is obviously not interested in the grains as values-in-use for his family, but he will resell them, possibly after they have been carried to high-value-regions (in space), say Athens, Rome, or Luoyang, or stored (in time) until the next famine. The economy consists of a great number of such exchanges of goods against money and of money against goods and whether they are the C–M-leg or M–C'-leg of C–M–C' or the M–C-leg or C–M'-leg of M–C–M' is often undistinguishable when viewed from the outside. M–C–M'-players only enter the circuits at a different point and with a different motive.

The motive behind why M–C–M'-players would make the effort to exchange money into money through, the intervention of a commodity, is quite obviously, not a qualitative difference between their starting and end-position; rather it is merely quantitative. The input-money must become more output money – what Marx notated as M', with M'-M, ΔM, s or p representing the profit. This new motive revolutionizes the prior society and the prior world; it may well have been the most revolutionary "thing" in human history. In particular, it frees motives for production from motives for consumption as money frees the accumulation of wealth from

---

10   M–C–M'-players are a self-discovered, self-made, and self-selected group of players who offer counterparty services to C–M–C'-players in a "sandwich"-like manner. "You need to sell your labor or your produce? I am here to help!" ..." Now you want to spend your salary or other income? I am here again...– I am your complementary market-maker, whether you are seller or buyer in your C–M–C'-drive".

the need to store and maintain values-in-use. As the importance of both M–C–M'-players and their relative wealth grows, M–C–M' rises to the generally accepted and assumed motive of human behavior, even if the vast majority of the people remain outside of the game (much like how many back-yard football-players never reach the big leagues). One might question why wealth owners should, notwithstanding their already captured immense wealth, still pursue wealth accumulation. One motive may come from hitherto-non-wealth-owners, who aspire to rise into the wealth owners' ranks by increasing existing wealth owners' wealth. *Levitt/Dubner* have observed that it is the foot soldiers amongst drug dealers, who often still live with their moms, that start gang wars; while their bosses prefer peace, it is their only chance to advance in their career.[11] Similarly, continued aggressive wealth accumulation by the already wealthy which may not be a result of their endless greed, but from the greed of their foot soldiers, e.g., former Harvard, Stanford, Oxford, and Cambridge graduates who try to battle their way up to wealth too. Further increasing one's existing wealth, is, of course, also a matter of preventive defense, of consistency, and beauty. Even wealth owners who commit significant parts of their wealth to philanthropy continue to have other parts managed profitably.

If M'>M, the resulting M'-M or ΔM is the profit (we assume that M includes such other costs as storage, transportation, fees, taxes already, and hence is a *sum* of payouts). It does not matter whether the merchant resells at the spot or shifts the goods in space or in time or processes them before resale. Such physical alteration before resale can, however, be expressed by evolving the notation to M–C...C'–M'[12] with C...C' depicting the physical processing with value-in-use and value-in-exchange-effects.[13] It is not necessary for the second exchange to already reach the end-consumer; another capitalist as purchaser is good enough to allow for the first capitalists to realize his profit, even if he is, by the same token, starting a drive for profit. We could write M–C–M'–C'–M''–C''–M'''–... to notate a *chain of* several consecutive circuits (if the full profits are re-invested), given that the process can be reiterated if M' is reinvested by the same capitalist. To my knowledge, Marx never used this notation and we do not need it either.

M–C–M' (M–C...C'–M'), c, v and s, profit and loss, cashflow, and present values

M–C–M' expresses how M–C–M'-players intuitively think and act. Marx, though, kept his "general" "formula of capital" only transitorily in the center of his argument

---

11   *Levitt/Dubner* (2005) page 97, 83.

12   *Marx*, Capital, volume II, chapter 1.

13   The processing firm is then promoted from "merchant capital" to "industrial capital" or "productive capital" (*Marx*, Das Kapital, vol. II, MEW 24, page 56. As already stated, it is important for Marx that the profit is already there in C' and has only to be "realized" later. Surplus value *s*, as attached by workers in production, already "sticks" in C' before the C'–M'-"realization".

and moved quickly from "simple commodity production" and "merchant capital" to "industrial capital", where he could best set out his theory of surplus value and exploitation, which, after all, he saw this as the jewel in the crown of his analysis of capitalism. To get there, he splits up capitalists' outlays M into two parts, representing the used-up equipment and inventories, which he jointly calls *constant capital*, abbreviated c, and the wages or salaries for labor, which he calls *variable capital*, abbreviated v. In order for M' to be larger than M, M' must contain not only recoveries of $c + v$ but an additional amount on top. Marx calls this amount *surplus value*, abbreviated to s. Hence, while $M = c + v$, $M' = c + v + s$. Accordingly $M'-M = s$. s is also called surplus value by Marx, and, it is the same as profit, including in Marx.

Marx did not connect his terminology to accounting terms such as sales, revenues, profit, cash flow, etc. It is, however, clear that his constant capital c encompasses both costs for equipment and inventories and that c is fully recovered as part of M'. Accordingly, the costs for depreciation are included in c and Marx's profit M'-M or s must already be *after deduction of depreciation*, i.e., "pure" profit or profit in the meaning of a profit and loss-calculation. It is also clear that M' represents the sales prices or sales proceeds, sales, revenues or turnover in the sense of accounting. Accordingly, he either assumes (contra-factually) that the costs of depreciation have fully become cash-pay-outs as part of c when M' is collected or his M–C–M' operates at the level of profit and loss-analysis. Alternatively, we might say that Marx assumes circuits, whose "beats" are such that they condense all financial effects in the two transaction legs M–C and C–M' – and the difference between cash flow-analysis and accounting-analysis becomes meaningless.

This allows us to view M–C–M' like a retrospective profit and loss calculation or a prospective business plan. M is then conceived of as *the present value of a series of discrete and sequential outlays* (beyond the purchase of a single commodity) that do not have to be exclusively purchase prices, technically (but may also be salaries, interest, rent, maintenance, repair, substitution, and even administrative fees, taxes etc.) for many individual goods and services, which arrive at different times (including e.g., energy and transport services)[14] and M' is the *present value of a series of discrete and sequential consequential inflows of revenues*. This brings M–C–M' in full accord with modern business planning, today's value calculation, and corporate finance. The M–C–M'-analysis converging with business planning, business valuation, and corporate finance, speaks for both of them.

The origins of profits in M–C–M'

We have already claimed that, contra Marx, profit does not come from labor value. Profit, instead, comes from the seller *appropriating that part of the value-in-exchange that the buyer attributes*, in his subject-related way, to the good or service sold *beyond*

---

14   See *Marx*, Das Kapital, vol. II., MEW 24, page 346.

the seller's costs in the generalized form of money. This is even so if the buyer's attribution of value-in-use and value-in-exchange is rather bizarre or eccentric. Keeping in mind that all value is attributed by a subject in a way specific to that subject, one may say that *the buyer "objectively" pays for what he "subjectively" attributes* or that the seller gets the buyer to "objectively" pay for what he "subjectively" attributes. This is the clue to profit economies' economics. Profit, then, is possible, first, because a buyer-subject, attributes buyer's value-in-exchange to the commodity in his subject-related way, which is higher than the seller's costs (not the seller's value!); second, this is because the buyer politely, and in an understanding way, expresses his valuation in the inter-subjectively valid and generalized form of money. It must also be presupposed, third, that the buyer has the money and is willing to sacrifice it for the purchased good.

This opens a corridor where seller and buyer may agree on a deal. A price will be acceptable to the seller, if it is reasonably higher than his costs and allows for a proper profit, and to the buyer if the price is reasonably lower than his subjectively attributed value-in-exchange. No exploitation is involved. If the sold commodity is a consumption good, then the buyer feels happy to consume what he gets (which can only be expressed on an ordinal scale), if the commodity sold is an investment good, a wealth asset, equipment, or inventories, then, both, buyer and seller expect a quantitative increase of wealth. This can even be expressed in cardinal numbers: For instance, if inventories, equipment, a building, or a business are worth $100m in the hands of a low concept and low synergies seller, but are worth $200m in the hands of a high concept and high synergies buyer, and the sale is made at $150m, then the deal enriches both parties by $50m. The buyer's higher concept and higher synergies allow the seller to appropriate some of the value-in-exchange that the object has for the buyer.

The result for the seller is, thus, the same in all C–M' or C'–M'-legs, whether with private consumers or firms as buyers. The value-in-use sold, and with it the value-in-exchange sold, are gone, but the seller receives the amount M' as a claim or immediately in cash. With it comes a profit M'-M, i.e., an increase of the seller's wealth. If a private consumer, a consumer, who does not invest the good, is the buyer – a worker buys a meal – he is interested in utility, and if he consumes the good, then both its utility and value-in-use are destroyed – and with it its value-in-exchange. By far the greatest number of purchased objects or services are the means of subsistence, e.g., whoever buys food, shelter, clothing, drugs, positional goods, sex, or a health service may (and likely will) be better nourished, protected from the weather, clothed, stoned, or drunk, might enjoy the positional goods, may be satisfied, and even be healthier. However, the value given away to the seller is gone for good...[15].

---

15   Of course, by being fed, sheltered, clothed, healthier, satisfied, etc. the worker-consumer will re-strengthen his capacity to work and to offer his work in his further C–M-exchanges.

This is different if the buyer is not a private consumer (not a worker or a consuming wealth owner), but a productive or sterile wealth owner who uses the object as C in an intended new M–C–M'-drive. In this case, the buyer's initial money-loss is not final. The buying wealth owner will, rather, if everything goes as planned, recuperate what it paid out as M and will pocket M'-M, a profit on top, and their wealth will increase thereby. One side consumes or invests; the other side gets richer.

It is noteworthy that C–M–C' and M–C–M'-transactions are insensitive to the past and future of the money and commodities. Firms sell as easily to buyers who earned their income honestly through work and exchanges as they sell to buyers who robbed the money or received transfer payments. Even freshly created money will be willingly accepted and digested. Similarly, goods and services sell indiscriminately well whether they were bought, robbed or expropriated by the state or criminals. Goods procured by violence in a *praeter-economic way* are not rejected if they are introduced in the economic system. Getting to a M'-M difference neither requires the goods to be procured within the economic system through free and "unimpaired", fair exchanges, on the left supply side, nor that the money paid on the right sales side arises from proper market-compliant trades.

A metaphor for M–C–M'

It is interesting to try to look out a metaphor for M–C–M'. The economic system is not comparable to the blood system of mammals, given that blood is pumped into the body and it is not sucked in by the body. The metaphor of a jet engine (sucking in air on one side and blowing it out on the other side) or of a gun (arming on one side and firing at the other) do not fit either. They move pressurized air out of the jet engine or the bullet out of the gun following a push by the engine or the gun, while the customers must actively pull or suck in an M–C–M'-circuit. Marketing, advertising, and selling can lure the customer to do so, but ultimately everything depends on him attributing value, having the money required, and being willing to take the pain to sacrifice it. If customers do not actively pull, suck in, or absorb commodities by actively sacrificing money, then the circuit cannot be completed.

M–C–M', thus, is like a *two-chamber-system*, where both movements, the initial M–C-investment and the final C–M'-collection, come from the *sucking-activity* of those on the right edge of the chamber. Firms sitting on right edge of the left chamber bring about the M–C-transmutation by sucking in commodities, including labor, and by paying M-outlays to them, and customers sitting on the right edge of the right chamber bring about the C–M'-transformation by also actively sucking the commodities produced (by paying M'-validations to them). *M–C–M' is about double-sucking* and the unfortunate units on the left can only try to lure the others to suck. This means that sucking must always be paid for by money payment-sacrifices.

Figure 4: M–C-chamber and C–M'-chamber

M–C-chamber	C–M'-chamber
>>>>> flow of supplies >>>>>	>>>>>> flow of produced goods >>>>>
firms absorb goods and services from suppliers by their money sacrifices M (named from perspective of firms in the center)	firms and final consumers absorb goods and services from firms by their money sacrifices M' (named from perspective of firms in the center)
<<<<< flow of money sacrifices <<<<<	<<<<< flow of money sacrifices <<<<<

It is noteworthy that the two forces that suck, pull, or absorb, are normally not causally related. The proceeds for the firms from the sucking of the customers are normally not yet available when the firms must do their sucking and payments to their suppliers for equipment and inventories and workers for labor. The relationship is only final. Firms must make their sucking before they could suck from their customers and they must pre-finance their sucking. At that point they mostly have no guarantee that their hopeful customers will also suck in their to-be-made products.

Causation vs teleology; the objectivation of subject-related and subjective value attributions

It is astonishing to watch the 1987 video by *Fischli* and *Weiss* "Der Lauf der Dinge" or "*The way things go*". To give a rough idea, it is like an almost 30 minutes observation of a chain reaction through a very long line of falling domino pieces that knock each other down. However, it is much more complex, and no single domino piece is involved. Rather tires, trash bags, ropes, pieces of wood, ladders, soap, candles, shoes, fuses, water, foam, gasoline, chemicals, and pyrotechnics are used to show an uninterrupted play of cause and effect. It begins with a trash bag hanging on a rope that untwists. The rope becomes longer, the bag reaches a truck tire and gives a turning impulse to it. The tire rolls down a small slope, hits something else and sets it into motion... Almost a half an hour later, and still following the initial impulse, some moving object knocks a bottle over, the water pours out of it and fills a container hanging on a balance beam; when the other side of the balance beam moves upwards it brings a burning candle close enough to ignite a fuse that leads to a small explosion, which again pushes a small carriage forward, etc. While the movie is full of creativity and surprising ideas, in the end they are all correlated in a *simple order of physical or chemical causes and effects* following one another in time.

"The way things go", hence, does not include conscience, observation, mutual observation, intentionality (teleology, purposeful behavior) or strategic behavior anywhere as a means of transmission of the impulse, not even in the sense that a water bottle would try to get out of the way of a truck tire rolling towards it (as a dog might).

Unlike *Fischli/Weiss'* installation, the economic system only partly operates via causes and effects. Catching a fish, yes, is a condition of the possibility to later sell it in the market and a factory owner paying a week's pay to a worker is a condition of the possibility for the worker to go to an alehouse and spend their salary; hence, the catching of the fish and the payment may be called "causes" of the later sale or purchase, which can then be called "effects". However, the economy largely operates *via expectations of what others will do in the future and reactions to these expectations by the observers*, i.e., via purposeful behavior, by motives, or teleologically. Ultimately, as systems theoretical economic sociology teaches, the economic system is created by expectations of future payments or non-payments, which lead (backwards) to earlier payments or non-payments.[16] Purposes, goals, needs, desires, and factual expectations, by dominating the realm of the future, feed back into the present and shape it, thereby, also changing the expectations of the future and even the future itself, following the next round of feedback. *Expectations of the future make the present and the future.* Expectations as to the future's sucking-in of goods particularly affect the present sucking-in, which will in turn affect the expectation of future sucking-in and of future sucks-in. The main causation in the economy are not physical forces from the past, but present mental images of the future influencing the future. The expectation of the future wags the present.

The time-structure is: An expectation for the future, t2, is created in t1. An appropriate payment/non-payment-behavior is implemented and, in t3, its appropriateness is either verified or a new expectation is created for the future. There is, thus, also a sequenced overlap of flows of actual payments, which provide money resources for further payments, and of expectation-building and resulting decisions of how to use or not to use the money resources now available. The mutual anticipation of everybody's future behavior will – in both "chambers" – address two issues: Will Alter have money and will it spend it on me? Both moments are unreliable. Subjective value attribution is always subject-related on the one side (as concepts and synergies are different depending on the subject, see page 42 et seq.) and, by the same token, subjective (in the sense of open to bias and error, see footnote 9 on page 42). However, as they are anticipated and even implemented and materialized by selling or buying, they get "objectivized" for the parties involved and their observers through the generally accepted medium of exchange, money. Thus, the economy's extremely shaky subjectivity also endlessly creates hard objectivity. Reflexive mutual observations, including in the 2nd and 3rd degrees, may bring about a, temporarily, rather solid bottom. *George Soros* speaks of two functions, a cognitive and a participating or manipulative of human thinking: "When both

---

16   See *Luhmann* (1988) page 53; *Baecker* (1988) page 105 ff.

functions operate at the same time, they can interfere with each other. How? By depriving each function of the independent variable that would be needed to determine the value of the dependent variable: when the independent variable of one function is the dependent variable of the other, neither has a genuinely independent variable"[17] There, is, thus "slippage" and "uncertainty".[18]

Things can become even crazier. One can either maintain that the reflexive witchcraft, which superimposes itself over what would determine values and prices without it, remains false, a deception, illusionary, ideological, etc. and ascribe truth only to the covered-up underlying reality; in this case, one ought to admit that one can get rich by making "false" investments and "poor" by making correct investments. Alternatively, one can acknowledge that where reflexivity applies, it may cancel out the possibility to conventionally distinguish between truth and falsehood. "Knowledge", *Soros* says in the latter sense, comes from a traditional correspondence idea of truth and true statements. "A statement is true if it corresponds to facts." However, reflexivity tricks us concerning the correspondence idea of truth. "The facts no longer serve as an independent criterion, by which the truth of a statement can be judged because the correspondence may have been brought about by the statement changing facts."[19] Reflexive witchcraft in the form of positive self-reinforcing feedback loops may operate as "fertile fallacies", "interpretations of reality that are distorted, but produce results that reinforce the distortion."[20] Reflection of reflection bends the space in which we can decide on truth. Should we draw a parallel to relativity theory? Or to the even more frantic behavior of parts in quantum theory? Gödel, Escher, and Bach, of course, are certainly also not far away.[21]

A Balance sheet view of M–C–M'

Although the M–C–M'-notation (or the C–M–C'-notation) require and presuppose transactions and exchanges and presuppose further exchanges and flows to take place, they do not depict transactions, exchanges, actions, or flows themselves. Rather, they *fixate intermediate moments of tranquility between transactions*. Like balance sheets, they look at what the same person or player owns at certain moments, here at three different sequential moments in time, and show changes in the *form* of their property and, possibly, its *value* at these junctures. The transmutations lie between these moments.

---

17   *Soros* (2010) page 12.
18   *Soros* (2010) page 13.
19   *Soros* (2010) page 13. Soros gives the example that the statement "it is raining" is not reflexive, but the statement "this is a revolutionary situation" is reflexive.
20   *Soros* (2010) page 16, 29. See also *Soros* (1995) page 65 et seq.
21   See *Hofstadter* (1985).

In the case of C–M–C', this occurs from the perspective of a person in want of a special value-in-use for consumption: C–M–C' spells out "now I have the wrong commodity for consumption, now I have money, for god's sake, finally I now also have the right commodity for consumption!" In the case of M–C–M', the perspective is from a person for whom the exchange of money into a commodity is a means to make more money; it spells out "now I have money, now I have commodities, now I have more money". We have, thus, *two* legs or steps (each with a flow of goods and an inverse flow of money[22]) and *three* moments of relative tranquility, in each C–M–C' and M–C–M', when C, M, C' or YM' can be envisaged as an entry (on the assets side [23]) in a balance sheet.

M–C–M' and supply and sales peripheries

The two transformations in M–C–M', M–C, and C–M', imply two different peripheries[24], a *supply periphery* and a *sales periphery* (Absatz, débit, off-sale) around each firm, which can be envisaged as being at the center of the transaction. Capitalist firms want to have many, good, and cheap suppliers on their (figuratively) left side and appreciate a continuously increasing efficiency and increased productivity of these suppliers, which reduces their costs. On their (figuratively) right side, capitalist firms wish to sell as much of their produce at prices as high as possible; hence, they wish their prospective customers to be hungry, in need, or desirous of their produce and to have many valuable uses or utilities for the produce. These customers should also be as rich as possible. While the counterparties on both sides must be smart to economically produce or to have made a lot of money, they should still act somewhat stupidly towards the firm by undercharging or overpaying. The more these prerequisites are fulfilled, the better the firms in the middle can absorb cheap commodities from the left and successfully lure those on the right to absorb them at a maximum margin.[25]

---

22   We also, accordingly, have *four flows*: First money M flows to suppliers of goods, second, C, the purchased goods flow to the firm; third, C (or C', if processed), goods, flow to purchasers; fourth, the money M' flows to the firm again as the sales price.

23   Only C–M' touches upon the liabilities' side, as equity goes up.

24   On this occasion we might ask: How can trade be productive? Merchants render commodities produced elsewhere available at places *where* they are needed, store them *till when* they are needed, adjust their sizes, volumes and certain properties to specific needs of markets, etc., and prospective users attribute additional value-in-use and value-in-exchange to these changes.

25   To complete the picture: Firms wish *competing* firms, which attempt to also install themselves between the potentially same suppliers and customers, to be as few, as inefficient, unprodutive, poor, and as dumb as possible.

M–C–M' as driver of economic and technical evolution

If consumption-oriented C–M–C'-players made exchanges with other consumption-oriented C–M–C'-players, then this would lead to what Keynes called a *"co-operative"* or *"real-exchange economy"*.[26] Such an economy, as it is bereaved of the main capitalist motive of profit, while it will likely bring about more equality, social security, and social cohesion than capitalism, would unavoidably slow down technological and economic progress and restrict the quality and quantity of procured values-in-use. This is because the motive for the C–M–C'-player is only a change of values-in-use, a relinquishment of certain utilities connected to one object or capacity (his labor) in favor of other utilities. The dash in C–M–C', behind the second C, accordingly, only means "another" or "a preferred" value-in-use; the preference for another value-in-use is, though – see Plato above –always finite and exhaustible. Only the emergence, by self-selection, and the success of specialized M–C–M'-units, who provide "counterpart services" to the consumption-oriented mass of C–M–C'-players, propels the strongest and most effective economic motive, the profit motive, into being. If capitalism finds it proper to operate in the productive economy, it will generate a powerful motive to develop new products sellable at a high M' and reduce the costs of production (of M) and in both cases stimulate technological and economic progress.

Societies that have allowed and incentivized M–C–M' at a large scale were the historic winners in periods of peaceful technical and economic competition and, in fact, also during most wars. Those who slowed down and hampered M–C–M', on the contrary, were the losers. In this sense Sparta (although it won the Peloponnesian war) languished behind Athens, the European Middle Ages remained behind 15th century Renaissance Italy, the China of the 19th century fell behind the West of the industrial revolution or the countries of soviet style socialism in the 20th century never reached the economic level of the US, Japan, and Western Europe (although the USSR won the war against Germany).

Segregating effects of M–C–M'

M–C–M' has two heavy segregating effects. In M–C–M'-circuits, consumptive side C–M–C'-players are always net wealth-transferors who attribute value-in-exchange to the good offered in excess of the production costs and transfer this value-in-exchange to the selling wealth-accumulating M–C–M'-players. The M–C–M'-players "cash in" profits M'-M, while their customers only consume. Their wealth is not only reduced if the goods are for immediate consumption, but also if endurable goods are purchased, the value of which will dwindle as time goes by. Only in exceptional and negligible cases, if for example a used car becomes an antique car, does it increase

---

26   *Keynes*, Collected Writings, volume XIII, page 408 f. On M–C–M' and Keynes, see also *Keen* (2011) page 217 et seq.

again. The effect of M–C–M' is, accordingly, always a transfer, absorption, or sucking off of wealth from the C–M–C'-player as wealth-transferor to the M–C–M'-player as wealth-transferee.

The most voluminous version of C–M–C' in modern capitalism consists of workers selling their working power to purchase consumables. As human beings, if healthy, they are equipped with labor through their biological existence and may have qualified it through education and training; then they sell their labor C for M. Hereafter, they use M to purchase everyday nutrition, shelter, clothing, cheap thrills (alcohol, drugs), or a few positional goods. Following this, they are, at best and if they have not fallen ill, suffered an accident, or become too old etc., prepared for an "eternal recurrence of the same" and are capable of offering their labor again. However, M, what they have received as their wage income, disappears without any wealth left. Workers may go through several hundreds of such C–M–C'-circuits – selling their labor, working, obtaining wage, buying consumables, consuming them – only reproducing their labor power, but without any wealth build-up. Workers, who are not able to work or to generate income otherwise, are worse off. This is the *first segregating effect* of M–C–M', which operates *between the parties of the exchange*.

Of course, it is possible that C–M–C'-players in some circuits may also become M–C–M'-players, entrepreneurs, capitalists, or firm in other circuits, where they may also collect a profit. This can compensate or even overcompensate for the loss of wealth suffered in consumptive C–M–C'-circuits. Wealth owners do this all the time and quite obviously. They spend a part of their wealth on consumption. There are also ex-workers who may join the ranks of wealth owners, as inventors, entrepreneurs, artists, sports and movies stars, talented and hardworking professionals, managers, etc. However, millennia of history of profit economies show that this possibility never substantially changed the overall course of events towards a progressive segregation between wealth owners and non-wealth-owners. In summary, it suffices for M–C–M'-players to be at least predominantly M–C–M'-players (in terms of numbers and volume of transactions) to likely materially increase their wealth, while it suffices for C–M–C'-players to remain predominantly C–M–C'-players (in the same sense) to see their original wealth, if there was any, fade away without being able to make up for it. If M–C–M' operates for some time in an area, it will, thus, pump away purchasing power from the C–M–C'-players and, normally, bring about an increasingly unequal wealth distribution.

The *second segregating effect of M–C–M'* works *between M–C–M'-players themselves*. It results from the different profitability of M–C–M-circuits. As some M–C–M'-players realize higher and others lower profits, or even end up with losses (if M>M'), this has the potential to annihilate their firms.

To explain why few grow rich and richer, while many others remain poor, we, only need M–C–M', which by itself creates an increasingly superior center of financially strong and rich wealth owners, which look left, right, and down to a periphery of much poorer C–M–C'-players. This is the result of the normal operation of profit economies and capitalism, as old as they are, and is not a consequence of Marxian "exploitation", of accidental circumstances, or even of deplorable austerity-policies of states.

"Circuit-relatedness" versus "time-periodicity"; C–M–C'- and M–C–M' as circuits, not period-flows

Firms think in circuits when they invest. They call their benchmarks "profit", "return on investment" (ROI), or "internal rate of return (IRR)" which are all expressions for the ratio (M'–M)/M. They may also call it "net present value" (NPV), which is M'-M with M and M' when viewed as present values of a series of payments. These terms, even if firms are unaware of them, are circuit-related or "Umschlag"-related terms.

They presuppose an idea of an "aggregate investment", a sum of outlays in the first movement, and of an "aggregate return", a sum of revenues in a second movement. What belongs to the outflowing and incoming series of flows depends upon the type of investment. A money market dealer's time horizon may only be seconds, minutes or days; the time horizon of a car dealer may be weeks or months, whereas the time horizon for a real estate developer or for an energy plant operator may be years or decades. However, firms condense them into "investment" and "return on investment" (as Marx condensed them into M and M').

As we have seen, investment outlays may even occur *after* the last return has been pocketed, e.g., if mine or plant operators underlie re-cultivation obligations. *Firms can never, thus, attribute much significance to the results in a discretionary time interval*, e.g., the usual annual reporting period. Accordingly, the *thinking in circuits, "circuit relatedness", expresses the heartbeat of business and of investment.* "Time-periodicity", on the other hand, even if it governs reporting, national accounts and statistical data will, by necessity, discretionarily chop off economic events, which are important to assess an investment as a whole. Flows must be chopped off where M–C–M'-circuits end, but M–C–M' circuits may not be chopped off because time periods end accidentally.[27]

Quesnay's tableau économique took the "circuit-relatedness" of business into account by simply surreptitiously presuming that the circuits in his *royaume agricole* would all close in one year; the predominantly annual rhythm of his predominantly agricultural economy allowed for this assumption. Quesnay, thereby, implicitly acknowledged the need to maintain the purity of "circuit-relatedness" in economic analysis. Our effort has to be stricter, methodologically speaking. It maintains the

---

27   Accounting is, of course, aware of this problem. Therefore, time-periodical reporting uses liabilities and provisions to show future M-outlays. The risk-adverse purpose of accounting, though, normally forbids showing future M'-rewards. Macroeconomics is not subjected to that restriction.

purity of circuits, which alone allows for meaningful results, by dealing with circuits solely on the abstract, theoretical level of circuit analysis – and by completely disregarding time periodicity. A circuit, in this book, as already seen, encompasses M-outlays as its first leg, which can be split up into c-outlays (encompassing sterile outlays, such as i-outlays and r-outlays[28], and producive outlays into equipment and inventories) and v-outlays. The second leg of circuits consist in M' rewards that recuperate M with M'-M (or s,) coming on top as profit. Circuit-analysis considers these abstract processes. "Time periodical flows", which belong to the empirical surface level, have no direct relevance and allow for no direct statistical tests.

M–C–M' in product markets and asset markets

Whether there is a market for something, depends on what parties chose to sell. Now, in their M–C–M'-drives, parties cannot only sell things that stand side by side at the same level, such as vine, Coca Cola, automobiles and computers, but also things at a higher level, such as the *capacity to produce* vine, Coca Cola, automobiles or computers. Or, while it is possible to build houses to rent them out, with the aggregate collected rent being M', it is also possible to sell houses. Therefore, it makes sense to distinguish between product markets and asset markets. Businesses produce tangible or intangible goods for sale in product markets, yet firms, i.e., the "M–C–M'-machines", can be sold in asset markets, either in the stock market or M&A etc., as well. Product markets differ according to what kind of commodities are transferred and on the applied legal technique, e.g., whether only a right to a temporary use is sold, e.g., for rent or interest, whether a service is sold, for a service fee, or whether ownership is transferred by a sales contract, for a sales price. Of course, players also consider asset sales and purchases to make a profit. In other words, the process of M–C–M' is capable of applying to itself and *to becoming reflexive*. The "M–C–M'-machine", an organized capacity to generate future financial surpluses, which we call an "asset", is valued by the present value of its future surpluses, and traded in the "meta-markets", which asset markets are.[29] Like profits from the operation of the asset in its "home"-product-markets, these present values can only be estimated (guessed, in a way); in fact, as they depend on a much longer time period and on more circumstances, the uncertainty involved is higher.[30] How

---

28   Interest-outlays, rent-outlays, variable-capital-outlays (salary payments), and constant capital-outlays (outlays on equipment and inventories). Sterile and producive spending components will be explained later. See pages 123 and 351 et seq.

29   This view has provided new means of securing loans, e.g., by pledging and mortgaging assets, which allowed to extend credit to owners of such assets. New means to secure credit were combined with new sources of money when money creation came into being.

30   Assets may be taken back to product markets and used as equipment of another asset again. E.g., buildings, which had been rented out, can be purchased by a firm for use as an office or by a worker for use as a dwelling.

an asset performs, e.g., a business is being run, depends upon the concepts and synergies, of its owners; there are high concept and high synergy and low concept and low synergy users. In asset markets the potentials to generate future financial surpluses – debt, real estate, businesses or other assets – are normally forwarded to their most efficient users. Being regarded as an asset does not disenable the asset from possibly generating uses that may remain sellable in product markets. While the land is a sellable asset, its temporal use may still be purchased in product markets. Therefore, the borderline between product markets and asset markets is sometimes fuzzy.

M–C–M' and social anthropology

We have mentioned that a feeling existed that it was "bad" – against custom, tradition, good spirits, religion, morals etc. – to subject the procurement of goods for humans to profiteering and that many mystical men and great thinkers spoke out against it. It is beyond the possibilities of this book to pursue this as much as the issue would deserve, but just as we know that profiteering played no role in goods procurement in primitive society, so too can we be certain that the rise of profiteering and M–C–M' in the early profit economies of ancient Greece, Rome, and China contributed greatly to the horrors of classical Greece (6th to 4th century BC), the empire of Alexander the Great, the Roman Republic and the Roman Empire, Principate, and Dominate, and Chinese history from the "Spring and Autumn"-period, via the "Warring States-Period" through the Ch'in and Han-dynasties to just short of the T'ang dynasty, hence roughly the period between 800 BC to 600 AD.

It may surprise many readers that we must assess the Middle Ages as generally more "human" and particularly more bearable for the lower classes. The improvement affected all major civilizations and was due to the astonishing parallel success of religions and philosophies in putting the bad ghost of M–C–M' – at least partially – back into the box, with the prohibition of interest-bearing loans being their signature case. If it got worse again, with the "enclosures" and the "original accumulation", then this was in fact caused by the resurrection of M–C–M' during the European Renaissance. Accordingly, M–C–M' was not only criticized as a cause of evil at the historic times before the Middle Ages, but was also retrospectively used by theoreticians as an explanation for the resurrection of the evils of antique profit economies. We shall briefly mention four authors, who make use of M–C–M' in this sense; these authors are Karl Polanyi, Karl Jaspers, Stanley Diamond, and David Graeber. *Polanyi* presents his reasoning more like a critique of markets rather than as a critique of profit economies. He writes, "...never before our own time were markets more than accessories of economic life. As a rule, the economic system was absorbed in the social system, and whatever principle of behavior predominated in the economy, the presence of the market pattern was found to be compatible with it ...

[and] ... revealed no tendency to expand at the expense of the rest".[31] He views pre-market-economies as mostly dominated by reciprocity and redistribution.[32] There is, thus, "the absence of the motive of gain, the absence of the principle of laboring for remuneration [and] ... the absence of any separate and distinct institution based on economic motives".[33] A "divorce of the economic motive from all concrete social relationships which would by their very nature set a limit to that motive" did not exist at that time, therefore.[34] Markets are limited and controlled, whether in primitive society[35] or in feudalism or mercantilism. There was even little difference between primitive society, feudalism, and mercantilism in this regard. "They disagreed only on the method of regulating; guilds, towns and provinces appealed to the force of custom and tradition while the new state authority favored statute and ordinance. But they were equally averse to the odea of commercializing labor and land – the precondition of market economy."[36] Yet, arrives the "utopia"[37] of self-regulating markets and with it an "extreme artificiality of market economy",[38] which, if it succeeded against resistance, only did so as "the outcome of a conscious and often violent intervention on the part of government".[39] "No market economy was conceivable that did not include a market for labor; but to establish such a market, especially in England's rural civilization, implied no less than the wholesale destruction of the traditional fabric of society."[40] A competitive labor market did not really exist in industrial capitalism in England before 1834, according *Polanyi*, when the *Speenhamland Law* was substituted by new poor laws.[41],[42] While he declaredly puts forward a criticism of the ideology of self-regulating markets, decades before the neoliberal ecstasy came over us, he actually "hits the sack and means the donkey". That becomes quite clear when he writes: "The transformation implies a change in the motive of actions on the part of members of society; for the motive of subsistence that

---

31 *Polanyi* (1944) page 71.

32 *Polanyi* (1944) page 53.

33 *Polanyi* (1944) page 49.

34 *Polanyi* (1944) page 57.

35 Where "the individual... is not threatened by starvation unless the community as a whole is in a like predicament" (*Polanyi* (1944) page 171). See Polanyi (1944) page 167 on starvation in market economies.

36 *Polanyi* (1944) page 73. Mercantilism, according to Polanyi, liberated trade from particularism, but simultaneously expanded the scope of regulation (page 70).

37 *Polanyi* (1944) page 144, 258.

38 *Polanyi* (1944) page 77.

39 *Polanyi* (1944) page 258. See also page 146 "The road to the free market was opened and kept open by an enormous increase in continuous, centrally organized and controlled interventionism."

40 *Polanyi* (1944) page 81.

41 *Polanyi* (1944) page 82.

42 *Polanyi* (1944) page 81–84.

of gain must be substituted."[43] While this clearly refers to M–C–M' and expresses a substantive understanding, it remains a weaker point in Polanyi's great work that he officially uses "too much self-regulated market", rather than "profit economy" or M–C–M' as his main *explanans. Stanley Diamond*,[44] in his important article on "the order of custom and the rule of law"[45] and throughout his other work, offers a distinction that could become the most fundamental for the theory of social evolution. The overall-distinction between primitive society and civilization is clearly preferable to the Marxian sequence primitive society – slavery – feudalism – capitalism – socialism, etc., which is, in the last instance, derived from a retro-projection of the false Marxian theory of exploitation in combination with an "economistic" reading of a Hegelian concept of evolution. While it is true that in times where there were no (or not too many) "twofold free laborers"[46] (but slaves or feudal dependent peasants), wealth owners would obtain access to their labor not via modern employment contracts, but otherwise, this difference is overstressed if it is elevated to the key to understand evolution. Moreover, the dichotomy primitive society vs civilization transgresses the economic dimension. It entails custom vs law, primitive organization vs statehood, mythical thinking vs rational thinking *and* C–M–C vs M–C–M', etc. *David Graeber in his* work "Debt", employs *a* term coined by *Karl Jaspers* for the aforementioned period, which was "*Achsenzeit*" ("Axial Age")[47] and leaves no doubt that the "Axial Age", hence ancient capitalism, was a very ugly period,[48] but does not, unfortunately, address economic issues and M–C–M' extensively. Still, the importance assigned to M–C–M' as a central tenet of economic theory is clearly also indirectly supported by his work.

As a second social-anthropological aspect, it is noteworthy that there were material frictions in getting modern capitalism off the ground, not only in terms of

---

43   *Polanyi* (1944) page 43 et seq.

44   As a law student and political thinker, one grows up considering the "rule of law" as a great achievement. Rightly so! Nothing apart from the state can and should rule and it is best for everybody if the state's rule takes the form of predetermined, known, general, objectively administered and court-controlled laws (rather than discretionary, impulsive orders following the spur of the moment of a weird ruler). As children of today, we even appreciate the "rule of law" if we do not like the contents of the laws at the time. *Diamond's* use of the term "rule of law", however, places the emphasis on the laws, which the state authoritatively pushed into primitive society – based on abstract reasoning, philosophy, religion – displacing the order of custom.

45   *Diamond*, The rule of law versus the order of custom, Social Research, Vol. 38, No. 1 (Spring 1971), pages 42–72.

46   The second feature, apart from laborers being freed of land, consists in their being freed of feudal bonds, hence a legal person that may freely contract (*Marx*, Capital, volume 1, chapter 4, section 3).

47   *Jaspers* (1949) page 251.

48   *Graeber* (2011) page 224, 251.

the lack of capital or money, but also in terms of the lack of willing workers. Even if workers were bereaved of the chance to subsist, as they had before, outside of manufactures and factories, they still at all needed some "education" to become capable and willing to endure employment in capitalist production (rather than emigrating, becoming bandits, or dying off). Social-historical, anthropological and psychological studies found significant resistance of early workers against manufactures and factories. It appears that the *"pull"* coming from firms' job offers (including to lure with goods, which could only be bought with salaries), and the *"push"* from the loss of more primitive income opportunities were very often *not* enough to draw the expropriated peasants, their children, and other rural residents into wage labor. The reason may have been the unaccustomed long working hours, compared to the indolence of the prospective laborers, at which e.g., Malthus points with regard to South American or Irish workers,[49] or a reluctance of early workers to bow to the discipline in manufactures or factories. It often also appears that men were, quite simply, also not psychologically fit for this purpose. Therefore, a second artificial "push" had to be exerted through foreclosing of even second- and third-class ways of alternative subsistence. Marx describes the English enclosures in this sense[50] – the termination of poor laws ought also to be mentioned here[51] – and analyzed the German *Holzdiebstahlsgesetz*, a law against the gathering of wood in forest,[52] in this context, too. The period of the creation of a mass proletariat is also the period at which stories about poachers appear everywhere and the police and criminal law began to levy much heavier sanctions against petty property offenses of the poor. Simple theft and pickpocketing, indeed, became capital crimes in England in the 18th century.[53] Sometimes, raising taxes in money may also have been a purposeful instrument by which to force lower classes to seek work in manufactures, factories, or mines.[54]

Predator-prey interdependence and M–C–M'-governed macro-transmissions

We have presented M–C–M' as a crucial concept for the economic analysis of profit economies and already seen, to some extent, how it *builds and shapes* the economic system, almost like a DNA, by selecting which economic events occur or do not occur. We shall later use M–C–M' to examine deficient employment-generating spending and the problem of the closure of M–C–M'-circuits. In the upcoming section, we

---

49   *Malthus* (1836) volume II, page 382–398.

50   *Marx*, Capital volume I, chap. 24.

51   *Polanyi* (1944) page 81 et seq.

52   *Marx* (2008) page 109 et seq.

53   I refer to my further treatment of the subject in my doctoral thesis (Wächter (1987)). See also *Thompson* (1975), *Hay* (1975) page 17 et seq.; *Ignatieff* (1978); *Lea* in: *Fine* (1979) page 76: *Linebaugh* (1976); *Spitzer/Scull* in: *Greenberg* (1977) page 276; *Rusche/Kirchheimer* (1974); *Treiber/Steinert*, (1980).

54   *Graeber* (2011) page 51.

shall try to draw a *line from biology, i.e., from social biology, to M–C–M' and the economic system*. This line will teach us two important lessons: First, while it largely consists of communication, the economic system still has a "materialistic" kernel, *a mechanic of biological life and death*. Second, while the economic system inserts itself between human predators and nature, it not only safeguards within itself the old type of socio-biological predator-prey-interdependencies in a modified form, but also adds new interdependencies in a similar predator-prey-style.

Animals, as we already stated with regard to humans, have a multitude of necessary relationships to their environment. Aside oxygen, water, sun beams, land or water to live on or in etc., they need food as nutrition and materials from the animated and unanimated nature, humans also for clothing, housing and other production. If all these necessities are the "prey" of zoological systems, the latter, in turn, are the "predators" of their prey. The manner, in which prey is produced and reproduced, matters greatly for predators. Some prey – other zoological systems – are predators themselves, while others – botanic systems and minerals – are not.

In predator-prey-relations of primitive stages, predators take *the body of the prey*, which they mostly disassemble to eat it up, use it for clothing or for shelter etc., thereby *destroying* or *killing the prey*. There are different predator and prey species with specific characteristics, which determine the predators' preferences for prey, e.g., what plants or meat they can chew, digest and they like and whether they can gather or hunt them. Insofar primitive predator-prey systems emerge around a *twofold complementarity*: value-in-use of the prey for the predator (e.g., measured in nutritional value) and superior power of the predator over the prey (e.g., measured in kills per effort). Both moments need to unite: For a hyena to become a predator over a lion, it does not suffice for the hyena to like the tasty lion's meat…

Predator-prey relations between species are not static but can change. E.g., if a species migrates into a new habitat, another species in that habitat may discover the newcomer as tasty prey. Normally, of course, a species will only migrate into a new habitat, if it expects to find prey underneath it there. Hence, for prey to be available for a predator, it must first have found other prey underneath it. In practice, there will often be a basic low mineral level, one or several botanic levels, and then a series of upper zoological layers of predators and prey, which each built on the next lower level. Short cuts and jumps across levels are, though, possible. Humanity thrones at the top. While the levels have in common that the upper depends on the lower and influences it, of course, the character of the relationship between plants and the mineral world or between animals and plants and minerals or between animals and animals and the rest differs greatly. The term "predator-prey-relation", thus, has a different meaning on different levels to which it is applied.[55]

---

55   Often reference is made to a so-called "nutritional chain". Small fish eat plankton, big fish eat small fish, humans eat big fish, like tuna and whales. Small land animals eat gras and

Looking at nutrition, if there are no predators above, the destiny of the top-predator depends exclusively on its prey, hence on the prey's number, how many kills the predator can make, how many other predators for the prey are around and how many kills they make. Furthermore, the top-predator depends on the prey's reproduction rate, and whether the prey population is exhausted by the kills it suffers. If a predator is also prey to a predator of another level, its destiny also depends on the number of kills it suffers itself. The relation to prey underneath is the most important moment of the biological existence of species, the avoidance of being captured as prey on a higher predators should be the second important one.

Predator-prey-relations mostly exist in parallel between a number of predators and a number of preys, and this over several stories, so that two species often have only little impact on each other. However, sometimes stronger interdependencies evolve between two species, and veritable predator-prey-systems emerge. We have already seen one moment, which intensifies predator-prey-interdependencies: If a predator has *no other predator on top*, its fate will largely depend on its prey underneath. Interdependencies become more intense if one species becomes the sole or overwhelming nutrition supplier to a predator, i.e., if the nutritional value of killed units from the prey species covers most of the predator's species aggregate nutritional demand. This implies that no or only few alternative prey is around. Such *exclusivity of supply* will rise the impact of a falling or growing prey population onto the predators; if there is far too little supply, the demanding predators will simply die out. Contrary to what we know from the theory of market forms in capitalism, exclusivity of supply will, though – we are in the realm of values-in-use-procurement by violence and not in the realm of freely negotiated contracts – not convey market power to the prey.

The interdependencies become very intense in the other direction, if a predator species becomes the overwhelming or sole demander for a prey species, i.e., if the number of kills by a predator in relation to the prey population grows particularly high. This implies that no or few alternative predators are around. *Exclusivity of demand* will, thus, even if it does, again, not convey market power to the predator – we continue to be outside of the realm of freely negotiated contracts – rise the impact of a falling or growing predator population onto the prey population. If *exclusive supply combines with exclusive demand*, we find ourselves in a particularly highly integrated predator-prey-system. The Specific properties of the predator and prey populations

leaves, big animals eat small animals, humans eat big animals, like pigs, cows, lambs etc. Sometimes there are jumps across levels and humans also eats small fish, mussels, oysters (which are too well protected against less clever inhabitants of the oceans), chicken and other birds. Inversions occur rarely. Small animals seldom manage to procure the power to kill an animal on a higher level; occasionally there is group hunting though, or they can steal the kills from superior animals or are scavengers.

and their prey and predators underneath as well as of the habitat, in which they live, determine the story of such relations.[56]

Initially, humans are just one predator and prey species amongst others. As predators, they take the body or parts of the body of their prey mostly killing or, occasionally, only crippling it. Sometimes they also take kills made by the prey. As prey they suffer the same fate. As the human species elevates itself above all other species, it more seldom becomes prey to them and the effort to defend against predators can be reduced, allowing to transfer time and energy to improve and refine the capabilities of human preying. They first improve their gathering and hunting skills, but then – once more, the Neolithic meant the crucial jump forward – become sedentary and substitute the gathering of plants by planting and harvesting them and the hunting of animals by capturing and breeding them. The increased control over their prey allows mankind to also deal more efficiently and economically with it. E.g., they can now avoid unnecessary killing and collateral damage to their prey if they only need *fruits of the body of their domesticated prey*, e.g., its hair, wool, eggs or milk. Or they only kill and eat *offspring* of prey, thereby preserving valuable breeding capacities. Furthermore, mankind learned to use *services of prey*, such as having domesticated oxen or horses pull chars or plows or as using slaves in neolithic plantations. This early form of industrialization in the relationship of mankind to its human-helots, animal-helots and plant-helots further raises its superiority over all other species.

With the increasing dominance of humanity intertwined revolutionary changes occur. Proto-states and states are erected and invent and administer property and other laws. Property laws basically consist in foreclosing opportunities as predators for some while monopolizing these opportunities in favor of others. This is particularly evident with hunting rights, by which the appropriation of non-domesticated animals becomes an exclusive right of the title holders. But ownership of land, too, means that non-owners are excluded from using it to farm or pasture botanic or zoological prey. In other words, while the human species rises to become the dominant species, humans invent, amongst themselves, rules and practices, which systematically limit the "direct preying" of human individuals to specific channels, by which an increasing number of humans lose all access to such "direct preying". Humanity risen to the top of the pyramid, erects barriers for its individuals to profit from its

---

56   We shall not further pursue the specifics in this book. They are, amongst others, the life expectancy and fertility of predators and prey, the nutritional value of one kill for the predators, the killing effectivity of the predator, whether mostly "just-in-time-delivery" of the needed amount of prey is available or whether a significant percentage of the nutritional value out of a kill rot before consumption, the effects of the peripheral species etc. They render the matter over-complicated very quickly and may diffuse the interdependencies within the system. As we are interested in the evolution of predator-prey-structures in the economic system, where more generalized structures prevail, they do not greatly matter for us here.

victory and their fighting spirit is redirected to battling for a share of the aggregate prey, which human society has become capable to strike; human individual predators meet again to battle this out on a novel intra-societal fighting ground.

As hinted at the beginning of this section, we propose to conceive of this mediated intra-societal distribution of killed or to-be-killed prey (which we may now again think of as including minerals) in terms of predator-prey-relations, too. Insofar the prey, which has been or can be socially made available, *remains* prey and predators continue to fight for it. But, as seen, society also enlarges the term of "prey" by discovering the human *capacity to work*, i.e., *labor power*, as a fantastic utility, which is worthwhile to be chased. This rendered preying reflexive: human predators, since, procure for themselves not only the booty of other human predators but also their capacity of future preying. But it does not even stop here. The human society went on to elevate a wholly original and very specific produce of human labor to the most consequential *super-prey* of human history: media of exchange and, ultimately, *money*. Gold, silver and copper, commodity money, first conquered this role, but soon states would soon establish fiat money (without value-in-exchange if demonetized) as instrument to pay taxes and as legal tender, and this wholly artificial "fiat prey" joined commodity money as super-prey.

This evolution was accompanied by several remarkable formal changes: *First*, prey changed its character from to-be-gathered "free" and "wild" plants or to-be-hunted "free" and "wild" animals to *inner-social appropriation rights* regarding the socially domesticated botanic and zoological prey. These appropriation rights were mostly already *owned* by somebody who related to them as his *property*. As physical violence of privates was largely forbidden, one could only appropriate these appropriation rights with their owners' consent; hence, one needed to agree on an *exchange* with owners who *traded* their prey. In fact, the owners were rather often willing to enter into trades or exchanges. To prepare them, which was facilitated as states now protected the property by laws, the owners now even dared to *parade their prey on markets* to invite predators to trades.

Second, as regards money as the new and single most important generalized and standardized super-prey, *the need of a specific complementarity between predators and prey disappeared*. The money-prey had utility in its value-in-exchange, and this utility attracted all predators equally. This was connected to a differentiation in the human predators. Aside their specific stomach for values-in-uses, which reflected their complementary position in biology and social production – e.g., as general humans they need medicine to overcome illness and as farmers they need agricultural tools –, they build a second stomach, which was now *identical in all predators*. Aside needing or liking specific different things, they began to like money, too. Money insofar resembled sunbeams and oxygen. Yet, beyond what sunbeams and oxygen were capable of, money, could mostly be exchanged into specific complementary prey, too. Finally, it was remarkably different insofar as humans could absorb it *without limits.* The overkilling of botanic and zoological prey, beyond present needs, would only lead to stores with rotten plants and meat and unnecessarily reduce the living prey. Yet, the money-prey does not rot. It can be stored in any quantity, and it can even be multiplied.

Third, while old-fashioned predator-prey structures – e.g., big fish had to always look out for small fish, and small fish had to always look out for plankton etc. – possessed an inflexible "directedness" to specific suppliers, which created a hierarchical "chain"-or "string"-structure, this was different with money. This men-produced standard prey, money, as an exception, rendered the playing field for predators *equal and polycentric.* Predators could now watch out for this prey everywhere, at 360 degrees around them. Everybody, even those with little money, became a possible supplier of the money prey – as everybody had become its demander.[57]

Fourth, we not only have, as far as money is concerned, a polycentric mutual supply of and demand for a standard prey, aside the continued hunting of specific predators for specific complementary prey, but the "kills", which we already have observed to have become consensual, also *integrate into pairs.* One kill of prey, which was offered by providers of a specific complementarity and one kill of prey out of the atomistic pool of the standard prey money now always had to occur simultaneously in an intertwined (do ut des) manner.

Fifth, the substantial and formal changes that "predators", "prey" and "predator-prey"-relation have undergone in their transformation from social-biological to intra-societal predator-prey-relations – new forms of prey, consensual trades or exchanges instead of violence, polycentricity and paring up of kills in trades or exchanges –, do *not annihilate the predator-prey-interdependencies as such but safeguard them. This is the most important point for us.* The point is obvious with regard to old-fashioned biologically based dependencies: Priests in the Palace of Nestor near Pylos, even if their access to plants and cattle is now mediated by "inner-social prey", such as money, which they receive for their priestly services, will still need vegetables and meat to survive. Furthermore, even if money is available to them, if the prospective sellers, the owners of farm land and pasturages, have carelessly exhausted their reservoirs, in case of natural catastrophes or if domesticated prey was captured by other predators, the priests will not be able to buy anything. Yet, in addition to such still essentially social-biological dependencies, novel interdependencies arise, which emerge out of the intermediation of the economic system and are essentially social. E.g., Nestor may no longer be interested in the services of so many priests and send some away who may not be able to find new exchange partners who will buy their labor and allow them to lay grip on money as intermediate prey. Or somebody who even has the money must learn that others have bought the

---

57   Note that through money not every human became prey for everybody, but that every human could *own* prey for every human.

specific goods away, which he wanted to buy, e.g., to later resell them at a higher profit.

Most moments of our discussion of the transformation of predator-prey-inter-dependencies during social, economic and political evolution, which we now conclude, are, as such, not new in substance. Yet it allows us to conceive of C–M–C' and of M–C–M' as a bond or type of entanglement in capitalism, which has been inherited from social biology and only been transformed. C–M–C' and M–C–M', in particular the latter, may be something like the Lotka-Volterra-Formula of capitalism.

Section 2. The productive and the sterile economy

As stated, this book assigns a great importance to the distinction between a sterile wealth economy and a productive economy. With this distinction we first refer to intuitions that everybody already has – even if based, at the moment, on too simplifying abstractions. We shall leave it that way for the time being and only later make comments about how the flows of the two economies have to be separated more cleanly. The reader is asked to follow the argument with that in mind.[58]

Today, probably most people feel that the productive economy is the "rule" and the sterile economy is the "exception" in capitalism. From a wealth owners' perspective, and to better understand what really goes on, it may make sense to turn this around. Renting out land, giving land to feudal vassals for a share of the harvest, making loans to generate interest, or equipping firms with equity for a share of the profit has been the first and preferred way to draw revenues for millennia; these revenues are sterile revenues, though. Productive activity, on the contrary, inventing a new technology, discovering markets, engineering production, building factories, employing workers, mass-producing something, etc. appeared artificial and unnecessarily complicated and burdensome to many wealth owners. You had to understand something about a lot of things, show focus, intelligence, competence, organization, endurance, resilience, recklessness, *and* needed a good deal of luck in the productive economy – and all of this only to turn money you already had into (often many and tiny) claims against customers, whose sum, if you could collect it, would hopefully exceed that which you had possessed previously. The productive economy, may, thus, more properly be seen as a series of exceptional expeditions, a rare and risky activity for the particularly braves and merchant heroes, like war times compared to peace times.

---

58   The later delineation will show that what at first glance appears to typically belong into the sterile wealth economy has almost always a component of producive spending, and that what appears to typically belong in the productive economy also almost always has a sterile component. See on page 123 et seq. and 351 et seq.

The wealth economy: Sterile revenues and sterile spending

Wealth owners make use of this their owner power, which states secure through the rule of law, in an evolved and civilized stage of society, by using their ownership of money, real estate, and other wealth to draw revenues. The wealth economy consists in drawing recurring income from wealth assets in product markets and from buying and selling assets with capital gains in asset markets. The sterile wealth owners' only job, as sterile wealth owners (not as business manager or philanthropist), involves overseeing this and occasionally making changes to their portfolio.

Imagine you had grown up in a wealthy family. You learned about the existence of foreign countries and other cities by learning about the wealth that your family owned there: Twenty hotels in Europe, a glamorous and famous department store in Barcelona, a series of apartment buildings in Ottawa and Toronto, a significant stock holding in a car manufacturer in the US and, of course, your family offices in New York and London taking care of a large portfolio of bonds, stock, and real estate. You would have learned that your family receives ongoing payments from these investments; on occasion, you would visit some of the hotels as a privileged guest and, as you became a teenager, you would sometimes be invited to join meetings in which people report to your family about the status of the investments. At times, consultants would advise your parents to sell an investment and to buy a new one, e.g., after your uncle who spoke Spanish and had lived in Barcelona had passed away. When you once proposed that all hotels should have tennis courts, your mother would smile at you and say "leave that to the people who understand something about it." You and your parents would not have to deal with suppliers or customers of your family's possessions, not have to get up early and to drive, not even in a limousine with a chauffeur, through polluted, noisy, and crowded roads to factories at the outskirts of ugly cities. You would also not have to deal with blue collar workers or other employees; indeed, you would mostly not even deal with those who do deal with them.[59] You would, hence, grow up looking at the wealth economy from a *family office perspective*. Note this is a story *above* the "City perspective" or "Wall Street perspective" taken by Keynes or Minsky[60] as it includes asset classes not even traded in the London City or on Wallstreet. All sterile revenues flow to wealth owners; they arrive at what we shall call their *"sterile arrival port"*. The main sub-categories of sterile revenues in the wealth economy, in product, and asset markets, are:

---

59   Of course, many young men and women who are lucky to be born in a wealthy family take pride in learning some trade from scratch.

60   *Minsky* (1975) page 55, 70.

Sterile wealth owners' sterile debt revenues

Debt enables the simplification of M–C–M'-investments into M–M'-investments, the shortest way to generate income out of existing wealth. Once you own debt, you normally need to not do anything more to increase your wealth, but to collect the debt service (interest payments and repayment of the principal) on the agreed dates in the agreed amounts.

Social obligations played an important role in early and innocent primitive societies, before money and profit emerged. Fathers wished to have as many sons as possible because sons "owed"– on the basis of an order of custom, not on law or contract, hence, in a mythical or traditional sense – them to work for them and to maintain them in their (short) old age. Such social obligations were superseded and re-shaped by law and their contents changed in more advanced ancient social structures with proto-states or central states.[61] We saw that it became a perfectly accepted method to make war on neighbors, to subjugate them and to draw tributes from them. The most "signature debt" of antiquity, though, was internal: It was the debt of small farmers to local grandees or to grand merchants. The smaller and poorer their land, the worse their equipment, the less they could self-insure against the risks of agriculture, the more they had to take on such debt. Or if the state insisted on collecting taxes in money, small peasants would be forced to take out loans, thereby losing a smaller or exorbitant part of its value as interest.[62] Almost everything could drive them into their creditors' arms. If bad weather hit or only a daughter was to marry, then they needed money to finance the time until the next harvest, to purchase seed or to provide a dowry.

This kind of debt, in fact, became infamously brutal in the early profit economies of the "Axial Age", e.g., in Greece, Rome, and China. The creditors of such loans did not need to worry about whether the loan and interest could be repaid, as long as they could execute in the land, animals, tools, or even in family members of their farmer-debtors, e.g., by selling them or their daughters into slavery. In the Middle Ages, with the dominance of great religions – Christianity, Islam, and Buddhism – and feudal structures, through usury laws and personal bonds of feudalism, the situation became more bearable (as we already saw). *David Graeber* writes: "Yet for most of the earth's inhabitants, it (the Middle Ages) could only be seen as an extraordinary improvement over the terrors of the 'Axial Age'." Tougher practices remerged only with upcoming capitalism, the abolition of usury laws, abstract private property and with Protestantism (in Europe).[63] Still, just as in farmers' monetary debt, feudal bondage conveyed sterile revenues.

---

61   See *Diamond* (1971) pages 42–72.

62   *Sadao*, The economic and social history of former Han, page 600 et seq. Or they would sell their produce at a disadvantageous price to them.

63   *Graeber* (2011) page 250; see also pages 210 and 250 et seqs.

Sovereign debt emerged as a new type of debt with central states. It either came into being to finance luxury desires of groups courted by the reigning dynasty or because sovereigns had to finance wars. It was a great means to finance the 500 years of fighting between the new-born countries to establish their supremacy in Europe, after the Middle Ages.[64] Sovereign debt emerged in Renaissance North Italian city states. The Holy Roman Empire of the German Nation of Charles V soon followed suit. At first, the loans were paid out in commodity money, silver or gold, by the wealth-owning merchant families, the Medici in Florence or the Fugger in Augsburg. Later the Spanish wealth elite followed, who – to the extent they had not already wasted their riches – supported the Spanish emperors against the Netherlands and Great Britain. Other great merchants and bankers stood behind the warring parties of the Thirty Years War, Louis XIV, and the British, who had become rich with their colonial possessions, and who also partially debt-financed the wars to defend and extend their possessions. The amounts of money needed, and the sovereign indebtedness, grew from war to war. What the English colonial merchants, manufacturers, or factory owners had to lent out to finance the British army in the American Independence War was far less than what the subsequent Napoleonic wars would cost;[65] a further rise came with the arrival of the states of the second wave of capitalist development, the US, Germany, Japan, Austria, Russia, etc. through their wars, the US civil war, the Crimean war, the German unification wars, World War I, and World War II.

The worth behind state debt was not so much the present assets of the state, or of their populations, but the future flow of assessable taxes and other contributions – basically the same worth which is behind tribute debt of subjugated tribes or states. However, while the subjugated only work obstinately, avoid tribute payments where possible, and throw liberation wars from time to time, state citizens normally

---

64   See *Kennedy* (1987). The rivalry between a significant number of units in Europe with the financial and military means to maintain their independence (page 55), fewer impediments than elsewhere and others opening the door wide, e.g., China and Japan by withdrawing from sailing the oceans in 1433 in 1636, allowed these European units to compete for the top of the world. Doing so, they pushed military technology and financial practices to their limits, resulting in frequent old-fashioned over indebtedness and illiquidity of states, but also in the invention of new financial practices of state financing. These included not only the obvious robbing and mining of silver and gold, particularly by the Spaniards in South America between 1560 and the late 1630s or the confiscation of church or other land, including under false accusations, e.g., by *Cromwell* in England in 1530 (page 110), but also serious modernizations, such as putting the tax system into order by *Sully* under *Henri IV.* in the early 17th century in France (page 122), or in England around the Napoleonic wars (page 138, 212), setting up an early sovereign debt market in Amsterdam or England the early 17th century (page 123) or with the foundation of the Bank of England in 1694 (page 139–141).

65   *Ferguson* (2008) page 70 et seq. "Without wars", Ferguson writes, "nineteenth-century states would have little needs to issue bonds" (page 92).

pay their own state's taxes more willingly and states are better at executing tax debt against their own subjects.

Initially, when a king called the feudal lords and great merchants to make financial contributions, they primarily acquiesced with the motive to support their sovereign's cause. They did so if the war was in their interest and/or as they, e.g., in the case of the Fugger, intended to use the loans to gain political influence over their sovereign. Soon, though, the financial investment motive split away from other motives and wealth owners would simply "invest" in war financing, including by making loans to or by buying debt from their countries' enemies (as arms manufacturers would sometimes supply both sides of a war). In the 20th century, sovereign debt evolved from an exceptional means of war financing to a more regular means by which to also finance infra structural, social policies, and prosthetics, i.e., macroeconomic policies. Sovereign debt, since, also finances roads, ports, airports, canals, protection against natural catastrophes, education, and social transfers.

The opportunities to invest in debt rose with the growth of corporations (corporate debt is like a war bond on success in business) and, later, even extended into small household debt (housing debt, student loans, automobile debt, other consumer utilities debt, subsistence debt, e.g., credit cards debt), which became available at large scale. They can also be re-packaged and structured, collateralized, and be protected by insurances, e.g., credit default swaps. Today, debt includes not only bonds, but also options, futures, and certain derivatives.[66] Debt investments got more abundant with private bank credit money creation and state fiat money creation. Creditors no longer had to lay out scarce gold or silver to debtors but they could at least partly use fractional reserves bank credit money creation.

---

66 Many people find it difficult to understand debt. If they had wealth, they think, they would not give it away and expose it to the risk of not being repaid. They would rather keep it safe or invest it in a venture, which they could control, themeselves. Apart from seriously wealthy people simply not having the time to invest all their wealth themselves, there are several other errors in this. First, all wealth, not just debt, is always at risk. Land was often exhausted, destroyed by natural catastrophes or wars (in recent times polluted), expropriated, or it lost value because nobody would pay rent. Businesses may go bankrupt or may also be expropriated. Money held in banks may be lost if banks go bust; paper money hoarded in safes at home may be robbed, be burned, or lose its value in inflations or currency reforms. Furthermore, in fact, most debt is less risky than people believe. If a wealth owner buys a stock and the corporation falls into bankruptcy, then the investment is lost, if the wealth owner loans the money to somebody who buys the stock with the loan, then the wealth owner at least still has a claim for repayment against the debtor *in persona*. Furthermore, many loans – e.g., real estate loans of banks – are against additional collateral. In this case, creditors need not worry too much about the business merits of the intended investment or about the general solvency of the debtor, but only need to watch the value of the collateral. After all, wealth owners are not mistaken if they continue to do what they have done for millennia – loan out money.

Sterile wealth owners' sterile rent revenues

The second asset class encompasses revenues from allowing the use of real estate. Real estate encompasses naked land and land with buildings and other structures on it or only such buildings or structures. Rent is for real estate what interest is for loaned money; the debtor has to repay the principal of the loan on top and the tenant has to return the rented real estate on top of paying rent. Rent revenues or spending flow into product markets for consumptive and investive purposes.

Land is, normally, not produced. That is different only if new islands are built, e.g., in Dubai, if cost lines are extended, or if land has been destroyed by flooding, volcano eruption or chemical, nuclear or other waste before. Under the *conditio humana*, land, which provides a resistant surface and keeps you from sinking away, is needed underneath every activity. "Mother earth" is the *causa causans, the conditio sine qua non* of human existence. It is needed for simply being around, eating, sleeping, consuming, and relaxing, but also for all investive activities, e.g., artisans' ateliers, shops, agriculture, factory production, even asset administration. The ground's specific physical properties (allowing to grow rice or for foresting or pasturage) or what is underneath the land (raw materials, coal, oil, gas, precious metals) may enable additional value attributions. Land is a rather robust asset, destructible only in few situations (losses to oceans, rivers, volcanic activity, atomic pollution). As it cannot be carried away or hidden, it is easy to recover if somebody has taken it away from you (by expropriation or by illegal force). You only need to build up sufficient strength to reconquer it, e.g., by finding allies or in a political restauration. Land can be used as a factor of production by the owner directly by employing laborers, dependent peasants or slaves on it who produce something to be sold. However, owners only use a small part themselves and lease out the largest part for rent. That was a big thing in history as renting land became the means of survival for otherwise property-less farmers; it sometimes even allowed them to prosper. Self-employed artisans also rented shops; they were smaller in square meters but were situated in more expensive neighborhoods, closer to centers of villages, towns, or city centers. Land and buildings were later rented to manufacture and factory operators. More recently, urban land became great to rent out as office space to service firms or as dwelling, including even to workers. Its value depends on its rent-generating capacity, which in turn depends on the higher or lower profitability of businesses, for which it is used, or of the incomes of the people who want to live there and on what they can spend.

Sterile wealth owners' sterile profit revenues

Firms, entrepreneurs, or capitalists that produce goods and services through a combination of money, land, labor, etc., realize employment-generating revenues and profits in product markets. They pay interest to creditors and repay, eventually, the principal to them for their invested borrowed capital. For their equity capital, they pay ongoing profits and, at some time or other, liquidation surpluses. Instead of liquidation, equity owners may also sell businesses in M&A or on the stock market. If a business is run as a sole proprietorship, then the sole proprietor pockets the profits, liquidation surpluses, or sales prices. There is only one legal entity and no transfer of profits between legal entities is necessary. If, as more commonly occurs, the business is run as a separate legal entity, e.g., a limited liability company or stock corporation, then the equity providing wealth owner draws the profits through a legal transfer of dividends, of a liquidation surplus, or through collecting sales prices for shares.

While the firms' original M'-revenues in product markets, and their profits as a part of these revenues (M'-M), were productive as money had been spent productively in their expectation, the "transfer" of the dividends and of liquidations surpluses, based on equity contracts, is no longer an employment-generating spending. The opposite view would mislead us into falsely counting employment-generating revenues and profits, which have already been counted at the level of the equity-using firms, twice.

Sterile wealth owners' sterile asset sales revenues

We have already seen that what enables profit in product markets, assets, can also be sold. Since, people have learned to intellectually recognize a capacity to generate future surpluses as itself being a value-in-exchange (valued in the amount of its present value) and to practically transfer it (after proper legal techniques have been invented for this purpose), wealth owners have acquired an additional option to realize sterile profits, by "exiting" an investment in an asset through selling the asset.[67]

The productive economy: Producive revenues and spending

Most people identify capitalism with the age of industry, technology, and mass production. We prefer to consider capitalism as generally using owner power to draw profits in M–C–M'-circuits, irrespective of whether commodities are produced, industrially or otherwise, or whether sterile profits are generated. Still, it remains true that capitalism has unleashed an enormous explosion in production that has led to a productive economy of a hitherto unknown power.

---

67   There is other sterile spending, e.g., on renting mobiles, paying license fees for patents, or other intellectual property rights, e.g., in software, music or movies or on commodities (such gold, silver, copper, platinum, other precious metals, rare earths, grains, pig halves, art, jewels, classic cars, antiques and foreign exchange. Often, the commodities traded possess the character of assets in assets markets but they can, like pig halves, grains, copper, or antiques, swapped into productive investment or consumption.

Productive wealth owners' employment-generating consumptive revenues

Quesnay put his *"classe des propriétaires"* at the top of his tableau. The reason for this cannot possibly have been on the basis of their productive output, given that they produce nothing; it may have been because of their rank in a stratified society or it may have been because of their crucial role as the "big" consumptive spender in Quesnay's tableau. The *cl. des propriétaires*, in fact, saved Quesnay's royaume agricole and allowed the productive circuits in his tableau to close.

Not only do they consume *more* units (number of goods, liters, kilograms) *per capita*, but they also consume the up-market share, the top agricultural products, the best vines, the most delicious pieces of calves and pigs, the fattest ducks, the largest chicken and the tastiest tomatoes and apples, the finest silk, teas and spices, which end up in in their pantries, wine cellars, kitchens, and on their tables. Wealth owners have the most beautiful houses, and attract and employ the best architects, brick-layers, carpenters, painters, and artists and buy the most comfortable and stylish furniture. The hire the most intelligent philosophers and teachers for their kids, the best golf-professionals, and have the prettier housemaids, more pleasant and better menial servants, and the most attractive courtesans and boys for erotic plea-sures. They also typically pay higher unit prices; accordingly; after all, their relative per capita contribution to consumptive employment-generating spending is much higher than of the remainder of the population.

Already ancient and medieval farmers, merchants, artisans, servants, cour-tesans, and entertainers, if they could, turned to the castles, country estates, monasteries, and clergy, whether Christian, Islamic, or Buddhist, and to the courts of princes, kings, and emperors in order to sell their goods and services. It was the wealth owners' desire for luxury, which led to inventing these products, induced their manufacturing and created trade systems to distribute them. Thus, merchant adventurers, shipping companies, transport agents, storehouse keepers, customs collectors, the captains and sailor on the ships, and the camel owners and their staff of caravans, bankers, and lawyers, who facilitated the trade, and even the pub and hotel owners, doctors, haircutters, and prostitutes along the lines of far-distance luxury trade also received their livelihood through wealth owners' luxury consumption; many cities along the caravan routes to Egypt, at the Silk Road and the cities of the Hanseatic League and ports in Oman or at the naval lines between the Americas, Spain, Portugal, France, the Netherlands, and Britain owe their very existence mainly to luxury trade. The same applies to others, with whom the readers would not like to change places, to toilers in diamond, gold, silver, and marble mines or even slaves in plantations for tea, coffee, spice, and opium etc. Quesnay still ex-aggerated: Wealth owners do consume a lot, but they unfortunately do not consume enough to close the productive circuits of capitalism; still, they deserve praise for their important contribution to circuit closure through their consumption (if you wish: from Marx's department II.a.).[68]

We do not have to worry about the financing of wealth owners' consumption. They sit on stores of wealth and their consumption is very resilient. They will still be able to finance their consumption long after the economy has fallen on hard times. If the wealth of an individual wealth owner is ever exhausted, which happens from time to time of course, he simply drops into the workers' class and others take over.

Other than from wealth owners, consumptive employment-generating spending to firms can only come workers (firms do not consume). While, workers do not appear in Quesnay's model or the household-firms-model of mainstreams economics, they are, nevertheless, the class of the greatest majority of mankind with significant consumption needs for food, health, and other services and with a significant contribution to employment-generating consumptive spending. As they no longer own land, they cannot directly sustain themselves from nature, and as they own nothing else instead, they cannot generate income via investment either. Their survival and prosperity – the modern social master drama – thus, solely depends upon their being employed in firms' first M–C-leg and upon being paid salaries.[69] As others, e.g., Marx and Kalecki, have observed before us, workers are very reliant as consumers because they spend all of their salaries. We shall be able to uphold this principle even with top earning CEOs, employed lawyers, etc., as we shall split them into workers, who consume all of their workers' salaries, and wealth owners who invest them or who spend a part on more luxurious wealth owners' consumption.

Wealth owners and workers consumption is largely productive, but also contains splitters or components of sterile spending, e.g., purchase prices for old countryside castles, rent for dwelling, or workers' consumptive debt service.

Productive wealth owners' employment-generating investive revenues

Firms buy from firms to make profits (M–C) and, thereby, enable other firms to close their circuits and to realize profits (C–M'). If this spending is productive, then firms receive employment-generating investive revenues. These revenues consist of purchases of equipment and inventories. Some splitters or components of purchases of equipment and inventories, e.g., of naked land, may be sterile.

---

68   See the discussion of the reproduction schemes on page 271 et seq.

69   Transfer payments are only considered later.

Section 3. A tableau économique of modern capitalism

While the terms of employment-generating and sterile spending or revenues, and of a productive and a sterile economy will still need some cleansing and purification, it makes sense to already give the basic idea of our model's result.

Arrival and departure ports of wealth owners

Quesnay modelled his tableau with three classes. Given that he falsely split off artisans, manufacturers, and commerce from his cl. productive and mislabeled them as "sterile", these three classes can no longer be used. Marx's model, which is based on ownership and non-ownership of the means of production, has only two classes (workers and capitalists). At this point, we agree with Marx. However, Marx did not assign a systematic role to sterile wealth and the Marxian model has no place in which to properly deal with it. Quesnay, in contrary, we may suggest, at least foreshadows the distinction between sterile wealth and productive wealth in opposing his *classe des propriétaires* to his two other classes. Mainstreams economists mostly use another two-units model, based on the distinction between investment and consumption: households, which consume, and firms, which do not, at least not in the narrow sense. Households also sometimes make sterile investments by buying assets in their model. Households, accordingly, are not too remote from Quesnay's classe des propriétaires, but they unfortunately mix up wealth owners and non-wealth owners and thereby, in a way, make the opposite mistake to Marx.

To overcome the weakness of Quesnay, Marx, and the mainstream model, our tableau, at first much like Marx, operates with two classes. They are, as in Marx, wealth owners and non-wealth-owning workers (non-wealth owners and workers are the same) and their existence is the result of the social differentiation that has occurred since antiquity. This highlights that capitalism is an owner economy with yet a large majority of embedded non-owners. However, we need more than just two players to show how the distinctions of sterile vs productive and investive vs consumptive[70] become operative in our tableau. For this purpose, we figuratively equip the wealth owners' class with *four "ports"*. It has *two "arrival ports"* through which it *receives* revenues, a sterile arrival port for sterile spending of others, and an employment-generating arrival port for employment-generating spending of others. The employment-generating arrival port collects the whole employment-generating spending of the society, hence of all wealth owners and of workers. The sterile arrival port collects sterile spending from all wealth owners and workers. The distinction between the sterile and employment-generating arrival ports reflects dif-

---

70   See Foreword page 23

ferent *effects* of revenues or spending, in particular with a view to the employment induced by it.

The distinction between *motives* of the spending, which can be either investive or consumptive, leads to two *"departure ports"* of the wealth owners. Wealth owners have a *consumptive* and an *investive departure port*. If they consume (whether their consumption is productive or sterile), then they emit payments via their consumptive port; if they invest (whether their investment is productive or sterile), then they dispatch them via their investive departure port. Flows leaving from there will be partly sterile and partly productive and, accordingly, will arrive at other wealth owners' sterile or employment-generating ports.

Workers need *only one in-and-out-port*; their departures are only consumptive (sometimes sterile and sometimes productive)[71] and their arrivals are only productive (as firms made them to induce them to work). Wealth owners make salary payments to workers from either their consumptive or investive departure port.[72]

Figure 5: Arrival and departure ports of wealth owners

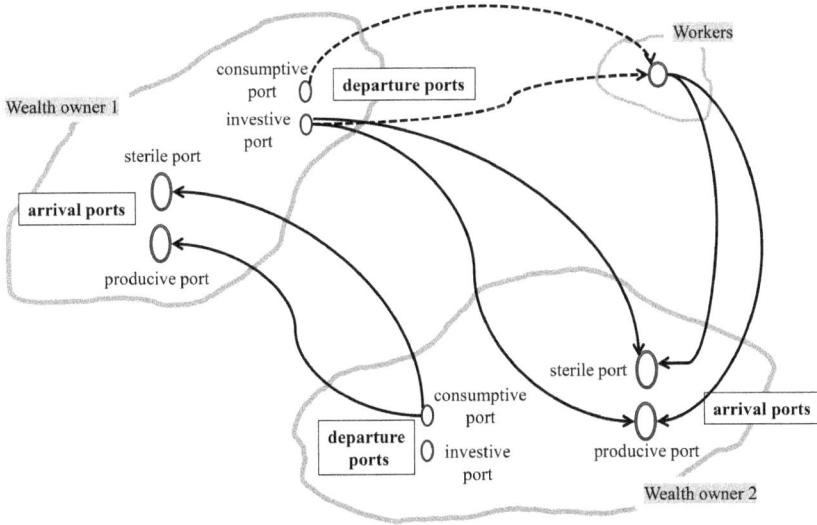

---

71   If workers make investive spending, then they do so not as workers but as wealth owners, see page 120. Workers, contrary to what may appear as implied in Marx's reproductions schemes, mostly cannot use their full salaries for consumptive producive spending, i.e., consumption to Marx's II.b.-department, as they also have to make sterile spending in the form of rent and debt services.

72   Wealth owners sometimes pay salaries for consumptive reasons, e.g., for menial services etc. These leave through their consumptive departure port.

Quite importantly, the models used in this book part with the idea, that an individual, physical or legal entity, *belongs exclusively to only one single category or class*. Instead, we hold that individuals can simultaneously belong to several categories in a functionally differentiated system, such as in the economy. As such, they can participate in different processes or they can change their roles between processes. Workers in particular can sometimes be wealth owners aside of also being workers. They cannot only move up, leave one class and join another, much like wealth owners can drop into the workers class, but workers can also sometimes, at the same time, be wealth owners with a part of their wealth.[73]

A three-unit- tableau économique of "original" capitalism (without prosthetics)

The preceding graph represented how the distinctions of the Matrix I (producive vs sterile and investive vs consumptive, on page 23) affects the flows of the economy and separates flows with different macroeconomic properties into distinguishable flows between specific ports. Yet, we also envisage a Quesnay-like tableau flow model with sterile wealth owners (our heirs of Quesnay's classe des propriétaires), productive wealth owners (firms, entrepreneurs, or capitalists) and workers. This tableau, with, thus, three subjects, positions, or units, only shows the productive economy in a first version.

---

73   The idea that an individual ought to belong to one class was "natural" in stratified societies and was upheld by Marx for the purposes of social analysis and political practice; the working class was supposed to be the revolutionary subject and Marx wanted economic classes to correspond with social classes and even, if possible, political forces. Giving up this artificial postulate frees economic analysis and renders it more plausible. Of course, some workers are also wealth owners and if we, thus, add workers and wealth owners up, the total will exceed the number of citizens in a state. But that is neither a theoretical problem nor does it alter the distinction between non-wealth-owners and wealth-owners.

Figure 6: Tableau with productive economy without wealth economy and prosthetics

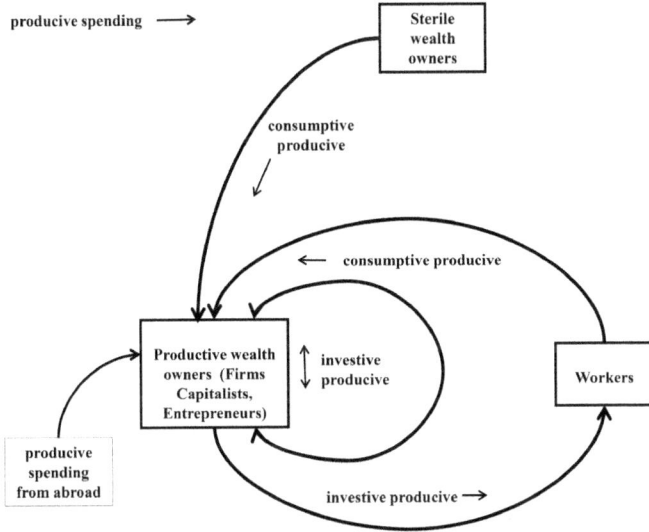

On hast to look at it from the workers' perspective with the question in mind: "What employment-generating spending must be forthcoming to induce salary flows to workers?". Just as in *Quesnay's* tableau, it is also helpful to imagine economic activity as commencing with sterile wealth owners making employment-generating consumptive spending, e.g., by ordering meat and wine or having a new countryside mansion constructed. This spending, as only expected or already contracted spending, will trigger productive wealth owners (firms, entrepreneurs, capitalists) to hire workers and to make salary outlays thereto. These salaries partly flow back, as employment-generating consumptive spending, to firms. Furthermore, the expected or contracted spending induces employment-generating spending of firms to other firms for the purchasing of equipment and inventories (including services), which will again partly flow back to firms or workers.[74]

The *second* tableau now also includes the wealth economy, i.e., sterile spending or sterile revenues.

---

74   Marx's reproduction schemes split up firms into departments that produce production goods (dept. I) and consumption goods (dept. II). This is helpful and allows to describe transactions amongst capitalists and between capitalists and workers as asymmetrical processes. The reproduction schemes are introduced later in more detail, see on page 271 et seq., but they are not crucial for the argument of this book.

Figure 7: Tableau showing productive and sterile economy

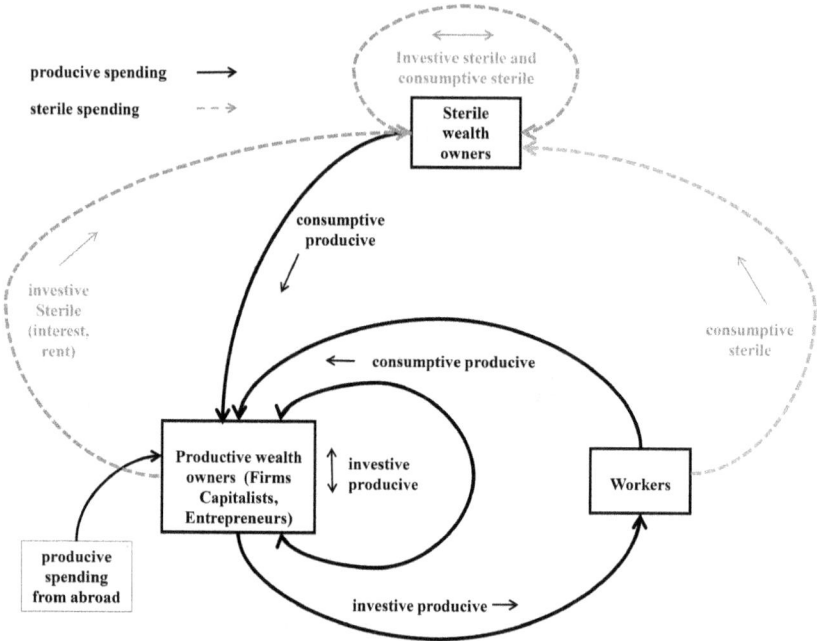

The dotted grey curve at the top with arrows on both sides, beginning and ending at sterile wealth owners, shows sterile spending between them, e.g., sterile (purified) interest and rent, paid in product markets, for investive and consumptive purposes, and purchase prices in asset markets, i.e., in transactions regarding debt (bonds), real estate, and businesses (in stock market, private equity, etc.).

Firms and workers in the productive economy also have to make sterile "tributes" to the wealth economy.[75] Firms have to make investive sterile spending to sterile wealth owners, e.g., interest on money borrowed for productive investments (i), rent paid to use buildings for productive purposes (r), or even sterile purchase prices ($stpp$) for real estate, etc. for productive purposes, e.g., to build a factory. Workers have to pay interest on debt and rent for dwellings to sterile wealth owners as sterile consumptive spending. This is shown in the dotted grey downward lines on the left and right on the outsides. The solid black lines, showing employment-generating spending are a copy of the first tableau.

Verbally expressed, the capitalist sterile and productive economy have the following units, stations or subjects with the following spending/revenues:

---

75   Note that it is not normally possible to make producive spending without at least some sterile spending. "Tributes" must be paid into the wealth economy to be allowed to be otherwise productive. This point will be elaborated on pages 123 et seq. and 351 et seq.

Productive wealth owners or *firms, entrepreneurs, capitalists*: They receive employ-ment-generating consumptive spending from other wealth owners and workers and investive employment-generating spending from other productive wealth own-ers or firms, entrepreneurs, and capitalists (each via their employment-generating arrival ports). They dispatch investive employment-generating spending to other productive wealth owners or firms, entrepreneurs, capitalists, salary spending to workers, and investive sterile spending (each via their respective investive departure port).

Sterile wealth owners: They receive sterile investive spending from productive wealth owners', the "tributes to the sterile economy", sterile consumptive spending from sterile wealth owners and from workers, each through their sterile arrival port ($i, r, stpp$). They also make consumptive sterile spending to other wealth owners, productive and sterile, via their consumptive departure port.

Workers: They receive investive salary payments from productive wealth owners and consumptive salary payments from sterile wealth owners.[76]

While the state is already assumed to exist as guarantor of the ownership-struc-ture, taxes or protectionist state policies are still not yet considered as a factor influ-encing the flows in both tableaux. There are no relevant social transfers or fiscal or monetary policies. Private banks and a central bank are still missing. They will only come into play as our investigations progress.

Elaborating sterile and employment-generating spending

We noted that the distinction between the sterile wealth economy and the produc-tive economy is not intrinsic to the economic system. E.g., if a building is sold, it does not at all matter for the participating economic entities – not the vendor seek-ing capital gains, not the purchaser seeking investive or consumptive value-in-use or future capital gains – what part of the sales price rewards recent productive in-vestment in the building and what part is merely for the transfer of the property-title to the God-given land.[77] The economic system, in its operations and self-obser-vation, does not care about circuit closure and about whether its operations provide employment opportunities for the non-owners, i.e., only-owners of labor power – as little as whether a band of bagpipe musicians can sell out all of their gigs. The dis-tinction between the sterile wealth economy and the productive economy is rather a distinction *post factum* made by scientists for the purpose of analyzing effects of the economic system upon society at large and for the state to possibly act.

---

76   The flows derived, using the distinction between the productive and sterile economies, could obviously be used for national accounts (which reflect "time periodical" flows), yet this possibility is not pursued further in this book.

77   It may only, in certain regards, be relevant for balance sheet and tax laws.

Furthermore, the distinction is not a distinction, which is manifest and readily visible in the operations of the economic system. There is no physical borderline between the productive and sterile economy. Unlike blood with and without oxygen in humans, which are nicely separated in arteries and veins, flows of sterile and employment-generating spending, like vitamins and cancerous particles in food, *travel together in a blended mix.* Imagine the desks of employees of a big firm being still connected by an old-fashioned pneumatic tubes system, through which they exchange official and private messages. They do that sometimes even in one and the same capsule – the tube system does not care about the character of the messages and this character is not visible from the outside.

Figure 8: Production, expenditure, income

Production	Expenditure	Income
Sterile revenues	Workers' consumption	Workers' salaries
Producive revenues	Wealth owners' consumption	Firms' productive profits
(minus "intermediate consumption")	Firms' productive investment (gross)	Wealth owners' sterile profits
	Wealth owners' sterile investment (gross)	Increases of productive stock
output	output	output

So far, we have used the distinction between the productive and sterile economy in an intuitive *prima vista*-sense, which gave us a preliminary list of sterile and productive economic activities. We regarded in particular loaning out money and renting out real estate or selling real estate and debt, as well as selling existing productive businesses (in M&A or in the stock market), as a sterile activity. Constructing houses or building factories anew and the daily running of factories or service firms were productive on the other side. This now needs elaboration. We need to acknowledge that rent and interest (or revenues for loaning out money) as well as purchases prices for real estate, debt and businesses contain productive components while the construction of buildings and businesses contains sterile components.

To begin with the *first case*: At some time, the original planning, managing and physical construction of buildings and businesses, e.g., of factories, which are later rented out or sold, lead to a high of productive activity. In fact, even the creation of debt does not only consist in handing over money but involves employment-generating marketing, administrative, legal, bookkeeping and tax-related activities, which cannot be denied to be productive. Afterwards, physical assets require ongoing care, maintenance, administration, repair and occasional remodeling. The ultimate sale of real estate, debt or of business (through M&A or in the stock market) leads to a second high of productive activities of the seller in regard of the respective asset, e.g., marketing, due diligence, negotiations, legal work, banking, tax work, bookkeeping etc... Even if the buyer is not interested in these activities as such – but only in the value-in-use or value-in-exchange accruing to him – the seller engages in them because they are necessary to realize his M', these spending are employment-generating. The buyer too has similar costs, which he also incurs because he expects a later higher M' of his. This spending, a part of his M, is obviously employment-generating, and it is, also rewarded by a employment-generating spending, his later M', e.g., higher rent, which tenants, or higher purchaser prices, which buyers of the asset will pay.

We must, thus, notionally identify and *carve out* certain productive components or splitters in what we have so far regarded as solely sterile spending (as interest, rent, purchase prices for real estate and businesses etc.), and assign them as employment-generating spending to the productive economy.

How can this "carving out" be properly achieved? We return to the fact that all prices result from a play of ownership power, utilities, value-in-use-ascriptions, value-in-exchange-ascriptions and budget limitations. From this perspective, the amount of an expected M', including of any component and splitter thereof, which induces an investment on the seller's side, does not depend upon the amount of costs spent on a good but only upon whether the result of the application leads to a higher ascription of value-in-use and value-in-exchange by the buyer. Accordingly, no investor would have spent any amount of M, had he not expected a value-in-exchange increase, ascribed and paid by a prospective customer, which would allow him to recover his costs and to make a profit. Furthermore, we cannot deny that causal chains are running from e.g., the investment decision of a builder to erect a beautiful house at the "Grote Markt" in Brussels in the 17th century to today's existence of the building and its phantastic present value (discounted future rent surpluses or its market price, which, due to today's high multiples, is likely even higher than the discounted rent surpluses). We can also take for granted that every investor goes after the maximum profit and may even assume that some investors of the 17th century were so greedy and crazy to dream of the aggregate surpluses, which the building at the "Grote Markt" actually afforded since its construction.

Still, we only carve out a small part of these aggregate surpluses and assign them as employment-generating spending to the productive economy. The purpose of the distinction between employment-generating and sterile spending is *to point at those expected future revenues M', which actually induced employment*, and these are not all surpluses, which are ultimately *caused* by an investment. The later M', which induces the investment are, thus, neither the surpluses in the wildest dreams of investors nor the surpluses, which were luckily realized, but *only the surpluses, which would have sufficed for the investment decision of the historic investor at the time.* This turns the task of splitting up M' into a sterile and employment-generating revenue-component into the task of setting a minimum profitability for employment-generating spending. If ever needed, a quantification of the produive component could, hence, be derived by a "cost-plus"- approach.[78] All M' is sterile, except for the recovery of costs and a profit add-on, which an investor would reasonably demand to make the investment. This implies that not only the revenues, which the investor could have expected without any employment-generating spending remain sterile (this anyhow), but also such revenues which he could only expect after he made the investment remain sterile to the extent they lead to an extra high profit. The method, thereby, ascertains that extra-profits due to, e.g., location or timing, remain sterile.[79]

If we look at the homogenous flow of revenues (or spending, looked at from the other side) and try to tell an employment-generating from a sterile part, we may find the two parts either distributed in time or in space. There could be a "revenue-history" of an asset with a (first) phase, in which the asset only earns its employment-generating revenues, recovering its production costs plus a reasonable profit, and, after this is achieved, a second phase when the asset is promoted to the heaven or demoted to the hell of the sterile economy, where it merely draws sterile revenues.[80] Alternatively, we could imagine the asset as drawing a sterile and a employment-generating revenue component, in a certain proportion, in parallel for some time, until the collected M' will no longer contain any employment-generating revenue

---

78   Contrary to Marx's labor value and exploitation theory, there is nowhere in the economic system an intrinsic objective relationship between outlays or costs and the value-in-exchange or price of a product. Accordingly, such a relationship can not be used to isolate the produive spending-component in M'. We are also not attempting to re-introduce some kind of *justum pretium* through the backdoor into economics. Rather, we view prices result from a power play between ownership power, subjective value-ascriptions of prospective customers and budgets. For the macroeconomic purpose of splitting up an expected M' into an expected sterile spending and an expected produive spending of a customer, we only assume that the productive investor expects average profitability on his *c*-outlays or *v*-outlays, but no more, and that profits beyond are sterile.

79   The construction of the building was, microeconomically and legally, a *conditio sine qua non* for all later rent revenues for the structure in the high valuation area and time and, in that sense, the production of the structure has "caused" the high rent revenues (or sales price) M' to flow. Yet, macroeconomics is not *causal*, but *teleological*; it must seek to understand what motives and expectations move the economy. As mostly profit-making-expectations bring about ongoing system building, the macroeconomic character of a flow must depend on what expectation ignited the flow. A later collected M'- revenue is, thus, to repeat the point, not produive because it was caused by a productive investment, but only in the amount which would already have sufficed to induce the investment in low valuation conditions.

80   The time period, in which revenues are still considered to reward and have motivated the productive investment could be called "pre-maturation", the time afterwards, when all collected revenues are wholly sterile, could be called "post-maturation".

component and be wholly sterile. If, during the existence of an asset, e.g., a building at the "Grote Markt", maintenance, repair, remodeling or administrative work is being executed, as it will frequently, this will always lead to re-assign a part of the incoming future M' to employment-generating revenues. Overall, the employment-generating revenue component in the aggregate M' will, hence, show eruptive jumps upward and slow falls afterwards, comparable to depreciation in bookkeeping.

The *second case* of carve-outs relates to revenues for *prima vista productive activities, which yet contain sterile components*. Productive firms make M-outlays (*c*-outlays) which include interest, rent and purchases prices for real estate and businesses, which are sterile. If they draw revenues for commodities or services produced using rented real estate, debt-financed equipment or inventories or purchased assets, a certain component recovering these costs and allowing a certain profit is sterile. E.g., the price for an espresso in a café on the Champs Elysée will contain a component that rewards the sterile ownership of the building and may contain a component that rewards the taking out of a loan by the restaurant operator. That component, as great it may be to sit in that café, may even be significant. There is no difference with service fees paid to education, medical and care services or production industries.

Only after carve-outs" will there be a "purely" sterile economy and an equally pure productive economy. The suggested method to split up employment-generating and sterile spending of customers or revenues M' replicates the actual way, in which real investment decisions are made, insofar as they, too, can only made on the basis of rough, vague, and uncertain guesses and estimations of M' realizable in the future, or of increases of M' attainable by additional productive investment inputs. We close the theoretical elaboration on sterile and employment-generating spending here.

Lack of a proper distinction between wealth economy and productive economy in mainstreams economics

Most mainstreams economists hate the idea of distinguishing between exchanges, which are somehow economically (or socially, politically, culturally, aesthetically, intellectually, biologically, morally, etc.) "valuable", "beneficial" or "salutogenetic" etc. and which are not. They consider such attempts as unscientific and insidious attacks on economic freedom. While we have already acquiesced that the operations of the economic system *itself* do not use such distinctions, we hold that observing the economic system from the perspective of society may use whatever distinctions it considers useful.[81] The distinction, which this book will apply between employment-generating spending (consumptive or investive) and sterile spending (consumptive or investive) and a corresponding productive economy and sterile economy, will, indeed, be the crucial tool to analyze the precondition of circuit closure in productive economy.

Mainstreams and other economists sometimes use distinctions, which are similar to our distinction. For instance, they make a distinction between a so-called *"real economy"* and a *"finance economy"* (or simply "finance"). This distinction ignores that land, real estate, commodities, gold, antiques, art, classic cars and businesses, which ought to belong to the "finance economy", are utterly physical or otherwise "real". There is nothing more "real" than real estate, but even bonds are "real" as they represent legal claims, which enable, in the last instance, to attach assets of the debtor in case of default. In other words, this distinction between "real economy" and "finance economy" is misleading and fallacious.[82] The distinction between the wealth economy and the productive economy avoids the calamity of attaching the label of "real" or "physical" to one of its sides. It rather distinguishes between tangible or intangible (the development of ideas, know how, strategies, advice, software, designs, inventions, scripts etc. are included) products being produced *anew*, either completely anew, or *being altered*, on the one side, and transactions taking place without this being the case. The wealth economy only draws revenues from pre-existing old tangible or intangible assets or from shifting such pre-existing assets around, the productive makes new tangible or intangible things.

The distinction between the wealth economy and the productive economy must also be distinguished from the distinction between *"productive"* and *"speculative"* economic behavior. While it is true that purchases in the wealth economy are very often made for "speculative" reasons (in a way all M–C–M'-motives are "speculative"), e.g., to later resell the purchased bonds, land, buildings, stock, businesses, commodities, art, antiques, etc. with a capital gain, we must note that there are also a significant number of purchases of old, pre-existing wealth assets, such as land, city apartments, suburb homes, art, or antique cars, gold, commodities, etc., which are not or not predominantly motivated by speculation, but are motivated instead (1) by consuming the respective values-in-use, e.g. by living in an apartment, or (2) using them in an investive way in a productive business, e.g. to build a factory on land,

81   Neue "wirtschaftswissenschaftlichen Reflexionstheorien" writes *Luhmann* (1988, page 83) müssen "gegenüber der Differenz von reich und arm kühles Blut bewahren…, während die gesamtgesellschaftliche Reflexion genau dieses nicht kann…"

82   That something is wrong between the distinction between "real economy" and "finance" can already be recognized in the fact that if "real economy" is the "marked space", then the opposite of the "unmarked space" ought to be "irreal", "surreal", "virtual" etc. The distinction applies different criteria to each side in order to define what belongs to that side.

open a call-center (a particularly sad job!) in an office building, or to decorate a board room with a piece of art. Consumers and firms, in other words, often have to "trade" with the wealth economy and pay a "tribute" $(i, r, stpp)$ to sterile wealth owners if they only want to consume or make a productive investment, but without any or a predominant speculative motive.[83] The riches of the wealth economy, in other words, are sometimes needed for consumption or for productive investment. Insofar, the distinction occasionally made in mainstreams economics between "productive" and "speculative" gives worse marks to the wealth economy than it deserves.

Thomas Piketty's book *Le capital aux XXIe siècle* of 2013 has recently stirred significant debate.[84] Written from a classical social-democrat perspective, it analyzes and criticizes today's increasing wealth inequality and considers ways and policies to slow and to reverse the trend; it also looks to generate greater employment and productive growth. In this context, Piketty examines the question of the relationship between wealth and employment-generating production. We set out the differences between his approach and ours as follows: First, we neither consider inequality as a rather recent phenomenon nor do we think that recently a significant "qualitative jump" in inequality took place. Mrs. Thatcher, Ronald Reagan, financialization and globalization and the neoliberal 1980s or later austerity policies are *not* the historic culprits for social inequality. Rather, income and wealth inequality emerged already with the economic specialization into C–M–C'-players and M–C–M'-players in profit economies. This has reigned since antiquity, e.g., in China, Greece, or Rome, and recuperated vigor after the lazy Middle Ages in Venice, Florence, Genova, Spain, the Netherlands, the UK, etc. It is true that capitalism has a general tendency to always increase inequality, because its ongoing operation increases inequality, but beyond it is useless to ruminate on whether Greek, Roman, Spanish, or US slaves, laborers in Spain's silver mines, children-workers in Manchester, the unemployed in the Great Depression or German or French workers of today are "more unequal". It also does not really matter for the present social master drama whether the Fuggers, Rothschilds, Rockefellers, etc. were relatively "richer" in relation to the middle and lower classes at their times than Elon Musk, Jeff Bezos, Bill Gates, Warren Buffett, or George Soros are today. Employment depends upon motives for wealth to "go productive" and not on wealth or income ratios. In fact, there is a strong counter-narrative against the narrative of generally increasing inequality: If we compare the income level of the broad masses in developed Western countries to the income level of the broad masses in BRICS-countries over the last thirty years, then we cannot

---

83   He who purchases a wealth asset, if for consumptive or investive use, will often be aware of its potential to generate capital gains and that may even co-motivate the acquisition. But if the expected value-in use or return without capital gains are high enough, the acquisition would also take place for the consumptive or investive motives alone.

84   See also *Piketty* (2019).

but observe a significantly *rising equality*, e.g., hundred millions of people having ben catapulted into middle classes in China, India, Brazil, and other countries in the last decades – capitalism's self-praise to unleash economic development and to bring wealth retains some truth even today! In other words, Piketty's concept of rising inequality is too unspecific, too general, and not targeted enough to explain the deficient closure of productive circuits.

We also differ from Piketty by positing the necessity of a distinction between a sterile wealth economy and productive economy while Piketty does not.[85] Piketty's treatment of rising wealth inequality, in what he calls the "general contradiction of capital" and his "two basic laws of capitalism", consistently puts productive apples and sterile oranges into one basket. If he calls "r > g", (rentability of capital[86] > growth) "la contradiction centrale du capitalisme" and summarizes "la principale force déstabilisatrice est liée au fait que le taux de rendement privé du capital r peut être fortement et durablement plus élevé que le taux du croissance du revenu de la production g ", and if he, finally, states "l'inégalité r > g implique que les patrimoines issus du passé se recapitalisent plus vite que le rythme de progression de la production et des salaires ", he gives no thought to the question of whether the continued high-flying of profit, compared to growth, could have to do with the existence of a sterile and productive economy. He is on a good track, but does not follow through nearly enough. Moreover, if he puts forward the view that the average rentability of capital is lastingly 4 %-5 %, while long term annual average growth in countries at the frontline of technological progress hardly exceeds 1 %-1.5 %,[87] then this ought to raise the question: How can this work? There are two possibilities: either capital in general reaps an ever-significantly larger share of whatever growth or the profits of capital, which could explain the higher-than-growth-rentability, are reaped *outside* of production. This is similar to what occurs in something like our sterile economy. Piketty even points to this possibility by saying: "Le capital se reproduit tout seul, plus vite que ne s'accroît la production",[88] but he still makes no attempt to follow this trace and to attack the issue of what this production-independent and growth-independent profit-growth economy might be.

The terms that Piketty uses to state his "deux lois fondamentales du capitalisme" permanently intermingle the two economies. His "première loi fondamentale du capitalisme" relates the stock of capital of an economy to the flow of revenues from

---

85 See already Foreword page 21.
86 The rentability of capital or the "taux de rendement de capital", encompasses not only productive profit but also rent, interest, capital gains, royalties, etc. See *Piketty* (2013) page 93. Piketty also mentions profit and dividends in his list (also on page 94)
87 Unlike China or Europe in their respective "thirty glorious years" from 1990 onwards and from 1940 to 1970 (*Piketty* (2013) page 161, 166).
88 *Piketty* (2013) page 942 (all prior quotes).

capital. It reads $\alpha = r \times \beta$[89] and means that α, a fraction of revenue of the capital to the aggregate national revenue (Piketty states that this is around 30 %),[90] equals the fraction of the profits to invested capital, i.e., the rentability of capital, which is **r** (often, says Piketty, around 5 %),[91] multiplied with the multiple of the national capital over the annual national revenue, which is β (often, Piketty claims, around 6).[92] This first law, which Piketty says is a "pure égalité comptable" and "tautologique",[93] clearly involves no distinction between different components of the revenues of capital related to sterile and productive activities.

Piketty's "deuxième loi fondamentale du capitalisme", $= s/g$,[94] means that β, which is in both equations and connects them, the multiple of the national capital over the annual national revenue (which Piketty often sees as around 6) equals the fraction of the saving rate (often, Piketty states, around 12 %) over the growth rate (often, Piketty states, around 2 %). The second law, *Piketty* claims, is not tautological, but "le résultat d'un processus dynamique; elle représente un état d'équilibre vers lequel tend une économie épargnant à taux s et croissant à taux g... "[95] Again, Piketty neither splits up β nor the growth rate g into a productive or sterile component. In other words, he skips the option to pursue his research interest – where does increasing inequality come from? – by considering that profits could arise outside of production and, hence, in a sterile manner.

Silvio Gesell deserves a special mention in the present context, too. He was interested in employment-generating spending and closure of productive circuits more directly than Piketty. He was also looking for moments in capitalism itself that stood in the way and picked wealth stored in the form of hoarded money as its maleficent flow-interrupter. This track was well-selected, but his choice was too narrow. It was not solely excessive intermediary hoarding of money that lay in the way of investment in the productive economy, but long-term investment in the wealth economy within a far broader meaning and in far more forms than just in cash holdings. Accordingly, *Gesell's* recipe of "expiring money", money which would automatically lose value (which aimed at discouraging hoarding), remained inadequate too.

In summary: The widely used distinctions between a "real economy" and "finance" or between "production" and "speculation", Piketty's finding of r > g and Gesell's finding of money hoarding blocking production and employment, while

---

89 *Piketty* (2013) page 92 et seq.
90 *Piketty* (2013) page 92: "la part des revenus du capital dans le revenu national, part qui sera noté α,...".
91 *Piketty* (2013) page 92: "Ou r est le taux de rendement moyen du capital ...".
92 *Piketty* (2013) page 92: "le rapport capital/revenu β...".
93 *Piketty* (2013) page 93, 266.
94 *Piketty* (2013) page 262 et seq.
95 *Piketty* (2013) page 266 et seq.

they confirm the project of this book and the necessity to distinguish a productive and sterile sector in the economy, all fall far short of solving the task.

Section 4. An original assembly

The introductory elementary economics of profit economies, which will now be concluded, has equipped us for the further journey undertaken in this book. We deny "objective value" and shall not be misled by the theory of labor value and exploitation. We possess a basic concept of money, and specifically the idea of the importance of money creation, and understand its difference to fiat money (fiat money being only one, if the most efficient, form of money creation). We have, furthermore, come to appreciate that the economic system must be regarded as a temporalized system that is created and re-created by elementary events in time, more like a dance, where dancers swap partners in between, which have exchanges. Classes or units, including our two classes and their ports, are only spatial representations of where players take roles as sellers or buyers in exchanges in time as part of their strategic two-leg-behavior, which aims beyond the single exchange. Marx's C–M–C' and M–C–M' are these two-leg-circuits, but only if we also lay the distinction between sterile or employment-generating (or the wealth economy and productive economy) across the distinction of consumptive (M–C' in C–M–C') and investive (M–C in M–C-M'), we are truly equipped to analyze the problems of circuit closure in capitalism and to ultimately combine it with a theory of prosthetics.

We shall close the elementary economics of profit economies with a romantic moment: Contrary to natural law theories, the state was *not* founded by social contract. Capitalism was likewise not introduced following deliberations in an original assembly.[96] Yet, *imagine*, contra-factually, capitalism *had* been erected per resolution after such an original assembly and assume that the speakers (contrary to what we know from democracies from ancient Athens to the present) had only made honest and reasonable arguments. In this case, proponents of capitalism could still have possessed strong and intelligent arguments in its favor (which would have somewhat resembled Hobbes' honest and true arguments in favor of Leviathan). They could have argued: "See, we all like values-in-use and produce them to consume them or to exchange them against other values-in-use. This (C–M–C') works, more

---

96   Social institutions are normally not founded neither to serve a commonly agreed purpose, such as to fulfill a social function, nor do they, e.g., states, owe their existence to an insight or teleological intervention of a steering god or a social contract in the sense of Hobbes, Locke or Rousseau. They rather come into being because a political entrepreneur with some mix of financial means, political allies and hard and soft power in the background has successfully established them for certain purposes. They, then, become part of the social landscape and are later appropriated for other purposes.

or less. However, what happens if we invite, in addition to these value-in-use-related motives for production and exchange, an additional and much more powerful artificial motive, a motive which is not interested in values-in-use, but only in value-in-exchange, profits, and wealth?" The pro-capitalist speaker could then have gone on to claim: "If we let this ghost out of the bottle, we shall see value-in-exchange-production drive value-in-use-production to levels otherwise impossible...". "That is wholly true..." an anti-capitalist opponent might have replied, "but we must also know that while profit-seeking (M–C–M') will massively push value-in-use-production, it will also ignite other activities, irrespective of whether they generate truly useful values-in-use and – and this will be reckless to humans, animals and the environment in general." "Furthermore", he could have added, "we should know that, as time goes by, those successful in profit-making, the winners of the game, which we would invite in, will monopolize the means of production and the non-winners will become dependent on them. There will be no other option for the non-owners to draw incomes but from the winners, and the winners will only employ them if they need them to produce goods, which promise further profits for the winners!" The honest proponent of capitalism would not deny this. And he would not deny either if the anti-capitalist proponent adds "As a result of capitalism, there will, thus, be stronger than otherwise social segregation between wealthy and non-owners and we will antagonize against each other in society, in politics and sometimes in civil war. Worse, a new strong motive[97] for foreign wars will arise – to mitigate the condition of the non-winners to the detriment of foreign people." This too, the honest proponent of capitalism may not renounce. But he will now raise his voice and arrive at his strongest point. "Yes, I admit", he will add, "it is a devil's pact. But it is a devil's pact, we *have* to enter – simply because if *we* don't, our neighbors will. Yes, the world will become richer, more advanced and uglier by the same time. But no country has a real alternative." And he will go on painting a dark scenario: "See, these others will then – in this more advanced, wealthier and uglier world – use their newly gained superiority to build the armament and military organization to put us at a disadvantage, they will be equipped to take away our riches, colonize us possibly enslave it in a violent way." "Let us...", the pro-capitalist speaker might, thus, conclude, "take the risk of inviting a guest, who will be stronger than we are and may control of us – all alternatives are worse!"

Arguments along these lines (which resemble the prisoner's dilemma) can be expected to have ended most debates in original assemblies in favor of capitalism. And everything we have learned since confirmed their soundness. Even if capitalism, in a world of a plurality of capitalist countries, was no guaranty for lasting wealth and dominance, those who first "used" it (by surrendering to it!) enjoyed the greatest advantages – not only in the exchange economy but also in the realm of wealth pro-

---

97   Apart from the old motive to rob and subjugate neighbors.

curement by violence. And those, who renounced to allow capitalist dynamics in, as China in the 19th century, the most progressed country by then, the Middle Ages and soviet style communism, had to pay a heavy price. But capitalism appearing to be without alternative does not mean that what is strong in it can stay without significant antinomies, which were not yet elaborated in the debates in the original assembly. We shall secure the insights of great economist about these antinomies and circuit closure. But before that, we enter a bit deeper into history and the ancient social master drama.

Part II:
Ancient capitalism, the ascent of ancient prosthetics and their dilemmas

Since the Renaissance, European intellectual elites upheld that the main political, legal, cultural, philosophical and other ideological features of modernity, and to a lesser extent even its economic features, already existed in ancient Greece or Rome – in the world of Plato and Aristotle, the Greek polis and the Roman republic and empire. This idea was weakened as the European elites stopped learning Greek and Latin in the 20th century and the Marxian evolutionary scheme primitive society – slaveholder society – feudalism – capitalism (and then, as some hoped, socialism – communism) gained ground. Even if, quite obviously, antiquity was very different from modernity, this book sympathizes with the old view: There are significant similarities between ancient profit economies and modern capitalism.

The consecutive brief examination of profit economies of antiquity, which we shall, quite recklessly, also call "ancient capitalism", will emphasize these similarities between the ancient master drama, which was the loss of the land of small farmers to large latifundia owners, leading to a call for "land for peasants" and the master drama of modern capitalism, which is the lack of employment, leading to a call for "jobs for workers". The evolutionary relationship is obvious: The solution of the ancient master drama to the detriment of the small peasants created the modern master drama; workers today need jobs because their predecessor-peasants lost their land. (What Marx described as "original accumulation", e.g., with a view to the English "enclosures", was largely a repetition of what had already happened in antiquity, in particular with regard to land, which had been recuperated by small peasants during the Middle Ages).

We shall see that originally, the economic, social and political demands emerging out of the ancient master drama, were conservative and restorative. They were conservative in the sense to protect the small peasantry against the loss of land and restorative in the twofold sense of either demands for the restitution of specific lost plots of land owner or for the assignment of new, alternative land, e.g., of state land or of land in colonies. But such conservative-restorative policies, aimed at maintaining the structure of a land-owning small peasantry, only succeeded locally and transitorily. Overall, they failed. Instead, the rich imperial hubs of antiquity, Athens, Sparta, Rome or the centers of the Chinese Empire, which had the necessary financial means, experimented with progressive methods – by generating prosthetic demand and by direct prosthetic transfers. This included military or infrastructure spending, from the construction of the Chinese Great Wall to the construction of roads, canals or capitals, like in Shang an, Luoyang, Beijing, Athens or Rome, payments to citizens for serving in the army, in the civil service or as judges, and social transfers, e.g., to the Roman lumpenproletariat. The ancient prosthetics became the predecessors of the modern prosthetics that states would use in their dealings with the modern master drama.

Chapter IV. Primitive society, civilization and the ancient master drama

Section 1. Goods procurement in primitive society

Nutrition procurement, storage and rhythms in primitive life

Zoological systems, animals and humans, need oxygen to survive; this was normally no problem. They also need, as we stated, nutrition; this was a sizable problem and animals and humans were almost permanently preoccupied with procuring the next in-soak of nutrition. Humans also have certain narrative needs and desires, e.g., for symbolic and positional representation, included already in "that early and rude state of society",[1] which Adam Smith used as a theoretical oppositional starting point to the modern economy (in much the same way as social philosophers, e.g., Hobbes, Locke, and Kant, used the *status naturalis* as opposed to the civilized state). In the "natural" state, there was still a direct relationship between each man, or rather between original groups of men – families and tribes – and nature. Survival depended upon a favorable habitat, in terms of geography and climate. Edible goods (or goods usable for clothing or shelter) were offered by nature, but they first had to be found, gathered, or hunted. Supply was often unreliable, sometimes through catastrophes, weather, and competing animal or human nutrition seekers. Putrefaction occurred. The greatest danger came from *humans* or from neighboring tribes robbing stored food and animals, or even taking over the territory.

If habitats were rich and generous, primitive hunters and gatherers could, like animals, hunt or gather depending on whether their bellies were full or empty. Habitats in which such permanent richness existed were, though, few. Mostly food procurement rhythms followed necessities dictated by the hunted prey and the gathered plants. As in this case food did not come in just-in-time to be consumed, preservation and storing technologies – keeping it from spoilage, protecting it against unwelcome guests like insects and animals – became a great issue. The nature of the prey and plants (and, sometimes, predator-prey-dynamics) and the combined skills

---

1   *Smith*, Wealth of Nations, book I chapter VI first line.

of hunting, gathering, and storage would at this evolutionary stage determine the rhythms of expeditions of nutrition procurement and of idleness or leisure, as well as the capacity of a horde, tribe, or settlement to survive.

Impact of the neolithic

People have been drawn together in small settlements since the Neolithic revolution; gatherers became farmers, and hunters became cattle breeders etc. As food was now being grown or pastured, its arrival could be more reliably planed for. More importantly, compared to itinerant hordes, nutrition production grew in quantity and quality thanks to technical improvements and to the division of labor. Craftsmanship developed and discoveries, innovations, and inventions wer made, if terribly slowly compared to the speed they acquired since the 18th century. Nutrition production also became less dependent on individual success when making a kill or finding plants. As prey were domesticated, bred, raised, and slaughtered and plants were seeded, cultivated and harvested, nutrition production became, yet, more dependent on the rhythms resulting from the inclination of the earth axis, i.e., seasons, and from the different stages of animal life. Farmers must normally work on their fields and with their domesticated animals throughout the whole year, but what they are doing – preparing and fertilizing the soil, building and repairing irrigation systems, seeding, fighting against pests and vermin, harvesting, and further processing grains or vegetables – is seasonal or determined by stages of animal growth, accidental weather or natural catastrophes.

Section 2. Primitive society and civilization

The small step from exchange to capitalism

Societies did not remain consigned to small villages of families and tribes after the Neolithic Age. Larger towns and cities evolved at many places, e.g., the bronze-age Egyptian Civilization around the Nile River, the Harappa Civilization (or IVC, Indus Valley Civilization), and the Mesopotamia civilization in the Tigris-Euphrates-river-system, each around the third and second millennium BC. The Greek, Roman, or Chinese civilizations were born somewhat thereafter. Roughly in parallel, private ownership of the means of production, and of land in particular, was established, and exchange, money, profit economies, the state, law, philosophy, and monotheistic religions surfaced.

In particular, the economic system took off and quickly transmuted into ancient capitalism. We have defined the economic system not by a purpose or a physical result – goods procurement – but by a certain *mode of operation*, negatively in terms of the absence of violence, and positively by exchange and the use of money. The use of money arose shortly after exchange, or with it, and there is, in fact, not much difference between these two moments. Exchange may have, to some extent, emerged "bottom up", even though markets probably did not commonly have the innocent background of proverbial "village markets". As long as village life, family, and tribal structures remained intact, the exchange of values-in-exchanges probably played no big role, and when markets came into play, they probably did not naturally grow out of village life but were superimposed following severe *disturbances* of locally integrated communities, e.g., to sustain mass armies, often by force. Alternatively, markets came up with long-distance luxury trade that served the early Neolithic elites. Long- and medium-distance trade in basic goods developed only thereafter, e.g., from south of the Yangtse to the changing Chinese capitals in the North near the Yellow River (Huanghe) via inland canals, mostly with rice,[2] or from the 15th century onwards via the Baltic Sea with wood, grains and wine in the European Hanseatic League.[3]

What could not be procured directly from nature, or via traditional kinship or tribal bonds or by way of violence, could, thus, be obtained by instigating the consent of suppliers by offering other goods.[4] This practice somehow became more and more frequent and the "market" became a metaphor, first for the expectation of a recurring local gathering of possible exchange partners, and then for the reachability of exchange partners via long distance communication and transport. Thus, from the perspective of goods procurement, e.g., the feeding of a community, the "market", or rather the economic system, could assume the functions of either nature or of store houses. If I did not find what I needed to feed my community members in nearby gardens of nature and if I had not taken care of filling up my storehouses in due time, or if my surplus then had been insufficient, what could bail me out? Somebody ought to bring the needed goods to me... Yet, as *Peter J. Golas* reasons with a view to

---

2   The Grand Canal whose origins date back to the 5th century BC with a final length of around 1.800 kilometers, which ultimately connected Hangzhou with Beijing or other Chinese capitals, stands out as the longest and most important one. During the Sung dynasty China had internal waterways of 50.000 kilometers in the aggregate (see *Vogelsang* (2013) page 238 et seq., 299 et seqs. and *Gernet* (1972 tome I) page 303 et seqs.

3   *Kennedy* (1987) page 51, 65. *Polanyi* (1944) page 66 sees internal trade as being "created by the intervention of the state". "Right up to the time of the Commercial Revolution, what may appear to us as national trade was not national but municipal. The Hanse were not German merchants; they were a corporation of trading oligarchs... Far from "nationalizing" German economic life, the Hanse deliberately cut off the hinterland from trade" (page 66). Polanyi concludes: "Neither long distance trade nor local trade was the parent of the internal trade of modern times" (page 67).

4   *Boisguilbert* has already stated that "each member of the productive class only buys someone else's commodity under the implicit assumption that someone else, directly or indirectly, buys the commodity he sells." (*Faccarello* (2016) page 11).

the Chinese Sung dynasty: "Agricultural societies, even when relatively prosperous, inevitably have large numbers of people living near the subsistence level. Famine is therefore an ever-present thread. The problem is compounded by slow and erratic, transport systems, that impede distribution of goods from areas of plenty to areas of shortage."[5] Other issues are no less important. First, there may simply not be enough areas of plenty and such areas may not have enough of the specifically needed nutritional inputs to give them away... Second, if they do have some excess goods, what should motivate them to transfer them to somebody else and put themselves at risk? Here the economic system can come in to play. It offers a strong generalized motive to render help to those in need, money payments. The problem is, however, that the motive to procure goods and transport goods will only arise if *proper* money payments will be made. Worse, the economic system not only requires money payment as condition sine qua non to provide its helping hand, but it will sometimes even itself become a part of the problem by creating "artificial scarcity" through, as *Golas* puts it "refined commercial practices, including speculation and market manipulation...". The economic system relieves from finding the necessities when they are needed and from storing them, but not from having money or something else for exchange.

Once the economic system had been established, the following sequence unfolded almost automatically and did so rather quickly:

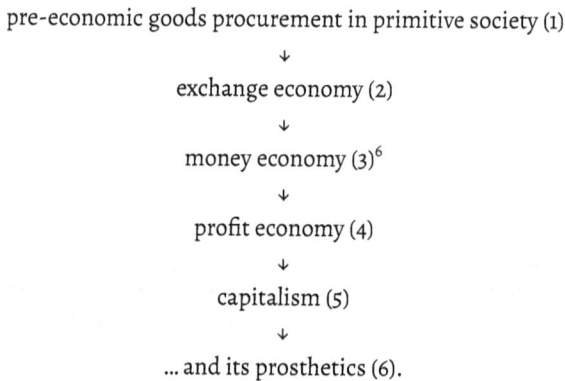

pre-economic goods procurement in primitive society (1)

↓

exchange economy (2)

↓

money economy (3)[6]

↓

profit economy (4)

↓

capitalism (5)

↓

... and its prosthetics (6).

Stages 2 to 4 may occur almost simultaneously; stage 5 may follow along, more or less quickly. With a view to the transition from a money economy to a profit economy, (2, 3) to (4), it is useful to consider the economic system as a "host system" earmarked by

5   *Golas*, The Sung fiscal administration, p. 204.
6   In *Luhmann* (1998) page 14, while in all social formations "...one has to agree on access to scarce goods,...the differentiation of a special functional system is only brought about by money as a medium of communication".

exchange and money, and the drive for profit or the dynamic of capital as its "guest system", which operates within the wider general economic system. The guest system relate to the first host system as a storm system relates to the atmosphere, an infectious disease to a population, or an ideology to a wider discourse. One can also say that it is like going hunting in a forest or like playing a soccer match on a playing field. Sure, there are markets, just as there is exchange, but they are only the playing field. The name of the game being played, however, is "profit economy" or "capitalism". Talking about a "market economy" is, accordingly, a bit like talking about "stadium sports". While this separates them from sailing, golf, mountaineering, and the Tour de France etc., it does not say anything about the game actually being played (javelin throwing, soccer, female pole-jumping, or boxing). Economic theory must, yet, name the game played, which includes the purposes of the exchanges and the systemic connections between them. This already explains why we generally prefer to speak about "capitalism", and not about a "market economy".

A profit economy and capitalism emerge, as we saw in the elementary economics of profit economies, in the economic system as soon as humans make a specific use of exchanges by not entering them to procure values-in-use for their consumption, but to turn money into more money. In so doing, they discover and use the internally available option of money – to generate exchange profit via M–C–M'-circuits. While the economic system as such takes regional control over goods procurement, M–C–M' (as guest-system) wrest control from the economic system. The guest-system's players become aware that they have the most powerful interest in the propagation of the economic system and give it a massive boost, extending it in space and into the depths of society. The growth of the money economy, as the host-system, is pushed not only by the interest to facilitate commodity exchange in C–M–C'-circuits, but also by the guest-system, to gain ground so that it can unfold additional M–C–M'-circuits.

Even if to the extent the economic system develops in a "bottom up" way, states will normally crucially support it. There are two sides of this: the more a domestic area is pacified, a monopoly of physical force is erected and laws and courts begin to operate; as we have seen, present values of future values-in-use increase. States, or even proto-states, are greatly interested in this process, in order to increase their territory's well-being, military power, and their tax revenue. However, the social classes represented by states also have a direct personal interest in evolving the economic system as they most immediately stand to profit from more and more voluminous M–C–M'-circuits.

Host system and guest system

What the guest-system seeks in the host-system is "profit"– and therefore, "profit economy" is the first plausible name for the host-system when it gets dominated by the guest system. "Profit" places the emphasis on the special motive or purpose of economic behavior (M–C–M' instead of C–M–C') and the logic behind it. As we have seen, this creates asymmetricity of the roles involved in the exchanges. The pursuance of this motive and the logic of profiteering will soon bear fruit and will lead to a significant enrichment and capital formation in favor of the M–C–M'-players. The emphasis now shifts from some self-selecting themselves to be M–C–M'-players (the "trade heroes") to its result, the accumulation of ownership of means for playing M–C–M' in one class; this, from thereon, justifies the term "capitalism". It is insofar correct to even already apply this term to economic systems that have existed as early as in Greek, Roman, and Chinese antiquity. Making a "profit", and the possession of "capital", do not require that those who work enter into free contracts; accordingly, the term "capitalism" is proper irrespective of whether or not the immediate producers are slaves (personally dependent unfree peasants), "twofold free" workers, or any mix of the above. Making a "profit" is also independent of the tremendously lower development of productive forces in antiquity.

Like there are only small nuances between an exchange and a money economy, and between a money economy and a profit economy, there is hardly a palpable difference between profit economies and capitalism. The more we become aware that ancient Greece, Rome, or China were profit economies or ancient capitalist economies, the less we will be surprised that the re-discovery of Roman law as the law of a "slaveholder-society", in Bologna in the 11th and 12th centuries, prepared the Renaissance and modern capitalism in Europe. We also need no longer be amazed by the relevance of Greek state theory (of another "slaveholder-society") today, even including in mass-democratic societies. If today's capitalism is not so remote from ancient capitalism, then this off course challenges the Marxist evolutionary scheme primitive society – slavery – feudalism – capitalism (and then socialism – communism). If we had capitalism already in ancient Greece, Rome, and China, and we still have it now, then the crucial historic "jump" or the great evolutionary and historic rupture must have happened much earlier. It happened precisely between primitive society and ancient profit economies or ancient capitalism, i.e., between primitive society and civilization.[7]

---

7   The Marxist evolutionary scheme is primitive society – slavery – feudalism – capitalism (and then, some hope, socialism – communism). It is ultimately based on the theory of labor value and exploitation as the three first production methods are distinguished by different "methods" or "forms" of exploitation (in slavery, exploitation takes place via ownership of the laborer, in feudalism via feudal bonds, and in capitalism via employment of free workers). The scheme was always misleading. E.g., Greek or Roman slavery could be well combined with otherwise capitalist forms. By massively using slave labor in the 16th to 19th centuries (slaves were used in Cuba until the end of the 19th century), Spain did also not regress into a "slave-holder society" and it would be beside the point to view the US, even if it maintained

A new view of the Middle Ages

Once we begin rewriting evolution and history around the two essential poles of primitive society and civilization, we open up the possibility to see the primitive society – slavery – feudalism – capitalism – sequence in a new light. Social anthropology has consistently taught that the antagonism between the profit economy and families, tribes, and the order of custom was most aggressive first in the "Axial Age" and, second, since the 15th century. In contradistinction, much social anthropology has portrayed the feudal Middle Ages, which are generally disparaged as being "dark", full of superstition, and cruelty, much *like an extended rest for the lower classes* between two tougher evils. Feudal societies not only had one hundred to one hundred and fifty holidays per year (of course, peasants had to do what it took on the fields in order to bring in a proper harvest, and often that was not enough) but peasants, in fact, appear to have often been better off than before or after the Middle Ages. Equally, the dynamics of the profit economy and of ancient capitalism – or of the debt, which David Graeber puts in the center of his book "Debt" – were partially set out of operation or greatly moderated by ideological, mostly religious, anti-capitalist movements. Catholicism, Buddhism, and Islam, which dominated the world at that time, *all* had very strong anti-usury and anti-debt contents that protected the peasantry from the destiny of their predecessors in antiquity.[8] Furthermore, there

---

slavery until the end of the civil war in its South, as having been a "slaveholder-society" until then.

8   *Luhmann* (1991) page 69 views the collapse of socialism in the early nineties of last century as a failure of a large-scale experiment of an ethical control of the economy. Quite surprisingly (or unsurprisingly), soviet style socialisms would then move closer to the Middle Ages as its predecessor-experiment of reducing the power of M–C–M' in favor of C–M–C', ethics and religion. On centrally planned and administered economies, see also *Luhmann* (1988) page 106 et seq. *Kornai* (1992) supplied an economic analysis of Luhmann's "large-scale experiment of an ethical control of the economy". He, in particular, juxtaposed the methods of "coordination" within a socialist economy to the methods of a market economy. Socialism, he finds, is only a "semi-monetized economy" (page 131), which. although it possesses a quasi "monobank" (page 132), is largely "centrally managed" (he prefers "centrally managed" to "centrally planned" because of ongoing interference, page 117) by bureaucratic coordination. The process begins with a policy decision on what output is desirable in the planning period and the nearly megalomaniacal effort to draw a mental picture of how technological development, resources, investment, labour, intermediary output, monetary matters and foreign trade should integrate into this picture. But direct bureaucratic control could only work if perfect information on the past and precise predictions of the future were available, commands were faultless and carried out with impeccable accuracy (page 118). Resources are nevertheless directed accordingly, leading to persistent "vertical negotiations" between the central planning committee and ministries, within ministries, between ministries and firms and between different firms (page 122), in which the lower levels typically demand higher inputs and lower output targets. The "vertical negotiations" are accompanied by a

were strong institutions that shared an anti-M–C–M'-bias, e.g., churches, convents, and universities. The feudal structures, through which feudal lords appropriated surpluses of the work of dependent peasants,[9] often, indeed, involved a seriously meant personal bond; this was very different from the relationship between masters and slaves in slavery or between capitalists and workers in capitalism. It accentuated the self-interest that feudal lords had in a certain well-being of "their" dependent peasants.[10]

Of course, religions, which had all emerged as anti-debt–movements in the "Axial Age", not only massively suppressed the development of money and profit economies, but they also depressed scientific, technological, and societal progress.[11] Stagnation reigned throughout the Middle Ages. This only changed when dynamical capitalism re-emerged alongside the Renaissance and Reformation. After all, it can be argued that it was not in the allegedly "dark" European Middle Ages that peasants suffered the most, but before the Middle Ages or afterwards, e.g., when large peasants' upheavals and peasants' wars, such as the great German peasants' wars, took place between 1524–1526, when an estimated 70,000 were killed. (This number of dead will appear ridiculously low compared to the millions of dead in Chinese peasant rebellions and wars, which we shall encounter later).

Section 3. The master drama of ancient capitalism: Land for peasants

Agriculture and small peasants' land ownership

Today's intellectuals tend to underestimate agriculture, but agriculture, and land, meant everything for more than 90 % of human history for almost 100 % of the peo-

---

systematic distortion of the upward flow of information (page 123) and lead to the already mentioned permanent central interference, which renders prices rather irrelevant. E.g., if socialist states wish to enable consumer prices below costs, they subsidize them by a "negative turn-over tax." (page 136). Kornai's results are largely sober and well-balanced. Many planning officials of the former GDR and managers of people owned businesses, to whom the author could talk to when he worked for the German privatization agency the early 1990ties, would likely have shared Kornai's views.

9   This expression does not imply a Marxian exploitation concept. The appropriated surplus is the difference of the value-in-exchange is attributed by markets and the costs.

10   Sometimes the case is made that the economics of slave economies convey stronger motives to take care of slaves than for capitalists to take care of free workers. However, ongoing supply of "fresh" slaves worked in the opposite direction.

11   Quite interestingly, *Graeber* explains patriarchalism, including prohibiting women and daughters from leaving the house and their wearing of veils, as an attempt to protect them against being enslaved and prostituted if the family's father should become overindebted. (*Graeber* (2011) page 182 et seq.)

ple. Many social philosophers assumed that primitive society – "that early and rude state of society"[12] – had rather equal rights of appropriation, or even a rather equal distribution of land and, apparently, this assumption was historically true over a longer period in many civilizations. After the Neolithic revolution, in many cases, tribes worked their fields and used their pasture jointly, and, given the slow speed of ancient history, this condition may have actually lasted for millennia.[13] However, it did come to an end everywhere, and inequality did emerge. The most powerful and noble families, magnates, "engrossers", latifundist, a local or regional landed nobility, a gentry or as they may have else been called, or, sometimes town-based grand merchants, got to own the largest share of agrarian and other land over great periods in history that followed. Of course, there were narratives, e.g., myths, that explained how this situation had come about, and normative ideas, which were promoted by these families and proto-states or states, which justified it. Often there were also laws, which protected it expressly.

Legal construction of land ownership, property etc.

In the present context "land ownership" etc. is supposed to mean primarily somebody having the right to appropriate the result of working the land. If the small peasants had that, there was no master drama. The legal construction is, economically, of lesser or little or no relevance. E.g., whether the land may officially have been owned (if at all the notion of ownership or property exists) by a god, emperor, king, or overlord was inconsequential if the peasants working the land could reliably appropriate the produce and could expect this to continue in the future. This situation was not be practically different from the peasants officially owning the land, having some title to it, as may have been evidenced by land registers etc. In fact, small peasants were often better protected if they had no title to the land – as they could then not pledge or mortgage it (and see creditors execute in it), or lose the land by selling it in distress. We also note that an attempt to apply modern legal terms to ancient conditions will mostly take us nowhere. E.g., it would be inadequate to construe the reliable, foreseeable use and the right to appropriate the produce of the land as "possession" or as *usus fructus* in the modern sense (which legal terms may, in fact, also not be the same in different legal systems). After this point is clarified, there is, though, now

---

12   Wealth of Nations, book I chapter VI first line.

13   In China this situation was mainly known as the *tsing tien* system (well field system). See *Bodde*, The state and empire of Ch'in, pages 27 et seq. 35 et seqs. In Rome, according to *Mommsen*, fields were initially in common property and "wealth" was identical with cattle and the possibility to use land. He argues that the word "pecunia" (meaning money *and* cattle) and "manucipatio" (meaning transfer of property) were not applied to the transfer of land, but only to movables (manus = hand). See *Mommsen* (1976) volume 1 page 197, 198.

no more reason to painstakingly avoid terms like ownership, property etc. related to land ownership.

The distribution of agrarian land, production, population, taxes, armies and state administration

Small peasant's land ownership, production and states' tax incomes etc.

The distribution of agrarian land matters greatly for the production output, for the size and character of the population, for the amount of taxes the states can collect, and hence for the state's fiscal situation. Thereby, it also matters for the number of state-functionaries and soldiers the state can recruit and its external might, whether it is used expansively or defensively, the size and volume of its construction projects and infrastructure and the luxury available to a court. High agrarian production output and high collected taxes will also support artisanry and finance intellectuals, e.g., philosophers, teachers, and artists, although they are normally rather cheap.

At the beginning of the book, we stressed that men are dependent upon their environment with regard to water, nutrition, housing etc. They need to, first, procure these goods from nature and then to defend them against other humans and animals who might take them away. This has the greatest impact in the motivational system of humans. *A given distribution of land directly connects to this.* If small farmers have land, which is usable for agriculture, *they will most likely work it* as they can then simply live from their harvests as largely autarchic units. Given proper soil, climate, no natural catastrophes, and no civil and external wars, that is mostly enough and they can survive rather independently of what is going on around them. In particular, they need not worry about there being somebody with effectual esoteric demand for their output and sufficient producive spending for it. Their autarky keeps them outside of the economic system and unaffected by its interdependencies, complexities, non-transparency, and frequent erratic behavior. Left alone, disturbances by humans, they have to worry about nature alone.

Peasants in Antiquity needed only few suppliers. They could mostly themselves generate their supplies directly from nature, e.g., seed, primitive tools, and water, or on a bartering basis with local artisans. Aside ownership of usable land and possible political restrictions, there were no serious entry barriers to becoming a peasant.

Customers were, thus, not crucial for small independent peasants. There was the state, though, presenting itself as their partner against their will, and requesting them to deliver a share of the harvest (either in kind or in money, which difference will matter later). Such requests are justified by traditions, myth, religion, other ideologies or the law, and they can widely also be enforced, at least against small peasants living in transparent conditions, and which have no army of their own. As peasants want to avoid not only imprisonment or other punishment but also execution in their land, the necessity to pay taxes enters in their motivational systems nearly as merciless as their physical necessities for food, water and housing. There is a strong transmission belt between land ownership and production, which does not only favor the immediate producer families but also distant other people, to whom the produce is redistributed by the state. Even if small peasants can initially self-supply with tools, seed, and water, after some time, if they run a small surplus beyond their immediate survival needs and their tax obligations, they will open up a market, at first small, then sizable, for equipment and inventories, consumption of food that they do not produce themselves, and occasionally even for a bit of symbolic, positional and luxury consumption.

If the respective plot of land was not owned by the small peasants who work it, they could not subsist from it, they wouldn't have as many children as now, and nobody would receive the share of the produce, which they forward to the state as taxes. They would also not generate employment for others.

Latifundists' land ownership, production and states' tax-incomes etc.

Assume now the land is taken over as private property by a latifundist. He will only have the land worked, if he can draw a profit out of this, meaning that he needs to find somebody to work the land for less than what somebody else will give for the produce or that he receives a proper share of the produce. In the simplest case, if the latifundist is lucky, he can keep the peasant family on the land, get rif of the state (the state ought not to accept this, but states were often not capable of enforcing tax payments against latifundists) and collect the state's former share (ceteris paribus, either in kind or in money) for himself. The state does not have to waive its claim wholly but the state and the latifundist may repartition the share of the produce they draw from of the peasant family. This would lead to tax-losses for the state and a meagre profit for the latifundist only. If the state insists on his full share, or if the latifundist ask for more than what would add up to the old tax, the share of the peasant family in what they produce has to fall or it has to work harder or more effectively. This will often ruin the peasant family. In this case, the latifundist may hire somebody to work the land as an agrarian laborer instead, which will, though, change very little. The latifundist still have to leave a significant share of the harvest with the employed laborers – if now as salary. Otherwise, the laborer, too, will leave or decay. And the latifundist will still have to deal with the state's request for a share...

Latifundists will, more generally than the state, not be interested in produce in kind, but in money. Depending on circumstances, they will try to sell the whole produce and pay their laborer in money, or they will sell the share of the produce they receive in kind. To whom will they sell the produce? Most certainly, they won't be able to sell the produce to the peasant families they displaced from the land or who were displaced elsewhere – they do not have the money to pay for it. The private owners will need to find *somebody else* with sufficient effectual demand, who must draw a sufficient income from somewhere else, This is, of course, possible, e.g., long-distance trade, armies, or urban hubs with state-functionaries may generate such income, but latifundists will have to compete for this demand against other latifundist and, may be, against some remaining small peasants.

The old simple and stable mechanism, which applied when a peasant family was working its own land, in which production, including of a part forwarded as taxes, was directly driven by survival necessities of the immediate producers, is gone. The higher the percentage of the land, which is owned by latifundists, and in respect of which they claim a share of the produce in addition to the state, the more conditional and precariat will motives for agricultural production be, and the more likely will a "surplus"-population of landless beggars, prostitutes, bandits, pirates, and social revolutionaries come into being. Of course, following this, the population will shrink, tax income and size and quality of the army and of the infrastructure and the administration of the state will fall. The decay of the small peasantry will, in particular, damage the military. The respective state's power of violent wealth procurement and to defend against violent wealth procurement of neighbors will be undermined to the extent it expropriates its fellow citizens who are to do the fighting and finance it.

We shall now take a historical look at the Greek, Roman and Chinese ancient history. The Greek history, which we examine, evolved over only a few centuries, from around 700 to 400 BC, until the end of classical Greece before the Hellenistic period. Or review is mainly focused on Athens, with a very brief look at Sparta. Rome was much larger than Greece, but the period examined also only extends over a similar period, from around 400 BC into the 1st century BC. Finally, this book will, very briefly, also look at an East-Eurasian variant of the ancient master drama. Our observations on China shall be more general and cursory then those before, but extend over more than two millennia.

Chapter V. Conservative-restorative policies and prosthetics in ancient capitalism

Section 1. Conservative-restorative policies and prosthetics in ancient Greece

Origins of the ancient master drama in Greece

Private ownership of land emerged in Minoan and Mycenae palace cultures after the Neolithic Age and during the late Bronze Age. The Minoan culture, mainly in Knossos on Crete, lasted from around 2600 to 1450 BC. The Mycenae culture, e.g., Mycenae, Pylos, and Tiryns, conquered the Minoan in its last centuries and lasted from around 1600 BC to around 1200 BC.[1] Appropriations of agricultural land from small farmers by latifundia owners are believed to have taken place and led to social conflict. Some authors connect the downfall of the Mycenae palace culture with earthquakes or the breakdown of trading systems with Phoenicia and social rebellions that followed agrarian conflicts.[2] A general regression into a more primitive stage of evolution occurred thereafter. Palaces, trade, bureaucracy, and the art of writing (Linear B) disappeared; tools and pottery became simpler. We enter into what historians call the Greek "dark ages" or the Greek "Middle Ages" (lasting from around 1100 BC to 700 BC). Migrations occurred at that time, e.g., the Dorians moved to the Peloponnese.[3] The migrating tribes would grab the land from their displaced predecessors; afterwards, an internal redistribution within the winning tribes occurred. Given Greece's geography, with many curvy coastlines, isthmuses, islands, peninsulas, and mountains, this took place in over a thousand[4] mostly small, en-

---

1   *Ober* (2016) page 119.
2   *Burn* (1990) page 56 attributes the decay of the Mycenae palace culture to the fact that "the palace people... had become so far removed from the peasantry that they could no longer trust them as soldiers." Other explanations, earthquakes, drought, and raids by sea people are given by *Waterfield* (2018) page 17.
3   On migrations within Greece, into Greece, and around Greece, see *Cartledge*, Historical Outline c. 1500 – 146 BCE, page 54–60, in Cartledge (1998) page 38. *Burn* (1990) page 61.
4   *Thommen* (2019) page 26.

capsulated, and separated poleis.[5] Attica, roughly the size of Luxemburg,[6] was the largest; Sparta on the Peloponnese followed; Syracuse in Sicily was later to become the third largest. Hesiod, born before 700 BC, in view of the land appropriations, recommended that farmers "always be in good time" in agriculture, then "you will buy another man's farm, not he buys yours".[7] Hesiod also recommends remaining free of debt and having only one son to keep the land together.[8] The ancient social master drama was, nevertheless, probably the main cause that triggered the Greek outbound colonization, which began between 750 and 600.[9] As everything in Greece, it was a small numbers game.[10] The families who had kept sufficient lots of land stayed in Greece while many who did not, approximately forty thousand adult males, left.[11] The colonists preferred costal places or offshore islands around the Aegean Sea, Black Sea, Adriatic Sea, and Mediterranean, from Spain,[12] North Africa, Southern France, Massilia, today's Marseille, to Sicily, the West cost of today's Turkey and Odessa. Plato coined the expression that they were sitting around the Mediterranean and the Black Sea "like ants or frogs around a lake".[13]

After the Greek "Middle Ages" we reach what historians call the "archaic period" of Greek history. This period lasted from around 800 to 500 BC; the "classical period" (479 BC to 323 BC) followed thereafter.[14] Like everywhere in ancient history, the two sides of our distinction, between wealth accumulation through robbing and through exchange (see Chapter 1 and 3), mutually influenced each other. The Greek land-owning citizen farmers, the *hoplites*, worked their fields and fought expansive

---

5   *Burn* notices: "...our maps usually *under*emphasize the disunity of classical Greece" (page 63).

6   See *Cartledge*, Power and State, page 149, in *Cartledge* (1998).

7   Hesiod's book was called in his *Works and Days*. Quoted from *Burn* (1990) page 76.

8   See *Thommen* (2019) page 26 and *Clauss* (1993) page 55.

9   The significant problem of displaced ("drifting") peasants moving from north China to the south following the second century AD was dealt with by assigning land to them and providing them with tools. They were also partially exempted from taxation and supported by relief measures if locusts, draught and floods hit. See *Ebrey*, The economic and social history of the later Han, page 618 et seq.

10   See *Cartledge*, Power and State, page 140, in Cartledge (1998). *Waterfield* (2018) page 20. *Graeber* (2011) page 182, sees Greek colonization as a means to forestall future debt crises.

11   See *Cartledge*, Historical Outline c. 1500 – 146 BCE, page 54–60, in *Cartledge* (1998). Attica seems to have had enough land to nourish the Athenians and Laconia to nourish the Spartans, so the Athenians and Spartans mostly stayed home. The colonists appear to have largely come from tighter places and islands. (*Thommen* (2019) page 50, 58; Burn (1990) page 118).

12   Burn (1990) page 111.

13   *Plato*, Phaidon, 109 St 1 A.

14   On the periodization of Ancient Greece, see *Cartledge*, Historical Outline c. 1500 – 146 BCE, page 54–73, in *Cartledge* (1998).

and defensive wars. How did these two ways of goods and wealth procurement (or of defense against foreign goods procurement by violence) affect each other?

Peaceful economics and violent prater-economics

Interestingly, we hear a lot about more about the negative impact of the peaceful exchange economy onto goods procurement by violence than the other way around. The dynamics of the peaceful exchange economy obviously greatly damaged the social base of the poleis' military. Athens had an average "gross" population of around 250,000 of which Athens' citizens, all males, who also supplied the core of the military, were around 30,000 to 50.000 in the 6th and 5th century, hence the time from Solon's reforms to the end of the Peloponnesian war. In bad times, e.g., during the Persian and Peloponnesian wars, it dropped,[15] in times of prosperity, e.g., after the Persian wars, the population grew and it may have doubled between 480 and 431.[16] We should assume that the number of Athens' free farmer warriors was still lower in the early sixth century, when Solon was archon, say at 30,000. According to a widespread opinion, the distribution of ownership of land in Athens was still comparatively equal in the 6th and 5th centuries BC. *Ober* reports that 20 % of Athens' citizens did not own land, 7.5 to 9 % owned 30–35 % of the land and the remaining 70–75 % owned 60–65 % of the land.[17] If we apply these percentages to 30,000 citizens of Athens, then we come to assume that approximately 6,000 citizen would not have owned land, and that 21,000 citizens would have owned 60 % of the land.

Hoplite warfare was introduced somewhere between the 7th and the end of the 6th century.[18] Allegedly, Athens and Platea had 10,000 hoplites in the battle of Marathon in 490 BC, of which the vast majority would have come from Athens,[19] say 9,000. If we assume the number of Athens' hoplites to be less a hundred years earlier, then they may have been around 6,000. Sparta mostly had around 5,000 hoplites.[20] As hoplites were "mostly middling peasants with some resources of their own",[21] or as Cartledge puts it, "citizen landowners, people who on average owned

---

15   This appears to be roughly the majority opinion of historians. A disease between 430 and
      425 BC may have claimed 75,000 lives (*Ober* (2016), page 302), 20,000 lives (*Thommen* (2019)
      page 205) or one quarter to a third of the population (*Günther* (2011) page 216).

16   *Grant* (1992) page 64. *Burn* (1990) sees it peaking at 70.000 under Pericles (page 215).

17   *Ober* (2016) page 143 with further references.

18   According to *Forest* (1986) page 25, it appears on vase painting in the middle of the 7th century
      BC. *Waterfield* (2018) page 62 argues that it was introduced only at the end of the 5th century
      BC.

19   *Forest* (1986) page 37 et seq.

20   Forest (1986) page 33.

21   *Grant* (1992) page 46; *Günther* (2011) page 177. Other authors argue that hoplite equipment
      was comparatively cheap (*Ober* (2016) page 202).

about 5 and 10 acres of land",[22] they must have constituted about 30–40 per cent of the adult male citizen population of a city state.[23] Accordingly, the fault line ran straight through the core of the Athens army apparatus between farmers who were at risk of losing their land and others who were likely to remain safe. A loss of a farm to a wealthy neighbor would, off course mean a loss of a hoplite for the army and weaken Athens' military might.

Farmer-hoplites were, sure enough, killed in military action, and had to be absent from their fields during campaigns. Astonishingly, this appears to have been less damaging to the hoplite army as such. While wars in the 6th and 5th centuries were more the rule than the exception, a number of factors moderated their effect. First, hoplite soldiers would normally have sons who would literally take over the hoplite equipment as well as the land from their fathers; the loss of the land would end the existence of a "farmer's position", the death of a senior farmer not necessarily. Second, in fact, the damage of warfare to agriculture was bearable as campaigns took mostly only place in midsummer, when there was no work to do on the fields,[24] and family members or slaves, which even small farmer sometimes had, took over the work in the absence of the hoplites. Third, if it came to battles, while hoplite phalanx fighting was an incredibly courageous face-to-face fighting, casualty-rates and killing-rates were nevertheless limited. This was partly due to conventions and symbolic elements. The battle began when both sides were properly deployed in formation and, more importantly, it was considered to be decided upon if one phalanx was pushed back or dissolved (there were no reserves). Consequently, some fights only lasted for minutes. Fourth, if a phalanx had been brought into disorder, then the hoplites would throw away their heavy equipment (weighing around 23 kilograms) and their helmet, which limited movability and sight, to run away. Dishonorable, as it was, it gave the advantage to the fleeing hoplites as the pursuing phalanx still had to carry their heavy weapons.[25] This was, perhaps, a practical reason for why pursuing dissolved phalanxes (absolutely contrary to Clausewitz' recommendations) never became a relevant factor in the 6th century and throughout most of the 5th century. However, it does not answer why lighter troupes or cavalry were not held in reserve to do the killing after the battle's culmination. The answer to this question may be found in symbolic moments or in the fact that escalation to "absolute war" (in Clausewitz's sense) was certainly not in the interest of hoplite-farmer armies. The victorious phalanx would, rather, only erect a symbol of its victory on the battlefield; the loser would carry their armor, their wounded, and their

---

22   *Cartledge*, War and Peace, page 168, in *Cartledge* (1998).
23   *Cartledge*, War and Peace, page 168, in *Cartledge* (1998).
24   *Ober* (2016) page 61. The Mediterranean was less dangerous in summer (loc. cit.).
25   *Clauss* (1993) page 90.

dead away – and that was it.[26] Accordingly, the winning side in hoplite warfare often had only as few as 5 % of its hoplites killed and the loser around 10 % or 15 % to 20 %.[27] As a consequence, heroic hoplite phalanx fighters could grow rather old. If a summer campaign occurred every second year, winning hoplites would statistically reach a 100 % probability of death only after 20 years; if they began campaigning at 18, then that would probably be at around the average life expectancy of the time.

It is for these reasons that the risk to hoplite farmers of losing their existence was indeed higher back home, where there were plenty of "other men" who wanted to "buy their land".[28] This may explain why Solon argued, in his report on his laws, that without these laws "the polis of Athens would have been bereaved of many men"[29] or why Burn explained compromises in conflicts between the aristocracy and poorer farmers as follows: "It was not so much the danger of revolt, for the rich had the best weapons; but what would become of a state with a dwindling army?"[30] A well-known event in the Peloponnesian war, around 170 years later, speaks volumes about the importance of hoplites in ancient Greece: In the Peloponnese war, the Athenians captured 120 Spartan hoplites in a coup at Pylos (on the small island opposite from modern Pylos). While this appears to be a very modest number, it seems that holding these few hostages enabled Athens to negotiate the interim Nicias peace in 422 BC.[31]

Draco, the reformer

Draco became archon in Athens in 621 and enacted what would later be called "Draconian laws". Little is left thereof, but his laws, which were displayed on wooden pillars,[32] must have strengthened the supremacy of statehood structures and the state monopoly of criminal prosecution, e.g., by prohibiting vendettas and feuds[33] (which normally works against the power of the old noble and wealthy families). Draco's laws, their harshness notwithstanding, may also have limited the discretion of the

---

26   It much limited the casualty rate. See *Waterfield* (2018) 160 et seq. Philipp II of Macedonia did away with this restriction and had his cavalry pursue dissolved enemy formations and kill them up to the last man (*Clauss* (1993) page 90).

27   *Waterfield* (2018) page 160 et seq: 5 % and 15 % to 20 %; *Cartledge*, War and Peace, in Cartledge (1998) page 168: 5 % and 10 %.

28   See again Hesiod's phrase "you will buy another man's farm, not he buys yours", quoted from *Burn* (1990) page 76.

29   Quoted in *Aristotle*, The State of the Athenians, 12.4, translated from German by the author based on a translation from Greek by M. *Dreher*, see *Günther* (2011) page 70.

30   Burn (1990) page 119.

31   *Thucydides*, The history of the Peloponnesian war, chap. XII; *Günther* (2011) page 203. According to *Cartledge*, War and Peace, in Cartledge (1998) page 179, two hundred and ninety-two Spartan hoplites were captured. See also *Fisher*, Rich and Poor, in Cartledge (1998) page 93.

32   *Thommen* (2019) page 59.

33   *Thommen* (2019) page 50, 59; *Clauss* (1993) page 61.

jurisdiction by the ruling aristocracy, the *eupatrids*. In the late 7th century BC, right after Draco, there was again great social discontent because small farmers, the *georgoi*, had either lost or were at risk of losing their land to their wealthier aristocratic neighbors.[34] Like everywhere, this appears to have happened after they had taken out debt in distress. They were then often sold into slavery abroad or their wives and daughters were made to become prostitutes.[35] Others had to accept long-term arrangements with rich landowners,[36] under which they were lastingly – until the repayment of debt with interest – obliged to deliver a share of their harvest. It appears that they were called *hektemoroi* (six-part-men), but it is not so clear whether it meant that they had to deliver one sixth[37] or five-sixth of their harvest[38] – although this is a dramatic difference.[39]

Solon, the reformer

The squeeze of small peasants, whatever aspect most contributed thereto, also led to the famous *reforms of Solon of 594 BC*. It appears that the small farmers and the

---

34 *Günther* (2011) page 60, reports of unrest and civil wars (*staseis*) in many poleis since the late 7th century BC, without connecting them to the agrarian question.

35 *Clauss* (1993) page 61.

36 *Fisher*, Rich and Poor, in *Cartledge* (1998) page 90.

37 *Waterfield* (2018) page 79. Waterfield appears to support the view that the *hektemoroi* had to give away one sixth of the harvest (with reference to *Aristotle*, The Athenian Constitution 6.1). However, later he seems to imply that one sixth was only the monthly interest. *Günther* (2011) page 71 and *Clauss* (1993) page 62, also believe that one sixth had to be given away.

38 *Grant* (1992) page 88 ("probably means that... they had to pay five-sixth of their produce to their creditors...").

39 One sixth seems moderate in relation to Sparta's helots (from the conquered area "Helos"). (*Thommen* (2019) page 84; *Waterfield* (2018) page 107), who had to deliver *half* of their harvest (*Grant* (1992) page 86. *Thommen* (2019) page 86). But the land worked by the Helots in Messenia was much better than the land in Attica. Possibly more importantly, the Athenian peasants were proud free hoplite-citizens; therefore, one sixth might have already caused a great stir-up. Allegedly, there was, at the time, also a switch from producing grains locally in Attica to importing grains from the Black Sea, especially from Crimea and today's Ukraine, as well as a prohibition of the export of grains. This shifted the production in Attica to olives and wines. Small peasants, however, the argument goes, did not have the capital to plant olive trees and grapevines (*Rohlfes/Rumpf* (1970) page 9). This is supported by olive trees requiring one generation before the olives could be reaped; vineyards also needed significant time (*Ober* (2016) page 200). If, thus, small peasant could not switch and stuck to grains, the imported grains could have lowered the market price and ruined them, particularly as they only had marginal land in remote hills (*Burn* (1990) page 119). Ultimately, Hesiod had already made the point that the lack of primogeniture heritage laws rendered allotments so small that they were no longer viable (*Grant* (1992) page 64, 88; *Fisher*, Rich and Poor, in *Cartledge* (1998) page 88).

aristocrats of Athens explicitly agreed to assign the task to work out a settlement to Solon when he was made archon in 594 BC. What he delivered, the laws of Solon, just as before Draco's laws, were publicly displayed on wooden pillars.[40] First, enslavement (of men, women and children) as a means of execution was prohibited. Greek citizens who had already suffered this fate were even repurchased, if they could be tracked down. The number affected, and resulting costs, must have been significant; Burn believes that the rich had to pay heavily for it.[41] Second, all outstanding debt was cancelled and, consequently, in symbolic acts, the boundary markers on mortgaged land were swept away (seisakhtheia).[42] Conversely, interest already paid or excessive interest had to be repaid.[43] Third, most argue that Solon abolished sharecropping.[44] That understood, there was, fourth, clearly no redistribution of land, which could only have been achieved through a partial expropriation of the Greek aristocrats and nothing was enacted, much like elsewhere, to disallow the future sale of the debt-free land to large landowners. Fifth, some argue that Solon set limits on the amount of land that one man could own in Attica.[45] Sixth, some also argue that large landowners had enclosed public land and that Solon ordered them to disenclose it.[46] Finally, there was no prohibition for small landowners to take out new loans and there was, if such new loans were not properly repaid, also no restriction for creditors to execute in the land again. Some authors believe that the interest rates were, though, limited to a more endurable level for the future.[47]

In summary, Solon's reforms greatly mitigated the problem for the then-victims for the moment and limited small farmers' downward risk in the future, but they did nothing to stop the decay of small peasants as such.[48] Solon either accepted that the effects of his reforms would only be very transitory or he was hoping for something surprising, new, and good to happen. He was actually not disappointed. The time

---

40 Cartledge, Power and the State, page 140, in Cartledge (1998)

41 Burn (1990) page 123 et seq.

42 Waterfield (2018) page 79.

43 Burn reports that this request was raised in Megara (1990) page 113). It was later also raised in Rome (Mommsen (1976) volume 1 page 315 et seq, volume 3 page 260).

44 Forest (1986) page 29. However, Waterfield (2018) page 79, argues that Solon did "not make debt-bondage illegal – a man may still have had to repay debt with labor or services – but he extracted the deadly sting of potential enslavement" (page 79).

45 Waterfield (2018) page 76.

46 Waterfield (2018) page 79 with reference to Solon F. 36 4–7 and Aristotle, Politics, 1266 b 17–19.

47 Grant (1992) page 88. According to Grant Solon restricted "the export of grain, by which large farmers had ruined the poor driving up the price of corn at home" (page 64). That is unclear. Exporting corns and a higher corn price should normally have helped small farmers. It might have damaged other poor, but hardly farmers.

48 Solon obviously obliged sons to support their fathers in their old age if the father had allowed them to learn a handicraft (Günther (2011) page 72). That seems like easing the way of small farmers out of peasantry, but not as a measure to maintain small farmers.

between Solon and the end of classical Greece was littered by a series of events and measures that, while they did not halt the centralization of land in the hands of the aristocracy, softened the social consequences thereof quite effectively.

Peisistratus and his sons, tyrants as reformers

Solon also made significant constitutional reforms, thereby giving stronger rights to the middle and poorer classes. In particular, he established a people's "council of hundred men", in addition to the archons, competing against the aristocratic Areopagus, and assigned more power to the general people's assembly, the *Ekklesia*. After Solon, it became customary to distinguish three areas in Athens with different social situations and political preferences: *pediakoi*, the inhabitants in the plains around Athens, mostly wealthy latifundia owners with aristocratic preferences; the *hyperakrioi* in the hills-districts further away from Athens, poor peasants, including marginal farmer-hoplites with democratic preferences, who often supported Peisistratus; and, finally, the *paralioi* in the coastal region, craftsmen, merchants, seamen, and salary workers who would later also be oarsmen of the trireme fleet, who had mixed political preferences.[49] This block-building and Solon's constitutional reforms strengthened popular opposition and opened up new channels to voice requests of threatened farmers.[50] This, in fact, eased the way for the tyrant *Peisistratus* who is said to have come to power mainly through the support of the *hyperakrioi*, the marginal hoplite-farmers, from the hill-districts.[51] Two attempts to grab power by Peisistratus, in 560 BC and 556 BC, had only succeeded for a few years,[52] but his third attempt in 546 BC made him, and later his sons, tyrants for altogether 36 years. He collected a direct ten percent tax on the produce and partially used it to grant loans to small farmers[53] to purchase ploughs and oxen.[54] It is plausible that these measures, together with Solon's prior debt releases, helped marginal peasants palpably for the time being. "Production soared", Burn optimistically writes and adds, with a view of small farmers, "...and the debts were easily repaid".[55] It is, yet, even more important that Peisistratus, and his sons Hipparchus and Hippias (ruling 546 until 510 BC), invented a new economic practice, which overlaid the ancient master drama at the end

49   *Thommen* (2019) page 68. Cleisthenes used the somewhat different three sectors, city (*asty*), mainland (mesogeion) and cost (*paralia*) and blended them in his *trittyes*, see *Thommen* (2019) page 113.
50   *Burn* (1990) page 123.
51   *Fisher*, Rich and Poor, in; *Cartledge* (1998) page 81.
52   *Waterfield* (2018) page 76 et seq.
53   *Ober* (2016) page 224. *Thommen* (2019) page 69.
54   *Burn* (1990) page 124 et seq.
55   *Burn* (1990) page 124.

of archaic Greece and in classical Greece. While Peisistratus and his sons did not engage in much warfare,[56] they made material construction investments in Athens' infrastructure, such as in water supply and in representative buildings, temples, and
public monuments, likely on the Acropolis, and in a public park north west of the
Acropolis,[57] which provided tangible employment and income alternatives outside
of agriculture. *In other words, prosthetic employment-generating spending made its appearance.* Undoubtedly, this increased production; for instance, we know of a flourishing
period in Athens' handicraft ceramics production and exportation of black and red
figure ceramics[58] and Hipparchus allegedly used private means to have Homer's Iliad and Odyssey written down for the first time.[59] Archaeologists believe that they
are able to detect an increase in the planting of olive trees in the period of Peisistratus and his sons, which they take to be a sign of a prevailing confident long-term
outlook;[60] hence, the exact opposite of high liquidity preference.

Ancient prosthetics and the Persian wars

After Peisistratus and his sons, we see further prosthetics mitigating the ancient
master drama, which were now often connected to warfare. The Athenian hoplite
force of 10,000 hoplites[61] under Miltiades won a surprise victory at Marathon
against Darius I in the first Persian war in 490 BC. Themistocles, expecting a further
Persian attack, thereafter brought the Athenian marine up, from merely twenty
ships in 500 BC,[62] to two hundred or even three hundred triremes for the second
Persian war.[63] Each trireme had around two hundred rowers at three levels. Even
based on only two hundred triremes, Athens, thus, paid up to a total of 40,000
people as oarsmen, officers, or other crew at campaign seasons' peaks. Triremes
were mainly ramming-tools and had little spare room. They could, thus, not stay
at sea for long and needed nearby harbors and a significant number of people to
support them in Piraeus and elsewhere. The triremes, of course, had to be built
before, and, prior to that, wood had to be procured and to be transported and new
docks and even a new harbor had to be constructed.[64] Themistocles had set into
motion an enormously huge investment, which healed the economic wounds of

---

56 *Burn* (1990) page 124 speaks of "a long generation of peace, which the tyrants gave to Athens
    (and which) saw the laying of strong economic foundations...".
57 *Waterfield* (2018) page 83.
58 *Ober* (2015) page 230.
59 *Günther* (2011) page 74.
60 *Burn* (1990) page 124.
61 *Ober* (2016) page 243.
62 *Günther* (2011) page 119.
63 *Cartledge*, Power and State, in: *Cartledge (1998)* page 179.
64 *Burn* (1990) page 159.

displaced small farmers' much like World War II created employment after the Great Depression.

Concerning the financing of these prosthetics: The operation of one trireme with 200 men is said to have cost one talent per month, which corresponds to 6,000 drachmae per month (1 silver talent = 60 minas = 6,000 drachmae = 36,000 obols) and to 200 drachma per day, hence one drachma per man per day.[65] This appears to also be the normal daily pay in the 5th century.[66] Other authors estimate the costs of a trireme to be lower than that. According to Cartledge, crew men in triremes were paid half a drachma a day and this was also the normal pay in the period prior to the Peloponnesian war. Accordingly, a trireme's crew would have cost half a talent per month[67] Waterfield estimates that 200 triremes with 40,000 men had cost "more than ten thousand drachmas a day",[68] which would mean that there had been only costs of a quarter of a drachma per man per day. Anyhow, the fleet of triremes created a very significant volume of employment.

Themistocles' investment had been well made. Darius' son Xerxes, in fact, gathered massive forces of likely 150,000 land troops, including 8,000 cavalry and 800 warships, constructed a bridge over the Hellespont, and, beginning in 483 BC, even built a 2,200 meters long canal through the Athos peninsula in Northern Greece (the Easternmost of the three "fingers" of the Chalcidice peninsula), to avoid a dangerous sea region, which had sunk a part of his father's fleet during the first Persian war.[69] The allied Greek forces under the Spartan leader Leonidas were, at first, not able to deny the Persian army entry through the *Thermophiles'* narrow in the north of Greece and had to withdraw to the south, near Corinth. This left Attica undefended and, accordingly, the Persians occupied and destroyed large parts of Attica, Boethia, and Euboae, including Athens. However, the unified Greek navy, to which Themistocles' new-built navy of Athens made the greatest contribution, delivered a crushing defeat over Xerxes at the sea battle of *Salamis* (between Piraeus and Corinth) in 480 BC. A year later, in 479 BC, the Greek, this time by its hoplites land army, won another great victory in the battle at *Plataea*, Aeschylus described the return of the defeated Persian's king Xerxes I. in his "The Persians".

---

65   *Waterfield* (2018) page 68, 164. Waterfield sees the nominal salaries increasing from one drachma for a day's manual labor, at the end or the 5th century, to 2,5 drachmae at the end of the 4th century BC (page 198).

66   *Ober* (2016) page 148.

67   *Cartledge*, Power and State, in: *Cartledge* (1998) page 179.

68   *Waterfield* (2018) page 147.

69   *Waterfield* (2018) page 148.

Conservatism, prosthetics and Athena's splendor

The following (approximately fifty years) prior to the Peloponnesian War (431 to 404 BC), became the heyday of classical Athens. Athens emerged from the Persian wars as the leading imperial power, mainly because of its trireme navy. But the question was how the Greeks sitting on the shores of Asia, in particular, could be protected against Persian revenge.[70] Athens' answer was the *Delian League*, which Athens founded in 478 BC with up to 1,000 partners;[71] these partners, given that most of them were unable to provide triremes themselves, had to make contribution payments in cash. After some time, membership in the Delian League was no longer voluntary and the payments resembled imperial tributes. When Naxos tried to leave in 467 BC, it was besieged and forced into re-joining.[72] "Free riding" – enjoying protection against the Persians by the Delian League, but not contributing thereto, was not allowed. Athens' imperial position widened its arsenal of prosthetics: First, if Athens conquered new land, including of former allies who had attempted to leave the Delian League (other examples included the Mytilene uproar or the conquest of Melos or Histiaia[73]), it could assign it to Athenian *klerouchoi*, poor citizen, often impoverished former hoplite farmers, who were reinstituted in an economically independent position. They would either move to their newly assigned land, and work it as a free farmer, or lease it back to its original owner.[74] In particular, Athens founded new colonies in Brea in Trakia in the mid-4th century BC.[75] (Similar practices were to become more relevant in ancient Rome.) These measures, based on state violence, generated prosthetic employment-generating spending at almost no cost. Second, huge amounts of contributions or tributes in money or in kind flew into Athens from its Delian League partners. As a further military investment, Themistocles had a wall built around Athens and the Piraeus harbor,[76] securing Athens' supplies, mainly corn, from the Black Sea. Archaeologists believe that fortifications of this kind were extremely expensive at the time and must, hence, have provided huge income opportunities for both firms and laborers who had to break

70   *Burn* (1990) page 195.
71   *Waterfield* (2018) page 174 et seq.
72   *Ober* (2016) page 280, *Waterfield* (2018) page 179.
73   *Günther* (2011) page 142.
74   *Ober* (2016) page 290 et seq., page 303, 306.
75   *Günther* (2011) page 142.
76   *Burn* (1990) page 193, 216. See also *Ober* (2016) page 274. Themistocles even travelled to Sparta to expressly assure the Spartans that Athens did not have the intention to build a wall – while it was secretly built. It is funny that the famous sentence by *Walter Ulbricht* on 15 June 1961 "Niemand hat die Absicht eine Mauer zu bauen" ("nobody has the intention to build a wall!") has, thus, likely been said already 2,400 years before in Sparta... .

the stones, carry them, cut them, and integrate them into the walls.[77] Third, as the Persians had destroyed Athens completely in 479 (and again 480 before Plataea), the city of Athens needed to be re-build. It was on this occasion that Pericles erected the Propylaea and the new Parthenon for the goddess Athena on the Acropolis, the remnants of which we admire today.[78] Thucydides, the politician, not the historian, though, denounced this as misusing the contributions of the Delian allies "decking our city like a vain woman with precious stones and thousand talent temples".[79]

Fourth, another sort of prosthetic employment-generating spending made its debut as imperial Athens became also more democratic. Under the influence of Ephialtes († 461 or 457 BC), and Pericles (490–429 BC), Athens began to make significant compensation payments to its citizens for the exercise of public office (from around 450 BC onwards). The stated purpose was, already then, to enable members of the lower property classes, particularly the thetes,[80] to share public responsibilities. Sources report on an astonishingly high number of positions, e.g., of remunerated judges, which can hardly be explained that way. It is said that e.g., two hundred to four hundred jurors decided upon one single private case and five hundred jurors decided upon larger public cases. Altogether, six thousand (!) jurors were reportedly drawn by lottery each year.[81] Clauss estimates the number of judges who were assigned to deciding a single case at between 200 to even 3,000 jurors, mostly likely 500, and believes that the number had been so enormous as to avoid bribery and deals.[82] Yet, he may have overlooked the more trivial effect: The state was mass-financing its poor citizenship.

The pay per day was certainly not just symbolic. Initially, around 450 BC, jurors received two obols or a third of a drachma per day; as from 426–425 BC, three obols or half a drachma was paid which was just enough, according to Waterfield, to supply a small family with its barley.[83] Aristophanes derided this practice as a means by which to re-distribute 10 % of the contributions or tributes from the Delian League's

---

77   Ober (2016)) page 77.
78   Burn (1990) page 221 presents "the public building program beginning with the great temple ...on the summit of the Acropolis" as a means to alleviate the situation of those, "who had never known a time when they could not earn a summer's income by rowing the triremes."
79   Burn (1990) page 229.
80   Solon's other property classes were the pentakosiomedimnoi, who had over 500 "bushels", the hippies, who served as cavalry, like the Roman equites, who had 300 "bushels", and the zeugitai, who had 200 "bushels". Yet, the thetes would be the core social basis of Athens imperial democracy in the fifth century as it had been organized by Ephialtes and Pericles (See Cartledge, Historical Outline c. 1500 – 146 BCE, in Cartledge (1998) page 65, and Waterfield (2018) page 80).
81   Günther (2011) page 182. Thommen (2019) page 123 gives slightly different numbers.
82   Clauss (1993) page 84.
83   Günther (2011) page 184; Waterfield (2018) page 209, 210.

allies, or of 2,000 talents, to the lower classes. Modern research stresses that not all 6,000 elected jurors served every day, but still they served an astonishing 150 days per annum (!), which would have led to a redistribution of 75 talents. The scope of public offices, for which remunerations were paid, was not limited to jurors. After 399 BC, even attendance of the *ekklesia*, the people's general assembly, was paid; the normal pay was 1 drachma for being there for a half day, attending exceptional meetings paid 11/2 drachmae. [84]

Now, where did the finance for all of these public investments and transfer payments come from? There were, indeed, already certain taxes in Athens, e.g., Peisistratus' aforementioned 10 %-tax on land or the poll-tax (*isoteleia*). Moreover, like hoplites had always financed their spears, sword, armor, and helmet and *hippeis* themselves, it was common for the wealthier Athenians to make occasional one-time contributions (*eisphora*) to the public. E.g., wealthy citizen who were desirous to stage honorable celebrations, such as the Panathenaea and Dionysus festival, had to pay a price for this.[85] Additionally, wealthy citizens would fund the construction of sanctuaries and monuments. When the navy was set up, this practice was extended to the financing of individual triremes, including the pay for the crew for some time.[86] State debt, on the other hand, does not appear to have been an important factor, although sometimes temples, e.g., the temple of Delphi, gave out loans more or less voluntarily.[87] Furthermore, Athens of the classical period continued to enjoy the same protection of goddess Athena that the Greeks had already enjoyed before Troy. When the Persian threat was greatest, in 483 BC, a new and extra-rich silver vein in the Athenian silver mines at Larium in south-east Attica[88] was fortunately discovered. Themistocles, then, convinced the *ekklesia* on the *pnyx* not to distribute the silver amongst the citizens – allegedly two and a half tons of silver was available[89] –, but to use it to finance the build-up of the fleet instead.[90] The new silver vein continued to contribute to Athens' public finances far beyond the Persian wars; it appears to have only been exhausted approx. around 100 BC.[91] This was sheer luck.

---

84   *Günther* (2011) page 185.

85   Most of the sacrificed animals' meat was eaten by humans. As *Waterfield* (2018) page 10, put it: "The gods usually received a smoke and smell, the bones and other inedible bits, but the rest was consumed by the humans...".

86   *Ober* (2016) page 345.

87   *Nack/Wägner* (1975) page 97 call the temple of Delphi "the central bank of all Greece". See also *Ober* (2016) page 339. Buddhist temples in China or monasteries and temples in Persia, Israel, Byzantium, elsewhere in Europe, or even in Japan would later do much the same (*Mandel* (2007) page 220).

88   *Burn* (1990) page 166.

89   *Waterfield* (2018) page 147.

90   *Burn* (1990) page 166.

91   *Waterfield* (2018) page 66 et seq.

In a commodity money regime, gold or silver mines are the best money creation glands. Finally, of course, as already mentioned, Athens' imperial goods procurement by violence contributed a great share to prosthetics financing, i.e., after 479, through contributions of the Delian League's members.

Spartans

Sparta, the second most-important Greek polis dealt with the ancient master drama through a blend of structural conservatism and progressive prosthetics. The Spartans had subjugated the population of neighboring Messenia in a particular form of state slaves, called *helots*. This subjugation, at the hands of the free Spartans, became the central axis of Spartan politics. The difference in rank between the helots and Spartan citizens was emphasized and culturally elaborated on many occasions. Strangely enough, the Spartans *formally declared war on their helots every year.* Worse still, young Spartans were expected to prove their courage by discretionarily attacking, injuring, and even killing helots in some kind of weird initiation rite following the completion of their state education.[92] Just as the distinction with helots was greatly emphasized, so were the distinctions in wealth, which, of course, existed between free Spartans de-emphasized and different measures were taken to hamper a further increase of inequality, e.g. by inheritance laws and through the prohibition of that which might dynamize the economy. In roughly that sense, *Hegel* wrote, "... the constitution of Lacedæmon is ... worthy of high esteem for it regulated and restrained the high Doric spirit, and its principal feature was that all personal peculiarity was subordinated, or rather sacrificed, to the general aim of the life of the State, and the individual had the consciousness of his honour and sufficiency only in the consciousness of working for the State. A people of such genuine unity, in whom the will of the individual had, properly speaking, quite disappeared, were united by an indestructible bond, and Lacedæmon was hence placed at the head of Greece, and obtained the leadership... This is a great principle which must exist in every true State, but which with the Lacedæmonians retained its one-sided character ... This abrogation of the rights of subjectivity, which, expressed in his own way, is also found in Plato's Republic, was carried very far with the Lacedæmonians." Hegel particularly stresses the interference in property relations to the aim of equality: "...it likewise ends in a harsh aristocracy, just as the fixed equilibrium of property (each family retaining its inheritance, and through forbidding the possession of money, or trade and commerce, preventing the possibility of inequality in riches) ...". While Hegel sees and understands the purposes behind these motives, Sparta did not stand exactly where he would have liked the world spirit to march. Ultimately, he observed that Sparta "passes into an avarice which, as opposed to

---

92   *Waterfield* (2018) page 62, 108. The issue is not undisputed amongst historians.

this universal [spirit of the Athenians], is brutal and mean".[93] Sparta, thus partly, dealt with its social master drama in a more conservative way than Athens. M–C–M' and the expropriation of free peasants was impeded, in the first place, by rigid social practices based on an egalitarian military *esprit de corps* – as if Solon had given up his moderation and taken over a perpetual Jacobin rule or as if the Roman Gracchi brothers had erected a slaveholder society, in which socialism ruled between the slaveholders. That certainly helped to maintain the fighting power of Spartan hoplites and reduced the need for prosthetics.

Hence, we find that when the master drama of antiquity raised its head in the 6th and 5th centuries in Greece there were, altogether, two different strategies to save the all-important armies from it. First, peremptory attempts were made by Solon, Peisistratus and others in Athens, to conservatively support small farmers to continue to survive as such. In Athens these conservative-restorative efforts ultimately capitulated in front of the economic dynamics, while in Sparta's militaristic society they were largely successful preserving the hoplite-farmer-army. In Athens, yet, a workable solution was discovered in a gigantic prosthetic employment-generating spending for the preparation and execution of two major wars, the reconstruction of Athens after the Persian wars, the further build-up of Athens as the Delian League's imperial center, and the continued military spending required to maintain Athens' hegemony. There was, in other words, already a lot of "big government" in the small polis of Athens, which handled the ancient master drama. The money needed in Athens was procured by tributes, plundering or requisitions, as well as by contributions and taxes of free Athenians at home, or the lucky discovery of a silver streak, a rare occurrence of just-in-time mass money creation in a system of commodity money.[94] In short, while massive expropriations of small farmers by M–C–M' was ultimately not avoided in Athens, taxation and expropriation, goods procurement by violence, and money creation, allowed to deal with the disintegrating effects of the ancient profit economy. We shall see that these forms of prosthetic employment-generating spending, and the ways of funding them, became the forerunners of prosthetic practices in Rome and in our times.

---

93   *Hegel*, Lectures on the History of Philosophy, volume One. The quotations are taken from
       the introduction to Anaxagoras.
94   The death of a great number of Athenians through the wars and outbreaks of diseases that
       took place from 430 to 425 may have helped to avoid an excess population.

Section 2. Conservative-restorative policies and prosthetics in ancient Rome

Origins of the ancient master drama in Rome

Rome's ancient master drama unfolded in two major stages. In the early Roman Republic, much like in Greece, small farmers, who were still free citizens and soldiers of the Roman armies, were displaced by large patricians from their farmer positions if they were hit by some unfortunate accident, such as lasting bad weather and several bad harvests. As even the early military campaigns of Rome lasted longer than in Greece, farmers often also had to take on debt and defaulted on it because of their extended absence. For the same reason, the death of soldiers in war was more frequent than in Greece. The second stage followed after the massive inflow of slave labor after the Punic and Macedonian wars in and after the 2nd century BC; this rendered plantations with slaves so profitable that it ignited a new hunger for land.[95]

In its early beginnings, when Rome was still a small town, Servius Tullius, the 6th Roman King (died 543 BC) allegedly erased a part of the plebeian debt and gave previously state-owned land to the poor.[96] In 494 BC, the *secessio plebis* followed which was a mythical withdrawal of the Roman plebs to a holy mountain (mons sacer), much like a general strike, to bolster demands for debt release.[97] The Twelve Tables Code was enacted in 450 as a result of these so-called "condition fights". It restricted archaic rights of patrician creditors to execute against the plebian debtors. Debtors were now granted 30 days to honor the debt and could then, and only then, be carried to the creditor's house by *manus iniectio*, and fettered "in iron chains of no less than 15 pounds for 60 days". The creditor had to feed the debtor and had to present him publicly on three consecutive market days; he was then permitted to sell him *trans Tiberim* or to kill him.[98] There was also debt slavery in which the debtor had to work for the creditor, called *nexus*. Around 120 years later, the *lex Poetelia Papiria des nexis* from 326 BC did away with the iron chains and private prison for debtors.[99]

Francesco de Martino mentions the proposal of a field law by Spurius Cassius in the 5th century BC and that there had been twenty-two further field laws between

---

95   When the "making" of new slaves, following the Roman empire's expansion, had dried up, great landowners discovered a new interest in keeping local peasant on their fields by turning them into dependent colons (colonati, coloni). This practice, which took place during the final centuries of the Roman empire, predated feudalism and at least granted some income opportunities to the *colons*. Our account of the Roman ancient master drama will end with the colons.

96   *Hegel* (1986) page 360.

97   *De Martino* (1991) page 45.

98   *De Martino* (1991) page 45, 46.

99   *De Martino* (1991) page 47, 48.

486 and 367 BC. He also reports that tribune Potelius unsuccessfully proposed to the consuls of the year 441 BC to examine advantages of distributing fields to the people. Apparently, the conquest of Veji by Rome in 396 BC led to the distribution of some conquered land, which relaxed the situation for a time.[100]

The Lex Licinia Sexta agraria

In 387 BC, Licinius enacted the famous *Lex Licinia Sexta agraria*; this limited the general size of land that could be owned by anybody to 500 jugera and forbade pastures with over 100 large livestock and 500 small livestock on the *ager publicus*.[101] The *Lex Licinia Sexta agraria* also had the option of land assignations. Yet it appears that nobody was willing or powerful enough to at least enforce the limitations of land possession or to implement land assignments.[102] At least the early Roman expansion within Italy generated some new farmer positions, after conquered land was distributed to soldiers, which mitigated the problem again. "Thus", writes Mommsen, "the war, which the money economy had waged on the peasantry over centuries, which was to end first with the ruin of the peasantry and then of the whole community, was discontinued without proper decision because of lucky wars and the huge and magnificent domanial distribution rendered possible thereby."[103]

Wars and plantations

After the Roman victory in the 2nd Punic War in 201 BC things worsened for the small peasantry. Expansive wars fought previously had been short, required an only a limited number of free peasants-soldiers, and had produced only a few slaves. This changed. The more the theaters of war lay remoter from Rome and outside of Italy, the more wars lasted longer, required a greater number of peasants-soldiers and, worse, after victorious wars Romans would turn inhabitants of conquered regions into slaves and use them in plantations as slave laborers.[104] Gigantic plantations, particularly in Sicily, Campania, and North Africa were opened. This ignited a novel motive for land appropriations back home. "With the help of slaves", de Martino

---

100   *De Martino* (1991) page 28–31, 40.

101   De *Martino* (1991) page 43–45.

102   Instead, we have reports once again that when Roman soldiers were away in Rome's subjugation wars, patricians, quite unpatriotically, used the opportunity to illegally occupy their land or to purchase it (*De Martino* (1991) page 131.)

103   *Mommsen* (1976) volume 3 page 82, translation by the author.

104   *De Martino* (1991) page 93, 99. In the 2nd century, the military campaigns of Marius, Sulla, Lucullus and Pompeius, specifically in the Eastern Mediterranean, supplied a great number of slaves that apparently added up between one million and three million in the 1st century BC.

writes, "the property owners worked the land from which they had displaced Roman citizens."[105] Equally imported slave corn outcompeted corn made by free Roman farmers. As Mommsen puts it, "now the small farmer was crushed by the overseas corn, in particular by the slaves' corn." Apart from the lower price of slave corn, slaves were not drafted into the army and slave production was, thus, steadier.[106] By the same token, the Roman Republic's expansion created a larger market for agrarian produce and a trade system consisting of latifundia with slave labor and employment-generating spending from the City of Rome and Roman armies was born. This system functioned for centuries. Most of the small independent peasants that had survived all previous distress, were finished off now. With it, the SPQR's original social foundation was dissolved.

Contrary to Greece, the conservative-restorative reaction to the ancient master drama in Rome consisted hardly in efforts to restitute the individual plots to the farmers who had lost them. Conservative-restorative attempts to protect the small peasanty rather primarily focused either on creating new farmer positions in conquered territories abroad or to distribute state-owned domanial land in Italy. State-owned domanial lands, mainly in Italy, were always mostly or wholly *de facto* occupied by the nobility or the *equites*, even though it was officially owned by the Republic[107] and popular demands for the distribution of this land to small peasants, became the central topic in the revolutionary years from 133 to Gaius Julius Caesar in 45 BC.

Tiberius Gracchus

The late Roman Republic's most famous upheaval was the attempted, and partially executed, reform by the Gracchi brothers, who descended from one of the finest Roman families. *Tiberius Gracchus* made a first effort in 133 BC, and, after he had been killed, his younger brother *Gaius Gracchus* followed in 123, – to be ultimately also killed. immediately after having become tribune, *Tiberius Gracchus*, proposed a field law, which largely consisted in a renewal of the *Lex Licinia Sexta agraria* of 387 BC (which had, as we saw, not been implemented). His proposal, once more, solely addressed state-owned domanial land. Truly private property, thus, remained wholly unaffected and the reform essentially only aimed at ending the unofficial occupation of state land by latifundia owners, without paying rent. The reform, accordingly, was quite far removed from a full-on attack on the private property of the landed nobility or landed equites as such. As Tiberius Gracchus foresaw that farmer, if they were given land as wholly free private property, would quickly lose it to grandees

---

105   *De Martino* (1991) page 131, translation by author.
106   *De Martino* (1991) page 122, 131.
107   *Mommsen* (1976) volume 3 page 89 et seq.

who would purchase it from them in the next crisis, he only assigned it as an *inalienable hereditary leasehold*. This was an important modification of the ancient *Lex Licinia Sexta agrarian*.

Secondly, Tiberius Gracchus deviated from prior bottom-down reform attempts insofar as he acted aggressively in a pre-emptive way. He knew that the ordinary government and administration would not implement the reform and managed to create a special executive and administrative body for this purpose, a commission of three men, who were loyal to the program and pushed through the actual land redistributions.[108] He also anticipated, as limited as his proposal was,[109] the nobility to oppose it very powerfully. Quite interestingly, this opposition also took the form of the second tribune of the plebs, *Marcus Octavius*, the colleague of Tiberius Gracchus as, using his *ius intercessionis* to block the reform proposal from being voted on in the people's assembly. Tiberius Gracchus took a very aggressive approach once more. A tribune of the plebs that acts against the plebs, he argued, forfeits its position. He thus applied to the people's assembly to remove Marcus Octavius from the bench of the tribunes. The people cheered and applauded, the motion found a majority, and was passed. Only by means of an open and rather clear breach of the Roman constitution could the reform, thus, advance. The radicality, by which Tiberius Gracchus moved on was regarded as a declaration of war by the latifundia owners and he thereafter always feared for his life, writes Mommsen, and only appeared in public with 3,000 or 4,000 followers. He sought to further strengthen his position with the plebs by proposing other laws in their favor, e.g., distributing the heritage of the king of Pergamon (which had fallen upon the state of Rome) to the new landowners to purchase equipment and tools. He also sought to have his office as tribune extended for another year, a second breach of the Roman constitution, as a preventive defense. This was undertaken to no avail. Noblemen killed him and three hundred of his supporters with wooden staves and threw their bodies into the Tiber River.[110]

Interestingly, even after the bloodbath and although the enacted law had been passed in clear violation of the Roman constitution, Tiberius' law itself was neither expressly set aside nor treated as null and void. On the contrary, the senate actually instructed the redistribution commission to begin its work. The result was impressive. 80,000 new farmer positions or new farms were created, the father of the law's death notwithstanding.[111]

---

108   *Mommsen* (1976) volume 3 page 95 et seq.
109   *Mommsen* (1976) volume 3 page 100.
110   *Mommsen* (1976) volume 3 page 98, 99.
111   *Mommsen* (1976) volume 3 page 109, 110.

Gaius Gracchus

Tiberius' younger brother Gaius, who was lucky not to have been killed in the slaughter of his brother, became tribune in 123 BC. He filled his brother's shoes and initiated colonization projects in Tarent, Capua, and in former Cartago, creating 6,000 peasant positions in Cartago alone. Foreseeing that he needed popular support, he granted new rights to Roman citizenship, on condition that the new Roman citizens personally appear in Rome – with they being attracted to Rome through the possibility to purchase corn at rock-bottom-prices. This founded not only the tradition of massive corn distributions in Rome,[112] but also the technique of luring voters into the city with financial promises. The senate responded brutally. After a new people's tribune was elected on 1 January 121 BC, the senate outweighed the head of Gaius Gracchus in gold to whoever would deliver it. 250 of his supporters were slain, his slave killed him, the gold reward was properly paid out, and his body was thrown in the Tiber River, same as his brother's. 3,000 of his supporters were later also prosecuted and hanged.[113] Twenty years of restoration followed. Gaius Gracchus' colonization projects in Capua and Cartago were discontinued. A similar project was initiated in Narbo, at least. Still, as Mommsen writes, "peasant's positions disappeared as rain drops in the sea".[114]

Slave riots, uprisings, and real slave wars broke out on slave plantations. The first Sicilian slave war lasted from 136 to 133 BC; others occurred between 104 and 101 BC. The third wave with the most famous slave war of all, led by Spartacus, came about between 78 and 71 BC. These uprisings attracted colorful and weird figures as their leaders. One such uprising was led by an overindebted *equite* who had declared himself "king" of his liberated slaves. In another rebellion, its Syrian leader, the slave Salvius, was appointed to "king Tryphon"[115] A third chief of a slave rebellion was called "Antiochos, King of Syria".[116] Slave armies sometimes had up to 70,000 soldiers, and when they were defeated, the slaves were all killed. Such was the case when Spartacus was defeated, 6,000 slaves were crucified at the via Appia in 71 BC.[117]

---

112 *Mommsen* (1976) volume 3 page 109, 114. The main means to finance the corn distributions – according to *Mommsen* volume 3, page 240, the costs were significant – was a new heavy taxation in the province of Asia. The right to collect these taxes was rented out to the *equites* and the right to select the jurors for the jury courts, who were in charge of controlling abuses of these rented-out right was also assigned to them (volume 3 page 120. 121, 125). A big loss for Asia financed a big win for the *equites*, proletarians, and for Gaius Gracchus.

113 *Mommsen* (1976) volume 3 page 129–132.

114 *Mommsen* (1976) volume 3 page 126, 142, 143.

115 *Mommsen* (1976) volume 3 page 142, 145, 147.

116 *Mommsen* (1976) volume 3 page 87.

117 *Mommsen* (1976) volume 3 page 87, volume 4 page 92.

Marius and Saturninus

The ancient master drama, which was not about slaves but about land losses of free peasants, did not pause either. After *Gaius Marius* won the war against the Cimbri at Aquae Sextae and Vercellae in 101, and after he had been consul for an unprecedented 6 years – another clear breach of the Roman constitution, of which now many more were to follow –, Marius joined forces with *Lucius Appulieius Saturninus*, who was a people's tribune and they undertook another attempt of an agrarian reform. A law was proposed under which Marius' former soldiers were to be given land (promised by Marius previously) and under which the general redistribution of land in Cartago, as had already been planned by Gaius Gracchus, was to recommence. The land, which Marius himself had won from the defeated Cimbri, was also to be distributed. The proposal went on to provide that the temple treasures of Tolosa should be used to finance fixtures and tools for the recipients of the land distributions. *Marius* himself was to manage these, as *Mommsen* puts it, "enormous conquest and distribution plans", for which he would have to become "monarch of Rome for the time of his life".[118] As a complementary measure, *Marius* and *Saturninus both* reduced the prices for the corn "sold" to poor citizens to such an extent that the prices became merely symbolic.[119]

The nobility, yet, somehow succeeded to antagonize Marius and Saturninus and when Saturninus' supporters resorted to physical violence and the senate asked Marius, still being consul, to intervene against old his ally militarily, he did so. On 10 December 100 BC the first battle between Romans since Rome's foundation was fought in Rome. The Populares were defeated on the market and Saturninus and his closest allies were taken prisoner and arrested. While Marius probably contemplated how to save his ally and how they might go on with their joint project, the nobility's youth pre-empted him. They climbed the roof of the building in which Saturninus and his followers were arrested, unroofed the bricks and stoned Saturninus and his followers to death. This was the end of that attempt at reform.[120]

Marcus Livius Drusus

The next example of a land reformer was *Marcus Livius Drusus*, a man of colossal wealth indeed and with a firm commitment to the cause of the oligarchy.[121] He became people's tribune in 91 BC and proposed a law that once more aimed at rebuilding of a strong small peasantry by distributing state-owned lands in Campania and

---

118   *Mommsen* (1976) volume 3 page 211, 212.
119   *Mommsen* (1976) volume 3 page 211, 213.
120   *Mommsen* (1976) volume 3 page 211, 217, 218.
121   *Mommsen* (1976) volume 3, page 223 et seq.

Sicily. Much like others before him, he sought support through the votes of the general Roman poor (including those who would not have wanted to work in fields) by further increasing corn distributions.[122] His law also suggested restituting juror positions to the *nobiles*, to the detriment of the *equites*,[123] which comprised an attempt to lure parts of the oligarchy into his coalition. Yet, the Roman constitution forbade such clever maneuvers and this time the unconstitutional law was quickly repealed. Nevertheless, he was murdered like the Gracchus brothers and Saturninus before him.[124] The efforts of yet another far-sighted member of the oligarchy who wanted to halt the undermining of the Roman peasantry ended with his death.[125]

Publius Sulpicius Rufus

We now enter the times of Sulla and Cinna, leading up to Pompey and Caesar, the end of the republic and of the beginning of the Roman empire. Free peasants had largely disappeared, rather completely in Etruria and Umbria; only some were still existent, e.g., in the valleys of the Abruzzees,[126] when *Publius Sulpicius Rufus* came up with reform projects in the first century BC. After the destinies of the Gracchi, Saturninus and Drusus he sought to protect himself militarily from the outset and for this aim he reactivated, once again, the now-old-but-still-great *Gaius Marius*. Publius Sulpicius Rufus had a people's resolution passed that assigned command for the upcoming Asiatic war with Mithridates to Marius. The resolution also included a request to Sulla to hand over his six legions of 35,000 soldiers to Marius. Two tribunes were sent to Sulla's army camp with this instruction in hand, yet Sulla had them, as *Mommsen* puts it, "torn into pieces". Sulla then marched on Rome to breach the city's peace. Marius was unable to resist militarily and so Sulla took power, decapitated Publius Sulpicius Rufus, and exposed his head atop the market's speaker's stage. Rome remained a bad place for noble social reformers. Marius was also taken to prison and he was even supposed to be murdered. Yet, the German slave, who had the job to do, so the saying goes, collapsed when he saw into the eyes of the famous war hero of Aquae Sextae and Vercellae, and Marius used that moment to escape.[127]

122 They were financed by money creation through the emissions of copper-clad dinars.
123 *Mommsen* (1976) volume 3 page 224.
124 *Mommsen* (1976) volume 3 page 220, 226.
125 There were also a number of reformers who were atrociously killed, in China, e.g., the Emperor *Wang Mang* (9–23 AD). See *Vogelsang* (2013) page 169.
126 *Mommsen* (1976) volume 3 page 229, 238.
127 *Mommsen* (1976) volume 3 page 264–268.

Cinna

Mission completed, Sulla himself took his army to Asia in 87 BC to fight Mithridates. His temporary absence, yet, opened the door for another reformer, *Lucius Cornelius Cinna*. Cinna became consul and proposed a law to reverse Sulla's restauration. Both parties, in wise foresight, appeared armed at the voting place on the day of the voting on the proposal and Cinna's co-consul, Octavius, interceded against Cinna's proposal. The situation escalated and arms were put to use; the market ran red with blood and the oligarchy's party killed 10,000 democrats. The event was later called "*Octavius-day*". Cinna escaped, though, and reactivated Gaius Marius again, now for a third time. While Sulla was away, Marius raised an army, once again took Rome, and set up a democratic terror regime. The consecutive killing by the democrats lasted five days and nights and included all of the senate party's leaders. It was now the democrats' turn to expose the oligarchy's decapitated heads on the market's speaker's stage. Marius even became consul for the seventh time and Cinna remained consul for four years, up until 84 BC. The democratic regime also restored the Gracchi brothers' old colonization and land distribution project in Capua and granted debt releases (by $\frac{3}{4}$ of the nominal amounts).[128] Yet, the emphasized reprisals from the Gracchi brothers' programs notwithstanding, the situation had totally changed. Agrarian reform proposals, like corn distribution, were no more than a calculated move in a civil war between army commanders (might we say warlords?), demagogues, and other modern-style politicians seeking mass support for their power aspirations.

Irrespective of their ecstasy, the democratic party was always aware that Sulla could soon return from Asia with a strong, victorious army. And return Sulla did; he marched on Rome a second time and once again defeated the defendants in the "Battle of the Colline Gate" (of Rome) in 82 BC. This put an end to democratic rule. Cinna himself had already been killed in a mutiny by his soldiers previously. Marius had preferred to die a natural death prior to Sulla's return; all that Sulla could do was to exhume Marius' corpse and throw it into Arno River. Sulla now ignited a period of terror by the oligarchic party, with Sulla's proscriptions becoming famous. Sulla still even made some land distributions, mostly to his retired soldiers; but the times at which free farmers had been the basis of the Roman republic and its war machine had long gone. This dynamic was broken for good; because Sulla's army's mercenaries had no land of their own, they had joined the army and the share of the booty that they received afterwards bore only superficial resemblance to previous reform attempts. In fact, ex-soldiers who received land assignments after their service could no longer use it because they no longer knew how to work land. They either sold it or rented it out.

---

128   *Mommsen* (1976) volume 3 page 316–327.

The end of the republic

The republic ended and Rome moved towards Principate and Dominate. Some emperors made assignments of land thereafter, but battles over land reforms no longer appear to have become significant throughout the empire's history. The military success of the Roman empire's further expansion probably enabled it to feed its soldiers and *proletarii*, and if it did not then there was at least no way for them to become farmers once again. Yet, just as the Roman economy now largely depended on a slave-based agriculture, it also depended on a continued influx of new slaves, which necessitated ongoing new conquests. *Stability, thus, required steady expansion.* Yet, the circumference of the Roman empire had become too stretched after it had made the Mediterranean a *mare nostrum* and reached Spain, France, Britain, Germany, Odessa, Greece, Turkey, Persia and even Egypt and North Africa. Now geometry became its destiny. The empire's borders and its connecting lines had become longer and longer, indefensible ultimately, and the Roman expansion came to an almost natural end (much like biological organisms cannot grow limitless in size). Consequentially, the influx of slave labor stopped, leading to what was to be called the crisis of the 3rd century AD. The crisis undermined the slave-based Roman economy. Not only the foreign people who, thus, avoided to be enslaved profited, but also the Romans themselves: Free labor (at least freer than slave labor) was in demand again. The leasing of land (*locatio conductio rei*) by latifundia-owners to peasants had been known since the middle Republic, but it had only been occasionally practiced. Now working leased land by "colons" (*coloni, colonati*) moved up to become the dominant form of agrarian production. *Cicero* mentions *colons* for the first time in a speech in 69 or 68 BC, but *colons* were already as important or more important than slaves in the 2nd century AD.[129] Initially, they were seemingly free men, which, though, began to change in the 4th century AD. Their relative power had obviously weakened once again.[130] The ancient social master drama had obviously been transformed into a semi-feudal structure, and prosthetic spending played no major role at that time.

***

---

129   *Johne* (1994) page 5.
130   Colons could no longer terminate lease agreements, were bound to the land as were their children, and could even be sold with the land. They needed their landlord's consent to marry and concerning certain legal transactions and their procedural rights were restricted. In the Codex Justinianus 11, 52, 1 they were described as free men, but slaves to the ground on which they were born "...licet condicione videantur ingenui, servi tamen terrae ipsius cui nati sunt aestimentur" (quoted after Johne page 8). Their position worsened further to such a degree that emperor *Justinian* asked wherein the difference between a slave and a *colonatus* would consist of in 530 AD, see Codex Justinianus 11, 48, 21 (quoted after Johne page 8). Indebtedness, as always, played a role in this demotion (*Savigny* (1822) 1–26).

As a summary: The social master drama consisted in free farmers of antiquity losing their land to the nobility, or to other latifundists at a large scale. A segregation
between owners and non-owners resulted therefrom in ancient Greece and ancient
Rome. We have examined attempts to maintain the small peasantry as a social base,
first by trying to secure the individual land for them, where their families had often
worked for generations and second by assignments of new lots of conquered land to
army veterans, to displaced farmers or to other poor people. Ultimately, both types
of conservative-restorative policies, which were quite often or mostly initiated by
members of the nobility or by other wealth owners, were typically thwarted by their
classmates. A great many ex-farmers were, thus, demoted to the ranks of *proletarii*
and were propelled forward, in fact, already into the social master drama of modern capitalism, and now depended on being employed by firms or became reliant
upon transfer payments. At this juncture, at least the polis of Athens and the Roman empire that were both holding imperial positions were able mitigate the fate of
their own demoted peasants by extending significant prosthetic employment-generating spending. Prosthetic employment-generating spending to firms consisted
of purchasing weapons, carriages, and boats, thereby leading to employment in either manufactures, workshops, or shipyards or in the construction of representative
architecture or events, such as festivities and circuses. In Rome, private luxury, e.g.,
countryside or city villas with fancy baths, heating, and water systems and mosaics
also played a material role. The less free farmer-soldiers there were, the more the
sons of former farmers at least, could find jobs as mercenaries. There were also many
paid public offices in Athens (the true purpose of which were transfer payments, not
the services actually rendered) and corn distributions in Rome. All substitute income
options for displaced farmers, yet, except for the lucky discovery of a new streak in
a silver mine in Laurium by Athens, depended upon the possibilities of a successful
imperial robber-state and were no generally available means to deal with the ancient
master drama. Ultimately, external violence mostly financed prosthetics in one way
or another, even in the erection of the Acropolis or the Pantheon. Money creation
existed only as uncontrollable finding and mining of gold or silver, as robbing it, or
as debasing commodity money, which one occasionally crossed the border into fiat
money in Greece and Rome and became no relevant source of financing in the aggregate. Hence, if control over the subjugated prosthetics financiers was lost, then the
society would internally get into great stress and the social order might collapse. Dependency on the subjugation of others was prosthetics' first dilemma in antiquity;
the absence of controllable larger-scale money creation was the second.

Nothing of what Solon or Roman social reformers asked for essentially contra-
dicted the economic and political rule of the Greek or Roman nobility as such. Never
had the reformers demanded a socialist utopia, the ending private agrarian land
ownership or only the expropriation of a significant part of the existing *latifundia*.
But limiting *latifundia* growth, or giving parts of domanial state land to small farm-

ers, was already too much for the narrow-minded nobility. One could, thus, argue that the fights between reformers and anti-reformers were actually battles between short-sightedness and long-termism or between individual class members' greed and the ruling class's general interest. Or one could argue that the ruling classes of Greece and Rome were enchained by the prisoners' dilemma (where a single player, by allowing space for their particular interest, works towards the ruination of his class). States, even as small as Athens, or as large as Rome, with a large sector of goods procurement by violence would do better not to eliminate those who did most of the physical robbing. Accordingly, one might surmise that it was a fault of the Greece nobility not to pay heed to Solon and the likes and Rome should have listened more to its Cassius, Potelius, Licinius, the Gracchi, Drusus, Rufus, Saturninus, or even to Cinna. One may also doubt this consideration and ask: Could Rome at all have become Rome, including the stretched and over-stretched empire, with an army of only farmer-soldiers and a rather egalitarian society? Did not a similar attempt fail in Sparta? Did not Alexander the Great triumph with a project that more closely resembled Rome? These questions are outside of the scope of this book. From antiquity we return to modernity and to the modern master drama.

Section 3. China: A glance at 2000 years of East-Eurasian ancient master drama

Constituents of the ancient master drama in China

No other country has a history as long and coherent and with a size and mass like China. It is as if Rome had remained a unified world empire from the Punic wars to today, yet at several times its historic extension and population. Still, in the West, Chinese history has remained a field of interest for a small group of specialists, mostly sinologists, only, and is normally not exploited for general theoretical endeavors. The author had the intention to break that pattern. After he had worked out major lines of the ancient master drama in Western Eurasia, he wanted to spend some time in China to examine its ancient master drama more length. This original intention fell victim to the travel restrictions in the Corona pandemic and to the increasing awareness of the author that an account written by someone not capable of reading Chinese would have to remain of limited value. Therefore, the original intent shrunk to a short glance at the Chinese ancient master drama. Here are the insights:

First, readers of books on Chinese history are stricken with the observation that the ancient master drama is significantly more present and explicit there than in historic writing on Western Eurasia. Rural property relations, the de-facto or de-jure land-owning by a small peasantry, or its loss of the land to "engrossing" latifundia owners, are almost everywhere outspokenly treated not only as causes of abundant or meagre state finances, of social unrest, banditry, rebellions, civil wars, dynasty changes, revolutions and external wars but also as central historic themes. There is not much difference in this regard between the dynasties. The awareness obviously already existed in antiquity itself. Debates, which connected agricultural policies and taxation with the domestic strength and the international and military status of the empire, or domestic, international and military weakness, are omnipresent, certainly since the Ch'in in the late 3nd century BC. This awareness was never lost and, thus, state policies rather consciously oscillated between the protection and support of the small independent peasantry via redistribution of land, state loan programs, the provision of tools, oxen, seed and of agricultural knowledge to small farmers and tax releases in their favor,[131] and the promotion of private property of agricultural land as the alternative. Both were hailed to allow the Chinese people to better subsist, generate growth, and to finance internal and external strength of the state,

Second, while it is often argued that Chinese history knows a period resembling to the European Middle Ages or to feudalism, ruptures nearly as sharp as the one between the dynamic capitalist times of European Greek and Roman Antiquity and the stagnant European Middle Ages and back from them to modern capitalism with the rise of Venice and in the Renaissance cannot be found in China. On the one hand, Confucian and Taoist thought, as well as an idealized memory of the agrarian situation in the Ch'ou dynasty (1046–256 BC), which will be explained below, and, somewhat later, Buddhist thought, were ever-present and often moderated capitalist M–C–M'-dynamics. On the other hand, what could have been the Chinese Middle Ages – the period from the Late Han to the Sui – did not improve the situation of the small peasantry so thoroughly as the European Middle Ages did. The agricultural question, state financing and social rebellions etc., more equally than in Europe, pervade almost all historic periods .[132]

Third, in China there appear to have been even more personalities, arising out of the emperor's administrative elite or noble families, of the type of a Solon, Peisistratus, the Gracchi brothers and their likes, that promoted top-down reforms in favor of the peasantry. Still, these reforms, which were, as we shall not tire to stress,

---

131 It is noteworthy that taxes were generally often rather low. During the Ming dynasty land was, e.g., often taxed at only about 3 % percent of its yield and the tax was, quite favorably, payable in kind. (Huang, The Ming fiscal administration, page 107.)

132 E.g., while most Chinese Marxist historians appear to believe that the transition from slavery to feudalism in China history occurred in the final two and a half centuries of the Ch'ou dynasty, most Soviet Marxists only placed it at the end of the 3rd century AD. Some Non-Marxist historians even consider the first four or five centuries of the Ch'ou as feudalist (Bodde, The state and empire of Ch'in, p. 22).

always *also* reforms in favor of the central states, its tax-income and its war-machinery[133] and, furthermore, like in Europe, against the gentry, mostly shared the destiny of their European brothers and failed and their proponents were ultimately similarly frequently killed as in Europe. Chinese history also has significantly more large peasant rebellions, which were rather successful for some time than Europe, e.g., with the German Peasants Wars of the 16th century. In fact, they quite often evolved into real "rebel-regimes", which controlled great parts of China over longer periods, sometimes decades, and were connected to fierce, lasting and very bloody civil wars. Some of the rebellions also triggered the demise of a ruling dynasty. E.g., the social rebellions during the later (Eastern) Han strengthened independent military commanders which ultimately overthrew the Han. Or, a main leader of the "Red Turban"-rebellion, which greatly contributed to the fall of the Yüan dynasty, became himself the founder of the consecutive Ming dynasty and the first Ming emperor in 1368.[134]

Fourth, the Chinese, more clearly than the European variant of the ancient master drama, exposes the factors, which determine the course of the master drama: (i) the existence of private sellable ownership of agrarian land or not; (ii) there being natural catastrophes (river floodings, rivers changing their bed, locust, several periods of particular cold, bad harvests, draughts etc.), civil wars and wars destroying the precariat base of the small peasantry or not; (iii) states providing land, tools, seed, knowledge or other aid to small peasants or not, in particular after catastrophes, or not; (iv) states overtaxing peasants and demanding excessive labor and military services from them (required for war, the building or maintenance of the Chinese Wall, canals, roads, other buildings-projects or the luxury of the court) or not and waving or cutting taxes, granting loans or making transfer payments or not; finally, (v), there being a strong, independent gentry or merchant class, which aggressively exploited the small peasantry and appropriates its land or not. The effect of certain policies could change depending on the time after it was unleashed. E.g., it appears, that the introduction or re-introduction of private sellable property of agricultural land always initially often stimulated and raised production, while it later, almost unavoidably, later led to the opposite, the decay of the small peasantry and its displacement by the gentry, followed by a weakening of the central state's tax-base and the central state itself.

---

133   *Sadao*, The economic and social history of former Han, page 556 et seq. As *Wright* comments: "No Chinese empire could prosper without adequate arrangements for the distribution of agricultural land, and the collecting to taxes based on agricultural production" (*Wright*, The Sui dynasty (581–617), page 93.)

134   The founder of the Hand dynasty, which displaced the Ch'in dynasty, Liu Pang or Kao-ti, was also of peasant origin, *Sadao*, The economic and social history of former Han, page 552.

Fifth, quite interestingly and not greatly different from Europe, more lasting peasant rebellions that attempted some sort of state-building, almost always promoted not only general equality of possession, equality of status and of the sexes but were also connected to eclectic utopian and religious ideologies and often bizarre practices, e.g., ritual sexual orgies etc. As the peasants-rebellions in China were longer-lasting, this is more visible than in Europe.

The ancient master drama throughout the main Chinese dynasties

In the following, we shall look at some major episodes of the Chinese ancient master drama. Over large part of Chinese history, the agrarian situation as it was alleged to have been in the Ch'ou dynasty (1000 to 771 BC), indeed, served as idealistic benchmark for agrarian policies. Already Confucius (551–479 B.C?) had praised the Ch'ou's agrarian policies, his disciples followed suit and hardly ever were requests for agricultural reforms made, including in bloody uprisals, which did not refer to it. The so-called *"tsing tien"*-system ("well field"-system), which was said to have even already existed around 2500 BC, and to have survived from there until into the Ch'ou dynasty 1500 years later, was in the center of these romanticized memories. One unit of a "well field" consisted of eight families, four roads and a well which was dug in the center. The whole concept was derived from practical, value-in-use-oriented or technical considerations. The politically and socially important implication was in the background: The value-in-use-orientation could prevail because private property and the law of private property were no factors, neither in the sense that interests flowing out of private ownership would influence the organization of the daily life in the countryside, nor in the sense that peasant families were at risk to lose their land. Historic research appears to confirm that the image largely corresponds to actual practices in the Ch'ou dynasty.[135]

However, the break was to come. While the accumulation "of landholdings by local clans or families was probably well under way in the Warring States",[136] it was under the *Ch'in* rule, who would later unify China, when the "legalist", Han Fei-oriented and "modernist" reformer *Shang Yang* established general private ownership of agricultural land in the fourth century BC.[137] This initially increased productivity and raised the production;[138] it contributed to render the Ch'in fit to end the "War-

---

135   "The *tsing tien* system is the most important element in Chinese economic history", writes
       Chen Huan-Chang. See on this system *Chen Huan-Chang* (2015) page 497 et seqs., page 497,
       501, 506. On the "checkerboard"-fashion design of the *tsing tien* system, see also *Bodde*, The
       state and empire of Ch'in, page 27 et seq.
136   *Sadao*, The economic and social history of former Han, page 548.
137   *Bodde*, The state and empire of Ch'in, page 28, 35.
138   Both *Twitchett*, Introduction, page 25, and *McDermott/Yoshinobu*, Economic change in China,
       960–1279, page 347 et seqs., stress this point with regard to the later privatization of agrarian

ring States"-period and to unify China in the late third century. It would, however, at longer term, even if legalist policies to some extent repressed trade and merchants,[139] enrich the latifundia owners, impoverish the small peasantry and drive the state into collapse. In 206 BC, immediately after the death of the First Emperor of the *Ch'in* and before two decades of its nationwide rule had lapsed, major peasant revolts broke out,[140] which already ended the Ch'in dynasty, [141]

The *Han dynasty* succeeded the Ch'in dynasty, yet the situation for the peasants did not improve. "Ownership of great tracts of land developed in conjunction with natural calamities and the Han taxation system. The peasant farmer lived on the margin of subsistence... Even though the burden of year-round cultivation and labor service was very heavy, this would be greatly increased in times of flood and drought or of exceptionally high taxation. The peasants were then forced to sell their crops at half the market price or to borrow money at high interest rates. Entrapped in a spiral of debt, they ultimately had to dispose of their land, their houses and even their children. Land sold in this way came into the hands of local wealthy people, merchants or usurers, mostly members of powerful families, who thus build up large holdings."[142] Like in Greek and Roman history this led to ever-present claims and proposals for the redistribution of land, the revival of the *tsing tien* system (well field-system), or even to a certain amount of practical measures to that aim (including the Solon-style liberation of enslaved peasants). In 44 BC the "reformist" (pro Ch'ou and pro Confucius) *Kung Yü* became advisor to Han Emperor *Yüan ti* and implemented several anti-modernist (anti-Han Fei, anti-Shang Yang, anti-Ch'in), economic reforms. He even asked to return to a pre-monetary economy. This was, yet, of course, not put into practice. At the same time, at the instigation of *Shih Tan*, a proposal to redistribute large land holdings and to limit the maximum size of land holdings was accepted in principle, yet never implemented.[143]

The Han-emperor *Wang Mang* (9–23 AD) attempted a land reform under which all able-bodied men were to receive a standard allotment of land. Families with more land would, thus, be obliged to distribute the surplus to land-poor relatives

---

land following the An Lushan rebellion in the T'ang dynasty (following 755 AD). *McDermott/ Yoshinobu*, ibidem, page 348, also note that "virtually all signs of grain production and productivity increases come from the south of China", where private agrarian property had been accepted for a longer time.

139   *Bodde*, The state and empire of Ch'in, page 59.

140   *Vogelsang* (2013) page 125.

141   See *Sadao*, The economic and social history of former Han, page 548 et seq. The First Emperor of the Ch'in is the emperor who was buried with the terracotta soldiers near modern Xi'an, around 210 BC.

142   *Loewe*, The former Han dynasty, page 204.

143   see *Loewe*, The former Han dynasty, page 204, 205.

or neighbors.[144] Of course, the execution of this policy was opposed and blocked by wealthy "magnate" families in state offices. They preferred to pursue their personal interests in continued land accumulation.[145] Wang Mang's reforms failed and he was killed. While the heads of failed Roman reformers were sometimes exposed at the forum Romanum, Wang Mang's head was allegedly kicked around in Shang'an (today's Xi'an).[146] In general, "by the middle of Later Han the growth of large landed estates was becoming a dominant characteristic of some of the provinces".[147] This greatly weakened the Han government's possibilities to exert control over the peasantry, "from whom it required tax revenues and labor services, and resulted in considerable decentralization towards the end of the later Han."[148] Unsurprisingly, the final period of the *later Han*, thus, saw decades of civil conflict and near anarchy under the *Yellow Turbans* and other popular rebellions, leading to the end of the Han in 220 AD [149]

China had now lost its unity and was split up in several regions. The reign of the *Northern Wei* and of the *Jin* dynasties, again, saw distributions of 3 or 3,5 hectares of agrarian land to adult men and of 1,5 hectares to adult women for lifetime use. The short-lived *Sui dynasty* (581–618 AD), which reunified the country again after more than three hundred fifty years, too, executed an egalitarian agrarian policy and centralized the state against the opposition of the nobility. It, furthermore made war against the Turks and in Korea and unleashed gigantic building projects. It build the Emperor's Canal, two nearly new capitals, Daxing and Luoyang, and initiated extensive reconstructions of the Chinese Wall. It appears, however, that the good it had done to the small peasantry with one hand was more than compensated by excessive taxation and corvée services, which enabled these projects. Unluckily, a major flooding of the Huanghe (Yellow River) worsened the situation, which led to insurrections of both the small peasantry and of the nobility. A member of the nobility, Li Huan, took Daxing by force and erected the T'ang dynasty.[150]

The *T'ang dynasty* was to last longer, from 619 – 907 AD. Alike the Jin, Wei and Sui, it initially pursued an equal land distribution policy. It also created hundreds of self-sufficient military settlements, erected granaries, and otherwise supported the small peasantry. In addition, the economy generally flourishes in the "Golden Age" of the T'ang (Emperor Xuangzong 713–756 AD). Yet, a rebellion of general *An Lushan* and of *Li Shimin* following 755 AD caused a severe rupture. The rebellion depopulated

---

144 *Bielenstein*, Wang Mang, the restoration of the Han dynasty and, later Han, page 232.

145 *Sadao*, The economic and social history of former Han, page 558.

146 *Vogelsang* (2013) page 169.

147 *Loewe*, The structure and practice of government, page 490. See also *Sadao*, The economic and social history of former Han, page 555.

148 *Sadao*, The economic and social history of former Han, page 559.

149 *Twitchett*, Introduction to volume 3, page 2 et seq.

150 *Vogelsang* (2013) page 233–243.

many of the largest and richest provinces and put an end to the control of the central state over the provinces and, thereby, also to the official claim of the emperor owning the agricultural land and of it prerogative to carry out recurrent land redistributions. The loss of control of the central state, because of the destruction of local land registers,[151] finished off its grip on local land taxation and its funding. Local and regional autonomous units, which grow out of former state commanderies, erected independent power centers and administrations. Afterwards, the central state could only undertake "spasmodic efforts to distribute vacant lands amongst dispossessed households, and to limit the accumulation of land. While after the An Lushan rebellion "lip service" is still paid "to the Confucian maxim that all land remain(s) the emperor's land", a "de-facto-recognition is given to individual landholders".[152] This privatization was basically to last. Since "the mid-eighth century… most of the Chinese economy would operate (on private economic arrangements) for the remaining twelve hundred years of its imperial history."[153] Between 820 to 884 AD disorder and social banditry turned into an almost general popular rebellion of immense proportions. The rebel leader *Huang Ch'ao* even captured the T'ang-capital Sh'ang an in 880, slaughtered state officials, looted the city, and held it for more two years.[154] Foreign powers conquered more and more former T'ang territories and the T'ang central state and its order collapsed in 907 AD.

The *Sung dynasty* (960–1279 AD) reunified large parts of China in 960 AD and moved its center to the south. It saw a series of popular rebellions since its establishment and several ministers made attempts to strengthen the small peasantry through land distributions. After the so-called *Ch'ing-Li* reforms (1043–1045) had failed or been revoked,[155] *Wang An-shih* (1021–86) was to become the most notable Sung reformer. As he explains himself in his own manifesto, the so-called "Myriad word memorial", he pursued the purpose of enriching the nation and strengthening its military power by, as *Smith* puts it, a "tentacular multi-level effort".[156] Once more, with reference to an idealized Ch'ou dynasty, he redistributed agrarian land to revitalize the peasant economy and supported the success of the new peasants with parallel water-control and irrigation projects. To give a number, it is known that between 1070 and 1076 the reform administration under Wang initiated 10.793 water control and land reclamation projects, reclaiming a total of… approximately 38.829.779 acres of land.[157] Wang also implemented a state-run rural credit system,

---

151   *McDermott/Yoshinobu*, Economic change in China, 960–1279, page 347.

152   *Twitchett*, Introduction, page 25.

153   *McDermott/Yoshinobu*, Economic change in China, 960–1279, page 322.

154   *Somers*, The end of the T'ang, page 683 et seq. (746).

155   *McGrath*, The reigns of Jen-Tsung (1022–1063) and Ying-Tsung (1063–1067), page 316–323.

156   See the extensive account by *Smith*, Sheng Tsung's reign and the new policies of Wang An-shih, 1067–1085, page 347 et seqs.

157   *Smith*, Sheng Tsung's reign and the new policies of Wang An-shih, 1067–1085, page 393.

called "green sprouts", which enabled the purchase of tools and seed, and specifically helped to bridge the vulnerable period of the agrarian year after the consumption of last year's harvest. Furthermore, Wang An-shih had technical tutoring provided to peasants promoted the favorable early ripening Champa rice.[158] Following the early Han and the Tang, he settled farmer-soldiers in Northern border regions on state farmlands (*pao-chia*-system).[159]

Like *Tiberius Gracchus*, more than a thousand years before him, Wang An-shih expected opposition and was highly power-conscient. He publicly denounced the "engrosser families", who appropriated the land of small peasants[160] and "who do nothing but collect interest of tens of thousands of strings of cash each year".[161] In a further similarity with the Gracchi brothers, he distrusted the normal bureaucracy and set up a "specific apparatus" to execute his reforms, staffed it with his followers, and tried to tilt the odds in the expected power struggle by placing people loyal to him in key posts and seeking control over the council of the state.[162] Ultimately, though, his reforms also failed, if, as it appears, less because of the resistance of the gentry but because they were sacrificed, like in the case of the Sui, for the state's own short-term fiscal imperatives. As *Paul Jakov Smith* puts it, the reform policies "one after another... were metamorphosed into the claws of a predatory bureaucracy whose sole purpose was to gouge new revenues out of the economy."[163]

Accordingly, the ancient social master drama continued to haunt the *Sung dynasty* two hundred years later. By then *Chia Ssu-tao* (1273–75) made a new effort of reforms. He set a ceiling on total land holdings and the state reserved the right to buy up to one third of land above it and to transform it into public land in support of the army. When the state began to exercise this right, the policy, foreseeably, met, fierce opposition from the latifundia owners. Historians surmise that this resulted in an estrangement between the latifundia owners and the Sung dynasty, which helped to bring the Sung down in favor of the Yüan dynasty a few years later.[164]

---

158   *Smith*, Sheng Tsung's reign and the new policies of Wang An-shih, 1067–1085, page 395 et seqs and *Golas*, The Sung fiscal administration, page 170 et seqs. See also *McDermott/Yoshinobu*, Economic change in China 960–1279, pages 363 and 394.

159   *Golas*, The Sung fiscal administration, page 174, 199.

160   *Smith*, Sheng Tsung's reign and the new policies of Wang An-shih, 1067–1085, page 392. (This contribution contains a particularly elaborate study of the reform policies of Wang An-shih and of their problems).

161   For references and extensive account of Wang An-shih see *Smith*, Sheng Tsung's reign and the new policies of Wang An-shih, 1067–1085, page 348 et seqs. (390).

162   *Smith*, Sheng Tsung's reign and the new policies of Wang An-shih, page 368.

163   *Smith*, Sheng Tsung's reign and the new policies of Wang An-shih, page 394. Once more, the state collecting taxes in money rather than in kind, combined with currency shortage and deflation, proved especially ruinous for the small peasantry, which often had to resort to selling its working capital to honor its tax obligations (ibidem page 442).

164   *Golas*, The Sung fiscal administration, page 167.

The Mongol *Yüan dynasty* (1271–1368 AD), too, began with policies supporting the small peasantry, e.g., by agricultural communities and by efforts to limit the financial burden placed on them.[165] After the conquest of South China by the Yüan, lots of agrarian land were given to the small peasantry. However, caused by warfare, building projects, e.g., the prolongation of the Emperor's Canal from the Huai river to Dadu (later Beijing), the Yüan resumed to heavily tax the small peasantry. A climate change and bad harvests worsened their situation, which led to several peasant insurrections, from the so-called "White Lotus" to the "Red Turban-Rebellion" of 1351–1366. The latte ultimately brought the Yüan dynasty down.

Often peasant revolts had only paved the way for the formation of a new dynasty by a nobleman, a bureaucrat or a political entrepreneur out of the old ruling elite. The *Ming dynasty* (1368–1644 AD), yet, was, in fact directly erected by one of the very leaders of the insurrection that had taken down the Yüan dynasty. *Zhu Yuanzhang*, leader of the "Red Turban-Rebellion", became the first Ming-emperor Hongwu. He, at first, also supported the small peasantry. While it initially continued to enjoy protection under *Hongwu's* successor *Yongle*, who moved the capital to Beijing, this policy was, though. not upheld for long. It appears that financial demands resulting from the military defense against the Mongols and the Manchu, and a major war in Korea against Japan, led to immense costs for mercenary armies. Furthermore, later Ming emperors seem to have, indeed, lost control over their own court and its luxury spending. The situation was amplified by the rigid effects of a *de facto* commodity money-regime, specifically of Spanish and Portuguese silver, which came to China in the 16th and 17th century.[166] While the silver stimulated trade, it rendered tax-payments for small peasants often unbearable. Nature, too, was unsupportive. A "Small Ice Age", a significant drop of the average temperature, and a series of poor harvests, ultimately led to years of great popular insurrections between 1627 and 1644.[167] After one insurrection army, under *Li Zicheng*, had conquered Luoyang and Xi'an, pillaged Kaifeng, and taken Beijing in 1644, where his troupes plundered private homes and killed Ming state functionaries in a savage frenzy, this ended with Ming emperor Chong Zen famously hanging himself near the imperial palace. A Ming general, *Wu Sangui*, decided to now join forces with the Manchu against the peasants' rebellion. Together with the Manchu, he drove the peasants' "Great Shun-regime" and Li Zicheng out of Beijing, and the Manchu established a new rule as the Ch'ing dynasty.[168]

---

165   *Endicott-West*, The Yüan government and society, page 599. *Rossabi*, The reign of Khubilai khan, page 448, 475.

166   See *Gernet* (1972) tome 2, page 210.

167   *Gernet* (1972) tome 2, page 173 et seq.; *Vogelsang* (2013) page 408, 409.

168   See *Shouyi* (2010) page 329–332 and 337 et seq.

Even after the Ch'ing dynasty had been established in Beijing, the actual assumption of control by the Manchu in all of China took further 39 years until 1683,[169] with the terrible price of, as often estimated, around twenty million dead. These wars, in which the remnants of the Ming dynasty were often supported by peasant rebellions, led to the formation of many small independent farms, in particular in the southern Yangtse-region. The Ch'ing supported them by water–control and irrigation projects and reduced taxes for small peasants, in fact several times, to a rather low level. The taxes initially still sufficed the central state's needs as Chi'ng were comparatively effective in collecting them. The Ch'ing , once more, also established military-agrarian settlements, and, thus, their dynasty flourished.[170]Unfortunately, this was to change. The *Ch'ing* increasingly lost control over their military apparatus, the provinces, and the central state's spending and the fiscal situation worsened. Following attempts to now raise taxes again, the agrarian situation aggravated as well and the Ch'ing, consequently, saw large peasant and other rebellions, of which the White Lotus, the Nien war and the Taiping peasant war were the most notable. The *Taiping peasant war* became the most extensive and enduring peasant rebellion in Chinese history and world history . Growing out of over hundred local uprisings, it lasted from 1850 to 1864, mostly dominated the Yangtze valley, and led to the formation of the "Taiping Heavenly Kingdom", which controlled significant parts of Southern China. The rebel army grew quickly to 120.000[171] or even 500.000 troops, as they claimed,[172] captured Nanjing, renamed it into Tianjing, the heavenly capital, and held it until their final defeat. They fought huge battles against armies of the Ch'ing and marched to Beijing, where they, yet, failed. Although the Taiping rebellion was a civil war, it was one of the largest and most bloody wars in human history with an aggregate number of dead around 20–30 million (more than WW I). Like many peasant rebellions, the Taiping had eclectic sectarian beliefs and practices – one of its leaders declared himself younger brother of Jesus Christ. The Sectarianism of the Taiping rebellion made it difficult to unite it with other simultaneous rebellions; otherwise, the insurrectionists' might have grown even larger and their power might have lasted longer.[173] These rebellions contributed greatly to disarming the Ch'ing dynasty to Western attacks, in particular since the First Opium War of 1840.

---

169   See *Shouyi* (2010) page 329–332 and 337 et seq.

170   *Vogelsang* (2013) page 427–430.

171   *Kuhn*, The Taiping rebellion, page 275.

172   Chungqiang/Nierui (2014) page 1942.

173   Taiping means "great peace". For accounts of the Taiping rebellion see *Chungqiang/Nierui* (2014) page 1938 et seqs.; *Shouyi* (2010) page 393 et seqs., page 403 et seqs. *Kuhn*, The Taiping rebellion, page 264 et seqs.

Figure 9: Simplified table of dynasties, agrarian situation, reforms and revolts (Part I: From Ch'ou to T'ang)

Dynasty	Capital	Agrarian situation, reforms and revolts
Xia before 1700 BC... – Shang 1700 to 1000 BC...		
Western Ch'ou 1000 to 771 BC	Shang'an (today Xi'an)	"*Well field-system*" (Tsing tien) widely applied. Rather equal plots of land available for peasants' families who pay taxes.
Spring and Autumn 722- 481 BC; Warring States 453–221 BC...		
Ch'in 221–206 BC	Xianyang (near today's Xi'an)	Shang Yang, advisor to the Ch'in king, ends "well field-system" around 361 BC. Agrarian land privatized. Landless peasants are settled on fallow land, of which they become owner. Initial strengthening of peasantry. However, small peasants soon lose their land to gentry. Major peasants' revolt follow after death of First Emperor, which allow the Han dynasty to conquer power.
Western Han 202 BC-9 AD	Shang'an (today Xi'an)	Han dynasty establishes military-agrarian colonies in connection with defense against the Xiongnu and its expansion, but they later collapse. *Wang Mang (9–23 AD)* nationalizes agrarian land and prohibits private property to protect the small peasantry. He fails, also following natural catastrophes, and is killed. The Decay of small peasantry contributes to Fall of Western Han.
Eastern Han 9 AD-220 AD	Luoyang	A Gentry dominated economy and society. Initial measures to support small peasants. But peasants later lose their land. Peasants' rebellions as "*Yellow turban*" (184–196 AD) and "*Five-bushel rice-sect*"-revolts (188–215 AD). Fighting these revolts strengthens military commanders. One of them, Dong Zhuo, burns down Luoyang ends Eastern Han dynasty.
Jin, Southern and Northern Dynasties 209–581 AD partially apply land distribution policies		
Sui 581–618 AD	Daxing (today Xi'an), Luoyang	The *Sui dynasty*, too, executes land distribution policies, but huge costs of wars, building projects and a flooding of the Huanghe river lead to insurrections of small peasants and the nobility, ending the Sui-dynasty.

Dynasty	Capital	Agrarian situation, reforms and revolts
T'ang 619–907 AD	Shang'an	The T'ang dynasty, too, initially pursues equal land distribution and other policies in favor of the small peasantry. After the rebellion of General *An Lushan* and *Li Shiming* in 755, local separatists gain power and foreign states conquer territories. This leads to the collapse of the T'ang.
Five Dynasties 907–960 AD...		

Figure 10: Simplified table of dynasties, agrarian situation, reforms and revolts (Part II: From Song to Ch'ing)

Dynasty	Capital	Agrarian and fiscal situation, reforms and revolts
Sung 960–1279 AD	Kaifeng, Hangzhou	After the Sung dynasty largely reunites China, it sees a series of popular rebellions. The reformer *Wang An-shih (1021–86)* initiates land redistributions, water-control and irrigation projects, a state-run rural credit system, and technical tutoring for peasants. The reform fails – probably because of the state's own short-term fiscal imperatives. *Chia Ssu-tao (1273–75)* makes a new effort for reforms by setting a ceiling on total allowed holdings of agrarian land and claims a right of the state to buy up land above this limit as public land. The consecutive opposition from the latifundia owners may have contributed to the fall of the Sung to the Yüan dynasty.
Yüan (Mongols) 1271–1368 AD	Dadu (today Beijing)	The Yüan dynasty initially supports the small peasantry. Later excessive taxation, partially caused by warfare and building projects, and bad harvests, worsen its condition and peasant rebellions, e.g., the *"White Lotus"-movement* and the *"Red Turban-Rebellion"* bring down the Yüan dynasty.

Dynasty	Capital	Agrarian and fiscal situation, reforms and revolts
Ming 1368–1644 AD	Nanking, Beijing (1421)	The *Ming dynasty* was erected by one of the leaders of the "Red Turban-Rebellion", which had brought down the Yüan dynasty. The small peasantry initially enjoyed significant protection under him as emperor *Hongwu* and his successor *Yongle*. Financial demands from the military and wars and the loss of control of the court's luxury spending as well as the effects of a *de facto* commodity money-regime, together with a "Small Ice Age" made the situation for the small peasantry unbearable. Following years of great popular insurrections between 1627 and 1644 Ming general *Wu Sangui* joined forces with the Manchu and helped to establish the Ch'ing dynasty.
Ch'ing (Manchu) 1635–1911 AD	Beijing	The establishment of *Ch'ing dynasty* all over China involved, particular in the southern Yangtse-region, the widespread formation of small independent farmers. The Ch'ing erected military-agrarian set-tlements, organized water–control and irrigation projects, lowered taxes for peasants and established an effective system to collect them. The flourishment of the Ch'ing dynasty ended with is ongoing loss of control over its military apparatus, its provinces, the state's spending and the agrarian and fiscal situation: This resulted in large peasant and other rebellions, with the *Taiping peasant war (1850–1864)*, with an aggregate number of dead of around 20–30 million, as the most terrible. These internal evolutions contributed to disarming the Ch'ing dynasty to Western attacks, in particular since the First Opium War of 1840.

Section 4. The failure of conservatism/restoration, ancient prosthetics and their dilemmas

A story with a result known in advance

The general result of the ancient master drama

The story, which the ancient master drama tells, is of the type of a tragedy. Its result is everywhere the same: It ends with the appropriation of the small peasantry's land by large wealth owners and with the small peasants' successive social annihilation. They are ejected from what had previously been the one and only large landowning class. Following this, they may, in Greece and Rome in particular, lose their citizenship or become bandits or fall into slavery. Not seldom, they join rebellious movements, whose characters oscillate between banditry, social revolutionaries and religious sects. This outcome resulted from the general failure or conservative-restorative policies vis-à-vis the social master drama. It showed the "incompleteness" of capitalism, if it is superimposed with the task to provide means of subsistence and other values-in-use to the human environment of the economy. The drama unfolded differently depending on the circumstances, regions and time. It sometimes expedited or slowed down its pace, sometimes it changed its course for a while and peasants won transitorily.

Circumstances particularly damaging to small peasants

If large landowners wanted to lay grip on the land of small farmers, then almost everything worked in their favor. The agricultural surplus of small farmers was mostly too marginal for them to maintain significant stores with reserves of seed or food. Thus, a little bad luck – droughts, flooding, bad weather, locust or epidemics could ruin their precariat existences. Small peasants could also not self-protect against even smaller detachments of armies in wars or civil war, or if the social and political order had collapsed and bandits attacked. Great landowners, while exposed to the same risks, could better self-protect and were better self-insured. Moreover, great landowners normally had more knowledge and more means to avoid or to minimize the damage wrought by adverse events. The extent to which central states squeezed the farmers through taxes or whether they granted tax reliefs would also often decide their fate.[174] Similarly, whether taxes were allowed to be paid in kind, by grains, or whether they had to be paid in cash,[175] mattered a great deal. If taxes had to be paid in cash, that allowed merchants, or again latifundia owners, underpay for the peasants produce. Central states, who should have been the allies of small farmers, also often dealt them crucial blows out of ignorance, negligent control of the tax collectors at place. The next step for peasants in distress was to take out the murderous debt that is so representative of antiquity. In the event of their likely default, great

---

174   We already mentioned briefly that the tax rates in normal times were often insignificant compared to modern democratic states. E.g., in 205 BC, the land tax, which was levied on actual crop yields, was at 1/15 of the yield and later reduced to 1/30, which remained the standard under the former Han. Following military expenditures, it was increased to 1/10, but reduced to 1/30 again in 30 AD. See *Sadao*, The economic and social history of former Han, page 596, 597.

175   *Sadao*, The economic and social history of former Han, page 594, 595 on the "later Han". Except for the obligation to pay taxes in cash, small peasants found themselves still mostly outside of the money economy. Yet, their need to avail themselves with cash to pay these taxes subjected them to abuses by merchants and money lenders. (*Sadao*, The economic and social history of former Han, page 594, 600 et seqs.).

land owners would execute by seizing their land and, often, their wives, children and themselves too.[176] Loans, which appeared to help at first, became the crucial step to the final fall.

But not only extraordinary shocks from outside damaged small farmers, if the economy evolved smoothly and quiet, that too could put them at a disadvantage and often eliminate them. Latifundist were typically able to outsell the small farmers with cheaper or better products, given that they normally had the better land, the better seed and used more advanced technical means, such as iron ploughs, animal power, flood control, or irrigation.[177] They were also often able to influence large buyers to buy their products in non-economic ways, e.g., through marriage alliances of for political or other career support. Who do you do business with if one supplier can get your son a desired post at the Chinese emperor's court while the other cannot?

The aggressivity of large landowners in displacing small landowners was exacerbated by money and special situations. First, the emergence of money unleashed more motives to appropriate land and, allowing to store of wealth, made the accumulation of land more reasonable. As stated previously, this mechanism ignited probably the ugliest and most reckless period of human economic history so far, the "Axial Age".[178] Second, if new trade systems emerged, in which grand landowners could link in with newly appropriated land, they would often also occupy it and displace small peasants with naked violence.[179] For instance, as we saw, this was so after the arrival of great numbers of slaves after the Punic and Macedonian wars in ancient Rome, which not only rendered the produce of many thousands independent small peasant uncompetitive, but also generated opportunities for latifundists to use the appropriated land for slave agriculture. Such changes often also carried the needed markets along: The produce of the plantations could be sold to the Roman army and the Roman proletarians, or to the City of Rome who distributed the corn. A prosthetic measure created a market for large plantation owners that were just creating the need for more prosthetics! Equally, fertile cropland, which could be used for pasturage to supply textile manufactures and factories with wool (much like the textile manufactures and factories in England in the "enclosures" around the second half of the 15th century[180]) motivated the appropriation of the land of small owner-farmers or the termination of lessee-farmers.

---

176   As an example, see *Sadao*, The economic and social history of former Han, page 545 et.seq., 557–559, describing the Spring and Autumn and Warring States periods.

177   See *Sadao*, The economic and social history of former Han, page 545 et seq.

178   *Graeber* (2011) page 251, 119.

179   See *Twitchett*, Introduction, page 25 on predatory landowners driving out small peasants by simple intimidation.

180   See *Marx*, Capital, volume I, chapter 24; *Polanyi* (1944) pages 36, 73, 79.

Circumstances allowing small peasants to recuperate land

If natural agricultural crises, negative climate changes, pandemics, wars, civil wars, social unrest disorder have caused a material decline of population and a collapse of state and local order, mostly not only those who formerly worked the land but also the local grandees, who owned it, are dead. So are most state-functionaries who protected the interests of the local grandees. Landless peasants or the recovering state can, thus, simply occupy the land, often without much resistance.[181] Furthermore, central states, if they seek to re-establish order after war, catastrophe or anomy, are mostly not only clearly aware that the small peasantry is their natural ally, but they are back in a position to act on this knowledge. There is no relevant difference here, whether these states are despotic, a free republic or a social rebellion... Furthermore, for a significant re-establishment of a small peasantry to occur, it does, in fact, not matter whether the states declare themselves to be owner of the land (and only factually allow peasants to work it)[182], whether they officially distribute the land as private property to the peasants, or whether they, via some intermediary level, give the land as a feud to them. In the sense the sinologist *Kai Vogelsang* writes on Chinese History after Wang Mang (ruling 9–23 AD): "From thereon all new rulers – up to the communists in the 20th century – began their rule with a land reform; the abolition of large latifundia and the strengthening of tax-paying small peasants formed the base of the central state."[183] It became almost normal that the small peasantry would florish if order was re-established by a new regime, at least at first. The largest lasting period of such an improvement of the small peasants' condition was to become the Middle Ages.

The failure of conservative-restorative policies and the meaning of the defeat of the small peasantry

Interests of central states in a strong small peasantry

Central states emerged after a local noble chief had successfully led a battle of an alliance of tribes, feudal grandees, or regions against a foreign foe. After victory, this chief would, of course, not relinquish power but seek to move on and to become king or emperor. In other cases, central states were simply formed, without foreplay, by a local noble militarily attacking and defeating other nobles, or, finally, by taking over an existing, but defunct central power. Such drives for power were mostly justified as religious or other ideological crusades. Any such state formation required

---

181   This, e.g., frequently happened in medieval Europe following 1300 (see *Gilomen*, Wirtschaftsgeschichte des Mittelalters, 2014, page 100 et seq.).

182   As was officially the case during most of Chinese history, from the Ch'ou to the T'ang – with certain specifics after the reforms of Shang Yang under the Ch'in.

183   *Vogelsang* (2013) page 168.

bureaucrats and soldiers, which had to be financed. Yet, even if wealthy supporter financed the war effort against a foreign attacker or the aspirant's rise to power, their willingness to provide money typically ended after the enemy was defeated or the new regime secured.[184] The "propensity to pay taxes" of greater wealth owners, so to speak, was constantly poor in ancient history, much below the propensity of less wealthy citizens and of the small peasantry in particular.[185]

Accordingly, aspiring new central powers in need of finance, and in need of equipping their bureaucracies and armies, should have regarded small farmers as their natural allies and protected them, if only as a reliable source of taxes. The should have done this after conquering power as, then in particular, they had simple and effective means to this effect: "Give peasants land!" was the natural recipe of "supply-side" state intervention after regime foundation. New free farmers, of course, would stimulate trade and growth, too, and, most importantly, make the best soldiers and strengthen states both offensively and defensively. The stated correlation was widely known and a significant share of politicians and the most intelligent advisors in antiquity were well aware of it. We find discourses at courts and in bureaucracies on the subject everywhere, throughout Greek, Roman, and Chinese history, and the most famous philosophers, religious men, and political and economic thinkers all addressed this issue. If new regimes seized power, as we saw, they very often, in fact, did undertake serious efforts to support the small peasantry initially – irrespective of whether they were Greek "tyrants",[186] democracies, or brutal despotic regimes. Additional state policies in support of the small peasantry consisted in lowering tax rates, in particular in years of bad harvests, allowing taxes to be paid in kind (taking away profits from intermediate merchants), distributing agrarian tools or granting loans to small peasants for acquiring tolls, promoting agrarian knowledge amongst them and throwing state-managed irrigation programs etc. Furthermore, new regimes often sharpened usury laws and mitigated laws on debt execution, fixed maximum interest rates, or even distributed land conquered from foreign foes. Occasionally, as the ultimate means, they even took appropriated land away again from the local wealthy and

---

184 Sometimes, though, they would also enter into alliances with their foes.

185 This was no different in ancient China. See, as one example for many, *Shen*, The move to the south and the reign of Kao-Tsung (1127–1162), page 644 et seqs., page 701).

186 The word "tyrant" was given its negative connotation, like "despotism", only later. In ancient Greece, it is said to have only meant "not elected" and to have been seen as enviable by most men. (*Waterfield* (2018) page 64 et seq.).

returned it to small peasants.[187] If implemented early, when the dynasties were strong, or after severe crises, such measures had significant positive effects.

Contradictions within ancient states and the failure of conservative-restorative policies

However, not only were conservative-restorative policies of central states to maintain a large land-owning small peasantry an uphill battle against an entropic, near-automatic economic process (in which the decay of the small peasantry would immediately pick up speed as soon as the efforts ceased for moment), but the state, the ruling nobility and state-functionaries were *caught in intrinsic contradictions*. The overall historic failure of conservative-restorative state policies, which aimed at securing the small peasantry's[188] ownership of their land, can only be understood before this background. The contradictions had several aspects: First, yes, states were interested in independent peasants as both taxpayers and soldiers, but there was often just no feasible alternative to raising taxes of the small peasantry. Second, the supporters of the ruling king, dynasty or oligarchy, in particular the courted aristocratic families, who might otherwise rebel, and, of course, the emperor's own family, had to be entertained and pleased – at often immense costs. For these reasons alone, the central state often could not but kill the cow of small independent farmers, instead of milking it. Third, the central state's personnel came from the great landowners' class itself, and it was as natural to them, just as with their non-bureaucrat landowner colleagues, to try to round off their properties. All these aspects contributed to the failure of policies supporting small farmers. Historians sometimes point even to a fourth way of escalation: Displacement of small peasants, which had already taken place, with such ex-peasants joining bandit gangs or social rebellions and formed sizeable armies that the central states had to fight, drew further on its finances.[189] Actually, even states that already pursued prosthetic policies, which may have been triggered by the decay of the small peasantry, would use the remaining

---

187   Land redistribution "generally work best at the beginning of any regime when land confiscated from rival pretenders and from the ruined elite of the previous regime give the emperor large supply of land available for distribution." (*Wright*, The Sui dynasty (581–617), page 94.)

188   Writes *Gernet* (1972, tome I, page 192) on Han-China: "Les premiers décrets qui visent à limiter l'étendue des propriétés privées, datent du dernières années du Ier siècle avant notre ère. Ils seront suivis jusqu'à la fin du IIIe par une longue série d'autres décrets analogues, qui semblent avoir été généralement inefficaces, témoignant ainsi des difficultés que rencontre l'État à maintenir son contrôle et sa protection sur la petite paysannerie."

189   Wang Shih, a formidable T'ang military commander, was entrusted to crush Ch'iu Fu's bandit rebellion in the south in 860. He opened government storehouses to the peasantry to discontinue to not further feed the rebellion (*Somers*, The end of the T'ang, page 691).

small peasants to finance these prosthetics – and often overused it. Ultimately, central states would annihilate small peasants to fund prosthetics in favor of other already annihilated small peasants and to fund armies to fight rebellions of displaced small peasants. One way or the other, they would often deliver the final blow against their former ally.

The meaning of the defeat of the small peasantry

The defeat of the small peasantry – its expropriation – meant that owners were turned into non-owners. This did away with their option to subsist independently from the economic system in a self-sufficient autarch manner. Moreover, no longer would displaced farmers be capable of offering grains or other agrarian products on markets. They had only their working power left – and whether they could sell it, on labor markets, would now depend on somebody else being willing to sacrifice money for it, either because he could make profit out of it or, more seldom, consume it.

As regards the respective piece of land, with one strike, whether it was worked and whether agrarian products would at all be drawn out of it, began to depend on a more demanding algorithm. Before it was worked if its produce sufficed to feed the family working it and allowed a tax payment etc. to the state and human physical needs, via the human motivational system, directly steered humans to the work land. Now a third "stakeholder", the land's new private owner, entered the game and claimed a share of the produce, too. Hence, unless the state waived a part of its share or productivity grew, the peasant family had either to work harder or to consume less. Furthermore, there was a consequential formal aspect: The new land owner was mostly not interested in piling up produce in kind (and see it rotting), but he wanted to accumulate money.[190] It, thus, became crucial for him, how much the market paid for his share of the harvest and whether there was a market. If there was no market or it paid too little, he would have no interest in the land being worked and not allow the peasants to work it at all. The private land owner was an M–C–M'-player and, thus, imposed the profit-criterion on the whole enterprise.

Private land ownership of small peasants themselves, while they remained dependent on nature, had been able to keep their survival and subsistence indepen-

---

190   For the economic principle it does not matter whether the land-owner expected to receive his share in kind (and would sell it himself) or he already receives a money payment (with the peasant having to sell his share or the produce). It also does not even make a difference relevant for the economic principle whether the peasant family has to a pay a money rent and retains the whole produce for itself. Some forms look more "capitalist", others more "feudal" than others, but the economic necessities are the same. However, if the peasants are obliged to pay the shares of the private owner (or of the state) in money, that opens the door to their additional abuse by local merchants, usurer or others when they have to sell that share of the produce.

dent of the economic system. Only if they were additionally trying to exchange a part of their agrarian produce in local markets, they came in touch with the economic system at all, and only with that part. The land appropriation by latifundia owners changed all this. By the same token, humans were made non-owners and fully subjected to the logic of an owner-society. The very idea of ownership, was in fact, brought up not to make owners, but non-owners.

The failure of conservative-restorative policies and the rise of prosthetics

The issue of the small peasantry was most intimately connected with wealth accumulation by violence (see chapter I). If the ancient master drama was allowed to run its course, the peaceful, economic method of wealth procurement by exchange would undermine the inner coherence of ancient warrior states, which would destroy the prerequisites of their future success in the realm of wealth accumulation by violence – by weakening the core of their armies. The option to integrate displaced farmers as salary workers did not practically exist in a sufficient degree. Yes, workshops, e.g., where agricultural tools, carts and carriages, pottery, furniture for the wealthy, were manufactured, existed, but the effective demand for these commodities was far too low to employ a significant number of the displaced peasantry. To maintain military supremacy or at least competitiveness in warfare, the top robber states of antiquity had, thus, only two options: The *first option* was to halt and "roll back" the expropriation of the small peasantry, i.e., to turn the economic and social evolution around, to go back to the past and to reinstitute displaced peasants into their lost land or to, at least to create new "peasant positions" for them. We saw that a multitude of efforts in the sense of the first option, e.g., the assignment of land to landless soldiers after conquests of new territories, were made. But even if they no half-hearted window-dressing, they were, quite simply, not enough. If a "vessel empties", writes *Theodor Mommsen*, "by a steady outflow, even pouring considerable masses into it is not sufficient; a steady inflow must be fabricated...".[191] Yet, the ancient ruling classes never managed to fabricate a sufficient steady inflow. The most effective retarding or reversing moments, in fact, appear to have been the unintended or accidental natural or social catastrophes of which we spoke. The first, conservative-restorative option ultimately failed altogether.

The *second option*, was to move forward and to invent something new, an artificial, i.e., a prosthetic solution. But in what should prosthetics consist and how should they be financed? Transfer payments funded by money creation were impossible; money creation existed only as clumsy commodity money creation and this was far too marginal and unreliable to fund regularly needed prosthetics – and if it accidentally occurred, the ruling classes of antiquity would rather appropriate the new

---

191   *Mommsen* (1976) volume 3 page 406.

wealth themselves rather than to forward it to expropriated former peasants... Taxing the still surviving small peasants would not suffice to support their expelled former comrades either and the ruling elites had, of course, not appropriated the land of small peasants to have these lands worked to finance social transfers to the very same displaced peasants! Of course, the latifundists also had the possibility to escape such additional taxation, if the state at all attempted it. Furthermore, central states normally had better use for collected tax money... Debt was no workable solution either. If wealthowners could at all be convinced to loan money to the state, that money would have to be repaid to them; if it was given to proletarized former peasants to feed them, it would, though, normally never return.

At the crossroads of the two options – conservatism or prosthetics –, of which none appeared to function, the ancient top robber states ultimately came up with a rather clear generally used solution: Was not the original problem the loss of the displaced farmers as soldiers for the army? And was not, indeed, a substitute for the lost peasant-soldiers quite urgent anyhow – if the respective robber state wanted to maintain its capacity to procure wealth by violence and to, equally important, defend against such projects by its neighbors? Hence, why not keep the displaced peasants in the military, but *now for pay* instead of, as before, a show of free-farmer-owners' patriotism and act of self-interest of then still members of the owners-class? This specific use of the surplus population brought with it the method to finance it, too: If things went well, the mercenary or clientele soldiers would generate the wealth needed to maintain themselves through the success of their campaigns, be it, after a victory, through jobs in the ongoing policing and exploitation of the defeated (including transportation or the like), be it as former Roman soldiers were assigned land taken away from the defeated, or be it through the customary distribution of bread etc. to the sub-proletariat in Rome. If things went very well, a profit would remain left-over for the narrowed wealth owners' class. If the warfare only led to a stalemate or defeat, yet, it had at least kept one's surplus population busy for the moment and had, hopefully, provided prevention against a subjugation by the neighbors. Moreover, the warfare, by itself, would probably have eliminated a good share of the surplus-population through illness and deaths in action. If the robber states took into account – as they ought to: see the debates in the original assembly –, that in a world of imperial rivals there is no alternative to having an army anyhow, the solution found was close to genial.

Yet, it war, too, led into dilemmas. First, it could never work as a universal solution, The economic trick was to externalize the subsistence cost for the displaced former peasants to a third foreign party, but two countries cannot mutually rob each other. The solution could always only work for one side, while the loser ought to be enslaved or the like. The loser would obviously dislike the situation, seek to free himself, and, in fact, aspire to become the oppressor himself. People in two neighboring countries can well live peacefully alongside each other if they both have land, work it, and engage in exchange. If the people within the two countries, have, however, partially mutually displaced each other from their land, and they seek a subsistence for the displaced group by subjugating a foreign country, this can only work for one side and will never be stable. Second, the displaced former peasants who conquer foreign tribes or countries, police and control them, throw down upheavals and organize the transports to the homeland, become a *lasting mass-reality as such*. From thereon, their very existence forces their home robber states to continuously seek to subjugate other countries, including to find new victims if old ones are exhausted. Prosthetics by warfare are, thus, a standing cause for new wars; they are, as such, *bellogenetic* by necessity.[192]

---

192 *Herfried Münkler* (Münkler (2017) makes a similar argument with regard to the war of Thirty Years.

Part III:
The deficiency of employment-generating spending in modern capitalism

After having dealt with general doctrinal issues of profit economies in Part I and with dynamics and prosthetics of ancient capitalism in Part II, now modern capitalism is examined in two parts, Part III and Part IV of the book. Part III studies the dynamics of the modern capitalist economy without prosthetics, hence in its most abstract and purest form, with a view to the closure of the circuits of the productive economy, which only generate employment. It, thereby, also describes the basis for the modern social master drama. We shall find that, even if non-owners are now, in contrary to ancient capitalism, employed by capitalist firms in significant numbers, the circuits will often enough not close and that, thus, the necessity of prosthetics continues to exist. Chapter VI secures the paradigm in the background. Chapter VII, which is the book's longest and most theoretical, examines economic approaches adopted to circuit closure throughout the history of economic theory by outstanding economists, from Quesnay to Minsky. Chapter VIII presents the resulting explanation for deficient employment-generating or deficient producive spending in the capitalist productive economy. Part IV will later deal with the prosthetics of modern capitalism.

Chapter VI. The master drama of modern capitalism: Employment for workers

"Die Entstehung der Armut ist überhaupt eine Folge der bürgerlichen Gesellschaft, und sie ergibt sich im ganzen notwendig aus derselben" … "Es ist in der bürgerlichen Gesellschaft nicht eine bloße Naturnot, mit der der Arme zu kämpfen hat. Die Natur, welche der Arme sich gegenüber hat, ist nicht ein bloßen Sein, sondern mein Wille. Der Arme fühlt sich als sich verhaltend zur Willkür, zur menschlichen Zufälligkeit, und das ist das Empörende in der letzten Analyse, dass er durch die Willkür in diesen Zwiespalt gesetzt ist." … "Der Mangel an Arbeit ist, wie bemerkt wurde, ein Hauptumstand, der die Armut herbeiführt. Es tritt bei einem gedeihlichen Zustand der Kultur immer eine Überbevölkerung ein. Wenn der Armut Gelegenheit zur Arbeit gegeben wird, so wird dadurch nur die Menge der Waren vermehrt. Nun aber ist es gerade der Überfluss von Waren, der den Mangel an Arbeit herbeigeführt hat…"[1]

We saw that the ancient master drama ended with the general loss of land of the largest part of the population. Thereby, the subsistence of the new-born non-owners or workers became dependent on the new-born owners. The non-owners either needed the owners to offer jobs or to make gifts to the former. But whether owners offered jobs depended on whether they could use the non-owners' work to close profitable M–C–M'-circuits. That was the result of the social system having allowed the economic subsystem, dominated by capitalism as its guest system, to take charge of social goods procurement. Now, even if the economic system, in its crisp beauty,

---

1   *Hegel* (1983) page 193. Translation by the author: "The origination of poverty is, as such, a consequence of civil society, and in the whole results from it by necessity." … "In civil society it is not a mere natural hardship, with which the poor has to fight. The nature, which the poor has as its opposite, is not only a factual existence, but my will. The poor feels himself as behaving himself to arbitrariness, to human randomness, and the outrageous, in the last analysis, is being put into this discord by arbitrariness." … "The lack of work is, as has been observed, a main circumstance, which causes poverty. In an advantageous condition of culture always a surplus population occurs. If the poor are offered an opportunity to work, thereby only the plenty of commodities is augmented. It is, however, just the excess of commodities, which has brought about the lack of work.…".

does not care about about the excretion of human surplus populations and their suffering and processes on unshattered, the social systems cannot let go.... If things go badly, then individual biological systems, which men are, will be put under stress. Individuals will, first, starve and become physically and mentally ill. Then, the cultural system will react: Writers will write novels, artists paint pictures, singers sing songs, directors shoot movies, priests will pray, etc. and all that will spill over into the political system. Now political ideologists and social reformers will write articles and give speeches, people will discuss and rally on the streets, party leaders will make demands, and there will be upheaval, rebellion, revolution, physical force and civil war. The powerful elites will, of course, as they did before, seek to defend their positions and there will be fights.

In fact, in parallel with the renaissance of capitalism in modernity, the social system had become much more sensitive and irritable to human suffering, including to even the suffering of the lower classes. The European Middle Ages left over Christianity with the idea, which had appeared so unspeakably weird initially, that *all* humans were created in God's likeness, and each cultural wave after the Middle Ages, from humanism, via Protestantism to the natural law, the Enlightenment, and, certainly, socialism, had only put more emphasis on this idea and claimed a more generous applicability for it. Yes, in everyday life, the lower classes were still trained and drilled to look up to the "hochwohlgeborene" nobility, like the upper classes continued to look down onto the "pauvre fol peuple" as something essentially different from them, but increasingly the contradiction between the *imago dei*-concept and the philosophies of modernity, on the one side, and the practices of every day's life, on the other, came to the forefront. When *Frederick the Great* of Prussia declared himself as *"first servant of his people"* 250 years ago, he "officially", so to speak, rebased the legitimacy of government on a functional role directed to the well-being of the people, even if he did not talked about equality within "the" people, his statement admitted at least that severe sufferings of the lower classes were a bad thing. The French Revolution of 1789 drew the first drastic corollaries from all this. It followed the French revolution of 1848, the Chinese Taiping rebellion from 1850 to 1864, the Paris Commune of 1871, the Russian and the Chinese revolution, "people-democratic" regimes in Eastern Europe, and revolutionary attempts and regimes in Africa and South America. The world entered into an era of "mass politics", with Communism and Fascism, becoming the two main novel political offers after the carnages of WWI. Whether, they will turn out to have been transitory stages to a universal "mass democracy",[2] we shall see. The relevance of the modern master drama, which we shall examine now, for society was greatly amplified by these developments. It is the true sting behind all macroeconomics.

---

2   For the argument of this book, we do not need a more developed concept of "mass- democracy". See, however, *Kondylis* (1991) and *Furth* (2008) and *Furth* (2015).

Chapter VII. The structural deficiency of employment-generating spending in modern capitalism

Section 1. Circuit closure analysis

The relationship between production and consumption in primitive autarch families or tribes can be imagined in the simplest case that a search of new subsidies, either by gathering plants or hunting prey, takes only place after all available subsidies have been consumed. Foresight comes into play, the search begins some time before new goods are needed, but this is limited by available storage technologies. Seasonal change and whether or not hunting, fishing or gathering is good or bad must be taken into account. If pastorage and agriculture have emerged, the seasons of seed and harvest, or the necessities from cattle life, determine the course. In this situation, an insufficiency in a group's means of consumption can result from miscalculating nature, from too little or ineptly executed human work or bad surprises: weather, catastrophes, locust, earthquakes, disease, war, etc.

The emergence of exchange and a money economy alters that greatly. It inserts itself between human collectives and nature as a new steering system. It enables higher and better production and distribution, but at the cost of a higher level of contingency and complexity that the intermediate system brings about. It also changes what matters for the producers. Weather conditions, animal migration and storing technology remain relevant, but the foresight is no longer directed to the consumption needs of the own families or the own tribe but to the esoteric demands of prospective exchange partners and their capability and will to pay.

The relationship between production and expected employment-generating spending in an exchange economy, money economy or capitalism is, in fact, the main subject of the writing of the above-mentioned examined authors. While they do not use the term "productive circuit", they all had it clearly in mind. The authors had three different options to approach the subject: First, to view employment-generating spending as *wholly independent of production*. This implies that incomes resulting from the production of commodities (the salaries and supplier firms' revenues) are not relevant for being able to sell them. The money to buy the produce is rather exogenously generated, at least in such volumes that the lack of money will never be a restricting factor. (This does not exclude that salaries and supplier firms' revenues may support circuit closure, yet, they are not necessary). This view reminds of the innocent times when humanity believed that its garbage, emissions etc. were so minute, when compared to the atmosphere, that they were actually negligible. There is a primordial ocean around us and we do not have to worry about the purchaser of our productions. We take A. Smith as an example of this view.

The second view does see a positive and necessary contribution of the outlays for the production of commodities to workers and supplier firms upon the employment-generating spending needed to buy them; it in fact considers this contribution as *guaranty for circuit closure*. The most famous representative of this view is the so-called "Law of Say" (we shall see that this "law" belongs more to Ricardo than to Say.)[1] "Ricardo's law of Say", as we will thus call it, is either stated, without any further justification, as "supply creates its own demand" (second interpretation). Or the argument is that because suppliers and workers are paid for their inputs to a production, they would automatically be sufficiently equipped to buy the produce and would also just do that (third interpretation). In other words, the point of the third interpretation of Ricardo's Law of Say is that the origination of the problem contains a sufficient solution in itself. The problem, as we shall see, will be the profit-add-on.

A third group of authors, while they, certainly, do not ignore a sourcing contributing of production outlays upon employment-generating spending, *deny* that these outlays *will be sufficient to close the circuits*. Following different lines of thought and offering different degrees of elucidation they doubt that the exploited can buy their produce (Sismondi), that costs can buy value (Malthus), or that M can buy M' etc. The point is: If capitalism is driven by profit, which means that the central players strive for more incoming money than outgoing money, production outlays must always be less than the collections for the produced commodities. How can that gap be filled to enable that produced commodities are fully sold at adequate profits – if this is at all possible?

Historically, different notional strategies have been employed to analyze problems of circuit closure. The first strategy, the one adopted by Ricardo and his followers, used "supply" and "demand". Other writers applied the distinction between "consumption" and "investment", or sub-categories thereof (e.g., Kalecki considered capitalists' consumption plus investment). Keynes, in turn, used investment, which he partially identified with saving. This book, instead, uses the breakdown of Marx's M into c-outlays and v-outlays in the first leg of the circuit and Marx's surplus value or s, which brings about the difference between the aggregate outlays M and the revenues M'. This allows to split the flows into smaller parts; it thereby also allows to make the contributions of authors who use prior notional strategies comparable. As Sismondi and Malthus have already shown, every reasoning about circuit closure

---

1   See on page 233 et seq.

has to grapple with the asymmetricity that is connected to the profit criterion. *More value-in-exchange/money must be sucked-in by capitalists, on their sales side, than they emitted to workers and supplier firms before on the sourcing side.* The driving force of profit economies is to create a gap between M' and M, the challenge to its ability to close its circuits is the very same gap. Our analysis will ultimately show that a closure of the gap – using value-in-exchange generated in the first leg of M–C–M'-circuits and the *expected* profits – is theoretically possible. *However, it is conditional.* Accordingly, a full and adequate understanding of the problem of capitalist circuit closure can only be achieved by understanding the structure of this conditionality. When can the conditions be met? And why is what ought to happen for circuit closure in the productive economy normally not happening? We shall find the answer in the flight of investment into the sterile economy. The reader who is only interested in the results of our review of the selected economists but not in their individual treatment may re-join in Chapter VIII. The deficient-producive-spending-syndrome .

Section 2. Quesnay's dépenses-integrated "royaume agricole"

An organism reproduced by just the right "dépenses"

Quesnay, the physician,[2] thought of the economy, of his "royaume agricole", in much the same way as of the body of his patient Louis XV. What happens at one place must have consequences at another place and in order for it to be possible something else must have happened before or be happening at yet other places. A biological or zoological system, Quesnay knew, has a built-in *telos* or an *entelecheia*, which works towards a healthy state. It takes care that juices of the right composition and volume will be produced and find their way to the right destinations at the right time; it also takes care that they will be welcomed and not rejected. Why should God not have arranged for the economy, which Quesnay "dissected",[3] to operate in a basically reliably way, predetermined by Platonian ideas or by a God-imbued spirit? So, he believed: "L'ordre et la marche de cette machine admirable sont fixés décisivement par

---

2   Noteworthily, *William Petty* (1623–1687), the English economist, who was writing earlier than Quesnay, was also a professor of anatomy.

3   He himself uses the word "disséquer" (*Quesnay* in: *Cartelier* (2008) page 154). Marx calls the tableau économique "einen höchst genialen Einfall, unstreitig der genialste, dessen sich die politische Ökonomie bisher schuldig gemacht hat". (*Marx*, Theorien über den Mehrwert, MEW 26.1, page 319). Marx also states that Smith would "hardly have executed and interpreted the totality of the movement so correctly as indicated in the Tableau Économique, notwithstanding the wrong predictions of Quesnay" (loc. cit. page 319).

son Auteur".[4] The "royaume agricole", thus it appeared, was a machine which, after it had come into existence and was set into motion, continued to run, except
when it was abused, indefinitely. The "royaume agricole", says Quesnay, is an "ordre des dépenses régulières,[5] (qui) assure perpétuellement la même reproduction
annuelle".[6] The supreme rule-setter of Quesnay was, in fact, a "dieu juste";[7] yet, as
we know from other religious or metaphysical concepts about society, that is no absolute guaranty against things getting out of hand. Misunderstandings, egocentric
short-term interests and sins may throw them out of their rhythm and the order
may fall apart.[8] In other words, Quesnay did not approach the systems integration
he observed with the modern question whether the system observed its own operation and elements, how it would do that and what means it had to interfere. His
religious-metaphysical approach also relieved him of the question of how his wonderful foresightful and well-meaning system had come into being; he has no theory
of economic evolution to his "royaume agricole". This pre-modern and pre-scientific
methodology is a weak spot in his economics.

It appears, though, that this deficit is the price paid for an otherwise extremely
strong and clear and, indeed, absolutely modern concept of the economic system.
Quesnay gives us statements, which, until today shine with insightfulness and precision. He wants to understand the "constitution économique", which has an "ordre
réciproque des causes et effets" and announces his intention to expose "toutes les
pièces de rapport qui entrent dans la construction de la machine économique", to

---

4   Quote in *Quesnay* in: *Cartelier* (2008) page 154. Cartelier also reads this "argumentation
     économique du type finaliste" in this sense (*Cartelier* (2008) page 19, and summarizes "Les
     règles doivent donc se déduire d'une loi naturelle volue par dieu." (page 17)

5   *Quesnay* in: *Cartelier* (2008) page 165, 190.

6   Quesnay in: Cartelier (2008) page 216.

7   Quesnay in: Cartelier (2008) page 344.

8   Quesnay examines forgetfulness of one's duties and lack of insight by the parts, e.g., sons
     of farmers desiring to move to Paris (*Quesnay* in: *Cartelier* (2008) page 107 et seq.), the pur-
     suance of excessive decorative luxuries (loc. cit. page 92) or excessive thrift in this regard:
     "Que les propriétaires et ceux qui exercent les professions lucratives, ne soient portés par
     quelque inquiétude qui ne sera pas prévu par le gouvernement, à se livrer à des épargnes
     stériles qui retrancheraient de la circulation et de la distribution une portion de leurs reve-
     nus ou de leur gains." (loc. cit. page 105). Quesnay, furthermore, speaks out against sovereign
     debt with the argument that it creates a sterile market. "Que L'État évite des emprunts,
     qui forment des rentes financières, qui chargent l'État des dettes dévorantes, et qui oc-
     casionnent un commerce ou trafic de finance, par l'entremise des papiers commerçables,
     *où l'escompte augmente de plus en plus les fortunes pécuniaires stériles, qui séparent la finance de
     l'agriculture, et qui la privent des richesses nécessaires pour l'amélioration des biens-fonds et pour la
     culture des terres.*" (loc. cit. page 117, italics added). On both occasions, Quesnay, noteworthily,
     uses the term "sterile" not with a view to his unfortunate cl. sterile, which, even if it can pro-
     duce goods, including services, and sell them above their costs, cannot be "productive"; he
     rather uses "sterile" it in a sense, which comes close to its use in this book.

understand "le jeu de cette machine régénératrice." For this purpose, he undertakes a "démonstration anatomique des toutes ses parties et par le développement de leurs entrelacements, de leur connexion et du concours de leur action mutuelle"[9] He finds a two-sidedness, a functional double character of flows. "Par la circulation on entend ici les achats payés par le revenu...".[10] There is a "...débit réciproque d'une classe à l'autre".[11] "...tout doit être dépensé pour pouvoir être reproduit."[12] And as in Quesnay what needs to happen *will* happen, he can also write "...l'ordre de la distribution de de la dépense du revenu..." shows that "la reproduction du revenu y est égale au revenu dépensé...".[13] "De la vient que l'on dit que consommation et revenu sont synonymes".[14]

The price for the stability of the "royaume agricole" is not necessarily an absence of growth. Quesnay's machine can run at any level, hence also at greater volumes. He even advocates policies, which allow production to rise – e.g., by the sale of agricultural produce to foreign markets.[15] Hence, we find a contradiction in Quesnay, methodologically speaking. On the one hand, we have an advanced understanding of a necessity of capitalist circuits to close and of the preconditions of their closure, on the other hand, we have a pre-modern Platonian, Aristotelian (Catholic even), explanation for why these preconditions will be automatically fulfilled. The exceptional contribution of Quesnay to the history of economic thinking resides in the first dimension, in speaking out about the existence of the necessary discipline of circuit closure in the economy[16] – as strict as any of those found in biological systems – and in requiring a style of economic reasoning, which is compatible with this request. By elevating that "the right amount of money will always be where needed to buy the produce" to an axiom of economics, he drew the attention of economists to the buried question if it happens why it happens. He moved the question *where employment-generating spending come from, how they are financed and how circuits of exchanges between units prepare the ground for a next round of circuits* to the center of economics. We should not criticize Quesnay that his answer falsely misconceived the economy as a teleological system by bringing God and happily fitting numbers into play, but admire him for discovering that capitalist circuits must close by assuming that they do close.

---

9   *Quesnay in: Cartelier* (2008) page 153 et seq. (both quotes).

10   *Quesnay in: Cartelier* (2008) page 137.

11   *Quesnay in: Cartelier* (2008) page 94.

12   *Quesnay in: Cartelier* (2008) page 165.

13   *Quesnay in: Cartelier* (2008) page 165.

14   *Quesnay in: Cartelier* (2008) page 165.

15   *Quesnay in: Cartelier* (2008) page 144.

16   One might say this about logistics and motivation of the elements or classes. In another context, Quesnay writes "Tout est assujetti ici à des règles rigoureuses...". (*Quesnay in: Cartelier* (2008) page 392.

Tableau économique as quantitative flow diagram

Quesnay's teleology lies in the match of God-chosen quantities. By putting numbers on flows that enable circuit closure, he tells what is needed for the circuits to close. The circuits close because of the fit of the quantities; hence the quantities will allow to understand why they close. Here is our leading theoretical interest in Quesnay – to understand how the quantities can be as they are or how employment-generating spending is created in the tableau in such numbers as to enable the flows of "dépenses" to integrate.

Quesnay presents several versions of his *tableau*, in the format of a zigzag-drawing or of a table. We have chosen to use the version from 1766[17] and represent it in this book as a flow diagram.

Figure 11: Quesnay's tableau économique (graphic by author)

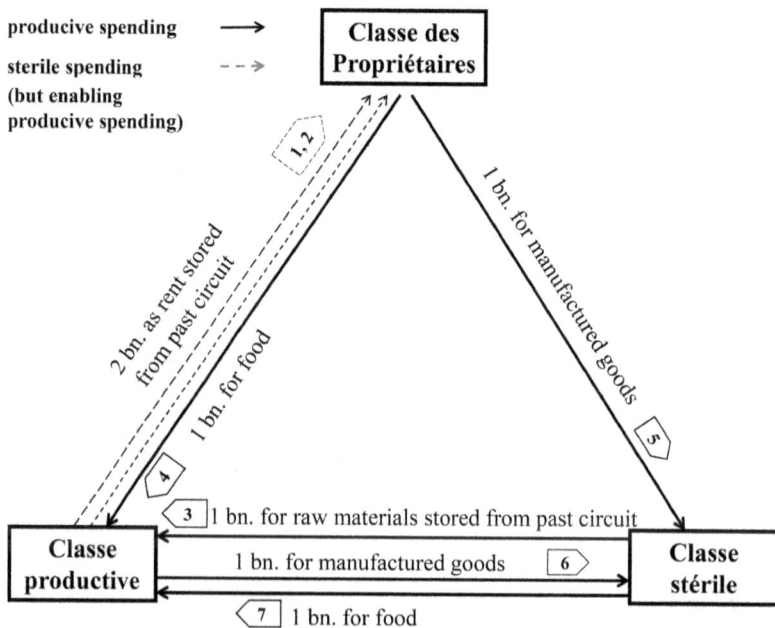

Cl. productive pays 2 bn. to cl. des prop., pays 1 bn. to cl. sterile and receives 3bn.

The flows require stocks as preconditions. There must be "avances primitives" of approx. Livres 10 bn. and additional "avances annuelles" of approximately Livres

---

17   *Quesnay* in: *Cartelier* (2008) page 207 et seq. (first published in Journal de l'agriculture, du commerce et des finances, June 1766).

2 bn. of the *"classe productive"*[18] (cl. productive) and Livres 1 bn. of the *"classe stérile"*[19] (cl. stérile) and there must be both labor[20] and money. No credit, no private banking, and no central banking are required and no state and no taxation appear as separate elements or flows in the tableau.[21]

In a biological system the flow of blood from the heart to an organ or peripheral place, which it will nurture, does not depend on the simultaneous flow of something else in the opposite direction. Muscles do not make "payments" to the heart for the nutrition they receive.[22] However, in the economy we have flows of goods or services in one direction and of money in the opposite direction, which mutually do depend upon one another; as jurists say *do ut des* or *quid pro quo*. Quesnay uses the word "dépenses",[23] which corresponds to our "spending", for the money flows being emitted by purchasers of goods or services for them.[24] His perspective, much like

---

18   Quesnay in: *Cartelier* (2008) page 212.

19   *Quesnay in: Cartelier (2008)* page 97. The "classe stérile" includes the producers of handicraft, housing, clothing, those who give loans, domestics, commerce, foreign trade etc. (*Quesnay in: Cartelier* (2008) page 139).

20   *Quesnay in: Cartelier* (2008) page 94. He mentions that half of the "avances annuelles" would be used for feeding animals and half for the salaries of the workers.

21   Even if the Banque de France was only formed in 1800, Quesnay was certainly aware of the activities of the Banque Générale of Paris under John Law from 1716 to 1720. He mentions "emprunts", "rentes financières", "la finance", and "papiers commerçables" a few times in a critical sense (*Quesnay in: Cartelier* (2008) page 117).

22   One might contend that a muscle, like everything in a organistic biological system, contributes to the survival and reproduction of the whole, including the heart. While this is true, the heart will not immediately withhold nutrition for the muscle, if the muscle no longer makes valuable contributions for the body as a whole.

23   He even occasionally uses "dépenses" to name two of his three classes when he speaks of the "classe des dépenses productives" and the "classe des dépenses stériles" (e.g., *Quesnay in: Cartelier* (2008) page 92). It is noteworthy, though, that only the cl. productive makes rent-"dépenses" to the cl. des propriétaires, thereby transferring the "revenu net" of the economy, which enables the cl. des propriétaires to close the circuits.

24   We can obviously look at each exchange, first, in terms of the flow of goods or services or in terms of the flow of money and, second, from the perspective of the seller or from the perspective of the buyer. The word *"supply"* covers produced goods or services from the seller's perspective, the word *"demand"* covers the need or desire for goods or services from the purchaser's perspective. *"Purchasing power"* (or "produive spending", "effective demand", and "effectual demand", etc.) points to the capability of the prospective recipients of the goods and services to make money payments for them. The desire to exchange goods or services against money, when looked at from the seller's perspective, is well expressed by the German word "Absatz". The French word "débit" evokes a book-keeping perspective (entering a debit). In English dictionaries, we mostly find the less specific words "distribution", "sales", or "offer" . Sometimes we also find "off-sale", which is less customary but comes closest to "Absatz" or "débit". A flow of money, when considered as incoming, is called "sales price", "revenue", or "income", while the same flow considered as outgoing is a "purchase price" spend-

ours, thus, focuses on (i) the *flow of money* (not so much of goods and services), and (ii) from the point of view of the *dispatcher of money* (who must first have it and then be ready to make the sacrifice and depart therefrom).[25] Furthermore, Quesnay (iii) looks at *actual* flows in executed transactions, not only at potential transactions. In other words, his "ordre des dépenses régulières" is rendered possible by there being people *capable and ready to give money away*. These money-"dépenses" re-appear somewhere else as "revenues" or income and integrate the economy as a whole.

The stocks, flows, quantities and action in the tableau

Quesnay's "dépenses" flow in a *triangle* between the "classe des propriétaires", the "classe productive" and the "classe stérile". Each class has certain physical stock and may also have a certain monetary stock. The cl. des propriétaires owns the land and rents it out to the cl. productive who uses it for production. The cl. productive has made "avances primitives" and "avances annuelles" and sits on money earned from the past year. It produces agricultural goods (grains, plants, animals, meat, wine) and other primary products (wood, minerals, other raw materials) with rented land and supplies them to both the cl. des propriétaires and to the cl. stérile. The cl. stérile also has certain physical "avances primitives"[26] (equipment, tools etc.) and some money and processes the primary goods further (e.g., to construct buildings or to produce clothes or furniture) with handicraft; it distributes them via trade to the cl. des propriétaires and to the cl. productive or renders services to them (as domestic servants, craftspeople, artists, lawyers, generals, priests, forwarders etc.) including by trading the produce of the cl. productive as merchants.

All three classes receive "dépenses" as a consideration for the goods or services delivered, which are their revenues, the cl. des propriétaires receives rent, and the other classes purchase prices or other payments for their services. These "dépenses" motivate and reward either production or, with regards to the cl. des propriétaires, the permission to use their land; they transport "purchasing power" and, in so doing, build the economic system and allow it to go on.

The quantities used by Quesnay in his *tableau* from 1766 have already been outlined in the flow chart above. They show how his system operates. At the beginning of a year, the cl. productive sits on Livres 2 bn. in cash from last year, which it pays as rent to the cl. des propriétaires in exchange for land. The cl. productive also sits on its "avances primitives" of Livres 10 bn., which were made on the land (irrigation

---

ing, expenses, or costs. These multiple terms for connected, or the same things, occasionally cause confusion.

25   This corresponds to Minsky's and Mehrling's observation that capitalism is essentially a financial system (*Mehrling* (2011) page 11).

26   See footnotes 18, 19 on page 207.

systems, fences etc.)[27] and on "avances annuelles" of Livres 2 bn. (seed, horses, oxen, food for laborers, etc.) also from the previous year.

The productivity of the cl. productive allows it to generate an output (in agricultural products and products of primary production) of Livres 5 bn. The cl. stérile sits, aside its physical "avances", on Livres 1 bn. as a stock of money from the preceding year. It uses this money as "avances annuelles" to purchase "matières premières" (primary materials) from the cl. productive and turns them into products and services, which are worth Livres 2 bn.[28] Hence, the cl. productive made Livres 5 bn. worth out of Livres 2 bn., the cl. stérile made Livres 2 bn. worth out of Livres 1 bn and an annual produce of Livres 7 bn. worth comes out of "avances annuelles" of Livres 3 bn in total. The cl. des propriétaires does not produce anything.

The annual produce of commodities and services exists only in kind at this point, e.g., in the storehouses and shops, and the aforementioned Livres values express only *anticipated* sales value ("valeur vénale"). Luckily, the system is set in motion, and everything goes as planned. The sequence is not crucial, but all processes can easily be thought of as financing themselves without additional money stocks as follows: The cl. productive makes "dépenses" of Livres 2 bn. as rent to the cl. propriétaires (flows 1, 2 in the tableau). The cl. stérile makes "dépenses" of Livres 1 bn. for raw materials to the cl. productive out of its stock of Livres 1 bn (flow 3 in the tableau). The cl. des propriétaires' spends the whole rent just received in two directions; it makes "dépenses" of Livres 1 bn. on agricultural produce (meat, grains, wine etc.) to the cl. productive (flow 4) and of Livres 1 bn. to the cl. stérile for processed goods or services (see flow 5), which the cl. stérile has produced in the meantime with the raw materials purchased from the cl. productive previously. The cl. productive can now fill up both its "avances primitives" and "avances annuelles" with purchases of equipment, tools. and maintenance and repair services, etc. from the cl. stérile for Livres 1 bn (flow 6) thereby providing the cash to the latter class, who in turn buys grains, meat, and wine for consumption from the cl. productive (flow 7).[29]

As a result of this round of mutual spending, the class productive still has a significant remainder of its original produce (agricultural and primary products) left, worth Livres 2 bn.; it will use this produce for its own consumption, for the consumption of its laborers, or as seed or for feeding and breeding animals, etc. the following

---

27 It is not completely clear in Quesnay's work whether they were made by the cl. des propriétaires or by the cl. productive. But this is not important for our argument.

28 This shows that the "sterility" of the "classe stérile" cannot possibly mean that it does not produce anything, which is salable for more that its production cost. Quesnay makes this especially clear in two dialogues. See the reprint in: *Cartelier* (2008) page 297 et seq., 357 et seq.

29 See also a somewhat more complicated, and more detailed summary by Marx, based on a "zigzag"-model (Theorien über den Mehrwert, MEW volume 16.1, page 282–290, 304–318.

year. It also still sits on the processed goods and services it bought for Livres 1 bn. from the cl. stérile.

Quesnay calls the Livres 1 bn. of the cl. productive, which is used to purchase processed goods and services from the cl. stérile the "interest" of the cl. productive. He argues that the percentage of this amount of the "avances primitives" (Livres 1 bn./ Livres 10 bn.), i.e., 10 %, would be fair and appropriate and tries to convince the cl. des propriétaires that it ought not to try to infringe upon this amount, given that this would do great damage to agriculture.[30]

If everybody were to concede to Quesnay's prescription, the cl. productive would be able to use the 1 bn. from the cl. stérile to pay for maintenance, repair and to substitute its "avances primitive" or "avances annuelles" and it could reinvest or consume the goods and services, worth Livres 2 bn., which it still holds from its own production. However, the other cash, which the cl. productive has left after the round, i.e., Livres 2 bn., must be paid in full to the cl. propriétaires as rent once again. The cl. stérile keeps the Livres 1 bn. it has left from the sale of processed goods etc. for Livres 2 bn. to purchase primary materials from the cl. productive in the next year (as it did in the present round, flow 3) and consumes the agricultural products purchased. The cl. des propriétaires[31] consumes the purchased agricultural and processed goods and services, including the services of domestics, and expects the rent of Livres 2 bn. to re-start the process the following year once again.

In summary, all classes are restituted into the monetary and other position, including stocks, that they had at the outset after a full round and after having been all fed and entertained throughout the year (to a greater or lesser extent).

As already mentioned, Quesnay, of course, knew about the "quart état" as part of the cl. productive and of the cl. sterile,[32] but he does not go into the internal relations within these two classes, i.e., between farmers, miners, foresters, etc. and their workers or between owners of manufacturing plants, handicraft firms, transport agents, or merchants and their workers. In fact, the quart état or the working class does not appear in the tableau at all, neither as recipient nor expedient of goods or services or money payments. It should also be noted that Quesnay, contrary to Marx's reproduction schemes, does not distinguish between a sector that produces goods for consumption and a sector producing goods for investment.[33]

---

30   E.g. Quesnay in: *Cartelier* (2008) page 96, page 166, page 216.

31   This is also referred to as "la classe des propriétaires du revenue" Quesnay in: *Cartelier* (2008) page 220).

32   See Footnote 20 on page 207.

33   If he had, then both sectors should have been present in the cl. productive as well as in the "cl. stérile".

Quesnay's macro transmissions

Quesnay's macro transmissions indicate the sources of the flows in the tableau, connect profit-making and employment-generating spending and imply a certain complementarity between the productive economy and the wealth economy. As quoted previously, Quesnay's tableau shows "l'ordre de la distribution des dépenses et de la reproduction du revenu par la dépense *même* du revenue"[34] and, in effect, as just seen, all seven flows of "dépenses" were not only financed by what flew to the respective class before, but also reproduce the prior starting positions for the following round. Coming from the basic insight "il ne peut y avoir d'acheteur qu'autant qu'ils sont payés eux-mêmes pour pouvoir acheter...",[35] Quesnay sets up a circular financial flows-structure, which is built on this requirement and closes all circuits. Other wealth – wealth from abroad, credit, and fiat-wealth – is not necessary to close the circuits of the tableau.

If we apply the M–C–M' or C–M–C'-scheme, the rent-"dépenses" by the cl. productive to the cl. des propriétaires (flows 1, 2), the "dépenses" by the cl. stérile to the cl. productive of Livres 1bn. (flow 3), and the dépenses of Livres 1bn. by the cl. productive to the cl. stérile for processed goods and services are, from the perspective of the respective dispatchers, investive M–C-spending. From the perspective of the recipients, they are C–M'-collections or revenues following investive outlays. The "dépenses" of Livres 2 bn. for food, wine, etc. by the cl. propriétaires and by the cl. sterile to the cl. productive are consumptive M–C'-spending (flows 4, 7). The same applies to the "dépenses" of Livres 1bn. by the cl. des propriétaires to the cl. sterile for processed goods and services for consumption (flow 5).

Under the distinction between employment-generating and sterile spending, of the Livres 7 bn "dépenses" of a year in the tableau, the Livres 2 bn. of investive M–C-payments (from the cl. sterile to the cl. productive for raw materials and from the cl. productive to the cl. sterile for processed goods and services of each 1 bn. Livres)[36] are employment-generating spending. Equally, the payments of Livres 3 bn. of consumptive M–C-payments are employment-generating spending (from the cl. des propriétaires to the two other classes for agricultural products and processed goods and services and from the cl. sterile to the cl. productive for agricultural products). The tableau's final flow in are the rent payments of Livres 2 bn. from the cl. productive to the cl. des propriétaires. Assuming that they have no component rewarding the erection of buildings, improvements, repair, and maintenance and they would, thus, be "pure" sterile rent. That, as Quesnay's tableau exemplifies, does not exclude

34   *Quesnay in: Cartelier* (2008) page 190, emphasis added.
35   Including the Livre 2 bn. of rent and the "avances annuelles" of the cl. stérile, which waits in cash as stocks to be transformed into flows." *Quesnay* in: *Cartelier* (2008) page 345.
36   After "carve-outs", as we view it. See on page 123 et seq. and 351 et seq.

that they are highly beneficial and integrative. Without them, the cl. des propriétaires could not keep the wheal turning so generously as it does. It takes the royaume
agricole's "revenu net", consumes it for luxuries and *immediately puts it fully back into
the productive economy*.

Surplus or profit in the tableau is sufficient to nourish all three classes. The cl.
productive begins the years with annual "avances" in kind and Livres 2 bn. and ends
the year with them. During the year, it nourishes itself and draws some enjoyments,
by consuming in kind a part of the difference between its gross produce worth Livres
5 bn. and the sold produce of Livres 3 bn. Equally, the cl. stérile, begins with Livres
1 bn. in cash and some "avances" in kind, consumes purchased agricultural products, say food and wine, but ends where it began, with Livres 1 bn. in cash and some
"avances" in kind. Finally, the cl. des propriétaires begins with its land and a claim for
the rent for the previous year and ends with them again. In between it has fully consumed the preceding year's rent, the "produit net". Hence, all classes in the tableau
finish as they began; none has accumulated additional capital or wealth. The royaume agricole is neither shrinking nor growing; it is, as we have stated previously, a
stationary economy, simple rather than extended reproduction.

Quesnay's cl. des propriétaires deserves special attention. As we already know,
according to Quesnay: "Les propriétaires ... ne produisent rien"[37], and: "les propriétaires sont utiles à l'état que par leur consumation...".[38] While it is quite true that the
cl. des proprietaries does not produce anything, the most astonishing thing about it
in Quesnay's tableau, is the marvelous fact that the cl. des propriétaires *immediately
and fully* consumes its rental income. Whether by benevolence, forward guidance by
a "dieu juste", decadent addiction to luxury, or for whatever reason, we do not know;
but they do the right thing and fill the gap by this maximum generous consumption,
thereby vindicating the toil of the cl. productive and of the cl. stérile, allowing them
to close their circuits. *Quesnay's wealth owners, in fact, do almost exactly the opposite of
what normal wealth owners do*. Normal wealth owners even shift employment-generating revenues into sterile investments; Quesnay's wealth owners immediately and
fully re-inject sterile wealth revenues into the productive economy. There is no flight
of Quesnay's wealth owners from the productive economy by acquiring wealth assets, not of sovereign debt, not of stock, firms, gold or other valuables, not even of
land and of existing country side chateaux. Quesnay's wealth owners also do not

---

37 *Quesnay* in: *Cartelier* (2008) page 3.
38 The quotation continues: "...si leurs revenues n'étaient pas distribués au professions lucra-
    tives, l'État se dépeuplerait par l'avarice de ses propriétaires injustes et perfides" cited after
    Cartelier (2008) page 36. Providing land is immensely important from a value-in-use per-
    spective and it is remarkable that Quesnay, writing in an absolute monarchy and handing
    over his work to the king, misses the opportunity to mention this contribution, at least in
    addition to their consumption.

speculate to seek capital gains. What will become a political request of utmost importance in Sismondi's, Malthus' and Keynes' thinking, the wealth owners in the organism contrived by Docteur Quesnay already silently comply with. This, the immediate re-injection of everything, which leaves the productive economy as a sterile "tribute" to wealth owners, together with the cl. productive and the cl. stérile also immediately spending the full amounts of their revenues in the productive economy, is the secret of Quesnay's circuits closure. In real life, unfortunately, a significant part of what moves in the sterile economy, stays there.

Disorder and growth in the tableau

Quesnay exposes the problem of whether sufficient "dépenses" can be generated to integrate and reproduce the capitalist spending flows, by showing that the problem is automatically taken care of. This built-in teleology or the *entelechia* in his tableau (or should we speak about *nomoi* or his *universalia in res?*) do, though, not forestall the possibility of deviations. Given that Quesnay, following the design of his theory, does not have a philosophy of history or a theory of economic evolution, such deviations must, yet, be perceived as disorder or like an illness. This is precisely why Quesnay tries to lobby and educate his classes to behave as they should behave.[39] The tableau not only shows how things are, but it is also a proscriptive plan for behavior.

Furthermore, it allows us to reflect on the possible origins and consequences of disorder and on possible remedies thereto: If the cl. des propriétaires were, against Quesnay's guidance, to increase the rent payable by the cl. productive to Livres 3 bn. (and infringe upon what Quesnay considers the fair "interest" of the cl. productive on their "avances primitives"), then the cl. productive would lose Livres 1 bn., which it could spend on maintenance, repair and spare parts and its "avances primitives" would degenerate. The productivity and output of the cl. productive would, accordingly, soon fall. Of course, it could also only buy less from the cl. stérile. Alternatively, the cl. des propriétaires might buy luxury goods and services from suppliers outside of the tableau, e.g., from abroad. This would diminish the money flows to the domestic cl. stérile who would then have to cut back its "dépenses" to the cl. productive, whose reduced income would lead to reduced production and consumption of the cl. stérile. Disturbances can also originate from the sphere of the cl. productive. Natural catastrophes or war can either reduce or destroy harvests or seeds needed for the years to come. Cattle needed for breeding can be eaten up, thereby bringing the production down and leading to the human population's undernourishment.

If the cl. des proprietaries were to engage in war, financed by a reduction of food or luxury consumption, conversely, this might only lead to a repartitioning of his purchases from both the cl. productive and the cl. stérile. The cl. des proprietaries

---

39   See footnote 8 on page 204.

would possibly buy fewer agricultural luxury consumption goods, but likely more simple food for soldiers from the cl. productive. It would also likely buy additional armament, and have more castles and ships, etc., built by the cl. stérile, but would purchase less silk, furniture, artwork, and domestic services from it. If there is an aggregate increase of "dépenses" to the cl. stérile, then it should, in turn, increase its "dépenses" to the cl. productive for raw materials (which may thereby be enabled to pay higher rent to the cl. des proprietaries). The tableau, thus, not only allows for changes between a more Spartan or Puritan and a more luxurious or decadent or catholic lifestyle, but also for aggregate overall growth, provided this can be financed from available stocks of wealth, credit, or from fiat wealth. The economy may grow and re-settle in "sync" at a higher output level.

***

Quesnay's tableau gives us several important introductory insights upon circuit closure. *First*, it teaches us that subjecting the biological and cultural reproduction of mankind to an economic system, even one subjected to the profit criterion (the M–C–M'-requirement), *can* function like an integrated organism *if* certain numeric preconditions are met. *Second*, he shows that the value-in-use-side poses no un-solvable problem. Frictions might arise if the cl. proprietaries had no land, or no good land at least, or if the cl. productive or if the cl. stérile were incompetent or unwilling to produce the primary goods or processed goods or services in proper quality and quantity in relation to the effectual demand of the other classes. (This is basically in agreement with Marx's reproduction schemes, in which the value-in-use-dimension appears to be even more of a concern.) The *third* requirement – the integration must be achieved through exchanges that fulfill the demands of the M–C–M'-logic, hence, enabling profit – is stickier. This was, in fact, the crucial hurdle for Quesnay. How can the circuits close and, simultaneously, profit be made? Or, more specifically, how can the three classes make "dépenses" to each other, which equip each other to make their "dépenses", yet still allow them all to make profit?

We studied what his numbers and his numeric narrative implied on how profit-making and circuit closure could coexist. The finding can be expressed in sober terms in the following way: If no additional money arrives, to enable circuit closure, then those who generate new value-in-exchange *in the form of produce* must give the same amount of value-in-exchange *in the form of money* to somebody who will use the money received to buy produce in its full amount therewith.[40] For the "revenu net" (in money form) to be able to buy the "produit net" (in kind, in commodity-

---

40 "Quoi qu'il en soit, le point essentiel est l'existence d'un flux de paiements qui ne sont pas représentatif d'un coût... Pour que se forme un revenu monétaire net au plan global, il est

form) money must, thus, travel from the value-in-exchange-creating class to the vindicating and rewarding classes that buy the produce in the very same amount. This is quite similar to the producing class having to buy the produce from itself, except for the being one change of money ownership in between. Quesnay uses legal property relations, the owner-power of the cl. des propriétaires over their land to justify this critical transfer rent-payments. Thereby, his solution comes mostly from the land-owning and rent-absorbing (but not producing) cl. des propriétaires, which, very gratefully, if unproductive, turns out to be a class of very hungry big spenders.[41]

Quesnay has posed the eternal question of macroeconomics of capitalism in the paradoxical way of presenting it as being solved for eternity. When he gave his answer, he reverted from a high-concept-question to a rather naïve pre-ordained numeric solution,[42] which was metaphysical and premodern methodologically. Of course, Quesnay's answer was, unfortunately, false in substance: Landowners (or sterile wealth owners in general) do *not* save capitalist circuit closure by using their sterile revenues for consumptive employment-generating spending. Quesnay was still happy with his answer, not only because it pleased his organistic theoretical bias, but also because it supported corollaries which pleased his political preferences in favor of capitalist agriculture.[43] Sismondi, Malthus, Keynes, Luxemburg, Kalecki, and others adopted Quesnay's modern and systemic question, but freed

---

nécessaire qu'une partie de la dépense consiste en l'anticipation de ce revenu net." (*Cartelier* (2008) page 45, italics in the original).

41   Marx would later attack Malthus for allowing for the existence of such a class, see on page 257 et seq. There is, actually, a very similar structure in Marx's work: In Marx, the working class is the class that solely generates new value-in-exchange, a sub-component of Quesnay's classe productive and of his classe stérile, if You like. The value-in-exchange generated is appropriated by the capitalist class by legally acquiring ownership of the produce, which results, as in Quesnay, from owners' power and social rules (the inventories remain in the ownership of the capitalists even after having been processed by the workers). Marx's capitalist class, though, receives the new value-in-exchange, the surplus, not already as monetary rent (as in Quesnay), but still in kind, as produce C'. Therefore, the capitalists has to go through an additional stage to enable themselves to assume the role of Quesnay's classe des propriétaires. They must – paradoxically – sell their produce C', in particular its part representing the surplus (C'-C), which they can only sell to each other, in order to enable themselves to buy just this surplus-part C'-C (or M'-M) from each other.

42   He had access to statistical data and must have adjusted them so that they matched, either by trial and error or some kind of interpolation.

43   Marx saw the physiocrats as preparing the French Revolution. Particularly, he saw *Turgot* as a radical "bourgeois-minister" who "preluded the French Revolution". With all their "false feudal appearance, the physiocrats worked hand in hand with the encyclopaedists." (*Marx*, Theorien über den Mehrwert, MEW 26.1 page 24, 37, translated by the author).

themselves from his methodological and substantial limitations in trying to answer it.

Section 3. Smith: An invisible hand over suppliers and customers

Because he made no progress beyond Quesnay in the matter of circuit closure Adam Smith plays no major role in this book. He is still considered at some length for two reasons. First, unlike most economists today, being a man of great historic and philosophic knowledge, he was able to show what freedom and liberty (or, in our words: owner power) did in the economic realm; insofar he stands in the great natural law tradition of, e.g., Hobbes, Pufendorf, or Montesquieu, which already guarantees his historical longevity. In particular, he described how owners' power transforms into an abstract discipline of economic liberty, which not only keeps the greed of merchants within bearable limits, but also erects a benevolent automatic general motivational and steering system that favors productivity, consumer orientation, economic growth, and prosperity. Second, Smith stood between Quesnay and Ricardo with regards to the problem of circuit closure. Quesnay had seen the problem and he had set up the just introduced model, which is has remained valid for reflecting on it up to today. Ricardo also saw the problem, but used what he falsely called the "Law of Say" to pseudo-solve it.[44] Smith found himself between the two. He either did not see the problem or somehow considered it as solved; at least it played no relevant role in his work. Note that Smith's famous "invisible hand" was *not* meant to be a solution to the problem; the "invisible hand" was only meant to solve another, smaller problem, as we shall see.

Smith, as an economist, supported the physiocrats. Smith spoke of their work with admiration as the "agricultural system".[45] When Quesnay and the physiocrats had been pro-economic liberty, such economic liberty was, to a good deal, a conscient means to play merchants off against other merchants, about whom

---

44   We shall give three interpretations of, what we will call "Ricardo's Law of Say" below. Two are false statements while the third one is a valuable reformulation of the question the "law" is supposed to answer.

45   *Smith* (1776) page 1–3. As Smith says, all major European powers had adhered to the mercantile system since at least the colonization of the Americas, while the agricultural system (the physiocrats who called themselves "les économistes") would have "never been adopted by any nation and... exists only in the speculation of a few men of great learning and ingenuity in France." (Book IV chapter IX, volume II page 157). Smith rightly mentions that Egypt, Indostan, and China (and even Greece and Rome) often pursued policies akin to the agricultural system several times (Book IV chapter IX, volume II page 173–181). *Leon Walras* noted that the word "physiocray"" contains the Greek word for rule. It means "gouvernement naturel de la société" (*Walras* (1874) page 3).

physiocrats, like certain policies in ancient China, had always been quite suspicious. Economic liberty enabled competition and competition helped to discipline merchants to remain in the pre-conceived plan of the tableau and not to grow too wealthy or too powerful.[46] Smith embraced the physiocrats preference for economic liberty, but took it out of its narrow context. "Perfect economic liberty", was to be fully let out of the bottle and invited to take general control over the economy.[47] The economy was, as von Hayek would later say, a "discovery procedure" (Entdeckungsverfahren), a permanent auto-adjustment-process or, in the later wording of *Walras* a (progressive, multi-level, and multi-place) "tâtonnement".[48] Even the word "plan" or Quesnay's "ordre", which could be modeled in an idealized macroeconomic blueprint were, thus, improper in a formal sense. Men observe prices and try to maximize utility and profit conscientiously in their elementary exchanges and "markets" turn thousands or millions of such conscientious actions into an automatic play of liberty. When Smith speaks of an "invisible hand", thus, he not only means "invisible", but also "thoughtless", "mind-free", "automatic", or "blind" – resembling blindfolded Justitia. Nevertheless, the system will move towards a common good. Free markets, Smith believed, give better guidance to production than family, clan, or tribe traditions, religion, morals, philosophical convictions, or even paternalistic mercantilist bureaucrats. Economic liberty and competition bring about the greatest increase of effectivity, efficiency, and wealth, provided that it was simply left alone!

While Smith departed from the suspicion of physiocracy against merchants and from the narrow intent of using competition as a tool to control them, Smith, nevertheless, put great emphasis on the market's disciplinary power. The old method of disciplining (by state power, morals, and tradition) can be substituted by a new anonymous market discipline. Much less communicative, administrative, or legal state guidance will be required; instead, the (rather brutal) discipline of economic success and failure, purely economic sanctions, will largely take its place. The dark and nasty force behind the discipline of liberty, which definitively goes into men's Benthamian calculus of pleasure and pain, is the risk of failure. The terror-side of economic liberty, the "hand" if you will, is the threat of falling out of the upper

---

46   "Qu'on maintienne l'entière liberté du commerce; car LA POLICE DU COMMERCE INTÉRIEUR ET EXTÉRIEUR, LA PLUS SÛRE, LA PLUS EXACTE, LA PLUS PROFITABLE À LA NATION ET À L'ÉTAT, CONSISTE DANS LA PLAINE LIBERTÉ DE LA CONCURRENCE" (Quesnay in: *Cartelier* (2008) page 244).

47   At least in principle. Smith did not deny occasional mercantilist or pro-colonialist restrictive state interference.

48   *Walras* (1874) page 127 ("Il s'agit de fonder sur le fait de cette détermination sans calcul une méthode de résolution par tâtonnement des équitations d'égalité de l'offre et de la demande totale." The term "tâtonnement" was used previously by Turgot. See *Faccarello* in: *Faccarello/ Kurz* (2016) page 80.

society into being disrespected, suffering, hunger, and death, the lower world of losers. In "a civilized society" in which this discipline operates, Smith writes, "men stand at all times in the need of cooperation and assistance of great multitudes".[49] This awareness of their (abstract) dependency (to great multitudes) very effectively directs each player's self-interest to contributions that supply necessities, conveniences, and amusements to others. This view culminates in the famous words: "[I]t is not from the benevolence of the butcher, the baker or the brewer that we expect our dinner, but from their regard to their own interest. We address ourselves, not to their humanity but to their self-love, and never talk to them about our necessities but of their advantages."[50]

Smith's discipline is not limited to villages, small towns, or even cities like Manchester or London, though. It subjugates human behavior in countries, continents, and the world market. Smith has particularly become famous for the aforementioned metaphor of an "invisible hand". He analyzes: "Every individual is continually exerting himself to find out the most advantageous employment for whatever capital he can command. It is his advantage, indeed, and not that of the society, which he has in view. But the study of his own advantage, naturally, or rather necessarily, leads him to prefer the employment which is most advantageous to the society."[51] He then writes that "... he intends only his own gain, and he is... led by an invisible hand to promote an end which was no part of his intention".[52] So much for Smith's analysis of economic liberty.

Unfortunately, Smith also abandoned the theoretical interest of physiocracy in capitalism's capacity for macroeconomic circuit closure. Smith wrote twenty years after the physiocrats and had the luck to live through the industrial revolution in the most advanced capitalist country, which dominated the world technologically, politically, militarily, economically and culturally. Britain and the British Commonwealth, it may have appeared to him, would be able not only to secure much-needed imports of cheap raw materials, but also to export the processed goods in the whatever quantities. In this context he expressly speaks of the discovery of America as "opening a new and *inexhaustible* (sic!) market to all the commodities of Europe".[53] Smith, obviously, did not share Quesnay's worries concerning sufficient dépenses. If he at all ever thought about them, he might at least have felt that they should not be an issue for advanced and world-dominating Britain.

The problem of circuit closure, accordingly, is not present in Smith's work. Smith' famous term "invisible hand" does not prove the opposite. Smith's "hand" is defini-

---

49   *Smith* (1776) page 12.
50   *Smith* (1776) page 13.
51   *Smith* (1776) page 398.
52   *Smith* (1776) page 400.
53   *Smith* (1776) page 393.

tively not a forerunner of Ricardo's law of Say and does not secure that there are no non-owners, which cannot be employed. Smith is, of course, aware that supply must be demanded, that produce must be bought, and that only this will engender the employment of workers, but he neither presented this as a limiting factor for employment, nor his "hand" as the assurance that such limits would be overcome. This can be further explained in two ways. We may, first, consider the playing field, to which Smith' theory of social discipline through economic liberty applies, and where the invisible hand operates so benevolently (assigning the highest profits to those suppliers who serve customers best), as being, from the outset, silently limited to the *beati possidentes*. Hence, to those who, as customers, have sufficient money or, as suppliers, are owners of sufficiently valued goods. Would-be-customers and would-be-suppliers, who don't make it to become customers or suppliers, are systematically forgotten. The invisible hand rules markets – but in markets they are not, or they do not matter there. When Smith speaks of markets, and about the direct production of what is "most advantageous to society",[54] he only has in mind those who are at least marginal and occasional customers and suppliers. They certainly get better goods at more places, faster and more cheaply (or low-priced and low-quality-goods at all). Smith also has sellers in mind. They were buyers once, before they sold, and could buy their supplies at more places, faster and more cheaply and at reduced costs of transportation, etc. They can also use their owner power and buyer's competition to sell their goods to high value-ascribers with money at higher prices. The general increase in productivity will render countries of economic liberty richer than others, from which the public, including the poorer classes, will profit – as a spill over. There will be more and better roads and bridges and sidewalks in muddy city streets as well as more and better military barracks, uniforms and riffles for drawn conscripts. There will be nicer administration buildings and more modern prisons (of the Benthamian style?) and, hopefully, even better water and energy supplies to working class neighborhoods, improved public schools, medical treatment and more generous social security. Yet, just because the invisible hand cannot see money coming from the "have nots", it will not direct production to them, e.g., of housing or food to unemployed.

Or, second, we may view the "invisible hand" as also applying to the have nots. If it reacted to the "haves" through the inclusive and luring algorithm of "I give you more profit, the better you adjust to customer needs", what is its algorithm for the "have nots"? What does it tell the underworld of incapables, failures, the continuous inflow of losers, and what does it do with them? Well, if the "invisible hand" at all takes cares of them, it applies some sort of "to each his own" (suum cuique) to them. They get all the negative and bad stuff. Quite simply, it tells them in an exclusive and

---

54   In the above quote.

rejective way: "You are out. Go to hell and stay there!". There is no point in producing food or clothes (or even in constructing dwellings) for those who cannot pay a profitable price. Nobody will employ an old unskilled worker...The "no haves" get the hard stuff from the invisible hand. They are damned like the *non-electi* in Manichaean religions. That may seal the fate of whole social strata or even of continents.

Smith' "invisible hand", thus, does not state that circuit closure will be achieved, but only describes the – more or less pleasant – mechanism of markets discipline. E.g., where he thinks of a "proportion of those who are annually employed in useful labour, and ... of those who are not so employed....", he observes the "number of useful and productive labourers, it will hereafter appear, is everywhere in proportion to the *quantity of capital stock* which is applied to setting them to work and to the particular way in which it is so employed."[55] That is all. But he neither states that the capital stock will grow so large nor that it will be activated to such an extent as to generally achieve full employment. Nevertheless, he generally assumes that the produce can be sold by British firms somewhere and insofar Smith's "invisible hand" operates before a background of primordial inexhaustible sales markets, at least for English firms. He is not seriously interested in how certain benevolent hinterlands render this possible. Where he touches upon the issue, this appears to have happened by chance. Smith makes no attempt at a systematic theorical investigation in this question,[56] and his few dispersed remarks on it remain superficial.[57]

---

55   *Smith* (1776) page 2 (both quotes).

56   A more abstract reflection by Smith reads: "The extent of the home-trade and of the capital which can be employed in it, is necessarily limited by the value of the surplus produce of all those distant places within the country which have occasion to exchange their respective productions with another: that of the foreign trade of consumption, by the value of the surplus produce of the whole country and of what can be purchased with it: that of the carrying trade by the value of the surplus produce of all the different countries in the world. Its possible extent, therefore, is in a manner infinite in comparison of that of the other two, and is capable of absorbing the greatest capitals" (*Smith* (1776) page 334). Apart from a lack of clarity about the notion of "surplus" in the context, the quote does not provide any insight into the dependencies between the production of exchangeable value. Smith discusses the distribution of the annual produce among the three classes in Quesnay's tableau économique in a manner that "each class enjoys its proper share", even though he considers the possibility of encroachments of "that natural distribution", but he shows no interest in preoccupying himself more deeply with the interrelations between Quesnay's system of supply creation and demand creation (*Smith* (1776) page 167).

57   E.g. he says: "The great affair, we always find, is to get money. When that is obtained, there is no difficulty in making any subsequent purchase" (*Smith* (1776) page 375). He also mentions public mournings as increasing demand for black clothes (*Smith* (1776) page 104) and he points to high duties or prohibitions of trade impairing the demand for British produce: "By diminishing the number of sellers, therefore, we necessarily diminish that of buyers, and are thus likely not only to buy foreign goods dearer, but to sell our own cheaper, than if there was a more perfect freedom of trade." (*Smith* (1776) page 408). He is also aware that there is

After Smith had died in 1790, the economic situation in the UK and in Europe changed significantly. 15 years of Napoleonic wars incited a build-up of production, especially in the UK and France, and when the armament demand discontinued, in the absence of some kind of Marshall plan and of other expansion options, capacities were far too large for peace production. Ricardo, Say, Sismondi, and Malthus, accordingly, voiced unanimous complaints about a great "engorgement" of markets. The impression of these post-war years, a good decade, must have been similarly important for economic thinking of the time as the Great Depression would be 110 years later. It contributed, as in the 20th century, to shape two camps in macroeconomics, one camp, Ricardo and Mill in particular, remained convinced that missing employment-generating spending still did not have to be a systematic concern, and an opposing camp, Proudhon, Sismondi and Malthus in particular, that took the opposite view. The camps developed in parallel and argued against each other. The camp of Proudhon, Sismondi, and Malthus, in essence, aimed to set free the analytical potential of Quesnay's circuit analysis by giving up the catechism-like numeric preordainment that circuit would close and to consider whether or not circuits would close as a conscient contingent problem. The other camp, Ricardo and Mill, too, could no longer sidestep the question of where sufficient demand would come from, as Smith had. They tackled it by throwing in something for economists and the public to chew on; Ricardo invented the "Law of Say".

Section 4. Proudhon and Sismondi: Producers cannot buy their produce

But we first turn to Proudhon and Sismondi. In the *Grundrisse*, Marx labeled *Pierre Joseph Proudhon* as somebody "who certainly hears the bells ringing but never knows where". Marx therewith reacted to Proudhon explaining overproduction with the fact "that the worker cannot buy back his product".[58] We do not pursue Proudhon, Robert Owen, or other early utopian socialists any further, but will instead turn to *Jean Charles L. Simonde de Sismondi* (1773–1842), a man of higher intellectual caliber. Like Adam Smith, he was of deep historic knowledge and developed his economic ideas in a concise and scientific way. The first edition of his *Nouveaux Principes*

---

a feedback from investment to demand and that "...a capital employed in home trade...puts into motion a greater quantity of domestic industry, and gives revenue and employment to a greater number of the inhabitants of the country..." (*Smith* (1776) page 399). Marx wrote much to the point about Smith: "Die Widersprüche A. Smith's haben das Bedeutende, dass sie Probleme enthalten, die er zwar nicht löst, aber dadurch ausspricht, dass er sich widerspricht". *Marx*, Theorien über den Mehrwert, MEW 26.1, page 121. E.g. Smith's theory of value oscillates between a labor theory of value and something else.

58   *Marx*, Grundrisse, MEW 42, page 338.

d'Économie politique ou de la Richesse dans ses Rapports avec la Population was published in 1819[59], one year before Malthus' *Principles of Political Economy*. Both authors have great similarities in important regards and saw themselves as jointly battling against Ricardo and his disciples. Sismondi wrote three articles that were republished in the second edition of his *Nouveaux Principes* of 1827 and that he collectively entitled "Clarifications concerning the balance of consumptions with productions".[60] These articles and chapter VI of volume I of the *Nouveaux Principes* contain the essence of Sismondi's contribution to the question of employment-generating spending, which he called "the fundamental question of political economy".[61]

In his first article,[62] he states a "universal congestion" of the markets after the end of the Napoleonic wars and explains it by the fact that only revenue may or may not put "everybody into the position to buy his part of the annual produce" as "the revenue of all is not the same thing as the produce of the work of all". It is "possible that the produce increases and that the revenue is diminished, that the stores fill up, but that purses empty...".[63] More generally, Sismondi reproaches Ricardo and his disciples in the second article for falsely believing that by "creating objects of exchange one creates exchanges".[64] Against McCulloch's statement that "the production of one kind of a good constitutes the demand for another"[65] he contends that the price of a commodity is influenced by two elements: "He who wants to dispose of a product certainly calculates what it costs him; but he who wants to buy the product...

---

59   *Sismondi* (1827).

60   *Sismondi* (1827) page 369 et seq

61   *Sismondi* (1827) page 439 "...la question fondamentale de l'économie politique est ... la balance de la consommation avec la production...".

62   Originally published under the title "Examen de cette question: Le pouvoir de consommer s'accroît-il toujours dans las société avec le pouvoir de produire?" in "Annales de jurisprudence de docteur Rossi" of 1820. The article critized an anomimous article in the Edinburg Review (volume XXXII, 1819) by, as Sismondi later learned, John Ramsey McCulloch (*Sismondi* (1827) page 376). McCulloch became a leader of the Ricardo school after Ricardo's death. In Schumpeter's words, he was "roughly handled", did not add "anything substantial" and the "touches" that he did add were of "doubtful value" (*Schumpeter* (1954) page 477, 478).

63   *Sismondi* (1827) page 375 (translation by author). The original reads: "Je l'ai expliqué par une théorie, que je crois nouvelle, sur la nature du revenue, qui met chacun en état d'acheter sa part du produit annuel. J'ai cherché à faire voire comme le revenu de tous n'est pas la même chose que le produit du travail de tous; en sorte qu'il est possible que le produit s'accroisse, et que le revenu se diminue, que les magasins se remplissent, et que le bourses se vident...".

64   "Aux yieux de MM. Say et Ricardo, en créant des objets à échanger on crée des échanges...". (*Sismondi* (1827) page 414).

65   Retranslated by the author into English from French. Sismondi's French translation reads: "La production d'une espèce de bien constitue la demande de l'autre". (*Sismondi* (1827) page 378). McCulloch's quote already states "Ricardo's Law of Say". "*Une* demande" would be correct, "*la* demande" ist overstretched.

decides by two motives, which do not have any relationship with the costs of production, i.e., his need first and then his means to pay. The combination of these two elements and their proportion with the product built a demand that may be stronger or weaker than the price of production." There will be no demand in either case if a prospective counter-party has no desire for the product or if it cannot or does not want to make the "sacrifice" of the money payment.[66] We are in full agreement with Sismondi here.

Sismondi attacks McCulloch and Ricardo for creating a "hypothetical world" that only makes their argument appear to work. McCulloch, Sismondi claims, "supposes work without profit, a reproduction, which just only replaces the consumption of workers". He "supposes masters and workers, but he does not leave anything left for the masters", but, "if those do not have any part, do not have any profit, they can't either have any interest to make the work continue... This false supposition affects the base of the whole reasoning. In the moment we seek what will become the surplus of the production of the workers over their consumption, one cannot make abstraction of this surplus, which forms the necessary profit of the work and the necessary part of the masters."[67] This is the deepest thought in Sismondi's argument. The motivational structure in the economic system, which is superimposed over goods procurement in a profit economy, requires a reward, the profit, for those – the "maîtres" – who invest capital and keep the system chugging along. However, that profit must come from somewhere – and it can only come from selling produce that the workers alone cannot buy. Their salaries reflect only a component of the produce and cannot be high enough to buy the whole produce. For completeness, outlays to other capitalists must be included. Thus, it must be left to the capitalist to buy the produce

---

66 *Sismondi* (1827) page 379, as translated by the author. The original reads: "Celui qui veut se défaire d'un produit fait bien son compte d'après ce qu'il a coûté; mais celui qui veut acheter ce produit, celui qui le *demande*, se détermine par deux motifs qui n'ont aucune relation avec les frais de production, savoir, son besoin d'abord, puis son moyen de payer. La combinaison de ces deux éléments et leur proportion avec le produit composent une demande qui peut être ou plus forte ou plus faible que le prix de production." "Il n'y a non plus aucune demande quand celui qui désire la chose produite n'a aucun superflu a donner en échange, ou ne veut pas faire, pour l'avoir, le le sacrifice qu'on exige de lui" (italics in the original). Sismondi uses the word "sacrifice" several times in this context, e.g. again on page 381 and 385.

67 The French original reads: "Et, d'abord l'auteur suppose un travail sans bénéfice, une reproduction qui ne fait que remplacer tout juste la consommation *des ouvriers*...il suppose des maîtres et des ouvriers, mais il ne laisse rien pour la part des maîtres. Cependant, si ceux-ci n'ont aucune part, n'ont aucun bénéfice, ils ne peuvent avoir non plus aucun intérêt à faire continuer le travail.... Cette fausse supposition porte sur la base de tout le raisonnement. Au moment où nous cherchons ce qui devient le surplus de la production des ouvriers, il ne faut pas faire l'abstraction de ce surplus qui forme le bénéfice nécessaire du travail et la part nécessaire du maître." (*Sismondi* (1827) page 384).

representing an add-up beyond their outlays; the surplus-part of commodities must be bought by the masters to provide the masters with a surplus in money.

These purchases alone (necessary for a profit and to motivate the system to go on) cannot be explained as easily as the purchases by the workers. Quite obviously, Sismondi's reasoning here foreshadows the reasoning of others that followed. Demand, esoteric, effective, and effectual, for the v-part and c-part of the produce (or the part for which recovery of M will be sought) can be explained by workers' demand (the v-component) and suppliers' demand (the c-component), but the expected excess s (= M'-M), which alone allows profit, cannot be explained that way. Sismondi debunks insufficient demand of "masters", i.e., insufficient spending of M'-M, as the problem and tries to explain it mostly from value-in-use-related aspects. However, he does not yet use a distinction between the productive and the wealth economy and does not discover the hunt for profit in the wealth economy as the main cause for deficient circuit closure in the productive economy.

In the second article,[68] Sismondi further addresses the views of Say and Ricardo that "by creating objects for exchange, one creates exchanges".[69] In essence, he gives two arguments for why their views are wrong. First, the "created objects for exchange" (on the other side of the markets, the produce of Alter, which Say and Ricardo expect to buy the products of Ego) may, unfortunately, not be attributed with sufficient value-in-use and value-in-exchange by Ego. It depends on value-attribution by Ego how much Alter can buy with his products and the production of Alter may create less purchase power than for what Alter would be happy to sell. However, if Ego does not buy the whole produce from Alter at a price, which is profitable and, thus, acceptable for Alter, Alter's M', then Alter will also be unable to buy Ego's produce at Ego's M'. In other words: Because Alter does not attribute enough value-in-exchange to Ego's produce to reach Ego's M', which only validates Ego's investment, Ego will be unable to exchange his produce for Alter's M', which only validates Alter's investment. Economists who hold the power of market adjustments very highly may contend that Alter will simply take the loss, sell at a lower price, and go on to new investments. It is true that the profit principle will induce Alter to further investments (albeit possibly more carefully and more in the sterile economy). Yet, the contention oversees that Ego is already infected and that the damage has already happened: Alter's bad investment has compromised the chances for (even a possibly sounder) investment of Ego and already initiated a depressing wave in the economy (other depressing moments will arise from other aspects that we will consider later). Second,

---

68   Originally "Sur la balance des consommations avec les productions", Revue encyclodpédique, Mai 1824, tome XXII.

69   *Sismondi* (1827) page 414, translated by the author. The transformation of Say's Law of Say into Ricardo's Law of Say is now more explicit.

Sismondi reiterates his point that if a production by Alter happily enjoys the ascription of its target value-in-exchange M' by some Egos, then that may not be the Egos with the money. The money M' must be in the hands of the Ego who has the "needs"; needs must be "united with means of exchange". Accordingly, it does not "suffice to only create these means of exchange" but that they must "also pass into the hands of those who (have) the desires or needs...". Sismondi, in particular, points to a problem concerning the procurement of means of exchange for the most reliable of all would-be-consumers: "Rather it often happened that the means of exchange were increased in the society while the demand for labor or the wages were diminished; accordingly the desires and needs of one part of the population could not be satisfied, and the consumption also diminished."[70] If we stipulate that "esoteric" demand cannot attribute value-in-exchange, then the second argument obviously merges with the first one. The crucial point here is the circular dependency.

Sismondi also develops the idea of a circular dependency at the level of a national economy in Chapter VI of volume I of his *Nouveaux Principes*. This resembles Quesnay's tableau, but Sismondi does not use fixed classes, only functional roles. In the positive case, "a prompt and complete consumption determines always a superior reproduction"[71] and the "circle can extend itself and can change to a spiral";[72] hence, growth occurs. In the negative case, "riches that have not found their destination [to be purchased by the market, G.W.] stop the reproduction of an equal quantity which it must replace".[73] Sismondi compares this to a lonely individual, who stops working once he has the food, clothing, and housing he needs.[74] "Society is exactly like this man...it does not want food any more if there is nobody to eat it...". Yet, he knows that things are worse in a profit economy: "...the limits that consumption sets to the reproduction makes themselves even much more felt in society than in a lonely man: even if society may count a great number of individuals malnourished, poorly dressed and poorly housed, ... it only can buy with its revenue".[75] The immediate connection, which existed in a single Robinson Crusoe, and of which we are reminded by Sismondi's example, is cut through. Hunger, the need for clothing, and for housing are no longer immediately felt reasons, at the societal level, to produce more. Rather,

---

70 *Sismondi* (1827) page 409, quotes translated by the author.
71 *Sismondi* (1827) page 113, translated by the author.
72 *Sismondi* (1827) page 120, translated by the author.
73 *Sismondi* (1827) page 177, translated by the author.
74 Sismondi (1827) page 177.
75 *Sismondi* (1827) page 117. The original reads: "Mais la borne que la consommation met à la reproduction se fait encore bien plus sentir dans la société que dans l'individu isolé; alore même que la société compte un très-grand nombre d'individus mal nourris, mal vêtus, mal logés, elle ne veut que ce qu'elle peut acheter; et comme nous l'avons vu, elle ne peut acheter que avec son revenu."

a new system of incentives is established between value-in-use-needs and production. Production is now only moved by profit expectations; hence, expectations of sufficient employment-generating spending – not by hunger or the need for either clothing or shelter. Production decisions are only made with a view to people being able to pay for them, not with a view to people in need of products. Therefore, it is particularly important whether non-owners (or only-owners-of-working-capacity) can manage to procure the means of exchange. They can only consume if they draw a revenue; this, however, they can only do if wealth owners use their capital for investments and buy their labor by paying salaries to them in order to generate profits.[76]

***

In summary, we have a market or buyer-determined theory of value in Sismondi (attribution of value-in-exchange based on utilities and value-in-use), and the insight that prospective value-attributers need sufficient value-in-exchange or money to make purchases. Sismondi explicitly pronounces what was implicit in Quesnay's work. Quesnay's axiomatic machine solved the problem, albeit without talking about it explicitly, by moving sufficient value-in-exchange to the place where it was needed when it was needed. Sismondi (and Proudhon, etc.) hit the nail on the head of what happens when Quesnay's axioms stop working. The idea comes to the fore that capitalism's profit motive could turn itself against the peaceful closure of the circuits in Quesnay's tableau. In this way, of course, the profit motive turns against one condition of its success and against itself and an antinomy opens up. Sismondi already sees that this antinomy will drive its way into prosthetics and into seeking complementary demand from abroad: "Toutes les grandes demandes sont venues de L'Amérique espagnole, ou aucun obstacle n'empêche point plus introduction des marchandises Européennes, où la guerre, allumée dans toutes les provinces, consomme beaucoup et produit peu, où de fortes passions populaires, excitées en même temps, font consacrer les capitaux, au lieu des revenus, à l'achat des armes et des marchandises que fournit L'Angleterre." At this point, Sismondi adds a footnote: "Nous avons vu… quels ont été les résultats de cette activité artificelle; comment les Anglais ont fourni eux-mêmes l'argent avec lequel leurs marchandises ont été achetées et consommées par les étrangers, et comment, depuis qu'ils ont cessé de prêter à leurs chalands, ceux-ci ont cessé d'acheter."[77] As this quotation shows, Sismondi not only develops prosthetics out of deficient employment-generating spending, but also even anticipates their dilemmas and exhaustion at cases.

---

76   Sismondi places great emphaisis on this point. "La détresse des manufacturiers est la plus cruelle, parce qu'à la différence des agriculteurs leur subsistance tout entière dépend des échanges." (*Sismondi* (1827) page 405).

77   *Sismondi* (1827) page 415.

Section 5. Malthus: Costs cannot buy value[78]

Principle of Population: needed food supply vs production

In his 1798 *Essay on the Principle of Population*, Thomas Malthus (1776 – 1834) developed the idea of mankind being a predator, while food (grains, plants, animals) was the prey. Mankind can multiply faster than food and, hence, its growth will be unavoidably limited, or as Malthus says "checked", by the food supply. This gap is growing. An "arithmetical" increase of food supplies (prey) will be less and less sufficient to the increased number of humans, who grow "geometrically".[79] While this mechanism is rabiate in principle, its practical operation is less so. Significant work is undertaken early and invisibly by "preventive checks". People marry late, have fewer children, or have no children at all. Emigration is another undramatic way to do the job. Some "positive checks", though, materialize in a form that is so brutal as to correspond to the unforgiving character of the law: abortion, infant mortality, and deaths due to malnutrition, infections, unhealthy housing, etc. Wars, accidents, natural catastrophes, and epidemics, etc. are also factual unpleasant "checks" to populations, but they arise out of other backgrounds without, mostly, having the goal in mind. In fact, they may even sometimes pave the way to a transitorily more abundant state of nourishment.

Thus, the Malthusian mechanism operates via men finding no food and dying of hunger or illness only in its most extreme form; more often, humans are simple not being procreated or born or disappear from places for other reasons. Malthus' population law, hence, neither implies that there will be hunger revolts and hundred thousand or millions of desperate adults robbing and killing each other for food or even cannibalism,[80] nor does it "apologetically" justify such horrors.

"Checks", though, there will be, and in an unequal society, like ours, they will also be unequally distributed. They will not fall on the powerful and wealthy, but on the weak and poor. This is true for the sacrifice of parents to abstain from having children, thereby affecting the poor with more providence, and for "checks" on humans born who will suffer hunger, become ill, and may die early and who may sometimes be said to have less providence. Belief in God and in a better life after death always enabled religious thinkers to face and to endure sad news about life on earth, and

---

78 A fall in price can sink the value of a product below the cost of production. See *Malthus* (1820) chapter 7 sect. 3, page 355

79 "...I say that the power of population is indefinitely greater than the power in the earth to produce subsistence for men. Population, when unchecked, increases in a geometrical ratio. Subsistence increases only in a arithmetical ratio." (*Malthus* (1798) page 71).

80 While human history sadly also went through such bad periods (see for instance *Davis*, The reign of Li-Tsung, page 881, 902), it will normally not get that far.

so too could Malthus, the clergy man, live with his concept's corollaries. If there are 17 chairs and 20 want to sit, then it would be nonsensical to embark on a charitable campaign in favor of those who have to stand, given that every success at such an attempt would only produce a new have not, a new patient for the next charitable campaign – this is a dumb Sisyphus-activity. A social security, inspired by lofty philanthropic motives, was nonsensical, given the objective shortage of food supply in Malthus' reasoning; it could only redistribute the evil, change the victims, but never remedy the problem. Only the course of the "fault line" may be redrawn, in favor of some and to the disadvantage of others. However, on the bad side of this line, and in the aggregate, there would always be poverty, sickness, and misfortune. God, obviously, wanted these bad destinies to happen.

Principles of political economy: potential and real production

Twenty-two years later, in his *Principles of Political economy* of 1820, Malthus again used the idea that two growth processes, which some pre-ordained necessity required to be complementary, are actually not. Now, it is not biological growth versus the growth of social production, but the social or, in fact, the economic is on both sides. The lack of complementarity between two dynamics now explains the limited food supply that already went into his population law as one side of the problem. "In a former work", he writes, "I endeavoured to trace the causes which practically keep down the population of a country to the level of its actual supplies. It is now my object to shew what are the causes which chiefly influence these supplies, or call the powers of production forth into the shape of increasing wealth."[81] He uses the distinction between the potential and the real to frame his investigation. Actual production will always be lower or at best equal to the maximum potential of production. Where it ends up matters greatly. There is, says Malthus, "scarcely any inquiry more curious, or, from its importance, more worthy of attention, than that which traces the causes which practically check the progress of wealth in different countries, and stop it, or make it proceed very slowly, while the power of production remains comparatively undiminished, or at least would furnish the means of a great and abundant increase of produce and population".[82]

Four stimuli of supply

Malthus espouses his view on the issue in the final, eighth chapter of his *Principles of Political economy* (1. ed. 1820, 2nd. ed. 1836) "On the immediate causes of the progress of wealth". In it, he specifically examines whether the development of four factors

---

81   *Malthus* (1820) page 345.
82   *Malthus* (1820) page 345.

(population growth, accumulation or saving, fertility of the soil, and inventions to save labor) suffice to stimulate production up to its theoretical maximum. He shows that these factors, individually and jointly, are unable to achieve this result both in theory and by experience.

To begin with, the growth of the population has intertwined effects on both supply and on demand. Even if there is a greater number of people, the "desire of any individual to possess the necessaries, conveniences and luxuries of life, however intense, will avail nothing towards their production, if there be nowhere a reciprocal demand for something which he possesses", which would attribute value thereto and promote his economically irrelevant "physical demand" to an "effective" or "effectual"[83] demand. As we know, only the two latter actually attribute value. However, this "reciprocal demand", e.g., for labor, depends upon the possibility of a profitable use of this labor and "...no productive labour can ever be in demand with a view to profit unless the produce when obtained is of greater value than the labour which obtained it." Accordingly: "A man whose only possession is his labour has, or has not, an effective demand for produce according as his labour is, or is not, in demand by those who have the disposal of produce."[84] Hence, the economy will only be receptive to those supplies of new labor (or other goods or services) that follow a growth in population if they can be used profitably and if the bearers of labor in the increased population are able to increase demand under the same prerequisite. In fact, experience shows, says Malthus, that "the slowest progress in wealth is made where the stimulus arising from population is the greatest."[85]

Malthus' treatment of the second factor, saving, the accumulation of capital, once again emphasizes demand. Admitting that there is "hardly a country in the four quarters of the globe, where capital is not deficient ... compared with the territory and even the number of people, and fully allowing (for)... the extreme desirableness of an increase of capital", he still judges the relation between capital and demand as more important than the relation of capital to the territory and to the population: "...I should say where the demand for commodities was not such as to afford fair profits to the producer, and the capitalists were at a loss where and how to employ their capitals to advantage, the saving from revenue to add still more to these capitals would only tend prematurely to diminish the motive to accumulation, and still further to distress the capitalists..."[86] Rather: "The first thing wanted in both these cases of deficient capital and deficient population, is an effective demand for

---

83   Malthus uses both terms with no visible difference between them.
84   *Malthus* (1820) page 348.
85   *Malthus* (1820) page 350.
86   *Malthus* (1820) page 372.

commodities, that is a demand by those who are able and willing to pay an adequate price for them...”[87]

For the third factor, Malthus relies on *Alexander von Humboldt's* reports on the Spanish dominions and Malthus' own observations on Ireland. He infers from them “that the fertility of soil alone is not an adequate stimulus to the continued increase of wealth”[88] Malthus quotes von Humboldt saying, with reference to the banana: “Je doute qu'il existe une autre plante sur le globe qui, sur un si petit espace de terrain, puisse produire une masse de substance nourrissante aussi considérable.”[89] Similarly, “la fécondité du *thaolli* ou mais Mexicain est au-delà de tout ce que l'on peut imaginer en Europe”[90] and von Humboldt calculates that half a hectare planted with bananas can feed 50 people, while half a hectare planted with corn can feed two people[91] or that a maize harvest below 130 to 150 times the seed is considered as bad around Valladolid in Mexico.[92] Accordingly, even in towns in which the provisions are dearer, even “the very dregs” of the people are able to earn their maintenance by only one or two days of labor in a week.[93] However, nowhere does this enormous large-scale facilitation, to procure food, lead to a significant increase of agricultural production or to other conveniences or luxuries, e.g., by manufacturing. Rather, the “extreme fertility” of this privileged region generally goes along with great indolence and improvidence. As von Humboldt says, “si les plaines fertiles d'Atalisco, de Cholula et de Puebla ne produisent pas des récoltes plus abondantes, la cause principale doit être cherchée dans le manque des consommateurs, et dans les entraves que les inégalités du sol opposent au commerce intérieur des grains, surtout à leur transport vers les côtes qui sont baignées par la mer des Antilles”. Malthus supports this view: “...the main and immediate cause which retards ... cultivation is indeed the want of consumers, that is, the want of power to sell the produce at such a price as will at once encourage good cultivation, and enable the farmers to give the landlords something that they want, for the use of their land.”[94] “Except in the neighborhood of the mines and near the great towns, the effective demand for produce is not such as to induce the great proprietors to bring their immense tracts of land properly into

---

87   *Malthus* (1820) page 372 and 341.
88   Malhus uses this identical summary twice after his treatment of the Spanish dominions and of Ireland (*Malthus* (1820) page 393 and 401).
89   *von Humboldt* (1811) tom. iii. l. iv. c. ix page 28, quoted after *Malthus* (1820) page 382.
90   *von Humboldt* (1811) tom. i. l. ii. c. v page 358, quoted after *Malthus* (1820) page 385.
91   *von Humboldt* (1811) tom. iii. l. iv. c. ix page 28, quoted after *Malthus* (1820) page 382.
92   *von Humboldt* (1811) tom. i. l. ii. c. v page 358, quoted after *Malthus* (1820) page 385.
93   *von Humboldt* (1811) tom. ii. l. ii. c. vii page 37, quoted after *Malthus* (1820) page 386.
94   *von Humboldt* (1811) tom. iii. l. iv. c. ix page 89, quoted after *Malthus* (1820) page 392.

cultivation...".[95] Accordingly, only sufficient foreign commerce, e.g., trade with the mother country, he notes, could "give value to the raw produce of the land."[96]

Malthus treats inventions to save labor as a possible fourth factor for the progress of wealth. He summarizes on this subject: "The presumption always is, that it [an invention to save labor, G.W.] will lead to a great extension both of wealth and value. But still we must allow that the pre-eminent advantages derived from the substitution of machinery for manual labour, depend upon the extension of the market for the commodities produced, and the increased stimulus given to consumption....".[97] In the end, Malthus finds that all four of the factors reviewed are, singly or jointly, not sufficient causes for the progress of wealth.

The requirement of a union between production and distribution

As Malthus argues in the sixth section of Chapter VIII of his *Principles of Political Economy*, a "union" only of the "powers of production", which includes the four factors examined previously, with "means of distribution", can help us to move actual production to its theoretical technical maximum. A certain "due proportion" is needed.[98] "Demand", Malthus says, "... is quite as necessary to the increase of capital as the increase of capital is to demand. They mutually act upon and encourage each other, and neither of them can proceed with vigour if the other be left far behind."[99]

Three factors in particular serve as "occasioning" for an improved distribution[100]: the *division of landed property*, *commerce*, and *unproductive consumers*. In the seventh

---

95   *Malthus* (1820) page 389.

96   *Malthus* (1820) page 390. Malthus attaches similar considerations to the adoption of the potato as general food of the lower classes in Ireland and to the low wages owing to the potato's cheapness, which we do not pursue (*Malthus* (1820) page 394 and 399 et seqs).

97   *Malthus* (1820) page 394 and 412 et seqs.

98   *Malthus* (1820) page 426.

99   *Malthus* (1820) page 399.

100 Malthus uses the notion of "distribution" but distribution certainly means more to him than just physical transportation or the existence of established trade channels, e.g., with wholesalers and retail traders etc. but rather "mission accomplished", in the sense the German word "Absatz", the French word "débit" or the uncustomary English word "off-sale". Sismondi even stressed that sales to intermediaries should not be confused with sales to ultimate consumers. If book publishers, he says, meet at the Leipzig book fare and bring each four or five dozen copies of four or five books, which they sell to each other (or barter amongst them), then relevant demand and consumption have not yet even commenced. Only if the bookstores at home find end-customers who are willing to make a sacrifice of a payment, this constitutes the needed demand. (*Sismondi* (1827) page 380–382). This may require a qualification. If the books are paid for, or bartered into valuable other books, hence, books in good demand, then their producers have in fact already realized the value-in-exchange that they were looking for.

through ninth sections of Chapter VIII, Malthus shows how they increase the exchangeable value of the produce. Malthus, in the nominalist catholic Salamanca or natural law traditions, considers exchangeable value as ascribed by people with purchase power, distribution, and value move together and become almost the same.[101] Whether a commodity or service has a "value" (physiocrats said "valeur vénale") is hardly distinguishable from it being properly "distributed" or from there being effectual demand for it. Value being ascribed to commodities in this way vindicates the entrepreneur's investment. The economy is in "proportion" (we may say that the economic machine is in "sync"), if its products reach a customer who pays a price that is sufficiently greater than the "costs" and allows for an appropriate profit for the entrepreneur. The more products enjoy this favorable situation, the more the social production will approach its maximum.[102] This is, however, mostly not so, and "this deficiency must have arisen from the want of an adequate stimulus to continued production".[103]

When Malthus talks about the importance of demand, e.g., by saying: "The first thing wanted... is an effective demand for commodities, that is, a demand by those who are able and willing to pay an adequate price for them",[104] he never allows for any doubt not only concerning the costs of production, but also about the entrepreneur's profit, which must both be covered by the sales price. A "commodity will not be produced, unless the estimation in which it is held by the society or its intrinsic value in exchange be such, as not only to replace all the advances of labour and other articles which have been made for its attainment, but likewise to pay the usual profits upon those advances".[105]

***

If the produce were sellable only at the price of its costs, then that would leave the central motive of the profit economy frustrated. Hence, even if such unprofitable sales may sometimes occur – as it may be a lesser evil to recuperate (at least) the costs of already existing products than to see them decay in storehouses –, certainly such production will be discontinued. Costs cannot buy value; costs are less than value. Only costs plus an amount equal to profit can buy the produce in a well-oiled profit economy. Three factors may help to achieve this: division of landed property,

---

101   See already on page 40.

102   Even if the "geometrical" growth of the population will nevertheless affect this maximum, it will still be too little for the growing population and poverty and depravation will remain or re-emerge because of the Malthusian population theory.

103   *Malthus* (1820) page 347.

104   *Malthus* (1820) page 372.

105   *Malthus* (1820) page 341.

commerce, and unproductive consumers, but whether they suffice remains indeterminable. Malthus spells out quite clearly the idea here that the profit motive itself poses the main problem for the closure of circuits in capitalism and points to "unproductive consumers" as *ultima ratio*. Malthus, like Sismondi and others before him, looks towards prosthetics to close the gap.

Section 6. What Say said and Ricardo's Law of Say

Malthus was a close personal friend of Ricardo. For the sake of faster progress in economic theory, it might have been better if the two had become enemies and Malthus would then have been less moderate and polite in his criticism of Ricardo.

Ricardo and Say

The years following the Napoleonic Wars had disproven Smith's earlier optimism (from fifty years previously) concerning a lasting sufficient demand being available, which would buy the capitalist firms' output. David Ricardo (1772 – 1823) was fully aware of the problem and was in constant discussions with his friend Malthus and others that occasionally included Sismondi, about the reasons why sales markets rejected the absorption of the produce,[106] which undermined confidence that future production would be sellable, and led to the underemployment of equipment and workers. The problem that Quesnay had axiomatically solved, and which Smith had ignored, Ricardo, though, felt could be explained with special and transitory circumstances. Capitalism, he felt, had no general problem. When he needed a formula to express his view, he began to generously refer to a formula of a European disciple of his, *Jean-Baptiste Say* (1776 – 1832). Say, according to Ricardo, was "not only the first, or amongst the first, of continental writers who justly appreciated and applied the principles of Smith..." (meaning the teaching of Ricardo himself) and did "more than all other continental writers together, to recommend the principles... to the nations of Europe", but, Ricardo went on, even "succeeded in placing the science in a more logical, and more instructive order and enriched it by several discussions, original, accurate, and profound."[107] One of these "enrichments" were a few sentences that Ricardo himself elevated to the "Law of Say" or "Say's Law". It provided a new, more

---

106 One year before Ricardo's death, in 1822, he visited Sismondi in Geneva. Sismondi reports that the two began their two or three meetings by agreeing that "all sorts of industry, agriculture and manufacture, complain, one alike the other, in all European countries of a congestion of the markets and the impossibility to sell or to only sell at a loss". (*Sismondi* (1827) page 411, translation by author).

107 Preface page 6. Ricardo leaves not doubt who is the master and who the disciple.

general, more abstract and, as it appeared, eternal reason for the automatic closure of capitalist circuits; this could replace the specific numeric argument found in Quesnay's tableau.

What Say said

Ricardo's Law of Say is most commonly stated as "*supply creates its own demand*",[108] but it is difficult to find a quote in Say's own words that corresponds to the statement. In disputes, it is common to refer to quotations from either Ricardo or John Stuart Mill[109] instead (not to be confused with James Mill, a direct Ricardian) or even to modern statements, e.g., by B.M. Anderson.[110] When searching for the origins of the "Law of Say" in Say's writing, we found the following reasoning in chapter XV of Say's *Traité de l'économie politique* (first ed. 1803). Here, Say actually deals with "débauchés."[111] He tells us that from entrepreneurs' views the problem is not producing, but selling; "money is rare" is their complaint. Say undertakes the task of clarifying the issue as follows: "L'homme dont l'industrie s'applique à donner de la valeur aux choses en leur créant un usage quelconque, ne peut espérer que cette valeur sera appréciée et payée, que là ou d'autres hommes auront les moyens d'en faire l'acquisition. Ces moyens, en quoi consistent-ils? En d'autres valeurs, d'autres produits, fruits de leur industrie, de leurs capitaux, de leurs terres: d'où il résulte, quoiqu'au premier aperçu cela semble un paradoxe, que c'est la production qui ouvre des débauchés aux produits. Que si un marchand d'étoffes s'avisait de dire: ce ne sont pas d'autres produits que je demande en échange des miens, c'est de l'argent, on lui prouverait aisément que son acheteur n'est mis en état de le payer en argent que par des marchandises qu'il vend de son côté. 'Tel fermier', peut-on lui répondre, achètera vos étoffes si ses récoltes sont bonnes; il achètera d'autant plus qu'il aura produit davantage. Il ne pourra rien acheter, s'il ne produit rien."[112] "L'argent n'est que la voiture de la valeur des produits".[113] Money fulfils only an "office passager".[114] "C'est donc avec la valeur de vos produits, transformée momentanément en une somme d'argent, que vous achetez, que tout le monde achète les choses dont chacun à besoin".[115] "Lors donc qu'on dit: la vente ne va pas, parce que l'argent est

---

E.g., for an Austrian adherent of Ricaordo's Law of Say see *Hazlitt* (1959) page 35.

Mill (1848) Book III, Chap. xiv. Sect. 2.

Hazlitt (1959) page 33, gives a statement of almost a full page with arguments and examples

Say (1803). In the preface of the *Principles* Ricardo refers to this chapter as follows: "Chapter xv part I, "Ses Débauchés", contains, in particular, some very important principles, which, I believe, were first explained by this very distinguished writer" (*Ricardo* (1961) page 7).

Say (1803) chap. XV 3rd and 4th para.

Say (1803) chap. XV 5th para.

Say (1803) chap. XV 11th para.

Say (1803) chap. XV 6th para.

rare, on prend le moyen pour la cause... On ne devrait pas dire: la vente ne va pas, parce que l'argent est rare, mais parce que les autres produits le sont."[116] Say goes on to explain that this also applies to classes that do not materially reproduce themselves, such as clergymen, lawyers, or state functionaries: "C'est pour cela qu'une bonne récolte n'est pas seulement favorable aux cultivateurs, et qu'elle l'est en même temps aux marchands de tous les autres produits. On achète davantage toutes les fois qu'on recueille davantage. Une mauvaise récolte, au contraire, nuit à toutes les ventes."[117] "Un homme à talent, que vous voyez tristement végéter dans un pays qui décline, trouverait mille emplois de ses facultés dans un pays productif, où l'on pourrait employer et payer sa capacité."[118] "Une ville entourée de riches campagnes, y trouve de nombreux et riches acheteurs, et dans le voisinage d'une ville opulente, les produits de la campagne ont bien plus de valeur."[119]

Now, these quotes are impeccable and correct, by and large, [120] but what is normally called "the Law of Say" is not found therein. Commodities always and only exchange either directly against other commodities, including labor, or against money, which has been exchanged against such commodities previously (that is certainly true – against what else might commodities be exchanged?). The more commodities have been produced, the more exchanges can take place (true again), given that they are possible ammunition of exchange partners. Still, though, there is no statement about what Ricardo presents as the "Law of Say". Yes, Say states that supply creates demand, but nowhere does he state that "supply creates *its* own demand", certainly not in the sense that there will *always* be *sufficient* demand to buy the entire produce supplied at a price that allows for a reasonable profit. Nowhere (not in these aforecited quotations and nowhere else to our knowledge) does he claim that a preordained quantitative match to this effect actually exists. On the contrary, Say explicitly casts this into doubt by making the following points:

"Cela étant ainsi, d'où vient, demandera-t-on, cette quantité de marchandises qui, à certaines époques, encombrent la circulation, sans pouvoir trouver d'acheteurs ? Pourquoi ces marchandises ne s'achètent-elles pas les unes les autres ?
Je répondrai que des marchandises qui ne se vendent pas, ou qui se vendent à perte, excèdent la somme des besoins qu'on a de ces marchandises, soit parce qu'on en a produit des quantités trop considérables, **soit plutôt parce que d'autres productions ont souffert. Certains produits surabondent, parce que**

Say (1803) chap. XV 7th para.
Say (1803) chap. XV 13th para.
Say (1803) chap. XV 18th para.
Say (1803) chap. XV 19th para.
120   The only objection, which could be raised: Say does not seem to be aware of the paradox mentioned by Malthus that easily accessible markets with many firms are sometimes favorable and sometimes unfavorable for other firms, see on page 56 et seq.

d'autres sont venus à manquer. En termes plus vulgaires, beaucoup de gens ont moins acheté, parce qu'ils ont moins gagné; et ils ont moins gagné, parce qu'ils ont trouvé des difficultés dans l'emploi de leurs moyens de production, ou bien parce que ces moyens leur ont manqué."[121]

Only the beginning (before the first "soit parce que...") considers insufficient eso-teric demand for specific values-in-use as the cause for deficient demand. Yet, Say clearly provides a second cause, which is not founded in firms' misreading of the needs and tastes of their customers. Accordingly, it cannot be removed by produc-ing other, more desired values-in-use. This second explanation is that the value-in-exchange-generation, through other productions, has suffered and the "counter-supply" of values-in-exchange, needed to pay for desired produce, is not sufficiently present. Say "vulgarizes" this, as he says, to make it utterly clear: Potential deman-ders have earned too little, as they had difficulties in either employing their means of production or because they did not have means of production or because they did not have salary incomes at all. In other words, the lack of esoteric demand and because prospective demanders lack means of payment (or ways to procure them) will shrink exchanges and, thereby, reduce future exchanges and future income opportunities. When examined properly, all of this is very close to the works of both Sismondi and Malthus. While Say's first reason for deficient demand (no "esoteric" demand, Say says no "physical demand") can be easily remedied[122] by shifting production,[123] the second (esoteric demanders cannot procure money) is much more difficult or even impossible to remedy. In other words, Say, the alleged inventor of "Say's Law", does,

---

121 *Say* (1803) chap. XV 14–16th para (bold print added).

122 It is actually not so easy to adjust output even to "physical demand". Why, if the needs of the public have been missed out on in the first place, should the second attempt be reliably so much better? It was a strong argument against central planning economies that they would not be able to successfully adjust production to existing needs – why should private firms be so much better? Furthermore, will not every true discovery of specific consumer needs or desires unleash a stampede of entrepreneurs all running into the same direction and will they, thus, not almost by necessity mutually frustrate their efforts, at least after some time? It is true that economic liberty and markets punish missing the consumer needs (hard), but they also excite far too many firms to run after the the same opportunity.

123 Say goes on to discuss this in the next 17th para. Ricardo and Hazlitt put great emphasis on this point. Ricardo writes: "It is not to be supposed that he should, for any length of time, be ill-informed of the commodities which he can most advantageously produce, to attain the object which he has in view, namely, the possession of other goods; and, therefore, it is not probable that he will continually produce a commodity for which there is no demand." (*Ricardo* (1961) chap. XXI, early, page 290). Ricardo also wrote: "Mistakes may be made, and commodities not suited to the demand may be produced—of these there may be a glut; they may not sell at their usual price; but then this is owing to the mistake, and not to the want of demand for productions." (*Ricardo* (1991) page 305).

indeed, not proclaim that supply *always* find its *full* demand. Products buy products *if* there happens to be desires for just the right special values-in-use and, in addition, *if* one has enough money. "Say's Law" is, thus, based on a misinterpretation by Ricardo and we must acquit Say of being the inventor of what is conventionally called the "Law of Say".

Ricardo's Law of Say

Hence, Ricardo overinterpreted and changed what Say actually said. "M. Say has", Ricardo writes, "... most satisfactorily shewn[124], that there is no amount of capital which may not be employed in a country, because demand is only limited by production...There cannot, then, be accumulated in a country any amount of capital which cannot be employed productively, until wages rise so high in consequence of the rise of necessaries, and so little consequently remains for the profits of stocks, that the motive for accumulation ceases,"[125] but Say, as we have seen, did not say this. We do not know how Ricardo came to "enhance" Say's work. Was he conscientious of the fact that he was reading something alien into him or not? If he was, why would he hope that his disciple would accept the fatherhood of a bastard baby? In fact, Say neither rejected Ricardo's interpretation, nor rephrased and repeated it in a way so as to better correspond to Ricardo's reading. It appears that *nobody* wanted to be too closely associated with Ricardo's Law of Say[126] and that everybody wanted to keep all of his options nevertheless.

Ricardo's Law of Say in ideological battles

When Smith wrote in 1776, he was authentically optimistic about there being sufficient demand for Albion's produce. When Say, Ricardo and Sismondi, and Malthus wrote, at the end of the first quarter of the 19th century, that was history and the "encombrement général de tous les marchés de l'univers, où l'on porte incessamment des marchandises que ne se vendent à perte"[127] was reality. Ricardo's Law of Say was, thus, irreconcilable with reality from the very day of its invention. The Communist Manifesto was published 25 years after Ricardo's death, and trade unions and socialist, social democratic or communist parties and philanthropes complained about

---

124 Ricardo does not provide a quotation in which Say is supposed to have made the statement, which Ricardo in an adjacent footnote calls "M. Say's principle".

125 *Ricardo* (1961) chap. XXI, early, page 290. Emphasis added. The condition "until ..." also already points beyond Ricardo's Law of Say.

126 *Keen* (2011) page 205, states that "'Walras Law' is simply Say's Law in a more formal guise...".

127 *Jean Baptiste Say*, Lettres à M. Malthus, Lettre première, in: *Jean Baptiste Say*, Cours d'économie politique, Paris 1996, page 224.

"poverty amidst of plenty" all throughout the 19th and the first part of the 20th centuries; Manchester capitalism, unemployment after the Great Depression and what was then called the "Third World" were all ongoing disproof of Ricardo's Law of Say.

The years between 1848 and 1989 centered around battles between socialist or communist ideologies on the one and liberal or "laissez faire"[128] ideologies on the other side. Imperial world powers partly subscribed to either the one or the other side. This lifted "Ricardo's Law of Say" to a mass-ideological relevance, which Ricardo himself had probably not foreseen. The "law," which Say never stated, "supply creates its own demand", became as important for political hegemony as doctrines of Catholicism and Protestantism had been in the religious civil wars of the 16th and 17th centuries; believers in economic liberty defended it as fervently as Catholics had defended the virginity of mother Mary. It is the destiny of economic theory, alike religious credence, if it becomes relevant in a mass ideological debate to be fully subdued to battle logic. It does no longer matter what the opponent truly states or means any more. Rather both sides portray their opponents' doctrines as overshooting what they really meant and, accordingly, both sides can justly claim that their positions are misrepresented by the other side.[129] As Ricardo's Law of Say had neither a clear father nor a clear content, and still tried to assert control over a basic macroeconomic question, no wonder it became a particularly fuzzy plaything.

Macro transmissions in the interpretations of Ricardo's Law of Say

This, Ricardo's Law of Say's sad destiny, does not relieve us from thinking hard about whether it may still have a sensible meaning. Three interpretations are possible and each are examined one by one.

First interpretation of Ricardo's Law of Say
The "Law of Say" could, first, wish to abbreviate what Say really stated and what we have quoted extensively: As produce exchanges against other produce, there will be more opportunities for exchange with those who have more of the other produce.

---

128   The author is not aware of the origins of the French expression "laisser faire". Given the adoration China enjoyed in the "siècle des lumières", Lao Tse's "Wu wei", might well be looming in the background.

129   E.g. Hazlitt, in its defense against Keynes, restricts the meaning of "Say's Law". The "doctrine that supply creates its own demand, in other words, is based on the assumption that a proper equilibrium exists among the different kinds of production, and among prices of different products and services. And it of course assumes proper relationships between prices and costs, between prices and wage-rates. It assumes the existence of competition and free and fluid markets by which these proportions, price relations, and other equilibria will be brought about." A lot of preconditions he presupposes! (Hazlitt (1959) page 36, 35).

Yet, as stated previously, this interpretation by no means implies that there will always be sufficient demand for all produce. This first interpretation would demote Ricardo's Law of Say to a true, albeit trite macroeconomic insight.

Second interpretation of Ricardo's Law of Say

The second interpretation stipulates – as a self-evident truth – that all produce can indeed be securely sold in full – without giving specific verifiable or falsifiable reasons for it. In other words, everybody remains free to figure out their own explanatory mechanism. This may be a notional identity or equality between to flows (such as I = S?), a mechanical transmission belt, like a law of gravity, a magic or mystical relationship, some math, or whatever. Why not quantum entanglement? It also could be a Platonic idea *(ante res* or *in rebus)*... – we are not told.[130]

If stubborn unbelievers continue to ask how the "law" can possibly function, they will soon have to understand that Ricardo's Law of Say cannot conclusively be thought of as relating to only two groups, those who want to sell and those who are expected to buy. Instead, the latter group of expected purchasers can only buy because they were or are already successful sellers. Hence, Ricardo's Law of Say must be anticipating the result of a circular process, a *regressio ad infinitum*, with everyone and with all involved. The following can also be stated: Not only must a first firm find customers who attribute some esoteric value-in-use to its commodities – which is obvious, without value-in-use-attribution they would not attribute any value-in-exchange –, but there is a quantitative issue, too. The esoteric value-in-use-attributers must attribute *more* value-in-exchange to the commodities than the firm has spent as costs on the production of the to-be-purchased product and they must be willing and able to make the sacrifice in this full amount. They will, however, only be capable of doing the latter if Ricardo's Law of Say is simultaneously also working in their favor (or has done so before) and if it equips them/has equipped them with the needed money. This condition, now, is exactly what Ricardo's Law of Say teaches us will always be fulfilled: Do not worry, it seems to state, everybody can sell because everybody can and has succeeded or will succeed when they do the same thing. Ricardo's Law of Say has the structure of, first, acknowledging a mutual dependency and of, second, foretelling that this mutual dependency will always resolve itself, without neither explaining why, nor dealing with quantities.

---

130   Sismondi writes: "C'est avec regret que nous voyons l'économie politique adopter en Angleterre un langage chaque jour plus sentencieux, s'envelopper dans des calculs plus difficiles à suivre, se perdre dans des abstractions, et devenir, en quelque sorte, une science occulte." (*Sismondi* (1827) page 373, 374). As chief of this "école nouvelle", which has "un esprit de secte", Sismondi names "Mr. Ricardo" (page 374).

Third interpretation of Ricardo's "Law of Say"

The third possible interpretation of the "Law of Say" intricates the "law" in a world of causality in which rational argument can now, indeed, take place. It begins with the idea that those involved in producing a product *acquire income* for their involvement, as outlays from a firm, and that they should be able to (re)purchase their product with it. Is this the case though? If we use Marx's splitting-up of M into c and v and his splitting-up of M' into c, v, and s in order to consider this question, the answer is rather simple: Yes, if the producing firms were to sell their produce at M, then their suppliers, supplier firms alike workers, could (re)purchase the produce with the money they got from the producing firm. However, it was certainly not the producing firm's idea to produce things to only recover the costs; they want a profit because that is what capitalism is about. Hence, the capitalist profit principle stands in the way of Ricardo's Law of Say working by the suppliers of the production inputs (re)buying the produce at M or for c plus v. What if the firms were to sell at M', hence at the profit s? Now, the aggregate of c-outlays and v-pay-outs can never suffice to buy M' (as M' > M or as $c+v+s > c+v$); we saw this already in Proudhon ("costs cannot buy value"), Sismondi, and Malthus.[131] Only M' could obviously buy M'. Only if all of a firm's suppliers and all of its employees use the outlays that they received for their contribution to the production, *and* if the firms themselves were also to use the profits from their produce for this purpose, then the whole produce should be sellable for M' i.e., even with the profit M'-M or s.[132]

In this reasoning, though, we assume that firms can use the profits they *intend* to realize to pay their own profits or to pay other firms M'-M crosswise. In the latter case, then, the precondition for all capitalists getting their intended M' would be that they *all* spend their entire profits (their M'-M) to mutually purchase each-others' products. This paradox has several sides.

Let us, first, do away with an innocent, benign side. The involved liquidity issue will willingly resolve itself in several ways. Assistance already comes from M–C–M' itself. We have seen that M represents not only pay-outs actually made by a firm but also includes future pay-outs the firm will have to make for the respective circuit,

---

131   Assume an entrepreneur has, all in all, invested 7 money units in equipment and inventories and 8 money units in salaries (no rent, no interest) and intends to sell the produce at 20 money units. He can obviously not buy "back" his own produce for the created value-in-exchange of 20 money units. Out of the production he has the produce, but no money at all. He cannot even have his suppliers and workers buy the produce; they received only 7 and 8 money units, 15 in total, which would not suffice to buy the produce at 20. At best the entrepreneur's suppliers and workers could buy a part of the produce for 15, but that would not satisfy the entrepreneur; if they (very unlikely) would at all do that, the entrepreneur would certainly not initiate a second circuit.

132   In this sense also *Foley* (1986) page 150 et seq.

e.g., what accounting would call depreciation or provisions. Accordingly, rather often a firm will initially not pay out the full amount of M but only a lower amount and accordingly it will retain the excess of M over the amount actually paid and can use it to pay for other firms' profit. A second means would be to take out loans, to buy the produce at the other firms M' and repay the loan from later incoming sales prices, their own M' (if at a loss of interest and bank fees). Firms could also, third, mutually grant credit to each other and repay them out of received purchase prices or setting them off against counterclaims for purchase prices, e.g., in some kind of clearing house.[133] As a fourth means, if worse comes to worst, they might even barter their produce amongst themselves. Hence, we see that it will be easy for all capitalists somehow buy each-others produce. Liquidity is not in the way of all produce being able to sell.

But here is the malign side of the paradox: Capitalists will only go out and organize the liquidity needed to buy their colleagues' produce if they have good uses for the offered values-in-use and if they have the needed money and are ready to sacrifice it. The utility of values-in-use for firms is not consumption but to use them in profitable investments; they will, thus, only ascribe value-in-use and value-in-exchange to other firms' produce, it they expect to be able to use it for their own profits. And the investment, for which other firms' output can be used, must beat other investments. If liquidity is normally not, the limitation of firms' capital and the need to maintain and to increase it is a serious factor. Accordingly. Each firm, which considers to close other firms' circuits by buying their produce, must be able to expect other firms to act alike and to dispatch the yet expected M'-M to it.

If we, accordingly, begin with assuming that supplier firms and workers "repurchase" their produce, to exceed M and to get to M', we need to bring in the producing firms as crosswise buyers of their produce. There is a necessity of a circularity, which can, ultimately, only deliver the result stated by the alleged law. This third interpretation of Ricardo's Law of Say has still significant worth for the progress of economic thinking. Unfortunately, though, as the proposition in which it evolves is *conditional* – all produce of all firms can be purchased at a profit, *if* all firms use their expected profits to purchase all of other firms produce. This is not a final answer but poses the question of macroeconomics only in a new form: Can capitalism maintain something like a permanent moderate bubble?

***

---

133   There are many historic examples of such practices. E.g., as *Sismondi* (1827) chap. VII, page 74 et seq. reports, the merchants of Lyon settled payments amongst them only four times a year.

Already in Malthus, we met the situation that an amount of demand was needed, beyond costs, which corresponded to the to-be-generated profit; otherwise, the circuit could not close. Accordingly, Malthus looked out for a union of production and distribution supported by division of landed property, commerce and at prosthetics (unproductive consumers coming from anywhere) as solution. The third interpretation of Ricardo's Law of Say (which is the only relevant) goes back and re-considers whether there is truly insufficient demand. It ends up by intricating the reader to think about, whether those who caused the problem – firms, by posing the profit condition – could not also deliver the crucial[134] blow to solve it. This is an important proposition to think about. Unfortunately, it does not take the reader to enlightenment but only gets him into a difficult bewitched circular territory, through which, ever since, writers of all camps, including Marx, Keynes, Kalecki and Minsky, would have to battle their way. The third interpretation of Ricardo's Law of Say, insofar, remains in the background of their attempts and of our attempt.

Section 7. Marx's insufficient theory on insufficient employment-generating spending

Karl Marx

Marx saw Newtonian mechanics govern astronomy and Hegelian dialectics – after being turned upside down by Marx himself – govern history. Marx's goal, like Ricardo's, was to discover laws, which explain the motions of the capitalist economy in a similar way. He started up with classical social philosophy, e.g., of Hobbes, Montesquieu and, again, Hegel, added what he liked in existing economic theory and tried to move further towards an integrated social, political, economic and historical theory. His approach conceived the economy as an interdependent sub system, which evolved over the time axis (within modes of production and beyond modes of production), the evolution being driven by a dialectic of the economic system itself (an endogenous dynamic) and dialectical mutual influences between the economic system and its non-economic (exogenous) environment, such as science, technology, ideology, society, politics, culture, religion etc. Insofar, Marx anticipated systems theory, yet, unlike most systems theory, Marx, the materialist, assumed a dominance of the economy as of one particular social sub-system. He famously expressed this asymmetry in his base-superstructure-metaphor. An ideological, legal, cultural etc. "superstructure", he said, "raised" or "elevated itself" ("erhebt sich") over the economic "structure" (or base, "Basis"). Truly, a "metaphor"

---

134 Supplier firms that delivered equipment and inventories and workers who gave labor inputs are assumed to comply anyhow.

that was. Marx and Engels never worked out what the metaphor meant more specifically. It could entail simple mechanistic bottom-up causation, pattern reflection, e.g., of the "commodity form" into law or art, or a conspiracy-like purposeful instrumentalism or other transmission forms.[135] As, in a world of dialectic, it was remarkable that there was to be asymmetry and dominance in favor of the economy, Marx at least quickly admitted feedback and a "relative independence" of the superstructure. That was no concession contre cœur: Marx, in fact, needed the "relative independence of the superstructure" anyhow to explain – in a non-mechanical – way how politics, a "superstructure-inhabitant," could turn against the "base" – in the future proletarian revolution. Probably, systems theory was not far enough for more progress at the time. How this may have been, ultimately the limits of the base-superstructure-metaphor did not damage Marx's social theory. To the contrary It opened the way to seeing social systems influencing each other, a path which coalesced with ideology critiques of Freud or Nietzsche, and which is further pursued by modern sociology. Marx also used Hegelian dialectic to describe social and historical dynamics, which allowed to conceptualize social systems as moving through time, hence, evolution and history. After having stripped off eschatology, philosophy of history and the idea of an avantgarde party, this part of Marxism too, "historical materialism", has in the meantime become a widely accepted moment of modern social sciences.[136]

Marx's approach to economics is also rich in two other regards: First, he saw grandiosity in capitalism; he found it great *and* ugly, enormously productive *and* destructive, a god *and* a devil. Second, his approach was close to Quesnay systems view without falling victim to Quesnay's pre-ordained axiomatic harmony. Third, via his social theory and historical materialism he projected the idea of a contradictory system evolving over time.[137] Fourth, as already expressed, a first crucial step of Marx analysis of capitalism, his "general formula of capital" M–C–M', and his concept of a "twofold free laborer" remain valuable economic observations. But, nevertheless, we cannot but remember Marx's theory of labor value and exploitation, a center piece in his *opus magnum*, but as a huge and crucial mistake. We shall treat this flaw of the theoretical giant rather mercilessly. He largely took over the labor theory of value as

---

135   On the different applications of the Marxian structure-superstructure-metaphor to the theory of criminal law, see *Wächter* (1983) page 161 et seq.; *Wächter* (1987) page 8–31.

136   *Furth* (2008) page 324.

137   In this regard there are some parallels with *Irvin Fisher* and *Knut Wicksell*. In a combination between contradictions and evolution, there are also visible methodological parallels with *Schumpeter* and even with the former US-security-adviser *W. W. Rostow*, who wrote a worthwhile economics book in 1960 (*Rostow* (1990)).

ready-made from Ricardo and attached the exploitation theory thereto.[138] As his understanding of surplus, profit and profit rate, including his theory of the tendential fall of the profit rate, were derived from them, their fallacy infected the heart-piece of economic Marxism and collapsed as a whole. There were reasons for Marx to end up in this mess: On the one side, he seriously pursued the honorable goal of an ambitious theory design between Newton and Hegel and to detect contradictions at the deepest possible level, yet on the other side, he also pursued revolution and needed a theory with moral and political appeal to workers and other progressive circles. But both goals conflicted, and in Marx, in the end, the politician won over the economist or the necessities or the political battle crippled his theoretical search for truth.

It is terribly difficult to analyze and explain something, e.g., of human physiology or of a combustion engine, if you invent an *additional mechanism, which is just not there*. The fictitious thing, which you want people to acknowledge and use in their thinking, will unavoidably shift itself between the elements, whose functioning might otherwise be easily explained, and thereby render sound explanations impossible. Wherever it finds a little space, the made-up implant will creep in, cancerously take root and mercilessly defend its footholds against more enlightened (and simpler) analysis. It is this *add-on of a non-existing fictive mechanism*, and the quasi-religious character of it, which gave Marxist labor-value-driven economics its distinctly sad character. Once committed to it, Marxists had to be permanently on the watch that nothing was stated about capitalism without using it as an explanans; anything else would mean surrender. This made Marxism cumbersome, awkward, unintuitive, clumsy, petty and doctrinal (in the negative sense of the word) – and, by the same time, moralizing and always on the jump from a scientific debate into a political attack of the opponent. The self-infliction of this millstone also condemned Marxist economists to devote an enormous part of their time to the frustrating high energy task to invent and defend explanations, which would allow undeniable facts to co-exist with the labor value and exploitation credo; as much as two third of their energy may have gone into this.[139]

---

138 Marx, as Schumpeter says, did much to keep Ricardian thought alive (*Schumpeter* (1954) page 478). Thereby, Marx kept Malthus down. Marx decision for Ricardo and against Malthus may have been the most consequential decision in the history of economic thinking.

139 E.g. the theory of labor and of exploitation implies that capitalists, before anything, need to increase the *mass of labor* employed to obtain the maximum of surplus labor, surplus value and profit. They, thus, ought to hate increases of the "constant" component of capital ("constant" as it generates no surplus value) and of the so-called "technical" and "organic composition of capital", which bereave them of the miraculous exclusively value-generating power of living labor. Accordingly, to keep up or even increase the exploitation rate s/v and the profit rate s/c+v, the main thrive of capitalist businesses should have been to *fight* and *retard machinery*. But that is not what happened; rather capitalism always pushed for an explosive increase of machinery. The core-element of Marxism, at least at the most abstract and basis

It is yet telling that Marx himself, in his later writing, which he did not publish himself but became the third volume of *Capital* through Engels' hands, mostly no longer bothered to maintain the awkward exploitation-loaded notations "variable capital" v, "constant capital" c, and surplus value s in central places, but substituted them with "exploitation-neutral" notations. "The formula $C = c + v + s$", he wrote "turns into the formula $C = k + s$, that is, the commodity-value = cost-price + surplus-value"[140]; later "... the formula $C = c + v + s = k + s$ turns into the formula $C = k + p$, or the *value of a commodity = cost-price + profit*."[141] He, thus, came dangerously close to treating profit as no more than an add-on or margin on costs, which he elsewhere did not tire to condemn as utmost vulgarism. He wrote: "Hence, if a commodity is sold at its value, a profit is realised which is equal to the excess of its value over its cost-price, and therefore equal to the entire surplus-value incorporated in the value of the commodity. But the capitalist may sell a commodity at a profit even when he sells it below its value. So long as its selling price is higher than its cost-price, though it may be lower than its value, a portion of the surplus-value incorporated in it is always realised, thus always yielding a profit."[142]

The 175 years of economic history, which passed by since the *Communist manifesto* of 1848, were merciless with the labor theory of value. The period offered an abundance of fascinating developments and crises for Marxist economics to explain: There was imperialism, two world wars, the end of colonialism, fascism, the rise and fall of soviet socialism, a Keynesian period of capitalism, a neoliberal ecstasy

---

level of Marxian analysis, being in a full-fledged contradiction to the most visible and undisputed trend of capitalism since the 18th century necessitated later Marxists to invent all sorts of artifical contructions to reconcile the facts with the theory of labor value. This problem in Marxist economic theory also affects its only semi-clear long-term theorem on capitalist evolution, the so-called law of the "tendential fall of the profit rate" (Capital volume III chap. XXIIII). This law says in principle: If the so-called technical and organic composition of capital increases with the growing use of machinery, c will grow relative to v, whatever s/v does, the rate of surplus value s/c+v will tendentially go down ($\uparrow$c/v $\downarrow$s/(c+v)). That "law", taken seriously, would have meant that the heydays of capitalism were in the decades of primitive manufacture capitalism, and that capitalism was already set to dry out for the lack of sufficient profit when Marx wrote *Capital*. This was so visibly nonsense that Marx himself undertook to tame his "law" through the invention of not less than six "counter-tendencies". Yet, here he stumbled from one problem into the next one. If the world can only be explained by a bundel of "tendencies" and "counter-tendencies", dialectical materialism with "historic laws" etc. capitulates to eclecticist theories.

140   *Marx*, Capital volume III chap. I.
141   *Marx*, Capital volume III chap. I.
142   *Marx*, Capital volume III chap. I. Much ado about nothing! This apparent change, of course, to save "labor value" and "exploitation"- theory, occupied many Marxians over more than a century with "proving" that Marx's change was no change. The different terminology only resulted from a higher level of analysis, they said.

with a "great moderation", a "subprime-crisis" and a "Eurozone crisis" and a war in Ukraine. China, the most important country of the history before the industrial revolution, and still the most populous country, is propelling itself back to the top of the world; other large countries, such as India, are progressing quickly. And capitalism has proven capable, in many countries, of delivering dwelling, food and many thrills, such as cars, electrical household equipment, mobile phones, computers and the internet, even partially in Sub-Sahara Africa, to the working classes, even often to unemployed, at affordable prices. Social security had been improved in most countries, while inequality is, nevertheless, rising. A lot to analyze for critical economics committed to the position of the laboring classes! But Marxist economics, because it raised high the banner of its labor value and exploitation approach, proved utterly useless at the whole front, with regard to each and every period. If at all orthodox Marxist, Maoist or Trotskyist economists, or leftists in general, came close to making a constructive theoretical contribution, they silently skipped labor value or only paid lip service to it. It was neither a constituent factor in Hilferding's or Lenin's theory of imperialism or in Rosa Luxemburg's contribution, nor even in the orthodox theory of "state-monopolistic capitalism."[143]

The theory of labor value and exploitation had another telling impact on the history of economic thought. Because it was mystical itself, it helped to hide the mystical moments in mainstreams economic theory (e.g., of Ricardo's Law of Say) and made the latter appear much smarter than it really was. Marx offered a weak spot to

---

143   The damage, the theory of labor value does, can also be seen at the Anti-Stalinist end of the spectrum. The work of the Belgian Trotskyist economist *Ernest Mandel* (1923–1995) combines sovereign command of Marx and the Marxian tradition with significant knowledge of non-Marxian economists. He undertook a study of the relationship between the "general laws of motion of capital" and "the history of the capitalist mode of production" from the 19th century to the 1960ties (*Mandel* (1972) page 11). He asked: "Wie kann die wirkliche Geschichte der kapitalistischen Produktionsweise der letzten hundert Jahre als die Geschichte der Entfaltung der inneren Widersprüche dieser Produktionsweise, d.h. als letztes Endes durch ihre "abstrakten Bewegungsgesetze" bestimmt, dargelegt werden? Welche "Mittelglieder" sind dabei operativ, um die Einheit des Abstrakten und Konkreten in der Analyse zu verwirklichen?" (page 20). He then used non-Marxian content, like *Leontief's* "long waves" and demand issues, for his journey, but nothing or little came out of the labor value and exploitation theory, in which he believed, for his project. While *Hegel* could explain the world history and history of philosophy rather well by means of his dialectics, Mandel could not explain the history of capitalism using labor value, exploitation and profit rate dialectics, not even with the help of non-Marxian add-ons. In this context, Mandel noteworthily refutes attempts to explain periods of capitalist development and of their problems, including by *Rosa Luxemburg*, with Marx' reproduction schemes page 22–40, page 27. He prefers to use limitations of consumption as a "Mittelglied" (pages 64, 257, 395, 508 et seq.) but achieves close to nothing in the end.

his opponents and, in a way, helped to turn the ideological battle between pro-capitalist and anti-capitalist economics into a battle between *two* dumb things. Marx was too smart not to somehow becoming aware of being captured in his own labor-value-credo during his lifetime. Like a lion behind bars, he continued to move around the same spots – from the "Grundrisse" or "Rohentwurf" (1857–1858), "Kritik der politischen Ökonomie" (1859), "Theorien über den Mehrwert" (1861–1863), *Capital* volume I (1867) to the writings that Engels would later condense into volumes II and III of *Capital*. That contradiction between Marx's honest aspiration to analyze capitalism at the deepest possible level and being fettered by his value and exploitation theory may explain why, in full 16 years, he could live after *Capital* volume I was published in 1867, until 1883, he did *not* himself publish any further volume of *Capital* or anything on the subjects, which he had planned or announced before. And it may explain why he did not longer use his exploitation-oriented notation from the first volume of *Capital* in his later writing (to become the third volume of *Capital* by Engels). Marxists often say that Marx only "laid foundations", but could not himself work out his theory. But wait! If he worked out his theory of exploitation already in the *Communist Manifesto* of 1848 (35 years before his death), deepened and extended his understanding on the theory of value in the *"Theorien über den Mehrwert"* between 1861 to 1863 and presented *Capital* volume I in 1867, why should he not have *somehow* made theoretical use of the centerpiece of his theory – labor value and exploitation –, in the many remaining years? Marx's unfortunate recurring periods of illness may also be no satisfactory explanation. Perhaps, Marx illnesses did not keep him from further working out his theory, but he became ill because he sensed that he was on the wrong track in an essential point.

Little can be said as an excuse for the labor theory of value and the attached exploitation theory. If the labor theory of value still became a major signature-element of orthodox revolutionary socialism and communism, then, as stated, because it was a great propaganda-tool. It distinguished orthodox communists from other leftists and stated, in most simple terms, why capitalism was bad. The labor value and exploitation theory offered something, whose essentials everybody could understand and it became a belief functionally comparable to the Catholics' credence in the virginity of mother Marry or the resurrection of Jesus Christ. Marx would likely not have become the greatest hero of the proletariat and revolutionaries around the world (and one of the most famous persons to have lived on earth) without it. He may have a smile for that from Highgate Cemetery in London.

***

Marx's economics offers three main points of departure, which Marx *could* have used for a theory of employment-generating spending in capitalism, M–C–M', the reproduction schemes and, again, his theory of labor value and exploitation. Marx made no use of either of them to describe the behavior of capitalism over time. He gave us no worked-out theory of crises (no short or medium-term theory of capitalism) and no worked-out theory of the grand trends of capitalism, e.g., concerning decay or breakdown (no long-term theory of capitalism). In fact, he gave us nothing, which was nearly worked out. He also made not much of a use of his theory of tendential fall of the profit rate (which is almost a mathematical corollary of the labor theory of value). His most often quoted statement on crises "Der letzte Grund aller wirklichen Krisen bleibt immer die Armut und Konsumbeschränkung der Massen gegenüber dem Trieb der kapitalistischen Produktion, die Produktivkräfte so zu entwickeln, als ob nur die absolute Konsumtionsbeschränkung der Gesellschaft ihre Grenze bilde"[144] is almost an admittance of that. The un-Marxian vague terms of "poverty" and "restrictions on consumptions" of the masses and considering even these terms only as being the "*final*" reason for crises admits that Marx has nothing to say about the *intermediate* steps. But in causation, even dialectical, intermediation is what matters. We shall, thus, without permission of the inventor or even against his verdict, check the potential of the three mentioned theorems for a possibly theory of employment-generating spending.

M–C–M′ and employment-generating spending

M–C–M′ as theory of wealth accumulation and segregation
We have left no doubt that M–C–M′ is an insightful description of the main economic processes in profit economies and capitalism; this notwithstanding its simplicity, its proximity to what merchants know intuitively or expressly and what religious men, philosophers, social movements and state leaders had attacked as deformations of the proper way to produce and distribute goods. M–C–M′ is also in line with Sismondi and Malthus[145] and even Keynes is much closer to M–C–M′ than he admitted in the *General Theory*.[146]

Some, the M–C–M′-players, exchange with a profit, their complementary counterparties, C–M–C′-players, don't. One side is after profits (and they normally realize them), the other side is after value-in-use-consumption (and they normally also achieve their goal): that is the gist of M–C–M′. M–C–M′, as we saw, has a segregating effect. It generates and accumulates wealth on one side and leaves the other side, after it has enjoyed the pleasures of values-in-use-consumption, dry and empty. Units predominantly playing C–M–C′ (entering transactions with the goal to consume) transfer wealth to units predominantly playing M–C–M′ (entering transactions with the goal to make a financial gain). As there is always unequal wealth distribution, to

---

144   *Marx*, Das Kapital, MEW volume 25, page 501.
145   His costs would be M, his value M′.
146   See below on page 290 et seq.

begin with, the wealth transfer will typically be upwards to the already richer, who are further enriched by the poorer, who, after having consumed, will stay as poor as before or worse. One side to M–C–M' collects and accumulates additional value-in-exchange, while others don't; the other side dispatches value-in-exchange to the first – with a doubly segregating effect. M–C–M' was introduced to express the essence of the operation of profit economies or capitalism and in many regards succeeds in doing so. Will it also work as a tool for the analysis of socially available employment-generating spending?

M–C–M' and a theory of employment-generating spending

Can the circular movement M–C–M' can be financed out of itself? An entrepreneur starts with a stock of money, either as he owns wealth himself or as he borrowed it from a wealth owner (in a Schumpeterian sense). He pays the money M out to the factors of production (other firms and laborer-consumers) who may pass it on amongst themselves; from there it may return to the firm who made the initial outlays. One thing is already clear here: M remains M, and it can never suffice to pay M' (M' being higher than M by the amount of the entrepreneur's profits). This was already captured in Proudhon's "the workers cannot buy their produce"[147] or in our review of Malthus ("cost cannot buy value"). The idea could even be further reduced to the yet simpler agrarian image "seed cannot pay harvest" (at least under normal circumstances). Hence, we must say that the incomes of the factors of production resulting from their contribution to the production will never suffice to buy the produce at a profit from the capitalist. This is an important insight, which we already owe to Sismondi and Malthus and which is the moment of truth in the 3rd interpretation of Ricardo's Law of Say.[148]

The entrepreneur, yet, does not want to only get M back for M. He plans to receive M'. He wants to close the circuit with M', with *more* than he gave to his suppliers. But before he can get M'-M on top, somebody must have had it (to give it to him). But initially this M'-M is not here. If we stubbornly and mechanically only think of the already existing, it accordingly can't work. But production creates something new. If we take into consideration not only newly created value-in-use, but the fact that new value-in-exchange may also be attached to the new values-in-use – if we view production as source of value-in-exchange – there is hope. But step by step: The factors of production receive their M early in the process. Assume they use their M to buy the M/M'-part of the produce.[149] The workers buy the v/M'- part of their produce,

---

147   Proudhon's statement ignores other suppliers, who receive c, $M = c + v$.

148   See on page 240 et seq

149   Note this possibility is independent of the pricing by firms. Those who received M can always but buy the produce for an amount of M. If the prices are very high, they can only buy a small part of the produce.

which is sold for the wages v (in other words, "labor costs can buy the labor costs-part of the produce"). Also, suppliers-firms can buy the c/M'-part of the produce. All in all, seed can buy the same volume of harvest.... So far, we found an explanation, why entrepreneurs can make "break even". Yet, they still sit on produce representing the money amount of $M'-M$ or on the $M'-M/M'$ part of their produce (or its s/M'-part) and they must also sell that to realize their planned profit, the purpose of their whole operation.[150] Assume first, the entrepreneur would be happy to keep the $M'-M$-part of the produce in kind, e.g., for him, his family and his servants, slaves or helots to consume it; in this case he does not need to turn the surplus into money via an exchange. Assume second, the entrepreneur's business is mining gold or silver. Again, he does not need to exchange his produce into money, as gold or silver are – essentially – money already and can spare a final $C'-M'$-leg. There is, third, the already mentioned, old-fashioned possibility for entrepreneurs (after having sold the c/M'-part to supplying firms and the v/M'-part to their workers) to barter their left-over $M'-M$-parts or the surplus-parts of their produce in kind amongst themselves. Whether this works, depends on whether all capitalists mutually attribute value to their respective produce. If so, after some "tâtonnement" and with a little luck, they may all march home happily. If all entrepreneurs only attribute enough value-in-use and value-in-exchange to the produce of their fellow-entrepreneurs, newly produced commodities will clear the market of newly produced commodities.

A fourth, also already mentioned, possibility, would be for all entrepreneurs to take out loans from banks, buy the produce they wish to buy, and, if they have later been able to sell their own produce, e.g., by virtue of the same mechanism, repay the loans. The prerequisite for this is again that the buying colleagues mutually attribute value to their products and that banks have money and do loan out money.[151] With allowing banks to provide liquidity, we have opened the door to using money coming from outside the circuits. Of course, they could also come, fifth, from reserve-stocks of money of entrepreneurs themselves. (Actually, if only one or a few entrepreneurs have such reserve stocks and start spending them, this may suffice to set into motion a wave of payments wandering through the whole group and eventually enabling

---

150   Marx puts this that the capitalist "durch seine Ware dem Markt mehr Wert wieder entzieht, als er ursprünglich hineinwarf ..., weil er größern Warenwert hineinwirft, als er ursprünglich entzog. Er warf den Wert G hinein und entzog den Gleichwert W; er wirft W + w hinein und entzieht den Gleichwert G + g." (*Marx*, Das Kapital, vol. II., MEW 24, page 47).

151   The banks, in order to hand out loans, will be mostly interested in the general creditworthiness of the capitalists, but may still like to ask for the existing surplus produce and future claims for purchase prices as collateral. Capitalists would have to give away a share of their $M'-M$ as interest and bank fees (as they would have incurred bartering costs if they had opted for the bartering solution). Alternatively the capitalists could use drafts on each other or set up a clearing house.

everybody to sell his surplus produce – as the money can do its job serval times one after another).

As a summary, it is generally possible to mobilize the finance and liquidity needed to complete the circuits of a capitalists through selling the surplus part of their produce (representing M'-M) to each other, assuming value is attributed to the produce, or to achieve the same by bartering. Already Marx said, if the value is there, the money is not the problem.[152] When Marx wrote, banks' credit money creation or states' fiat money creation was much scarcer than today; in our world of permanent private and state money creation and banking, it has become far less likely that circuits should not be able to close, if the value is there, for the lack of money to pay with. Hence, we have the noteworthy (surprising?) result that following the path of Marx's M–C–M'-analysis, in general, nothing stands in the way a closure of M–C–M'-circuits. Rather, to the opposite: After entrepreneurs have sold the M/M' part of their produce to their factors of production, they should be able to sell (distribute, "absetzen") the remaining M'-M/M' or surplus part amongst themselves.

This must, however, also be stated in the opposite way to stress the possible immanent barrier (which will rise to a fully-fledged antinomy): *Only* if all capitalists barter against each other or buy from each other their respective M'-M/M'-part of the produce, which is left over after the purchasing power distributed in the circuit has been recovered,[153] will they generate the necessary additional employment-generating spending to close all their circuits (the expectation of which induced them to initiate the circuits). Closing this reasoning, we note that much of it, now coming out of M–C–M', was already recognizable in our attempt to make sense of Ricardo's Law of Say in its third interpretation.[154]

A dialectical feast with M–C–M' and employment-generating spending in the "Grundrisse"

We have so far looked at the problems of circuit closure in a rather traditional limitational, rationalist and mechanical style of thinking. In the *Grundrisse*, Marx approached the same issue like a dialectical feast, if not like a spiritual orgy. He uses notions from his theory of capital, which reflect *supra-personal subjects* and observes how they move through M–C...C'–M'-transformations (it makes sense to use the extended version here, with C...C' representing production).

---

152 See *Marx*, Das Kapital, vol. II., MEW 24, page 331–334, and 346 et seq. *Foley* (1986) page 87 et seq., page 151 discusses gold production and loans as means to fund the purchasing power required by extended reproduction.

153 Of course, one capitalist can also sell to a factor of production of another capitalist if there is a settling "repurchase" somewhere else.

154 See page 240 et seq.

We already know the names of these notable and special spiritual characters, which transcend the phases of the "valorization process". The first one is "constant capital" or *c*, the second is "variable capital" or *v*. They not only move but proliferate and give birth to a new third character, already in the intermediate production phase C...C'; the result is the "surplus" *s*, which we also already know. A part of M, the money which the capitalist *will* use for the purchase of equipment and inventories, not only already knows its future, bears a stamp coming from its future use, but Marx also allows it to already transubstantiate: This part of the money M, the constant capital *c*, is already *its future* –in the form of *equipment and inventories*, then *in commodity-form* and at the end *in money-form* again. It is money as well as non-money as well as later money again. This subject *c* remains the same and only changes its form in its journey through M–C–M'. In the second stage, after the money bought equipment and inventories as input-commodities, it appears as machinery, oil, energy and chickens; *c* is then no longer a part of the money M but a part of C as equipment and inventories.[155] Follows production, and the constant part-subject of C now transforms into a part of the output, which is still physical produce in kind, a part of C' in commodity-form. C' is, on the one side, physically different from C as value-in use. We may have less chickens and less oil for heating and salt and pepper in storing facilities but chicken sausage instead. There will also be wear and tear. After the production we shall have less functioning equipment; parts of the machines are broken or torn down. But luckily, these parts have transubstantiated into more chicken sausage. Furthermore, the part of M, which was "variable capital", the money, which was meant go into salary payments, and did go into salaries, was eaten up by workers, but it also, as sweating human labor physically produced new tangible or intangible values-in-use. Capitalists, of course, were only induced to enter into these complexities by the hope that third parties would later attribute value-in-use and value-in-exchange to the result C', which is higher than the total costs of their c-inputs and v-inputs. This is, at least, the way non-believers in the labor value theory could describe it.[156]

---

155   Remember the capital letter C stands for commodities in M–**C**–M' and is not to be confused with *c* for constant capital.

156   Marx and other believers in the labor value theory will describe the gain of value-in-exchange over the initially purchased equipment and inventories as accruing to the produce not via *value-attribution by prospective customers*, but as result from the *specific capacity of labor to create value-in-exchange*. That is the crucial difference. Marx also stresses that already C' – not only M' after a sale– represents a higher value-in-exchange than C and reminds us that C' and C are also not only representing values-in-use but also values-in-exchange. We could, hence, instead of the customary expression M'-M = *s* also write C'-C = *s*. Non-believers in the labor-value-theory may even agree with the observation that value-in-exchange *may* already be present in the produce before it is sold (if it can be sold later), rather than only in the sales proceeds. But they cannot agree how this gain of value-in-exchange originated in

In Marx, in the aggregate, our supra-individual subject c, the used-up energy, the used-up oil, the chickens and the used-up part of machinery (or wear and tear, depreciation[157]), have wandered into the chicken sausage at exactly the same value-in-exchange. After all chicken sausages have hopefully been sold, the capitalist sits on the money M', collected sales proceeds or revenues on his bank account or in his cashier. Our c has changed its form once more and resurrected in money-form, again without a change in quantity, for every future use.[158] The same is true for the "variable capital" v. The salaries paid became sweating human labor, then this labor incarnated in the switch from chickens to chicken sausage, and then they were recovered in their full amount in cash. Surplus value s, which did not already exist at the first stage M or in the first transformation M–C, of course, must have a different biography. Its generation, the surplus-creation, occurred in production C...C'. In terms of value-in-use, it consists in the physical difference between chickens and chicken sausage; in terms of value-in-exchange it consists in the additional value-component s in the produce C', which joins c and v. According to Marx's belief, whether the capitalist succeeds to sell C' and collect M', nothing changes at the level of value-in-exchange. If the capitalist manages to sell the whole produce, the surplus-value s, which was already in C' has only transformed from the commodity-form to the money form. Marx calls this swap, in which the capitalist is crucially interested, rather than keeping his output in kind, "realization" of surplus value. If the capitalist can't sell the whole produce, he has a "realization problem", but it is important for Marx that, as the labor-power has already been applied in production and exploitation has already happened ($v + s > v$), surplus value already sticks in the unsold (or even unsellable) produce.

We have so far observed two supra-personal subjects, "constant capital"[159] and "variable' capital"[160] travel together from the beginning and being joined by an "infant element" s, which they beget in production.[161] But in Hegel and Marx, supra-

---

the produce (value-in-exchange-attribution by prospective customers vs value-in-exchange-imbuement by workers).

157   The term "depreciation", of course, comes from accounting and taxation and is not Marxian. But it meets the Marxian intention pretty close.

158   We name four stages here as we have split up C into C...C'.

159   To repeat: "constant", as it remains the same in value-in-exchange notwithstanding the alteration of its value-in-use-appearance.

160   To repeat: "variable", as it only carries the magic wand or sperm to create s.

161   Capital, in Marx, is not only a supra-personal subject, but a process, a dynamic, a relationship in action, a moving and processing contradiction. The up-coming comparison of variable and constant capital with males and females, jointly giving birth to babies in the barn of factories, in fact, even overrates the role of constant capital in Marx. The female gender is certainly regarded as fertile in biology and the earth is mythically celebrated as "mother earth"; however, constant capital in Marx, while it is almost always present in production, does not possess such attributes. He often calls it "dead labor" as opposed to "living labor".

personal spirits cannot only transubstantiate and proliferate but also "double", and after they have moved around separated for a while, re-unite. While c and v operate in production as machines, oil and chickens, c also travels to suppliers of equipment and inventories as their money revenues, while v in addition to make chicken sausage out of chickens as sweating labor, also travels to workers as their wages in money form. The ghosts c and v, thus, have *doubled and gone different ways*: c is not only there as equipment and inventory and v not only as living labor in the sphere of the capitalist, but c is also there as cash in the suppliers' cashiers and v in the working-class family's purses. If dancing couples split up on a dance floor, the partners move lonely for some time, the couples should be able to find their partners again. What splits up can also re-unite in the dialectical dances of Marx's spirits. The c in money-form in the pockets of the supplier firms and the v in money-form in the worker families' purses are ready to re-unite by buying parts of the chicken sausage. We have already seen how this happens, the c, which is in money form in the sphere of suppliers, purchases the c-part of the produce, the v, which is in money form in the sphere of the workers, purchases its v-part. The two dancing ghosts, thereby, also confirm in a mystical sense, that there should be no problem, in the aggregate, to sell the M-part of C' (or C) and to collect the M-part of M'.

The M'-M-part, though, or the C'-C-part, i.e., s, so far remained out of the picture. Let us see whether Marx's dialectics generates new insights this baby-ghost, and whether it, too, can double and whether the surplus can be realized. "Those economists", Marx wrote in the *Grundrisse*, "who, like Ricardo... were heedless of the barriers to consumption or of the existing barriers of circulation itself... – supply without regard to demand – have... grasped the positive essence of capital more correctly and deeply than those who, like Sismondi, emphasized the barriers of consumption and of the available circle of counter-values,[162] although the latter has better grasped the limited nature of production based on capital, its negative one-sidedness."[163] So both have their point, "the former more its universal tendency, the latter its particular restrictedness".[164] Marx then works his way through these contradictions:[165] "The whole dispute as to whether overproduction is possible and neces-

---

162   A good expression for the problem: "barriers of the available circle of counter-values"!

163   *Marx* (1973) page 410.

164   *Marx* (1973) page 410.

165   He is aware that he is analyzing a model, which is incomplete and abstracts from wealth outside of the considered circuits and credit. "The point here, of course, is not yet to develop overproduction specifically, but only the predisposition to it, such as it is posited in primitive form in the capital relation itself. We must also, therefore, omit here any regard for the other possessing and consuming etc. classes, which do not produce but live from their revenue....". This abstraction takes place here although these classes, in Marx' own words, "are most important for the historic formation of capital." Marx also admittedly abstracts from "[t]he entire credit system, and the over-trading, over-speculation etc. connected with

sary in capitalist production revolves around the point whether the process of the re-alization of capital[166] within production directly posits its realization in circulation whether its realization posited in the production process *is* its real realization."[167] Marx calls Ricardo as witness: "Ricardo himself has a suspicion that the exchange value of a commodity is not a value apart from exchange, and that it proves itself as a value only in exchange...".[168] Marx allows the contradiction to survive for the moment and adds that "Sismondi... emphasizes... the encounter with the barriers" and "their creation by capital itself...".[169] Then he returns to the dialectical dance floor: "So far in the realization process, we have only the indifference of the individual moments towards one another; that they determine each other internally and search for each other externally; but that they may or may not find each other"[170] "... Still, we are by no means finished. The contradiction between production and realization – of which capital, by its concept, is the unity – has to be grasped more intrinsically than merely as the indifferent, seemingly reciprocally independent appearance of the individual moments of the process, or rather of the totality of processes...".[171] Marx now shows how capitalism imposes ("posits") a condition on dancers, which complicates their re-uniting; they may only come together again, if they have a baby, profit, and that baby also needs to find somebody else to unite. To find a match for the baby is the "barrier" to the re-union of the parents. We will forgive Marx here that he expresses his thoughts enchained in his theory of labor value and exploitation. He says "...cap-ital forces the workers beyond necessary labour to surplus labour (the baby in Marx theory of labor value, G.W.). Only in this way does it realize itself, and create surplus value. But on the other hand, it posits necessary labour only to the extent *and* in so far as its surplus labour and the latter is realizable *as* surplus value. It posits surplus labour, then, as the condition of the necessary, and surplus value as the limit of ob-jectified labour, of value as such. As soon as it cannot posit value, it does not posit necessary labour... It therefore restricts labour and the creation of value – by an ar-tificial check... – and it does so on the same grounds as and to the same extent that

---

it, [which] rests on the necessity of expanding and leaping over the barrier to circulation and the sphere of exchange." (Quotes from *Marx* (1973) page 419, 416)

166   Marx normally uses "realization" in connection with surplus for the sale of the M'-M-part of the produce or the transformation of the surplus part of the produce into cash.

167   *Marx* (1973) page 410 et seq.

168   *Marx* (1973) page 411. Marx appears to be, and actually is, very close to giving up the labor theory of value: "The exchange value of a commodity is not a value apart from exchange" and the exchange value "proves itself as a value only in exchange".

169   *Marx* (1973) page 411.

170   The c-dancer and v-dancer find complementary partners of the other sex, the s-dancer must dance with another s-dancer.

171   *Marx* (1973) page 415.

it posits surplus labour and surplus value. By its nature, therefore, it posits a barrier to labour and value-creation, in contradiction to its tendency to expand them boundlessly...". [172]

The preceding quotations are rendered difficult and uncustomary not only because of their dialectics but also because of their focus on labor and labor time. Gratefully, Marx also expresses the same substance in terms of values–in–exchange, which is easier to come to grips with for non-believers in the theory of labor value: "In one and the same moment, it [capital, G.W.] posits the values on hand in circulation – or, what is the same, the proportion of values posited by it to the values contained in it and presupposed in circulation – as the barrier, the necessary barrier to its value-creation; on the other hand, its productivity as the only barrier and creatrix of values."[173] There is no guaranteed baby-dancer waiting for the baby. Therefore: "Overall, capital has a "tendency... to relate to every limit on its self-realization as to a barrier. The boundless enlargement of its value – boundless creation of value – therefore absolutely identical here with the positing of barriers to the sphere of exchange, i.e., the possibility of realization – the realization of the value posited in the production process."[174] Or, Marx writes, capital "posits the exchange of surplus values as the barrier to the exchange of necessary value"[175] "...overproduction", had Marx said before, is "the sudden recall of all these necessary moments of production founded on capital; hence general devaluation in consequence of forgetting them."[176]

So much for Marx's dialectical treatment of M–C–M', c, v and s, or "capital". We now see more clearly that in Marx M–C–M', c, v and s are moments in capital's motion and that it lies in the nature of the "over-ghost", which capital is, that, while it is able to transubstantiate, split up and to re-unite, to be also caught in conflict, in particular, *by relating "to every limit on its self-realization as to a barrier".*[177] In particular, capital – as the relation and process, which has taken control of the economic system, "...posits the values on hand in circulation... as the barrier, the necessary barrier to its value-creation".[178] In the end, Marx's analysis here has no definitive answer *where* capitalisms' barriers are exactly "posited", *how* they operate and, whether, in particular, they generally exclude the realization of the surplus part of the produce and, thereby, stand in the way of circuit closure and capitalist integration. The dialectics of M–C–M', thus, confirm that the realization of the surplus part of the pro-

---

172   *Marx* (1973) page 421.
173   *Marx* (1973) page 423.
174   *Marx* (1973) page 422.
175   *Marx* (1973) page 423.
176   *Marx* (1973) page 416.
177   *Marx* (1973) page 422.
178   *Marx* (1973) page 423.

duce is the critical issue, which can lead to overproduction and crisis. Integration is not impossible, but conditional upon babies finding a mate. What about the babies coupling and dancing with other babies?

The Theories of Surplus Value: Marx's critique of Malthus theory of "mutual swindling"

The Malthus-Section of Marx's *Theorien über den Mehrwert*, written between 1861 and 1863, also deals with barriers to production posed by capitalism itself. As already stated, Marx adores capitalism for it being powerful, forward-driving dynamics, before he unveils it as contradictory, ugly and in need to be overcome. He has an aesthetic preference to first embrace paradoxical situations before he dissolves them by dialectics. Even though Marx "inverted" Hegel's idealistic dialectics by putting it "on its feed", he could not protect himself against Plato's notional idealism, which stuck in Hegel. This, and Ricardo's labor value theory, which both resemble "realist" Catholicism, alienated Marx from the nominalist catholic tradition, in whose footsteps Malthus, a sober Anglican clergyman, who satisfied his spiritual desires outside of economics, was travelling. Marx expected and liked the central moment of capitalism to be sitting at a deeper level; hence, pivotal surplus or profit could not be a trivial mark-up on costs, which capitalists would discretionarily add out of greed, if they had the power, and which their victims would only endure because of their weakness. Rather than being a swindle or pushed through by force, *surplus value had to be a miracle*. This miracle, Marx himself aspired to solve. Already for these aesthetical reasons, Malthus must have greatly displeased Marx before he had even studied him thoroughly and he generally portrayed Malthus in an negative and aggressive way: Malthus was a plagiarist of Sismondi[179] and Marx used the arsenal of "ideology-critique" on him, e.g. by debunking him as an apologist of landed wealth.[180] The negative attitude remains present, even if Marx sometimes follows Malthus' thoughts with evident interest and applause and joins Malthus' for a part of his voyage.

Marx, particularly, treats with disgust what Malthus had to say on profit in his section on Malthus in volume 3 of the *Theories of Surplus Value*. We quote extensively: "In fact", Marx writes, "it comes to this: the value of a commodity consists of the value paid for it by the purchaser, and this value is equal to the equivalent (the value) of the commodity plus a surplus over and above this value, surplus-value. Thus, we

179 *Marx*, Theorien über den Mehrwert, MEW 26.3, page 8, similar on page 47. While Marx blamed Malthus for a "skillful" plagiarism of Sismondi. Sismondi himself did not raise any accusations against Malthus, but treated him as an equal in a joint battle against Ricardo and Say. "...mais presque tous les hommes d'affaires se conduisent d'après les principes exposés par M. Malthus et moi...c'est le débit qui leur parait être la cause immédiate de leur prospérité ou de leur souffrance..." (page 410). He even apologized for an early criticism of Malthus population theory (See *Sismondi* (1827) page 388, 389, 409, 410).

180 *Marx*, Theories of surplus value, chap. XIX, 14.

have the vulgarized view that profit consists in a commodity being sold more dearly than it was bought."[181] It is worthwhile to look at this argument in more detail. To repeat the quotation: "it comes to this: the *value of a commodity* consists of the *value paid for it by the purchaser* [hence, the price paid, G.W.], and *this value* [still the price paid, G.W.] is equal to the equivalent (the *value* [this must be less than the price paid, G.W.]) *of the commodity* plus a surplus *over and above this value* [this must, again, be less than the price paid, G.W.], surplus-value".[182] Marx is, thus saying: In Malthus, the value equals the value plus the surplus value – but he is not following up on this contradiction (not even in a book on *Theories on Surplus Value*) – so much he despised Malthus. Now, of course, in Malthus, the value does *not* equal the value plus the surplus value added in production. Malthus adheres to a subjective theory of value (in-use and in-exchange), which is attributed by customers. And, as there is more than one subject in the world, there can be different values. This applies in a specific way in a sale. A sale being concluded proves instantly that, at this moment, the subjective value-in-exchange of the seller is not higher than the sales price and that the subjective value-in-exchange of the buyer is at least the sales price. The subjective value-in-exchange of the seller may either come from either keeping the sales object and using its value-in-use (e.g., a car, an apartment house) or by selling it at a certain price or by renting it out to somebody else. The subjective value-in-exchange of the buyer comes either from a rather discretionary attribution of value-in-exchange based on his consumptive desires, e.g., from the qualities of the commodity as a positional good, or from the money he can draw by using it as a money-making machine. Ultimately, neither the costs of production nor the time of application of a specific productive force (such as labor) matter on any side of the trade to determine value-in-use or value-in-exchange. Setting values-in-exchange for a commodity is, thus, an independent act of the market, and if *nobody* attributes higher value-in-exchange than the costs, there is no possibility to make a profit.

Marx also obviously gets the emotional and moral connotation wrong. The negative touch connected to his interpretation of Malthus' view as "profit by mutual swindling" (violation of *iustitia commutativa*) is unjustified. Sellers who sell at a margin seek a profit, true – but that has nothing to do with "swindling". A seller or producer

---

181   *Marx*, Theorien über den Mehrwert, MEW 26. 3, page 14 (translation taken from https://www.marxists.org/archive/marx/works/1863/theories-surplus-value/), italics added. We repeat for reasons of precision that profit arises by selling at a value-in-exchange, attributed by customers, which, as hoped by firms, is higher than their costs. This is so as the value-in-exchange attributed by customers reflects their attributed value-in-use. Hence, whether there is surplus value or profit in the produce is not predetermined by anything, but if it emerges ou of what markets can use the produce for. It is the difference between properties of the produce, which reflect costs, and later and externally attributed value-in-exchange.
182   Quotation above, emphasis and comments added.

is only openly asking for an advantage, which he stipulates as a condition for a transfer of a commodity of his. Marx is concerned that by acknowledging this – profit in capitalism being based on owner power – the apparent "objective level" of the analysis, which Ricardo brought into play with his theory of labor value, and which Marx could use so conveniently to explain capitalism with exploitation, was disappearing. How different would the history of economic though have been if Marx had accepted the dismay of this false deep structure!

Marx believed to be able to show that the idea of a mark-up was particularly nonsensical if capitalists sold commodities to other capitalists: "But if the purchaser is himself a capitalist, a seller of commodities, and his money, his means of purchase, represents only goods which have been sold, then it follows that both have sold their goods too dearly and are consequently swindling each other, moreover they are swindling each other to the same extent, provided they both merely secure the average rate of profit." Marx tries to show the consequence to be "...that each loses as a buyer what he gained as a seller." No profit can be made, Marx believes, if capitalists merely mutually "swindle each other". Accordingly, profit by "swindling" could only be made by selling to the working class. "The only exception is the working class." It cannot "counter-swindle" as it does not sell commodities to capitalists (other than their labor) to capitalists. But there is another problem with it. "Since the price of the product is increased beyond its cost, they can only buy back a part of that product..." – here Marx, quite correctly, meets Proudhon, Sismondi and Malthus – but that cannot be sufficient. "... as profit arises precisely from the fact that the workers can only buy back part of the product, the capitalist... cannot realize [his profit] by exchanging the whole product against the workers' wage, but rather by exchanging the whole of the workers' wage against only part of the product." We have: Contrary to Malthus, capitalists can't make a profit by exchanges with capitalists by "swindling" as they mutually "counter-swindle" and they also can't make a profit in exchanges with workers as workers, while there is no risk of "counter-swindling", have too little salary income. After all, Marx refutes Malthus' theory of profit, which uses owner's power to get customers to pay more than the producers' costs for value-in-exchange attributed beyond these costs, on false grounds.

Still Marx continues to follow Malthus' argument. "...additional demand and additional buyers apart from the workers themselves are... necessary, otherwise there could not be any profit". Accordingly, Marx asks within the parameters of Malthus' thinking: "Where do they come from? If they themselves are capitalists, sellers, then the mutual swindling within the capitalist class mentioned earlier occurs, since they mutually raise the nominal prices of their commodities and each gains as a seller what he loses as a buyer. What is required therefore are *buyers who are not sellers*, so that the capitalist can realize his profit and sell his commodities 'at their value'. Hence the necessity for landlords, pensioners, sinecurists, priests, etc., not to forget their menial servants and retainers. How these 'purchasers' come into possession of their means of purchase, how they must first take part of the product from the capitalists without giving any equivalent in order to buy back less than an equivalent with the means thus obtained, Mr. Malthus does not explain."[183]

Marx believes to have found here – aside the disliked subjective theory of value – a second reason to refute Malthus: If circuit closure depends on some ominous "third class", how would this class finance its spending? Unfortunately, Marx plays unfair here: Malthus is working hard to understand the operation of a system of goods provision to society, which depends on profit-enabling M–C–M'-drives. Only such production will take place, which promises sufficiently profitable revenues; and only such production will generate employment for non-owners. Yet, there may not be enough of such required revenues/spending in the system. Malthus ponders if anything could close the gap – and finds something like what we call "prosthetics". Marx now skips the part whether Malthus is right with his discovery of the deficiency of circuit closure and shifts the attention only to the question that the artificial means may not be sufficient ("Mr. Malthus does not explain."). Yet, even *if they were not sufficient*, the importance of the original discovery of Malthus – *that they are needed* – would not be affected.

Still, Marx continues to pivot around Malthus' problem for some time, and even rather often, notwithstanding his negative attitude to Malthus, gives authentic accounts of Malthus reasoning: "It is difficult to understand", he writes, "how any profit at all can be derived if those who engage in mutual exchange sell their commodities by overcharging one another at the same rate and cheating one another in the same proportion." But then "This incongruity would be remedied if, in addition to exchange by one class of capitalists with its workers and the mutual exchange between the capitalists of the different classes, there also existed a *third class of purchasers*[184] — a deus ex machine — a class which paid the nominal value of commodities without itself selling any commodities, without itself playing the same trick in return; that is a class which transacted one phase only: M—C, but not M—C—M; [a class] which bought not in order to get its capital back plus a profit, but in order to consume the commodities: a class which bought without selling. In this case the capitalists would realize a profit not by exchange amongst themselves but 1) by exchange between them and the workers, by selling back to them a portion of the total product for the same amount of money as they paid the workers for the total product (after deducting the constant capital) and 2) from the portion of luxuries as well as necessaries sold to the third sort of purchaser....The profit would be made in dual fashion by selling as little as possible of the total product back to the workers and as much as possible to the third class, who pay ready money, who, without themselves selling, buy in order to consume." This cannot be read otherwise

---

183   *Marx*, Theorien über den Mehrwert, MEW 26. 3, page 14–16, italics added.

184   One might add, a third class who functions like the cl. des proprietaries in Quesnay's tableau.

than as Marx at least being in agreement with the logic in which Malthus poses his problem. He goes on: "But buyers who are not at the same time sellers, must be consumers who are not at the same time producers, that is unproductive consumers, and it is this class of unproductive consumers which, according to Malthus, solves the problem. But these unproductive consumers must, at the same time, be consumers able to pay, constituting real demand, and the money they possess and spend annually must, moreover, suffice to pay not only the production value of the commodities they buy and consume, but also the nominal profit surcharge, the surplus-value, the difference between the market value and the production value. This class will represent consumption for consumption's sake in society, in the same way as the capitalist class represents production for production's sake, the one representing 'the passion for expenditure', the other 'the passion for accumulation'.[185] The urge for accumulation is kept alive in the capitalist class by the fact that their returns are constantly larger than their outlays, and profit is indeed the stimulus to accumulation. In spite of this enthusiasm for accumulation, they are not driven to over-production, or at least, not at all easily, since the unproductive consumers not only constitute a gigantic outlet for the products thrown on to the market, but do not themselves throw any commodities on to the market, and therefore, no matter how numerous they may be, they constitute no competition for the capitalists, but, on the contrary, all represent demand without supply and thus help to make up for the preponderance of supply over demand on the part of the capitalists."[186]

Unfortunately, thereafter Marx reverts to the old killing argument: He lets the fact that Malthus did not convincingly explain where the financing of the prosthetic purchases is to come from, fire back on Malthus' discovery of the problem. Here is Marx's second reprisal, we quote at some length: "But where do the annual financial resources of this class come from? There are, in the first place, the landed proprietors, who collect a great part of the value of the annual product under the title of rent and spend the money thus taken from the capitalists in consuming the goods produced by the capitalists, in the purchase of which they are cheated. These landed proprietors do not have to engage in production and do not on the average do so. It is significant, that insofar as they spend money on labour, they do not employ productive workers but menial servants, mere fellow-consumers of their fortune, who help to keep the prices of necessaries up, since they buy without helping to increase their supply or the supply of any other kind of commodity. But these landed proprietors do not suffice to create "an adequate demand". Artificial means must be resorted to. These consist of heavy taxation, of a mass of sinecurists in State and Church, of large armies, pensions, tithes for the priests, an impressive national debt, and

---

185   Marx quotes Malthus' Principles of Political Economy, [second ed.,] page 326.
186   *Marx*, Theorien über den Mehrwert, MEW 26. 3. Page 44 et seq. (translation taken from htt ps://www.marxists.org/archive/marx/works/1863/theories-surplus-value/).

from time to time, expensive wars. These are the "remedies"".[187] Marx continues: "The third class, proposed by Malthus as a "remedy", the class which buys without selling and consumes without producing, thus receives first of all an important part of the value of the annual product without paying for it and enriches the producers by the fact that the latter must first of all advance the third class money gratis for the purchase of their commodities, in order to draw it back again by selling the third class commodities above their value, or by receiving more value in money than is embodied in the commodities they supply to this class. And this transaction is repeated every year."[188] "At any rate, what *follows from this*[189] is his plea for the greatest possible increase in the unproductive classes in order that the sellers may find a market, a demand for the goods they supply. And so it turns out further that the author of the pamphlet on population preaches continuous over-consumption and the maximum possible appropriation of the annual product by idlers, as a condition of production. In addition to the plea arising inevitably out of this theory, comes the argument that capital represents the drive for abstract wealth, the drive to expand its value, which can only be put into effect by means of a class of buyers representing the drive to spend, to consume, to squander, namely, the unproductive classes, who are buyers without being sellers."[190]

Marx, torn apart between polemics and honest interest, ultimately misses the gist of Malthus' argument: If a "third class of purchasers" is needed, but cannot not be found in a Quesnay-like insatiable and annually re-financed class des propriétaires, *that by no means speaks against the analysis that such third class or its spending is needed!* Malthus, like Sismondi, dissected, what would be required in the abstract for a circuit closure (what already Quesnay had shown implicitly), but Marx, although he seems to understand the argument, convulsively declines to accept it as fact. Marx rejects to acknowledge that Malthus is primarily giving a *theory of a problem* which is independent on whether Malthus' considered prosthetic solutions for it can work, in particular be funded. But Marx uses the lack of prosthetic solutions in Malthus, sufficiently convincing to Marx, to rebury the statement of the problem altogether.

Quite remarkably, Marx also fails to see that he is actually not so much criticizing Malthus but, indeed, mainly his admired Quesnay. For it was Quesnay, who, without justifying why, simply ordained that the cl. des propriétaires would exactly do what Malthus saw what *had* to be done if the capitalist circuits were to close. In Quesnay, the cl. des propriétaires was financed by the cl. productive – under the label of rent, hence based on ownership power – and the cl. des propriétaires used this

---

187   Marx again quotes Malthus' Principles of Political Economy, [second ed.], page 408 et seq.
188   *Marx*, Theorien über den Mehrwert, MEW 26. 3, page 44 et seq.
189   Emphasis added.
190   *Marx*, Theorien über den Mehrwert, MEW 26. 3, page 14–16.

rent, very noteworthily, fully and immediately for employment-generating spending – and thereby closed the productive circuits. Quesnay, thus, avoided the problem, Malthus was after. Malthus stipulated in contrary, that circuit closure does not emerge by itself. Rather, prosthetics are needed, and even then, it may not work. Marx should accordingly have recognized Malthus as a brother in arms, who, while accepting the great systemic framework of Quesnay that spending of the one is income of the other, challenged Quesnay's axiomatic harmonic outcome and sought to understand the conditions under which, if at all, a solution could arise. Instead of appreciating this valuable contribution of Malthus, though, the political beast in Marx went down on the clergymen and foreclosed another chance for progressing with a sober and realistic understanding of capitalism. Marx's treatment of Malthus was another great opportunity lost.

The labor theory of value and employment-generating spending

In order to examine whether the Ricardo-Marx labor theory of value, notwithstanding its essential fallacies, can still contribute to a theory of employment-generating spending, it must be set apart from two similar concepts. Labor, as other factors of production, carries costs; hence, there is a possibility of a *labor cost theory of value*. Furthermore, if you own commodities, you can trade them against labor just as against other commodities or money (as remuneration). Some commodities will trade against more labor than others or they "command" more labor. Hence, there is also a possibility of a *labor commanded theory of value*. Both are different from the Ricardo-Marx labor theory of value, which is a *labor quantity employed theory of value*.

Value as costs of labor employed?
Not much is needed to determine the costs of production. They can be counted and added up. Wages will account for a significant share of the costs. Furthermore, if equipment and inventory are used in production (in Marxian nomenclature both are constant capital or c), a significant share of the costs of equipment and inventory are salaries for the production of this equipment and inventory. This is so as what from the perspective of a capitalist buying equipment and inventory is c dissolves itself into $c + v + s$ from the perspective of the supplying capitalist. Yet, how far this analysis may ever be pushed, it will remain in the *realm of costs calculation*, on the supply side, and, it will therefore remain a "labor theory of *costs*". True, if an entrepreneur knows his costs of production, he may use this knowledge to calculate what sales prices he needs for a profit – but that does not give us a theory of value.

Sometimes it is argued that the value of a commodity is the *total of all claims for a share of the sales price* of a commodity or the *total of all incomes derived from it for the involved "stakeholders"* (wages, rent and profits).[191] However, the investment of any amount of costs combined with *hopes* to recover the costs plus a profit mark-up does by no means ascertain that the commodity can be sold at such price. A producer learns about his costs of production, when he makes the investment. Whether the produce is attributed enough value-in-exchange to allow a profit, he only learns if he brings the product to the market. Accomplices of a planned robbery incur costs to prepare it, which they "invest" (together with the risk to later go to prison); they, then, also mostly *expect* a certain value of the loot and of their share. But these expectations do not bring about or determine the loot. Equally, the expectation of a capitalist (or of all factors of production jointly) to obtain a satisfactory sales price in the market does neither create value-in-use nor value-in-exchange. We may only say that a robbery/production would not have taken place had the "accomplices"/factors of production not expected a certain value of the loot/produce enabling a proper reward. But that is a theory of investment, not a theory of value.

Value as labor commanded by exchange?

Subjective theories of value look at the opposing side of the market and observe whether buyers with purchasing power attribute value-in-use and, hence, value-in-exchange. If they desire to buy a thing, but do not have the money, then this can be expressed by saying, as we do, that they attribute "esoteric value". Yet, the only relevant way through which to attribute value comes from people who also have the money to pay. This is why, as we have already seen, the attribution of value to a thing can often almost be equated with purchasing the thing. Value, then, is nothing other than the expectation "will be bought for x very soon" or "will be bought in such a near future that the discounted present value is x."[192] Value is the *anticipated* reachable price, a prognosis at t1 of a price received at t2. To use the notion of value, hence, always implies bridging the present and the future, and always has a speculative moment.

Now, money is normally the unit in which the expectation or hope is expressed and by which it is made measurable. If the expectation is measured in terms of labor units instead (commanded by the commodity offered for exchange: men at such and such qualification will work 10 hours in exchange for my product), then this is only a negligible modification; it is like expressing an expected sales price in Dollars rather than in Euros and remains fully within the subjective theory of value, which expresses the value of a thing by what people will give for it, if no longer in terms of money, but in terms of labor.

---

191   "Wages, profit and rent are the three original sources ...of all exchangeable value" (*Smith* (1776) chapter VI).

192   See already footnote 4 on page 40.

Value as quantity of labor employed: the Ricardo-Marx labor theory of value

We have now arrived at the "real" Ricardo-Marx labor theory of value, which has pre-occupied so many minds and which is as different from the theories treated previously as it is wrong.

Marx wanted his theory of value to explain *surplus value* or *profit*. As we have observed, a mere theory of costs can never do this. Therefore, he is also not interested in the costs of the labor employed (the salaries), but in the amount, mass, quantity, of volume, i.e., in the *time and quality*, of the labor employed, or, as is sometimes rightly stressed, in the *socially necessary* amount of such labor employed.[193] Marx said that labor power is the single commodity whose value-in-use has the "eigentümliche" (particular) property to be a source of value in-exchange.[194]

We *first*, impolitely, note that the mechanism of value generation in this labor theory of value is *one-sided* (suppliers or producers alone exert control), *autistic* and *reified*; value comes over a thing in a similar way to how the holy spirit imbues a worshiper or as water fills a bottle. Marx's general conviction that value, the "commodity form", capital, and so forth are *social relations* remains wholly invisible at this core place of his economics. Subjective theories of value, on the contrary, look at prospective buyers with their attributions of value-in-use and value-in-exchange in the first instance; they are relational up to observations of the 2nd or 3rd, degree (reflections of reflections, and reflections of reflections of reflections). *Second*, a credence is often attached to the Ricardo-Marx labor theory of value, which is that commodities will not only have, inconsequentially, such or such amount of value "in them" because of the labor incorporated within them, but that they will *indeed exchange according to the amount of labor with which they were endowed*. Marx called this the "Wertgesetz" ("Law of value"), which he sometimes even labels as "ehern"[195] ("brazen"). Theories of value themselves decide on their claim as to their reach – and the labor theory of value is challenged at this point: Does it, in combination with the "law of value", only mean that commodities exchange at their labor value, *if* they exchange at all? Alternatively, does the labor theory of value in combination with the "law of value" mean that it is pre-ordained at a deep level of economics that everything what has labor value *will* exchange at its labor value? If the latter is true, then we ought to understand the labor theory of value in conjunction with the "law of value" also as a *theory of effectual demand*. In fact, it would be a theory, which in essence re-states Ricardo's law of

---

193   On labor embodied vs labor commanded, see also: *Keen* (2011) page 419.

194   *Marx*, Das Kapital, vol. I., MEW 23, page 181.

195   *Marx*, Das Kapital, vol. I., MEW 23, page 12. Marx speaks there of "Naturgesetzen der kapitalistischen Produktion" as with "eherner Notwendigkeit wirkenden und sich durchsetzenden Tendenzen", i.e. of "natural laws of capitalist production" as "trends operating and prevailing with brazen necessity".

Say, that there will always be sufficient employment-generating spending. If the latter applies, then the most important macroeconomic question (will there be enough employment-generating spending to buy the produce?) would have become a non-issue and, the prerequisite of economic integration could be taken for granted as a corollary from the theory of value. As we have already seen, Ricardo fathered "the Law of Say". We have now found an additional reason why a "law" with this substance should have been particularly convincing to the labor-value-theorist, which he was: It can be directly derived from his labor theory of value! We saw that Say's original statements only said, quite correctly that produce buys produce, without committing to the view that this produce would buy *all* produce. Ricardo's labor theory of value could have been the hidden missing link, which induced him to promote Say's innocent and correct observations to Ricardo's Law of Say. Why would produce be able to buy all other produce? It is because it all contained labor and was therefore valuable! Marx was an express opponent of Ricardo's Law of Say; however, through his labor theory of labor value, at least combining it with a "brazen law of value", he found himself on a slippery, downhill path and could have glided into something very close to Ricardo's Law of Say himself.

Marx's parade against gliding into Ricardo's Law of Say: value creation vs value realization

But Marx was too good an observer of real capitalism to fall into that trap. Much like how he had done elsewhere, the historian and critic saved the speculative economic thinker and, in the end, he avoided the labor theory of value and the "Law of value" from flipping into Ricardo's Law of Say. He did so by introducing a distinction between *value creation* and *value realization*. Labor can create value, but that does not already mean that the value will always exchange itself against other value. This can already be shown through M–C...C'–M'. The surplus value, created by labor, is already there in C' (C' expresses value in the form of commodities, which is higher than the amount C). Hence, the surplus value (C'–C) exists in the commodities produced before they are sold, if this ever comes to pass. If commodities endowed with labor value cannot be sold, but instead rot in storehouses, then surplus value has still been produced (value creation) but it cannot be "realized" (no value realization). Marx, thereby, kept the labor theory of value and the "law of value" separate from the macroeconomic theory of demand and of employment-generating spending. What remained was the claim that *if* commodities exchange, then they exchange at prices somewhere near the "deeper level" labor values. Hereby, Marx himself declared his labor theory of value and the "law of value'" as irrelevant to a theory of demand or employment-generating spending.

Marx's exploitation theory and employment-generating spending

Marx's exploitation theory

What about Marx's exploitation theory? Does it open a path to understanding the problems of circuit closure? Marx had regarded his own "general formula of capitalism" M–C–M' (or M–C...C'–M') as being too unspecific. In his opinion, it did not yet fully express the essence of capitalism, given that it allowed us to conceive of surplus value only as a mark-up that sellers were able to get buyers to pay because of their owner's power. Yet, Marx wanted the difference between M' and M to not be created only in exchange, but already in production. And he was also looking for another reason why M' would be greater than M; the reason should not only trivially be owner's power but better suit his superior taste for theory design: The searched for explanation had to operate at a deeper level, in a Newtonian or, even better, a Hegelian style.

The industrial revolution had developed the productive forces and had allowed for a larger surplus produce than ever before. Marx moved this observation, from the realm of *values-in-use* into the realm of *values-in-exchange*, and combined it with the Ricardo-Marx labor theory of value for his exploitation theory. Thus, he could progress from M–C–M' or M–C...C'–M' in the 1st section of the 4th chapter of volume I of *Capital* volume I to the 3rd section of the 4th chapter of *Capital* volume I. We have already quoted Marx as stating that labor power is the single commodity the value-in-use of which has the "eigentümliche" (peculiar) property of being a source of value in-exchange.[196] Marx now added that "the specific value-in-use of this commodity [labor power, G.W.] [is] to be source of value,[197] and of *more value than it has itself.*"[198] The old insight that a new value-in-use is created by labor was conquered by value-in-exchange-thinking and the new, physical or otherwise, properties resulting from the employment of labor were demoted to only being one side of the result. The more important aspect became the imbuement of the product with abstract labor power as a creator of new value-in-exchange. As we have already touched upon several times, for this purpose Marx splits up the value of finished commodities into three parts representing the used-up equipment and inventories, which he calls *constant capital c*, the wages for labor, which he calls *variable capital v*, and, finally, *surplus value s*, which is the value-in-exchange expression for the surplus produce, which has been created during production. He can now easily show that while labor power was purchased at its value, the variable capital *v*, its use or application, due to the

---

196   *Marx*, Das Kapital, vol. I., MEW 23, page 181.
197   *Marx*, Das Kapital, vol. I., MEW 23, page 208, translation by author.
198   *Marx*, Das Kapital, vol. I., MEW 23, page 181. Italics added.

aforementioned fantastic "eigentümliche" property, not only reproduces its ingoing value-component v (its costs or the wages), but also generates surplus value s.[199]

In this terminology Marx, thus, arrives at $c + v + s$ as the value of the whole produce, which corresponds to his M'. Accordingly, he can point to the surplus value s as the new part, which is identical with M'-M, and can argue that, as labor was only applied in production, that s must also have been created by labor in production. He has achieved what he wanted to achieve. He can now provide a theory for the observable fact that M'>M, which relies on production and not on exchange, and does no longer need owner's power to explain surplus value or profit as a discretionary mark-up. From there, he moves forward to draw banal corollaries in mathematical forms. E.g., he can now express degrees of exploitation as "exploitation rate" s/v[200] or as "profit rate" $s/(c + v)$,[201] etc.

Marx's exploitation theory and employment-generating spending

Marx's labor exploitation doctrine, based on the Ricardo-Marx labor theory of value, was to become Marxism's brand essence and is often seen as Marx's greatest achievement. What is more surprising is that Marx, as little as he tried to use M–C–M' for this purpose, made a serious effort to unfold this exploitation theory into a theory of employment-generating spending of business cycles, of crisis, or into a theory of trends in capitalism (with one minor exception, which will be discussed in due course). In Quesnay, the system had been in sync and there was unity between the exchange relations in the tableau: e.g., the Livres 2 bn., which the cl. des proprietaries received, enabled it to crucially purchase the respective parts of the produce of the cl. productive and of the cl. stérile. In Proudhon and Sismondi, where the system was not in sync; the exploitation, which they observed, naturally transformed into insufficient employment-generating spending. One might have expected that Marx would also make an effort to use his more elaborate exploitation theory with this intent. E.g., he could have expressed Proudhon's, Sismondi's, or Malthus' skepticism in terms of v not being sufficient to buy v plus s. Alternatively, he could have used $c+v/c+v+s$ to try to examine quantitatively how exploitation must leave workers without sufficient means to buy the produce and to show that it must, thus, backfire on capitalists' attempts to sell their whole produce. But Marx did not do that. We may, one more time, attribute this omission to the fact that his historical knowledge

---

199 Remember: In Marx, the value of the equipment and inventories is only *reproduced* in production in the amount of the value of the ingoing equipment and inventories; therefore, equipment, and inventories called "constant" capital c. The labor input purchased for v, in contrary, does not only re-appear in the same amount v in the produce, but causes a new value-component, the surplus value s, to emerge; therefore, it is called "variable" capital v.

200 *Marx*, Capital, volume I chapter 7.

201 *Marx*, Das Kapital, vol. I., MEW 23, page 428, footnote 150 and Capital, volume III, chapter II. We do not need to pursue this issue any further.

and intuitive understanding of capitalism was better than his labor value and exploitation theory. That compliment for the beardy man, but not for his pet-theories, may, yet, not please him very much.

Many Marxists from later generations would probably explain the omission by arguing that it was not at all the purpose of the exploitation theory to evolve into a theory of demand or employment-generating spending. But, what purpose, then, did the exploitation theory have beyond anchoring who is the good guy and who is the bad guy in history? And we might also ask: Should we not be entitled to expect such an effort from a theory that goes after the core contradictions in capitalism? Marx is often credited by Marxists for having spared them the troubles of a *"pauperization theory"*. But whether the result would have been pauperization, or whatever, could we not expect, from somebody who claimed to have discovered the "laws of motion of capitalism", at least a rough description of where the journey will go? If we are told to live in a non-Quesnayian world, in which things are not in sync and not in good order but where evil exploitation rules, should we not be told where its alleged wrong will drive the economy? It is quite weird, but in a way, Marx left Marxism open to the same criticism that Minsky and others raised against neo-classic economics: It cannot explain depressions and crisis. In the case of Marxism, this is even more difficult to understand as it has forged all sorts of tool, which appear to be made for the purpose, but which are left idle.

Marx's "Law of the tendential fall of the profit rate" and employment-generating spending

There is a section on the "tendential fall of the profit rate" in what Engels would later publish as *Capital volume III*. Does Marx give us a theory of employment-generating spending or of a trend of capitalism here? In the end, he does not.

The "tendential fall of the profit rate" is a mathematical corollary from the formula for the profit rate under conditions of an ongoing development of productive forces. Profit is nothing other than the surplus value s, but now it is put in relation to constant capital *plus* variable capital rate, $s/(c+v)$. The continued development of productive forces will unavoidably increase the mass of equipment and inventories applied in production in relation to labor, first on a value-in-use-level. Marx calls this an increased "technical composition" of capital. The trend can also be looked at from a value-in-exchange perspective, then called an increased "organic composition" of capital; this means that c will go up relatively in terms of money outlays in relation to v[202] when capitalists purchase the inputs for production. E.g., if producing 1,000 shirts by manual labor in a manufacture costs a manufacture owner 70 money units for labor v and 30 money units for equipment and inventory c, in a mechanized factory the same 1,000 shirts may cost him only 30 money units for labor v but, perhaps,

---

202 *Marx*, Das Kapital, vol. I., MEW 23, page 640.

40 money units for equipment and inventory c. If robots are used, then 5,000 shirts may be produced at the cost of only 15 money units for labor and maybe 50 money units for equipment and inventory c etc. Hence, the applied input of variable capital "tendentially" falls in relation to the constant capital applied and it also falls relative to output. Increases of productivity cut back on the mass of "living labor" v used, which alone, as we know by now, has the property to be source of surplus value and profit.

Marx thought a lot about causes of all sorts, including superficial, individual, and unsystematic causes (whereby he methodologically almost dropped his preference for "deep structure"-causes), which would counteract the "law of the tendential fall of the profit rate", and he listed a significant number of such "factors" (e.g., a rise in the exploitation rate s/v, a fall in prices of constant capital inputs...). In the end, though, the profit rate s/(c+v) must still fall tendentially. Nevertheless, he once again did not attempt to use this "law of the tendential fall of the profit rate" as an entry route into a general theory of demand, employment-generating spending, or of capitalist development (cycles, crises, long-term trends). This precaution did not keep Marxist writers from pointing out that the "law of the tendential fall of the profit rate" was Marx's most developed concept, which not only contained all of the elements found in his exploitation theory (c, v, and s coming out of v), but was also already formulated on the level of the "process of capitalist production as a whole" (subtitle of volume III of Capital). E.g., *Rudolf Hickel* once argued that the "law of the tendential fall of the profit rate" should be the "corner pillar" of the Marxian theory of crisis:[203] Marxism derives the need to overcome capitalism from capitalism's contradiction to the development of productive forces. The "tendential fall of the profit rate" expresses exactly this kind of conflict. The productive forces, which drive towards a higher "technical" and then "organic" composition of capital, turn against the relations of production, a capitalist profit economy, as they spoil profit generation by forcing capitalists to apply lower and lower relative inputs of "living labor", which can only give rise to profit.[204] However, Marx and Marxists after him made no serious effort to develop the limits of the markets to absorb production out of the

---

203   This argument is made in *Hickel* (1979) page XXXVII – LV.

204   There was a nice discussion in Marxism on whether the "law of the tendential fall of the profit rate" resides in the "production-sphere" or in the "circulation-sphere". *Hickel* supports the view that it already operates in the production sphere: The same output of goods, which capitalists can produce more easily, due to higher organic composition of capital, contains less surplus value as fewer workers have touched it with their magic wand of labor value creation. (E.g., 1,000 shirts produced in a mechanized factory contain much less surplus value than 1,000 shirts produced at a manufacture). Capitalists react by increasing the absolute labor input, which means that they also have to increase their absolute output. They, thus, try to solve the contradiction, which emerged in the production sphere, in the circulation sphere (*Hickel* (1979) page XXXVII – LV.)

tendential fall of the profit rate.[205] They deny the benevolent operation of Ricardo's Law of Say, but they do not use the tendential fall of the profit rate to explain to us why.

We, thus, as already happened with the Marxian theory of labor value and the exploitation theory, abort our attempt to detect useful insights for a theory of employment-generating spending in the "law of the tendential fall of the profit rate". All these theories are inconsequential rump theories, useful to draw young trade union members into communist parties, but not to explain capitalism. We move further to the famous reproduction schemes.

Marx's macro transmissions – the reproduction schemes and employment-generating spending

When Marx died in March of 1883, he left behind him a major stack of unpublished drafts. Engels reports that shortly before his death, Marx had told his daughter Eleanor that Engels should make "something" out of them.[206] Engels did and volume II of *Capital*, with its chapters 18–21 (roughly 170 pages) containing the reproductions schemes, was published in 1885.[207] In the "reproduction schemes", or as they may also be called, "accumulation schemes",[208] Marx undertakes a serious and interesting effort to come to grips with the question whether at all and under what preconditions capitalist reproduction or accumulation is possible. In a way, this was only a consequential step after having conceived the main motion in capitalism as M–C–M' and after having split up M into $c + v$ and M' into $c + v + s$. Given this, the task was to examine who can purchase the constituents $c + v + s$, once they exist as produce in kind, with the moneys either received as original investment pay-outs M $(c + v)$ or with the expected profits M'–M (s).

We have already seen a propaedeutic effort in Marx's dialectical treatment of how the ghosts of c and v can double, separate, dance, and re-unite again in the *Grundrisse*.[209] However, working this out in a more systematic and math-like way required distinguishing between different departments of capitalists and between the scenarios of simple reproduction (stagnation) and of extended reproduction (growth,

---

205 There is, by the way, another method by which capitalists could have logically reacted to the law of the tendential fall of the profit rate, namely by simply blocking the progress of productive forces. The theory of labor value, if it were true, should have driven capitalists into machine-wrecking. Obviously, that is not what happened.

206 *Engels* (1885) page 12).

207 *Marx*, Das Kapital, volume II, MEW 24, page 351–520. Marx's legacy also encompassed what was later edited as the third volume of *Capital*, the *Grundrisse*, and the *Theorien über den Mehrwert*.

208 *Hoffmann* (1971) page 75.

209 See page 251 et seq.

accumulation). This led directly to the reproduction schemes. They require more intellectual work than watching dancers, they are more of a number cruncher's job.

The result of Marx's analysis appears broken-off, unfinished, and without an express conclusion. It still shines through that he would have probably answered the question, whether extended reproduction is possible in capitalism, even if only employment-generating spending is considered which is generated in the observed production itself, in the affirmative. Yet, once more, he made this dependent upon preconditions, now in particular of a proportionality being observed. As little as Marx attempted to use M–C–M' as such as a means to examine whether capitalism can generate sufficient employment-generating spending, does he, though, seek to use the reproduction schemes, which evolve out of M–C–M', for this purpose. He neither announces that he will pursue this question, nor does he in fact undertake this. He even missed several clear opportunities to expand his analysis in the direction. Furthermore, if he had regarded his reproduction schemes as possessing fundamental relevance, concerning the closure of capitalist circuits (and hence undisturbed dynamical evolution or crises of capitalism), then why did he not publish them during his lifetime?[210]

Departments, sub-departments and flows in the reproduction schemes

The description of capitalism in the reproduction schemes found in *Capital* volume II is more concrete than the description of M–C–M' found in *Capital* volume I. M–C–M' allowed us to observe how M grows into M' and, from the perspective of circuit closure, to deal with Malthus' question "how can costs buy value?" in the more evolved way of "how can M buy M'?" For this purpose, M was split up into c and v and M'-M or s, and it became possible to pursue these value-components distinctly in circulation. The further treatment of this in the reproduction schemes is based on certain axioms: *First*, there are no other classes or categories who make purchases or supply labor or produce except for capitalists and workers; hence, there are only two units, not three. *Second*, only income earned in the observed circuits themselves, i.e., from investment outlays to factors of production, other capitalists supplying equipment and inventories, or from wages outlays to workers can be used to buy produce. *Third*, it is yet still assumed that enough money is technically available (in the right places) for the initial M-outlays, including if production is extended, i.e., in growth, to buy the additionally generated produce. Other financial means, pre-existing old wealth,

---

210   The author continues to remain unconvinced of the story that Marx's illness kept him from finalizing Capital volumes II and III. Engels tells us that Marx filled the pause, when Marx suffered from illness between 1870 and 1877, with studies of e.g., the "money market and banking,...natural sciences...geology and physiology, and namely autonomous mathematical works" (MEW volume 24, page 12, translation by author). If that is true, why did he not continue his economic work?

or wealth generated outside of the observed circuits is not a factor. *Fourth*, it is also still assumed that physical labor power and natural resources are available in the volumes needed for simple or extended reproduction; the reproduction schemes involve no theory of the origination of natural resources or of population and do not imply a restriction of production from either of these vantage points. *Fifth*, the exclusion of wealth not being generated in the observed circuits (the aforementioned exceptions notwithstanding) implies that workers also have no other means of subsistence than the wages they draw; furthermore, it is assumed that they spend their wages wholly and completely. Laborers receive what they need for their subsistence and reproduction, and they neither save nor invest.

Marx gives up his prior only "formelle Manier der Darstellung" (formal manner of presentation) in the reproduction schemes and now acknowledges the view that the movements are actually "nicht nur Wertersatz, sondern Stoffersatz".[211] He does not go so far to distinguish different branches and trades (mining, agriculture, manufacture, transport, services, foreign trade, etc.), but, based on *Smith*,[212] he uses one specific value-in-use-related distinction, namely the one between the *production of means of production* and the *production of means of consumption*.[213] The tableau-like-character of the reproduction schemes comes from this in conjunction with the splitting-up of M' into c, v, and s. There is, thus, capital producing means of production and capital producing means of consumption. The means of production are purchased by other capitalists, consumption goods are not purchased by either capital producing means of production or by capital-producing consumption goods, but only by consumers, whether it be capitalists or workers.[214] Marx speaks of two "Abteilungen" or "departments" and baptizes the producers of investment goods "Abteilung I", (*department I*), and the producers of consumption goods "Abteilung II" (*department II*); investment comes first.

A further differentiation follows that gives even more of a tableau-character to the reproduction schemes: The production of investment goods for the production of investment goods can be conceived of as occurring in a distinct *sub-department I.a.* of department I and the production of investment goods for the production of

---

211 *Marx*, Das Kapital, vol. II., MEW 24, page 393. Marx gives up the "formal manner of presentation". The movements are "not only a substitution of value, but also of material" (translation by the author).

212 *Marx*, Das Kapital, vol. II., MEW 24, page 365–369 ff. Notice that the distinction had already been implicit in Quesnay, where the "classe sterile" depended on the cl. Productive with regards to raw materials and the cl. Productive on the cl. Stérile with regards to equipment and tools.

213 *Marx*, Das Kapital, vol. II., MEW 24, page 394.

214 Hence, one cannot tell from the good's physical properties what category it belongs to. Chickens may be consumption goods or production goods, depending on their use.

consumption goods can be conceived as occurring in its *sub-department I.b.* Furthermore, the production of luxury consumption goods for capitalists and of more mundane consumption goods for workers can also be conceived of as occurring in two different sub-departments of department II; the production of luxury consumption goods for capitalists happens in *sub-department II.a.* and the production of consumption goods for laborers in *sub-department II.b.*[215] The distinctions mentioned previously are partly explicit and partly implicit in Marx. Marxian literature has sometimes further elaborated upon them. It may use two or three departments or two departments with each two sub-departments, as this book mostly does. Finally, while Quesnay did not make a distinction between the laborers and the capitalists in the cl. productive and the cl. stérile, Marx made this distinction at least implicitly. We believe that it is helpful, which results in eight elements[216] and the following asymmetric flows between them:

- Money will flow for *means of production* from department I.a-capitalists to department I.a-capitalists (themselves), from department I.b-capitalists to department I.a-capitalists, and from department II.a and II.b.-capitalists to department I.b-capitalists;
- Money will flow for *luxury means of consumptions for capitalists* from capitalists of all departments (I.a, I.b., II.a and II.b) to II.a.-capitalists;
- Money will flow *for necessary means of consumption for workers* from laborers of all four departments to department II.b.-capitalists;
- Money will flow *for wages* from capitalists of all departments (I.a, I.b., II.a and II.b) to laborers of all departments (I.a, I.b., II.a and II.b).

Beginning with M–C–M', splitting up M into $c + v$ and M' into $c + v + s$, the notation can easily be applied to the two main departments, i.e., I $(c + v + s)$ and II $(c + v + s)$, or, to the two sub-departments as well, i.e., I.a $(c + v + s)$, I.b $(c + v + s)$, II.a $(c + v + s)$, and II.b $(c + v + s)$. Alternatively, we might speak, as Marx sometimes does, of $c_1 + v_1 + s_1$ or create sums of values of different departments, e.g., $c_1 + c_2$, or of $c_{1a} + v_{1a} + s_{1a}$ or of $c_{1a} + c_{1b}$, (subscript Arabic numbers and letters indicate the departments). Similarly, equations can be given, e.g. I $(v + s)$ = II c which is the same statement as $v_1 + s_1 = c_2$,

---

215   The borderline between the two categories is rather unclear: Is the distinction based on *who buys* the produce (capitalists, workers) or on the *qualitative* nature of the produce (e.g., simple necessary means of reproduction or luxury goods)? Given that it is possible for the same firms to partly belong to I.a. and partly to I.b. or even partly to department I. and partly to department II., there is, of course, no problem with one firm partly being in sub-department II.a and sub-department II.b.

216   This is the maximum number that can be derived from Marx who, apart from treating the laborers mostly as one class, has sometimes two and sometimes three or, implicitly, four departments. Kalecki uses three (with one single department for investment goods).

the latter setting out the requirements for balanced reproduction, as we shall see. While Marx did not use a special notation for the different departments' workers, we have amended the notation in this regard and name the workers of the four sub-departments L1a, L1b, L2a, and L2b. The following flow graph is the outcome of this process:

Figure 12: Marx's reproduction schemes (graphic by author)

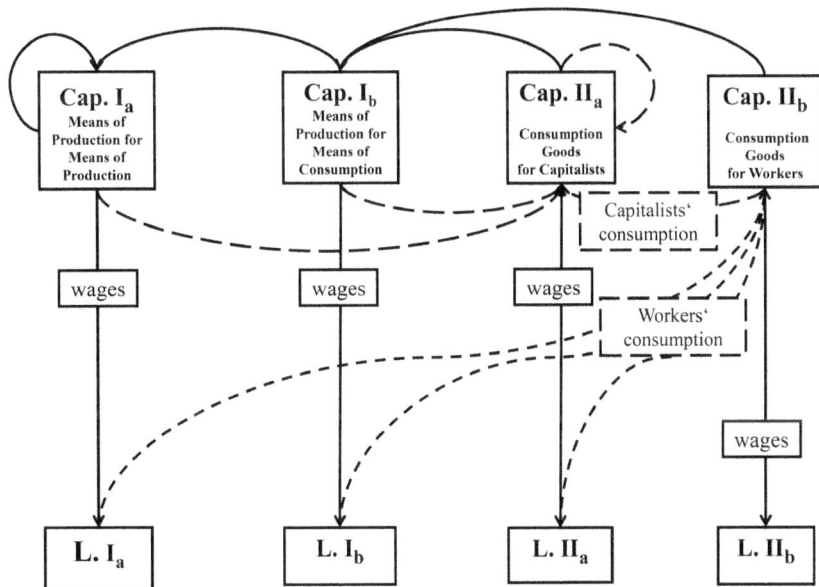

Simple reproduction

Simple reproduction means reproducing a stationary economy without accumulation, which goes on by operating on the same level forever; it could also be called no-growth or stagnant. In real life, there is mostly growth or, sometimes, shrinkage; therefore, simple reproduction is more of a theoretical starting point than it is a practical thing. The existing production facilities, equipment, and inventories are only "refilled" out of production in simple reproduction, but equipment or inventories are never increased beyond what has been used up, or needs repair or substitution. In bookkeeping terms, we may say that only the amount of depreciation of equipment is re-invested and that the working capital is kept at the same level. When looked at from the other side, this means that the part of the annual produce, which is not needed for the substitution of the used-up equipment and inventories, is consumed (unproductively), e.g., eaten up, worn as clothing, sacrificed to gods, destroyed in wars, or otherwise annihilated or at least taken out of the productive context and transferred into the wealth economy.

Here, Marx's reproduction schemes already make us aware of interdependences in the sense that certain quantitative relationships will prevail (as a tautology or identity) or must prevail (as a requirement) if simple reproduction is to function frictionlessly. *First*, the sales by the department II.b-capitalists, of necessary consumer goods to workers, will automatically be equal with the total of the wages received by all laborers (hence of workers of both departments or of the four sub-departments I.a., I.b., II.a. and II.b., i.e., by the laborers L1a, L1b, L2a and L2b., all being the same thing). This must be the case, given that the wages received (whether we refer to them as $I v + II v$, $v1 + v2$ or as $v1a + v1b + v2a + v2b$) are everything that the workers receive and is all they can spend, given that they have no further wealth. It follows that all paid-out salaries will end up with the department II.b.-capitalists because we have also assumed that workers spend their wages completely and exclusively on consumption and because the workers of all departments (L1a, L1b, L2a and L2b), while they receive wages from four different sources, have only have one address in which to spend them. The purchases from II.b.-capitalists, hence, must be equal with the total of wages earned. Accordingly, we must conclude that if the II.b-capitalists were to produce more necessary means of consumption for workers than the total of all wages, then they would not be able to sell them – at least not at the planned profits. Department II.b-capitalists can only collect what all capitalists together pay to their workers L1a, L1b, L2a, and L2b as wages. All of these relationships are logical or tautological conclusions from our axioms that reflect identities.

Second, the total sales of I.b-capitalists of investment goods for the production of consumption goods to II.a and II.b-capitalists will automatically be equal with the total purchases by II.a and II.b-capitalists. There is, simply and per definition, nobody else to possibly buy investment goods from for the production of consumption goods; this is yet another logical or tautological conclusion from the axioms that reflects an identity.

Third, the total sales of I.a-capitalists of investment goods for the production of investment goods will automatically be equal with the sum of their own purchases (by I.a-capitalists) and of the purchases made by I.b.-capitalists who produce investment-goods for department II.a and II.b; this is yet another logical or tautological conclusion that reflects an identity.

Fourth, we now come to the critical relationship, which is no longer a logical or tautological conclusion from axioms reflecting an identity appearing as automatism, but is actually a *requirement or a precondition for the flows to integrate and to reproduce the state of the economic departure* in simple reproduction. It can be met or not met and there will be simple reproduction, friction, shrinking or growth of the economy depending on that. This requirement expresses a *cross-relationship* between the departments: All capitalists and workers of the investment department I, taken together (the capitalists I.a and I.b and workers La1 and La2) can only receive as income that which department II-capitalists, without department II-workers,[217] purchase from department I. Marx stated the requirement as:

$$Iv + Is = IIc \text{ or}$$

$$I(v+s) = IIc.$$

The requirement of this equality, which must be fulfilled for the flows to integrate without friction, can also be written:

$$v_1 + s_1 = c_2,$$

which is even more transparent and which we know already.[218] Marx commented: "Es ergibt sich, daß bei einfacher Reproduktion die Wertsumme v + m des Warenkapitals I (also auch ein entsprechender proportioneller Teil des Gesamtwarenprodukts I) *gleich sein muß* dem ebenfalls als proportioneller Teil des gesamten Warenprodukts der Klasse II ausgeschiednen konstanten Kapital IIc; oder I(v+m) = IIc."[219] "Der Tausch I(v+m) gegen IIc bezeichnet die ökonomische Klammer, die beide Abteilungen zusammenhält."[220]

Summarizing simple reproduction, then, the surplus value of department I-capitalists (i.e., their profit, which, in simple reproduction, they consume completely) plus the wages (or "variable capital") of department I-workers must be

---

217 This is because department II-workers, like all workers, only purchase from department II.b.-capitalists.

218 Following *Hofmann* (1979) page 69. Marx's equations were possible for Marx because he considered the value sums of his expressions as equal. In Marx, this was so by necessity, given that the respective values-in-exchange either came out of production while the same values that had gone into production (*c*, *v*), or had originated in production (*s*). However, the reproduction schemes do not become futile for non-believers in the labor value theory if one assumes that the value attributed by the market to the processed commodities is *c + v + s* (or M'). Always remember that the notations can easily mislead a reader: The express *values-in-exchange* incorporated in values-in-use, e.g., c_2, in the last version of the equation, points to goods that, before they have been sold to department I and transformed into money, exist *in the physical form of consumption goods* (department II only produces consumption goods) even though the subscript "c" stands for constant capital, equipment, and inventory, i.e., means of production. $v_1 + s_1 = c_2$ means that the *value-in-exchange* of these *consumption goods produced by department II* is equal with the value-in-exchange of the investment goods needed by department II, against which they will exchange.

219 Marx, Das Kapital, vol. II., MEW 24, page 401. Italics added.

220 Quoted according to the concise summary of *Hofmann* (1979) page 67. In the German language "*m*" stands for "Mehrwert" which is surplus value or *s*.

equal to the "constant capital" produced by department I-capitalists and purchased by department II-capitalists. Less technically phrased, we might say: That which department I-capitalists produce beyond what they need to maintain their level of equipment and inventory must be equal to that which department II-capitalists need to maintain theirs and it must exchange against what department II-capitalists produce as a means of consumption beyond what they need themselves; this excess must also suffice to feed and otherwise provide subsistence to all members of department I, capitalists and workers alike. Rosa Luxemburg quite correctly observed that this quantitative relationship *applies to every and all economies*, including pre-capitalist ones. The amount of labor must *always* be distributed between producing investment goods and producing consumption goods in such a way that enough consumption goods are being produced for those preoccupied with producing investment goods; nobody else can do it apart from those producing consumption goods. The amount of investment goods produced by the producer of investment goods must be sufficient for those producing investment goods and consumption goods. So, what Marx found was that $Iv + Is = IIc$ or $I(v+s) = IIc$ or $v1 + s1 = c2$ expresses a "general absolute fundament of social reproduction".[221] The tribes of the Neolithic must have had some method, e.g., by tradition or myth, to allocate their labor accordingly; otherwise, even if there are no floods, no droughts, and no locusts and even if the weather was good, they would have suffered hunger at first or not have had the necessary tools or seed later. Of course, if more is produced than required, disregard for the "general absolute fundament of social reproduction" will be less detrimental; it will only mean that unnecessary excess production took place in the respective department.

We can already say that it is quite nice to be able to express this abstract economically and socially necessary relationship, which gained prominence in Marxian theory, in math – but will it also help us to understand whether enough employment-generating spending is generated? Before we think about a conclusion, we must look at "extended reproduction".

Extended reproduction

We know that M'-M or ΔM in the M–C–M'-notation is equal to s, Marx's surplus value. In simple reproduction it was assumed that capitalist behave like workers and completely "eat up" s or their profits or that they, at least, refrain from investing a part of them in additional equipment, inventory, or labor in the next circuit. In extended reproduction, capitalists change this behavior and reinject a part of s into the next circuit as c or v. There may be different reasons for why this is. They may have become less attached to luxury, more parsimonious for religious reasons (in the sense of *Max Weber's* "protestant ethics"), greedier to increase their future profits, or they

---

221   *Luxemburg* (1966) page 56.

may have been forced to do so to remain competitive. Whatever the reason, re-investment of parts of prior profits in additional equipment, inventory, and labor is good news for employment and for the productive economy. Technically, s is then split up *into three parts*, one part which goes into new additional equipment and inventory,[222] one part which goes into additional labor, and the remaining part which they still consume.

This shift to extended production (accumulation or growth) puts the *basic equation of simple reproduction*, which we already know, (Iv + Is = IIc, *or* I (v+s) = IIc *or* v1+ s1 = c2), which defines the preconditions for integration in simple reproduction, *under stress*. The obvious question is whether a similar integration of flows can be achieved in extended reproduction. In order to examine this, we give labels to the aforementioned three parts of s, whose use changes:[223] The first part, the part capitalists might add to investment in additional equipment and inventory beyond the old level c, is sac (ac standing for accumulated constant capital, s reminds us that surplus value is being used). The second part, the part of s that capitalists might use for *additional* labor, i.e., wages beyond the old level of v, is sav (av now standing for accumulated variable capital). Finally, the third part, the reduced remainder of capitalist consumption funds, which the capitalists will continue to use for consumption (or at least not reinject) in the subsequent circuit, is scr (cr standing for consumption remainder). We can now insert this split-off with the new labels into the produce of department I before accumulation begins. Instead of c1 + v1 + s1 this becomes:

on a departmental level:
c1 + v1 + sac1 + sav1 + scr1 (for department I) and
c2 + v2 + sac2 + sav2 + scr2 (for department II) or

on a sub-departmental level:
(sub-department I.a): c1a + v1a + sac1a + sav1a + scr1a
(sub-department I.b): c1b + v1b + sac1b + sav1b + scr1b
(sub-department II.a): c2a + v2a + sac2a + sav2a + scr2a
(sub-department II.b): c2b + v2b + sac2b + sav2b + scr2b.

---

222 As already noted on page 273, the reproduction schemes assume that requirements for money, labor, and materials, etc. resulting from their operation will be available; hence, an increase of production by capitalists will not be frustrated by a shortage of money, materials, or labor.

223 We use Hoffmann's notation here, see: *Hoffmann* (1971) page 69. Please remember once more that the produce of department I, including $v_1 + s_1$, is *always* "physically" ("stofflich") existing in the form of means of production and the produce of department II, including $c_2 + s_2$, is always "physically" existing completely in the form of means of consumption.

We can now also describe what happens when departments I and II attempt to accumulate or grow, hence to reproduce at an extended scale; we will do this on the sub-departmental level. While the sub-departments do not absolutely have to accumulate simultaneously, we shall initially assume that they try to do so. As stated, we do not assume a shortage in natural resources, money, or labor, which would impair this attempt:

Department I: Department I.a continues to buy its means of production, equipment, and inventors, which must be substituted, c_{1a}, as in simple reproduction, from itself, i.e., also from within department I.a – there is no other place from to buy them. However, it buys *more* from itself than it used to by the amount of sac_{1a} because it wants to grow in this circuit. In total, it thus buys $c_{1a} + sac_{1a}$. Department I.b. also likes to grow in the same circuit. For this purpose, it would also have to buy more from department I.a; it would buy what it also bought in simple reproduction, c_{1b}, but in order to grow, it would have to increase its purchases by sac_{1b} to obtain $c_{1b} + sac_{1b}$. Furthermore, the two sub-departments of department I would have to hire more workers; they would, in addition to v_{1a} and v_{1b}, have to also spend $sav_{1a} + sav_{1b}$ on salaries for workers L_{1a} and L_{1b}; the workers, who receive these increased salaries, stand ready to spend them in department II.b. Finally, the capitalists from department I.a and I.b consume at the reduced amounts of scr_{1a} and scr_{1b} by buying luxury consumption from department II.a.

Altogether, department I would have funds available for purchases from department II (added up on the aggregated departmental level) of $v_1 + sav_1 + scr_1$.[224]

Department II: Department II cannot accumulate or grow except with the purpose of producing more consumption goods, either for workers (department II.b) of for capitalists (department II.a). For this purpose, department II-capitalists hire new workers for both sub-departments II.a and II.b. and pay additional wages for the (now larger) number of workers L_{2a} and L_{2b}. The amounts of single reproduction of v_{2a} and v_{2b} will, thus, be increased by sav_{2a} plus sav_{2b}. To pay these additional wages, department II-capitalists must reduce their own consumption by the same amount of sav_{2a} plus sav_{2b}. Of course, the additional workers need additional equipment and inventory and department II.a and 2.b-capitalists will, beyond c_2, spend more money for the means of production by which to produce the means of consumption. The additional amount, which they intend to purchase from department I.b.-capitalists, will be sac_{2a} plus sac_{2b}. Department II.a and II.b-capitalists will continue to consume, but less; their consumption is reduced to scr_{2a} and scr_{2b}. These lesser amounts flow to department II.a. Altogether, department II will have

---

224   $V_1 + S_{av1} + S_{r1} = V_{1a} + V_{1b} + S_{av1a} + S_{av1b} + S_{r1a} + S_{r1b}$. The original or accumulated v-payments, of course, flow there via the workers of department I who used them for the purchases of consumption goods in department II.b.

funds available left for purchases from department I of c2 + sac2 on the aggregated departmental level.[225]

We have now set out the capitalists' program from both departments who want to accumulate simultaneously and will go on to investigate whether this fits together without conflict or friction crosswise: As observed previously, department I would have v_1, sav_1 and scr_1 left in the physical form of the means of production, while department II would have c2 and savc2 left in the physical form of consumption goods. Accordingly, v_1, sav_1 and scr_1, which are means of production, still in the hands of department I-capitalists, would have to exchange against c2 und sac2, which are consumption goods that are still in the hands of department's II-capitalists. Marx expressed this *necessity of extended reproduction*, which is now neither an identity or tautology nor an automatism, but a true requirement, in what he called the *basic equation of extended reproduction*:[226]

$$v1 + sav1 + scr1 = c2 + sac2.^{227}$$

Here comes the problem:

First, what department I wishes to give away in kind as means of production (the left side) *goes down* in extended reproduction; it is reduced by what department I itself wishes to use more of its self-produced means of production, hence, by sac1. However, what department II wishes to buy in kind as a means of production (the right side, its demand) *goes up* by the additional investment it desires to carry out by purchasing more means of production for the production of means of consumption, hence, by sac2. There is, thus, a conflict: Department II wants more means of production in kind; department I wants to give away less.

Second, what department I desires to buy as consumption goods *goes* down in extended reproduction. In simple reproduction, department I bought consumption goods in the value of v_1 + s_1 or of v_1 + sac1 + sav1 + scr1. However, department I's capitalists now only want to consume scr1. Even if they must enable their workers to consume more than in simple reproduction, v_1 plus sav1, there remains an overall reduction of department I's consumption by sac1[228] (the same amount which department I invests in more additional means of production) in the end.

---

225 $C_2 + S_{ac2} = C_{2a} + C_{2b} + S_{ac2a} + S_{ac2b}$.

226 See *Hoffmann* (1971) page 69.

227 It corresponds to the basic equation of simple reproduction of $I_v + I_s = II_c$, see on page 276 et seq.

228 Department I's reduced consumption is redirected; there is an increase in the share of workers' consumption going to department II.b. and a (greater) loss of capitalists' consumption going to department II.a.

And there is a *third* conflict as well: Department I wants less means of consumption in kind; department II wants to give away more. That is not then end of trouble: *Fourth*, department II wants more means of production for means of consumption from department II.b, but more resources are already absorbed within department I by department I.a. the production of means of production for the means of production.

There is, thus, conflict, friction, and stuttering everywhere instead of smooth accumulation and growth. We shall leave the issue here for the moment and will consider how bad the problem really is only later.

Russian revolutionaries, Rosa Luxemburg, and the reproduction schemes

The issue of whether, beyond analyzing proportionality matches, the reproduction schemes could be used to examine limits to capitalist circuit closure became prominent particularly in Russia at the turn from the 19th to the 20th century. Given the underdeveloped state of its capitalism, Russian revolutionaries doubted whether it could ever find sufficient employment-generating spending to take off and to grow. The poor peasantry was not capable of buying a significant mass of products from capitalist factories; the layers of capitalists themselves and the bureaucracy of the tsar were too small. Hence, the *narodniki* believed that Russian capitalism would need foreign markets or it would fail. *Woronzov* claimed the futility of capitalism in Russia because of a lack of export markets. *Nikolai-on*, a personal friend of both Marx and Engels, even observed that the role played by workers and by peasants as consumers had decreased because of a reduction in the labor force and because capitalist production had deprived peasants of income opportunities from side activities. He too considered foreign exports as a necessity, but doubted that Russian products could be so well-positioned as to find sufficient buyers.[229] Some Russian Marxists also supported reasoning of this style with Marx's reproduction schemes.

Russian "*legal Marxists*" opposed this view and believed in a successful development of Russian capitalism. *Struve* believed that a sufficient number of "third persons" existed, between capitalists and laborers, who would buy the products representing the surplus value, thereby allowing sufficient profit for capitalists. *Bulgakov* also believed in Russian capitalism's ability to develop independently of foreign markets. He tried to support this with the same reproduction schemes that the *narodniki* had used for the opposite purpose. He particularly pointed to the increase of department I relative to department II, which would render capitalism partly independent of demand for consumption goods and set into motion a self-sustaining closed circle, in which "the sole market for the products of capitalist production would be this production itself".[230]

---

229   *Luxemburg* (1966) page 244 – 260.
230   *Bulgakov* (1897) page 238, quoted after *Luxemburg* (1966) page 276, translation by the author.

However, *Bulgakov*, does not, as *Rosa Luxemburg* remarks, explain where suffi-cient buyers for the means of production, who would have to substitute the produce of department II, are supposed to come from.[231] *Michail Tugan-Baranovsky*, a third Russian "legal Marxist", even went beyond *Bulgakow* and saw Marx's reproduction schemes as the proof that "capitalist production creates a market for itself".[232] Crises in capitalism could, thus, ultimately only result from a lack of proportionality in ac-cumulation.[233] *Baranowsky*, thus, almost came close to reading Ricardo's Law of Say into Marx's reproduction schemes. This called *Rosa Luxemburg* to the forefront. She mocked "legal Marxists" who "showed the capacity of capitalist development in Rus-sia so thoroughly that, by the same token, they proved the possibility of it existing in perpetuity."[234]

Rosa Luxemburg, instead, proposed a theory, which she places between the *naro-dniki* and Sismondi on the one side and the Russian "legal Marxists" and Ricardo and Say on the other.[235] Both groups, she argued, did not explain "for whom extended reproduction takes place".[236] She answers this question that, even if other theoreti-cians "up to Marx" assumed the opposite, "the to-be-capitalized part of the surplus value... cannot possibly be realized by the workers and capitalists themselves".[237] Rather the "romantic" skeptics of the possibility of capitalist accumulation had the right feeling to look for "third persons", for feudal landowners, militarism, the lib-eral professions, or for foreign trade as "safety relief valve."[238] The "solution lies ... in the dialectical contradiction that for its movements capitalist accumulation re-quires non-capitalist social formations as its environment, progresses in permanent metabolism with them and can only exist as long as it finds this milieu."[239] Luxem-burg, thus, in the end[240] explains the limits to what, with Marx, she calls the "realiza-

231   Luxemburg (1966) page 269, 280.
232   *Tugan-Baranovsky* (1901) page 25, quoted after *Luxemburg* (1966) page 281, translation by the author.
233   *Tugan-Baranovsky* (1901) page 231, quoted after *Luxemburg* (1966) page 283.
234   *Luxemburg* (1966) page 296, translation by the author.
235   Luxemburg (1966) page 338.
236   *Luxemburg* (1966) page 299.
237   *Luxemburg* (1966) page 320, 321.
238   *Luxemburg* (1966) page 321.
239   *Luxemburg* (1966) page 338, translation by author. She emphasizes also that the products sold or "abgesetzt" outside of the two departments (op. cit. page 325) in a "non-capitalist social environment" (op. cit. page 338) may take any form and will "correspond to the needs of those non-capitalist circles, which help to realize it", e.g., it may equally appear as cotton or material for railways (op. cit. page 325). Luxemburg runs into the problem of how to dis-tinguish "inside capitalism" from its outside environment; see e.g., op. cit. 322–324, 327–329.
240   To Luxemburg this limitation appears to be valid only with regards to the produce represent-ing surplus value in extended reproduction, not to such produce in simple reproduction. In her view, in "extended reproduction" all surplus value *must* be realized "abroad" or "outside

tion" of a part of "the surplus value" with a limited absorption capacity of capitalists and workers.[241] This is, indeed, close to the interpretations provided by Sismondi and Malthus.

The reproduction schemes and employment-generating spending

We now return to the reproduction schemes and ask: Can the challenges of the mental exercises, which they entail, in extended reproduction in particular, ultimately teach us anything new about employment-generating spending beyond what M–C–M' could not? More specifically: From the study of M–C–M' we learned that if capitalists buy from each other that which represents the selling capitalist's surplus product, and pay for it by that which represents the buying capitalists' surplus product, there would be no shortage of employment-generating spending. This was confirmed by the study of simple reproduction at a more sophisticated level, using split-offs of M' into c, m, and s. Only in extended reproduction things got more complicated because extended reproduction proved impossible in all departments at the same time

But what happens if we jettison the assumption that accumulation or extended reproduction must take place simultaneously? What happens if different departments or sub-departments are *allowed to accumulate in an oscillating sequence*? And what if *a certain amount of friction is admitted*? Assume e.g., that sub-department I.a has a technical lead and sub-department I.b. has to wait until department I.a. is ready to sell its higher output to sub-department I.b.; why should that be a high-caliber-problem? Furthermore, if, while department I, as a whole, accumulates and employment-generating spending from department I to department II shrinks for some time (resulting in an overproduction of consumption goods in department II in the amount in which both departments refrain from consumption, i.e., by sac1 + sac2), why should this shortfall of demand for consumption goods not possibly be recuperated later after department I-capitalists have become more consumption-friendly again? Even if some overproduced food is to rot, so be it!

In the end, it thus appears that Marxists have exaggerated the additional problems of circuit closure in extended reproduction (beyond the problem which also exists in M–C–M' and in simple reproduction) and, in a way, fallen victim to their own strict mathematized notation. It is true that the observation of exchanges in the reproduction schemes is less abstract than in M–C–M' and that there are more

---

of capitalist circles" (op. cit. pages 339, 330), while the produce representing "constant' and variable" capital may not necessarily have to have the problem (op. cit. page 338, 339, 330)
241   Immediately after it was published, Rosa Luxemburg's "Accumulation of Capital" got bad grades from the most famous Marxist theoreticians of her time, e.g., *Bucharin, Lenin, Hilferding*, and *Bauer*. She answered in her "Antikritik", written in prison, which was only published in 1921, after her death.

possibilities of conflicts and frictions. However, do we not know – even without the exercise of the reproduction schemes – that baby animals can only grow into adult animals by eating more and breathing more and that their stomach, digestion organs, and lungs somehow manage to grow, *even if not completely in lockstep*, but in some zigzag-motion? Systems do come under stress when they grow and they, thus, need the capability to grow in a fluctuating, and unequal way and to endure transitory overcapacities at one place and under-capacities at others. Why should the extremely resilient capitalism be an exception? It is also an evident fact that capitalism managed extended reproduction quite well, did it not? After all, while Marx's reproduction schemes are helpful as a mental exercise in Quesnayian analysis, Marx was right not to try to use his departmental analysis to close the door for circuit closure.

***

At the end of our treatment of Marx we conclude that neither his labor value and exploitation theory, nor his theory of the tendential fall of the profit rate, but his early "general formula of capitalism" and his notation M–C–M', whether in the split up of M into $c + v$ and of M' into $c + v + s$, and in the language of the reproduction schemes or not, offer the best connection point to a theory of employment-generating spending. These notations at least allows to phrase the problem hidden by Quesnay's axiomatic numbers, which surfaced in Sismondi's and Malthus', and which was chewed back and forth in the third interpretation of Ricardo's Law of Say, in a more concise way: In a two-classes-model, capitalists must mobilize their *expected* M'-M themselves in order to pay for their collective M'-M or profit; in a two-classes-world, they are the only ones who can do this. From here we jump after the Great Depression.

Section 8. Keynes: Firms' deficient employment-generating spending as deficient remedy for consumers' deficient employment-generating spending

John Maynard Keynes

With *John Maynard Keynes, Michal Kalecki*, and *Hyman P. Minsky* we come to the final part of our journey through historic contributions to the theory of employment-generating spending. The three authors jointly treat firms' productive investment spending as the critical component and determinant for the activity in the economy and employment. Their theories have to deal with microeconomic motives, expectations, and decision making because individual firms, entrepreneurs, or capitalists decide upon their investment based on their individual profit considerations.

Keynes provided a macroeconomic basis by working out a novel liquidity-pref-erence-theory of interest derived from uncertainty. Kalecki and Minsky enriched and specified Keynes' insights. Minsky, in particular, emphasized the relevance of a broader spectrum of alternative investment opportunities and by adding his financial instability hypothesis; therefore, today, Minsky probably represents the most advanced theory of firms' productive investment spending. Although all three writers mainly think of the productive economy, and expect employment-gener-ating spending and employment from it, all three have no sufficient distinction between the wealth economy and productive economy or between investment in the productive economy and investment in the wealth economy. For this reason, their efforts do not come to full fruition.

Since the author got his first copy of the *General Theory* in a bookstore in Shibuya (Tokyo) in 1986, he has always enjoyed reading Keynes. He felt included in an in-tellectual dream of another person with a great mind where ideas flow easily and generously. Yet, unfortunately, as happens after dreams, it later often turns out that not everything was as clear as it had appeared in the dream. Perhaps a bit sadly, it also turned out that Keynes was, in fact, sometimes too easily satisfied with the first treacherous clarity or he was so deeply in love with his spontaneous and cre-ative thoughts that he did not want to expose them to the suffering brought about by tough scrutiny in the cold light of day. Keynes was a man of great intelligence; he lived a privileged, affluent, and respected life in a dandy-world amidst his at-tractive Russian wife (a ballerina dancer, who had been painted by Picasso), elite social groupings, such as the "circle", occasional top level political responsibilities and sometimes, so they say, gay love affairs. He may, thus, have considered him-self relieved from the pedantic standards of schooled consistency which apply only to lesser minds. What Hegel called the "Anstrengung des Begriffes" (roughly "no-tional toiling") and to what Marx appeared to have subjected himself desperately in his search of recognition from the official academic world, was not something with which Lord Keynes preoccupied himself a lot,[242] in fact, not even in a book, which he called *The General Theory of Employment, Interest and Money* and which he announced to shatter the science of economics. So, Keynes' *General Theory* became yet another un-finished great work, like Mahler's 10th symphony, Heidegger's *Sein und Zeit* or, yes, Marx's *Capital*. But what a great unfinished work it is!

Right wing libertarian, Austrian economists, *von Mises* and *von Hayek*,[243] opposed the *General Theory* from the beginning. *Henry Hazlitt*, an Austrian economist and a leading US economic journalist of the time, attacked it fervently in a systematic com-

---

242   *King* (2015) page 77, writes "Keynes was never greatly interested in economic theory for its own sake..."

243   E.g., *von Hayek* (1944).

mentary in 1959.[244] Having lived a professional life as a trial lawyer, the author cannot but appreciate argumentation which combines surgical attentiveness to detail with a killer instinct and the application of heavy weaponry where circumstances allow. That is what Hazlitt did to Keynes (leaving malevolent misunderstandings, which are also there, aside). After Hazlitt was done wreaking carnage on Keynes' *opus magnum*, it looked as if an iron door had fallen onto it. Unfortunately, apparent followers, such as *John R. Hicks*, were not much more helpful to the reception of Keynes' work. Hicks' influential interpretation of Keynes, which appeared a year after the *General Theory*, only served to pull Keynes back into the neoclassical camp. This direction, which was further pursued by *Alvin Harvey Hansen* in the US, indeed, remained the main line of Keynes-interpretation even if, somewhat embarrassingly, Hicks largely revoked the IS-LM-diagram,[245] the main result of his Keynes-interpretation, himself.[246]

With a view to notional, logical, argumentative consistency, admirers of Keynes, *Hyman Minsky* for instance, did not give much better grades to Keynes than his arch-enemy Hazlitt had. Keynes' work was partly "muddled",[247] Minsky wrote and his "seeds never reached full fruition". Instead, Keynes "embryonic scientific revolution was aborted".[248] Or: "The General Theory is a very clumsy statement. Much of the old theory is still there, and a great deal of the new is imprecisely stated and poorly explained." Apart from a general lack of consistency, several other moments at the time were not favorable to Keynes as a theoretician. States had always "interfered" in the economy, even in the earliest days, e.g., in ancient Athens, Rome, and China, long before programs of state interference had been systematized into "cameralism" or "mercantilism". Heavy state interference did not disappear in the heydays of British economic liberalism, but went together smoothly alongside British Colonialism.[249] Equally, the mass slaughter of World War I had only been possible because of massive state intervention in the economy and in what states mostly did, on the international and national scenes, after World War I, e.g., the reparation obligations in the Versailles treaty or the German government's policies favoring inflation,[250] continued that route. World War I had discredited the liberal po-

---

244 Hazlitt's work was published in 1959. Keynes had already died by 1946.

245 *Hicks* (1937) pages 147–159.

246 *Hicks* (1976) pages 135–151 (quoted after *Minsky* (1977) page 70, footnote 10). *Hicks* (1980) page 139. The IS-LM-diagram is, nevertheless, still taught in many textbooks of today. See *Keen* (2011) page 229–242.

247 *Minsky* (1975) page 67.

248 *Minsky* (1975) page 3.

249 As we shall see on page 394, even Smith praised the protectionist "Navigation Act".

250 Piketty writes "...l'inflation est dans une large mesure une invention du XXe siècle. Au cours des siècles précédents, et jusqu'à la Première Guerre mondiale, l'inflation était nulle ou quasi nulle. " Even after the introduction of new currencies, such as the Dollar in 1776 or the mark in 1873 "...une foi les parités métalliques fixées, plus rien ne bouge. Au XIXe et au

288 Gerhard H. Wächter: The Capitalist Economy and its Prosthetics

litical world view; rebellious mass movements grew, and the social catastrophes of the German/Hungarian inflation 1923 as well as of the Great Depression in 1929[251] encouraged more traditional political parties to shrug off limitations of economic liberalism. In fact, many state bureaucrats had never fully believed in economic liberalism in the first place. All of this evolved independently of Keynes' book. The UK, the US, imperial Japan as well as Hitler's Germany and even the Soviet union, which Keynes visited both,[252] would have applied Keynes's recipes, or similar ones, if the *General Theory* had never been written. This widespread acceptance of Keynes' proposals rendered any in-depth scrutiny of his analysis superfluous – or at least, it was not undertaken. War came. The practice of state-sponsored deficit-financed spending, thence, did not longer consist in innocently burying bottles with bank-notes and digging them up again,[253] but in destroying and burying cities (which would only later be rebuilt again), all of this occurred in a tenfold, probably, "investment"-volume than Keynes may have hoped for. A lot of things, thus, became more urgent than checking the consistency of Keynes' theory. That remained so until after WWII was over, but Keynes' recipes appeared now to be vindicated by the state-led reconstruction of the economies of the war-participants. The upcoming Cold War also necessitated new, massive state interventions in the West and in the East. Shortly before the Cold War was won, anti-interventionist or less interventionist or differently interventionist concepts, Monetarism, Thatcherism, Reaganomics, and Neoliberalism, raised their heads and Keynesianism ran out of steam. It lost its popularity for the same reasons that it had gained it forty years previously, because it no longer worked politically for the elites in a world of financialization and globalization. Keynes was already dead for a long time and could not do anything about it.

So once more, there was no push towards "hammer(ing) out" a "transition from the clumsy original [of Keynes' theory] to the better, more elegant, and polished statement of the new theory",[254] which Minsky had aspired. Nevertheless, Hyman Minsky now basically took over the responsibility himself to "fill out what Keynes

---

début du XXᵉ siècle, chacun sait bien une livre sterling vaut environ 5 dollars, 20 marks et 25 francs." (*Piketty* (2013) page 171, details page 174).

251   In the Great Depression, Chicago-economists argued for expansionist monetary and fiscal policies without this being integrated into the formulation of a theoretical concept of the capitalist process (*Minsky* (1975) page 5).

252   *Harrod* (1982) page 365, 394 and 478. Keynes visited the Soviet Union together with his Russian wife in 1925, 1928, and 1937.

253   *Keynes* (1936) page 129. Keynes also mentions earthquakes and pyramid and cathedral building (pages 129, 131) and points to a problem of modern substitutes, which underly a more functional rationality: "Two pyramids, two masses for the dead, are twice as good as one; but not so two railways from London to York." (page 131).

254   *Minsky* (1975) page 12, 13.

discussed in a fragmentary and casual manner".[255] Keynes, he said, had changed the focus of economic analysis. He had shifted it from a pre-crisis perspective on resource allocation to the problems of aggregate demand.[256] Keynes had found that until full employment rules, aggregate demand defines the ratio of employed to employable resources[257] and that investment demand, i.e., firms' employment-generating spending, is the crucial part of aggregate demand. The "level of output and employment as a whole depends on the amount of investment," said Keynes and Minsky labels investment in Keynes as "causa causans".[258] Or, as Minsky claims: "...the core of *The General Theory* is the theory of investment".[259] This insight brings the financial system into play. The financial system is necessary for "capitalist vitality and vigor" and "translates entrepreneurial animal spirits into effective demand for investment" (or it does not).[260] Therefore, in Minsky's view, beyond what Marx did, we need to take a step back to behind the investment M–C to the very procurement of the money M in the M–C–M'-sequence, and to pass over from a mere "investment theory of fluctuations in real demand", as helpful as it already is, to a "financial theory of fluctuations in real investment". Minsky, thus, accentuated the role played by wealth owner's "desired portfolio composition and ...financial relations in general" and elevated portfolio composition to the "areas of decision where changing views about the future can most quickly affect current behavior".[261] This is what Keynes was already aiming at when taking a "Wall Street-perspective" or by resting his theory "on a speculative-financial paradigm".[262] Accordingly, uncertainty must enter into the argument, not only with regard to investors' views concerning the prospective yields of the newly produced capital assets but also, and possibly more crucially, with regard to the liquidity preference and interest rate and their influence on alternative investment opportunities and portfolio decisions.[263] We are mainly interested in the aggregate theoretical contribution of the thoughts of Keynes, Kalecki, and Minsky (rather than in separating out their individual innovations), but shall still begin with Keynes' original argument.

255 *Minsky* (1975) page 60.
256 Minsky (1975) page 2, 7.
257 Minsky (1975) page 8.
258 *Keynes* (1937) page 221, reprinted in: Collected Writings XIV page 109 et seq.
259 See also *Minsky* (1975) page 92.
260 *Minsky* (1975) page 11.
261 *Minsky* (1975) page 55 and (1986) page 133.
262 *Minsky* (1975) page 55.
263 *Minsky* (1975) page 55.

Entrepreneur economy, capitalism, and M–C–M'

Keynes starts his investigation, which he connects to Book VII of Malthus' *Principles*, with the "economic organization" of society *as it really is*. It consists, as he says, "on the one hand, of a number of firms or entrepreneurs possessing a capital equipment and a command over resources in the shape of money, and, on the other hand, a number of workers seeking to be employed."[264] Keynes refers to this situation as an "entrepreneur economy".[265] In the entrepreneur economy, "the starting up of productive processes largely depends on a class of entrepreneurs who hire the factors of production for money and look for their recoupment from selling the output for money..."[266] Or: "A process of production will not be started up, unless the money proceeds expected from the sale of the output are at least equal to de money costs which could be avoided by not starting up to process."[267] In other words: "The firm... has no object in the world except to end up with more money than it has started with. That is the essential characteristics of an entrepreneurial economy."[268]

What Keynes describes here hardly differs from what Smith, Ricardo, Sismondi, Malthus, and Marx had more customarily (and in a little less friendly a tone) called "capitalism"; nevertheless, Keynes' observations are utterly correct. Indeed, Keynes' definition of the essential characteristics of his entrepreneur economy is *very* close to Marx's M–C–M'-analysis. While Keynes kept a clear distance from Marx in the *General Theory* or even overstated his distance – his main reference was negative –[269], in lectures held in 1932, he more frankly acknowledged his theory's material parallelisms with Marx's: "The distinction between co-operative economy and an entrepreneur economy bears some relation to a pregnant observation made by Karl Marx... He pointed out that the nature of production in the actual world is not, as economists often seem to suppose, a case of C–M–C', i.e., exchanging commodity (or effort) for money in order to obtain another commodity (or effort). That may be

---

264   *Keynes*, Collected Writings, volume XXIX, page 63 et seq.

265   Keynes was partly working on a set of classifications for economies, such as barter-economy, real wage economy, real-exchange economy, cooperative economy, entrepreneur economy, etc. shortly before he published the *General Theory*, which he did, however, not use in the end. See *Keynes*, Collected Writing, volume XIII, page 382 et seq., 408 et seq.; XXIX page 63 et seqs. 76 et seq., 87 et seq., 101 et seq.

266   *Keynes*, Collected Writings, XXIX, volume page 77.

267   *Keynes*, Collected Writings, volume XXIX, page 78.

268   *Keynes*, Collected Writings, volume XXIX, page 89. This forces Keynes to allow for the possibility of "a situation in which the marginal utility of output is greater than the marginal disutility of effort", which he regards as "a failure of organization which prevents a man from producing something, the equivalent of which he would value more highly than the effort it cost him" (loc. cit. page 101).

269   *Keynes* (1936) page 32 ("...underworlds of Karl Marx").

the standpoint of the private consumer. But it is not the attitude of *business*, which is a case of M–C–M', i.e., with parting with money for commodity (or effort) in order to obtain more money."[270]

Keynes "entrepreneur economy"[271] and Marx's "capitalism", thus, both see firms, entrepreneurs, or capitalists as complementarily intertwining consumption-driven C–M–C'-circuits with a second type of circuit, i.e., profit-driven M–C–M'-circuits, with a different entry point. They also both look at the circuits dynamically and on a time axis. Moreover, in Keynes as in Marx, the entrepreneur's first practical activities are M–outlays for equipment and inventories or to workers. They also still agree that the capitalist or entrepreneur make their M–outlays to receive the revenues of M' in return. Yet differences develop at this point. Keynes is much more interested in the exact calculus, which operates in the entrepreneur mind and all circumstances which may be of relevance here. Marx, of course, knew that not every investment is profitable and even if surplus value was generated in production, that it only physically "stuck" in the produce and still had to be "realized" through a sale, i.e., turned into money form. Marx knew about crises too; he had lived through a few of them in London, analyzed them, and was aware that they had to do with excessive production in relation to demand. Nevertheless, Marx's capitalists were basically only focused on exploiting laborers, on increasing the technical composition of capital, on increasing the absolute and relative surplus-value, etc. and they were not too concerned about selling their produce, ultimately. Keynes had just experienced the Great Depression of 1929, a category of crisis that Marx had not witnessed and saw the entrepreneur's mind as the critical place: How would this mind function when the entrepreneur made decisions about investments? How would he build his expectations – including on the salability and profitability of his produce? How would he benchmark his expected profits against alternative investment opportunities? Keynes developed a new theoretical repertoire to attack these questions; he,

---

270   *Keynes*, Collected Writings XXIX, page 81. The omitted part of the quotation reads "– though the subsequent use to which he put this observation was highly illogical". Even though we have omitted it, as Keynes obviously refers to the theory of labor value and exploitation, which Marx uses to explain the M'-M gap, we fully agree with Keynes' critical insertion. A good rule of thumb to identify truth in economics might be: Look out where Malthus, Marx, and Keynes agree! *Steven Keen* holds that if Keynes had used this argument from his lecture in the *General Theory* that his argument against "Say's Law" would have been so much stronger that this could have changed Keynes' reception and avoided the "Hicksian neoclassical counter-revolution" (Keen (2011) page 218). Keen's book appears to be the strongest left-wing economics book in decades.

271   The fact that Keynes, eventually, did not mention the influence of Marx's M–C–M' in the *General Theory* induces the comment that Kalecki and Minsky were equally rather shy to admit Marx's influence upon their thinking – sometimes to a degree that violates scientific rules and good taste. (Of course, a gentleman by the name of McCarthy or similar fears may explain this). *Keen* (2011) page 218 makes a similar remark.

in particular, had a "marginal efficiency of capital (m.e.c.)" battle against "liquidity preference" leading to a strong or weak "inducement to invest".

Keynes' theory of firms' investment: the inducement to invest

Rejection of "Say's law"

In Book I of the *General Theory*, Keynes refers to what we called "Ricardo's Law of Say". He calls it conventionally "Say's law" and summarizes it as "supply creates its own demand".[272] As this law was "equivalent to the proposition that there's no obstacle to full employment",[273] Keynes needed to do away with it to gain the space to develop the *General Theory*, which was exactly to examine and explain what happens if the alleged law does not miraculously generate full employment. Ricardo's victory over Malthus (and, hence, the triumph of "Say's law"[274]), said Keynes, was as complete "as the Holy Inquisition conquered Spain".[275] Keynes sided with losing Malthus and deplored the results of Ricardo's victory: "The great puzzle of effective demand with which Malthus had wrestled vanished from economic literature...It could only live on furtively, below the surface, in the underworlds of Karl Marx, Silvio Gesell, or Major Douglas".[276] Keynes then preoccupied himself with what would have been a non-issue under the dismissed law: "the pure theory of what determines the actual employment of available resources", which has only "seldom been examined in great detail."[277] On this journey, Keynes redefined, as *Minsky* would put it later, "the problems of economic theory as the determination of aggregate demand".[278]

---

272   *Keynes* (1936) page 18. He quotes John Stuart Mill's, Principles of Political Economy, Book III, chap. Xiv § 2: "What constitutes the means of payments for commodities is simply commodities. Each person's means of paying for the productions of other people consists of those which he himself possesses. All sellers are inevitably, and by the meaning of the word, buyers."

273   *Keynes* (1936) page 26, Collected Writings XXIX, page 78.

274   *Keynes* (1936) page 18 et seq See also *Keynes*, Collected Writings XIII page 422; Collected Writings XXIX page 256 et seq Keynes wrote to Lerner on 16 June 1936 concerning an article by Lerner on the General Theory: "There are two points which layed a considerable part in my own mental development, which you scarcely touch on. The first of these concerns the breaking away from the assumption in some shape or form of Say's law. This could be described as a re-discovery of there being a problem of the equilibrium of the supply and demand of output as a whole, in short of effective demand" (*Keynes*, Collected Writings XXIX page 215). Keynes also referred to the "powerful arguments" made by Malthus both inside and outside of the General Theory, e.g., *Keynes*, Collected Writings XXIX page 81.

275   *Keynes* (1936) page 32.

276   *Keynes* (1936) page 32.

277   See *Keynes* (1936) page 4. Exceptions include Sismondi and Malthus. See on pages 221 and seq. and 227 and seq.

278   *Minsky* (1975) page 2, 7.

The marginal propensity to consume, the consumption gap, and investment as a (dubitable) savior

If demand cannot be assumed to be available in sufficient volume *per se*, Keynes asks: where does demand come from?[279] Keynes begins with *consumption demand*: "The outline of our theory can be expressed as follows. When employment increases, aggregate real income is increased. The psychology of the community is such that when aggregate real income is increased aggregate consumption is increased, but not by so much as income...".[280] Increase in workers' incomes, be it because formerly unemployed people are brought into jobs or because of salary raises, will pretty much wholly go into increased consumption spending, for more and better food, presents to kids, new cars, furniture, travel, etc. If incomes fall, consumption spending will be equally directly reduced. "Dis-hoarding depends", Keynes rightly observes elsewhere, "not on businessmen trying to get out of money into goods but on widows trying to evade starvation".[281] Yet, well-earning humans will unlikely buy a second or third gourmet dish per day, or a fourth, sixth or seventh private computer, car, yacht, or residence etc., if their incomes rise, which will loosen the connection between rising income and rising consumption.

Now, what should the recipients of income increases, who do not consume more, do with their additional money? Keynes' answer is: They should make investments.

---

279 Particularly in Books I and III of the *General Theory*.

280 *Keynes* (1936) page 27.

281 *Keynes*, Collected Writings XIII, page 33. Keynes almost appears to wish to define what the community is expected to consume and to invest as its "effective demand". Why is expected demand effective demand? It is because only expectations have effects on the investments of entrepreneurs who derive their business plans and production plans from it. These are the most important and quite real effects of expectations. What the community, sometime later, in the C–M'-metamorphoses really buys or does not buy only vindicates (or not) the amount of past investment, but has no more effect on past employment or unemployment. That understanding of "effective demand" would, hence, be more specific than only pointing to the fact that purchase power must join the esoteric desire to consume a commodity or service. In this book, we have decided to use "effective demand" and "effectual demand" with two different meanings: "Effective demand" is expected demand only with effects on business and production plans, investment-outlays M, and employment at the beginning of a circuit. "Effectual demand" is real demand at the end of the circuit which vindicates (or does not) such investments. Its "effectual" effects are the procurement of M' or of the cash in the entrepreneur's pocket at the end. There are several clues that Keynes may have understood "effective demand" in this sense too. "The demand, which determines the decision to employ people must necessarily concern itself with expectations" (*Keynes*, Collected Writings XIII, page 602) or "Effective demand on this reflects the current expectation of actual amount..." (*Keynes*, Collected Writings XIII, page 603); however, we do not insist to impute our uses of "effective" and "effectual" demand onto Keynes who was neither seriously interested in notional issues nor, normally, consistent in the use of his terms.

"Thus, to justify any given amount of employment there must be an amount of current investments sufficient to absorb the excess of total output over what the community chooses to consume..."[282] Investment demand must fill the gap. Effective demand D, says Keynes, is "the sum of two quantities, namely D_1, the amount which the community is expected to spend on consumption, and D_2, the amount which it is expected to devote to new investment".[283] "Hence the volume of employment in equilibrium depends on (i) the aggregate supply function Φ, (ii) the propensity to consume, x, and (iii) the volume of investment D_2. This is the essence of the General Theory of Employment."[284] Keynes elaborated on this issue quite often. On 16 June 1936, he wrote to Lerner: "The second point which was important to my own thought was the discovery that, as income increases, the gap between income and consumption may be expected to widen ... A higher level of income will only be possible without loss to the entrepreneur, if the widening gap between income and consumption can be filled. This can only be filled by investment. Yet it is evident that the requisite volume of investment is not necessarily there."[285] In 1934, Keynes wrote: "Consequently, our habit of withholding from consumption an increasing sum as our incomes increase means that it is impossible for incomes to increase unless either we change our habits so as to consume more or the business world calculates that it is worthwhile to produce more capital goods."[286] Keynes attributed the great depression to a lack of investment. He lectured in Chicago in 1931: "...I feel, then, no serious doubt or hesitation whatever as to the causes of the world slump. I trace it totally to the breakdown of investment throughout the world."[287] However, entrepreneurs being as they are, he also lectured in Chicago in 1931: "If our object is to remedy unemployment it is obvious that we must first of all make business more profitable. In other words, the problem is to cause business receipts to rise relativity to business costs."[288] Or: "And nothing, obviously, can restore employment which does not first restore business profits. Yet nothing, in my judgment, can restore business profits which does not first restore the volume of investment, that is to say ... the volume of orders for new capital goods".[289] Or, in February 1935 he wrote: "My solution, put in a sentence, it is that, given the propensity to spend, *demand is a function of the amount of investment.*"[290]

---

282   *Keynes* (1936) page 27.

283   *Keynes* (1936) page 29.

284   *Keynes* (1936) page 29.

285   *Keynes*, Collected Writings XXIX, page 215.

286   *Keynes*, Collected Writings XIII, page 490.

287   *Keynes*, Collected Writings XIII, page 358.

288   *Keynes*, Collected Writings XIII, page 362.

289   *Keynes*, Collected Writings XIII, page 355.

290   *Keynes*, Collected Writings XIII, page 516, emphasis added. In Keynes, thus, investment is the savior of demand. But what if investment does not fulfil its responsibility as, e.g., "the

Keynes is aware that a very serious problem is attached to trying to solve the consumption gap with investment. We may only be kicking the can down the road. He acknowledged: "Each time we secure to-day's equilibrium by increased investment we are aggravating the difficulty to secure equilibrium tomorrow".[291] The more investment is used to create demand in order to maintain employment, the more it will later crucially surface that investment ultimately serves consumption only; the equipment and inventories produced may be hopelessly excessive compared to the necessities of consumption and of producing consumption goods. Now, we must ask: Is not this dilemma touched upon by Keynes here, so high-caliber and so poisonous that it fatally renders all hope in investment as savior obsolete? Keynes left this question, as others, unanswered, and did not venture further into this nightmare scenario. He ignored that he had ultimately not solved the problem. Would it not have to be paid for with later brutal drops of employment at the day of reckoning – when firms find no buyers for the increased volume of consumption goods, which they will have to try to produce with the additional investment goods some day? Is investment, thus, only an unsustainable, short-term strategy, that comes at a high price?[292] A concept not thought-through? Keynes moves on without ever answering these questions.

In the entrepreneur's mind before his investment decision

The General Theory describes circuits and there are several points at which circuits can be entered. In book III, Keynes chooses an entry point a bit earlier than Marx. In his "general formula of capital" M–C–M', Marx picked the moment at which the capitalist or entrepreneur departs with a sum of money as an investment, his M; Keynes goes a step back to when the entrepreneur ponders about what to do with his money[293] and looks into the entrepreneur's mind before the entrepreneur makes the

---

propensity to invest has been chronically weak"? *Martin Wolf*, in a *Financial Times*-commentary, then points at "the bottom 90 percent" of the society and at "persistent fiscal deficits" to do the job, both requiring to be "fueled by debt" (*Wolf*, Inequality is behind central bank dilemma, in: *Financial Times* of 22 September 2021). We are back, where Keynes started: The consumption gap results from the marginal propensity to consume with increasing income, investment is the savior, but does not do the job, so we revert to those who have a high marginal propensity to consume (approaching 100 %) but lack money and procure them with money via debt.

291   *Keynes* (1936) page 105.
292   In this sense, Foley argues, with reference to Rosa Luxemburg, that: "Investment in productive capacity can be justified in the end only as way of producing consumption goods". However, as workers' "consumption becomes less and less important relative to total production. How ...can we imagine that capitalists will continue to invest large sums of money to create productive capacity to meet shrinking final demand?" (*Foley* (1986) page 151).
293   Keynes is primarily thinking of an investment in the productive economy. This is apparent when he speaks of "current investment" as "current addition to the value of capital equip-

money-outlays.[294] Humans, to make decisions, need a rationale underneath which they can subsume information. The rationale for a merchant hero is to make profit and to accumulate wealth. Starting with a money amount M, which is available to him, he will venture through the oceans of values-in-uses (equipment, inventories, labor), only to return home with his ship filled with more cash, M'.[295] When he plans this mission, he will have to deal with uncertainty and interest twice. Higher interest raises the costs of the investment by increasing his financing costs and, generally, raises the price level of supplies. Uncertainty affects the revenues of the venture and its relation to the costs of the investment, Keynes' m.e.c. However, uncertainty and interest will also play a second role as the interest, which the investor *could draw* by loaning out the equity-part of M and which he *foregoes by investing it in his productive business* (risk adjusted), will benchmark the attractivity of his results, e.g., by discounting future surpluses.[296] Thus, higher rates of interest work twofold against investment in the productive economy.

---

ment which has resulted from the productive activity of the period." (*Keynes* (1936) page 62). When he has "exchanges of old investment" cancel each other out, and defines "investment" as "increment of capital equipment, whether it consists of fixed capital, working capital..." that, too, confirms his general view of investment in the sense of a produive, employment-generating investment. However, the above quoted expression reads in full "...increment of capital equipment, whether it consists of fixed capital, working capital or liquid capital" (*Keynes* (1936) page 75), which renders things less clear again. What is, in particular, "liquid capital" supposed to be? Normally any money injection into a firm would qualify as "liquid capital", yet a money injection could also be used to merely buy a pre-existing asset. Unfortunately, we encounter this opacity at exactly the worst moment in Keynes, namely in chapters 11 and 12 of the *General Theory*, which are elementary for his theory of investment and his theory of firms' contribution to produive spending.

294   We shall see that Minsky begins his observations even further backwards by examining of how an entrepreneur got the money for prior investive drives.

295   With reference to *Slotederdijk* (2005) page 134: "Als Ware wirft sich das Geld auf das offene Meer der Märkte und muss, vergleichbar den Schiffen, auf das glückliche Einlaufen in den Heimathafen, das Besitzerkonto, hoffen; in der Warenmetamorphose is die Erdumrundung latent mitgedacht...Durch die Rückkehr des schwimmenden Kapitals von der Fernreise wird der Expansionswahnsinn zur Profitvernunft. Die Flotte des Kolumbus und seiner Nachfoger besteht aus Narrenschiffen, die zu Vernunftschiffen umgerüstet werden."

296   "It seems", according to Keynes, "then, that the rate of interest on money plays a peculiar part in setting a limit to the level of employment, since it sets a standard to which the marginal efficiency of a capital-asset must attain if it is to be newly produced." (*Keynes* (1936) page 222). Turgot already knew that investors in the productive economy will demand a surplus of profit equivalent to their effort and risk over e.g., a sterile investment in land. See *Faccarello* in: *Faccarello/ Kurz* (2016) page 76.

Marginal efficiency of capital (m.e.c.): the numerator of the fraction

While Marx's M–C–M' departs from individual commodities, Keynes thinks bigger. In book IV of the *General Theory*, he deals with machines who spit out M–C–M'-circuits straight away, i.e., with investments in assets that already generate a series of yields or quasi-rents.[297] Once planning for such assets is completed, Keynes compares the *costs* (which he calls the "supply price") of the production of the M–C–M'-machine or asset with the expected future "annuities" resulting from the investment (which he calls the "demand price" of the asset).[298] Compared to Marx, Keynes' two money amounts, a smaller one, which is outflowing, and a larger one, which is inflowing, are aggregated and are capitalized to present values.[299] Keynes then calculates the rate, by which the value (Keynes' demand price) of the investment can be discounted to its costs (Keynes' supply price) and calls the calculated discount rate the *"marginal efficiency or capital"*, often abbreviated as "m.e.c.", including by Keynes himself.[300]

Uncertainty, liquidity preference and interest rate: the denominator of the fraction

While knowing the *m.e.c.* of an investment may already suffice for an entrepreneur to say "this sounds good – let's go ahead" or "this is poor – let's forget it", Keynes, though, adds a very significant moment. In book IV of the *General Theory*, he assumes that investors' decision-making is normally more complex than that. Before they come to a definite conclusion, they also consider alternative investment opportunities. This obviously corresponds to today's valuation theory, and here, once more, Keynes moves beyond Marx. In the *General Theory*, Keynes' considers mainly that an entrepreneur will benchmark his *m.e.c.* against receiving interest for loaning out money (mainly the equity-part of his M): "It is here that the rate of interest comes in. The series of annuities in prospect can be compared, after allowance for risk, with the series of annuities over a similar term which could be obtained by lending out a sum of money at interest."[301]

In order for interest to take the crucial role it is afforded in Keynes' work, the theory of interest, though, had to be revolutionized: The classical school (in Keynes'

---

297 Although this is not explicit, we shall continue to assume that Keynes mostly means investments in the productive economy.

298 Keynes' terms are a bit unfortunate and misleading. In our terminology, they would be *costs* or *value*, if derived from Malthus, or *M* or *M'*, if derived from Marx.

299 This is also true for the asset's "supply price", at least if a new business is founded, as that will take time and require a discounting of the costs as well. The discounting effect is less material here.

300 *Keynes*, Collected Writings, volume XIX, page 113.

301 *Keynes*, Collected Writings XIII, page 452.

298 Gerhard H. Wächter: The Capitalist Economy and its Prosthetics

use of the word) had held that the supply of capital and demand for capital regulate the interest rate as the price of capital. If economic activity was slow, such as when in a slump, then demand for capital would drop, supply would increase and, accordingly, interest rates would eventually fall. The classical school, thus, assumed a *benevolent built-in negative feedback-mechanism*, through which a downturn itself induced a recovery. Keynes challenged this idea of self-correction with his novel theory of interest. He begins by distinguishing different motives for why people hold money in cash (which bears no interest). There is a *transaction motive* (people may need the cash at times for transactions), there is a *precautionary motive* to hold reserves in case planned incoming cash flows do not arrive in time, but commitments from financial obligations must still be met. There is also a third, Keynes' most important and critical motive, which he called *speculative motive*. It attaches itself to a third part of moneys, the part which is *held in reserve in the expectation that financial assets drop in value*. This part of cash holding protects not only against suffering losses, but may also allow for profit. He who has uncommitted money available in a slump has the means to buy assets at fallen prices – in the hope to profit from a later rise in the price level. Keynes calls the advantage of holding this cash, although it does not earn interest or other cash inflows, *liquidity premium*, and he calls the inclination to hold money for the speculative motive the *propensity to hoard or to save*. Now: The higher the uncertainty, the higher the advantage of holding cash (in the expectation of falling asset prices); the higher the liquidity premium, the higher the liquidity preference and the higher the interest rate will be too. *Liquidity preference at a moment in time determines the interest rate*. Hence, in a slump, only a decrease in the liquidity preference could pave the way to new investment. Quite unfortunately, though, liquidity preference increases in a slump (at least until the bottom has definitively been reached). This is the most important point for Keynes. It gives his (formerly actually rather conventional and non-controversial) theory of investment a surprising and worrying macroeconomic turn: ↑uncertainty ↑liquidity preference ↑interest rate ↓inducement to invest.[302] It follows that depressions and unemployment can become rather stationary. In fact, positive feedback downwards can build up. The classical school's benevolent self-healing mechanism is an illusion, it needs a drop of liquidity preference for a recovery. Uncertainty, in this context, is a purely qualitative phenomenon that is affected by social psychology and all sorts of weird reflexive mechanisms. It is not as foreseeable as risk is (which can be dealt with via expectation values and

---

302 We also mentioned the first effect of higher interest rates, which Keynes placed less emphasis upon. This effect, though – increasing the cost of the investment or M – will also reduce the *m.e.c.* thereby also reducing the inducement to invest: ↑Uncertainty ↓expected future excesses ↓m.e.c ↓inducement to invest.

probability math[303]), but knows abrupt discontinuous changes; it is strictly nonlinear and, if not outright chaotic, at least potentially fast-moving.[304]

The inducement to invest: the value of the fraction

In the *General Theory*, the famous "inducement to invest"[305] is the place in which the *marginal efficiency of capital (m.e.c.)*, representing the expected profitability of the productive investment considered meets *the interest rate*, representing the profitability of the best alternative debt-investment (granting a new loan, buying an existing loan, or possibly other alternatives). It can be seen as a ratio or as a fraction. The *m.e.c.* is the numerator and the best possible alternative debt-investments, the benchmark, is the denominator. Keynes has his entrepreneur, accordingly, calculate the value of the fraction:

$$\frac{m.e.c}{interest\,rate}$$

That can be seen as a simple governor: The higher the value of the fraction, the more likely the entrepreneur will be to venture into the contemplated investment (of which Keynes primarily thinks of as a productive economy investment[306]). Keynes does not elaborate on by how much the fraction must increase over 1 for there to be an effective or strong inducement to invest, so we leave it with ↑m.e.c. / interest rate ↑inducement to invest.

The *General Theory* only and solely treats the interest rate as the denominator of the fraction, but why should a prospective productive economy investor only look at loaning out money at interest (or at buying existing debt) as possible alternative investment, *even* though there are clearly several other sterile investment-alternatives? For instance, why would he not consider purchasing *pre-existing assets* such as *land, real estate, stock or businesses, art, antiques, gold, crypto, etc.* and benchmark the rentability of the contemplated productive investment against their surpluses? Minsky will later make this point very big. He will argue that Keynes, in the *General Theory*, still "phrased his argument in terms of interest rates", instead of "introducing both the price of capital assets and the terms of money loans in his discussion...".[307]

---

303   See *Keynes* (1937) page 109 et seq., page 112 et seq.
304   *Keynes* (1936) page 154–159.
305   *Keynes* (1936) Book IV. Obviously, there must be a risk adjustment in the calculation of the planned surpluses leading to the marginal efficiency of capital.
306   To repeat: Keynes is not being very clear and consistent on this. See footnote 293 on page 295.
307   *Minsky* (1975) page 67.

But Keynes himself, as Minsky acknowledged, would already somewhat move into this direction very shortly after the *General Theory* was published.

Keynes' evolution of the inducement to invest in the Viner-Rebuttal

In November 1936, only months after the *General Theory* first appeared, *Jacob Viner* published a review in the *Quarterly Journal of Economics*.[308] Keynes rebutted the argument in the same journal in February 1937.[309] On this occasion he also shaped his theory in the direction that Minsky would later want him to go in. Accordingly, Minsky makes a great deal of Keynes' response and refers to it as the "Viner-Rebuttal". But it is true, Keynes indeed gives a clear signal of the need for an evolution, a broadening, of the "inducement to invest" in this rebuttal.

Viner had read Keynes' novel theory of liquidity preference and interest against the background of the conventional quantity theory of money. Based on it ($M^*V = P^*T$; M = money volume, V = velocity, P = price level and T = number of transactions), Viner interpreted Keynes in the sense that the liquidity preference would block some money and that, consequently, the price level would fall according to the math of this quantity theory. There was, then, according to Viner, not much new in Keynes. Keynes replied that his point had not been that the propensity to hoard or the liquidity preference would necessarily stock up idle money amounts as hoards, which would only operate through the quantity of money-theory. Rather, his mechanism would operate in a different manner: "(F)luctuations in the degree of confidence are capable of having quite a different effect, namely, not in modifying the *amount that is actually being hoarded*, but the *amount of the premium* which has to be offered to induce people not to hoard."[310] Keynes would not expect "so much in increased hoards", but that increased hoards would be avoided by "a sharp rise in the rate of interest". "A rise in the rate of interest is a means *alternative* to an increase of hoards for satisfying an increased liquidity-preference."[311] The effect or increased uncertainty and higher liquidity premium and interest rates, hence, is that "...securities fall in price until those, who would now like to get liquid if they could so at the previous price, are persuaded to give up the idea as being no longer practicable on reasonable terms."[312]

On the occasion of this clarification, Keynes generally rephrased his argument in terms of "asset prices", as demanded by Minsky, by "introducing both the price of capital assets and the terms of money loans in his discussion", at least in part. [313] Keynes now sees rising interest rates' influence on investments in the produc-

---

308   *Viner* (1936) page 109 et seq.
309   *Keynes* (1937) page 209 et seq.
310   *Keynes* (1937) page 216. Italics added.
311   *Keynes* (1937) page 211. Italics by Keynes.
312   *Keynes* (1937) page 211.
313   *Minsky* (1975) page 67.

tive economy in an indirect way not yet mentioned in the *General Theory*. Comparatively high market interest rates would not only compete against productive economy investments, through the fraction *m.e.c. / interest rate* (assuming the alternative investment would consist in making a loan or buying debt), *but they would also force asset market prices of pre-existing assets down*, not so much the prices for competimg investments in the denominator, but the prices for the considered investments in the numerator, expressed in the *m.e.c.* Keynes had calculated the *m.e.c.* as the "rate of discount which would make the *present value of the series of annuities* given by the returns expected from the capital-asset during its life just equal to its supply price",[314] he now added that the present value of the annuities could *never be higher than the "market capitalization" or the "prices of capital-assets"*[315] and, thus, allowed the fall of market prices to indirectly influence the *m.e.c.* "The mischief is done", Keynes said in the Viner-Rebuttal, "when the rate of interest corresponding to the degree of liquidity of a given asset leads to a market capitalization of that asset which is less than its costs of production".[316] Or: "Capital assets are capable...of being newly produced. The scale on which they are produced depends ...on the relation between theirs costs of production and the prices, which they are expected to realize in the market. Thus, if the rate of interest taken in conjunction with opinion about their prospective yield raise the prices of capital-assets, the volume of current investment will be increased; while if, on the other hand, these influences reduce the prices of capital-assets, the volume of current investment will be diminished."[317]

Hence, if present market asset prices fall, due to an increase of interest rates, then the lowered asset prices will operate like a "ceiling" or a "cap" for the present value of the future yields and the present value of the series of annuities will be limited by the present prices of capital assets.[318] This has the effect that lowered market prices of pre-existing old assets demotivate new productive investment, even irrespective of their nominal future yields. Keynes, thereby, opens a new devastating inroad for rising interest rates to depress investment, not only via a competing higher rentability of loaning out money, or another sterile investment in the denominator, but already through a poorer *m.e.c.* in the numerator.

---

314 *Keynes* (1936) page 135. Keynes' "supply price" is equal to "replacement costs" or production costs of the investment, see ibidem. Italics added.

315 See *Keynes* (1937), to which we have also referred to as the "Viner-Rebuttal", on page 211. Keynes refers to "the prices, which they are expected to yield in the market" when the decision of the investment was made (ibidem).

316 *Keynes* (1937) page 211.

317 *Keynes* (1937) page 217, 218.

318 He also made the formal change to switch from comparing rentabilities to comparing asset prices to costs. This formal change had no relevance as the old equation *m.e.c. / interest* rate could also have been expressed as a fraction between two present values.

The investment multiplier k

Yet another famous term found in Keynes' *General theory* is the "multiplier" or "investment multiplier *k*". We saw that Keynes believed that consumption does not suffice to reward investment and employment. When employment does increase, he wrote, "aggregate consumption is increased, but not by so much as income."[319] Accordingly, he was looking for ways for the "unused" income to return and to raise demand. He came, like the Russian "Legal Marxist" *Tugan-Baranovsky*,[320] probably without Keynes awareness, to hope for capitalists' exuberant investment demand to substitute ailing consumption demand. However, Keynes added an interesting idea here: Might investment not contain *a turbo-charger-like mechanism*, a positive feedback-mechanism which would enable a small increment of investment to, ultimately, bring about much more income, more consumption, and more investment?

Reasoning of this type is plausible and justified in principle because the economy is a reflexive system in time. Exchanges may not exhaust their effects with the consumption, and early small differences may, indeed, induce larger differences later. Let us see what Keynes makes out of his idea: If there is increased income, then some part of the increase goes into consumption. Initially, Keynes appears to see this part as the best one (if all income went into consumption, as in the case of Quesnay's *classe des propriétaires*, then circuit closure was guaranteed). Keynes defines the ratio between this more beneficial, albeit deficient, consumption increment and the whole increment of income as *"marginal propensity to consume" (mpc)*.[321] This is a fraction with a value < 1. He then takes this *mpc* to derive his "investment multiplier *k*" from it. This multiplier is simply the inverse of the shortfall of *mpc* to 1, i.e., *1/(1-mpc)*. We note that the multiplier is, thus, defined by a moment coming out of the past, which is relatively constant and which does not change much from circuit to circuit.[322] The investment multiplier's effect on aggregate investment, hence, depends on (i) the relatively constant marginal propensity to consume and (ii) the volume of investment. Accordingly, in Keynes' words, the multiplier "tells us that if there is an increase in aggregate investment, income will increase k times the amount of the increment of investment."[323]

---

319   *Keynes* (1936) page 27.

320   See on page 283 et seq.

321   *Keynes* (1936) page 115. He sometimes also uses the marginal propensity to save; the marginal propensity to consume and the marginal propensity to save add up to 1 (mps = 1 – mpc; mpc = 1 – mps).

322   We can also foresee that the investment multiplier *k* will fall with increasing income because we already know that the marginal propensity to consume falls with increasing income; this is less relevant in our argument, but it remains relevant for Keynes' original idea.

323   *Keynes* (1936) page 115. Note that while the original problem is a shortfall of consumption to income, a further increase of income is considered as solution. However, we know that this secondary increase of income will only go into consumption to an even lesser degree as

Let us, first, try to draw corollaries from this statement: If firms spend c-outlays for equipment and inventories to supplier firms and v-outlays, salaries, to workers (we assume that Keynes' investment encompasses both), then it is evident that the income of the two recipients goes up – by the precise amount of either c or v. The multiplier can only operate if workers and firms do something with their additionally received incomes in new circuits. In the first circuit, firms may give income to other firms and workers. In the second circuit, the receiving firms may give income to other firms[324] and to other workers. Workers, with their incomes from the first circuit, may also give secondary income to firms, but workers give no income to other workers. There is, thus, asymmetricity. Workers only play ping-pong at one table; firms play at two tables. The overall value of the multiplier must yet capture the aggregate effect, which results from these asymmetrical exchanges (intra-exchanges being possible for one class, but not for the other) over a series of circuits. The multiplier k has to express the aggregate income effect that investment will have over time or over a series of consecutive circuits, indeed over all future circuits, *ad infinitum*.

This means that everything is pure causality, like a wave leads to smaller consecutive waves which add up to a certain series of movements or in video *"The way things go"*. Nothing has to do with the anticipation of the future, teleology. Moreover, the Keynes' multiplier appears to unspecifically apply to all kind of "investment". Every Pound, Dollar, Euro, Yen, or Renminbi seems as good as any other and there is no care for the qualities of the investment, e.g., whether it is in newly produced goods or whether it consists in purchases of stock, land, or debt, etc. (in our terms, it does not matter whether the investment is in the productive or sterile economy).

Keynes' statements about the quantitative power of the multiplier are mixed. He partially says that the investment multiplier might multiply the initial increase of investment in employment, as salary income,[325] by a factor around 2, 3, or 5[326] and might theoretically go up to 10.[327] Firms, hence, could create an additional amount of income of 20, 30, 50, or even 100 million money units by employing new workers for 10 million money units; this is very material. Such a leverage would, indeed, flow

---

multiplier-generated income will not have a higher mpc, but a lower one. (The issue is not crucial for our argument).

324 One must here abstract from the possibility that the first firm, where everything started, makes a new additional investment, which sets into motion a second wave extending from this firm. That second wave would have to be captured by applying the multiplier *again*, which should be kept separate from the observation of the first wave's journey.

325 Keynes speaks of the multiplier being 2 or 3 times the employment provided by a specific new investment. *Keynes* (1936) page 121 et seq.

326 *Keynes* (1936) page 121 et seq., 128.

327 *Keynes* (1936) page 116.

from the pockets of workers into consumption and, even if Keynes lacks that distinction, it would also largely go into employment-generating consumption spending. On other occasions, Keynes is more skeptical about the multiplier's effect. Just as Marx domesticated his "tendential fall or the rate of profit",[328] which pointed to disaster in order to accommodate it to the fact that capitalism was visibly not collapsing, Keynes domesticated his multiplier, which points to salvation, to accommodate it to the inverse fact that capitalism had, in the Great Depression, not shown the powerful self-healing capacity which the investment multiplier promised. Certain "adverse reactions", he argued, often keep the "average value of the multiplier" much lower than 2, 3, 5, or 10. He mentions increases of the rate of interest, confused psychology of the public, the increment going to the benefit of foreign countries, the loss of debt service of re-employed workers after they come out of debt-financed unemployment, the lower propensity to consume of entrepreneurs, or even the worker's propensity to consume falling quickly with raising income as examples of such adverse effects.[329] He also says that the investment multiplier will work the better, the lower the saving rates are, or the "poorer" the society is; thereby he reduces expectations as to what the multiplier can do for more developed countries, like the UK or US, e.g. to avoid a second Great Depression.[330]

Another point is worth noting here: Whilst one would expect that the investment multiplier, to the extent that it works at all, should primarily increase income following *original private investment*, Keynes mainly mentions it in connection with *public investment*. So, he appears to consider his multiplier-mechanism not so much as a mechanism of capitalist self-healing (which would render prosthetic public investment less necessary or obsolete), but as a mechanism that adds fuel to the fire power for (the obviously still necessary) prosthetic state intervention. That leads to the question of whether the multiplier applies to original, private investment at all. This question must be answered in the positive (why not?). If so, though, Keynes would be telling us something like: *Support from the multiplier notwithstanding*, which creates more than the same amount of income out of an original increment of original, private investment, investment in capitalism, is not powerful enough to close the gap left by deficient consumption. However, the same multiplier still, which is insufficient when applied to private investment, is a significant help to additional "artificial" public investment. Is that what is left over? Finally, Keynes emphasizes that the multiplier multiplies only *the increment* of investment, and the overall effect may, thus, remain a "comparatively small amount of the national income".[331] After this, the investment multiplier k remarkably transmutes from a big theoretical thing

328   See *Marx*, Capital, volume III, chapter 13 et seq.
329   *Keynes* (1936) page 119, 120.
330   *Keynes* (1936) page 120, 121, 127.
331   *Keynes* (1936) page 122.

and great promise into a modest amplification of the benevolent effects of public investment.

We shall still take a further look at "the multiplier" to see what is wrong with it, including at a deeper theoretical level. We refer to our examination of instances in which economic units spend money.[332] We saw that in order for an economic unit to make the sacrifice of spending money, at least two conditions must be simultaneously met; the unit must have money *and* it must have esoteric demand which involves the attribution of sufficient value-in-use to a commodity. It should be clear that, except for money creation, money does *not* multiply in circulation, neither on the way from a normal emitter to a recipient nor during its stopovers in the pockets of either of them. There are things that multiply, i.e., which can be retained by the emitter, but can still be forwarded to one or several recipients, e.g., knowledge, information, infections, or illness. They can be given to others, but can still be retained by the dispatcher. Even life can be shared without its emitters having to die, but money can*not* multiply or propagate. It is an "either I have it or you have it" type of thing. Actually, as systems theoretical sociology points out, this limitation alone enables money to fulfill its function of dealing with scarcity.[333] Payments increase money-scarcity on the side of the emitter and reduce money-scarcity on the side of the recipient;[334] the sender loses the purchasing power in exchange for a commodity; the same purchasing power is picked up by the receiver. Accordingly, we may say that money, in one circuit, has a "multiplier" of exactly 1.

Now, money can of course be used and is meant to be used *many times* by different people to enable a series of transactions, one after another, in sequence. What can be multiplied, is the *frequency of the use of an existing money-stock*. The multiplier could, thus, work via keeping money active for a greater number of circuits, in which it serves, or by re-activating idle money. The multiplier would, accordingly, be greater where money is channeled into uses *with more income-generating follow up re-uses*. We might also say that a multiplier might work through an increase of the "*velocity of money*" (which obviously depends not on the physical travelling speed of coins, bank notes, or of credit money entries, but on the *quickness of the decisions* to relaunch them over several decision points or holders). This quickness in decision-making, however, depends upon properties of the recipients of money after each circuit, on their

---

332 See on page 39 through 54.

333 Only money creation is an exception. Commodity money can be created by finding and mining or by otherwise procuring gold or silver; credit money can be created by merchants or private banks or the central bank and fiat money can only be created by the state or central banks. If that happens, then money multiplies; beyond that, its stock and the spending-enabling capacity of money, cannot multiply.

334 *Luhmann* (1988) page 194 et seq.

"propensity" to forward money quickly to other units.[335] Had Keynes thought along these lines (which appears to be the only sound option), he ought to have to search for the "rapid-re-dispatchment units" and into what makes them inclined to re-dispatch money fast. As such, by examining fast re-dispatchment-favorable and employment-favorable uses, he might have discovered what this book calls employment-generating or producive spending, and unfavorable uses in what this book calls sterile spending. However, Keynes does not offer a distinction between employment-generating and sterile spending and he cannot use it to explain different velocities of money, from which a meaningful idea of a multiplier could be derived. That is also why Keynes does not attempt a systematic analysis of why and how an increment of initial investment is supposed to bring about significant additional quantitative effects. He cannot do this because he has no tools for that and he has no such tools as he does not possess anything similar to our Matrix I (on page 23) (consumptive-investive and sterile-producive). Furthermore, Keynes blocked himself off from seeing the issue through the way he structured his model: As everything depends on society's aggregate "propensity to consume", which comes out of the past, and, while it is slowly falling with increased income, remains rather constant for the moment, there is just no place for expectations and motivations of entrepreneurs here. Keynes greatly emphasized the role played by expectation (anticipation, prognosis, motivation etc.) as the engine of the economic system elsewhere, yet, with his multiplier he falls back into a solely causal narrative. Ultimately, as investment is neither primarily ruled from the past nor by one single moment, there cannot be one singly past-determined multiplier.

One prospect of an alternative conception of a "future-pulled" multiplier was partially already implied in our critique. It might be possible to conceive of *"productive investment multipliers"* to reflect how *special kinds* of productive investment generate more productive investment in future circuits. In fact, one could even include consumption and conceive of aggregate *"producive spending multipliers"* or *"employment-generating spending multipliers"*. These ought to be either derived from *marginal propensities of different types of producive, i.e., employment-generating spending* or from *different marginal propensities of different types of consumptive spending*, e.g., to erect new houses or factories or to employ menial servants, artists, greenkeepers and the like.[336] Mathematically, an aggregate "producive spending multiplier" or "employment-generating spending multiplier" could be conceived of as the inverse of the shortfall of the marginal propensy of producive spending (mpps) to 1, i.e., as $1/(1-mpps)$. This producive spending multiplier or employment-generating spend-

---

335 Workers with an assumed need to buy subsistence goods are the signature example – although they also make sterile spending for debt service and rent.

336 Unless hoarded money is already a wealth asset.

ing multiplier, thus, would increase in value with the marginal propensity to bring about producive or employment-generating spending.

We still do not believe that even that kind of "multiplier-thinking" would be a great theoretical aid to reflect on the economy's systemic and reflexive moments for the reasons already given. In addition, as is implied in the numbers for the multiplier used by Keynes, the "waves" that the multiplier might generate, collapse rather quickly, so that we have to – depending on the "aggregate propensity to generate producive (or employment-generating) spending" – expect multiplier's effects to exhaust in a short time. This is so because ine ach circuit a certain part is sucked away as "tribute" in the sterile economy and not consumptively or investively re-spend in the productive economy. Worse still, some of the money, which stops at firms, may be called back by wealth-owners and dispatched into the sterile economy, as a sterile investment or for sterile consumption. The wave, ignited by initial investment, quickly gets smaller and smaller and only a few circuits, say 3, will be relevant for practical purposes. Whether wealth-owners might simultaneously equip firms with the ability to make new productive investments is a different story; they certainly never fund productive investments "just because they have the money". The crucial moment is, as Keynes so rightly teaches with his "inducement to invest", whether there are enough profitable productive investment prospects, given alternative opportunities.

Our summary of Keynes' multiplier-reasoning is as follows: First, money does not multiply, but can only be used more frequently and re-used more quickly, so a multiplier-effect does not exist in the first circuit and can only come from subsequent circuits. Second, whether it comes has nothing to do with a near-constant "mpc", but continues to depend upon the theory of firms' employment-generating investive spending, i.e., on an (improved) version of Keynes' theory of the "inducement to invest". The multiplier cannot overrule the determination of investment by the inducement to invest, including in circuit 2 or 3 etc. Third, the sequential circuits, beginning with circuit 2, will generate less and less consumptive employment-generating or investive employment-generating spending in each case than the preceding circuits. This is best explained by the loss of tributes and other investitive and consumptive spending into the sterile economy. The multiplier comes down to observing how some outlays, which were dispatched from the wealth economy via firms' employment-generating ports, into the productive economy, hence to workers and supplier firms, will source future such investments and future income in future circuits, provided that they do not sink back into the wealth economy. Keynes' multiplier is intellectually fuzzy, practically immaterial, and the whole concept (spending being a simple function of income, rather than depending greatly on expectations) is fallacious.

Keynes' identity/equality of investment and saving

I=S

We have previously observed Keynes setting out the "inducement to invest" as his investment theory. Investment demand would be triggered by entrepreneurs' profit expectations and would fill the gap left by insufficient consumption demand, at least to some degree. More specifically, in this "investment theory of employment"[337] the decision about what part of financial funds available, or to be made available, went into an actual investment depended on a calculus influenced by the $m.e.c$ and the interest rate. Investment, thus, was a function of the profit motive and of the anticipation of an uncertain future in which alternative options to satisfy the profit motive were battling against each other.

Keynes' *General Theory* also deals with an identity/equality of investment and saving (I = S) repeatedly and at great length.[338] Quite obviously, if we split up this identity/equality into an I → S-direction and a S → I-direction, the latter direction may come into conflict with Keynes' prior "inducement to invest" theory of investment. If saving always *is*, or *becomes*, investment wholly and automatically (or it is and becomes it again, is the same thing wallowing around), then what do we do with the "inducement to invest" that appeared to explain when saving beomes investment? Therefore, the question arises: Is Keynes – like Rauschenberg undid a De Kooning-painting and Keynes himself, just moments ago, got into the risk of undoing his "inducement-to-invest"-based investment theory with the investment multiplier $k-$ now once more undoing his investment theory by his I = S? Is he filling the space,

---

337 See also "As I now think, the volume of employment (and consequently of output and real income) is fixed by the entrepreneur under the motive of seeking to maximise his present and prospective profits...; whilst the volume of employment which will maximise his profit depends on the aggregate demand function given by his expectations of the sum of the proceeds resulting from consumption and investment respectively on various hypotheses." (*Keynes* (1936) page 77).

338 The notions "identity" and "equality" are neither identical nor equal. They have a peculiar relationship. Identity is more encompassing. Things may be identical as such, in general, and they may be equal only in certain regards. The content of a container may be equal with the earlier content of a jug, e.g., after the jug was poured into the container; the volume is equal because the fluid is identical, but a volume of fluid in a container may also be equal with another (either present or measured previously) volume, thanks to a mechanism that measured the first volume and allowed the inflow of precisely the same volume of water from a river, which is not the same fluid and, thus, obviously is not identical. Keynes never clarifies whether he actually means identity or equality. If we can consider Keynes' I = S as resulting from his balance sheet or his national accounting view of an aggregated economy, then the identity/equality ought to be a mechanical result of the "bilancia"-axiom, which adjusts the volume of the capital side to a changed volume of assets on the asset side. Accordingly, this would be a matter of equality rather than Identity.

where his investment theory sits, with a second competing theory? Or is he modifying it? If so, in what sense is this taking place? Or is there no contradiction? Furthermore, what can we make out of I = S at all? We shall deal with these questions in the following sections. Before we begin, though, we shall admit that the answers will not be relevant for the progress of this book in either a positive or constructive sense. Rather, the insights, at which this book hopefully arrives, could have been laid down without anybody ever having stated that I was supposed to equal S. The sole, sound justification for the treatment of I = S is, thus, to possibly help the reader to *avoid getting lost in pitfalls and in confusion, in which one is easily drawn away by I = S*. Second, the author has to warn the reader that he will lay down Keynes I = S as he understands it best. My attempts to derive a fully consistent interpretation of quotes from Keynes on I = S have failed. I felt that I would have to pull or push his quotes in one or the other direction in order to ascribe a clear and precise content to his I = S or that I would have ended up with an over-complicated text, which would almost be unreadable. So, I shall put down my views on Keynes' I = S in straightforward theses and leave it up to the reader to determine whether they want to delve into the complexities and confusions in Keynes' definitions themselves and to check whether my treatment ultimately does justice to Keynes.

First, where Keynes discusses I = S, he is in fact, without keeping them clearly separated, *dealing with two issues in two worlds*. On the one hand, Keynes offers an elementary balance model of national economies. The invention and gist of this side of Keynes' treatment of I = S consists of combining double entry bookkeeping with substantial questions of national accounting in a consistent, albeit rudimentary, way. In this context, Keynes uses the terms "investment" and "saving" as a part of, as it is called today, some kind of "expenditure approach" to deriving the GDP, hence 'inflows accounting', similar to a profit and loss statement; in this context, he derives the identity/equality I = S from there. However, Keynes' main thread was to understand employment in capitalism, in particular as it was influenced by investment, and he also uses I = S here. In this second context, investment plays a crucial role as well (in fact, more so than saving even). Now, unfortunately, my thesis is that Keynes does not manage to obtain control over these two different uses of the term "investment" in the two different worlds. He does not define the "investment" of the national accounting context and does not keep it clearly separated from the "investment" of the theory-of-investment-and-employment-context. This is where the main confusion, created by I = S, stems from (confusion will also arise from to different uses of the term "saving", as we shall see).

The second thesis is that Keynes' identity/equality-theorem in the S → I direction is neither meant to undo Keynes investment theory nor does it result in this. Rather, the "inducement to invest" survives I = S and *remains* Keynes' main contribution to the analysis of employment in capitalism. Hence, our previous discussion of the "inducement to invest" remains valid too. It is, however, not easy to explain *why and how* the "inducement to invest" can survive the identity/equality as S → I. This was probably not even clear to Keynes himself.

Third, the identity/equality I = S looked at in the I → S-direction, as far as it does not belong into the realm of national accounting, but is actually meant as a theory of a macro-transmission, refers to an issue of *equipping and re-sourcing*. Yes, investment generates saving elsewhere and increases the possibility of investment elsewhere; invested money is not lost for the future of a capitalist economy; it returns and can be reinvested over and over again. However, already Malthus rightly observed that economic activity does not normally use the full capacities provided by the national capital stock anyhow and took this observation as his point of departure. If, though, too little is commonly made out of the saving that is already there, the most beneficial increases of the capital stock will not greatly matter and have no capacity to do away with the core-problem of the under-employment of the stock that existed previously.

We shall now briefly look at these three points, one at a time.

National accounting – where Keynes' identity/equality of "investment" and "saving" (I=S) belongs

Balance sheets are drawn up per unit and per a point in time; they show a unit's stocks (of assets and debt) at a point in time. The story of what happens between balance sheets dates is told by profit and loss statements. Balance sheets book transactions twice, as assets on the asset side and as equity or liabilities on the capital side. In national accounting, the profit-and-loss-view, looking at flows within time periods, via the three approaches to GDP-calculation (production approach, expenditure approach, and income approach) are even more important than stocks accounting. In order to set up a balance sheet, one must find, count, and value assets belonging, in a defined sense, to a subject at a moment: You can then deduct that subject's liabilities; what is left over is its equity in business accounting and its net worth in national accounting. In flows accounting, which must match stocks accounting in the result, you count and value outflows and inflows and the positive excess is the annual profit; in national accounting, the result is called – as influenced by the expenditure view – "saving". "Saving", thus, is like equity or increments in equity, bereaved of all substantial value-in-use properties. It is no more than a *counter-booking* to whatever is accepted as having had an impact on the asset side or on liabilities (with domestic liabilities being netted).[339]

---

339 National accounting automatically cancels out changes in ownership of assets and origination and destruction of liabilities, where the previous and subsequent owners or the creditor and debtor belong to the same economy. Keynes writes in chapter 7 of the *General Theory*: "If we reckon the sale of an investment as being negative investment, i.e., disinvestment, my own definition is in accordance with popular usage; since exchanges of old

In order for assets to appear in balance sheets, they must be considered as "exis-tent" in a specific sense of accounting. Accounting rules determine the meaning of such an "existence". Sometimes it is also difficult to say when assets appear for the first time (percentage of completion rules and other rules deal with this). Some use-ful things are generally not capable of being entered as assets, e.g., the work force, education, scientific or technological insights, etc. Rules also determine when as-sets must disappear from balance sheets, e.g., by consumption; depreciation is an-other way of consumption of equipment and inventories (and certain other posi-tions), rules on provisions are a third way of value-annihilation. What has been an-nihilated is no longer "there" on the balance sheet's date; it cannot be entered any longer, and down goes the equity or net worth as a right-hand-side-residual and so does the profit or saving as result of the period.

Apart from their formal structures, reflecting the methodology of double entry accounting, accounting rules, whether in commercial or national accounting, are directed towards generating specific information. States are interested in knowing their respective economy's aggregate wealth and the value of the produce of a cer-tain period, the GDP. The basic fact here is that what you have never produced (or found or even robbed) is as little there as that which you have eaten up or that which has been destroyed or depleted. If we look at a period, this leads to $Y - C = S$ (Income minus consumption equals saving). If the result S is positive, then this means that there was an aggregate increment of net worth on the capital side in the respective period because of the cumulative effect of changes in a great number of accounts.[340] There may now be more or less equipment, more or less inventories, and more or less other wealth assets and cash. There may also be changes in external liabilities on the capital side. Commercial profit and loss statements normally have no established

---

investments necessarily cancel out. We have, indeed, to adjust for the creation and dis-charge of debts (including changes in the quantity of credit or money); but since for the community as a whole the increase or decrease of the aggregate creditor position is al-ways exactly equal to the increase or decrease of the aggregate debtor position, this com-plication also cancels out when we are dealing with aggregate investment. Thus, assuming that income in the popular sense corresponds to my net income, aggregate investment in the popular sense coincides with my definition of net investment, namely the net addi-tion to all kinds of capital equipment, after allowing for those changes in the value of the old capital equipment which are taken into account in reckoning net income. Investment, thus defined, includes, therefore, the increment of capital equipment, whether it consists of fixed capital, working capital or liquid capital;" (*Keynes* (1936) page 75). We should note that, accordingly, the remaining cash – "liquid capital" is investment in Keynes.

340   Like equity in balance sheets of private businesses, "saving" is a counter-entry to all sorts of assets, such as money holdings, debt-claims, real estate, stocks, and equity participations in firms or other valuables. The only way to increase assets without increasing saving to also increase "liabilities to abroad". It is, thus, not justified to read into I = S that all assets entered into the national accounts beyond liabilities to abroad are *spent* on investment.

312 Gerhard H. Wächter: The Capitalist Economy and its Prosthetics

special aggregating word or term for these netted aggregate changes; commercial accounting is satisfied with the change being expressed as periodic profit or loss. This is different in national accounting. National accounting has a special second expression for the aggregated netted amount of changes on the asset side and in external liabilities. The same value, which is already known as "saving", is re-baptized from the perspective that it cannot be consumption (because then it would be no more), and hence as "investment".[341] If that is so, then it follows, by necessity, that if we deduct I from Y, we also receive C. If, however, Y − I = C and Y − C = S are both valid, then it follows that I = S.[342] So, Keynes can very plausibly state that I and S are "merely different names for the same phenomenon looked at from different points of view."[343]

From this balance sheet-origin of I = S, it should be clear that there is no way to use these terms "investment" (reflecting actions taken on the asset side and in external liabilities) and "savings" (showing their aggregate quantitative result on the capital side) for a theory of economic activity and employment in capitalism. Such a

---

341   If the "marked space" of the distinction called "consumption" is "consumption", then national accounting implies that its complementary "unmarked space" (non-consumption) is "investment".

342   $Y - I = C \rightarrow Y - I - C = 0 \rightarrow Y - C = I$. Hence, $I = S$. We prefer to show how the equality results from the axiom that C and I are complementary. This, of course, requires a wide definition of consumption. Not only must a voluntary or accidental destruction or decay of assets be consumption (in the form of depreciation), but also a sacrifice to goods, etc.

343   *Keynes*, Letter to Harrod of 27 August 1935, Collected Writings XIII, page 551. The abstract, notional, logical, and mathematical argument, which is normally given for the identity/equality, runs: "Provided it is agreed that income is equal to the value of current output, that current investment is equal to the value of that part of current output which is not consumed, and that saving is equal to the excess of income over consumption – all of which is conformable both to common sense and to the traditional usage of the great majority of economists – the equality of saving and investment necessarily follows. In short

Income = value of output = consumption + investment.
Saving = income— consumption.

Therefore saving = investment." (*Keynes* (1936) page 63). Rather openly, however, this argument does not tell us anything about a (possible) substantial macroeconomic relationship between whatever "investment" may be and whatever saving may be; it actually does not tell us anything about the economy and investment or saving in it at all, but it could apply to anything, given that it only draws conclusions from an axiomatic or definitional presentation of quantities. (E.g., If "world" minus "God" makes 500 and "world" minus "truth" also makes 500, then God must be identical truth, etc...). The "force" and "logic" of the argument come solely from the *in-built assumption* that the two amounts, which are deducted from the same other amount, are equal to one another.

theory cannot be derived from a self-manufactured tautology or bookkeeping identity, but only from analyzing how firms, driven by profit motives – in an environment of complex impulses –put existing stocks or arriving flows into employment-
relevant and productive uses – much like Keynes had attempted in his investment
theory.

S → I leaves Keynes' investment theory ("inducement to invest") intact

Accordingly, I = S, including as $S \to I$, is structurally incapable of undoing Keynes'
investment theory, his "inducement to invest". His insightful investment theory is
not endangered by I = S, but can instead be saved from self-demolition. This is what
Keynes wanted too. We have already given the main substantial reason why this is
so: *I = S belongs in the realm of national accounting; it follows from the principles set up there
and only and exclusively applies there.* It is not meant to state and, therefore, cannot
state, in the framework of a theory of investment and employment, that whatever
we call "saving" (alone or together with resources from other origins) automatically
becomes "investment" (of whatever type, productive or sterile).

Before the *General Theory*, e.g., in his *Treatise on Money*, Keynes saw the relationship of saving and investment just as most people on the street do: There are incoming flows of money, income Y, which merge with an already existing stock of money
or other wealth in a big basin, which stands ready for all kind of uses. A distinction
must then be drawn between a part of money, which is consumed out of this basin,
C, and the remainder of money, which is not consumed but instead stays there and
is saved for the moment, S. Saving means simply and only the negative act of not
consuming money for the time being (of, as Keynes correctly said, "not having dinner today").[344] Saving is, in fact, not a flow at all, particularly not a flow out of wealth,
but *an outflow, which does not happen*, a residual between a mixed stock of pre-existing wealth and a prior inflow of income and an outflow of money for consumption.
Saved money stays for later uses while consumed money is gone.[345]

Here is a quote by Keynes that expresses this view: "Of the resources of the community earned or available within a given year, a certain part is saved, a certain part
spent and a certain part is kept, so far as the individual is concerned, in suspense – it
is kept as free resources to be spend or saved according to future circumstances may
determine."[346] While the definition is, as unfortunately is often the case in Keynes'

---

344   This is still so in the *General Theory*, see *Keynes* (1936) page 210.
345   As already touched upon, if money is consumed for *long-lasting consumption goods*, such as
      cars or self-used dwellings, then one can argue that only the loss of value-in-exchange by
      wear and tear is consumed while the remainder has only changed its form from money-
      form into used car-form or resalable dwelling-form, but that is not decisive.
346   *Keynes*, How far are bankers responsible for the alternations of crisis and depression? in:
      Collected Writings XIII, page 4 et seq., italics added.

work, generally not very clear, it is at least clear in the regard, which is presently crucial: Keynes saw the aggregate of "saving" and of "resources kept in suspense" as a reservoir for future uses, including for employment-generating investments and he assigned freedom to the reservoir-owners to decide on these uses.[347] That already posited the structure that investors have access to and control over a larger sample of available money/wealth and that employment conditionally depends upon *how* the means in the reservoir are used by investors. Keynes maintained this reservoir-structure when he lectured that "I see no hope of a recovery except in the revival of the high level of investment... I suggest to you, therefore, that the questions to which we have to bend our intelligences are the causes of the collapse of investment and the means of reviving investment"[348] – implying a need to activate[349] more wealth in the reservoir (as potential investment into real, actual investment). In chapters 11–14 of the *General Theory*,[350] in which Keynes worked out his "inducement to invest"-theory, he continued to use the reservoir-and-subsample-concept as its base and showed no intention to give it up.

Even after he had presented the identity I = S, that did not change. He still wrote: "Saving and investment are merely alternative names for the difference between income and consumption"[351] Alternatively: "I regard them as being merely different names for the same phenomenon looked at from different points of view. Saving is the name given to a certain quantity looked at as the excess of income over consumption. Investment is the name given to the same quantity regarded as the constituent of income other than consumption...".[352] He did not want to pull out the rug from underneath his theory of the "inducement to invest". Rather, he expressly warned against this misinterpretation: "But we must not proceed from this inevitable equality to the plausible inference, which has been commonly drawn from it, that, when an individual saves, he necessarily increases investment by an equal amount".[353] Still

---

347 It is less clear in two other regards: What is the difference between the "part ...saved" and the "part... kept, so far as the individual is concerned, in suspense... as free resources to be spend or saved according to future circumstances may determine"? And where is "investment"? Is it part of "resources spent" or "part of resources saved"?

348 *Keynes*, An Economic Analysis of Unemployment. Lecture I "The Originating Causes of World-Unemployment", held in Chicago in June 1931 (Collected Writings XIII, page 349).

349 As we have stated previously, Keynes mostly thinks of investment as generally generating employment, without expressly saying so. See footnote 293 on page 295.

350 Keynes presents his change of mind as merely a definitional issue (see *Keynes* (1936) page 77). Keynes' novel identity/equality of investment and saving was also probably intended to counter the classical argument that both would be adjusted by changes in the interest rate. If they were identical or equal, then there would be no place for such an adjustment.

351 *Keynes*, Letter to Harrod of 27 August 1935, Collected Writings XIII, page 552.

352 *Keynes*, Letter to Harrod of 27 August 1935, Collected Writings XIII, page 551. Many similar statements can also be found in chapters 6 and 7 of the *General Theory*.

353 *Keynes*, Draft Chapter 8, Investment and Saving, in: Collected Writings XIII page 477.

Keynes does not give us a rational reason *why* we should not interpret I = S in the "forbidden" sense; the master instructs his audience "not (to) proceed" from his equality to the unwanted "plausible inference", to allow his theory of inducement to invest to survive, but he does not tell us how the apparent contradiction resolves.

Keynes returns to a discussion of saving in chapter 16 of the *General Theory*, now primarily in the theory-of-investment-and-employment-context. Here he gives us further comfort that he did not want I = S to undo his "inducement to invest". He writes: "An act of individual saving means – so to speak – a decision not to have dinner to-day. But it does not necessitate a decision to have dinner or to buy a pair of boots a week hence or a year hence or to consume any specified thing at any specified date. Thus, it depresses the business of preparing to-day's dinner without stimulating the business of making ready for some future act of consumption. It is not a substitution of future consumption-demand for present consumption-demand, – it is a net diminution of such demand. Moreover, the expectation of future consumption is so largely based on current experience of present consumption that a reduction in the latter is likely to depress the former, with the result that the act of saving will not merely depress the price of consumption-goods and leave the marginal efficiency of existing capital unaffected, but may actually tend to depress the latter also. In this event it may reduce present investment-demand as well as present consumption-demand. If saving consisted not merely in abstaining from present consumption but in placing simultaneously a specific order for future consumption, the effect might indeed be different."[354]

Keynes explains why the fact that "an individual decision to save does not... involve the placing of any specific forward order for consumption, but merely the cancellation of a present order"[355] is not overcome by some hidden abstract mechanism that operates in the background. Here is where Keynes also comes the closest to the distinction between sterile and productive investment, as suggested in our book. He declares "the absurd, though almost universal idea that an act of individual saving is just as good for effective demand as an act of individual consumption, has been fostered by the fallacy... that an increased desire to hold wealth, being much the same thing as an increased desire to hold investments, must, by increasing the demand for investments, provide a stimulus to their production; so that current investment is promoted by individual saving to the same extent as present consumption is diminished".[356] He gives us two reasons why this criticized view is fallacious, the second gets right to the heart of the matter: "Moreover, in order that an individual saver may attain his desired goal of the ownership of wealth, it is not necessary that a new capital-asset should be produced wherewith to satisfy him. The mere act of saving by

---

354 *Keynes* (1936) page 210.
355 *Keynes* (1936) page 211.
356 *Keynes* (1936) page 211.

one individual, being two-sided as we have shown above, forces some other individual to transfer to him some article of wealth old or new. ... These transfers of wealth do not require the creation of new wealth – indeed, as we have seen, they may be actively inimical to it."[357] After all, Keynes' employment theory, which is largely an investment theory of employment, clearly survives his I = S!

I → S: Investment enables more investment

If there is a way to save Keynes' investment theory from his identity/equality of S = I (in the S → I-direction), we still cannot acquit Keynes from having contributed to significant confusion. In fact, he has probably, at least partially, convinced himself that he could use I = S outside of its natural national accounting turf in the theory of capitalist investment and employment. If investment is triggered by an inducement to invest, then this gives us motives (interests and expectations as causes) for investment, but it does not tell us yet what investment *does*. However, investment does do something. It is made for profit (and cost recovery) and, where it is successful, investing firms will end up with just these recovered costs and the intended profit, which will better equip them for new investments in further circuits. Before that, supplier firms will have received c-outlays, which also has equipped them for more future investments. This was a line of thought that *Kalecki* pursued with his "profit quotation", more or less, which had investment plus capitalist consumption re-appear as profit.[358] Keynes also writes in this sense, "S' always and necessarily accommodates itself to I. Whether I consists in housing schemes or war finance, there need be nothing to hold us back, because I always tracks S' along with it at an equal pace. S' is not the voluntary result of virtuous decisions. In fact S' is no longer the dog, which common sense believes it to be, but the tail."[359] He concedes: "Thus it might be truer to say that the amount of savings over a period of time depends on the amount of investment, than the other way round".[360] In this sense, he also said

---

357   *Keynes* (1936) page 212. The first argument is: "It comes from believing that the owner of wealth desires a capital-asset as such, whereas what he really desires is its prospective yield. Now, prospective yield wholly depends on the expectation of future effective demand in relation to future conditions of supply. If, therefore, an act of saving does nothing to improve prospective yield, it does nothing to stimulate investment" (loc. cit.).

358   As we shall see, Kalecki will distinguish the two questions of a theory of investment and of a theory of profit very clearly. See on page 322 and seq. and 325 and seq.

359   In this quotation, S' is saving including the saving of entepreneurs from their Q. If E is the amount of earnings without entrepreneurs profits Q, then it follows that $E + Q = E'$ (total income) and E' - F = S' (see *Keynes*, Notes on the definition of Saving, in: Collected Writings XIII, page 275, 276.) The quotation is from *Keynes*, Collected Writings XIII, page 276. *King* (2015) page 6, writes "causation runs investment to saving, not vice versa".

360   *Keynes*, An Economic Analysis of Unemployment. Lecture II 'The Road to Recovery', held in Chicago in June 1931, Collected Writings XIII, page 388. Hawtrey, in a letter, proposed an example on how an increase of investment could create a tendency for savings to catch

(mentioning profit as a source of saving) that "... the entrepreneurs' profit increases when the increase in investment is greater than the current economy and decreases when the economy is greater than the increase in investment...the increment of investment is equal to the increment of profit plus current economy".[361]

Keynes rejected Ricardo's Law of Say, but he was still looking, in much the same way as everybody else in fact, for something better to substitute it with and to connect quantities in macroeconomic tubes. Specifically, he tried to connect employment to "aggregate demand". It is here that Keynes' expected to find his identity/equality of investment and saving to make the macroeconomic contribution, which could substitute Ricardo's Law of Say. He writes: "For the proposition that supply creates its own demand, I shall substitute the proposition that expenditure creates its own income, it is an income just sufficient to meet the expenditure."[362] Now, if it was not right to state that supply in general creates its own demand, then it might be possible to state that investive spending would – at least – generate *resources* for further circuits of investive spending, or that "investment creates its own refinancing". This was some kind of a *theory of saving* with a main thread that the saving could be used for investment again and was, thus, at least not macroeconomically lost after one use or circuit. Investment, Keynes observed, does not exhaust its power by generating employment in its first use; it can do the same again and generate employment once more. The money will flow from the pockets of the first-round-investing entrepreneurs into the pockets of the second-round-entrepreneurs: from there, it will probably become re-united with other financial means and can kick-start another beneficial employment-generating voyage – good news for employment.[363]

We have found similar reasoning in other authors. Quesnay, most certainly, saw the "dépenses" of all of his classes, investive plus consumptive, as simultaneously re-sourcing the employment-generating spending of the classe productive and stérile in future circuits. We have also abbreviated Malthus as saying that "costs cannot buy value". This formulation was put in a provocative, almost paradoxical, form in order to stress that cost-outlays can never be sufficient to finance profits; still, it silently implied that costs-outlays (payments of firms to supplier firms and to

---

up capital outlay and emphasized that there would be a discrepancy during an interval. Keynes did not answer this interjection in specific. See *Keynes*, Letters from Hawtrey from 12 March 1935 and reply by Keynes on 14 March 1935 in Collected Writings XIII page 565, 566.

361 *Keynes*, Collected Writings XIII, page 277. It does not matter for us that the notions used by Keynes are, once again, quite unclear.

362 *Keynes*, Collected Writings XXIX page 81 et seq.

363 In parallel, a similar beneficial process takes place with workers' salaries. It differs in so far as the laid-out salaries *v* will not go into investment, but into consumption.

workers) would at least suffice to re-fund costs. The same idea can be found in Sismondi and it could also be expressed in Marx's M–C–M' or reproduction schemes. There can be no doubt that M-outlays, which flow to suppliers, hence c-outlays, are their income, fill up their reservoirs, and that the aggregate reservoir of the capitalist class's savings enable new investive employment-generating spending.[364] The same is true of v-outlays, which enable workers' consumptive employment-generating spending (with less intermittent time – they appear as saving only very transitorily). The supplier firms and the workers receive money amounts c and v, which are equal with the firms' outlays, which can also be called M.[365] The sale of equipment or inventories by supplier firms and of labor by workers is also their purchase by investing firms; to that end, "sale" and "purchase" are only different names given thereto, only emphasizing the different views of either dispatchers or of recipients of flows. Thus, we will subscribe to the idea pursued by Keynes (or in Kalecki's profit equation, which will be discussed further below) that investment not only has conditional motives (and thus causes), but also consequences and results: The amounts that investors have paid for their investment arrive at supplier firms and workers with necessity and can be re-used.

This insight is, though, neither very new nor a great gain. Everybody who thought about macroeconomics was conscient that payments for investment are re-usable by the recipient for new investment once again. Moreover, the insight is not crucial for capitalist investment and employment, unfortunately. The problem with capitalist investment and employment is, as we said already, normally not a shortage of capital stock; therefore, it is not very material whether it is increased by "saving". We end on a terminological side note: If we look at investment outlays (c or v) in connection with a theory of investment, then it does not really make sense to call them, when looked at as incoming amounts, "saving". There is no objection, as far as supplier firms are concerned, to calling them *sales prices, sales receipts, turnover* or *revenues*; they are cost recovery plus profit, but what is left over to source new rounds of investment will be cut short by consumption because Keynes' entrepreneurs – much like Marx's capitalists – consume.

***

---

364   This does not imply that there cannot be other resources.

365   The equality solely comes from the convention to value the purchased equipment and inventories and labor at the sales or purchase price paid. If they were valued at the present value of the investment's expected future results, then they should normally be higher. If they were valued following usual bookkeeping convention, depending on capitalization of labor costs and depreciation, they might be, or soon become, lower.

After all, Keynes honorably reintroduced the problems of Sismondi and Malthus to economics after the Great Depression. He also offered a theory of a gap in aggregate demand, caused by a propensity to consume, which was declining with rising income or wealth and which had to be complemented with investment demand in order to stimulate employment. Things became self-referential at precisely this moment; investment, a means of consumption, had to emancipate itself from its serving function, thereby forgetting about this serving function, declaring its independence and autonomy, with only this erroneous hybris protecting the society against deficient consumption demand, for the moment. Keynes hoped that his entrepreneur economy, driven by profit, would manage to detach production from consumption to create employment.

Now, investing in the expectation of further investment, also made in the expectation of further investment, meant building trust on the future being able to build trust on the further-away-future, hence, on a virtuous cycle of trust. This, though, only works if all these future generations remain oblivious on productive investment ultimately only serving consumption, hence, that they will forget that the day of reckoning in terms of a brutal consumption-test will be coming. While Keynes honestly mentioned this fatal dilemma, which is innate in elevating investment being construed as the savior for deficient consumption, he, thereafter returned to ignoring it once again. But most problems do not go away by ignoring them, and there is particularly no way to get out of the haunting shadow of this one. Profit making with investment will run dry someday if the investment goods are not purchased by somebody who can use them to produce consumption goods. Therefore, the numerator-side of the fraction of the "inducement to invest", the marginal efficiency of capital in the business plans of Keynes' entrepreneurs in investments goods must someday be hit by a dramatic collapse. This will be the end of the bail-out by investment, debunking its remaining dependency on consumption; it will prove that the artists in the investment-spiral have all put their hope in hot air only.

Second, Keynes has no way to notionally and quantitatively grasp the gap by which "aggregate demand", as he calls it, is deficient because of insufficient employment-generating consumptive and investive spending. He neither relates the problem to Marx's notations M ($c+v$) and M'-M (s), nor, more crucially, applies a distinction between productive and sterile spending to these components. He also ignores the methodological issues of circuit analysis.

Other than that, third, Keynes "inducement to invest" offers a fine and valuable theory, one which uses his microeconomic observations of investors' calculus to develop a macroeconomic theory of firms' investment and, hence, of firms' employment-generating spending (as a sub-sample of overall employment-generating spending). It plausibly describes investors' decision-making and largely corresponds to today's insights in business valuation. In so doing, though, Keynes actually discovered a novel impediment to investment. He cancels out the possibility for a depression to benevolently induce a recovery through an automatic fall of the interest rate. Uncertainty, the new element operating via liquidity preference and rising interest rates, does away with the possibility of a self-healing and Keynes, through his innovation, actually worsened the prospects for investment to recover if it gets into trouble; investment, therefore, becomes even more unreliable as a substitute for consumption.

Keynes still underestimated the depressive effects of his discovery twofold. He cannot ascertain that only truly employment-generating-investment enters into his "marginal efficiency of capital" on the *numerator-side* of the "inducement to invest"-fraction. This is so because he did not clearly and strictly limit the numerator to productive investment but allows sterile investment to creep in; accordingly, his numerator is too loose. The *denominator-side* of his fraction, which reflects competing possible uses for money, which do not generate employment, on the other hand, is too narrow because it does not include all possible sterile investments. In particular, Keynes' denominator only looks at debt-investments, but forgets about investment in land, pre-existing buildings, stock, and pre-existing businesses (e.g., as private equity), gold, crypto, antiques, art, etc. For productive investments to come through, though, the numerator of the inducement to invest, i.e., the *m.e.c.* of a contemplated productive investment would also have to beat these. Therefore, overall, Keynes' theory, of when entrepreneurs will make employment-generating investments, if valuable and eyes-opening, is incomplete. Things are worse than he makes us believe.

Fourth, Keynes confronts his patient and willing reader with two irritating surprises by almost pulling the carpet out from under the place upon which his "inducement to invest" rests. All of a sudden, he proclaims a theory of a multiplier that explains the relationship of first and second circuit investments (and third and fourth circuits...) with a narrative that is essentially incompatible with the inducement to invest. He also posits the axiom of an identity or equality of investment and saving (I = S), which involves the same contradiction, albeit in an even more aggressive way in fact. So, he burdens us with two explanations too many of firms' investments and leaves it up to his reader to save his "inducement to invest" against destruction by the inventor himself. There is a clear parallel here to Marx overburdening his economics with the theory of labor value. After all, like Marx, Keynes cannot be said to have theoretically succeeded in the task that he set for himself, and like Marx, he became a hero mostly to those who aspire his political solutions.

Fifth, there is another problem in Keynes' thinking, which Keynes did not manage to control and which will be consequential for the remainder of this book. Just as Smith, in essence, has assumed markets for capitalist production to be inexhaustible primordial oceans, Keynes *assumed private debt financing for public deficit spending to be inexhaustible* and did not think through the question of where the money for the prosthetic employment-generating deficit spending would come from in the long run. Marx pointed to the problems and limits of prosthetics financing to unfairly fight Malthus' (and Sismondi's) theory of a *need* of prosthetics for circuit closure; Keynes made the opposite mistake and did not consider these limits.

Section 9. Kalecki: Only capitalists can save capitalists

Michal Kalecki

Michal Kalecki, a native Polish with Jewish origins, was an independent and cosmopolitical mind. He had a very interesting life as a scholar and world-touring economic adviser, in war and peace, to different capitalist and socialist countries, even if though his life also involved fleeing from the Nazis and leaving the US during McCarthyism. Born in 1899, he studied engineering and mathematics in Poland. After reading Marx, Rosa Luxemburg, and Tugan-Baranovsky,[366] without ever formally having studied economics, he first travelled through Europe on grants or self-financed his way by teaching. He was in Stockholm when the *General Theory* first appeared. Joan Robinson recollects what Kalecki told her: "Someone gave him Keynes' book. He began to read it – it was the book that he intended to write. He thought that perhaps further on there would be something different. No, all the way – it was his book. He said: "I confess, I was ill. Three days I lay in bed. Then I thought – Keynes is more known than I am. These ideas will get across much quicker with him and then we can get on to the interesting question, which is their application. Then I got up"."[367]

Soon afterwards, he arrived at the UK and spent time at several universities, including Cambridge and Oxford. Although he made friends with members of Keynes' Cambridge circle, Joan Robinson, Richard Kahn, Maurice Dobb, and Piero Sraffa, he had only one "cold" meeting with Keynes himself in 1937. Although she was close friends with Keynes, Joan Robinson still acknowledged a precedence of Kalecki's work over Keynes' work in major regards.[368] Kalecki remained in the UK during World War II, teaching and working as a statistician in the war economy. After the war, he took on tasks in Montreal and New York and worked for the UN and US institutions until McCarthyism made him return to communist Poland in

---

366 *López/Assous* (2010) footnote 2, page 226.
367 *Robinson* (1977) page 8, 9.
368 She writes on the major contents of Keynes' theory: "Michal Kaleck"s claim to priority of publication is indisputable. With proper scholarly dignity (which, however, is unfortunately rather rare among scholars) he never mentioned this fact. And, indeed, except for the authors concerned, it is not particularly interesting to know who first got into print. The interesting thing is that two thinkers, from completely different political and intellectual starting points, should come to the same conclusion. For us in Cambridge it was a great comfort." (*Robinson* (1966) page 337).

1955. Thereafter, he worked for Israel, Mexico, India,[369] France, and Cuba, partly from Poland and partly within these countries, until he died in 1970.

The theory of firms' investments as missing a "central *pièce* of... economics" and as a "central *pièce de résistance* of economics"

Like Keynes, Kalecki had incorporated Marx's contents (Keynes had used M–C–M', while Kalecki employed the evolutionary form of the reproduction schemes) and like him Keynes had avoided the pitfalls of Marx's labor value and exploitation theory. Both men had also remained outside of the circles of orthodox Marxism, communist, or socialist parties and of sectarian leftists. Alike Keynes, Kalecki saw investment as a crucial substitute for deficient consumption demand.

Furthermore, in Kalecki, much like in Sismondi, Malthus, and Marx,[370] the working class ultimately contributes nothing to capitalist's profits; it only pays back to capitalists, in an eternal recurrence of the same, the salaries, which it has received from them, for consumption goods. Let us follow Kalecki's argument in a bit more detail: Salaries are paid out to workers by *all* departments or capitalists, but as workers have to spend their whole salaries on consumption and can only do so to the department in charge of workers' consumption goods, the salary spending of the aggregate capitalist class rather promptly travels back to this specific department. The capitalist class, thus, as we already saw in Marx's reproduction schemes, in the aggregate, through all its departments, pays out an amount that is recollected by one of its departments. The costs are recovered and the contribution to aggregate profit is zero. Therefore, salaries can never increase capitalists' profits.[371]

---

369 *López/Assous* (2010). On Kalecki, see also *King* (2015) page 11.

370 In Marx, it contributes by creating surplus value, which capitalists can appropriate, but it does not crucially contribute to realizing the surplus value by buying the produce, which it represents.

371 "For the understanding of the problems considered it is useful to present the above from a somewhat different angle. Imagine that following the Marxian "schemes of reproduction" we subdivide all of the economy into three departments: department I producing investment goods, department II producing consumption goods for capitalists, and department III producing consumption goods for workers. The capitalists in department III, after having sold to workers [Kalecki means: to their workers of department III, GW] the amount of consumption goods corresponding to their wages, will still have left a surplus of consumption goods which will be the equivalent of their profits. These goods will be sold to the workers of department I and department II, and as the workers do not save it will be equal to their incomes. Thus, total profits will be equal to the sum of profits in department I, profits in department II, and wages in these two departments: or, total profits will be equal to the value of production of these two departments – in other words, to the value of production of investment goods and consumption goods for capitalists." Kalecki goes one step further, writing that "the production of department I and department II will also determine the

Salaries render profits possible for the dept. II.b-capitalists,[372] but they remain neutral in generating profits for the capitalist class in the aggregate. Even if workers spend their whole income reliably – as Kalecki said "workers spend all they receive"[373] or "workers don't save"[374] – they are not the ones to provide value to pay for the surplus produce. Thus, in Kalecki's work the capitalists are the only ones left charged with doing the critical buying, which enables profit. Others before him have stated this too, but thanks to his engineer-minded rereading of Marx's reproduction schemes, Kalecki makes the point more strongly and more stringently than expressed anywhere else. The solution to the problem of circuit closure definitively lies in the hands of capitalists alone. They must buy their own produce at profitable prices in order to validate their own investments. Capitalists must drag themselves out of the swamp by their own bootstraps.

Now, while Kalecki made this point very clear, he also admitted that during his lifetime no theory of firms' investment existed which would have convinced him. Let us look at his critique of Tugan-Baranovsky's investment theory: Even if *all* investment is rewarding for the capitalist class in the aggregate (because of Kalecki's profit equation – see the following section), this does not mean that all investment is also profitable for the individual capitalists who make it. They are only interested in their own profits, not in the profits of their fellow capitalists. What is "to the advantage of a single entrepreneur does not necessarily benefit all entrepreneurs as a class".[375] Therefore, the proof that investment is good for the capitalist class as a

---

production of department III if the distribution between profits and wages in all departments is given. The production of department III will be pushed up to the point where profits earned out of that production will be equal to the wages of departments I and II. Or, to put it differently, employment and production of department III will be pushed up to the point where the surplus of this production over what the workers of this department buy with their wages is equal to the wages of departments I and II."[787] *(Kalecki* (1933, 1954) page 80.) Note the following: We said that the reproduction schemes can be presented with two, three, or four units, while we have chosen four units [I.a.(means of production for means of production), I.b. (means of production for means of consumption), II.a. (means of consumption for capitalists) and II.b. means of consumption for workers). Kalecki uses a three-unit-model for capitalist firms here: producers of means of production (I), of means of consumption for capitalists (II) and of means of consumption for workers (III). This can be extended to a four-unit-model if we distinguish between producers of means of production for means of production (I.a.) and producers of means of production for means of consumption (I.b.), with departments II and III then becoming II.a and II.b In *Capital* volume II, Marx basically uses a two-unit-model only.

372 Kalecki calls our II.b.-department producing consumption goods for workers 'department III', but this difference is only terminological.

373 *Kalecki* (1937) page 35.

374 *Kalecki* (1937) page 36.

375 *Kalecki* (1935) page 26.

whole, is no theory of investment yet; such theory ought to explain why an *individual* capitalist might invest. Thus, writes Kalecki, Tugan-Baranovsky's theory "rests on an error that what *may* happen is actually happening..." and he blames Tugan-Baranovsky because he "does not show at all why capitalists in the long run are to invest to the extent which is necessary to contribute to full utilization of productive equipment."[376] Alternatively, as Kalecki states: "Tugan considers the *possible* use of the national product created by full employment of the productive forces as the actual fact ...". Therefore, his theory is not "wrong", but it is "completely unfounded". The challenge remains "in order to give an answer to this query... construct a theory of investment decision..., which I always considered to be the central problem of the political economy of capitalism."[377]

Kalecki did make efforts of his own towards a theory of investment.[378] He investigated capitalist's investment behavior in business cycles[379] and came to see a virtuous circle, in which the investment rate and the derivative of the previous investment rate from the past might determine the present: "It follows that investment at a given time is determined by the level and rate of change in the level of investment at some earlier time", he wrote.[380] He also reflected that "investment decisions (are determined) by, broadly speaking, the level and the rate of change of economic activity."[381] What Kalecki says here is certainly true, at a certain stage of analysis. The past does have an impact on future investments by establishing certain technological, economic, and social preconditions in industries, capital, institutions, consumer preferences, etc. These earth-grounded facts cannot help but influence expectations about the future, including those of investing firms. The speed and dynamics of economic activity witnessed yesterday – and of their changes and derivations – also matters here. However, Kalecki himself ultimately did not consider this effort satisfactory and quite rightly. He admittedly remained unhappy with the state of investment theory, including his own, until the end of his life and recapitulated that the "determination of investment decisions ... *remains* the central *pièce de résistance* of economics" (without even mentioning Keynes).[382]

---

376 *Kalecki* (1967) page 147 (italics by Kalecki).

377 *Kalecki* (1967) page 148 (italics by Kalecki).

378 *Kalecki* (1943, 1954) page 110 et seq.

379 These subjects appear in the titles of many of his articles and in the introduction to his *Selected Essays on the Dynamics of the Capitalist Economy* written shortly before his death. He admits that while his "theory of effective demand (was) already clearly formulated in the first papers (and) remains unchanged in all the relevant writings... there is a continuous search for new solutions in the theory of investment decisions" (*Kalecki* (1971) page viii).

380 *Kalecki* (1943, 1954) page 124.

381 *Kalecki* (1968) page 165.

382 In his last article on the subject, see *Kalecki* (1968) page 165.

We believe that Kalecki was misled, possibly by his engineering background, to look out for a theory of investment that would explain present investment from the past with the help of some complex function, e.g., one comparable with a theory of waves that build up and interact or a theory of the dynamics of gases. We believe that the interference of human minds dealing with uncertainty, including with the uncertainty resulting from the reflexivity that other humans deal with the exact same situation, is much stronger than any causation chains from the past. To this end, we side with Keynes' inducement to invest and Minsky's later evolution thereof, even though Keynes was not free of the same fallacy when he slipped into the idea of a multiplier and of an identity of I = S in the S → I-direction, as we observed, which also featured causation-style types of answers. But while the correct expectation-driven or motivation-driven style maintained the upper hand in Keynes, this approach is less undeveloped in Kalecki; he searches for the theory of investment in the wrong place of past-based causality and takes the insufficiency of his attempts there to signify his general defeat in a theory of investment.

Kalecki cannot have believed in Keynes' "inducement to invest"-theory either. Not only he continued to mourn the lack of a theory of firms' investment but, while he survived Keynes by 24 years, never made a attempt to use Keynes' "inducement"-theory, not even as raw material, to build such a hitherto outstanding investment theory. Unlike Minsky later, Kalecki also made no effort to further evolve the "inducement to invest" in the direction of the Viner-Rebuttal. The reasons for this are probably the same as those provided above: Kalecki was essentially going after a theory which would explain when the potentiality of investment becomes a reality of investment with engineer-like causes or mathematical functions, running from the past into the future and not, like Keynes, on the basis of uncertainty and expectations about the future. It is also telling that Kalecki made no effort to use Keynes' multiplier or Keynes' identity of saving and investment in the S → I-direction for a theory of investment, although they have mechanistic causal moments which were generally closer to Kalecki's preferred theory design. The reason for this omission may be found in Kalecki's aforementioned critique of Tugan-Baranovsky. It may have been clearer to Kalecki than it was even to Keynes that Keynes' identity of saving and investment, when read in the S → I-direction, was only a theory of refunding and had no potential to analyze whether the funds would actually be used for investment or not. Kalecki likely also felt that his own "profit equation", to which we turn in the following, provided a superior theory of the funding of investment.

Kalecki's macro-transmissions: "Investment plus capitalists' consumption equals gross profit"

Kalecki's famous profit equation is *investment plus capitalists' consumption equals gross profit*, which one might abbreviate (Concap + I = P). Here we encounter a sourcing-related style of teaching, which, as mentioned previously, is functionally close to Keynes' identity/equality of I = S in the I → S-direction. While Kalecki felt that a convincing theory of firms' productive investment had not been developed until the end of his life, which dealt with Keynes' identity/equality of I = S in the S → I-direction, he was still quite satisfied with his "profit equation" which dealt with it in the I → S-direction.

The profit equation certainly considers what happens *after* firms make actual investments. It looks at typical recurring exchanges of capitalists, and at their effects on a macroeconomic level. It does not reflect upon *when* capitalists will invest or how much – insofar it misses the most crucial macoeconomic question –, but it does tell us that it is good it they *have invested* and even quantitatively measures how good it is. Strangely enough, future investment, still comes into play, as the old investment fills the pot, like in poker, for other capitalists, which are lured to also invest. First movers must invest, to prepare the ground and to draw second movers into investing too; Early investments of some enable gross profits of the aggregate capitalists' class as a whole. This obviously must be read before the background, taught elsewhere by Kalecki, that only capitalists can provide the profits for capitalists and to keep the wheels turning.[383] However, Kalecki does not think in terms of teleology or motivation – capitalists have no interest in the profit of their colleagues – but rather in terms of mere factual effects: as the invested money arrives somewhere else, the financial means are supplied for others to profit. Therefore, even bad investments are good for the capitalist class in the aggregate; they too can be turned into other capitalists' additional profits. An investment, which goes wrong for the investor himself, who may have made no profit and even gone bust, still not only employed and fed workers, but also munitioned suppliers who will have their outlays returned and mostly also receive profit on top. Investment, which is bad for the investing capitalist as it is unprofitable, is still good for the capitalist class generally! Now, the same applies to capitalist consumption, which was never meant to generate profit for the consuming capitalist anyhow. Macroeconomically, it is always like a blown investment; the fact that consuming capitalists get satisfaction out of consumption, but not out of failing investments, is not a relevant economic factor.

In order to arrive at his profit equation, Kalecki used an approach similar to the "theory of business cycles", or so he at least said in an article written shortly before his death in 1970.[384] He identified proper flows, captured them in definitions, and determined the relationships and causal influences between them. In this way, he sought out macro-transmissions, like Keynes and Marx had, the latter in his reproduction schemes. Already in an article written in 1933, Kalecki had chosen "gross real profit" as the critical "output flow" and he would remain attached to this

---

383   See page 322.
384   *Kalecki* (1968) page 165.

term throughout his life. He then chose investment and capitalists' consumption as his most important "input flows"[385] and connected the three by his profit equation. Kalecki ran his profit equation, "gross profit equals investment and capitalists' consumption", in both simplified and in more developed versions. In his simplified version, he abstracts from taxes, government spending, and foreign exchange. "Indeed", he writes, "in our simplified model, profits in a given period are the direct outcome of capitalists' consumption and investment in that period. If investment increases by a certain amount, savings out of profit are *pro tanto* higher." Or "...investment, once carried out, automatically provides the savings necessary to finance it."[386] Capitalists forward to other capitalists the means for additional investment and for capitalists' consumption in several ways: "...if some capitalists increase their investment by using for this purpose their liquid reserves, the profits of other capitalists will rise pro tanto and thus the liquid reserves invested will pass into the possession of the latter"; accordingly some capitalists' profits may come directly from "liquid reserves" or from the prior saving of other capitalists. However, they may also come about indirectly through bank loans: "[A]dditional investment", Kalecki goes on to claim, "is financed out of bank credit [and] the spending of the amounts in question will cause equal amounts of saved profits to accumulate as bank credits".[387] What began as a bank loan to one capitalist, coming from the deposits of another capitalist,[388] ends up as profit for yet a third group of capitalists – and likely into their bank accounts again.

Kalecki asked himself expressly in what direction his equation "gross profit equals investment and capitalists' consumption" operates: "What is the significance of this equation? Does it mean that profits in a given period determine capitalists' consumption and investment, or the reverse of this? The answer to these questions depends on which of these items is directly subject to the decision of capitalists. Now, it is clear that capitalists may decide to consume and to invest more in a given period than in the preceding one, but they cannot decide to earn more. It is, therefore, their investment and consumption decisions, which determine the profits and not vice versa".[389] Hence, as implied in Keynes, albeit more clearly, in Kalecki, investment and consumption are the dog and profits are the tail. Alternatively, we might say that investment and capitalists' consumption are the call and profits are the answering echo, or that profits are the explosion in the cylinder and profits the rotations of the shaft, or that investment and capitalists' consumption

385   *Kalecki* (1933) page 1.
386   *Kalecki* (1933 1954) page 83.
387   Kalecki (1943, 1954) page 84.
388   Ignoring bank credit money creation for the moment.
389   *Kalecki*, The Determinants of Profit (1933, 1954), in: Selected Essays on the Dynamics of the Capitalist Economy, 1971, page 78.

328 Gerhard H. Wächter: The Capitalist Economy and its Prosthetics

are the rain and snow in the Himalayas and profit the swelling of the Ganges river, etc. Kalecki in his profit equation is clearly only concerned with what comes out of investment; hence, if we draw the comparison with Keynes' identity/equality in the I → S-direction again, he speaks about the Concap + I → P-direction of his profit equation, but it has no application vice versa. That direction ought to be covered by the (as yet lacking) theory of investment.

Evidently, the terms "investment", "capitalists' consumption", and "gross profit" require elucidation. Like Marx, Kalecki lived in a two-class world in which wealth owners and entrepreneurs are merged into capitalists. Wealth owners do not appear separately; they do not consume and do not draw wealth revenue of their own, e.g., rent. Everything happens either between capitalists (who also consume) or between capitalists and workers (exchanges between workers are also excluded). Every investment implies that capitalists take one of two roles, either as *investor-capitalists* (operating in the M–C-leg of their circuit) and or as *supplier-capitalists* (operating in the C–M' or C'–M'-leg of their circuit); the investors-capitalists' paid purchase prices will be the supplier-capitalists' collected sales prices. If we include consumption, we may say that one side's outlays, capitalist's investment and consumption, become *sales, turnover* or *revenues* of the other side. This way, we, though, do not yet arrive at "profits" and at the equation "*profits* = investment plus personal consumption of capitalists" or "*gross profits* = gross investment plus capitalists' consumption".[390] So far, we have rather justified why *sales* (turnover or revenues) equal investment plus personal consumption. This appears unavoidable because sales, turnover, or revenues are not profit but a part of sales prices only recover outlays or costs.

Yet, Kalecki uses a change of terminology to avoid a contradiction here. Profit in his equation is not simply taken to mean "profit" *but some extended, coarse, rough, or gross version of profit*: "Gross profit", he defines, is the "aggregate real income of capitalists including depreciation per unit of time consisting of their consumption and saving".[391] Hence, depreciation is included. Kalecki confirms this when he also defines "gross profits", from the perspective of an individual enterprise, as the "difference between the value of sales and prime costs".[392] Inventories should include "prime costs" – and they are to be deducted from sales in order to arrive at "gross profit".

Kalecki's equation, accordingly, is not dealing with "pure" profit, as in Marx's M–M', or with "earnings", e.g., in the sense of the conventional accounting and reporting-terms of "earnings", "earnings before taxes", EBT, etc., but he is instead talking about "pre-depreciation profits" or "earnings before depreciation". We may ask

---

390 *Kalecki* (1943, 1954) page 83 et seq Italics added.
390 *Kalecki* (1943, 1954) page 83 et seq Italics added.
391 *Kalecki* (1933) page 1.
392 *Kalecki* (1937) page 36.

whose depreciation Kalecki thinks of and try to relate it to Marx's *v*, *c*, and *s*. The supplier-capitalist receives a payment, which for him is M'. That is not his profit, given that he has had to incur labor costs *v*, which must be deducted. He also has costs for inventories, which must be deducted (we may call them *c/inv*). Then, there is a final part of *c* left, the part for depreciation of equipment (which we may call *c/dep*). Kalecki quite obviously wants the supplier-capitalist's *c/dep* to be a component of his "gross profit". What Kalecki is looking at, could, thus, alternatively be called the *supplier capitalist's cashflow minus costs for inventories and labor*. This is the value that Kalecki primarily uses to study the economy's macroeconomic wheels.

Kalecki moves from his simplified model to his general one by allowing for foreign trade, state taxation, budget deficit, state expenditures, and workers' saving. He emphasizes that only export surpluses (not just exports, but export minus imports)[393] increase capitalists' gross profits. Increases of government indebtedness also have this effect; they are like "domestic exports" and are functionally equal to trade surpluses.[394] The "general equation for profit" then becomes: gross profits net of taxes equals gross investment plus export surplus plus budget deficit minus workers' savings plus capitalists' consumption.[395]

Now, does Kalecki and his profit equation teach us something new about the theory of firms' investment (or about their employment-generating spending)? How does the equation relate to Keynes' identity/equality? Does it give us anything that goes beyond it? Kalecki teaches us that capitalists' investment and consumption are good – from the perspective of employment and the modern master drama – in the aggregate. Investments and capitalist consumption will never be lost, even if becomes useless for the individual capitalist who originally made it. This idea was already present in Keynes' identity/equality, partly more encompassing (as salaries and workers' income was included from the beginning), partly in a narrower sense (as capitalist consumption was not). Let us compare the situation to a pre-money, pre-economic form of subsistence procurement. Assume that a neolithic community makes an effort to erect a dam to irrigate an area for agriculture. The dam breaks, so the effort was in vain. Now translate the event into capitalism. In both cases, the physical results of the efforts are gone and the physical damage (in terms of deaths, resources used, etc.) is the same. Yet while It may be very difficult to re-build the motivation for a second effort in the neolithic subsistence community, that is quite different in capitalism. While the merchant heroes of the first effort are bankrupt, somebody else now sits on Keynes' saving or Kalecki's gross profits. The motivational system's independence from values-in-uses in a money economy

---

393   Kalecki criticizes Luxemburg for confusing the two. See *Kalecki* (1967) page 152.
394   *Kalecki* (1934) page 16, 18.
395   *Kalecki* (1943, 1954) page 82. If Kalecki were to assume, as he mostly does with justification, that workers do not save, then the deduction of such savings can be omitted.

proves utterly robust, one might even consider calling it "anti-fragile" with *Nassim Nicolas Taleb*.[396] Capitalists, it seems, hold an instrument in their hands (their consumption and their investment) which is able to perpetuate motivational power for production and employment and can both enrich their class and carry workers along (at least to some extent). Keynes and Kalecki are telling us that the stuff to motivate workers and supplier firms to turn the wheels is not likely to ever be scarce in capitalism. The problem rests in the investor firms: Their motivational stuff is not money but profit, more money – and that stuff is indeed scarce, certainly in the productive economy. Whether investor firms will actually make investments remains as conditional as it already was in the third interpretation of Ricardo's Law of Say, in Sismondi, Malthus, Marx, and in Keynes' theory of firms' investment.

Kalecki's profit equation runs a transmission gear through the economy at large, which allows investment and capitalist consumption to positively feedback on investment via enabling future profits. However, we need profit-enabling investment first in order for the transmission gear to operate and to allure second movers. But it remains in the realm of conditionality and potentiality when these second movers will be allured, as, according to Kalecki, a convincing theory of investment is still missing. Perhaps Kalecki, like Keynes and Marx before him, did not arrive at one because he remained caught in the productive economy and was, as little as Marx and Keynes, able to see the perpetual drain of the wealth economy on the productive economy's investment funds. They question whether or not Kalecki's potentiality of investment will, to a sufficient degree, become reality, may have to be answered from the perspective of the battle between the two economies for the money. There will always be, irrespective of what other circumstances affect firms' behavior, insufficient employment-generating spending and lack of circuit closure because of the drain of money into the sterile economy. Like Keynes, Kalecki ends by suggesting prosthetics through state intervention and, like Keynes once again, he does not appropriately reflect on the limits and consequences of such prosthetic spending in any great depth.

***

Kalecki very clearly sees the paradox, which was already present in Sismondi, Malthus, in the third interpretation of Ricardo's Law of Say, in Marx, and in Keynes: Will the capitalists save the capitalists by buying the M'-M-part of the produce of their colleagues for M', thereby allowing them to validate their investment M? He also expected that they would, aside consumption, only do it for investment purposes. He wrote "...profits, to put it paradoxically, are invested even before they come into being",[397] but he knew that the benevolent consequences of investments

---

396 In the sense of *Taleb* (2012).
397 *Kalecki* (1935) 29.

for the capitalist class in the aggregate are not a sufficient motive for investment for individual capitalists. His profit equation describes a macro-transmission through the economy, one comparable, if more concise, to Keynes' identity of S and I, but in the end he only gives us that capitalists' prior investment, and consumption will enable the receiving supplier capitalists to make new investments. Whether this potentiality becomes a reality remains open-ended.

Section 10. Minsky: Liquidity and firms' employment-generating spending

Hyman P. Minsky

Hyman Philip Minsky (1919 – 1996) was a student of both Henry Simmons and Josef Schumpeter, and influenced by their views on credit[398] and financial instability. Furthermore, he was influenced by Irving Fisher's debt-deflation theory.[399] Moreover, he was particularly impressed with Keynes. He must have known Marx, partly used his insights, but he was careful when referring to him; he commonly made reference to Marx's ideas via Kalecki.

Minsky's starting point was where Marx and Keynes agree: "For a capitalist system to function well, prices must carry profits. Prices are also vehicles for recovering costs... Firms try to build into their supply prices an excess of cashflows over operating costs...This building takes the form of markups on technologically determined costs...".[400] "The capital development of a capitalist economy is accompanied by exchanges of present money for future money, the present money pays for resources that go into the production of investment output, whereas the future money is the 'profits'"[401] "For output to be produced over a succession of periods, prices must exceed the per-unit costs of those inputs that directly vary with production"[402] "Business investment involves spending money to produce goods that are to be used in a production process that are expected to yield revenues in excess of current out-

---

398   Schumpeter writes, for instance, that: "Der Unternehmer "kann nur Unternehmer werden, in-
        dem er vorher Schuldner wird. Er wird zum Schuldner infolge einer innern Notwendigkeit...
        und ist nicht etwas abnormales, ein durch akzidentielle Umstände zu erklärendes, missli-
        ches Ereignis. Sein erstes Bedürfnis ist ein Kreditbedürfnis." (*Schumpeter* (1912) page 208). On
        Schumpeter see also *Beinhocker* (2006) page 39.
399   *Fisher* (1933) page 337.
400   *Minsky* (1986) page 158 et seq
401   *Minsky* (1993) page 2.
402   *Minsky* (1986) page 161.

of-pocket-costs....this excess is imputed to capital assets and becomes the return on investment... is like a bond... a money-now-for-a-money-later exchange"[403]

Minsky had been interested in business cycles and the dynamics of capitalism since the 1960ties, much like Schumpeter. In this context, he preoccupied himself especially with Keynes. In 1972, he published an article on him[404] and in 1975 a comprehensive book, *John Maynard Keynes*, followed. Minsky chose to play the role of the concise, systematic thinker, he would have wished to have been with Keynes as his aid and comrade-in-arms when Keynes originally phrased his ideas. Convinced that Keynes was basically right, he went through Keynes' text with the aim of clarifying loose and vague terms and reconciling contradictions. It was certainly to Minsky's advantage that he saw himself more as a diagnostician than a prescriber of remedies[405] – just the opposite of Keynes. Thus, he produced an improved, more consistent, and clarified Keynesian framework. But there was an additional wrinkle. Keynes had already thought of capitalism as a monetary economy. Minsky – on the tracks of Simmons, Schumpeter, and Irving Fisher – pulled Keynes further in this direction, in particular by connecting considerations on how finance, via limited budgets and liquidity, can impact firms' employment-generating spending – in the negative and in the positive. Here Minsky added material of his own and, as his article "The Financial Instability Hypothesis: An Interpretation of Keynes an Alternative to 'Standard" Theory' of 1977[406] shows, went beyond a precise reconstruction of Keynes only. Rather, he let Keynes' thoughts and his own financial contributions merge into something, which almost became one thing for Minsky, and which he baptized the "Financial Instability Hypothesis". He stayed on this track until his last book *Stabilizing an unstable economy* (1986) and his paper "The Financial Instability Hypothesis" (May 1992). He now admitted "... the Financial instability Hypothesis is an interpretation of the substance of Keynes' 'General Theory.'"[407]

In this Minsky's view, the financial system was not a peripheral, subservient, and neutral subsystem of the economy, which only emits disturbing waves of instability from the outside on the basis of occasional malfunctions, like bushfires in a countryside region, an erupting volcano, or the collapse of a network of computers. Rather, the financial system sits *in the center of the economy*, and it steers firms' investment both generally and permanently. It does this for the good or the bad of the economy, which becomes only especially visible in booms, crises, and busts. A theory of capitalism that accepted this central spot of finance, hence, had to be able to show how finance generates instability – something which the model of the neoclassical

---

403 *Minsky* (1986) page 192.
404 *Minsky* (1972).
405 *Minsky* (1982), Introduction, page viii.
406 Also reprinted in *Minsky* (1982). See also *Minsky* (1980).
407 *Minsky* (1993) page 1.

synthesis could not do.[408] Working this out was what Minsky saw as his task and he accepted this challenge.

The "Financial Instability Hypothesis I": Asset prices, interest rate, investment, and *soft* macro transmissions

"Keynes' system consists", Minsky generalized, "of an analysis of capitalist finance in the context of uncertainty and how capitalist finance affects the valuation of items in the stock of capital assets and thus affects the pace of investment."[409] The "core" of the *General Theory*, according to Minsky, "...is the theory of investment and why it is so prone to fluctuate..." (Note the difference to Kalecki who denied the existence of a theory of investment). In this regard, Minsky goes on, "...Keynes' theory of investment links the fluctuating pace of investment, which is an output (real sector) concept, to variables, which are determined in financial markets."[410] As we have seen, this line of argument began with Keynes in the *General Theory* with uncertainty, an increased propensity to hoard, liquidity preference, and interest rates; we have also seen how it was further evolved by Keynes himself in the Viner-rebuttal to capital assets' falling prices as a crucial intermediate step.[411] What Minsky now added, in order to arrive at his "Financial Instability Hypothesis", on the one side mainly consisted of an elaboration and systematization of Keynes' Viner-rebuttal: Values of capital assets are shown as being in juxtaposition to current production or replacement costs of such assets; their relationship determines the fate of the production of new assets. It does this on the positive upward side, by allowing and enabling creative "upward instability".[412] In the upswing, improved financing terms lead to higher profits, which lead to expected higher future annuities, and which lead to higher present values that again lead to improved financing terms. Better financial terms, enabled by almost any financial innovation whatsoever, raise the value/price of capital assets in two ways: They increase the future quasi-rents (through lower financing costs) and by the market's raised valuation of these quasi-rents.[413] Bankers are as ready and eager as firms to transition into euphoric states or even to "explode" and to jointly glide into irrational exuberances. Bankers tend to discover that in booms their "margin(s) of safety" grow higher than they had originally required.

---

408   *Minsky* (1982) Introduction, page xii.

409   *Minsky* (1975) page 129 (italics by Minsky).

410   *Minsky* (1975) page 92. Minsky silently, quite rightly, reads a focus on the productive economy into Keynes, although Keynes (like Minsky) did not apply the distinction between the productive and sterile economy.

411   *Viner* (1936); *Keynes* (1937).

412   *Minsky* (1977) page 66, 78, 83 and *Minsky* (1966) page 118. "Capitalism", says Minsky beautifully, "reacts to past success by trying to explode" (*Minsky* (1966) page 149).

413   See *Minsky* (1978) page 83. See also *Minsky* (1986) page 199.

Hence, even if they stay with the same "margin of safety"-requirement in the next round of loans, their financing will expand as they can calculate with higher asset values. It is very likely, though, that they will now, in the interest of increasing the profits of their banks, somewhat reduce their "margin of safety". This makes money even more abundant and adds a further impulse to low interest rates. The outlook onto new investments (including in the productive economy) becomes brighter. Entrepreneurs will, thus, be very eager to pick up newly offered money and to invest it, setting in motion further stimuli to employment and growth.

Much of the preceding Minsky narrative of the upswing-part of the business cycle is familiar and had already been present in Irving Fisher, Keynes, and others. Minsky spoke of it as a "peculiar circularity of a capitalist economy", which is "that sufficient investment to assure the economy does well now will be forthcoming only as it is believed that sufficient investment to assure the economy will be forthcoming in the future".[414] Here we are again: Firms must believe that firms will invest in the future in order for things to go smoothly in the present.

We have seen that Keynes, in the *General Theory*, introduced his marginal efficiency of capital (m.e.c.) as the discount rate that would make "the present value of a series of annuities given by the return expected from the capital asset" equal to its "supply price", which was the "replacement costs" for the capital asset or "costs of producing that unit"[415] and that Keynes compared this discount rate with the interest rate to derive the inducement to invest as some kind of a "governor" for investment. Minsky had, as mentioned previously, called the original *m.e.c.*/interest rate-version of the "inducement to invest" in the *General Theory* "muddled" because Keynes only "phrased his argument in terms of interest rates" and "...chose to suppress the price of capital assets in his statement of his liquidity-preference function".[416] Minsky even blamed Keynes for retrogressing from a "cyclical perspective" to an "equilibrium-growth perspective" here and in other parts of the *General Theory*, especially in chapter 17. "As a result of these flaws", according to Minsky, "the full power of his argument was obscured and lost..."[417] Yet, luckily, Keynes had already himself refined this deficient original view in the Viner-Rebuttal by redefining the ratio between the (fallen) prices of preexisting (productive) investments and the production costs of new (productive) investments as the critical value. Minsky supported this: "...it is necessary to explicitly introduce the price level of capital assets PK as a determinant for the demand for money so that changes in the quantity of money... or changes in uncertainty or speculative expectations can affect the price of

---

414 *Minsky* (1986) page 254.
415 *Keynes* (1936) page 135.
416 *Minsky* (1975) page 67.
417 *Minsky* (1975) page 67.

capital assets".[418] Accordingly, adjustments operate largely via values of "preexisting assets".[419] "An investment good, once delivered and 'at work' in a production process, is a capital asset. As a capital asset, its value is the present value of the anticipated gross profits after taxes (quasi rents) that are imputed to its participation in economic activity. The present value of a capital asset is an inverse function of the (long term) interest rate."[420] The problem are "market prices for reproducible assets that are far below their current cost of production."[421] "Investment consists of producing substitutes for items in the stock of real capital; the price of the units in the stock is the demand price for the units to be produced."[422] Accordingly, "...normal functioning requires that the price level, perhaps implicit, of the stock of real capital assets be consistent with the supply price of investment goods at the ongoing wage level. The euphoric boom occurs when portfolio preferences change so that the price level of the stock rises relatively to the wage level, causing an increase in the output of investment goods. A sharp fall in the price level of the stock of real capital assets will lead to a marked decline in investment and thus, in income..."[423]

Minsky also makes a distinction between safer "*outside assets*" (money and government bonds), the value of which is not likely to fall much, and riskier and more volatile "*inside assets*" (real capital, meaning land, valuables, real estate, businesses and equities),[424] whose value may fall drastically quickly. In any case, "the relative prices of different assets change." "An increase of uncertainty will see the price of inside assets – real capital and equities – fall relative to the price of outside assets – government debt – and money..."[425] This even allows to give a criterion for more and less stable economies as a whole: "The domain of stability of the system depends upon the ratio of the value of those assets whose market value is independent of system behavior to the value of those assets whose market value reflects expected system behavior."[426] While Minsky re-phrases Keynes' Viner-Rebuttal, and makes

---

418   *Minsky* (1975) page 72.

419   *Minsky* (1986) page 166.

420   *Minsky* (1980) page 107.

421   *Minsky* (1966) page 128.

422   *Minsky* (1966) page 134.

423   *Minsky* (1966) page 143.

424   *Minsky* (1966) page 130–132.

425   *Minsky* (1966) page 132. This is also supported by there being two different, albeit connected, "price levels" in capitalism, one for current output and one for capital assets; if the price level for current produce is low compared to the price level for capital assets, then conditions for investment are favorable; if the opposite is true, then they are unfavorable. (*Minsky* (1978) page 79 and 94; *Minsky* (1986) page 160 et seq., page 200 et seq).

426   *Minsky* (1966) page 149. One might challenge the implication that assets exist, the value of which are wholly and eternally independent of system behavior.

it much stronger, it is arguable whether he here adds much substance to Keynes' arguments.

"Financial instability hypothesis II": Asset prices, interest rates and *hard* macro transmissions

Minsky described how the generous availability of credit "softly" supports new investment. It does so as low rates reduce the costs of investment and raise the prices of competing old pre-exiting assets. The mechanism, of course, also works downwards. This was the main subject of our preceding treatment of Minsky, which we referred to as Minsky's "Financial instability hypothesis I". But Minsky, also regards *specific old debt of an individual firm*, inherited from its prior investment circuits, as affecting this firms' future investment. This operates via the debt service on the old debt, which must be paid out of the annuities from the individual firm's ongoing present operations. This debt service is a postponed part of M-outlays for prior circuits. Outlays, which had been cleverly avoided at the time of the investment, had first become patient balance sheet structures, but now, nastily, limit budgets and demand liquidity. They, too, co-determine whether new M-outlays in new circuits, i.e., new investments, are feasible. Minsky deals with them in what we call his "Financial instability hypothesis II".

Minsky says himself that he "makes much of the way in which ownership or operative control of the asset are financed" [427] and here he is adding new substance to Keynes. Old debt in balance sheets becomes the great downward amplifier and accelerator in depressions. Old "debt contracts", the inherited "debt structure" or "debt portfolio", which firms carry along and which express their financing-methods of earlier investments, cripple and block new investment in new circuits or even kill the firms. "The financial instability hypothesis", declares Minsky, "goes beyond what is explicit in the *General Theory* by integrating the liability structure and the cash payment commitments they imply into the analysis of the determination capital asset prices and the financing of investment". [428]

The debt obligations from the past now simply and straightforwardly absorb available cash flows and "physically" (in a "hard" way) disenable investment. Like workers must consume, firms must honor their debt. Minsky's interest in doing this is, of course, not so much that his old financing methods affect the individual entrepreneur in his individual investment decision (obviously borrowed money will enable him to invest more first, but the debt service on it will restrict his liquidity later), but he elevates the issue from a business schools subject into a macroeconomics subject. The existing financing structure upon asset values in the aggregate

427   *Minsky* (1986) page 194.
428   *Minsky* (1980) page 102.

has macroeconomic power, in particular, when the financing structure of firms is hit by a downswing. The liquidity effects of old debt boosts the "soft" effects of falls of asset values following increased uncertainty etc. Debt plus rising uncertainty is, in fact, a positive feedback-mechanism to render original losses of asset value more poisonous.[429] In chapter 4 of his *John Maynard Keynes*, Minsky gives a factual description of financial aspects of the corporate world. Economic units make portfolio decisions, which always encompass "what assets are to be held" on the one side and "how the position...is to be financed" on the other side. Both sides involve "annuities", which are cash flows, incoming and outgoing. "The well-being of an ordinary business firm depends not only on the behavior of the market for its output and the terms upon which it can hire inputs but also on the behavior of financial markets on the terms on which it can borrow, sell assets or float shares." [430] The financial market, together with the structure of the old debt. determine how costly the old debt is. The remnants of past financing thus become the main entry road for bad hard causal effects. Profits are not only "the signal for investments..." but also "that part of prices that supports the financial system and the structure of financial relations by providing the cash flows that validate past financial commitments"[431] Accordingly, if profits lack in a downswing, financial commitments of the past cannot be validated, and the "position making" of debtor-firms, in particular of (already) speculative and Ponzi financing firms, will be hit hard. [432] Minsky "by emphasizing the way in which investment demand is generated by the combination of the value of stock of assets,[433] the financing available from internal funds and financial markets, and the supply price of investment output..." shows "how a collapse of asset values, that occurs because of position making problems of units engaged in speculative and Ponzi finance, leads to a collapse of investment." [434] In other words, rising uncertainty and

---

429 The whole line of argument can be seen in the context of general considerations on complexity. Evolution builds up complex systems to deliver better results at lower costs. This, though, only comes at the price of higher fragility and of greater damage in cases of malfunction. Atomic plants are more effective than windmills and airplanes are more effective than horse-drawn carriages, but both entail more preconditions and have a higher potential for damage. Minsky applies that view in a specific way to the credit system, banking and the financial system as a whole. Increasing one potential for investment in good times becomes a millstone around one's neck in bad times.

430 *Minsky* (1975) page 68, 69 with the quote on page 69.

431 *Minsky* (1980) page 92.

432 One can see that here Minsky thinks of profit before interest payments ("earnings before interest"). They are also before principal repayment, but this is always so – taking out a loan is no expense and no revenue.

433 The mechanism runs via the existence of two price levels, the price level for current output and for capital assets and money (See *Minsky* (1986) page 160, 195) and via "the fall in the price level of the stock of real capital assets" (*Minsky* (1966) page 143).

434 *Minsky* (1980) page 101.

interest rates, falling asset values[435] not only dissolve "soft" pro-investment animal spirits by "soft" means – operating on the profit calculus of firms, but they disenable investment, in a brachial, causal manner, by blocking and sucking away financial means needed for it.

Minsky categorizes the quantitative relation between outgoing cashflows on old debt and incoming cashflows from firms' annuities in a famous triple terminological invention. There is *hedge financing* (interest and principle payment can be financed with current inflows), *speculative financing* (interest payment can be financed with current inflows, principle repayment cannot; hence, debt must be "rolled over" or financed out of the sale of other assets) or *Ponzi-financing* (neither interest payment nor principle repayment can be financed with current inflows – principle repayment is only possible by increases of the value of the financed asset, disposal of other assets, if at all). [436] As we already know, banks and the financial system as a whole show different degrees of acceptance of these types of financing depending on their momentary perception of a more favorable or unfavorable relation between expected incoming quasi-rents, asset values and debt-payment commitments.

Most children know that you need to honor due payment obligations or you will run into trouble. If there is no liquidity left and it cannot be created, very bad things happen. There will likely be executions against the debtor, which will force him to fire-sell assets below their market value and will burden him with additional costs. And, no doubt, the debtor will, partly because he is struggling to meet his existing payment obligations, and partly because his money is gone, cut back on his expenditures. Remarkably, these rather obvious children's insights appear to have been forgotten in mainstreams macroeconomics when Minsky pointed at them twenty or thirty years ago; astonishingly, but they were afterwards forgotten again – so that economists and bankers, in their desperation after the financial crisis of 2008, re-discovered Minsky as revelation. They spoke of a "Minsky moment" when uncertainty increased interest rates and the resulting lower business values made inherited finance structure unbearable and over-stretched old debt service. A formerly tolerated Ponzi financing or even a speculative financing will then be rapidly terminated by banks. Moreover, debt contracts, which had originally been conservative hedge financing instruments, may now degenerate into unsustainable speculative or Ponzi instruments. While asset values smelt away, the payment commitments

---

435   "A rise of investment, due to improved financing terms, leads to an increase in profits. As the level and trend of profits enter into the determination of the price of capital assets, the "evolutionary" expansion of financing forms increases the prices of capital assets in two ways: It increases both expected quasi rents and the price that will be paid on the market for a given time series of expected quasi rents." *Minsky* (1980/2) page 83. See also on the twofold negative effect of rising interest rates: *Minsky* (1980/2) page 27.

436   *Minsky* (1977) page 66 and *Minsky* (1980) page 105.

and the value of the debt, which financed them, unfortunately, do not. Firms, which are no longer able to finance their debt commitments out of normal current annuities, are forced to revert to alternative exceptional means, such as pledging, mortgaging, hypothecation or sale of assets. If you hold the wrong assets, "inside assets" (e.g., stock) instead of "outside assets" (e.g., state bonds) or "not protected assets" instead of "protected assets",[437] that will expedite your downwards glide as you will find the value of these assets particularly diminished. This is "hard" stuff, there are "hard" macro transmissions. Summarizes Minsky: "The adequacy of cash flows from income relative to debt, the adequacy of refinancing possibilities relative to position, and the ratio of unprotected to protected financial assets are determinants of the stability of the financial system."[438] Or: "The financial instability hypothesis by emphasizing the way in which investment demand is generated by the combination of the valuation of the stock of assets, the financing available from internal funds and financial markets and the supply price of investment output shows how a collapse of asset values, that occurs because of position making problems of units engaged in speculative and Ponzi-financing, leads to a collapse in investment." [439] The financial instability integrates "the liability structure and the cash payment commitments they imply into the analysis of the determination of capital asset prices and the financing of investment" [440] This hard downside transmission is the original contribution, which Minsky adds to Keynes.

Yet, there is also something, which could be called a "hard" upside macro transmission. Alike Sismondi and Malthus, Keynes was aware that salary outlays increase aggregate demand and exert positive feedback on the economy and future investment. Minsky starts from here and adds insights from Marx's reproduction schemes and shifts the perspective from the benevolent effect of salaries as employment-generating spending to their effects on profits. He is looking for a certain cross-wise numeric equality between a part of salary outlays and firms' profits. The argument goes as follows: All salary outlays of firms of investment and consumption industry departments become employment-generating spending of workers to consumption goods firms catering workers. However, as the salaries paid to workers by consumption goods firms are also costs of these firms, in the aggregate they offset. Yet, salaries paid out by investment goods firms to their workers also end up in the pockets of consumption goods firms, but they are no costs of consumption

---

437 "Protected assets" are money, gold, near money (as government debt), which he also extents to bank deposits with deposit insurance. Minsky also acknowledges different shades of protection, with even bank deposits without deposit insurance, depending on inter-bank markets and a central bank acting as lender of last resort. being factually more protected than corporate or consumer debt. (*Minsky* (1966) page 133).

438 *Minsky* (1966) page 128.

439 *Minsky* (1980) page 101.

440 *Minsky* (1980) page 102.

goods firms, but only of investment goods firms. Thus, consumption goods purchases by investment goods industry workers will be profits of consumption goods firms. "...the mark-up on labor costs in the production of consumer goods will be the wage bill in the production of investment goods,"[441] In other words, investment in investment industries – in the amount of salaries paid to workers in those investment industries – is macroeconomically transmitted, via consumption of these salaries for consumption goods by workers, into consumer goods industries firms profits. Investment industry salary pay-outs, thus, will – at least if inventories with stocks in consumption goods are exhausted – result in a positive hard macro-transmission increasing employment-generating spending and generating new investment and employment and enabling circuit closure. This is a noteworthy hard upside effect (while, of course, the hard downside transmission in crises is the more crucial one).

***

Although his insights are almost half a century old, Minsky still provides the most developed theory of firms' employment-generating spending. Accordingly, his thinking became the most important reference point for the debates on the "lost decade" in Japan and on the financial crisis of 2008, e.g., in authors such as *Richard Koo*, *Adair Turner*, or *Steve Keen*. Let us relate Minsky's insights, on the euphoric impact of low interest debt and high assets values in upswings and the depressing or crippling impact of the resulting unbearable debt-service in a downswing, to our standard question coming from the "third interpretation of Ricardo's Law of Say", Sismondi, Malthus, and Marx's M–C–M': Will firms mobilize/use their expected M'-M-profits to mutually buy their produce, thereby representing M'-M? The answer of the "financial instability hypothesis" reads: They may do it (or might even wish to overshoot) if, due to generous finance and low interest rates, asset prices are high in an upswing or boom, and firms will most likely not do it if asset prices fall in a downswing or bust due to rising interest rates and crippling debt structures. Concerning Minsky's insights, we might first add an *important time-moment* or *cyclical moment* to the analysis. Minsky, more than any of his predecessors, acknowledged the relevance of pre-existing assets for the productive economy, macroeconomically through the impact of lower or higher asset prices depressing or triggering investments, and at the level of individual firms through the impact of its own debt structures. The wealth economy is beginning to claim center stage as explanans for action in the productive economy. Yet, Minsky did neither posit nor work out the fundamental distinction between the productive economy and the wealth economy and did not pursue the trace of the wealth economy sucking away investment from the productive economy and why, apart from cyclical movements, there will be an

---

441 *Minsky* (1977) page 64 with reference to Kalecki (but not to Marx).

aggregate loss to the wealth economy which renders investment in the productive economy deficient, even across the cycles.

Chapter VIII. The deficient-producive-spending-syndrome

This chapter draws conclusions from the economists that were reviewed in the chapter VII and uses the distinction between the wealth economy and the productive economy to push beyond their insights. It also lays down our main result about the capitalist economy: the syndrome of deficient employment-generating spending, or *the deficient-producive-spending-syndrome.*

Section 1. A merely abstract possibility of circuit closure in capitalism

The economists reviewed in Chapter VII were, as we are, preoccupied with circuit closure and the role of firms' investive spending. The general result of the chapter was *a possibility of circuit closure* – depending on how the wealth owners behaved and on whether they reinvested M'-M in the productive economy. Some authors had the intuition of different types of investment, one of which would contribute more to circuit closure than the other, and some occasionally labeled or may have internally thought of the type, which was more favorable to circuit closure, as "productive". But this notion, whether outspoken or not outspoken, remained fuzzy and was not clearly distinguished from sterile investment. Therefore, the reviewed authors were not able to examine on what the materialization of the possibility of circuit closure depended; they could neither indicate the field nor the conflict of forces, which act upon them and draw them into the one or other direction.

Quesnay had solved the problem of employment-generating spending or circuit closure in the productive economy so quickly that one could miss that he had even posed it in the first place. He neither required the idea of conflicting forces, nor of programs or of a benevolent institution. Rather, his circuits, following his axioms, closed[1] *a priori* as his *royaume agricole,* and particularly his *cl. des propriétaires,* were

---

1   The reader is reminded that there are two meanings of "closure" in this book, which should not be confused. If systems theoretical sociology speaks of "closure" of the economic system it means that the economy, by necessity, is always closed to its environment – as it exists

344 Gerhard H. Wächter: The Capitalist Economy and its Prosthetics

infused with a benevolent supreme spirit of a "dieu juste". They did so by spending all of their revenues in an employment-generating manner.[2] Of course, that was a pre-enlightened, if not pre-rational, style of thinking, which could help nothing to understand the working mechanisms (if they had worked). But if we spell out what Quesnay implied in the background, then we can see that his teaching was based on a strict necessity of circuit closure. This was the main lasting, yet very important contribution of Quesnay: *drawing attention to a hidden step fulfilling a hidden necessity*.

Unfortunately, the great *Adam Smith* allowed Quesnay's problem to intermittently slip out of sight again. He thought in terms of liberty and competition and worked out, with fascination, how they improve the efficiency of production and steer it towards more consumer satisfaction. But, unfortunately, Smith did not care much about the closure of productive circuits *as a problem*. Actually, his famous "invisible hand", contrary to how it is sometimes portrayed, was not meant by him to solve the problem of macroeconomic circuit closure; it was something else, less demanding and only operated at the lower level of taking care of more, better, and cheaper supplies being carried to markets, hence, the beneficial effects of competition on supply. Smith focused so much on such benevolent effects on productivity, quality, and prices and advantages for consumers and others from them that he almost forgot that enough employment-generating spending had to emerge from somewhere in order to validate the production and feed the producers and their workers.

After the Napoleonic wars, this trust of Smith in inexhaustible markets (even for colonial powers) was lost and the subject of employment-generating spending and circuit closure rose back to the top of the economic reflection agenda. It now split scholars into two camps, and the schisma lasts until today: *Sismondi* and *Malthus* denied that there would be sufficient employment-generating spending for circuit closure in principle or considered it as unlikely at least. David Ricardo tried to get the ghost back into the bottle explaining the obvious lack of employment-generating spending by temporary, sectorial, or regional frictions, largely based on the mismatch of the value-in-uses produced and esoteric demand. If a short answer was needed to coney the latter view, Ricardo, not Say, provided such a short answer in the so-called "Law of Say". Born as a bastard, it, though, remained unclear what the "law" meant exactly. Of the three interpretations we listed previously, the second interpretation of "Ricardo's Law of Say", an abstract harmonious version, became the basis for a style of economic reasoning that dominates most neoclassical economics

---

only of elementary events of payments/non-payments in time. Circuits, as we use them, however, can either close or not close. They close if they validate M-outlays by a reflux of M', thereby allowing for a proper profit M'-M. The latter use of "closure" is more widespread in the book.

2   See the discussion of Quesnay on page 203 et seq.

until the present day. It was mathematized as a system of simultaneous equations by *Walras* and given a graphical expression of supply and demand curves by *Marshall*. Yet, there is also a *third interpretation* of Ricardo's Law of Say. One can read it, like Quesnay, albeit more abstract and generalized, as an attempt to understand *how* the circuits of the productive economy can find enough employment-generating spending to close: All capitalists, it could suggest, at least if we bring all its possible implications to daylight, should be able to close their circuits with a profit *provided that* all capitalists also spend the profits that they expect out of a circuit and mutually purchase their products. The critical point of this third interpretation of Ricardo's Law of Say is that all capitalists must spend their full profit to buy the part of other capitalists' products that represent their profit (C'-C or M'-M or s). While it was likely that they would spend c (of the prior circuit) on each other again and v (of the prior circuit) on workers again, the full spending of the profit was the big challenge. This third interpretation of Ricardo's Law of Say was quite useful as it was more general and abstract than Quesnay's numeric assumptions regarding the cl. des propriétaires and the cl. stérile and because it pointed to circuit closure as a *potentiality*. It necessitated research about the preconditions, a mechanism or benevolent spirit, which could induce wealth owners to do the right thing to embrace the roles assigned to them. It also implied the lasting insight that a theory of circuit closure would largely have to be a theory of firms' investments.

Marx's notations (c, v, s, M–C–M') and his reproduction schemes enabled him to present the problem-exposition by the third interpretation of Ricardo's Law of Say and Sismondi's and Malthus' reasoning in a more technical and concise way (even if the labeling of these notions is influenced by his false theory of labor value and exploitation). He was able to split up M into equipment and inventories (as constant capital c) and into salaries (as variable capital v) and to identify the surplus s with the M'-M-margin. This also allowed Marx to set c, v, and s (M'-M) into motion and to observe how they would travel through production and circulation assuming different shapes or putting on different clothes at each stage. The problems posed by Sismondi and Malthus and the necessity stipulated by the third interpretation of Ricardo's Law of Say did not go away, but they could now be laid down more precisely: If c-outlays are made in a circuit, then will they also buy the c-part of the produce? If v-outlays are made, then will they also buy the v-part of it? And: who should buy the s-part of the produce? As firms had paid out M or $c + v$ in the first M–C-leg of the circuit, M or $c + v$ should, in principle, still be available in other firms and in workers' pockets to "re-purchase" the M-part (or c-part plus v-part) of the produce in the second leg. One could, thus, point fingers at the likely culprit: All firms also obviously desire to sell the C'-C-part or M'-M-part (or s-part) of their produce in order to realize their planned profit M'-M, and *all* firms, entrepreneurs, or capitalists just have to mutually buy these very same C'-C-parts and M'-M-parts (or s-parts) from each other with their profits, which they *expect* from the circuit.

All this laid out in front of the observing economists that only a *circular activity, hence, the ignition of* a new, second-generation round of M–C–M'-expeditions, would enable the closure of the prior round of circuits. Capitalists could, *as a matter of potentiality*, bring the "open" circuits to a close and could save themselves (and others) by starting such new circuits (without using value-in exchange from pre-exiting stocks of wealth or from money-creation, which will only be considered in Part 2 of Book III). But would they? What would be required to get them there? While Marx's notation (M, c, v, s, M') was predestined to further examine the issue of circuit closure, Marx himself, almost stubbornly, did not want to use it for this purpose. He wanted to use it for a *different purpose*, i.e., to elaborate a theory of labor value and of exploitation and let M–C–M' lie fallow as a tool to analyze problems of circuit closure. Although the issue of employment-generating spending and circuit closure gained more urgency after Marx's death and in the first third of 20th century, with imperialism, World War I, the October Revolution, and the Great Depression, his later Marxian followers, if they pursued the issue of circuit closure at all, also hardly ever used M–C–M' for the purpose. They much rather used the distinction between consumption and investment as tools. Consumption was insufficient, *Tugan-Baranovsky* believed, but capitalists, driven by their profit motive, might so fiercely invest that this could close the circuits, at least in principle. This idea offered a possible answer to the question of whether capitalists would use their (planned) M'-M to buy each other's planned M'-M.[3] Tugan-Baranovsky also used Marx's reproduction schemes. They appeared to confirm that circuit closure was possible, on the condition that the beneficial gap-filling investment observed the proportions necessary for extended reproduction. *Rosa Luxemburg* objected. Investment would *not* be sufficient, even if it observed the proportionalities of the reproduction schemes. Rather, to close circuits in extended reproduction, employment-generating spending would have to come from *external sources*, pre-capitalist markets or from foreign countries or public spending. Luxemburg mentioned armaments in particular. Even if she was not greatly elaborating on its financing, now the use of pre-existing stocks of wealth or of wealth outside of the considered circuits definitively came into view. In other words, the motive of capitalists to increase profits with more investment would *not* suffice to get capitalists to buy the produce representing C'-C or M'-M with their planned M'-M. Some kind of a *deus ex machina* was needed; circuit closure, *R. Luxemburg* pointed out, could likely only be achieved artificially, i.e., prosthetically.

Lord Keynes may or may not have known about this discussion within what he called the "underworld" of Marxists and other leftists when he wrote the *General Theory*, but he too put the consumption/investment-distinction in the center of his reasoning. He gave an explicit alternative theory of why consumption was deficient – because of the falling propensity to consume with increased income – and then also

---

3   Again: M'-M is always equal with C'-C or s.

looked to investment to close the gap. His reasoning was more sophisticated than Tugan-Baranovsky's and in his result he was more skeptical; in fact, he took almost the opposite view of the latter. Keynes outrightly *denied* that investment would *automatically* come forth in the volumes required to substitute missing consumption (which he did not relate to M'-M or *s* etc.). Investment was rather conditional. To understand it better, he drafted a novel theory about *when* firms would make investments. This theory exceeded Marx and foreshadowed today's state-of-the-art business valuation. He did so, in particular, with the idea that an "inducement to invest" does not solely depend on the *expected rentability of a considered investment*, but that it also depends on the *lack of reasonably better alternatives*. In the *General Theory* he benchmarked a considered investment with a certain marginal efficiency of capital (m.e.c.) only against interest on loaned out money or on bonds, in the *Viner-rebuttal*, he made an adjustment and saw the bad effect of high or rising interest rates as *mainly operating indirectly* via *falling values of old, pre-existing assets*. If these fallen values come close to or drop lower than the production costs of similar newly to-be-produced assets, then that will stop investment. (Whether an investment to produce a new asset is made requires that the values of old, similar assets remained significantly higher than the production cost or replacement costs for new assets).

Ultimately, Keynes' theory of deficient aggregate employment-generating spending closure came down, first, to explaining deficient consumptive employment-generating spending by a falling propensity to consume and, second, to showing how substitutive investive spending would encounter problems *as there were systematic reasons for it to run out of good motives*. That could be taken as an answer to our question, again phrased in Marx's M–C–M'-notation, about whether capitalists would mutually spend their expected profits M'-M to buy each other's surplus produce C'-C for investment reasons. Keynes' result was similar to Rosa Luxemburg's: They would probably not! From this point onwards Keynes' analysis does not progress much further; instead, he turned to prosthetic recipes such as deficit spending, public works, etc.

Kalecki admitted that nobody (which expressly included himself and ought to have included Keynes as well) possessed a valid theory of investment at the time. Investment theory was rather a "central *pièce de résistance* of economics." *Minsky*, when he arrived on the scene, worked out the evolution of Keynes' theory of investment in the Viner-Rebuttal. He elaborated that investment decisions are not only affected in the negative by poor relations of the m.e.c. to interest rates (Keynes before the Viner-Rebuttal), but also by asset prices having fallen so low that there was no point in producing similar assets at higher costs (Keynes after the Viner-Rebuttal). While Keynes was more interested than Marx in whether entrepreneurs would make the original outlay M–C, Minsky was interested in a moment that occurred even prior to M–C. This moment was not even captured by Marx's notation M–C–M'. It lay before there was M, so it could only be expressed as "...M". He asked: "Where does the money for investment come from?", "when does it come?" and "in what form does it come?". Or: "Are there knots and twists that are connected to its origination?". He found that credit has a substantial impact upon investment and buttressed much more than Keynes that the decision about productive investment is not made in a "neutral" space of an interplay of esoteric demand, available employment-generating spending, and profit expectations. Rather, *finance is always already there – in the absolute center of investment and employment decisions*. So, in Minsky, the theory of circuit closure, which Keynes evolved into a theory of investment, extends into a *behavioral science of finance*. All investments, very plausible and sound investments, like very unplausible and unreasonable ones, owe their existence to the same, healthy or unhealthy, financially driven dynamics. And there are *cyclical moments* and *conjunctures* in finance... Whether its dynamics push towards circuit closure or not depends on the stage of the business cycle. Circuit closure is time-determined, given that it is cycle-determined. In Minsky, *everything* comes out of the discretionary and uncontrolled dynamics of finance, which almost wags the dog of the productive economy and plays havoc with it – for the good and for the bad. That is a huge difference to Quesnay's view where a boringly reliable cl. des propriétaires always will, year after year, unaffected by any conjunctures whatsoever, consistently spent the social surplus, which had been transferred to it previously, in the productive economy. Quesnay's productive economy is stomach-governed, Minsky's economy is Non-Quesnayian, erratically finance-governed.

Minsky, accordingly rendered things more complicated. If we confront his results with our central question of whether firms will spend their expected profit M'-M or s to buy each other's produce (thereby enabling circuit closure in the productive economy, rewarding investment and employment), then Minsky will tell us that there is no hard macro transmission to ascertain this benevolent outcome. The capitalist economy is a self-reflective world in which profit depends on anticipated future profit opportunities, investment depends on anticipated future investment opportunities, and the benchmark for profit on finance. The present not only comes out of anticipating the future, but also through a weird circular reflective business and financial psychology. What firms observe in mirrored mirrors calls the shots in this world of observations of the second and higher orders. Firms observe other firms, whether they anticipate future profits and will, via investments, create opportunities for other firms to invest too. Firms' investments depend on financing and on whether bankers (and later the state and central bank) join or exit the auto-reflective fever of productive firms. By easing or restricting the supply of money, bankers doubly improve or worsen the conditions for new investment. They raise or depress the values of the annuities of old capital assets, against which the quasi-rents or profits from new investments are checked, and the render the production of new assets cheaper or more expensive. Doing so, bankers have no better insights into the future than the employment-generating firms but err through the same mirror-cabinet. What they and firms do, which undoubtedly has hard effects on the economy, results from ghostly speculations. The only available means to observe what others will do in the future is to try to guess what their intentions are, by which they react to the expected intentions of others. But even those intentions are hard to read – they stick in human heads. Thus, one can only try to study external behavior to spot signals of intentions. What information do others possess? What information do they consider important? How carefully do they look at this information? What changes of public opinion do they expect? We have a highly complex process originating out of multi-level reflective observations and only utterly meager, ambiguous, and often deceptive facts. Trendwatchers watch trendwatchers betting on nebulous trifles and bagatelles.

Three moments aggravate the situation: *First*, while firms who observe firms and banks will possess some decision-making algorithms, these algorithms will not only often be unknown, non-linear, complex, reflective, or even chaotic, but they may also change over time. Thus, even if we could process the vague information from the mirror-cabinet into usable data and we had learned to work with the algorithms that other firms used previously, we would still not know which algorithms they will use in the future. What is pivotal today may no longer be relevant tomorrow, including at the level of algorithms used for reflection and action. Neuronic networks change all of the time. Gimbal frames, upon which other gimbal frames are hinged, are substituted quickly and suddenly.

Second, whatever data we may be able to get out of the mirror-cabinet, our own strong emotions, greed, and fear, animal spirits always sit on the side-lines ready to pounce. They do just the opposite of furthering rationality in the interpretation of the poor data. We need to distrust both ourselves and others.

Third, typically, decisions have to be made very quickly – time pressure increases the likelihood of unsound results in this environment of scarce information, uncertain algorithms, emotionality, and irrationality.

In the aggregate, all of this surrenders the steering centers of capitalism – on which the issue of whether capitalists will mutually validate their M'-M-expectations and close circuits ultimately depends – to circuses, which, while they hunger for facts, are actually, mostly only feverishly dependent upon themselves. They suffer so much from the instability they perceive that they are grateful if *any* direction is offered to them and throw themselves as quickly into exuberance as they do into crisis, panic, or depression, which may ultimately almost come as a relief.[4]

To this house of madness, Minsky even added a further "hard" macro-transmission, which only operated downwards. Not only could the (generally shrinking) investment and lack of easy credit disenable and dis-encourage firms from investing,

---

4   See *Kindleberger* (1978). Thus, crises become a factor in the theory of circuit closure. See also *Kiehling* (1991) page 24, et seq., *Mackay* (1841) and *de la Vega* (1688).

but the fall of asset prices and the rise of interest could also, brutally, irresistibly, and directly cut down on investment if the ongoing debt service absorbs the financial means, which firms could otherwise use for new investment (or if firms even went bankrupt). This is where Minsky's "survival constraint" pushes to the fore. If its time comes, this "check" totally overrules all normal investment-decision-making. The calculus of anticipating annuities from investments, calculating a m.e.c. and benchmarking it against interest rates or whatever, is displaced by the new simple rule: maintain liquidity at all costs! This rushes firms to sell or pledge assets, which precipitates further drops in assets prices. In this stampede, firms' contributions to investment and to other firms' circuit closure will die, even if the firms manage to save themselves. What Minsky exposed here is, unfortunately, *another bad thing for circuit closure*. If things get bad, that will automatically make things even worse. It will put firms' normal operation on hold and will establish an emergency regime that cares only for liquidity and about its own survival.[5]

Both, Keynes and Minsky supported the recipes on which states were operating for the longest time: Try to induce productive firms – by monetary or fiscal stimulus – to invest more and try to convince, manipulate or force firms into productive investments. Also guide and help banks to finance such investments. One problem is that a lot of the money that is poured-out will still go into the sterile economy and will, in both economies, cause booms and, ultimately, busts, which will often outweigh the previous benevolent prosthetic effects. Therefore, most recently, particularly after the financial crisis of 2008, states have raised the level of control over firms and banks and have introduced new legal means, compliance requests and supervision in order to moderate the bad "animal spirits" of firms, at least with regard to the money coming out of the prosthetic monetary and fiscal policies. Social control over top agents in firms and banks becomes a means of macroeconomics (as it occasionally had been in Quesnay, but much more stringently implemented today). This novel type of social control extends to not only to significantly policing and penalizing banks and firms,[6] but even to therapeutics (e.g., by setting limits to top-management salaries and bonus structures) and to outright moral re-education. Top managers and owners are, in fact, expected to bring about circuit closure in the productive economy by socially-minded, not profit-minded, investment de-

---

5   Minsky still saw one "hard" positive macro-transmission; he confirmed that workers will reliably re-spend salary outlays to them on consumption goods. Biological necessities and their being non-owners, with no means to obtain consumption goods from elsewhere, guarantees this. Like Kalecki, Marx, and others, Minsky also assumes that they will spend their whole salaries, but that is not enough, of course.

6   "US banks", reports *Wolf*, "have paid more than $200bn in fines". "But", he adds somewhat disappointed, "... almost nobody has gone to prison" (*Wolf*, How to defeat rightwing populism, in: Financial Times of 25 May 2016).

cisions. While socialism is off the table, at least for the time being, the organs of capitalists are often expected to act almost like socialists.[7]

In summary, most authors dealt with in chapter VII were looking into the direction also pursued by this book, but neither of them achieved a satisfactory grip on the problem. The capitalist wealth economy has a broader and deeper negative impact on investment in the productive economy than disturbances, cycles and bubbles. The problem is not just the role of finance in decisions on productive investment, the nature of the prevailing finance or the existence of a survival constraint, but *the problem is the capitalist wealth economy as such*. It persistently sucks away value-in-exchange before this value can enter the productive economy and flow into employment-generating uses. That is the main reason for deficient circuit closure in the productive economy. We shall now take up the distinction between the productive and sterile economy again and develop it further.

Section 2. The drain of wealth out of the productive economy

Producive/sterile and investive/consumptive further elaborated

Ultimately, from authors reviewed in chapter VII, Quesnay believed that the *classe des propriétaires* would clear the markets by its luxury consumption and Ricardo was confident that this result would at least somehow be achieved. The other authors looked at productive firms investments, but remained unconvinced. Nobody arrived at a usable conclusion as to why employment-generating spending was deficient and why circuit closure in the productive economy failed – if it failed. Consumption appeared to be good, they were aware, but perhaps some felt that consumption of wealth owners might include spending, which was not really generating employment. They hoped that investment would fill the gap, but some were also aware that investments in the stock, bond, or real estate market were mostly not useful either. They got stuck here and remained unable to elevate the intuitive difference between a "good" sector and a "bad" sector in consumption *and* in investment to a usable notional macroeconomic distinction.

We shall now try to make progress right here. For this purpose, we take up the distinctions between the wealth economy and the productive economy or sterile

---

7   These policies cannot nearly work, obviously. They are only attempts to find non-existent subtleties between having one foot on the accelerator and one foot on the brake. The prescriptions come from mass-democratic politicians who mostly do not remotely understand what they are doing, but know very well that, even if they understood, they could not even act on better knowledge. Their main effect will, thus, be an additional layer of hypocrisy. We are about to lose one of the true beauties of capitalism – its openly admitted rationality of profit-making.

spending and producive spending, which looks at the macroeconomic *effects and consequences* of the spending for the closure of capitalist circuits, again. This distinction was already introduced in the Foreword and laid crosswise over the more common, second distinction, second between investment and consumption, which looks at the *motives* for the spending or the *use* of the purchased goods. Their crosswise combination led to Matrix I on page 23 .[8] Following the examination of employment-generating spending in Chapter VIII, we shall now bring together the terminology of sterile and employment-generating spending with the terminology of M–C–M', as broken down into M (c, v) and M'-M (s) in to a new Matrix IV identifying the causes for deficient employment-generating spending in capitalism.

---

8   Good theoretical thinking – and all thinking is theoretical – consists in properly distinguishing distinctions. This is even so if one is not aware of what one is doing, but the awareness of it, of course, helps. *George Spencer Brown*, Laws of Form, first published in 1969, has made a very important contribution in this regard, particularly into systems theory, which proliferated via *Heinz von Foerster*, *Niklas Luhmann*, and others. See also: *Luhmann*, Zeichen als Form, in: *Baecker* (ed.), Problem der Form, 1993, page 45 et seq.; *Kaufmann*, Das Prinzip der Unterscheidung, in: *Baecker* (ed.), Schlüsselwerke der Systemtheorie, 2005, page 173 et seq.; *Schönwälder-Kuntze, Wille, Hölscher*, George Spencer Brown, 2. ed., 2009.

Figure 13: Matrix IV – Consumptive vs investive and producive vs sterile spending (developed)

	consumptive	investive
sterile	I. · Recipients: Sterile wealth owners · Emitter: Wealth owners and workers · Purpose: consumptive debt service, consumptive rent, consumptive asset purchases (e.g., dwelling)	II. · Recipients: Sterile wealth owners · Emitter: Productive and sterile wealth owners · Purpose: Productive and sterile wealth owners pay interest, rent, or asset purchase prices as "tributes" if they make productive or sterile investments
Producive or employment generating	III. · Recipients: Productive wealth owners · Emitter: Wealth owners and workers · Purpose: purchase of consumption goods and. services	IV. · Recipient: Productive wealth owners · Emitter: firms · Purpose: purchase of equipment and inventories (incl. services) for productive investment
All spending is after carve-outs of components of opposite type		

If we look at this Matrix IV, The *upper part* shows sterile spending, which always flows to sterile wealth owners. Quadrant I shows sterile consumptive spending, e.g., interest for consumptive debt and rental payments to landlords for dwelling. Quadrant II shows sterile investive spending. On the one hand, it includes "tributes" from productive to sterile wealth owners, e.g., interest, rent or profit spending for productive investment or asset purchases if assets are used for productive investments (e.g., the purchase of land). On the other hand, it includes interest and rent spending and asset purchases, which are (or which serve) sterile investments between sterile wealth owners. The *lower part* of the matrix consists of employment-generating or producive spending, which always flows to firms i.e., productive wealth owners. Quadrant III shows employment-generating or producive consumptive spending, e.g., purchases of goods (including services) by sterile wealth owners and workers (firms do not make consumptive spending) from firms. Payments, which are directly made by wealth owners to their private employees for consumption purposes, such as for menial services, cooks, housemaids, gardeners green-keepers, drivers etc. are also shown in quadrant III (imaging there being a fictive firm between the wealth owners and the workers).

All flows are after carve-outs; hence, the employment-generating, i.e., producive, investive spending in quadrant III or IV are already after deduction of
components, which belong in quadrant I or II and already encompasses components which were carved out from sterile spending in quadrants I or II.[9] Quadrant
I, alike, includes already sterile parts from the actual amounts paid by workers or
by wealth owners for food, other necessities or luxury and Quadrant II includes
a sterile part from firms c-outlays directly paid to sterile wealth owners and from
firms' sterile profit spending to wealth owners. Quadrants III and IV in the lower
part are the places in which reflows of spending from the wealth economy into the
productive economy, hence where consumptive or investive spending by wealth
owners are booked. In the following section, we shall take a more detailed look at
the different flows.

Flows from the productive economy into the wealth economy

A sterile part of firms' c-outlays

Reading volume I of Marx' *Capital*, or the reproduction schemes in volume II, one
would, at first, think that his c-part of M goes wholly into equipment and inventories and remains in the productive economy. *But that is not so.* While the spending
for equipment and inventories, c, may be innocently regarded as employment-generating, we must make a major exception for the spending of interest for interest
i, rent r, or asset purchase prices (*stpp*) for old, pre-existing assets (with the minor
counter-exception of our carve-outs for employment-generating spending-components in sterile spending). These "tributes" of firms to sterile wealth owners, without
which no productive investment is possible, are significant.

Therefore, one should not read out of Marx that *all* c-outlays, which are going to
supplier capitalists, are employment-generating spending that validate prior productive investments. Only c-outlays *minus* sterile "tributes" *plus* employment-generating spending-components in these payments are employment-generating spending. Accordingly, supplier firms are *not even able to mutually purchase the M-part of their
produce from each other* because they receive *less* than the whole of other firms' M-outlays. This goes on from circuit to circuit.[10] This drain is *different* from whether or not
firms are willing to mobilize their full, planned profits M'-M from a circuit to mutually purchase the M'-M-part of their produce (which has occupied center stage for
Sismondi, Malthus, Luxemburg, and others). Before firms even come to consider

---

9   See page on 123 et seq
10 What national accounting calls consumption of fixed capital, or what bookkeeping calls
    depreciation, are *construed flows* only. It may take several years and sometimes decades be-
    fore significant re-investment spending, beyond small maintenance payments, are actually
    made.

whether to fully reinvest their expected profits in their productive business, they have already done damage to each other through unavoidable misspending in the form of tributes to sterile wealth owners.

A sterile part of workers' salary spending

Workers make consumptive employment-generating and consumptive sterile spending from their salaries.[11] Many economists, even prior to Marx, saw salaries as a share given to workers of the revenues from the produce, which was roughly sufficient, but not much more, for them to physically and socially reproduce (including proliferating and raising children). The absolute amount of the salary, or its relative share, was often not specified further. Capitalists did not have lasting relationships with their workers – unlike feudal lords with their peasants or even masters had with their slaves in the past. Accordingly, from a pure economic perspective, there was no built-in interest in individual capitalist employers to maintain a minimum salary. However, there were religious, cultural, or other humanitarian ideas about men's dignity. While they could be bent significantly, as the re-introduction of slavery in the South of the US and examples of child labor, excessive working hours, lack of work-safety, and forced labor in camps has shown, humanitarian standards still worked towards raising salaries. The self-interest of employers, indeed, sometimes also played a role if there was tough competition amongst employers for workers. Finally, politics, trade unions, other workers' organizations, philanthropy, and social-democrat, socialist and communist parties contributed to salary increases. All this was basically known at the times at which Ricardo and Malthus were writing (even if social-democrat parties etc. did not exist yet). When Marx wrote, he added two novelties. First, he connected this state of insight to a concept which arose from the theory of economic evolution: the difference between a necessary work-product and a surplus work-product, with the necessary work-product being what individuals or social units (families, tribes etc.) need to produce to survive and with the surplus-product being what can be used for growth, i.e., extended reproduction, or excess consumption.[12] He taught that workers' salaries essentially stand for what the necessary work product is in the theory of economic evolution. Second, by introducing the term of "variable capital" v in non-concrete, highly abstract sense, he made it possible to let the variable capital travel through a series of economic events in a Hegelian way – as a part of the money in the pockets of capitalists willing to make productive investments, as salaries, which are paid to

---

11   If they make investive sterile spending, they do not so as workers, but are wealth owners from there on out; if they make investive producive spending, they are firms from there on out.

12   If low productivity or bad luck keep tribes from generating the necessary work product, they will die out.

workers, then in production, as additional value-in-exchange-component, which the workers transfer to the produce, hence, as a value-component of the produce, and, finally, as part of the sales prices collected.

As Marx saw paid salaries, even if they could occasionally be somewhat above or below the necessary work product, essentially necessary for the workers and their families to survive, he had to expect that workers would spend the "variable capital" v, i.e., their salaries, in full again. His theory of salaries, thus, became a theory of their use and a theory of a component of employment-generating spending by the same token.

Marx further confirmed this view throughout his reproduction schemes, which see the variable capital v flow *completely back* to the capitalist class (dept. II.b.-producers of consumption goods for workers), thereby affirming that all money paid out as salaries will contribute to buying the production. Kalecki, on the same track, later coined the almost-proverb that "workers spend what they earn",[13] which, while essentially true, did not go beyond Marx. After all, workers partly appeared as macroeconomically reliable chaps who would do their best to keep the productive economy's wheels turning by returning their salaries to productive firms so that they could recoup the v-part of their M-outlays in order to close their M–C–M'-circuits.[14]

Unfortunately, something had been overseen, which the distinction between employment-generating and sterile spending debunks: There is the a similar drain on the spending power of workers (conveyed to them by salary payments) as there is on firms c-outlays: Wages cannot fully flow back through workers' consumption to productive firms (even dept. II.b.-producers of consumption goods for workers)

---

13   While workers consume what they earn, capitalists earn what they spend. "Capitalists as a class gain exactly as much as they invest or consume, and if – in a closed system – they ceased to construct and consume they could not make any money at all" (*Kalecki*, Outline of a theory of the business cycle, 1933, in: Selected Essays on the Dynamics of the Capitalist Economy, 1971, page 12. Kalecki disregards the distinction between the productive and sterile economy here.

14   Salary taxation does not seem to fit in this picture. If salaries are taxed, is income not withdrawn where it is absolutely needed in that case? In fact, as Minsky writes: "(t)he personal income tax assures that the after-tax income of technologically determined labor is not sufficient to buy back the output it produces even at the prices even at the prices mandated solely by technologically determined labor costs" (*Minsky* (1986) page 184). The explanation ought to be that the state redistributes workers' income to the detriment of better earning workers and the benefit of lower earning or unemployed workers through salary taxation. It, thereby, infringes upon the self-praise of capitalism that better educated or more well-trained workers, who also work harder, have a chance to materially increase their incomes in an act of forced solidarity or socialism between the low-income-recipients. In exceptional circumstances, the not-redistributed excess taxation may even flow into other uses, such as warfare.

because workers, too, *have to make sterile spending to sterile wealth owners out of their salaries*. They pay the same categories of "tributes" to sterile wealth owners as firms pay, i.e., interest i, rent r and occasional purchases of old, pre-existing assets, as out of their collected salaries v, they have to inevitably make sterile consumptive spending of rent r, for interest payments i or if they purchase old dwellings (instead of paying rent). As sterile parts of the c-outlays of firms do not return into the productive economy, a part of the v-outlays of workers will not return there either.

The issue deserves a few amendments. In the past, rural workers in the countryside (being successors of their small peasant predecessors) mostly still owned little pieces of inherited land, forests, fields, or gardens, which often encompassed a dwelling where they lived. They, accordingly, had no rent to pay. As workers were drawn away from their home villages to industrialized regions that all changed; they became tenants and paid rent. However, this did not bring self-owned working-class dwellings to total extinction. If the economy did well (as it often did in the capitalist centers), workers sometimes managed to acquire self-owned dwellings anew, using loans, wage-income, mutual help, and the black economy. Furthermore, capitalists occasionally supported workers in acquiring dwellings – to attract workers to their factories and/or out of philanthropic motives. Many such settlements still exist today, e.g., in formerly coal mining centers of the German Ruhr or Saar, and still carry the names of the benefactors. Moreover, developed countries may have state programs to support the bank-financing of working-class homes; e.g., in the US Fannie Mae and Freddie Mac enabled working-class families to share "the American dream".[15]

Trying to acquire ownership of a self-used dwelling, whether newly built or pre-existing, is probably mostly a good microeconomic bet for individual workers who can afford it. However, from a macroeconomic perspective it involves turning away a part of workers' salary spending from bakers, butchers, farmers, clothes manufacturers, shopkeepers, alehouse owners, car-manufacturer, education, vacation, household and consumer electronics, etc. to payments for the new dwelling, whether as a purchase price or as interest. If the dwelling is newly built, then this only applies to the land component of the purchase price plus the interest paid on this component; if an old, pre-existing dwelling is purchased, it applies to the whole purchase price plus the whole interest paid (in each case, as always, after carve-outs). On the other side, workers save sterile rent payments as soon as they move into their new home. The aggregate macroeconomic effect will depend on

---

15   Such programs often lead to unsound financial practices and speculation, e.g., in the US-Savings and Loan crisis of the eighties and the US-subprime loan crises of 2007, when banks, real estate developers, construction firms, etc., and workers colluded in generating new credit. It cannot be denied, though, that the – ultimately prosthetic – activity had significant employment effect in the construction industry.

the relative price level of the different markets, but the sterile component of salary spending does neither dissolve nor is there a first-hand guaranty that it the percentage of sterile spending of workers' salaries will fall underneath the percentage in the situation in which workers paid rent. State support to finance workers' dwellings may, thus, sometimes even mean that overall sterile spending by workers is macroeconomically increased (with a share wandering from landlords' pockets to bankers' pockets). In any event, there is a hefty entrance fee for workers to join the club of homeowners,[16] which reduces their overall employment-generating spending over the medium term. In the long term, after debt service has come to an end, it will, of course, enable workers to raise the share of their employment-generating spending once again.

Workers also make sterile spending following *non-real-estate-consumer loans*. In the early times of capitalism, workers were ineligible for loans from banks in general (occasionally they obtained non-real-estate-debt from loan sharks, but that was small scale), and had no interest whatsoever to pay to banks. However, since the 20th century, in particular after World War II, banks have offered to debt-finance cars, motorcycles, endurable consumer goods, electronics, and even computers and mobile phones for workers, their spouses, or their kids. Interest rates are higher than for real-estate-loans as no collateral nearly as good as dwellings can be offered. Nowadays, renting-out or leasing-out has become a highly important distribution channel for such goods, particularly in the automobile industry (where insured cars work rather well as collateral); accordingly, in addition to the largely employment-generating spending of purchase-prices to the manufacturing capitalist, workers also pay significant sterile components to sterile wealth owners for the benefit of using the good earlier.

Educational loans have become extremely important in countries in which higher education and universities are privatized and in which (often outrageous) fees are demanded; here education is mostly subjected to M–C–M'-operations. Attempting to debt-finance these fees for their kids is a moment in the survival battles of former middle classes and in the social advancement dreams of gifted and ambitious members of the working class.[17] The fees of schools and universities are largely em-

---

16   If a worker buys a small house in the countryside or a modest apartment in a suburb of a city for around EUR 100,000 and takes out an annuity loan in this amount with the interest fixed at 4 % over 30 years and an initial annual repayment of 1 %, then he will have to pay interest in an amount of over EUR 70,000 until he owns his dwelling debt free.

17   The question is not whether privatized education is generally "better" than state-run education or a deplorable thing in general. This dispute, though, is certainly not settled in favor of privatization with the argument that top private US, UK, etc. universities can hire the crème of international scientists today and have more Nobel laureates etc. E.g., Germany, in the "Kaiserreich" from 1871 to 1914 set up a state university system with a worldwide reputation, out of which many leading theoreticians of relativity theory, quantum theory,

ployment-generating spending, but the interest paid on loans to finance these fees is largely not. The amounts of money withdrawn from the productive economy are also significant. Even worse, an increasing number of worker families finance their sheer subsistence for the present month by *subsistence debt*. I.e., they spend their expected wage incomes from a few months down the line with a *credit card, short term or an over-draft loan*. One more time, the wealth economy has managed to tighten its grasp on the available spending of workers, which macroeconomically further reduces the spending of workers in the productive economy. All this results in not even all amounts of the workers' salaries being fully circuited back into the productive economy.

A sterile part of firms' profits

The third and final drain into the wealth economy consists of the sterile spending of a part of business profits (M'-M). We have already seen that firms, which engage in productive investment, cannot avoid paying "tributes" to the sterile economy in the form of rent or interest payments or payments of purchase prices for pre-existing old assets. We saw them do this as part of their *c*-outlays, which ignited a circuit. Now we can see them doing it again, a few steps later down the road, *out of the profits* at the end of the circuit. This drain takes three forms: hoarding by wealth owners, sterile investment by wealth owners, or sterile consumption by wealth owners. In all three cases, the productive profits M'-M arrived, as part of employment-generating spending of others, through employment-generating ports of wealth owners and were intermingled with already existing sterile wealth and incoming sterile revenues. This transformation of profit from formerly employment-generating revenues (M'-M), does not have to involve a legal or microeconomic payment; it is, in particular, not necessary to turn business profits M'-M into dividends, declare dividends, and distribute them "physically" to sterile wealth owners, even though this is what normally happens. *Rather, the business profits M'-M collected become automatically macroeconomically sterile if they are not re-used for productive investment, i.e., if they are not re-dispatched again, via the investive departure port or via the consumptive departure port, to other firms' employment-generating arrival ports or to workers.* It does not matter either whether these profits remain on deposit accounts of firms, which is quite unlikely, whether they are transferred to accounts of holding companies or family offices, or whether, which is far more likely, they are re-invested in bonds, stock, including own shares, derivatives or real estate, whatever the firm's treasury deems best. If pre-existing luxurious city apartments or countryside homes are purchased for consump-

---

and in other sciences emerged. Even the universities of the USSR, which were also state-run, do not appear to have been so bad in general.

tive pleasure, the use of the profits is also sterile for the time being.[18] Profits re-enter the productive economy only if they are, indeed, re-used for employment-generating spending, productive consumption, or productive investment.

Deficient re-flows into the productive economy

Deficient consumptive employment-generating spending by wealth owners

Quesnay and Malthus held wealth owners dear. If they were, as Quesnay wrote, "utiles à l'État que... par leur consommation",[19] then *they were at least that* – and in significant volumes! Wealth owners certainly consume more and better, even "producively", than non-wealth owners. Historically, the old feudal classes were new-born capitalism's beginner's luck. Consumption-oriented and decadent as they were, they did not change their habits alongside the decaying of their position, but instead celebrated on the sinking ship and often spent their left-over wealth into exhaustion (as, e.g., Chekhov's plays show). Wealth owner's consumption is, quite advantageously for the economy, normally not affected by normal cyclical economic ups and downs of the productive economy to a significant degree.[20] Even if the economy shrinks, they mostly still draw sufficient incomes from interest, rent, dividends, and capital gains to maintain their living standard, without even diminishing their wealth stock much. Only a historically extreme decay will materially affect their consumptive employment-generating spending, e.g., the end of the Greek poleis, the fall of the Roman Empire, failures of major states, decades of civil war and anomy, such as in the Warring Wtates period or the many other interregnums in Chinese history or the Thirty Years War in Europe. This list also

---

18   Obviously, there is no sharp and stable line between consumptive spending and investive spending by the purchase of pre-existing old assets. Wealth owners can always change their minds freely.

19   Even if Quesnay added a "que" (only): "...les propriétaires sont utiles à l'État que par leur consommation" – proprietors are useful to the state only through their consumption –, see *Quesnay* (cited in *Cartelier* (2008) page 36). This statement is not only of great importance macroeconomically, but also remarkable regarding the ideological situation in France forty years before the French Revolution: You could obviously tell your prince (Louis XV), to whom Quesnay gave his tableau, that he was utterly useless (except for in terms of his consumption), but the prince would swallow this... The explanation could be that a dynastic legitimation of government, which was principally *in*dependent of making a functional contribution, was still largely intact. Look at Quesnay and the claim, which another, albeit smaller, absolutistic sovereign raised at the same time (Frederick the Great of Prussia declared himself as "first servant" of the state), and you can see the shadow of the guillotine.

20   As an ex-partner of my law firm, who used to be invited to dine with a well-known German wealthy family as a student, reported, if the stock market went down, they would immediately only serve margarine instead of butter. However, that was probably only a nice symbolic signal.

includes the aforementioned decay of the feudal nobility, which in Germany ended in the massive degradation and expropriation of its remnants (and significant parts of other traditional wealth owners) in the great inflation after World War I, which "wiped out the pre-war German Bonds".[21]

What sets limits to the absolute contribution of wealth owners' consumption to employment-generating spending, though, remains their *low absolute number*. They are simply too few and have too little aggregate belly space and time for greater employment-generating consumptive spending. Quesnay's tableau was not only wrong in the assumption that wealth owners would spend their circuit income (i) completely (ii) on consumption (iii) in the productive economy, he was also wrong in his estimation of wealth owners' consumption being 2/5 of the annual net produce; it is much less than that, at least today, and *far too low to save the day*.

Deficient investive spending by wealth owners

As soon as any value-in-exchange arrives in the wealth economy, it gets completely intermingled with the value-in-exchange, which is already there. The issue is solely about whether the *same amount* travels back. Circuit closure would require that the drains, from the productive economy into the wealth economy, are fully recovered by new employment-generating spending – but this does not normally happen. Once value-in-exchange has arrived in the wealth economy, it will only return after wealth owners have made a positive decision to re-channel it back into the productive economy by new employment-generating consumptive or by new employment-generating investive spending. In Quesnay's tableau, cl. des propriétaires received livres 2 bn. from the cl. productive and re-channeled this full amount into the productive economy.[22] They did what was macroeconomically necessary for circuit closure without Quesnay telling us why they did it. In reality, though, wealth owners have mostly not acted like that, and, in fact, *they have good reasons to refrain from reinvesting in the productive economy*.

Since profit economies exist, sterile wealth was primary. Wealth owners were sitting on massive amounts of wealth, of which they only put a small part to productive use. Wealth owners have retained this habit, even in modern capitalism. In particular, they have a bias for land. Land, as the premier non-produced good, existed prior to the beginning of human production and all successful wealth generators, either by violence or by exchange, Sparta's and Athens' ruling elites, Chinese emperors, the Roman patricians, equites and, if successful enough, even plebeians, merchants of the Han, T'ang and Ming dynasty, Islamic merchants since Mohammed, Christian merchant adventurers and feudal lords of the Middle Ages, the Medici, Fugger

---

21   *Graham/Dodd*, Security analysis, 5th ed., photographic reproduction of 1st ed. page 7.

22   Livres 1 bn. to cl. productive and livres 1 bn. to what Quesnay falsely called cl. stérile, which was actually quite productive.

and the Rothschilds, today's new-economy-stars, narco-traffickers, and successful lawyers, *always* desired and desire to possess real estate. Their prime interest goes to land and buildings in privileged urban or countryside locations, villas, castles, chateaux, etc. but the interest also goes to land that is usable for pasture, farming, hunting, foresting, vineyards, or the mining of cupper, tin, clay, iron, gold, silver, diamonds, jade, jewels and so forth. Indeed, wealth owners are even eager to own low-income apartment houses ("slum lording"). It is true that those successful in profit economies and capitalism, especially the "nouveaux riches", also desire to purchase *new* houses, new weapons (more so in the old days), new coaches, cars, airplanes and yachts and new furniture, clothing, electronics, and a lot of services, etc., but they never exchange their profits against such new produce in full. *Those who profit most from the production of new goods will spend most of their profits not on buying others' new production, but on buying what has long been there, from nature or previous generations' work.* The winners of the productive economy take their booty and walk away with it *without* caring about whether their fellow current producers are able to sell the M'-M-part of their produce. As they become successful, they become conservative and shift large chunks of their profits into the less thrilling or boring wealth economy; you might say that they are like narcotrafficker who do not consume their drugs themselves. There was and there is a general "propensity" to withdraw wealth from productive to sterile uses.

So far we have described this propensity as a fact only. Most unfortunately, though, the propensity is not only a nonsensical romantic remnant from the past, but it is based on hard microeconomic rationales. Keynes construed his "inducement to invest" as a battle of forces competing for entrepreneurs' investment. He quantified this battle of forces as a ratio between adverse "attraction-powers" on the entrepreneur's money. In the *General Theory*, in particular, the "inducement to invest" thence became a *fraction* between the marginal efficiency of capital (m.e.c.) of a considered investment in the numerator and the interest rate in the denominator. The *General Theory* not only left the issue of what kind of investment was to generate Keynes' m.e.c. unspecified (he saw it as beneficial without applying a more-than-intuitive distinction between productive and sterile) and, furthermore, impoverished the alternatives for the entrepreneur to one single form of sterile investment (lending out available money or buying a bond in this amount to draw market interest).[23] In the *Viner-Rebuttal*, Keynes extended the denominator to include the

---

23   This use of interest in the "inducement to invest" gained power by Keynes introducing a novel theory of interest. He abolished the "classical theory" that interest rates would necessarily fall in a depression and automatically initiate a recovery. Instead, he derived the interest rate from uncertainty and liquidity preference. However, uncertainty and liquidity preference would, as Keynes found, *rise* in a slump and *raise* interest rates (exactly the opposite of what the "classical theory" had held) and disfavor investments in the productive

purchasing of whatever pre-existing, old assets, the new production of which was considered in the numerator.

Two further amendments are necessary in order to combine Keynes' approach with our distinction between the wealth economy and the sterile economy: On the top-side of the fraction, the *numerator* has to be *narrowed down* so that *productive economy investments* are considered *exclusively*. On the bottom-side, to the contrary, the *denominator* must be extended beyond not only debt investment through new loans or bonds ot the purchase of pre-existing loans and bonds, but to include *all* sterile investments (hence, apart from loans, debt, pre-existing productive assets also naked land, gold, antiques, art, crypto, etc.). Only then will the numerator truly exclusively target productive investments and the denominator will encompass all competing sterile alternative investments.[24] Hence, Keynes' "inducement to invest" ought to be re-formulated into an *"inducement to firms' employment-generating investive spending"* to describe the conditions under which productive wealth owners will, in fact, macroeconomically "pay back" the tributes to the sterile economy and their profits into the productive economy. It will tell us that they will only re-invest tributes and profits (or invest the same amounts from other sources), provided that these productive investments promise to be *more profitable than the alternative sterile investments*.[25]

There is, of course, no general iron rule, which always gives an advantage to sterile economy investments. Yet, a few circumstances work to often tilt the decision in

---

economy even further. This aspect is secondary for the progression of this argument. See on page 292 et seq.

24 Keynes' imprecisely targeted terms obviously miss the purpose of his "inducement to invest". E.g., in a real estate or stock boom, sterile investment in these assets promises a significant return on investment and a high m.e.c., which, particularly if bond markets are booming simultaneously and showing ultralow interest rates; this will mathematically lead to a strong "inducement to invest", but only trigger sterile investments without employment effect. Keynes' unspecific term of "investment" even "sells" FOREX-speculation as beneficial. E.g., George Soros writes: "...keeping capital in liquid form in an appreciating currency is more rewarding than investing it in physical assets." (*Soros* (2003) page 82).

25 As an intuitive illustration from our times: Are we could observe in more than a decade after 2008, living in a world in which money interest rates are close to zero, does not mean that the productive economy goes crazy with new investment. Have great parts of Africa rushed forward into the computer age or at least industrial age in this decade? Has mankind invested in erecting settlements on the moon? Alternatively, do we not instead have to state that a significant part of infrastructure of even the most developed countries, from J.F.K-airport and US-highways, as *Larry Summers* does not tire to point out, and hundreds of bridges of private highway-operators in Italy etc. are close to falling apart? And have we not also lived through a decade of corporate stock repurchase programs, proving that the most successful corporations do not know how to apply their huge reserves in *new* productive investment? While low interest rates would have suggested tremendous investment activities under Keynes' "inducement to invest", that is not what happened, at least not in the productive economy.

favor of the sterile investments. The productive economy, indeed, is a *hostile habitat of fierce competition* for customers' (employment-generating) spending as well as for cheap supplies. Firms need a *competitive advantage* in order to succeed, which has mostly to come out better and cheaper products, or good luck, often both of them. In the productive economy, products compete against other products for scarce readiness to make money sacrifices, which will keep many circuits from closing. Accordingly, an excess of profit-seeking capital will push the profit rates in the productive economy down and a significant share of investors will end up with revenues which are not worth the effort. Or they may even be net losers. Ultimately demand, employment-generating spending, is limited as it depends on consumptive spending in the final instance, which is limited, as far as esoteric demand and values-in-use are concerned, by numbers of people and their needs and desires, and, worse, as far as effective demand and values-in exchange are concerned, by available incomes. We are in the world, which Adam Smith so much praised for necessitating firms to fall to their knees in serving their customers. The power behind this discipline, as we have seen, stems from a game of "musical chairs" or a "journey to Jerusalem". Firms in the productive economy each sit on a chair, music swells, and the firms have to raise themselves and wander around and seek new customers and supplier (i.e., new chairs). However, one chair is taken away after every iteration, and when the music stops one firm will not find enough customers and a systematic under-complementarity is created. The productive economy's game, thus, requires keen monitoring, attentiveness, quickness, determination, skill, and sometimes recklessness. This is a world of mostly *negative* feedback. The more products firms carry to market, the relatively fewer chairs there are, which will push down prices and still leave produce unsold. This situation needs Schumpeterian entrepreneurs, men like the merchant heroes of the Middle Ages, inventors or the 18th and 19th century, technological and conceptual innovators, who certainly do deserve our admiration – *but this Darwinian-Smithian survival of the fittest only is bad for the numerator of the fraction...*

Now, consider the world of the *wealth economy*. Here, just the opposite is true. The theoretically limitless demand for profit drives the demand for wealth investments. The wealth economy has the pleasant capacity that *the more money enters, the more prices go up also for positions you hold already.* More competition for assets creates – via benevolent *positive* feedback – bubbles and capital gains across the market.[26] Consumers with limited esoteric demand or with esoteric demand but without money, on the

---

26   Even the risk add-ons to discount rates for productive economy investments are normally higher than in the wealth economy, which also lowers the present values of productive investments compared to wealth investments. Thus, the *capital asset pricing model* (CAPM) will often support the wealth economy via the lower Betas that it normally applies to wealth investments; they help to outcompete investments in the productive economy.

other hand, are no factor. In the productive economy, the quest for profit of competitors, bids down prices and profits; the more productive wealth owners, via their firms, engage in transactions (at a given level of demand), by selling products, the lower prices fall. In the wealth economy, the more sterile wealth owners engage in transactions (at a given level of demand), by buying and holding assets, the higher prices rise. The more investors sell in the productive economy, the more the lesson becomes for most players: "You should no longer be here!", the more investors sell in the productive economy, the more the lesson becomes: "Be here big!". The productive economy rewards exquisite selections and original first movers, the wealth economy rewards cowards and herd behavior.[27]

In summary: By hosting M–C–M' and allowing it to take control, the economic system not only invited capitalism to seek profit in an often socially benevolent, at least growth and productivity generating, way within the productive economy, but also to seek profit *everywhere* in its reach – and capitalists found out quickly that the wealth economy is an awesome place to make money without production. Ultimately, *this* is the main reason for the net outflow of wealth from the productive into the wealth economy and why the general possibility of circuit closure in capitalism does not materialize. The attractive possibility of "opting-out" of the productive economy spoils the generally existing possibility of a closure of circuits of the productive economy and triggers deficient productive spending.

If we return to the debate in a fictive original assembly, regarding inviting capitalism into existence, we might hear an opponent of capitalism making a point in this regard. "I know", he might say, "capitalism can, much more fervently than mere natural consumptive motives, push value-in-use production... But capitalist investment always goes where the highest profits are, and if it is lured outside of value-in-use production, the investment will go there, become sterile, and betray production." The speaker might also make his final point: "The more capitalism turns everything upside down, the more it will make non-winners, and the more of them are around, the less it can rely on their employment-generating spending and the more it will depend on the spending of the winners itself. They, however, march into the sterile economy".

Section 3. The deficient-producive-spending-syndrome

The deficient-producive-spending-syndrome, accordingly, is a corollary of three insights. The first is that circuit closure would only be possible, if capitalist productive

---

27   In the wealth economy, you only need to go against the trend in the very last moment before the herd changes course too. See *George Soros* in footnote 26 on page 51.

firms were to reinvest their profits (M'-M) fully in the productive economy. The second insight is that, in addition, wealth owners ought to reinvest the different "tributes" (as explained above) they levy on the productive economy into the productive economy. The third insight is that there are strong reasons for wealth owners neither do the first nor to do the second.

Because of this, deficient employment-generating spending comes out of the deep-structural heart-beat-level of the capitalist economy. It is real, self-made, has its origins in capitalist circulation (not "production"), and is, in fact, ultimately only an aspect, which logically arises out of the profit motive of capitalism, i.e., of M–C–M', itself. Capitalism, in order to satisfy the profit motive has to absorb more value-in-exchange from circulation than it returns. Capitalism is, thus, inherently incomplete. It is like a slot machine that is programmed to pay out more than players throw into it. It needs somebody else to refill it. It is parasitic, yes, it is even vampire-like and needs fresh blood from the outside all the time.

While this character is hidden, it is still the final reason why the dynamics in the productive economy of profit economies often change from powerfully pushing towards more, better, and more efficient production and technological innovation to depression. Firms that anticipate that they will fail to close ongoing productive circuits avoid the initiation of new circuits in the first place. Not all firms give up all new circuits, but certainly *the less successful firms give up the less promising circuits*. Like in Malthus' population theory, competitive advantage *only distributes the unavoidable outfall* between different firms and decides on the primary victims of the depressing effects, but does not cause the outfall as such. The deficient-produce-spending-syndrome, conversely, does not dis-enable winner-firms – many well-known large firms amongst them – from showing tremendous success and touching tremendous profits down over centuries. The trouble allocates itself into the shadows of the less lucky or poorly managed firms that over-proportionally run out of employment-generating spending, shrink, underinvest, under-employ or even go bust. Even if all firms could perfectly target their products to esoteric consumer demand, if their products would all be of equal quality, if the buyers would intentionally place their purchases in a manner that a proper share of revenues accrues to all firms (or if a huge cartel, oligopoly, monopoly, or the state, including with perfect knowledge, would steer everything), employment-generating spending ought nevertheless to remain insufficient.

If we take the a Quesnayian world as an ideal starting point of a healthy economy, and if we view capitalist employment-generating spending as an *organic function* to supply the money needed for the purchases at the closing leg of the circuits,[28] then we will have to assess this organic function – in a medical term – as "hypo" and to

---

28   Of course, capitalism is *not* such a system with the built-in purpose of creating demand for profitable production and *no* machine with feedback-steering to secure such demand.

call capitalism itself *"hypo-spending"*. Alternatively, we might call capitalism's ill as *"hyper-collecting"*. The structurally given hypo-generation of employment-generating spending or hyper-collecting of revenues is the elementary antinomy of capitalism. It creates the deficient-producive-spending-syndrome. Stocks of pre-existing wealth initially mitigate things, as savings or inheritances do on the level of individuals. However, after the reserves are used up, iron will hit iron, and firms will anticipate that by lowering investment; this anticipation creeps back from circulation to depress production unless employment-generating prosthetic spending are added.

***

In principle, the purpose of this book is to lay out its propositions but not to give an overview on the views of mainstreams economics competing with or relevant for these propositions. Like we have briefly related the book's general theoretical approach to the approach of mainstreams economics in the Foreword, it may, yet, still be worthwhile to look at parallels and differences between the views, which we have now presented as the deficient-producive-spending-syndrome, and beliefs of mainstreams economics on the subject. We shall do this by looking at commentaries written in the *Financial Time* by one of the leading economics journalists of the world, *Martin Wolf,* in the last decade. Since the financial crisis of 2008, he has particularly reflected on deficient demand, deficient investment and deficient growth from almost all possible angles.

First, it is to be noted that the factual observations behind deficient employment-generating-spending are nearly uncontroversial. Hence, *Wolf,* too, observes in utter clarity and directness: "The principal high-income economies – the US, the eurozone, Japan, and the UK – have been suffering from 'chronic demand deficiency syndrome'". "More precisely", *Wolf* goes on, "their private sectors have failed to spend enough to bring output close to its potential without the inducements of ultra-aggressive monetary policies, large fiscal deficits or both". This factual statement is uncontentious.

Second, while most mainstreams economists would likely want to dispute our three above-mentioned insights, there is, in fact, no clear theoretical controversy either. Even *Wolf,* although he is bitterly aware of the relevance of the subject, makes no serious effort to offer anything, which could claim to coherently explain the reasons for his impeccable observation. Mainstreams economics is rather earmarked by a certain non-theory, a *theoretical hole*, at the place, where the subject ought to be dealt with. At best we find *traces of an eclectic multifactorial theory*, yet even without stating what the relevant factors are exactly supposed to be and how they are supposed to work together. Furthermore, like already Keynes had somewhere broken away from a theoretical analysis of deficient investment in favor of policy recipes, Wolf, too, mostly lets his theoretical explanations of the fact for deficient demand only appear implied in policy recommendations. For example, *Wolf* suggests: (i) "to distribute incomes from savers to spenders" – the theoretical implication is that it would be good for employment-generating spending if spenders, i.e., poorer classes and the state, had more money available. Or he suggests (ii) "unproductive savings should be discouraged"–the theoretical implication is that it would be good for relevant demand to redistribute spending from the sterile into the productive economy.[29] In a connected commentary *Wolf* gives three further explanations "of such weak demand", (iii) the "post-crisis overhang of private debt" after the financial crisis of 2008, (iv) that the pre-crisis demand was "unsustainable, because it relied on huge accumulations of private and public debt" and (v) "a slowdown in potential growth due to some combination of demographic changes, slowing rises in productivity and weak investment".[30] Wolf's explanation (iii) refers to a specific historic episode only and does not even attempt to explain this episode; it also, remarkably, only uses *consequences of prosthetics applied in this episode* to explain the present lack of demand. Explanation (iv), too, does not attempt to explain deficient demand out of "original" capitalism, but explains it with a medicine being taken away (as we shall observe the exhaustion of prosthetics in Book IV of this book). Insofar as Wolf's explanation (v) refers to "weak investment", it is, thus, no explanation at all but only a restatement of the fact of deficient investment demand. What is left over is an unclear combination of unclear observations (demographic changes, slowing rises in productivity) without any specifications; there is, thus, no serious explanation given.

In other articles, while repeating the aging of societies, *Wolf* also mentions (vi) globalization and the (vii) relocation of investment from the high-income to other countries, and (viii) investment being in IT and other intangibles (generating less employment).[31] The last point appears to be the most plausible at first sight, yet at the price that it restates the argument of the Luddites of the 19th century, which, most certainly, *Wolf* would generally not want to buy. Or does he believe that increases in productivity per se trigger unemployment? Probably not. In fact, should not the worker relieved from their prior jobs by IT and other intangibles-investments find new employment in, e.g., rendering services to those who draw higher salaries (v) or profits (M'-M) thanks to these IT and intangibles-investments? As that may ever be, most certainly Wolf does not give a theory of why, while what the Luddites argued

29   *Wolf*, Radical cures for unusual ills, in: *Financial Times* of 26 November 2014. Of course, Wolf does not possess and not use the distinction between a productive and a sterile economy.
30   *Wolf*, The curse of weak global demand, in: *Financial Times* of 19 November 2014.
31   *Wolf*, The corporate contribution to the savings glut, in: *Financial Times* of 18 November 2015 and *Wolf*, Challenges of a disembodied economy, in: *Financial Times* of 29 November 2017.

in regard of physical machinery in the 19th century was wrong, it is now right with regard to IT and intangibles (or where the borderline runs).[32]

Wolf also deals with the question of investment demand and states (ix) a "glut of savings relative to investment opportunities".[33] The same statement comes from his FT-colleague *Gemma Tetlow* who pronounces the "FT verdict" that "...a lack of worthwhile investments... must be playing a greater role in deterring companies from more capital spending". But why are there not enough worthwhile "investment opportunities",[34] meaning sufficiently profitable investment opportunities? This is so, in part again, because there is not enough investment demand, but also because there is not enough consumption demand (in our understanding only producive, employment-generating consumption demand would matter). But why is there not enough (producive) consumption demand? *Wolf* often argues with "inequality" or "rising inequality".[35] "There is no powerful reason", *Wolf* writes, "to expect income inequality, the fundamental driver of today's excess savings, to reverse...".[36] This mirrors Keynes argument of a falling propensity to consume with rising income,[37] which points into the right direction: Workers would consume more if they had higher incomes. Wolf, being in favor of less inequality, e.g., to generate more helpful demand, cannot possibly accept (x) "labour market reforms", also called "structural reforms", e.g., as implemented by the "Hartz-reforms" in Germany in the early 2000s, as inducive to more aggregate demand (meaning employment-generating, producive spending). While such reforms, which Germany and the EU also recommended to Greece and Spain etc. will lower the costs of labor, "the one thing those reforms did not do", *Wolf* rightly notes, "is create dynamic aggregate demand".[38] Labor market reforms only put certain countries, where they are applied, e.g., "the world's structural mercantilists: China, Germany and Japan",[39] in an (even) stronger competitive position, but are no general solution.

All in all, Wolf's argument regarding inequality is not only too unspecific, but also only this lack of specification allows *Wolf* to maintain the argument at all: If

---

32 We shall not conceal that, as "intangibles" encompass monopoly rights, which are sterile assets, we would even agree with Wolf if he meant that spending on intangibles as *sterile assets* is sucking away spending from the productive economy. (But he does not say so).

33 *Wolf,* Negative rates are a symptom of our ills, in: *Financial Times* of 15 April 2016.

34 *Tetlow,* Theories behind productivity woes range from tech troubles to zombies, in: *Financial Times* of 23 October 2016.

35 *Wolf,* Monetary policy has run its course, in: *Financial Times* of 13 March 2019.

36 *Wolf,* Inequality is behind central bank dilemma, in: *Financial Times* of 22 September 2021.

37 See on page 293.

38 *Wolf,* Reform alone is no solution for the eurozone, in: *Financial Times* of 22 October 2014.

39 *Wolf,* Trump's false promises to his supporters, in: *Financial Times* of 16 November 2016; see also *Wolf,* Germany is the eurozone's biggest problem, in: *Financial Times* of 11 May 2015.

Wolf specified the argument, he ought to say that such an increase of workers income was needed as to allow them, in the worldwide aggregate, to "re"-purchase products from capitalists in the amount of at least v (which would imply that they are relieved of any sterile spending) and that capitalists too are relieved of such need of sterile spending and, furthermore, only make producive, employment-generating spending out of their M'-M, which is impossible. Or: generating the employment-generating spending needed to close the circuits would require capitalists to wholly or largely waive profits – but then they would no longer be incentivized to employ workers at all....Thus, the mentioning of income inequality as cause for deficient consumptive demand, while pointing to the right direction (and while showing a social awareness of *Wolf*), is, ultimately, a naïve reference to a wasp nest: If it was taken seriously and thought through, it would end up in the abolishment of capitalism.

We close this section with a somewhat complicated quotation from *Arvind Subramanian*, which, if properly disentangled, admits that circuit closure is impossible if capitalist circuits are left to operate fallowing the original capitalist logic. *Subramanian* summarizes the views of the adherents of the secular stagnation hypothesis as follows: "...the essence of the macro-dilemma", he writes, "is that the equilibrium real rate of interest – the real rate of return required to keep the economy's output equal to potential output – has turned significantly negative, while nominal policy rates cannot be reduced much below zero". To repeat: *Subramanian* is saying, that the *equilibrium real rate of interest*, the real rate of return required to keep the economy's output equal to potential output, has turned "significantly negative"! In other words, he says that for circuits to close, real interest rates (after inflation) must be below zero. That, though, is *to admit that output cannot reach potential output,* unless the *unfulfillable* condition is met that somebody provides money to capitalists *instead* of normal profits, which they cannot gain out of their circuits. Yet, there is nobody in "original capitalism" who would make such money-presents to people to induce them to buy the output (including by loaning money to them, for which they have, after inflation, less to return than they received). Another way to read the quotation would be that as long as the logic of property, wealth accumulation and profit (M–C–M') prevails, there is no realistic possibility for capitalist circuits to close – as nobody will pay free lunches to others.[40] This, of course, is a near-mathematical reformulation of the results of the deficient-producive-spending syndrome and almost leads over to prosthetics. Before we go there, we shall, yet, acknowledge that the deficient-producive-spending-syndrome does not exclude the existence of secondary economic dynamics aside itself.

---

40   *Subramanian*, Secular stagnation's era may be drawing to close, in: *Financial Times* of 1 July 2021.

Section 4. Secondary dynamics and the deficient-producive-spending-syndrome

The deficient-producive-spending-syndrome, as we said, does not deny the existence of impressive massive regional, periodical, or sectoral growth and employment in the past, presence and future of capitalism. It does also not claim exclusivity for explaining the non-closure of circuits or of cyclical or structural movements or turbulences in employment-generating spending. Other theories of growth, decay, cycles or ruptures may, rather, be compatible with it. E.g., the deficient-producive-spending-syndrome does not deny that, in addition to its deep-seated effects, a lack of proper foresight, of communication and of joint planning, may conjointly lead to sectoral, regional or temporal overproduction, which will have to cyclically unload. Equally may discoveries, changes in technology, customer preferences, products or supply or distribution channels induce entrepreneurs to invest more or less in certain sectors, regions or at certain times the productive economy (as *Schumpeter* emphasized in his theory of economic development and of business cycles); this may well ignite significant sectoral, regional or temporal booms, which end in specific slumps. Demographic factors changing consumption and, thus, spending patterns, may be a factor, too. An important stream in economics uses the growth of volumes of available money, by discoveries or import of gold and silver, or other private or state fiat money creation, and consequentially abundant money and easy credit, as an explanation for growing investment in the productive economy and the shrinking of the volume of money, and the consequential restriction of credit as an explanation for depressions.[41] The deficient-producive-spending-syndrome does not deny such connections and is, accordingly, compatible with many theories of cyclical behavior and structural changes of the economy, including with *Minsky's* observation that consumers and firms will restrict spending to reduce their debt level after the bursting of bubbles following periods of expansive debt build-up, etc.[42] Most certainly, the deficient-producive-spending-syndrome also does not deny the relevance of exogenous shocks from nature (climate changes, flooding, diseases, differences in harvests, pandemics, etc.) or politics (wars, civil wars, expropriations, taxation, etc.).

Nevertheless, the deficient-producive-spending-syndrome does indeed claim to rule at a deeper level underneath these additional cyclical or structural movements and it also does claim to be more fundamental than they, like a powerful and ubiquitous "undercurrent" under regional, temporal, or sectoral "overcurrents". The de-

---

41   See, e.g., *Fisher* (1933) page 337. In this book, we already partially regard rendering additional money available via credit or money creation as a prosthetic reaction to the deficient-producive-spending-syndrome.

42   *Richard Koo* applied this theory to Japan. See *Koo* (2009) page 39 et seq

ficient-producive-spending-syndrome is, thus, the sad "grand" narrative of capitalism, whose ultimate appearance at the surface will be shaped by many short-term
and transitory, nice or particularly bad "overcurrents". The economy of the day is always a conjunction of both, a generally depression-inclined trend and of more of
less happy interim-episodes.

Part IV: The prosthetics of modern capitalism and their dilemmas

Part IV observes prosthetics that have been developed and are used in modern capitalism to deal with the deficient employment-generating spending posited in Part III. Some techniques were already invented in Antiquity and part of state policies ever since, e.g., spending financed by violent external goods procurement, protectionism, war, taxation and expropriation, commodity money creation by finding and mining gold and silver or by debasing precious money coins. Other techniques were only born, or only grew to relevance, in modern capitalism, e.g., credit money creation by private banks or state fiat money creation by states or central banks. Part IV considers these different instruments of prosthetic spending as they substitute the missing, original capitalist employment-generating spending, and their different dilemmas.

Figure 14: Ancient and modern social master drama and the funding of prosthetics

	Master drama	Prosthetics	Main forms of Funding
Ancient capitalism	Can owner-farmers keep their land so that they can subsist from their work?	Procurement of income opportunities or direct transfers of values to non-owners by the social, in particular the political system	Wealth procurement by violence, war, protectionism, expropriation, taxation and commodity money creation
Modern capitalism	Can enough producive spending be procured so that non-owner workers can subsist from their employment?		*additionally:* debt, private bank credit money and state fiat money creation

Chapter IX. Redistributive and expansive prosthetics

"Eben die Armut der Arbeitenden besteht darin, dass das, was sie produzieren, keine Abnehmer findet. Es ist so zu viel Kapital vorhanden, und es wird mehr produziert, als die Nation verzehren kann. Um dieses Überflusses willen, muss die bürgerliche Gesellschaft suchen, dass sie ihren Handel ausbreite. Damit kommen die Armen wieder zur Arbeit und zur Möglichkeit, ihre Substanz zu gewinnen. Die bürgerliche Gesellschaft strebt so überhaupt über sich hinaus, zunächst auf diese äußerliche Weise in Anlegung von Kolonien." (*Hegel* (1983) page 195, 199.)

"The entire credit system, and the over-trading, over-speculation etc. connected with it, rests on the necessity of expanding and leaping over the barrier to circulation and the sphere of exchange. This appears more colossally, classically, in the relations between peoples than in the relations between individuals. Thus, e.g., the English forced to lend to foreign nations, in order to have them as customers." (Marx, Grundrisse Foundations of the Critique of Political Economy (Rough Draft), Translation by Martin Nicolaus, in http://www.marxists.org/Arch ive/marx/works/ 1857/grundrisse, page 416)

There is *redistributive* and *expansive* prosthetic spending, which are distinguished by their sourcing. Funds for prosthetics may be sourced by either taking away *existing* money or other values (e.g., land) from somebody (with or without their consent) or by creating them *anew*. The first way of sourcing leads to redistributive prosthetic spending; the second, which is mostly only a practical option with regard to money, leads to expansive prosthetic spending.

These two ways do not differ regarding the *application of the funds*. Certain values-in-exchange, mostly money, must be transferred to a better place, where it will be spent productively. It must be channeled to somebody, hence, who has an original want of certain commodities, i.e., an esoteric – investive or consumptive – demand, but who does not have the financial means to fulfill it prior to the transfer. It is also imperative that this recipient must, in fact, make the employment-generating spending. We might say, to once more use a term of Keynes, that the money must go to somebody with a *high propensity for producive spending* (or employment-generating spending).[1] On the other hand, it does not matter whether the recipient of the prosthetically procured financial means makes the employment-generating spending directly itself or forwards the money to somebody else – via transfer payments or salaries – who will make the employment-generating spending. States are great addresses in both regards: The social security budget is as goods from this perspective as the military budget, even education works well.

Redistributive prosthetic spending without money creation can, though, only shift around existing funds in space or time without increasing them in the aggregate; redistributive prosthetic spending, thus, unfortunately remains a "zero sum game". However, it may still increase the total of employment-generating spending, given that it may transfer them from units with low propensity of employment-generating spending (but which own wealth) to units with a high propensity of employment-generating spending (with no money but high esoteric demand). Redistributive prosthetic spending will, accordingly, *spatially* "enrich" certain areas and "impoverish" others; it may also enrich *earlier* periods to the detriment of later periods. Accordingly, redistributive prosthetic spending accentuates highs and lows in areas (space) or cycles (time), such as the developed capitalist world versus the Third World or ecstatic spending after breakthrough inventions or in wars versus periods of normalcy.

All prosthetic spending, which goes beyond redistribution of funds and increases the available sum of funds, requires money creation and is *expansive*. Such expansive prosthetic spending is mostly connected with debt build-up, which will be dealt with in Chapters XI and XII.

---

1   See on a possible "producive spending multiplier" on page 306.

Chapter X. Redistributive prosthetics funded without money creation

Prosthetics without money creation, which can only reshuffle an existing amount of wealth, are always redistributive prosthetics. The three means of redistributive funding of prosthetic spending are taxation and expropriations, goods procurement by violence and protectionism, or, third, redistributive debt. They remain alive after the ascent of money creation, but their relevance will, at least in normal times, relatively go down the more powerful money-creation-based funding becomes. Still, even redistributive prosthetics funded without money creation already operate in a world, which knows money creation as such. A meager, irregular, and unreliable form of money creation existed already in commodity money, i.e., gold or silver regimes, as additional gold and silver could be found, mined, robbed or imported (with or without being embossed). For money to exist at all, it must have been created before and a monetary system without money creation is fictitious. However, redistributive prosthetics look at prosthetics, which do not themselves make use of money creation and in the following we shall initially simply – contra-factually – assume a world without money creation.

Section 1. Redistributive prosthetics funded with domestic taxation and expropriations

Domestic taxation and expropriations

Redistributive character of taxation and expropriations
State power enables states to arrange the transfer of things (land, firms, money) from one owner to a new owner, either directly or indirectly, as a triangle-transfer via the state. In order to effectuate such transfers, states use violence or the threat thereof. The transfers never increase the mass of the available things, but instead shifts wealth in space. Therefore, taxation and expropriations are only *redistributive* and the prosthetic employment-generating spending that they may generate is also only redistributive. They encompass, on the one hand, one-time changes of own-

ership, expropriations, which are often bloody and connected to civil or even for-eign wars,[1] and, on the other, regular and recurring changes of ownership mostly of money. e.g., i.e., taxes, fees (without services of the states or which are in excess of the value of the services), and social security contributions etc. They are a modest and legalized peacetime version of expropriations, which express a certain balance of power and longstanding social compromise. Expropriations and taxes have an advantage over debt-financed prosthetics (to be reviewed later) in that they fund ad-ditional employment-generating spending *without diminishing the state's employment-generating spending in the future*. This is different to debt, which will have to be repaid eventually by the state.

---

1   Examples of blunt, one-time-expropriations include the occupation of land of the catholic church and nobles, often using false pretexts, in the Reformation following 1518 by protes-tant miniature states in Germany and in the 1530s by Cromwell in England. In China, the central state occasionally expropriated land of generals or other state functionaries who grew to powerful, in particular in periods of low tax incomes (On the middle Sung see: Mc-Dermott/ Yoshinobu, Economic change in China 960–1279, page 409). Buddhist and Taoist temples were also frequently expropriated. The economic effect of expropriations also arose out of new settlements of the Spanish, the Portuguese, the Dutch or the British ap-propriating land in the Caribbean, in South or North America or in Australia, even if the native inhabitants, e.g., the "Red Indians" in the US or the Aborigines in Australia. The latter examples were, in fact, combined with the first-time and original creation of title and ownership in the modern sense. If appropriated land is put to use by poor peasants, then even land, which was considered as rather poor before, often proves good enough to allow their families to subsist and sometimes even to draw small profits through some selling. Both uses will generate additional productive spending, given that new farmers will buy cattle, seed, agricultural tools, build fences and irrigations, etc. and some consump-tion goods in the market. States can even expropriate the dead. *Sangha*, one of the "three villainous ministers" of Khubilai khan, entrusted the supervision of Buddhist teachings in south China to a Buddhist monk by the name of Yang. The latter, to finance Buddhist tem-ples and monasteries, possibly in revenge for earlier expropriations of Buddhist temples, too, "broke open the tombs of the Sung royal family and ransacked the valuables buried with emperors and empresses. He plundered 101 tombs and removed 1,700 ounces of gold, 6,800 ounces of silver, 111 jade vessels, 9 jade belts, 152, miscellaneous shells, and 50 ounces of pearls." Sangha was later executed by Khubilai (*Rossabi*, The reign of Khubilai khan, page 479).

Figure 15: Taxation and the funding of prosthetics

	taxpayer, expropriated subject	state
before	1	o
Tax paid or expropriation	o	1
nothing repaid	o	1
Result spending power	loss 1	gain 1

Only higher propensity of employment-generating spending make taxation and expropriation work

The loss for the taxpayer or for the expropriated state subject, of course, remains and this reduces their capacity for future employment-generating spending. Therefore, redistributive taxation and expropriations only increase aggregate employment-generating spending *if their final recipients have a higher propensity to bring about employment-generating spending*; however, that is typically so. Wealth in the orbit of sterile wealth owners, which is as committed to the profit condition as any wealth, only moves back into the productive economy if it is allured by profit expectations higher than in the sterile economy. Macroeconomically, thus, money is set free by being taken away from sterile wealth owners, where it underlies the profit condition, which is often favoring a sterile investment, and transferred to the high-propensity-to-make-producive-spending-area presided over by the state. The spending of the expropriated money follows a different algorithm than if the money had remained in private hands – and here is the net macroeconomic gain. The money will now be spent by the state (and mostly productively) *even if no profit can be made*. Sterile wealth owners do not use their profit (as *Quesnay's* tableau assumed or as *Malthus* wanted them to do) by wholly spending it on consumption. This sad reality is now sidestepped. The state, after it takes control of the money, acts almost like Quesnay's wealth owners did act or like Malthus expected his to act. Macroeconomically nobody cares about the penalty, which is implied for the taxpayers or the expropriated: Quesnay's and Malthus' wealth owners could fill *their own bellies*, collected tax money fills the bellies of state functionaries, soldiers, social security recipients, military and infra structure suppliers and their workers, etc.

Wealth owners' and productive firms' taxation

Wealth owners decide whether to financially equip their firms in the productive economy to initiate M–C–M'-drives or whether to keep their money in the wealth economy for sterile investments. Their money flows opportunistically back and forth between their employment-generating and sterile ports accordingly. They will make their decisions based on a comparison of the *expected risk adjusted after-tax-*

profitability[2] of investments in the two economies. Taxes on capital and profits in the productive economy will render such investments less attractive, compared to investments in the wealth economy. Tax money resulting from taxation of the productive economy will, thus, often backfire macroeconomically and only come at the price of diminishing productive investment. Conversely, taxing sterile wealth will normally not negatively affect investment in the productive economy, but, if taxation observes proper limits, it might in fact even improve the crucial comparative after-tax-profitability of productive economy investments. Accordingly, sourcing money for prosthetics from the wealth economy via taxation does not frustrate the purpose and will normally not reduce firms' future employment-generating spending.

Workers' taxation

Workers appear to be bad addressees of taxation, at least at first: Let us assume that workers still dwell in huts or in small houses inherited from their peasant forefathers in villages, pay no rent, have no debt, and – in agreement with the simplifying classical and Marxian-Kaleckian doctrine[3] – use their wages completely for the consumption of goods from the productive economy. In this case, their *propensity to consume* and their *propensity for producive spending* are identical. Accordingly, taking away any part of their wages and re-channeling it, via the state, into other places in the economy cannot possibly increase employment-generating spending. Taxing them ought to rather only throw them into poverty and despair (making them sick, homeless, undernourished, etc.). Accordingly, taxing workers would be, first, missing the point (no additional employment-generating spending) and, second, impossible (or, at least, the taxed away parts of salaries would have to be instantly filled-up by transfer payments or by increased worker indebtedness). This so far follows from the pure Marxian-Kaleckian doctrine.

Nevertheless, we obviously witness massive taxes, direct incomes taxes and indirect taxes, value-added or other consumption taxes (tobacco-taxes, fuel-taxes etc.), on workers in developed capitalist countries. In fact, we see a significant layer of workers who are, notwithstanding possible transfer receipts, net taxpayers. Conversely, we also see a layer of unemployed or low-income workers whose taxes (they unavoidably pay consumption taxes) are overcompensated by transfer receipts. How can these observations be reconciled with the findings of the previous section? First, we have to relax the assumption that workers always need the full amount of their salaries for subsistence. Marx already conceded that salaries depend upon market

---

2   See our discussion and amendment of Keynes' inducement to invest on page 299 et seq. and 313 and seq.

3   See on page 322 et seq.

conditions and regional and momentary power relations between workers and capitalists, which are influenced by political, social, and cultural aspects.[4] If salaries may be sometimes above the amount needed for necessary reproduction, this, though, already renders the taxation of workers partially possible. Furthermore, our expectation that workers' *propensity for producive spending* was 100 % depended upon the assumption that their *propensity to consume was also 100 %* because they earned so little that they would only buy daily consumption goods in the productive economy, still lived in inherited huts or houses in the countryside and were debt-free.

If we now relieve these assumptions and look at higher-earning people, who fall under the category of workers with their work income, e.g., technicians, middle managers,[5] employed doctors, employed lawyers, employed tax advisers, state functionaries, university professors, judges, military officers, etc., and at workers who earn significantly more than the average, e.g., in the automotive industry (being a worker in the automotive industry can be a fancy position nowadays), we find that their propensity for employment-generating spending has *fallen below 100 %*. They have excess income left, which they might put to two different kinds of sterile uses: sterile consumptive uses (in particular paying rent or purchasing and debt-financing dwellings) or sterile investments (to partly move out of their class). Taxing it away and channeling it back into productive consumption (of unemployed, sick, elderly, kids in education, etc.) or into productive investment via the state will, thus, indeed raise aggregate employment-generating spending.

In other words: Workers who earn more than what they need for their family's reproduction or their individual reproduction, if they are single,[6] are treated just as sterile wealth owners and their "excess income" is re-channeled into macroeconomically better uses. This involves a remarkable contradiction to modern capitalism's claim of social mobility. Modern states, in particular in European high taxation

---

4   Wealth owners' living standards cannot be the benchmark for minimum standards of humane life. Salaries cannot possibly suffice for the working class to purchase the same quality of healthy and delicious nutrition (caviar, lobster, foie gras, wine, Champagne, and Cognac *hors age* etc.), fancy clothing, horses (even dogs), cars, yachts, owning airplanes, first or business class travel, housing, villas, etc., which is enjoyed by wealth owners. The same applies to access to beauty care, cosmetic operations, membership in prestigious gyms and golf clubs, entertainment, more elevated cultural pleasures, even to cooler drugs (they use crack and opiate-substitutes instead of cocaine, etc.), and, worse, health services and education. He who does not like a clear gap between the living standards of workers and wealth owners ought either to revert to soviet style communism which, indeed, significantly closed the gap (the exceptions in favor of the party elites were mostly rather moderate) or has to give up intellectual consistency.

5   Top managers also belong to the category of worker, even if they normally use their salary income for investment and quickly become wealth owners aside being workers.

6   The difference is achieved through tax allowances in special cases, e.g., marriages.

countries, *tax away just what top performing workers would need to move up into the middle class* (the lower deciles of wealth owners). They do not reward the group of *best-performing* workers, but deny them climbing up the ladder and keep them in their treadmill. Taxation also redistributes incomes over lifetimes of individuals; it renders workers children richer, young adult workers in their best ages poorer, and retired workers richer again. States, thus, sacrifice the realization of capitalism's own promise of social mobility to keep their reservoir for prosthetics filled at a certain level; more successful workers finance social transfers to less successful workers, and workers in their best age finance transfers to themselves back into their own childhood and forward into their retirement or into periods of illness.[7] This also results in many middle layers of better off workers, e.g., technicians, middle managers, employed doctors, employed lawyers, employed tax advisers, state functionaries, university professors, judges, military officers, often having a hard time paying off their debt for a modest apartment or house over their lifetime.[8]

Privatizations of state property

If states have come to own wealth assets, which they cannot have acquired but by expropriations or taxation (only then they may have used them business-like), they can fund employment-generating spending also with their running profits or through a one-time sale or privatization of the asset. The latter was the destiny of many railways, airports, roads, energy suppliers, communications firm, utilities, large housing companies, schools, hospitals, etc. in many highly developed Western countries in recent decades. This move was largely ideologically based on the neoliberal credence that all economic activity should be left to the private sector and bringing the world closer to the ideal was regarded as a step to perfect happiness. *But it also momentarily filled the cashiers for prosthetics.* As privatizations undo earlier expropriations or liquidate earlier tax-financed investments, including capital gains, they may be regarded as postponed spending of proceeds from earlier taxation or expropriations.

The collapse of socialist countries in Eastern Europe, too, led to massive privatizations of businesses and real estate at the close of the last century. Such post-socialist privatizations, e.g., in Germany, were often connected with massive subsidies to the purchasers and resulted in net losses to the privatizing state. Their point, though, was not to source money for prosthetics, but they were rather themselves transfers – partially in kind and partially in money – to firms of the productive economy to ignite further employment-generating spending.

---

7   See *Wolf*, The welfare state is a piggy bank for life, in: Financial Times of 1 April 2016 (with reference to Nicholas Barr).

8   Taxes are normally only used by states in a sterile way to the extent they pay interest. But states normally do not purchase pre-existing sterile assets.

The dilemmas of domestic prosthetics funded by taxation and expropriations

The motive of M–C–M'-players in capitalism is profit and wealth accumulation; the sterile and the productive economy serve this purpose. Redistributions and taxation are hostile to this; income taxation takes away a larger or smaller part of M'-M; wealth taxation and other taxation encroach upon M and non-monetary forms of wealth, which can be used to make loans, be rented out or in production.

High-powered political dilemma: political and military defense of wealth owners against expropriations and taxation

The most attractive individuals to be expropriated and taxed can be found at the top of the wealth pyramid. They descend from great families, often with noble origins and famous names, many of these names were well-known down through the centuries. They are better educated and trained, know more, can do more things, and have better connections. In ancient times (today no more?), they were typically even taller, stronger, and more beautiful by and large, etc. and had better health and genes than the average person. If it there was a civil war against lower classes, then they were also the better fighters. Spartan hoplites were better than their helots. In modern civil wars, the elites mostly at least drew advantages from better leadership, more money, better weapons, and more mercenaries, and from more spies and traitors. The wealthy elites that we are talking about, were normally also able to establish hegemonic ideologies that supported their power.

While it is, as we said, a misleading paradigm to conceive of history primarily as "history of class struggle", class struggle does, nevertheless, sometimes rear its head. It is there when redistributions or expropriative taxations pose a threat and if wealth owners fight against this threat. In most countries, though, a certain *armistice level* is reached in the form of *ongoing partial expropriations by taxation* and other means (e.g., limiting employers' rights to terminate employment contracts or landowners' rights to terminate rental agreements or securing minimum salaries or maximum rents). This level may significantly differ between countries – the wealthier countries can afford a more generous compromise; the level of expectation is lower in poorer ones – but it often allows to maintain social peace for some time. If misguided politicians, bureaucrats, social rebellions, or organized revolutionary movements launch an attack beyond the armistice line, whether by "legal" and "constitutional" means or outright violence, then this typically re-ignites civil war again. We got to know such civil wars in Greek poleis ("stasis"), in Rome around the Gracchi brothers etc., in ancient China, in the French Revolution (1789), the French February Revolution of 1848, the Paris Commune (1871), the Russian October Revolution (1918), the German November Revolution (1918), the Chinese civil war (1927–1949), the Vietnamese civil and anticolonial war (1955–1975), or the over-throws of popular fronts or Peronist governments in Chile and Argentina in the 1970s.

It would be an interesting question to examine (which must remain outside of the scope of this book) what side was historically more responsible for bloodshed, i.e., whether there was more offensive revolutionary violence by the attacking lower classes or more preemptive defensive counter-revolutionary violence by the wealth owners. The only obvious thing is that in most cases the more reckless and brutal party won – while in retrospect most observers find the losers to be the more likeable.

Returning to taxation and expropriation as prosthetic means, we must accordingly conclude that these means are struck with a high-powered political dilemma: Taxation and expropriation always move around aggressively defended borderlines and their crossing may lead to civil war. Even today, the odds are mostly tilted in the favor of wealth owners in an "Ernstfall" (*Carl Schmitt*) because, in addition to their advantages already touched upon above, they also possess a great influence within the depths of the state apparatus, like the standing army, military in general, police, state bureaucracies, and in the "ideological state apparatuses" (*Antonio Gramsci*) like education, media political, and culture. This limit to taxation and expropriation cannot be taken lightly – if taxation (or even expropriations) are excessive, hell will break loose.[9] The ubiquitous final failure of social revolutions relaxes the aggressive defensiveness of wealth owners by no means; instead, they set their line of defense much earlier, much further "forward", than where revolutions become interesting for the more utopian dreamers and theoreticians. Thus, wealth owners will decidedly oppose revolutions and reforms even if they do not pursue the utopian "final goal" of a new society, a functioning socialism or some paradise on earth, etc. Wealth owners' concerns are not primarily in proving, as a matter of ideological battle, that there is no alternative to capitalism, and not even in avoiding the killing that is commonly connected to revolutions, but, ultimately, *mainly to avoid damage to their wealth and progressive wealth accumulation*. In other words: The political dilemma of taxation and of other forms of expropriation as prosthetic means is, quite simply: *Civil war lurks if they are pushed too far.*

Limited effectiveness of redistributions

A second, purely economic, dilemma lies in the limits of effectiveness of redistributions. To begin with, the most important expropriations historically were land redistributions: As we saw, land redistributions to the detriment of domestic latifundia

---

9   It should be noted that fierce opposition by wealth owners will not only unleash if red banners are waved or communist slogans are shouted, but they are smart enough to look at the substance of the matter. History knows many examples – we have touched upon some of them in our historical parts – where well-meaning, committed conservative politicians and bureaucrats, who believed to act in the best interest of nation as a whole or of the wealth owners in specific, were hit hardest and most brutally.

mostly failed, were undone, or remained marginal. Yet, land requisitions and redistributions of "empty" land (meaning land, which was sparsely populated and used by lower developed tribes), e.g. by Greek, Roman, or other European colonizers in Europe, Africa, the Caribbean, South America, within the US, or in Australia, typically combined by racial cleansing or genocide, were *very successful*.[10] Consider the colonization by ancient Greek poleis as a first example: Landless peasants from mainland Greece spread out to colonize places like Little Asia, the Black Sea, South Italy, Sicily, and even touched upon Spain and Southern France, where they became landowners and successful farmers. Unfortunately, following further population growth and land centralization back in Greece, new landless peasants emerged there soon after and the original problem repeated itself in the homeland. Alternatively, consider the US. Private lot-landownership of farmland became the basis of the tremendous success of US-agriculture in the 19th century. It gave birth to hundreds of thousands of new farms, which almost instantly went beyond subsistence farming and achieved significant profits.[11] These massive land redistributions greatly helped artisans, manufacturing, and early factory owners to ignite the industrialization in the US, e.g., by supplying these farms and the farmers. Yet, the deficiencies of employment-generating spending were not lastingly solved thereby. Although the land redistributions had a vivid initial effect, similar to Greek colonization, the problem later only reproduced itself at a higher level.

The experience of splitting up and privatizing larger entrepreneurial units, businesses, or firms, e.g., in post-socialist privatization or re-privatization campaigns, points in the same direction. Initially, the new units will make additional M-outlays

---

10   In a lecture from 1819/20 *Georg Friedrich Wilhelm Hegel* pointed to a twofold advantage of colonization: "Durch Kolonisation wird das Doppelte erreicht, dass die Verarmten Eigentum erhalten und dass durch diese zugleich für das Mutterland ein neuer Markt gebildet wird. ...Die Frage ist nun, wo Boden für Kolonien zu finden ist." (*Hegel* (1983) page 198 et seq.).

11   In the south, the initially innocent new American farmers even followed suit to their Spanish, Portuguese, Dutch and French predecessors and re-introduced slavery. Slavery can be seen as the expropriation of humans over their self-ownership and made M-outlays much cheaper. In a way, slaveowners' *v*-outlays disappeared at the cost of increased *c*-outlays (higher costs for "equipment", prices paid for slaves, and "inventories", payments for slaves' subsistence). In 1770, the slave population of the US was 400,000 and it grew to 4,000,000 by 1860. Between 1800 and 1860, about 40 % of the population in the south were slaves (given a growth of both the slave and of the non-slave-population). This "patrimoine négrier" is highly concentrated; e.g., Thomas Jefferson inherited over 600 slaves. The price of slaves was 10–12 times the annual salary for a free worker. *Piketty* assesses the value of the slaves in the first half of the 19th century to be around 1.5 times GDP, about the same as the value of agricultural land. See *Piketty* (2013) page 250, 251, 256. The French Revolution abolished slavery in France in 1792, while Napoléon re-introduced it in 1803; after the February Revolution of 1848 it was again abolished. Slavery, in France, was mainly a factor in the Antilles, La Réunion, and La Maurice.

and provide additional employment, but they will also immediately begin to compete for the ever-insufficient M'-M. If Amazon – a firm that seems to prove that the world can live with one wholesaler and detail-distributer – were broken up into smaller units again, while this would restitute income opportunities to middle-class firms (traditional detail traders, e.g., book stores), the deficient-producive-spending-syndrome would still reproduce itself at another level.

Redistributions of land, leading to more equal landownership, was demanded by the poor peasantry for millennia and, as we saw, often acclaimed by reform-politicians of the upper classes. The ideas behind the suggestion were mostly, first, to enable the receiving farmers to feed themselves and their families, thereby avoiding anomy, banditry, and rebellion, and, very importantly, to produce soldiers for the state's army. Second, new farms were expected to generate additional employment-generating spending – and did so. Whether or not money, agricultural tools and knowledge were also transferred to the new farmers, they still had at least the chance to use a surplus produce to purchase equipment and inventories (tools, ploughs, oxen, seed, etc.) or to finance improvement measures, e.g., irrigation – all of these being employment-generating spending. They could also use land or their expected harvest as security to finance such investments (although this was always risky). With a little progress of their farms, they would likely employ agricultural laborers and pay wages enabling these workers to make further employment-generating spending, too. Land redistributions, thus, are rightly regarded not only as a means for the poor peasantry to survive and to provide well-fed soldiers for the state, but also to generate prosthetic employment-generating spending and growth. This is why Alexander von Humboldt, Sismondi, Malthus, and others praised the equal land distribution and supported hereditary laws that would split up land possessions after each generation and opposed primogeniture.[12]

How severely do taxation and expropriations depress the economy – and does it matter?

If asked to comment on the limits of taxation and other expropriations in capitalism, most mainstreams-economists would probably argue that excessive taxation and other expropriations cancel out or severely diminish *the motives* of entrepreneurs or professionals *to work hard* and, thus, slow down growth or shrink the economy. They will go on to imply that this detrimental effect will somehow set "objective" limits to both taxation and other expropriations. In our view, though, such feared negative effects on production or growth are *no effective cause*, which actually limits taxation and other expropriations; this for two reasons: First, there are no economic mechanisms, which automatically stop policies that strangulate growth and do damage to the economy. Such mechanisms did neither exist in the Middle Ages,

---

12   See also footnote 39 on page 154 (at the end).

nor in Soviet style socialism or elsewhere where unsound state policies impede production and growth. That is why liberal and neoliberal economists had to (partially rightly) almost permanently denounce the existence of such bad policies and demand changes. It rather takes conscient action to stop these policies, which only the state can take. In other words, the very same state, which pursues the bad policies is needed to change them. The allegedly "objective" limits to taxation and expropriations are, thus, in fact, only proposals to the state to change its policies. If the state does not want to hear the proposals, e.g., because it is controlled by determined left-wing government, the arguments become, at best, additional reasons to take down the government and, ultimately, to throw civil war. Hence, we are referred back to the political level.

Secondly, at what point do taxation and other expropriations really become *so bad* as to materially depress the economy and impede growth and production? The reader will recall that in the discussion of working-class-taxation, we noted that states nowadays more or less tax away the part of the income of the elite of the working class (of particularly well earning blue and white color-workers, of technicians, middle managers, employed doctors, lawyers and tax advisers, state functionaries, university professors, judges and military officers), which they would need to significantly move up socially. Therefore, after having lived a somewhat more luxurious live than the average deciles of the working class in terms of inhabited appartements, cars driven, food cooked at home, visited restaurants, travelling, culture and education of their kids, they leave the planet with only a capital stock worth a nice urban apartment. Still, these social layers, with mainstreams-economics professors amongst them, are the most active and hard-working of society. Apparently, the heavy taxation, which they suffer and keeps them from materially moving up, does *not yet kill their motives* to make valuable economic contributions. If we look at even lower income deciles, we meet those who take care of kids and the sick and the elderly, such as kindergarten-nurses, teachers, hospital nurses etc. Their net income is only slightly above what most social security recipients have. Nevertheless, this small margin appears to suffice to keep their important social services alive. Maybe, we generally have to acknowledge that many human beings in the two layers we looked at are, contrary to the idea of *homo economicus*, are not wholly and not even crucially motivated by monetary income. Rather, many of them may close their eyes to the economic observation that "it is not really worth the effort" because they *want* to uphold a narrative of their live with a deeper meaning and beauty than just money.[13] Finally, if we consider owners of large wealth now, we may have to acknowledge that taxing away a more substantial part of their income or their wealth than customary

---

13   Purely money-interested investors in hospitals, private schools, universities etc., thus, may need an environment of not purely monetarily interested doctors, nurses, teachers, professors etc. for their goal attainment.

in even today's high taxation countries, may wholly not stop their investing. If 75 % percent of profits are taxed away – are the remaining 25 % not better than nothing? Even if fully-fledged expropriations take place somewhere, it may still make sense to continue other business operations or to set up new businesses in the hope that they will enjoy a more pleasant fate. Remember that creditors who have just lost loan repayment claims in an insolvency of a sovereign or private debtor, often immediately hand out new loans to the same creditor if the prospects of the future debt service appear improved? Or think of the Medieval bankers, who, after being expropriated, expelled and sometimes persecuted, often gladly returned to give new loans. Furthermore, it is not so easy to transfer wealth to foreign countries with assured better net profit and wealth preservation expectations. And wealth, which leaves a country, improves the conditions for the wealth that stays. Thus, we believe that ultimately, the true means that effectively stops excessive taxation and other expropriations, and the true dilemma of prosthetics funded with taxation and other expropriations, remains the political power of the wealth owners, including their capacity of throwing a civil war.[14]

Section 2. Redistributive prosthetics funded with war, external violent wealth procurement and protectionism

War, external violent wealth procurement and protectionism

War and violent goods procurement as means of prosthetics funding

Examining ancient capitalism, e.g., in Rome, we have already seen how war and violent wealth procurement were used as means to fund prosthetics by state might and praeter-economic means. Robbing riches of neighbors, e.g., land, cattle and

---

14   This is not the place to analyze capitalist states' taxation politics in greater depth. However, such analysis would have to preoccupy itself with the – somewhat astonishing – fact that taxation often disfavors incomes, profits, and salaries, in the productive economy and favors incomes in the wealth economy, in particular capital gains. Because wealth owners draw a mix of disfavored productive and favored sterile incomes, their average tax rate, thus, goes down. Better earning salary receivers and professionals, who do not draw sterile income, are, accordingly, worse off. It is also remarkable that, as rental markets for dwellings are largely controlled and impose hidden social transfers on landlords to their tenants', tax laws often allow landlords to make good for these sacrifices by leaving capital gains at the sale of properties largely untaxed. The clear (microeconomic) signal for the better earning players in the productive economy is to enter the wealth economy as soon as possible. Macroeconomically, of course, the wisdom of these taxation policies, which further drain wealth into the wealth economy, is dubitable.

tools, and subjugating them into forced labor or into paying tributes worked well to feed and preoccupy one's surplus population. It even oftentimes allowed additional wealth generation by violence for the domestic owner's class, too. (We ought to add that there was, of course, no institutional or other guaranty that the domestic wealth owner's class would not immediately begin to appropriate the wealth or the income opportunities just won by their surplus population once more, e.g., quite typically, to displace soldiers who had become farmers from their newly gained land, even if that reproduced the problem). Nevertheless, warfare was a great relief. It could also reduce the need of prosthetics by diminishing the number of the surplus population as such through illness, death, or by dispersing them abroad. Warfare possesses yet another peculiar property, which gains great impact in modern capitalism, and which helps to shrink the problem of deficient producive spending for the future: War destroys land, buildings, other equipment and inventories, too. It, thereby not only creates new esoteric demand for the destroyed or damaged objects, but also renders their production more profitable, so that they become more competitive compared to sterile investments once more. In other words, aside any war prosthetically feeding the soldiers during the war and a won war often funding prosthetics for a longer term thereafter, and aside reducing the number of people in need of prosthetics, wars will almost always also improve the odds for the productive economy in the future, which by itself, will generate more employment generating spending afterwards (for some time). War is, accordingly, not only a mono-instrument of prosthetics funding, but it is multi-functional and operates on several levels; like a debt jubilee does away with excessive debt, it frees an economy of excessive goods.

Protectionism as means of prosthetics funding

If prosthetics are funded externally through war and violent wealth procurement or domestically through expropriation and taxation, the increment of employment-generating spending over the "original" capitalist employment-generating spending had a clear individualizable source, the subject of the subjugation or the tribute-payment or the expropriated or taxable subject. This is different with prosthetic increases of employment-generating spending from protectionism. Protectionism operates via influencing the market and additionally generated or attracted volumes of employment-generating spending often have no visible individual emitter. Protected firms, which profit, may not know who suffers in consequence of their well-being, the victims may also not know that they lose specific amounts to concrete favored firms, and even the bureaucrats who conceive and implement protectionist policies may not know whom they punish. In fact, often protectionism only prohibits prospective competitors from entering the market – the victims never really come into being.

Protectionism: State power giving the edge

If firms make M-outlays to realize profits in circuits, then they generate employment-generating spending, which is "original" and not "prosthetic". If successful firms, or cities, countries, homelands of colonial empires, or imperialist countries can find employment-generating spending for their products, because their products are simply better or cheaper (or they more effectively supply them to markets in needed quantities etc.), then the M' that they receive is also "original" and not "prosthetic". Natural winners win because "natural" competitive advantages. They "pull" employment-generating spending towards themselves, without states influencing markets in their favor.

However, employment-generating spending becomes "prosthetic" when states use their state might to support protected firms selling commodities or purchasing supplies. The practice was known already in ancient Athens, Rome, and China, in medieval burger towns of the Holy Roman Empire of the German Nation and in Italian Renaissance city republics such as Venice. It also existed in what was later called "mercantilism" or "cameralism" in absolutistic states or princedoms and continues to exist until present times. Protectionism was at the center of economic policies of colonialism, imperialism, fascism and socialism. It also greatly helped catch-up developments of late-comers in capitalist development, e.g., of South-Korea, Japan and China. Previous state violence and war typically laid the foundations for the consecutive more moderate policies of protectionism.

While the worst practices of protectionism seem to have passed by with colonialism, imperialism, and fascism, protectionism as such has certainly not. It appears today in unilateral trade and foreign investment acts by states, treaties between states, and in acts by the World Trade Organization or other organizations. The employment-generating spending resulting from protectionist policies will increase employment-generating spending from abroad, which appear in the lower left corner of figures 6 and 7 on pages 121 and 122. Whatever its form, its essence is, to borrow an expression from *Clausewitz*, the continuation of firms' microeconomic search for competitive advantages by political means.

Protectionism needing a concise economic understanding

Protectionism begins with governments, city councils, duchies, kingdoms, and empires. They need to understand, first, what every merchant already knows about the economy: Economic self-enrichment works through selling the greatest possible number of commodities to the greatest possible number of purchasers with the highest possible profits, i.e., to maximize M'-M. Protectionism's core idea is a simple corollary from *correct* microeconomic insights of profit economies; therefore, it is and always was the most intuitive economic policy. *Protectionist policies only elevate how single firms think and operate anyhow on the level of state policy.* Market liberalism, conversely, becomes *counter-intuitive* for firms and well-meaning states as soon as strong competitors arrive upon the scene (as freedom of opinion becomes counter-intuitive if it is "abused" for the wrong opinions).

States, second, need to find ways to favor selected firms and to implement appropriate measures to ensure this. Sometimes, recognizing possibilities for protectionist policies and implementing them is far from easy. Proper points of attack must be chosen, circumstances, which favor protected firms (or disfavor the competition), and a toolkit of law, ideology, administration and violence, to which the respective state has access, have to be marshalled into action. Protectionism requires a lot of continuous decision-making; it requires selecting favored firms, products, and target markets. It requires the generation of a political will and maintaining it to help the favored firms and to contrive a series of strategically chosen measures to implement them. As markets move quickly, somebody must continuously monitor how the policies work and adjust them if necessary.

Supply periphery and sales periphery

The protectionist state, starting from a more or less conscient understanding of M–C–M' as its basic recipe, will specifically try to ascertain that there are as *many cheap* and *good supplies* as needed and that all resulting produce finds as *many and dear-paying customers* as possible. These two different purposes, as we have already seen in our initial discussion of M–C–M' on page 95, draw a distinction between two peripheries, a functional supply periphery and a functional sales periphery (Absatz, débit, off-sale) for each product, behind them. The supply universe, figuratively on the left, should be a *low-price sector,* while the sales periphery on the right should be a *high-price sector.* As prices reflect valuations, the sectors can also be called low value and high value sectors.[15] The favored firms (in the center) profit from *bridging* these sectors' value-differences. On page 91 et seq. we have used a two-chamber-metaphor for the role played by firms. The firms in the center can call the shots as long as they suck in or absorb goods, services, and labor in the left chamber. However, they have little control over the journey's crucial final leg. In chamber two, where they offer their products or services, they depend on prospective customers who must do the "sucking", but whether these prospective customers have the esoteric demand, the necessary money, and whether they are willing to make the financial sacrifice to the favored firms, is out of the firms' control. Protectionism, now, applies tools to improve the odds of favored firms (beyond seduction by marketing etc.). In fact, the protectionist tools are *grosso modo* negative imprints of everything, which antitrust

---

15   Clearly, these sectors are not solely defined in terms of geographical regions or political countries, but in terms of markets that may be independent of political or geographical borders. Africa may be a low value and low price sector for labor, agricultural products, and raw materials, but a high value and high price sector for certain luxury goods, etc.

laws forbid between competing firms and in the relations between firms and suppliers or customers. They consist in opening gates or filters that are advantageous for the favored firms, and in closing gates or filters that are bad for them or good for competitors.

Figure 16: The sun of the protectionist state shines over its favored firms

Supporting favored firms:	Damaging competing firms:
Force supplier sector of favored firms to supply them in sufficient volumes, at good quality, and at good prices	Force suppliers sector *not* to supply competing firms or to only supply them in limited quantities, at high prices or at lower qualities
Support supplier sector of favored firms, e.g., by pushing their labor costs down (e.g., slavery, maximum salaries) and granting them exemptions from taxes, fees, duties and customs	Damage supplier sector of competing firms, e.g., by trade restrictions, pushing up labor costs (e.g., minimum salaries) levying higher taxes, fees, duties and customs
Encourage, sometimes force, customers to buy minimum quantities or exclusively from favored firms	Prohibit or restrict customers from buying from competing firms

The logic of M–C–M' dictates that firms ought to show a softer and friendlier face to the customer than they do to the suppliers. Accordingly, the repertoire of protectionism on the left supply and on the right sales side are not equal. This is one of the (several) reasons why capitalism can be so wonderful and so ugly. Laws in the US south admitted negro slaves to be flogged in cotton plantations in Alabama to keep them under control, but never would the laws in England have allowed a lingerie supplier in Bond Street to flog British ladies if they did not buy their cotton lingerie.

Medieval and Renaissance Protectionism

The Swedish economic historian *Eli F. Heckscher* was a convinced free-trader and, energized thereby, wrote an impressive two-volume book entitled "Mercantilism" (1932). While the book suffers from an idealistic method,[16] Heckscher presented a

---

16   His stated goal, which he reiterates over and over, is to find "the" mercantilist "doctrine", "social idea", or even the mercantilist "mentality". E.g., Heckscher distinguishes three main types of mercantilist policies, which are either (i) directed towards commodities, ("staple policies", Stapel, entrepôt), (ii) directed towards procurement ("policies of provision"), or

very rich historic study of mercantilist practices. The first element of mercantilist policies, he found, was to prohibit high quality and low-price commodities from being exported to the disadvantage of the favored manufacturing or trading firms back home.[17] This applied to raw materials, semi-finished goods, tools and machinery, and also to labor. It ascertained that there were enough apt inputs as base for the favored firms adding value and also bereaved competitors of these same inputs.[18] Heckscher saw the medieval German "Bannmeilen"-laws, whereby cities forced the surrounding countryside to exclusively bring their products to the local city market, as a typical example of this.[19] Initially, the focus may have been on basic goods – grains, meat, bacon, butter, cheese, grease, oil, and other food –, but later, e.g., as cities (e.g. of the Hanseatic League, Brussels, or the North Italian city republics) entered into foreign trade, the mercantilist grip extended to raw materials, semi-finished products, tools, other means of production for export goods or, again, labor.[20]

While the preceding policies targeted the M–C-chamber, or, if the goods were processed, the M–C'-chamber, others addressed the sales-chamber, the C–M'-chamber (or C'–M'-chamber). A strong city-state, e.g., Venice, the first important European post-medieval robber and merchant-city-state, was powerful enough not

---

(iii) directed against competing products ("policies of protection" in a narrower sense) [see *Heckscher (1932)* German translation, page 64] or he uses notions like "commodity hunger" or "commodity fear" to describe the mercantilist "mentality". However, nothing really works and he only discovers that mercantilist firms are *sometimes* hungry (seeking cheap supplies) and have *at other times* "fear" of competing commodities (seeking sales monopolies) or even show both inclinations *at the same time*. Had Heckscher taken the contractionary capitalist process, which he, of course, was aware of, as a starting point ("buy cheap in order to sell dear" *(Heckscher (1932)* volume 2, page 43), everything would have fallen in its right place. As he did not, he blamed mercantilism for being more contradictory than it really is. Heckscher sometimes also confused politically and militarily guided policies, e.g., prohibitions against supplying strategically crucial material such as wood, horses, steal, and weapons, as mercantilist policies, while, in effect, they may even have been economic sacrifices on the geopolitical altar. That anti-trust-laws largely only developed after Heckscher's book was published partially excuses these conceptual weaknesses. The analysis of the different ways of market interference, on which anti-trust-laws are based, could have helped to better describe protectionist policies as well.

17   *Heckscher (1932)* page 71, page 131.
18   *Heckscher (1932)* page 134. "One could consider food as a factor of production, even as the most important of all" (translated from German by the author). Heckscher points out that mercantilism favored a large (page 142 et seq.) low income (page 148 et seq.) industrious (page 139 et seq.) working population and objects to the view that child labor had been an invention of the industrial revolution. According to Heckscher, mercantilists (like Colbert) supported child labor beginning at the age of four, five, or six (page 140 et seq.).
19   *Heckscher (1932)* page 72.
20   *Heckscher (1932)* page 74. 75.

only to prohibit foreign firms from importing commodities, e.g., salt, into what Venice considered her home market (Venice including in so-called *domini di terra ferma* around it), but also to force them to *open up their territories* to Venetian exports, e.g., again, salt.[21]

Colonialist protectionism and its end

Opening territories for the trade of superior (technologically and economically more developed) countries was also the first protectionist means applied by colonialist protectionism to support selling products from home abroad. England opened China up for English export and trade in the Opium wars between 1839 and 1868 (British cannon boats made Chinese authorities admit opium into their territory) and Perry opened Japan up for US supplies in 1853. Colonial powers often went further and forced territories, which they had opened for their commodities, to *exclusively* purchase them and to disallow competing foreign products. Furthermore, they established monopolies in their favor to render services connected to trades. E.g., England favored its own sea-related shipping and other services with the Navigation Act of 1660, which even Adam Smith, although the interfering hand was quite "visible" in that instance, praised as a masterwork of statesmanship.[22]

Britain, France, or other states set up and protected triangle trades, which, e.g., supplied low quality "jewelry", colorful glass pellets, to West Africa, exchanging them against robbed negroes, and took the latter as slaves to the US or the Caribbean, where they were traded against cotton for Europe. The British empire protected the other aforementioned triangle trade, which consisted of buying opium in India, selling it in China, buying tea and silk there and taking it, in addition to excess silver from the particularly profitable sale of opium, back to Europe.[23]

It did not stay this way, though. While founded by colonial powers, colonies forced their way out and thereby cut off the former's protectionist advantages. The countries of the first wave of colonialism, the Spanish and Portuguese kingdoms, had to accept the loss of Argentina, Brazil, Bolivia, Chile, Colombia, Ecuador, Mexico, Peru, Venezuela, etc., largely as results of liberation wars, in the first quarter of the 19th. century, and of Cuba after the Spanish-American war 1898. The most important powers of the second colonial wave were The Netherlands, England, and France. The Netherlands created a network of colonies, mostly in the form of trade posts, parallel to their war against Spain (1568–1648), of which the most important ones were lost again already in the 17th century. England saw its key colony in

---

21   *Heckscher* (1932) page 125.
22   *Smith* (1776) Book IV chapters 3, 5; *Heckscher* (1932) volume 2, page 6, 25.
23   Of course, triangle trades experience frictions; there is no guaranty that the volumes of goods always match.

North America, later the US, liberate itself in 1776. It was no accident that the US's rejection of England exporting its tea into the US, the Boston Tea Party, became a signature event of US independence. The British empire's colonial power went through several phases, but only appeared to grow more and more powerful for a long time. It enjoyed undisputed naval supremacy for over a century and was able to defend its interests in middle Asia against competing Russia in the Crimean War of 1856. In the end, though, it was also sacked and probably suffered more than any other country from the collapse of colonialism. India was lost in 1947, Hong Kong finally returned to China in 1997; other possessions had already become economically unimportant. After France had been stripped of its North American possession – Canada becoming British already in the 18th century, Louisiana was sold to the USA in 1803 –, its focus shifted to Africa, where it held most of the north western part. France also moved to the Far East, where it possessed today's Laos, Cambodia, and Vietnam. However, France lost fourteen French colonies in Africa in 1960; Algeria followed after a bloody war in 1962. By then, France had also already lost French Indochina in the battle of Dien Bien Phu in 1954.

Imperialist and fascist protectionism

Protectionist policies, though, as mentioned previously, did not end with classical colonialism. Neither M–C–M' had changed, nor had the search for sales markets become irrelevant. First, imperialism, as described by *Rudolf Hilferding*[24] and *Wladimir Lenin*,[25] continued to use protectionist policies – now with modern technology and mass-armies. Cheapening the national output through the input of unfree labor or robbed goods, thereby, of course, generating additional employment-generating spending, became an official state policy again – now the name of the "nation" (which sometimes included the national proletariat). Conquering countries to subjugate or even enslave them, as we have seen in the case of England and China, did not stop before previously culturally highly developed countries. In an even more tasteless and morally corrupt project, the late-comer Germany threw a grand scale attempt to degrade Russia, a former colonial power itself and the homeland of Tchaikovsky, Dostoyevsky, and Chekhov, into the status of a primitive colony in the middle of the 20th century. The attempted German eradication of the European Jews, too, had the economic dimension of a large-scale appropriation of Jewish wealth in Germany and the occupied territories, which would have improved Germany's economic position.

Protectionism after WW II

The end of even imperialism and fascism still did not imply the end of protectionism. The Marshall plan was protectionist in so far as it connected US-financing

---

24 *Hilferding* (1910).
25 *Lenin* (1917).

of European countries, largely by loans, with obligations to buy US-products. [26] Later the US allowed great volumes of foreign exports into its markets, partly in exchange for debt-financing its budget deficit by US-bond-purchases and partly in exchange for geopolitical favors in the Cold War. Thus, the US became a voluminous absorber of exports from Germany, Japan, and China (and other countries) and thereby nourished these competitors. The US has, though, recently attempted to turn this around and, e.g., re-conquer domestic and international markets for its productive firms, e.g., in the energy, semiconductor, automobile, steel, and tech sectors, including by protectionist means. Some measures, e.g., blocking technical supplies for gas pipelines from Russia (some allege the US even blew up Nordstream 1 and 2 in 2022) and general "sanctions" against Russia since the beginning of the Ukraine war, or an embargo against Iran, combine protectionist geopolitical and military objectives. Japan pursued protectionist policies when it kept foreigners from competing against Japanese firms, e.g., electronic industries, in Japan while it became a leading export power in the home markets of the dis-favored firms. China followed suit thirty years later. Socialist states had also run foreign trade monopolies, which, the different economic systems they backed notwithstanding, were protectionist in character.

Certain other state measures, which increase a country's competitiveness abroad, must also be seen as protectionist. E.g., Germany, under the chancellorship of the social democrat *Gerhard Schröder*, in a project called "agenda 2010", terminated previous political and legal measures in labor markets, which had raised salaries and thereby pushed down labor costs and secured cheap labor inputs for German productive firms. The agenda 2010 is believed to have significantly contributed to Germany's lasting export success in the second decade of the 21th century. Manipulating the foreign exchange rate has reemerged as major protectionist tool, too. Almost all countries have, moreover, pursued policies of pushing down their domestic interest rates, which has the same effect. Such policies improve the competitiveness of favored firms and prosthetically increase their access to employment-generating spending to the detriment of foreign competitors. [27]

As a summary, first, in contrast to what free traders still teach, there is overwhelming evidence for material protectionism almost everywhere, even today. Second, protectionism cannot be portrayed as an erroneous, nonsensical, fallacious, and illusionary misconception. Rather, protectionism offers proven recipes to microeconomically increase profits of favored firms and to macroeconomically help to

---

26   On the Marshall-plan: *Abelshauser* (2011) page 54 et seq.

27   The *International Bank for Settlement* (BIS) at Basel admits that monetary policies pursue the purpose of improving competitive positions abroad. It speaks of the "domestic transmission channel" of monetary policies in that sense (*International Bank for Settlement* (2016) pages 5, 13, 82 et seq.).

close domestic circuits – to the detriment of those abroad. We have a blatant contradiction between economic realities (over centuries and up to today) and the image painted of capitalism by liberals and neoliberals. Capitalist self-observation again admirably detaches itself from realities.

The dilemmas of funding prosthetics with external violent wealth procurement and protectionism

Nevertheless, protectionism was and is subjected to dilemmas, which severely limit its microeconomic and macroeconomic capacity. First, protectionism, *per se*, can at best shift deficient employment-generating spending around its space. However, as a "beggar-your-neighbor"-strategy, which it will always remain – it is asymmetrical by definition-, *it can never solve the worldwide deficiency* of employment-generating spending *as such;* it can only redistribute it. Second, like external violent wealth procurement, it generates displeased victims and opponents. These victims or opponents will apply defensive counterstrategies (I do not want to be your hinterland) and offensive protectionists strategies (you should be my hinterland). There will also be competition between protectionists to secure other countries as the hinterland (A-country should be *my* hinterland, not yours). All this will diminish the effectivity of protectionism. Third, and worse, protectionism will often lead to war, wars of liberation, and wars between protectionist pretenders. Fourth, protectionisms is an awkward and obstinate tool to handle in itself. In a world with complex nets of supply lines and trade systems, like that of today, it is very difficult to select macroeconomically relevant favored firms, products, and markets. Often hard and self-defeating choices have to be made, e.g., if a country's production includes primary products, intermediary products, and final products; protection of the final product may be damaging to earlier stages' products (or the other way around). What is good for sales of colored cloth, may not be good for the sales of cloth in general. When Jacob I, as Heckscher reports, in the early seventeenth century tried to enforce laws that *only* allowed the export of *colored cloth* from Britain to the continent to favor the dyers, he was challenged by a jurist (with the exquisite name of Julius Caesar) whether he wanted "in order to employ 10,000 dyers... render 100,000 spinners and weavers unemployed".[28] Favoring product A will often put product B at a disadvantage, favoring product C or products D and E. Fifth, each single product can only be favored by setting up a kind of a "nozzle pipe" (as in figure 4 on page 92), so if protectionist policies address more than one product market and install more than one "nozzle pipe", the more there are, the more likely it is that they will blow dust into each other's faces. With the scientific, technical, and economic progress and trade systems changing more quickly, the consequences of acts in one area for

---

28   *Heckscher* (1932) page 134.

other areas become more unforeseeable and difficult to manage and a protectionist central observer and gate keeper will quickly become overstrained. A protectionist mega-cockpit is not as easily to control as a Benthamian panopticon prison.

A sixth dilemma of protectionism could be ideological. Protectionism collides with central soft power contents of the main capitalist countries. The USA, the EU, and Japan, etc., no longer base their soft power on religion, dynasties, and nation, but on universal human rights, democracy and economic liberty. This does not fit together with protectionism, which is asymmetrical and recklessly egoistic instead of being caringly universal and altruistic. Conversely, states have always been very good at materially violating their official soft-power-claims without a great loss of consensus and legitimacy and without generating significant opposition back home. (Populations only tend to discover contradictions after hefty defeats – but not before). This is particularly true in a world, like ours, which marches into a generally bellicose international atmosphere and things get more and more subjected to military logic. We can, thus, eliminate the contradiction between protectionism and the ideology of the leading Western capitalist countries from the list of its dilemmas. To the contrary, the sharpening geopolitical antagonism and international bellicosity will probably give way to more protectionism between the blocks in within the blocks.

After all: Apart from being stuck in tricky practical intricacies, the main dilemmas of protectionism are that it is hopelessly insufficient in generating the necessary prosthetic spending at a world-wide level and that it will be opposed, by economic policies or militarily, by its victims. One the other hand, in an international situation of long-term and grand-scale confrontation between strategic blocs, such as between the West and Russia and the West and China (which may well merge into one, single confrontation), and where geopolitical hostility and military logic increasingly dominate, states care less about "making enemies". In fact, even the intrinsic inefficiencies of protectionism become less burdensome due to parallel sectorization and de-globalization of the world economy. Within blocks countries can also more easily be disciplined to accept protectionism and more political-economic trade-off become possible. While protectionism will, thus, remain at a great distance from solving the problems of world-wide capitalist circuit closure, it may experience a new spring as a prosthetic tool in a partly de-globalized world of militarized block-economies.

Section 3. Redistributive prosthetics funded with redistributive debt

Debt has played a major role in funding prosthetic employment-generating spending at least since the Renaissance.[29] Debt originates as redistributive debt, which is considered in this section, and rises to expansive debt, which is considered in the two following chapters. If we define redistributive debt as debt without money creation, as we do, we must be aware that even commodity money regimes knew some money creation, namely by finding and mining gold or silver. Still, it is useful to begin with this abstraction and to exclude debt, which is enabled by simultaneous money creation for the time being.

Redistributive debt generation

We analyze redistributive debt's prosthetic potential by looking out for preconditions for debt generation. These are: First, money exists; second, debtors are out there willing to take out debt and spend it but are still able, at least in principle, to repay the principal and the agreed-upon interest. Third, there must be debt holders, creditors, who own enough money and are willing to give it away for some time.

The creditors' side

Many people think that if they possessed a lot of money or other wealth, then they would not likely give it away as a money loan and expose it to the risk of not being repaid. They would rather keep it safe or at least invest it in a venture of their own, which they could oversee and manage themselves. There are, though, several errors in this. First, we have already touched upon the fact that *all* wealth, not just debt, is always at risk. Land may become useless if centers of living or of (agrarian or other) production move elsewhere, if the land is exhausted, polluted, destroyed by natural catastrophes or expropriated, or if the small peasants or tenants, who paid rent for the use of the land, die out. Businesses, too, may lose value, even going bust or may be expropriated, either in whole or in part. Even if money is held in bank deposits, it may be lost as banks may go bankrupt; fiat money may lose its value in inflations or currency reforms, or it too may be expropriated. Gold may be robbed or expropriated, and it may also lose value. The first error is, therefore, that all alternatives to giving loans are far from riskless – and what risk will materialize always depends on uncertain future circumstances. The second error: Debt is far less risky than people believe. Even a simple loan without any collateral (in the form of mortgages, pledges, or additional personal guarantors) always involves one build-in security: it involves a *claim for repayment against a debtor as a person*. This person is, regardless of what happens to the loaned money, obliged to repay the loan; in other words, the given away

---

29   See, e.g., *Ferguson* (2008) page 34 et seq., 42 et seq., 71 et seq

money is *secured by all other personal wealth* of the debtor and even by his capability to work or otherwise draw income in the future, including inheritances. Compare that to the risk-position of a wealth owner who poorly invests the money himself. If he opens up a restaurant that fails, then that money is gone for good; if he loans out the money to somebody who opens up a restaurant, then he retains a claim for repayment against the poor restaurant entrepreneur. Fourth, in fact, in many cases creditors can ask for and will receive additional collateral, e.g., pledges or mortgages of assets, assignments of claims for security or guarantees of third parties. A creditor who finances an investment under such circumstances need, then, not worry too much about the investment's merits, but may simply look at the other wealth and solvency of the debtor (and at how many other creditors there are that may compete for the wealth, of course). Fifth, creditors may still, in addition, select the recipient of the loan they hand out according to his experience and qualification and may prefer an experienced restaurant entrepreneur over an unexperienced one. People who are skeptical about debt, sixth, also tend to ignore that ultimately *all income must go through a stage where it has "only" the form of debt.* A private person or a firm making a sale receives a *claim* (bookkeeping entry: debit accounts receivable, credit sales); the same is true for a worker with regard to his wages, a lawyer with regard to his fees, a stockholder with regard to his dividends, and even for the state with regard to their tax claims. In this interim phase, the creditor is always and unavoidably exposed to the risks connected to owning debt, such as unwillingness of the debtor to pay or debtor insolvency. Debt is the pregnancy of new wealth and income comes only into this world through the transitory form of a debt claim. Wealth owners are, thus, ultimately *not* mistaken if they do what they have done for millennia – loan out a significant share of their wealth in money form. The issue on the creditor's side is not such much whether it is smart to give loans, but whether wealth owners have enough money. In the latter regard, as we shall see, the invention of new methods of money creation will greatly help.

The debtors' side

Microeconomically, borrowing in order to make an investment makes economic sense from both the borrower's or debtor's perspective, albeit under certain defined conditions. It makes sense if the additional costs of the loan (interest, fees, etc.) are exceeded by the *higher returns* resulting from the *investment being made earlier* (compared to saving up the required amount) or if a profitable investment is only possible because of the loan. Taking out a loan also makes sense if a spending is very urgent from a consumptive view, e.g., for medical treatment, to celebrate a marriage, for a burial[30] or to purchase an apartment in which to live. The financial surplus-sacrifice (of the interest or of fees) is then willingly accepted in exchange of

---

30 Big thing in history, see *Graeber* (2011) page 9, 131.

the possibility of an *earlier* fulfilment of the need or desire and in some cases, e.g., the purchase of an apartment, rent saved can be off-set against the interest paid.

States seldom borrow because they expect a profit from investing the borrowed money[31] and states do not consume. Why do they take out loans? State borrowing began for warfare in the Renaissance, e.g., in Venice or Florence. States also borrow in times of national catastrophes. Today, they also borrow, fully aware of what they are doing, not only to create new infrastructure values-in-use (built or repair bridges and highways etc.) but in view of the macroeconomic consequences of already the spending of the borrowed money. They borrow with a view to what good the spending of the borrowed money does to its recipients, not to what states get in return for the money.

States, thus, do not follow the normal microeconomic logic that debt financed expenses ought to have an increased return or, at least, be either necessary or urgent. In a world of egoistic M–C–M'-players, states act altruistically.[32] They can afford this as they own, even before money creation exists, a source of income that normal egoistic M–C–M'-players do not possess: The ability to confiscate and to tax their state subjects, and even to sometimes rob wealth or draw tributes from foreign states and tribes.

The money side

A large volume of money must be available for a great many debt contracts to come into being. Its scarcity will restrict debt contracts, but its abundance will propagate them. Quite obviously, if there is only commodity money (mainly gold and silver money), the basis for loans can only grow by finding, mining, or robbing new commodity money. The invention of credit money or state fiat money will, conversely,

---

31   If states borrow money for warfare, they improve their position to either defend against other countries taking away the wealth of their citizens or to appropriate other countries' wealth themselves. If states borrow to finance infrastructure, that improves the conditions for firms in their country. We still do not regard both cases as "investment" by states here as they are not M–C–M'-players themselves. In the case of war financing, the hoped-for advantages also do not accrue through exchange but outside of the economic system (wealth procurement by violence).

32   Private consumers sometimes borrow outside of, as it appears, reasonable economic logic as they borrow to finance their subsistence without a realistic chance to repay their debt. They, hence, take the resulting wave of reminders, threats, legal proceedings, execution, insolvency, penalty interest payment, extraordinary cancellation of loan contracts etc. into account, which involve significant additional costs and a loss of standing. Yet, we might also say that reasonable logic forces them to borrow, even though they cannot repay. Says Zen-Master *Taisen Deshimaru-Roshi*: "Time is the best solution for problems of money and love. If you climb into the coffin, nobody loves you anymore...". *Deshimaru-Roshi* (1994) page 40 (translation by author).

enable much more powerful money creation, thereby massively increasing the basis for loans.

Prosthetics funded by redistributive debt

Debt shifts funds for spending in space

We remind the reader that we still abstract from money creation. We assume the existence of a certain volume of money that only matters for prosthetics. We, e.g., live a commodity money or gold or silver money world, in which further growth of the physical base money is – fictitiously – excluded and where merchant and private bank credit money creation exist as little as state fiat money creation. Establishing a credit and debt relation, thus, can only make use of a temporarily limited and fix volume of gold or silver. Making a loan means moving scarce money from one unit to another, without the creditor possessing the possibility to fill up the resulting hole by easy-to-procure new money. [33]

Debt works via shifting funds for spending *in space*; spending power is directed away from where it originated "naturally" and might otherwise have been applied (or not) and is transferred to the borrower. As borrowers normally have intentions to use borrowed money (and not to hoard it), formerly lazy money is activated more quickly and spent earlier; therefore, redistributive credit also often brings about a shift of spending *in time*; it takes pace earlier. Furthermore, it is likely that the borrower will use it for a *different purpose* than the lender (if the lender were to have used it all). All three dimensions are interesting from the macro-perspective. Debt can increase spending at an earlier point in time; right now, it can redirect spending to a better place, e.g., in our domestic economy, and into better uses, in the productive economy rather than in the sterile economy. We already referred to the last dimension as differences in the *propensity for producive spending*.

Debt is easy because it is consensual – but must be repaid

The debt-based transfer of spending power differs from protectionist redistributive shifts of spending power and from taxation and from other forms of expropriation by being *consensual*. This avoids the dilemmas that enforced ways of money transfer trigger. He who would be an obstinate to-be-expropriated, taxpayer, or victim of protectionism, will be an easy-going voluntary lender and acquiescing creditor. Wealth owners, who would hate to be expropriated or taxed, compete against each other for the chance to give away the same money as a loan.

---

33   Without money creation, we would indeed live in a world similar to the one suggested by mainstreams economics' supply and demand-curves for money, a world in which banks are mere intermediaries of pre-existing money, and where they need to collect money on savings deposits to make loans.

The initial harmony between the givers and receivers[34], though, comes at the price that the loans must (normally) be *repaid*. The borrower/debtor only retains the advantage to *use liquidity for some time*. More present liquidity comes at the cost of a loss of liquidity in the future. The table shows this:

Figure 17: Redistributive debt and the funding of prosthetics I

	Lender	Borrower
Loan given	-1	+1
Loan repaid	+1	-1
Result spending power	±0	±0

Interest and fees further reduce macroeconomic usefulness of debt

But this is not yet the end. The table abstracts from interest and fees, which worsen the situation for the borrower. As interest and fees have to be paid in addition to the repayment of the principal, the total debt service is significantly higher than the amount of the loan and the isolated microeconomic result is often an *overall loss* for the borrower. That is not supposed to be the whole story, though. Microeconomically, as we already saw, if the loan is investive, then the borrower expects an increased profit from being able to make his investment earlier or at all, which he expects to overcompensate the interest and fees, etc. – or he accepts the additional costs to satisfy his consumption need or desire earlier. What happens macroeconomically? When does investive debt financing (of *productive* investments, which only matter for us here) add aggregate prosthetic employment-generating spending? First, if investive employment-generating spending is made out of loans, then their beneficial uses do not retroactively go away if the loan cannot be repaid. Microeconomic and macroeconomic rationality part company. Microeconomically, both the lender and the borrower have failed, but macroeconomically, a beneficial employment effect from the initial employment-generating spending has been achieved. Second, even if the borrower repays the loan and pays interest in full, then an aggregate residual gain in employment-generating spending may still survive – *under certain conditions*. Assume somewhere in ancient Greece, in the Middle Ages or in the industrial revolution, redistributive credit made "lazy" money available to a merchant hero, e.g., via a nautikon daneisma, f(a)enus nauticum, a commenda or

---

34   The borrowers who receive a loan from a hated latifundia owner or from a loan shark at excessive interest, are initially– at least growlingly – grateful for it.

societas maris (for a ship venture[35]) or a straightforward loan to a stock corporation (for a railway venture). If we allow our loan-recipient to complete his venture successfully, repay the loan, and then fail with a second venture, then we have a result roughly as shown in Figure 18.

This Figure shows that the (upper) scenario in which the loan is given has an aggregate producive (employment-generating) spending of 2.7, whereas the scenario in which the loan is not given has zero producive (employment-generating) spending. Even if we deduct the second project's investive producive spending of 1.7 and the entrepreneur's consumption out of the profits of 0.2, then we still have an original producive spending of 1 out of the remaining loan. Thus, debt service out of profits, while it reduces the microeconomic profitability of the investment, does not reduce the original beneficial effect of the loan on producive spending. Conversely, it is quite clear that *not paying interest* or *not repaying the loan* (e.g., by consecutive debt cancellation or partial debt cancellation) raises aggregate producive spending, given that it would allow for further producive spending (instead of sterile "tribute" spending) to be made.

If we look at redistributive *consumptive* debt we find again that the beneficial effects on employment-generating spending do not go away if the loan cannot be repaid. Loans to propertyless workers, e.g., to enable family celebrations, marriages etc., or which are needed in times of catastrophe, e.g., the Corona pandemic, do, thus, not lose their beneficial macroeconomic effects if they cannot be repaid. The loans taken out by decaying former feudal wealth owners to finance their ongoing luxury consumption also only, ultimately, added to aggregate employment-generating spending to the extent they were not repaid. Otherwise, while they allowed for the nobility to distribute the remnants of their wealth more flexibly in time, the interest and fees ate up a part of the value of the mortgaged mansions and drew it into the sterile economy.

---

35   See *Weber* (1980) page 51. These legal forms were mixes between loans, silent partnerships, and partnerships. Rather similar practices existed in Sung China a few centuries before (*McDermott/Yoshinobu*, Economic change in China, 960–1279, page 403).

Figure 18: Redistributive debt and the funding of prosthetics II

	Original loan	First project spend-ing (fully pro-ducive)	First Project revenues	Debt service (repay-ment prin-cipal, interest)	Con-sump-tion by Debtor (fully pro-ducive)	Second project spend-ing (fully pro-ducive)	Second Project revenues (failure)	Aggre-gate pro-ducive spend-ing
Loan given	1	1	3	1.3	0.2	1.5	0	2.7
Loan not given	0	0	0	0	0	0	0	0

The dilemmas of funding prosthetics with redistributive debt

In the above pages on redistributive debt, we have already encountered the first dilemma of funding prosthetics with debt (which applies generally to redistributive and expansive debt alike): *Debt normally has to be repaid* – with interest and fees on top. Yet, the best debt for macroeconomic purposes would be non-repayable debt! The problem with non-repayable debt is, though, the extreme scarcity of credi-tors who are willing to hand out such loans. Rather wealth owners will scrutinize prospective loan customers, force them to make disclosures on all sort of things that could constitute a risk for the debt service and torment them with score-systems, etc., all this with the purpose to deny loans to such applicants (non-repaying) who would macroeconomically best serve the purpose of funding prosthetics with re-distributive debt.[36] Thus, the "repayment-restriction" and "interest-restraint", i.e., ultimately the profit-criterion, pose a dilemma of using debt to generate macroe-conomic employment-generating spending. The profit-criterion also restricts the willingness of prospective debtors to take out loans.

On the other hand, if consumptive loans are handed out and used for employ-ment-generating consumptive spending, the principal is repaid and interest and fees are paid, future consumption will fall below the level where it would be without

---

36   It renders banks more generous towards their worker-customers if they can hope to sell their "NINJA"-loans to each other before their flaw becomes visible – as in the case of subprime loans – or to the central bank – who engages in "quantitative easing". But that normally only becomes a factor under conditions of money creation; hence, where debt is expansive.

the loan; there will, thus, be an aggregate loss of employment-generating spending in consequence of the loan, a macroeconomic loss. Only in the case of investive loans, which are turned into employment-generating and successful investive spending, will there be a significant macroeconomic gain, which will see all participants microeconomically happy. All this is true, as stated previously, for redistribute and expansive debt alike.

Yet, the macroeconomic use of redistributive debt incurs an additional dilemma. In a regime without money creation, e.g., in a commodity money regime (gold or silver money) without any inflows of new gold or silver, money is very scarce. The lending counterparties ought to possess tons or gold and silver (or credit entries covered with them) to serve all hypothetical requests to finance prosthetics, but they do not have them; *there are simply not enough creditors who will lastingly part with their money.* This will educate borrowers to observe traditional limits of borrowing, i.e., mostly to only borrow money transiently in particularly urgent value-in-use-needs or in the case of particularly promising profit expectations. And, of course, they will only borrow at comparatively high interest rates, which will additionally microeconomically shrink the number of debt contracts that come into being and work against a macroeconomic effect of redistributive debt.

The macroeconomic effect of redistributive debt, is, accordingly, restricted by the profit condition imposed upon granting and taking out repayable loans by lenders *and* borrowers, which two conditions can only be conjointly met in the case of a very successful investive spending of the loan by the borrower. It is, additionally, restricted by the limited volume of money available in a world without money creation. Redistributive debt, thus, never rose to the macroeconomic relevance that expansive debt – debt under conditions of money creation – would later acquire, especially in fiat money regimes.

Chapter XI. Expansive prosthetics funded with money creation in commodity money regimes

Money creation enables expansive prosthetics

The preceding chapter looked at monetary regimes, where fictitiously, money creation did not exist at all. The following chapter now examines prosthetic employment-generating spending in monetary regimes, which *do have money creation* – from initially a little money creation to abundant money creation without practical limits. Where newly created money is accepted by markets – otherwise there is no real money creation – it can be used to make purchases. If the money is channeled to the right places who have unfulfilled esoteric demand for goods of the productive economy, its spending spent in the pr effective demand or foreseeable employment-generating spending induces additional production and employment. We shall get to know private banks and the state (which includes its central bank) as the most important origins of new money, i.e., the most important *money creation glands*. From there, the new money is either distributed via loans, e.g., to productive or sterile wealth owners or workers. given to somebody for free, mainly to social security or firms as transfer recipients, or the state itself spends it for what it deems socially advantageous, for the military, for its functionaries, or for the infrastructure. That are the subjects to which this chapter is dedicated.

Higher volume-potential of money creation-boosted prosthetics

Prosthetic spending financed with money creation, has higher volume-potential than redistributive prosthetics. Money creation can be technically effected through a social-economic or evolutionary coming-into-use of new commodities, which are accepted for the purposes of indirect exchange, such as mussels, cows or precious metals. Later money creation may be brought about as an intentional act by a group of people, an institution or the state, who introduce *more* of what is already accepted as money or *some new version* of it, e.g., new, possibly debased, gold or silver coins, token coins made of wholly non-precious metals, merchant credit notes, bank notes, which convey a claim for conversion into gold or silver, notes, e.g., issued by central banks or states, which don't, hence, fiat money notes, entries of credits into bank accounts, or even digital money.

Money creation and fiat money

It is always important to remember that the historic period of money creation is not identical with the period of fiat money regimes. We reiterate once more that already in commodity money regimes there is a significant amount of money creation, by finding, mining and embossing or simply bringing into monetary use new gold or silver. There is also merchant credit money creation and even a very substantial fractional reserves bank credit money creation, before fiat money exists. If fiat money arrives, which only works as state fiat money or a state's central bank fiat money in practice, this only fires up a second stage of money creation, which throws all prior restrictions out the window and allows for the application of the alchemy of money creation at a much more voluminous, much more powerful and, so they say, unlimited scale. Money creation is freed from the fetters of an extrinsically determined base of commodity money, of tons of gold or silver available in vaults, of convertibility requirements, and of reserve fractions or multiples. It is, thus, not at all surprising that state fiat money became the means *par excellence* to – through debt or without it – ultimately fund prosthetic employment-generating spending after other forms of funding hit lasting or transient limits.

The crucial macroeconomic thing for prosthetics is money creation as such, in whatever shape. Money creation, in particular via merchant money creation (promissory notes and bills of exchange), via fractional reserves bank credit money creation, and via fractional reserves central bank or fractional reserves state money creation, was already massively used to mitigate deficient employment generating spending in commodity money regimes. To repeat the point once more: The advent of state fiat money is very important, not because allows money creation for the first time, but (only) because it enables greatly higher, indeed limitless, volumes of money creation than were possible previously.[1]

Combining the deficient-producive-spending-syndrome with insights into monetary history, and assuming that states wish or need to apply prosthetic policies, provides a general thread through economic history. In the present chapter XI, we look, in this sequence, at commodity money creation, merchant credit money

---

1   *Weber* (1980) page 113: "Bei Geldschaffung aus einem ... "beliebig" vermehrbaren Stoff, wie: Papier, gibt es eine solche mechanische Grenze *nicht*. Hier ist dann wirklich der freie Entschluss einer politischen Verbandsleitung ...die von jenen mechanischen Grenzen gelöste Regulator(i)n der Geldquantität."

creation, and private bank credit money creation, at first still in a world of commodity money as base money, and how it is used for prosthetics. We later follow the evolution to a regime of state fiat money as base money and initially examine how prosthetics can be funded by private bank credit money creation in the more abundant world of state fiat money. Ultimately, we shall see that state fiat money creation can fund prosthetic employment-generating spending even independent of private banks. The means of expansive prosthetics, thereby, theoretically, strip off all limitations.

Section 1. Expansive prosthetics funded with commodity money creation

Commodity money creation

In history, the appearance of new commodity money normally enabled new employment-generating spending and greatly pushed production. Had not the Greeks discovered a very rich streak in their silver mine in Laurium right prior thereto, they would likely not have been able to carry out the tremendous productive activity (construction of ports, shipyards, of the trireme fleet, and of weapons), which won them the second Persian war. Europe might be very different then, and we might, of course, not be able to admire the monuments of the classic Greek architectural heritage. Alexander the Great, too, might not have succeeded with his conquests had he not found the Persian kings' silver hoards, which he embossed into money coins.[2] The massive inflow of gold and silver following the Spanish and Portuguese conquests in South America, while it had very mixed results in both Spain and Portugal (the money went into the wealth economy and luxury consumption to a significant degree and caused inflation),[3] after it had travelled to Asia and China, though, helped out the economy of the Ming dynasty there.[4]

---

2   Clauss (1993) page 96.
3   *Graeber* (2011) page 309, 311 et seq.; *Bonn* (1896) page 180.
4   Previously, the Ming dynasty, under its first emperor Hung wu, the former rebellion leader of the Red Turbans, for the lack of sufficient gold or silver and, probably more so to procure itself a money creation gland, had attempted to introduce a fiat money system based on non-convertible paper money while suppressing the use of silver and copper. The attempt largely failed. Increasingly, though, silver arrived in China from Potosi via Spain. Between 1540 and 1600 these annual silver imports rose from 40.000 kilograms to at least 150.000 kilograms. The silver was used as un-minted money. See *Heijdra*, The socio-economic development of rural China during the Ming, page 453 et seqs. and *Huang*, The Ming fiscal adminstration, page 148, 149. According to Jacques Gernet, about half of the 400 Millions Silver Dollars imported from South America and Mexico between 1571 and 1821 was used to buy luxury goods in China (*Gernet* (1972) page 47).

The dilemmas of funding prosthetics with commodity money creation

Still, funding prosthetic employment-generating spending through commodity money creation is restricted by the difficulty or almost-impossibility of procuring new commodity money in a planned and controlled way in sufficient volumes at the times when it is needed. State organized campaigns to search for gold or silver were, overall, almost as unsuccessful as state-sponsored or private attempts to artificially produce gold or silver by alchemy. Gold rushes in California, Alaska, Australia, South Africa, and other places were insufficient and uncontrollable too.

Two early related practices in commodity money regimes anticipated fiat money. They consisted in either adding an open seignorage (raising the official nominal embossed value of a gold or silver coin beyond the market value of the precious metal in it) or by secretly reducing the precious metal content of coins, e.g., by adding lead.[5] A third practice was made possible by specifics of the Chinese monetary system. Since the Qu'in, cupper coins with a square hole in the middle were used, and, given the relatively low value of a single coin, it was customary to connect to large numbers by putting a string through their holes, whereby "strings" became the de facto units of payment. In periods of scarcity of cupper, the Sung fiscal administration would now allow the use of "short string" of only 770 coins rather than of normal strings with 1000 coins.[6] But all these methods only worked for a short time. They were resented by markets and led to inflation. Often their quantitative effects were also too limited to make them a powerful instrument of money creation.

It is quite noteworthy that the preceding forms of commodity money creation – finding and mining, debasement and seignorage – operated without any trace of debt being involved. That would all change with merchant credit money creation and fractional reserves credit money creation.

---

5   The practice of debasement is well known with regard to European princes, but it also already existed in the 2nd century BC in the Chinese Han dynasty, where we witness an oscillation between state monopolies for the minting of the square-holed cupper coins and private minting, and between aggressive an moderate debasement; occasionally, even undebased coins were minted. At the times we also see experiments with state fiat money in the form of deerskin (*Sadao*, The economic and social history of former Han, page 587). The social reformer Wang Mang (9–23 AD), too, resorted to the debasement of coins (*Bielenstein*, Wang Mang, The restoration of the Han dynasty, and later Han, page 232).

6   *Golas*, The Sung fiscal administration, page 208.

Section 2. Expansive prosthetics funded with merchant credit money creation

Merchant credit money creation

Trade as inventor of facilitations of trade

In a commercial deal, both parties cooperate to expedite its execution. The buyer wants the delivery of the goods as quickly as possible. And, if the seller can be secure to receive the purchase price, he will also support the buyer to become liquid again as quickly as possible. Merchants developed several techniques particularly addressed to further this goal. In fact, they were the first to create credit money, merchant credit money. It all begins with the debt moment that is already present in the simplest exchange contract. We start with this moment and see how merchants worked it out into a classic form of securitization.

A transactional analysis of exchange reveals that the parties must, before they factually exchange commodities against money, already be legally bound to carry through the exchange, as jurists say "a logical second" in advance. This avoids the possibility that a party can change its mind in the middle of the process; e.g., if the commodity is handed over before the payment, then the buyer can no longer say "I don't want it" or "I take it only as a gift", etc. The theoretical distinction between the closure of binding contractual obligations and their fulfillment even exists if the commodity and the money are exchanged instantly when the purchase contract is closed.

Legal claims as genes of merchant credit money

Beginning from this point, the parties may stipulate the lapse of a shorter or longer time between creation and fulfilment of the legal obligation. If the delivery of the commodity comes first, its use by the buyer may, thereby, be de-coupled from the payment by the buyer. *This trivial legal option of dated payment already has macroeconomic potential*; it opens up the possibility for a purchaser to receive a commodity today, even if he does not have the money yet. Received commodities can, thus, already be further forwarded or processed by the buyer before they are paid for and this expedites the circuits of the economy and employment, albeit only by a small margin. The silver coins for a payment by a Spaniard to a merchant in Rotterdam may still be on a ship from the Americas to Sevilla, but if the Spanish buyer is regarded as being solvent, then the trust that the money will later be forthcoming travels before the physical coins and the Spanish buyer's promise to pay later may cause the merchant in Rotterdam to already deliver goods today.

So far, this only expedites the M–C-leg of the circuit on the part of the Spanish buyer. Should merchant practices not also be capable of expediting the C–M'-leg and a future M–C-leg of the circuit of the seller, in the example of the selling Rotterdam merchant? As the Rotterdam seller already has the claim for the purchase price, and as his Spanish debtor is assumedly solvent, could he not *simply assign his claim* for the purchase price and use this assignment as payment for a new M–C-order, e.g., to an Edinburgh-based merchant? If this were possible, then the gold or silver coins, which are still gently rocking on the ship to Sevilla, could become instrumental to yet another circuit and could expedite the closing of the seller's M–C–M'.

Securization as promissory notes and bills of exchange

While this legal possibility undoubtedly always exists – it is necessary a moment of the logic of a sales transaction –, merely contractual claims are still very individualistic and insecure. Therefore, the assignment of claims for a purchase price as such did not rise to the status of becoming a general instrument of settling accounts between merchants in long distance commerce and no market developed in which such claims were traded. However, this very same transactional debt-moment, which is intrinsic in all exchange contracts, allowed to being *evolved into promissory notes and bills of exchange*, which carried more security and became tradable and negotiable instruments for merchants. They turned into merchant credit money, which grew crucially important in international commerce over centuries. Merchant credit money took three forms, the promissory note, the merchant's bill of exchange, and, ultimately, the bank cheque, too. The *promissory note* is the simplest form of merchant credit money, a signed written confirmation to owe money (an "I owe you", IOU), e.g., out of a sales contract or to settle a dispute, to a payee, either to any holder of the note or to a named person. E.g., our Spanish buyer, who received the delivery of commodities, might write out a promissory note to his supplier in Rotterdam if the gold is still rocking on the ocean or he wants to otherwise use it. The Rotterdam supplier takes the promissory note instead of waiting for cash (as he trusts in the solvency of his Spanish customer and in its liquidity when the note is due).[7] Moreover, by signing the promissory note, he who signs it assumes a *personal additional and legally separate liability to pay*, which is stronger than the mere payment debt out of

---

7   Already at the end of the Chinese T'ang dynasty (late 9th century AD) merchants engaged in long distance trade drew up and exchanged paper documents, probably like bills or drafts (see *McDermott/Yoshinobu*, Economic change in China, 960–1279, page 403). If *McDermott/Yoshinobu* speak of a "private use of paper money" in this context, it must be stressed that these papers were certainly no fiat money but probably merchants credit money. In the late 9th century A.D. certificates of deposit were also issued at Sh'ang An (ibidem), which resembled, in their function, to the original certificates of the Amsterdam Wisselbank 700 years later; yet they were issued by provincial government officials rather than by a private bank. The Chinese Sung dynasty, in 985, would hand over vouchers to its army provisioners far up in north China, which could either be redeemed in cash or exchanged for tea voucher, which could then be redeemed against tea in south China, or which would be traded amongst merchants (*Golas*, The Sung fiscal administration, page 198).

the purchase contract. The promissory note not only excludes the objection that the underlying commodities were not delivered or were defectiv, but is also subjected to special rules of civil procedure that expedite and ease enforcement; it is legally "stronger" than a mere claim for payment.

Instead of signing a promissory note, a recipient of a delivery, e.g., our Spanish buyer, may also involve other persons, who are not parties to the original sales contract, in the process of merchant credit money creation. For this purpose, he may "draw" a *bill of exchange* (or a "draft") on, say, his customer in Paris to whom he sells the commodities. Such a bill of exchange brings a triangle structure into being. It is an order by one person, the *drawer* (in our case the first recipient of the commodities, the Spanish buyer), to another person, the *drawee* (the customer in Paris), to pay money to a third person who is also called the *payee* (in our case the original supplier from Rotterdam). The drawee, the second recipient of the commodities in Paris, of course, only becomes liable to pay the bill if he himself makes a declaration of will to this effect. He typically does this by signing the bill as *"acceptor"*. The second recipient of the commodities, the person in Paris in our example, will often be ready to sign as acceptor as he will otherwise, quite simply, not receive the delivery just yet. By adding an acceptor as a further debtor, the bill becomes more secure and this increases the readiness of the first supplier in Rotterdam to accept it.

Third signatories adding security and tradability

Because they are detached from the original transaction (as mentioned, the objection that the underlying commodities were not delivered or were defective is excluded and their enforcement before civil courts is expedited), promissory notes and bills of exchange become *tradable or negotiable*. They may be *endorsed* by the payee (in Rotterdam) to third parties (in Edinburgh) who may in turn endorse it further (to parties in the US). Such endorsers normally also become liable to pay the bill like a *guarantor*. He who later holds the bill, may, thus, claim payment against the drawer, the acceptor, and all endorsers who are jointly and severally liable debtors when it becomes due; thus, a polygonal structure emerges.

As we mentioned already twice, a promissory note and a bill of exchange have the effect of improving the seller's legal and procedural position, compared to the mere assignment of a purchase price claim. Their main economic improvement is based on this and on the bill gaining security with each signatory and on promissory notes and bills being tradable or negotiable instruments. A supplier can already pay his own suppliers by endorsing a promissory note or bill and, therefore, can make new purchases and receive their delivery, typically inventories, for the next M–C–M'-circuit. To that end, bills of exchange de facto substitute gold or silver money and allow their holders to quasi "pay" with them instead of cash from a macroeconomic perspective. The gold or silver coins keep rocking on the ship to Sevilla, but merchant credit money creation has already made several uses of them in expediting their deal-making. There is no chance that new commodity money could have been created so conveniently to close the transactions.

Those who sign promissory notes or bills may *or may not* hold and maintain a 100 % reserve in commodity money somewhere. If they do, and as long the full amount of gold or silver is indeed in their possession, then no additional new money is created? If the gold or silver payment they promise is not already, or no longer kept in reserve, then the stock of pre-existing money is enlarged, *new money – merchant credit money – is created*. Such merchant credit money is comparable to von Mises' circulation credit[8] which is created by banks out of fiduciary media, or what we will call fractional reserve bank credit money. While fractional reserve bank credit money disappears again, when a loan is repaid, merchant credit money disappears with the final settlement of the promissory note or bill.

Banks: Discounting promissory note and bills – and signing checks

Banks developed roughly in parallel to merchants' promissory notes and bills of exchange. A first way for banks to come into play was by *discounting promissory notes and bills*. Instead of holders waiting until the promissory note or bill became due, or until they would find another merchant to take them as payment, holders would carry them to banks and immediately receive cash for them. This involved credit by the bank – the note was only due later – and the bank assumed the holder's risk. The bank also wanted a profit. Therefore, the bank paid less than the note's nominal amount, which was called *the discount*. A second way for banks to get involved was to allow their depositors to draw bills of exchange *on them*. A bill of exchange drawn on a bank (as *drawee*) is called *bank check* (or *bank cheque* or, simply, a check or cheque). Checks would be drawn on banks by bank customers. The very drawing of a check would only *entitle* the bank vis-à-vis to make a payment, e.g., out of money of the depositor's account, to the check-holder; thereby, the bank did not yet assume a legal obligation vis-à-vis the check-holder. In this case, banks' wealth would not increase the security of the check and the checks would not convey better security than notes or bills (without acceptor or other additional debtor). But banks could also accept checks (as *acceptor*), whereby they would personally become liable to the check-holder; these checks would become more secure. Checks, too, can be endorsed and endorsers, like drawers, normally become jointly and severally liable, further increasing the security of the check.

---

8   E.g.: "The fiduciary media affect the market phenomena in the same way as money does. Changes in their quantity influence the determination of money's purchasing power." (*von Mises* (1949) page 434) or: "It is important to realize that commodity credit cannot be expanded. The only vehicle of credit expansion is circulation credit." (*von Mises* (1949) page 434). Von Mises does not take finding new mines or robbing existing precious metals into account here.

Legislation on checks often prohibited or restricted the acceptance of checks by banks. States sought to, thereby, prevent checks from being used instead of bank notes and closed the door for banks to circumvent state regulations on the creation of bank fractional reserve credit money through bank notes. Today, for the emergence of bank deposit accounts, checks are very seldom used and bank laws have often become more liberal in this regard.

The dilemmas of funding prosthetics with merchant credit money creation

The dilemmas of prosthetic spending, enabled by merchant credit money creation in regimes of commodity money, result from notes, bills and checks only evolving out of specific commercial transactions, these possessing a significant level of complexity, involving significant information necessities for users, and carrying costs and unavoidable remaining risks.

The number of notes and bills is, in particular, limited by the number of the members of the merchant class with a rank and reputation of solvency that their notes, bills and checks are trusted. It is also limited by the volume of commercial transactions, in which such trustworthy merchants actually engage. Furthermore, there is a price for the "self-made-ness" of merchant credit money: The creation of merchant credit money takes a certain level of effort, coordination, information, communication, and persuasion– and even that will not always ascertain that it succeeds. It also often necessitates the help of lawyers. Not everybody will be equally capable of assessing the risks connected to taking or endorsing a note or bill and not everybody else will take it as payment because prospective holders may have different information.

Of course, the security of a promissory note, bill or check is of crucial importance. Even if it conveys a *strong* legal position, the security of payment still ultimately depends on the solvency of the drawer, drawee, acceptors, and endorsers or other guarantors. Merchants must, thus, take remaining risks and assess them. Time, once more, is an issue. A debtor-counter-party may be initially solvent, but no more by the time the promissory note, bill or check is due.[9] While a gold of silver payment is solid, the final word about a payment with an endorsed note, bill or check will only be spoken after they have been presented to the signatories. Bad surprises are especially possible if the solvability of several signatories depends on the fate of the same single trade system. A settlement by notes, drafts or checks, which appeared to have worked well and may almost be forgotten about, may retroactively turn badly sour and he who took one of these instruments, and who endorsed and forwarded

---

9   Indeed, few can dare to feel sure to be solvent and liquid at a future date as typically their solvency and liquidity, apart from natural, economic and political catastrophes, depends on whether the counterparties in their networks of exchanges are solvent or at least liquid.

it to his supplier in turn, may later even find that he thereby became jointly and severally liable to a successive holder for the full amount (plus interest and costs). This plunges merchant credit money into a *flickering uncertainty* in the otherwise brazen world of payments by gold and silver. That feeds back on the readiness of merchants to accept merchant credit money, etc.

Sometimes drawers and drawees were also known to consciously do things that render notes, bills or checks less secure. Thanks to their money creation effect, signing notes and accepting drafts became a means of survival for businesses in trouble, including to prolong the life of otherwise totally insolvent firms. And it sometimes was a gimmick in the hand of fraudsters. A note is normally signed or a bill drawn if a commodity is in production or already being transported to the buyer; in this case, the buyer gives credit (makes an advance of the promissory note or bill) to the seller. Alternatively, the commodity has already been delivered to the buyer; in this case, the seller gives credit (in the amount of the difference in value-in-exchange between the promissory note or bill and gold or silver money) to the buyer. Both cases, though, share in common that there is at least *a commodity around*, which normally has a certain value-in-exchange close to the original contractual debt, and to which the creditor has a legal claim (either for delivery or for return if it is not paid). This adds some security.[10] However, parties that have exhausted their reserves and are no longer eligible for bank loans or private credit or who commit fraud, may use notes and bills to "mine" merchant credit money *ex nihilo* without any legal claim for a valuable good existing. E.g., if A and B both sign promissory notes for each other, without an underlying commercial transaction, notes have been issued without such additional value-in-exchange of a given commodity in play. The same is true if two people, once more without an underlying commercial transaction, draw bills on each other and are able to endorse them.[11] This drawing and redrawing of bills ("bill jobbing") is, in fact, a classic example of the underworld of abusing notes and bills.[12] In the end, merchant credit money creation remained far too limited in

---

10   It is, at first, only comparable to a bank holding reserves in commodity money for credit money. Holding reserves and being solvent are entirely different things, but still, reserves will often increase the bank's solvency (see on page 72 et seq.) Furthermore, the travelling commodities can be legally used as collateral, e.g., by retention of title provisions, etc.

11   This does neither imply the creation of counterfeit bill (with a fake signature) nor necessarily a deception by the acceptor. There may have simply been a misjudgment about his future solvency, hence, e.g., about the solvency of others, the market, or the lack of adverse events.

12   If "bill jobbing" spells the pathology of merchants' bills of exchange, it neither necessarily implies that A or B must have fraudulent intentions nor that the bill will not be honored. A and B may feel sufficiently solvent and may expect to be liquid on the due date, independently of the underlying transaction-value and even the payee or endorsers may not be worried that no new value-in-exchange is created together with the bill in the form of a new commodity, e.g., in view of the abundant other wealth of the drawer, drawee, or

scope, transactionally too complex, and too risky to satisfy the macroeconomic desires of money creation for prosthetics. Of course, during the heyday of merchant credit money, the necessity of prosthetics was also mostly not as perceivable as it would become in modern capitalism when the modern master drama accentuated.

Section 3. Expansive prosthetics funded with private bank credit money creation

Fractional reserves bank credit money creation in commodity money regimes

A first artificial money creation gland being born

The invention of bank fractional reserve credit money creation was of the utmost historical importance as it gave birth to a first powerful money creation gland. It was in banking, not in laboratories and by chemistry, where the dream of the alchemists was fulfilled. No test tubes, no fire, and no bizarre technology was needed for the purpose, only bookkeeping and the printing of statements of accounts (or bank notes or, albeit to a less relevant extent, the embossing of aluminum, iron, or other low value metal token money).

The gland of banks' money creation enabled the creation of something to which people would attribute tremendously more value-in-exchange than the costs of its production. This pushed down the costs of the generation of new value-in-exchange to about the costs of generation of debt, of mere paperwork. We have seen that commodity money and state fiat money have no trace of debt in them. That is different with merchant credit money. Like merchant credit money, private bank credit money, involves debt. It is, indeed, the offspring of a noble and privileged segment of merchants: Bank credit money creation works by the state allowing this segment, banks, to *sell some of their debt as money*.[13]

---

acceptor. How the law on bills of exchanges and merchant practices deal with this, in a way, resembles how bank codes regulate banks.

13   *Luhmann* (1988) page 145: "Die Banken haben das Zentralprivileg, ihre eigenen Schulden mit Gewinn verkaufen zu können…". "Geldschöpfung seitens der Banken" erfolgt, sagt Schumpeter, "durch Konstituierung von Forderungen gegen sich selbst." *Schumpeter* (1912) page 202. Schumpeter also quotes *Fetter* saying that a bank is "a business whose income is mainly derived from lending its promises to pay" (page 203). This insight, which would probably still irritate a significant percentage of otherwise well-educated people, is widely accepted in economics. "…our money mostly consists of the transferrable debts of banks to account holders" (*Wolf*, The threat and the promise of digital money, in: *Financial Times* of 23 October 2019). Wolf also writes "What makes banks special is that their liabilities are money – a universally acceptable IOU" (*Wolf*, Fear of hyperinflation is a delusion of the ignorant, in: *Financial Times* of 11 April 2014).

There are *two forms* of debt involved in bank credit money creation: the entry of a *credit on the bank-customers' deposit account* (this bank-debt to the customer *is* already money and is transmutable into other forms of money, such as bank notes, central bank notes, or token coins)[14] and the entry of a *debit on the customers loan account*, which remains the customer's normal bastard debt to the bank.

The activities of banks connected to merchants' promissory notes, to bills of exchange or to bank checks, remained far less important than the monetary activities that banks would, in parallel or later, develop in the new field of bank notes, bank deposits, and token coins. As we are still in the world of commodity money, if banks wrote out bank notes, entered credits on deposit accounts, or issued token coins, then the positions gained by bank-customers were still comparable to promissory notes (thus *"bank note"*); they conveyed a hard claim against the bank for the delivery of gold or silver.

Credit money without money creation: The early Wisselbank

We shall look in greater detail at when bank credit money involves money creation. The premier way for credit money to come into being in the world of commodity money was for customers to pay gold or silver money "into" their own accounts with a bank, as they did with the *Amsterdam Wisselbank* (founded 1609), allegedly the first modern bank. This first allowed cash-free transfers between customer with accounts with the same bank. Customers who had physically carried gold or silver money (coins or bullion) to the Wisselbank received "receipts". These receipts were evidence for a claim against the bank for the money deposited and could be used to make payments like with bank notes. There was, thus, initially no differentiation yet between a ledger evidencing a claim against the Wisselbank and its banknotes.[15] For the bank,

---

14   Banks, of course, also have conventional "bastard debt", e.g., they may owe rent to landlords or salaries to their employees. Even then, though, they can normally honor that debt by paying with self-created money – through entering a credit on the landlord's or the employees' account.

15   Similarly, already in T'ang China a practice had developed to deposit goods or money in shops against "certificates of deposit". Early in the 11th century, the state established a private monopoly for accepting such deposits but shortly afterwards took over this monopoly itself as a "Paper Money Office". This office soon confused this Wisselbank-like loaning-business with the creation of naked or somewhat blurred state fiat money, but, by the middle of the 13th century, failed. They later Yüan dynasty (1279–1368 AD) and the Ming dynasty (1368–1644 AD) also experimented with fiat money, but largely failed, too. Luckily as from the 16th century, significant volumes of European silver, from increased mining in Europe itself, and South American silver, either via the Pacific and Manila or Spain or Portugal, found its way to China and enabled the necessary (commodity money) creation (as unminted silver). That did not help further efforts of the state to introduce state fiat money. Obviously, the monetary evolution in China never nearly as much as in Europe discovered private banks' fractional reserves credit money creation as a tool. See *Golas*, The Sung fiscal

the receipt of commodity money was a balance sheet extension; the incoming gold or silver extended their assets side, the claim of the depositor, evidenced by the receipt, extended the bank's liabilities' side.

At first, although credit money was issued at the Wisselbank, *no* money was created. The Wisselbank *generated credit money* that entered circulation, but as, by the same token, it *withdrew the same amount of commodity money* from circulation, which was brought to rest in the bank's vaults,[16] the aggregate volume of money was not increased.

We now leave the Wisselbank and look at banks in general: If a customer wants to make a payment from his deposit account with a bank, and if the intended recipient has an account with the *same bank*, then the first customer's account with the bank is debited and the recipient's account credited, but all customers' physical balance of gold or silver money with the bank remains untouched. If a customer wants to make a payment to a customer from another bank, the first bank can either physically forward commodity money to the second bank or there has to be some other institution in which both banks have accounts. Such institutions can be other banks, clearing houses, or the central bank. Still, much like before, as long as the commodity money remains blocked at the first bank and the bank credit money only moves to another balance sheet, then no new money is created. This situation could be captured by the image (which sometimes laymen have anyhow) that for each bank note, deposit account, or token there is a physical box in the bank with the number of the note, deposit account, or token on it, in which the gold or silver "covering" the note, token, or account is safeguarded and from which account-related money is moved to other boxes or to another bank after transfers or which is given to the customer if he presents his banknote or token coin for conversion. *Von Mises*, in this sense, compared keeping a physical reserve of commodity money with "coat tokens" handed out by a cloakroom attendant for coats deposited. This highlights the crucial macroeconomic point: The coat is either with the coat owner or in the cloakroom, but no doubling of coats takes place. This is the same when the bank note circulates instead of the commodity money; no money is doubled as the holder of the bank note cannot use the commodity money in the vaults while he holds the banknote.[17] Banks may

---

administration, page 210 et seq. and *Atwell*, Ming China and the emerging world economy c. 1470–1650, page 381 et seqs.

16   *Ferguson* (2008) page 49.

17   The comparison is not perfect from a legal point of view. The holder of a note or depositor of an account, even if they qualify as money certificate, are *not the owner* of the commodity money, to which it entitles. Without the – quite atypical and constructed – assumption that the legal claim of the note holder or depositor is completely independent of the debtors' economic fate, including insolvency, the claim represented by a note or account would also be less secure than the claim of the depositor of the coat. Even if a bank held a 100 % reserve of commodity money for every unit of commodity money owed because of an issued

of course, as they usually do, put all gold and silver money *together in one big vault* instead of allocating individual gold or silver coins to bank notes, deposits, or tokens by putting them into separate boxes. As long as they ensure that the volume of money in the commonly used vault remains equal to or higher than the credit money issued, then no money is created.[18]

Credit money involving money creation

Things, however, change fundamentally – from a microeconomic and macroeconomic perspective – if the bank gives away the gold or silver money for which it has issued notes or tokens or for which it has entered credit on deposit accounts, *even while these notes or credit entries or token coins are still outstanding.* Imagine that banks buy wealth assets with such gold or silver or lent it out. Then, the commodity money and the credit money, which conveys a claim for the commodity money, are *both used at the same time.* Commodity money and the credit money representing it are both simultaneously operative, a doubling of circulating money and money creation takes place.

Moreover, money creation can also take place if the bank keeps the commodity money in the vaults and simply issues more credit money – by bank notes, credit entries, on deposit accounts or token coins – *than its reserves in commodity money.* In this case, the amount of credit money created over the stock of commodity money sitting in the bank's vaults is newly created money.[19] In von Mises' terms, the bank exceeds the limits of a "money certificate" or of a "money substitute" and brings a "fiduciary media of exchange" or "circulation credit" into being.

---

bank note, credit entry or token, as it would normally also be liable with that commodity money to other creditors, the commodity could be lost if the bank suffers losses, in part or in whole. That would then only be credit money, no longer a money certificate in the sense of von Mises.

18   While a museum visitor would be alienated if he receives another coat for his token, it does not matter for bank customers which gold or silver pieces they get back.

19   *Myers/Wang*, Economic developments, 1644–1900, page 629, report that Chinese banks of the late 18th century, e.g., in Ningbo, applied both practices (to loan out the silver or cash deposits or to increase issued notes beyond deposits). Both methods involved money creation. Yet, while China even used "paper money", which was, in fact, fiat money, already in the Sung and Yüan dynasties, the potential of money creation, credit and fiat money, did not nearly evolve as dynamically as in Europe. This had already been true with regard to merchant credit money creation, which suffered from China's withdrawal from maritime trade after glorious times of Zheng He under the Sung. The record with regard to private banks' fractional reserves credit money creation is by no means better. Banking, and, thus, private credit money creation, was only made a material factor by colonial powers, in particular by the U.K. after 1840. The first central bank of China opened not before 1908. The underdevelopment of the monetary and credit system massively contributed to China economically falling back against the West in the 19th century.

To repeat, if fractional reserve credit money is issued, then money is created in the excess of the issued bank credit money over the gold or silver money held in the reserve.[20] Money creation by banks, while it involves exceeding the commodity money in their reserves by issuing credit money (which could be easily noted by an observer with full information after a bit of math), may remain invisible to the public for a while. For instance, the aforementioned Amsterdam Wisselbank could, ultimately, not withstand using its initially extremely good standing to later greatly exceed its reserves by issuing credit money; that was punished and it had to be dissolved.[21]

A cycle of credit money creation

Banks are M–C–M'-players motivated by profit themselves, more specifically M–M'-players. When they still only issue receipts (as initially the Wisselbank) or bank notes, for which full reserves are held, they learn quickly that it is normally[22] highly unlikely for a great number of receipt holders or banknote holders or other depositors to simultaneously demand conversion of their claims into deposited gold or silver money. It may be advisable to look at this process (which is basically the same for bank money creation in fiat money regimes) in greater detail: When banks create money by issuing credit money, "paying out" a loan, as we saw, normally only means *making two bookkeeping entries*, a credit in favor of the customer on their deposit account with the bank and a debit on their loan account with the bank; together, they are a balance sheet extension for the bank. On the side of the credit customer, there is a balance sheet extension too. If the loan finances purchasing a house and the seller of the house also has an account with the same bank, then the loan is "paid out" by deleting the credit on the buyer-customer's deposit account and by entering a credit of the same amount on the seller-customer's deposit account. This is an exchange of liabilities for the bank and its balance sheet remains as extended as before; it now has a debt to the seller-customer (rather than to the buyer-customer), but still a loan repayment-claim against the buyer-customer. If everything goes well, then the buyer-customer, uses parts of his income to "re"-pay the loan as time goes by, e.g., of rent

---

20   "Breaking the link between money creation and a metallic anchor has led to an unprecedented monetary expansion..." See *Ferguson* (2008) page 63. This can apply either to the introduction of fractional reserve banking or fiat money.

21   From 1609 to 1672, Sismondi tells us, the bank continued to execute "religieusement ses engagements, et à conserver intact, dans ses coffres, le dépôt immense qui lui avait été confié." In the middle of the 18th century, however, it began to abuse its credit and "à prêter le capital qui était mort dans ses coffres à la Compagnie des Indes, aux provinces de Hollande et de West-Frise, et à la ville d' Amsterdam". When the French invaded in 1794, it had to disclose the "secret longtemps caché" and went bankrupt. (*Sismondi* (1827) page 79).

22   The opposite is true in stampede-like bank runs.

he collects for the house. He could do this by actually carrying gold or silver money to the bank; the bank would then put this commodity money in its vaults and reduce the buyer-customer's debit on the loan account. What is more likely, though, is that the buyer-customer will receive bank transfers from other bank-customers, which are credited to his deposit account, and which they will use to run down the debit on the loan account. If the loan is fully repaid, then the bank may have partially more commodity money in its vault, partially less debt to other customers, and partially more claims against other customers. The new money was born with the extension of the credit side on the buyer-customer's deposit account and on the debit side of their loan account. The credit on the deposit account "wandered" into the seller-customer's deposit account and the debit on the loan account disappeared via reductions of credits on other customers' deposit accounts, increase of their debts on accounts, or by increased gold or silver in the bank's vaults. In addition, the bank has a profit left in the amount of the interest (plus fees etc. minus operating costs), which the buyer-customer also paid over the years as part of their annuities.

The course of events would not be much different if the seller has an account with another bank. If only a basic cooperation between banks exists, then the buyer's bank would not carry gold or silver money to the seller's bank, but the account of the seller's bank with another bank, a clearing house, or the central bank would be credited and banks would only pay peak amounts that remain after offset in gold or silver, if they pay anything at all.

The banks' power to create money, to repeat, is based on their stunning and miraculous capacity to *pay bastard debt, including their own bastard debt, with other own debt* of a special type and this is possible as this second and special type of their *debt is accepted as credit money.* The bank fulfills its legal obligation, one debt (the bastard debt) to pay "out" the loan by simply assuming *another* debt, first to its loan customer, then to other customers or other banks, with a little luck, without having to touch one ounce of commodity money. As the banking system proliferates and gets more mature, this *shifting around of bank debt* can go on for a long time without ever touching gold or silver.[23]

The security of credit money

So far, we have looked at bank credit money from the macroeconomic perspective of whether and when it involved money creation, which was the case when its amount exceeded reserves. As stated in the Foreword, the microeconomic question of the *value and security of bank credit money,* or of the value and security of a claim against a

---

23   Non-bank units, e.g., normal bank customers, conversely, cannot act the same way, of course. A non-bank unit, in order to relinquish payment debt, cannot generate other debt from itself; it has to either procure bank debt, which is bank credit money, or to deliver hard gold or silver.

bank for conversion of bank notes or credits on deposit accounts etc. in commodity money, is a different story. The person who holds commodity money in kind (like gold or silver coins or bullion), thanks to the possibility to sell it as demonetized gold or silver, enjoys the simplest imaginable downside-protection. In order to assess the minimum value of their commodity money, it only has to follow the market for the money-thing, which his commodity money is or what it carries "piggyback".[24] As long as the commodity money's value as money is higher, i.e., it is still traded at its nominal value with a seignorage, then he will continue to use it as commodity money; if not, he will de-monetize it and use it as simple gold or silver.

The holder of credit money in a commodity money regime, however, enjoys no such downwards-protection. Only if the bank is fully solvent, then the credit money holder can convert his credit money into commodity money and from there everything is as it was before. If the bank is only partially solvent or is insolvent, the credit money holder will lose a part of the amount at which the credit money was issued. The important point to grasp is that whether 100 % of reserves are held by the bank against the issued credit money or not does *not conclusively spell whether the bank is also solvent to honor the conversion claims or other claims of credit money holders*. Money creation depends on whether simultaneously with issuing credit money the same amount of commodity money is put to rest in vaults, solvency depends upon the relationship of the *aggregate of the assets side* to the *aggregate of due liabilities*. Solvency does *not* depend on whether there is an amount of gold or silver somewhere that adds up to amount of freshly created money.[25] While it seldom harms anyone to own gold or silver, holding 100 % reserves for issued credit money is, thus, no guarantee for credit money's security. Conversely, a bank may be highly solvent even if it holds gold and silver reserves well short of the credit money created.[26] This is so, at least, as long as the public trusts in this banks credit money – as long as this trust is there, its credit money is as good as the commodity money in its vaults.

Bank runs and bail-outs in commodity money regimes

Yet, fractional reserves banks in commodity money regimes still ultimately rely on the convertibility of their credit money into commodity money. If too many customers demand payment in commodity money, typically because they doubt, often even mistakenly, the bank's liquidity or solvency, then this is called a "bank run".

---

24   See on page 70 et seq.

25   See on page 72 et seq.

26   In monetary debates, economists who are critical of bank credit money creation mostly use both arguments and sometimes confuse them, e.g., the British Bullionists in their debate with Anti-Bullionists around 1810, who argued in favor of the convertibility of bank credit money into gold money, or the Currency School in its debate with the Banking School, who argued in favor of limiting the issuance of bank credit money to gold held in reserves.

Note that this may hit banks, which are perfectly solvent, hence, whose assets by far exceed their debts. Yet, they only have the problem that their credit money exceeds their commodity money – and this problem, they have by definition – because they are "fractional reserves" banks. This is when central banks come into play with bail-outs. Bail-outs classically took the form of commodity money lending, with the central bank acting, in the often-quoted words of *Walter Bagehot*, as the "lender of last resort". In bail-outs, private banks receive commodity money loans from central banks, secured by assets, which are obviously not commodity money, as collateral. The interest rate applied and the conditions reflect the availability of commodity money for central banks, the views on the risk of the general economic situation, and the views on the special risks of the assets that the bailed-out bank provides as collateral and of this bank.

The most critical problem of bail-outs in commodity money regimes, of course, was the commodity money; gold and silver was even scarce for the central bank.[27] Bailing-out private banks in a commodity money regime, accordingly, was not only a question of will, but crucially mainly a matter of available means. Central banks could be lucky, though, and the creditors of the troubled bank might accept credit money issued by other private banks or by the central bank. Nevertheless, the ultimate limit for central bank bail-outs was set by the volume of commodity money somewhere available. Therefore, the principle applied, as *Walter Bagehot* has famously put it in 1873, was that central banks should *lend freely but at a penalty*. This way, banks would be sanctioned for over-aggressive "over-lending".[28] The principle worked its way backwards into preventive regulation and policing of private banks' credit money creation and private banking in general. States knew that private banks' profit motive would drive them to over-use their money creation gland and did not want to risk the precious commodity money reserves on altruistic emergency missions in favor of overly greedy banks too often. The central bank had rather to maintain its lending power in commodity money for more urgent national missions, such as wars. On the other hand, states highly appreciated private banks' money creation gland – nothing got them closer to their alchemistic goal for the time being. It was, thus necessary to come up with calibrated ideas of how to regulate private banks' money creation properly, without strangling them too much, but also without leaving their reckless greed too great liberties. This calibrated view

---

27   State's commodity money was often pre-committed for warfare. E.g., in 1543, 65 % of Charles V of Spain's revenues were committed to interest payment on old sovereign debt. In the last years of Elisabeth I., around 1600, two third of state expenditure went into either interest or new military spending. See *Kennedy* (1987) page 102, 126. A similar situation existed for Phillip II. of Spain (loc. cit.).

28   Quoted after *Ferguson* (2008) page 56.

was to substitute the UK-politics erring back and forth between a 100 % reserves requirement or full suspension on gold convertibility, e.g., as necessitated by the costs of the Napoleonic wars (on 27 February 1797 by Act of Parliament). This calibration occurred in two famous debates.

Two famous English debates on private bank's credit money creation

After the Napoleonic wars had been won, a famous discussion between the Bullionists and the Anti-Bullionists arose. The *Bullionists*, amongst them Ricardo, Henry Thornton (1760–1815), and John Wheatley (1772–1830) requested the reintroduction of gold convertibility in order to avoid inflation. *Anti-Bullionists*, with Henry Boase (1763–1827) and Sir Coutts Trotter (1767–1837), supported their positions with Adam Smith and James Steuart (1713–1780), and argued against the reintroduction of gold convertibility. No inflation and no crisis were to be feared, they proposed, as long as loans were given to creditors with sufficient wealth only (Real Bills-doctrine). Inflation from 1800 to 1814 seemed to support the Bullionists and, indeed, the *Resumption Act* of 1821 reestablished gold convertibility. Subsequent deflation and crisis (1825, 1836/37, 1839), though, kept the debate alive. Twenty years later, the controversy was reproduced and deepened in the equally famous clash between the Currency School and the Banking School. The *Currency School* was led by Lord Overstone (1796–1833) and continued to argue for the Bullionists' view. The *Banking School* was mainly represented by Thomas Tooke, John Fullarton, and John Stuart Mill and basically followed the Anti-Bullionists' argument that has been presented previously.

The controversy was politically decided upon by Sir Robert Peel's (1788–1850) *Bank Charter Act* (or *Peel's Act*) from 1844, allegedly once more in favor of the more restrictive view, hence of the then Currency School. The *Bank Charter Act*, in particular, took away the right of private banks to issue bank notes and established a monopoly of bank note issue for the Bank of England. Yet, *fractional reserve money creation by credit entries on deposit accounts* remained with private banks and largely unrestricted. [29] Furthermore, the Bank of England was obligated to maintain, (according to the credence of the Currency School) 100 % reserves. But, while this appeared to spell the conservative and restrictive view of the Currency School, it was allowed to hold reserves not only in gold but also in sovereign debt. The practical result of the Bank Charter Act, thus, consisted in allowing private banks to continue to create all the money they dared to create as long as they did not print bank notes

---

29   Partly as a reaction to the expropriation of their power to create credit money *via banknote issuance*, the period after the Bank Charter Act saw many mergers between provincial private banks. The establishment of larger units increased private bank's remaining factual money creation power. The fewer banks there were, the more transactions could be consummated *within* a bank without the issuance of bank notes – and the more could private banks still create credit money and profit therefrom.

and in allowing the Bank of England to print all the money they state needed as long as it at least received IOUs signed by the state in return. If the central bank continued to be legally obliged to exchange its banknotes into gold, the created money remained credit money, i.e., *central bank credit money*. While mainstreams histography still holds that the more restrictive Currency School won the controversy, in fact, money creation was, first, generally upheld as fully legitimate and institutionalized at the level of private banks *and* of the central bank. Second, the restrictive arguments of the Currency School were largely used to appropriate the most valuable power creation powers of private banks (through the issuance of bank notes) by the central bank acting in conjunction with the government and to generally strengthen the grip of the central bank and the state over private banks in order to control and to police their money creation. [30]

The contribution of private banks' money creation to capitalist development by productive firms

Fractional reserves credit money creation allowed banks to create more money than merchants' promissory notes, bills of exchange, and bank checks and redistributive lending ever could have made available. Being able to create money *ex nihilo* also induced banks to being *much more generous in giving away credit money for longer periods, to allow loans to be rolled over, progressive debt build-up, and the total of outstanding debt to reach heights that were previously unthinkable* (when money was scarcer and when only redistribute loans were possible).[31] And, of course, the profit motive drove banks to make use of this possibility at large scale. Increased bank profit is, normally, a direct function of increased bank credit issued; hence, bank profit grows with the multiple of the credit money issued over the held gold or silver reserves. When, in the second half or the 19th century, most European capitalist states established structures similar to the English example, which allowed for significant fractional reserves credit money creation by private banks, this enabled long-time credit expansion throughout Europe and contributed to significant employment-generating spending for the productive economy, and greatly pushed financing in-

---

30   In crises, the Bank Charter Act even allowed the Bank of England's banknote issuance to surpass the limits of the sum of gold and government debt held by it. This exceptional power encouraged overall money creation as its allowed to bail out private banks, which had created private bank credit money and were hit by bad luck. It goes without saying that states never seriously considered the libertarian concept of "free banking", which would have subjected banks to competitive discipline and taught the public to critically observe the competing banks' reserves and their solvency. That would have been the opposite of what states wanted, i.e., of banks with extended credit money creation possibilities, for prosthetics and the military.

31   See page 405.

dustrial growth, the infrastructure and the military.[32] Germany's economic development between 1871 and 1914 (Germany's first catch-up-period), in particular, was strongly supported by expansive fractional bank credit money creation money.[33] The story repeated itself in Germany's reconstruction in its second catch-up period after 1945.[34] Equally, outside of Europe, Japan and Korea and other developing countries financed their growth-drives post World War II or after the Korean war largely with money creation through fractional reserve bank credit money; bank credit money was also widely used in the French post World War II "planification".[35] States often also gave guidance and supported certain investments, e.g., by tax advantages, selectively lowering banks' reserve requirements, by guaranteeing repayments or the like.

The contribution of private banks' money creation and wealth owner's debt

Wealth owners' consumer credit and wealth owners' consumer debt was already a significant factor in commodity money regimes; wealth owners especially used loans to successively convert their defunct feudal wealth into cash, smearing the economy with employment-generating consumptive spending. Country estates and castles served as collateral and were later sold in slices to nouveau-riches or turned into factories; this took place from the English countryside to St. Petersburg and up to Kazan. Fractional reserves bank credit money creation, e.g., by John Law's *Banque Royale*, already financed asset bubbles in the wealth economy.[36] Britain saw bank crises since the 18th century,[37] partially based on asset bubbles. Germany had its first major asset bubble in the "Gründerkrach" shortly after its first unification in 1871, i.e., in 1873.[38] Finally much later, asset bubbles massively contributed to the Great Depression, the Asian Crisis of 1997, the dot-com-bubble, and the financial crisis of 2008, etc.

Workers take out no debt in commodity money regimes

Consumptive loans to workers, though, were hardly a factor in commodity money regimes. One could imagine that banks simply felt too class-conscious and arrogant to consider workers as loan customers; they mostly did not even have deposit accounts and picked up their salaries in a paper envelope with their handwritten name on it (and were mostly trade-unionists and social democrats, etc.). Alternatively, one

---

32   *Turner* (2016) page 32, page 57–60. Moments of state fiat money creation became more and more visible over time.

33   *Turner* (2016) page 54 with reference to *Gerschenkron* (1962).

34   See *Schröter* (2005) page 369 et seq.

35   Again: Even while moments of state fiat money creation became more and more visible.

36   *Turner* (2016) page 61–73.

37   See *Kiehling* (1991) page 24, et seq and *Mackay* (1841), and *de la Vega* (1688).

38   See *Kiehling* (1991) page 72 et seq.

could surmise that workers were unacceptable as loan clients for their lack of collateral, as the legal system was not prepared to litigate and execute claims from mass loans, or as the banks did not have and not want to create the clerk capacities for the low volume, mass-business. Yet another view could take the lack of fiat money as a cause for the non-existence of mass bank loans to working class people. Anyhow, banks' consumer loans to workers only rose to importance after fiat money had substituted commodity money as the base money. Even if workers remained mostly excluded as loan-recipients, private banks' money creation greatly supported productive investment of firms and other employment-generating spending of wealth owners and the state. It was a major factor of prosthetic circuit closure right from its inception.[39]

The dilemmas of funding prosthetics with fractional reserves bank credit money creation in a commodity money-regime

Limits to money creation capabilities

Even if a first money creation-gland is discovered – fractional reserves bank credit money creation –, which conveys much more power than redistributive lending without money creation, some relationship between the created credit money and the barren mass of gold or silver money in the banks' vaults must be maintained. The stubborn requirement of convertibility of credit money into scarce precious metals does not go away and it, of course, microeconomically restricts banks' ability to create money. This ratio, fraction, or, looked at from the other side, the multiple of credit money created against the commodity base money, can be stretched and was sometimes over-stretched, but it remains a burden that still fetters the financing of prosthetic spending to a country's possession of gold and silver macroeconomically.[40] The shortage of money is not yet finally overcome and the prosthetic program

---

39   "Aggregate demand" Keen writes, "is...aggregate supply *plus the change in debt.*" (Keen (2011) page 219 et seq., page 337 et seq.) referring to Schumpeter and Minsky. Schumpeter speaks of the credit structure as not only projecting "beyond the existing gold basis, but also beyond the exiting commodity basis" (*Schumpeter*, The theory of economic development, 1934, page 101, quoted after Keen (2011) page 220 et seq.). Minsky is saying that growth is financed by "emitting debt *or* selling assets"[975] (*Minsky*, Can it happen again? page 6 quoted after Keen (2011) page 219 et seq., italics added). This allows a simple explanation of crises that would arise in the future – even after state fiat money had become an option: "The collapse of debt financed aggregate demand was the key factor behind both the Great Depression and the Great Recession." (Keen (2011) page 352 see also page 300).

40   While banks are desirous to lower the fraction of commodity money held, they are also at least careful enough to consider risks for their solvency following excessive credit money creation. Banks' microeconomic self-interest, which, on the one hand, drives money creation (to increase profit by interest revenues) thus might also occasionally set limits to such an increase (by the fear of bankruptcy).

to artificially increase employment-generating spending often hits the barrier of too little ammunition. The circle of potential borrowers is limited and this keeps interest rates high, whereby the circle of prospective borrowers who use loans for employment-generating spending is once more narrowed.

Furthermore, and not at all surprisingly, money creation by banks' fractional credit money proved insufficient where exceptionally large amounts were needed, which often slowed down peace time economic expansion in western economies and, more so, in always gold and silver-scarce underdeveloped countries. It also posed a heavily felt restriction on the wars waged by states with commodity money regimes. Apart from greater or lesser access to voluminous capital markets, such warring states that had the better cards who were the quickest to suspend the convertibility of bank and central bank notes, and who succeeded best at managing emergency state credit money creation, central bank credit money creation or even exceptional interim state fiat money creation, and to, thereby detach the financing of the war efforts from the available commodity money.[41]

Credit not used for employment-generating spending

The second dilemma of commodity money regimes is what *Adair Turner* refers to – with a view to present fiat money regimes – as the "wrong sort of credit"[42] being issued. Whenever banks create money, including in regimes of commodity money, they decide how the money is used together with the credit-applicant, specifically about whether it goes into employment-generating or sterile spending. Now, unfortunately, fractional reserves credit money creation is all too often used for prosthetic *sterile* spending. This is so as already in commodity money regimes numerous sound microeconomic motives push into this direction. It is much easier to anticipate the cashflows from an existing sterile asset than from a newly created asset, which is typically the result of a productive investment. Another strong motive for banks to prefer to finance the purchase of pre-existing, old debt, real estate, or stocks is that *these assets are already there* and can be used as a security and possess a core-value-in-exchange. Many productive investments are utterly different in the negative. The value-in-exchange of a newly set up plant will be its business value; it depends on future profitable sales of products over a significant period. However, if the loan turns sour, they will mostly do this because no such business value has been created. Then,

---

41   Interim state fiat money regimes work in a twofold way. First, they create the exceptional additional state fiat money and, second, this extends the base over which private banks can create additional fractional reserves credit money (as soon as it is accepted as the bank's reserves).

42   *Turner* (2016) page 61 et seq. As *Arnold* reports, Mario Draghi, after his time as ECB-President, also began to distinguish between "good debt", which is "used for productive purposes" and "bad debt" which is used for unproductive purposes (*Financial Times* of 19. August 2020 page 2).

only the remnants of the failed business – real estate, equipment, inventories, etc. –, which can be sold separately, represent some value-in-exchange. Furthermore, banks will often find their hands chained in crises: If they spot an attachable asset of a sizable value, for instance, account receivables or cash, this execution itself may ultimately trigger insolvency. Execution in a momentary value in a newly created asset often destroys the value of the overall asset...

Another reason why banks may prefer to give "the wrong sort of credit", results from the effects that credit financing of a new productive venture has on the profits in the market of the venture and on the value of the financed venture itself. As touched upon previously, the arrival of a new productive investor, who founds a new automobile firm, for example, will increase competition and *typically lower the profitability of the firms in the market;* it will generate negative feedback, including on the new productive firm. On the contrary, the arrival of new sterile investors in bonds, real estate, stock or commodities, etc., markets, will *typically bet up prices* and generate positive feedback. In product markets, arriving new investors are bad news, while leaving investors are good news. In asset markets, arriving investors are good news and leaving investors are bad news. Banks, thus, drive up their collateral's value-in-exchange by financing sterile investments in asset markets. These dilemmas, which are inherent in commodity money regimes, even with private bank credit money creation, have driven the evolution to state fiat money.

Chapter XII. Expansive prosthetics funded with money creation in state fiat money regimes

Section 1. From commodity money regimes to state fiat money regimes

Fickle origins of state fiat money

In the previous chapters, prosthetic spending was already being supported by money creation, but the money creation was primarily private bank fractional reserves credit money creation only. State and central bank credit money creation or even money creation by fiat money showed up experimentally and transitorily in war or other emergencies but disappeared again after the war was over. This remained so until even after World War I and World War II, at Bretton Woods, and was only to change in 1971, when Richard Nixon un-did the latter restoration of a commodity money regime. Only now fiat money became the exclusive base money of the US and of most of the world. This ultimately provided states and central banks with a permanent money creation gland of their own, which was utterly more powerful than private bank fractional reserves credit money creation. At first, states did not use state fiat money creation as the primary means to finance prosthetics but as a tool to support private bank fractional reserves money creation. They used it to push interest rates down and to bail out private banks out where required. States also set up new legal frameworks and institutions, to ease to manage the growing debt, which was enabled by state fiat money.[1]

---

[1] *John Law* was one of the first writers who connected the idea that an increase of money would further trade and employment with the conviction that money without intrinsic value could be used. See *Murphy*, John Law (1671–1729) in: *Faccarello/* (2016) page 17). Goethe had Mephistopheles present the advantages of state fiat money creation to the Kaiser in his Faust II, published 1832 (Erster Akt, Lustgarten, line 6120 et seq., 6075 et seq.): "Ein solch Papier an Gold und Perlen statt,/Ist so bequem, man weiß doch, was man hat, .../Beschämt den Zweifler, der uns frech verhöhnt,/Man will nichts anderes, ist daran gewöhnt./So bleibt von nun an allen Kaiserlanden,/An Kleinod, Gold, Papier genug vorhanden./Schatzmeister (to Kaiser): "Seht Eure Stadt sonst halb im Tod verschimmelt,/wie alles lebt und lustgenie-

Under a system of gold or silver money, without fractional credit money creation, states had very limited space to maneuver. When they minted coins out of precious metals, decided upon their weight, embossed a currency unit, and put a nominal amount and emblem on it, they were, as we observed,[2] only able to earn a very small seignorage. Yes, they could issue the coins at a face value slightly above their production costs (mainly the content of precious metals), but no more, and could, thus, realize only a meager add-on. Markets would typically accept such a small "honest" profit in view of the additional value-in-use, which accrued from the convenience of the coins being embossed. If, however, in war, catastrophe, or out of frivolity, states attempted to increase the seignorage to a quarter, half, or the full amount of the value-in-exchange of the precious metals used (or if they debased the precious metals by an eighth, a fourth or half of their weight with un-precious metals, which is the same thing), then markets would often no longer accept these coins at their full nominal value.[3] This problem wholly disappeared with the introduction of fiat money regimes. Markets would now willingly swallow huge amounts of coins, paper or bookkeeping entries *with zero percent* gold or silver content or backing! The small money-creation maneuvering space that states had during commodity money exploded with the advent of fiat money regimes.

A near 100 %-seignorage at the issuance-moment

In addition, before states could dream of putting a seignorage on commodity money coins or debasing them, they first needed tons of gold or silver as base material. If they could not get hold of them, then their only option was to withdraw existing coins from the circulation and reissuing them at the same or a superior nominal value, albeit with a lower gold or silver content. That did not only look bad, but again the overall re-issuance profits were limited. They depended on the volume of money in circulation in their territory, on the percentage states would get into their hands, what degree of debasement the money already had, and how much more debasement the market would tolerate. There could also be technical problems.[4]

    ßend wimmelt./Obschon dein Name längst die Welt beglückt,/man hat ihn nie so freundlich angeblickt."

2   See on page 63.

3   Some late Roman emperors earned a particular bad reputation for pushing such attempts too far. In particular the "soldier emperors", e.g., Valerian I and Gallienus, who lowered the silver content to only 5 % (*Beck/Bacher/Hermann* (2017) page 40).

4   If you want to withdraw commodity money from circulation, to reduce the precious metal content from 80 % to 66 %, you have to first check each coin, which you manage to get a hold of concerning its prior state of debasement. One could surmise that differences in the embossing of coins served the purpose to easily distinguish coins of different debasement in later debasement rounds. The coins have, then, to be carried to a mint to do the work.

States, moreover, ran into difficulties to get rid of the additionally debased coins at the unjustified higher nominal value: *The advantage for the state lies only in the singular moment of initial issue or initial re-issue.* To realize it, the state had to induce somebody to deliver commodities, including gold or silver, in the nominal value of the coins *without increasing the prices* of the goods delivered. Unfortunately, the recipients of payments from the state were often suppliers, which were close to the state and on whom the state depended, e.g., military suppliers, the state's construction firms,[5] the emperor's luxury suppliers, bureaucrats or soldiers, whom it needed to treat well and not to alienate. Still, to repeat, the first bringing-into-circulation of the debased coins was the only opportunity at which the state could make a profit from the debasement or the seignorage. Wealthy merchants and nobles around the state who were asked to accept the new bad money, thus, mostly had no option but to try to outsmart the state (pretending to have no goods to supply or trying to increase prices) while still swallowing the bad money in a first step. They would, then, of course, use their superior might to *forward it to others, which were weaker than themselves.* In the end, most certainly, the particularly debased money ended up in the hands of the lowest rank with the fewest alternatives, probably soldiers and poor peasants. All these options of states were unpleasant, but in a pure commodity regime no further options existed. No wonder that states desperately hoped for the alchemists to make progress in their laboratories.

States' simplified relations to banks in modern times

States had intense relationships already with the predecessors of modern banks, e.g., to money loaners, and usurers, the Lombard and, in particular, the Jews, as the most professional dealers in money, in the Middle Ages. States were their loan-customers, were indebted to them, were advised by them, partnered with them, regulated them, asked them gently to waive some of their repayment claims from time to time, and occasionally expelled them from their territory, or, if they were Jewish, expropriated them or even unleashed or supported pogroms or killed them. Then again, they called "their" expelled Jews or other money lenders back.[6] Once modern banking was established, states particularly admired the banking houses' power to create money through fractional reserve credit money. Warfare financing ignited boosts in the development of private banks and states forged alliances with them. Banks assumed a leading role in the financing of the warfare between the Italian city states in Renaissance Europe by organizing the issuance of bonds.[7] In Britain,

---

5   They tend to also be cheated often by the state, see the case of Faffner and Fasolt who were cheated by Wotan in Wagner's Ring.

6   See *Sombart* (1902) volume I, page 266, 267.

7   *Ferguson* (2008) page 70.

the need to finance the build-up of the Royal Navy even induced the formation of *The Governor and Company of the Bank of England*, the later Bank of England, as such in 1694. Against granting a loan of £1.2-million-pounds to the state at 8 % interest, the bank received the privilege of issuing (otherwise uncovered) banknotes in the same amount; in other words, it was authorized to create money in the amount in which it had loaned bullion to the state. During the Napoleonic wars, in 1797, the English cabinet released the bank from redeeming its bank notes in commodity money. This might lead to interpretational questions and legal considerations. The interpretational question was what the release meant precisely. Did it mean a switch into a temporary or even general fiat money regime or just some kind of an emergence law under which the opening of legal proceedings for the conversion of credit money bank notes and credit money account entries into commodity money was denied for the moment? This remained unspecified, but the British cabinet's actions pointed to what would become a widespread practice of states in extraordinary situations, de facto flipping what had been credit money into fiat money by ordinance while leaving the question of whether the fiat money would again be restored to credit money later an open one. The legal issue was whether a cabinet was at all entitled to "release" a debtor from a debt (normally the government cannot interfere in contractual relationships). The crucial motive for the state-granted exemption from the convertibility was, of course, not the fear for the security of existing banknotes-holders – the bank's solvency might already have been poor previously and the position of its existing creditors was not greatly improved by the exemption –, but *to protect the banks' capacity to create further money*, which the state needed for the war or for whatever crisis.

Dirty origins of state fiat money

Other countries aside the UK also ventured into credit money creation and slipped into de facto state fiat money creation from there. When Louis XIV died after decades of warfare in 1715, his state finances were in disrepair. The situation was so bad, indeed, that *John Law*, a Scotsman, was allowed to found the *Banque Générale privée* to bring relief in 1716. This bank with a stated capital of Livres 6 million could cover 3/4 of its stated capital with largely depreciated state notes (bonds), which had financed Louis XIV's wars; the actual paid-in capital was less than Livres 3 million.[8] The bank, which was to become the *Banque Royale* in 1719, issued bank notes, *monnaie papier*, in the amount of its stated capital of Livres 6 million. This resulted in a volume of fractional bank credit money creation in excess of the total *monnaie papier* over the sum paid in silver, plus the residual value of the old state notes.

---

8   *Ferguson* (2008) page 140.

Following 1862, the Union, in order to finance the US civil war for the North without the involvement of a central bank – the Fed was only founded in 1913 –, issued so-called *"Demand Notes"* which were redeemable against gold, hence state credit money, in the limited volume of fifty million dollars. Unlike most or all other notes in use, which were only printed on the face-side, they were printed in green on the reverse-side (hence the term "greenbacks"). Shortly thereafter, the Union issued several hundred million of so-called *"United States Notes"*, which also had a green back, and were also called "greenbacks", but which were *not* redeemable against gold. It was said that a significant part of the public believed that the second issue was as redeemable as the first. Nevertheless, this second issue helped the North to win the war. From a monetary point of view, the first issue of "Demand Notes", was clearly credit money because of its legal convertibility into gold money; whether it led to money creation would have depended on whether the claims were or were not fully backed by gold reserves held by the Union.[9] The second, larger issue of "United States Notes", given the lack of convertibility, was clearly fiat money. Whether it led to money creation depended, as above, on whether while fiat money was issued gold reserves were built up. As this was largely not so, it overwhelmingly constituted money creation once more. As to the "solvency-concern": "United States Notes" were fiat money and they would as such, without additional measures, never convey any security for their holders. However, Congress allowed holders to use them instead of gold to pay taxes and made it legal tender, thereby ascribing significant value to them. At least as long as the North remained stable, he who had subscribed to them, had a good chance not to be punished for his patriotism. "United States Notes" were crucial to pay for soldiers and to purchase military equipment to ascertain the win for the North. In fact, after its victory, the Union promoted the initially non-convertible notes to be redeemable against gold.[10]

Germany and Japan established central banks in the second half of the 19th century. Like other countries, their monetary regimes remained based on commodity money, but they allowed money creation by the central bank by issuing central bank credit money beyond what the central bank was obliged to hold as gold or silver reserves (in addition to the ongoing money creation by private banks through fractional reserve credit money).

As in prior wars and emergencies, these systems – commodity money regimes, but allowing a certain fraction of bank and state fractional reserves money creation

---

9   Most likely the larger part of the issue, indeed, also constituted money creation. Note once more that the "solvency-concern", as we know well, is a different issue. The security of the claim for conversion of the credit money into precious metals (or other good value) depended upon the Union's general solvency, on whether or not it would win the war in particular.

10   See https://en.wikipedia.org/wiki/Demand_Note.

– came under stress in World War I and World War II. Most warring states at first increased the volume of central bank notes, which were not backed by gold or silver reserves, and, as this did not suffice, either officially or factually suspended the convertibility or redeemability of their central bank notes in gold or silver. This may not even have made a tangible difference for the holders of the notes, as, whether they were holding notes representing central bank or state credit money or state fiat money, their value always depended on the victory of the respective issuing country. After both world wars, World War I and World War II, the main Western countries, in a way quite astonishingly, once more returned to commodity money, e.g., the UK through *Winston Churchill* in 1925 and, after World War II, as already mentioned, the US and the whole Western block, after the Bretton Woods conference of 1944.

Section 2. State fiat money creation aside private bank credit money creation

From occasional experiments with state fiat money to a new monetary regime

While the occasional suspensions of convertibility in regimes of commodity money during emergencies had always ended with the restoration of a commodity money regime, as a side-effect it had allowed states to experiment with state fiat money and to prepare the ultimate full transition to state fiat money. And this day came when state fiat money creation gland was ultimately established lastingly as the superior money creation gland. If a date is needed, many authors point to the announcement by Richard Nixon of 15 August 1971 to temporarily (!) suspend the conversion of US-Dollars into Gold (at the fixed rate of US$35 at the time) – likely with the immediate purpose of protecting the remaining US Gold reserves from being exchanged against fractional reserves bank credit money created in order to finance the Vietnam war. As we now know, that "temporary" suspension ignited a worldwide system-switch and represented the final departure from commodity money.

Technically, the swap to state fiat money regimes did not actually require much more than the declaration of "non-convertibility" of the already issued credit money (of banks, central banks, or states); indeed, the change could even lastingly officially remain "temporary". Moreover, existing notes and coins did not have to be taken out of circulation and the gold and silver, which was sitting in the vaults of the treasury, could stay there. Yes, theoretically, it *could* have been demonetized to realize its value-in-exchange as commodity in a one-time coup. (The transition to state fiat money had set free the value-in-exchange, which gold and silver coins carried "piggyback"). But there was no rush to use this newly accrued option, and, indeed, there were less reasons than ever before to touch the gold and silver – states had just acquired the possibility to create as much fiat money ex nihilo as they wished. Rather, states felt that if the commodity money in the vaults would "psychologically" stabilize the new fiat money, probably for good reasons.

Fiat money was generally accepted by the public without much-a-do. Almost all citizens have to pay taxes and that provided a first layer of value-in-use and value-in-exchange to the new explicit state fiat money. The second layer arose out of the fact that the state fiat money immediately became legal tender, so that you could also use it to settle your debts with other privates. Furthermore, many groups of the populations of the new fiat money states drew benefits from the additional spending that it enabled. The seventies were years of abundance in many countries.

State fiat money: a doctrinal revolution

Nevertheless, the new general state fiat money was a *doctrinal and social revolution* as it admits the possibility of money to function without the money thing containing any iota of value-in-exchange after demonetization. Many saw the revolution as yet another enlightened self-liberalization, in the Kantian sense of the "striping off of self-imposed immaturity", as an overdue consequence of having overcoming archaism, magic, and myth in the political economy. The money "code", systems theoretical sociology claimed (and others made similar statements), never really required value-in-exchange of the money-thing (outside of its being used as code). As it had appeared to be a great progress that states took away the power to create laws from tradition and Gods, it now appeared that they had also done well to take away the power to create money from physicists, miners, and carriers. Only a few anti-modernists, "Austrian" and other gold or silver "fetishists", who appeared hooked on a reified reactionary style of thinking, remained opposed. They emphasized that not only had state fiat money appropriated powers formerly held by physicists and miners etc., but also power, which were ultimately the market's powers. Nobody could halt the landslide, though. Fiat money was just too attractive for all political parties in mass democracies, even though they intended to use fiat money very different purposes, from social transfers to warfare.

State fiat money: a second artificial money creation gland aside bank credit money

The most important result of the introduction of fiat money, as stated previously, was its power to *push the possibilities of money creation to a much grander scale*. Fiat money was alchemy's dream come true, so grand in fact that fiat money may today have become a tool of stateship that is as important as physical violence and, most of the time, more important. States now finally achieved what they had always desired – a possibility to create money, value-in-exchange, wealth, in a convenient form at their discretion, at no significant cost and at practically any time. It meant independence from finding, mining, robbing, debasing, or faking gold and silver and it meant independence from private banks, too, with their restraints on fractional credit money creation, the risks this carried – and with the occasional obstinacy of private banks. States could now issue money with near a hundred percent of seignorage or without any grain of precious metal at their discretion. It is, once more, elucidating to compare the states' new "monetary sovereignty"[11] with the meager ammunition that was available to the states of antiquity when they wanted to deal with their ancient master drama.[12] Weapons and armies win on the spot against wealth, but access to fiat money can also buy consent and legitimacy, hearts and minds, at home and abroad. It can achieve objectives without violence, and if civils wars and wars become necessary in spite of this, it can still help to win them by buying soldiers and weaponry. Indeed, the great mass wars of modernity, from the Napoleonic wars to World War II, could not *nearly* have been as horrible in the numbers, firepower, and precision of the arms used, the masses of soldiers and in the duration of the wars had they solely been financed with fractional reserve credit money creation or even in a commodity money regime with redistributive credit.[13] Modern wars exploded not only because of progress in technology, growth in populations, and on the basis of modern mass ideologies, but also because of monetary and financial explosions and because fiat money boosted money creation.

---

11   This term also used by *Polanyi* (1944) page 261. It is quite interesting that as part of reflections on monetary policy in a low-rate- world, *Martin Wolf* particularly closely relates state control over money not to states as such but to *democracy*. "The lesson of history seems absolutely clear: a democracy will not accept that money is outside of purposeful control." Democracy, it appears, is more "totalitarian" towards money (and the economy as a whole) than absolute princes or kings ever dared to be (*Wolf*, Monetary policy in a low rate world, in *Financial Times* of 14 September 2019).

12   If states wanted to take measures to mitigate the master drama in antiquity, they mostly could only distribute land to small peasants. However, they had to take land away from somebody for this purpose, either from domestic latifundia owners or foreign countries or tribes. This typically led to opposition, civil unrest, and civil or external war, and also involved, in the latter case, displacing, enslaving, or eradicating the population who possessed the "desired land". Even if states in antiquity only sought temporary relief, e.g., through public spending enabling employment or direct transfer payments to the unemployed, they still needed to appropriate the gold or silver used for this purpose from somebody who would likely resist. "Fiat gold" or "fiat silver" existed as little as "fiat land".

13   See the observations of *Ferguson* (2008) page 70, on the Italian Renaissance city states (in their wars against each other – giving birth to the *condottieri*) and of Spain against the Netherlands. The worst was yet to come. In this sense, see also *von Mises* (2013) page 222.

Section 3. Expansive prosthetics funded with private bank credit money creation

Fractional reserves bank credit money creation in state fiat money regimes

The acceptance of state fiat money

The transition to fiat money regimes displaced commodity money as base money. "Base" is a metaphor stemming from architecture and refers to a foundation on which something airier is erected. State fiat money, though, is "artificial" and, thus, in some way airy itself, certainly airier than gold and silver. Still, as we saw, its general acceptance relies on two strong "material kernels". The state, the most powerful social institution and largest creditor, takes it for tax payments and the very same powerful social institution enforces its acceptance by privates for the payment of debt as legal tender. Normally, when using fiat money, people do not even think so far but rather feel comfortable to accept fiat money because of a mental shortcut. They simply ask themselves whether they still trust that they can unload their fiat money again to buy other wealth with it. If so, then they accept it. The *trust in the trust of others* emerges on top of the two material kernels – acceptance to pay taxes, legal tender – which convey the primary level of value-in-exchange to fiat money. The social use of fiat money triggers a reflexive social-psychological mechanism, a supportive emergent property of fiat money. Accordingly, while fiat money always remains an endangered species – states can undo their invention in a second by no longer accepting it for tax payments – as long as they don't and nobody expects them to, the new airy base money is rock-solid. So far so good.

No elimination of private bank money creation

After the magnificent arrival of the state fiat money gland, as it is capable of theoretically unlimited money creation, states *could* have eliminated bank credit money creation altogether and switched the whole money creation to state fiat money creation. They *could* also have taken an inventory of all sovereign debt and of even parts of private debt, and could have created enough fiat money to settle all parts of it that they wanted rid of. From there on out, they could have exclusively used their state fiat money gland to directly pay for new government expenses or to finance transfer payments (what is called, as we shall see, "overt monetary financing"). All prerequisites for a declaration of independency and practical independence from private bank credit money creation were fulfilled. Had states acted in this sense, sovereign debt would, by now, have disappeared (as a debt and as an asset) in one fell swoop and there would no longer be any more sovereign debt bond markets.

Obviously, this is *not* what happened. States and central banks did not abolish private banks' money creation gland and did not push them back to the level of the innocent early *Amsterdam Wisselbank* – into the realms merely redistributive credit. To be sure, there were plans and ideas in this direction. E.g., in the so-called *"Chicago Plan"* of 1993, a group of well-known economists at the University of Chicago, amongst them Henry C. Simons and Frank Knight; supported a 100 percent reserves requirement and, thereby, in fact, asked for the abolition of fractional reserves bank credit creation. Since then, the proposal has never been wholly off the table; in fact, the popularity of *"full-reserve banking"* grew after the crisis of 2008. The proponents of the restrictions argue with macroeconomic dangers involved in money creation, the risk of massive losses of GDP after the bursting of bubbles and that only "full-reserve banking" can prevent private banks from blackmailing states in financial crises to, effectively, socialize risks resulting from their prior excessive money and debt creation. While the proponents of full-reserve banking are by far no anti-capitalist radicals, states and central banks have still not taken the bait to eliminate their private "junior partners" in money creation or to strangle them too much.[14] Rather, while they use the state fiat money creation gland for the base money and as a reserve tool, they still prefer to leave the credit money creation by private banks on top largely untouched. Money continues to be created at *two* hierarchical levels,[15] yet, private banks only no longer create bank credit money in a second "story" over commodity money, but, now, in a second "story" over state fiat money. This enabled an extension of bank credit money creation, which was most welcome in the 70ties.[16]

Cooperation and policing in the private banks-central bank "tandem"

The two methods of money creation now began to play together and to cooperate in "tandem", much like commodity money creation and private banks' credit money creation had done before. There were two main aspects to that. As before in a commodity money regime, states – who need a functioning money creation for their

---

14   E.g., Deutsche Bundesbank makes disparaging comments on full-reserve banking in Deutsche Bundesbank (2017).

15   Central banks are private law institutions and/or they do not underlie direct commands by the state in some countries. While it is imaginable that central banks might discontinue to do what states expect from them in times of great stress, we generally assume that this does not happen. Theoretically, money could still be created as merchant credit money, hence on a third level, through notes and bills. However, this level has almost wholly lost its relevance.

16   E.g., to finance reforms, new schools and universities almost everywhere, and the Vietnam war. Actually, bank depositors do also yield advantages from state fiat money as base money. True, in a fiat money regime, the collapse of fiat money leaves the credit money-holders without a claim for precious metals against their bank and in this regard they are worse off than their predecessors who held credit money on a commodity money base. But another depositor risk is minimized: States and central banks are more willing and capable of bailing out banks in crises, if they can use state fiat money rather than scarce precious metals.

prosthetics – would still not want to allow private bank's money creation to be endangered by private banks' excessive greed in a regime with state fiat money as base money. States had always been able to control, if needed, obstinate bankers and they would certainly not want to relinquish this power now, after they had even secured their general predominance in the money creation playing field. They would now adjust their arsenal of intervention, "policing" and bailing-out in crises to the birth of state fiat money.[17] The fact that base money was no longer scarce commodity money but theoretically unlimited fiat money doubly affected the situation. New factual opportunities for private banks to "misbehave" as well as new opportunities for states and central banks to save "misbehaving" private banks arose and the question of whether or not the central bank would save private banks was generally re-framed from a question of the *availability of scarce commodity money* plus *of will* into a question of *will alone*. Both sides interacted and that knowledge fed back on banks and raised moral hazards, which in turn required a more "totalitarian" style of bank-policing.

At first, the unlimited availability of base money after the advent of state fiat money allowed to liberalize the traditionally narrow, reserve fractions. Lowering the reserves fractions (or increasing the multipliers of credit money over the fiat base money in the banks' possession, which is the same thing) allowed the further growth of private banks' credit money creation ability, which was, as we already said, quite welcome. But how to set limits to protect banks' money creation gland from banks' greed instead? The answer was to establish requirements as to the balance sheets of banks, beginning with minimum requirements concerning equity and different layers of better and less valuable equity to debt and different layers of more and less risky debt. These categories could be related to assets of banks and all sorts of ratios could were set, within the liability side of the balance sheet and crosswise. Furthermore, banks' liquidity and solvency management drew more attention and became key; banks were generally forbidden from certain particularly risky activities. *In fact, these policing-innovations were only implemented with a significant time gap after the state fiat money regimes, which necessitated them, were erected.* This was due to the wave of neoliberalism ("Thatcherism", "Reaganomics") in the eighties, which delayed the introduction of proper means of bank-policing until, in fact, after the financial crisis of

---

17   Very much like good old German "Gewerbe-Recht" or "Policey-Recht". Quite interestingly, well into the eighties of the last century, a belief was held in Europe that administrative law governing economic activity was a "paternalist" European, if not Prussian or German thing, while administrative law appeared to play a minor role in the advanced capitalism of the US. All of a sudden, things turned around and the US began to teach the Europeans "regulation", "compliance" and "governance", which was, in fact, only the policing of businesses in the old European tradition. Nevertheless, these teachings were willingly transformed into new rules and laws by the European Union and propagated throughout Europe. The regulation was macro-prudent, anti-corruption, environmental, and gender-based etc

2008.[18] Only then the regulatory framework for banks was adjusted to the conditions of a state fiat money regime.

The availability of quasi-unlimited base money affected states and central banks bail-out-policies. The only effective strategic answer for a prospective savior to over-reliance on being saved is to *occasionally disappoint* that very expectation. That means either consciously selecting individual banks who overplayed their hands and sacrificing them from time to time or to apply the game theoretical strategy of "brinkmanship" by allowing the situation to get a bit out of hand, thereby, in fact, delegating the decision who will be saved and who not to a random generator.[19]

States and central banks further helped the increased lending based on money and debt creation that this period witnessed by institutionally strengthening and furthering diversified, liquid, and deep debt markets, in which original lenders or second-hand debt investors could confidently unload their debt assets and re-finance themselves if they needed liquidity, such as inter-bank and repo-markets. As these markets were internationalized, investors became less dependent on national trends, too. States often created legal provisions that eased ongoing debt build-up, e.g., privileges for sovereign debt in accounting for bank regulation laws or tax provisions privileging debt financing. All of this helped to enable – without central banks already building up significant piles of debt themselves or without "overt monetary financing" – a substantial rise in the volumes of credit money created by banks, and of, consequentially, of new debt and of expansive prosthetic employment-generating spending.

The "tandem" of state fiat money and private bank money creation enables fall of interest rates

The general transition to state fiat money, and the active support by states and central banks for debt markets, resulted in a tremendous worldwide fall in interest

---

18   The reaction to the Great Depression in the US was still designed with a commodity money regime in mind. Nevertheless, certain moments of its policing, e.g., as contained in the *Glass-Steagall Act of 1933*, could be revived in the years following 2008. After the Great Depression, World War II, on the one hand, "solved" macroeconomic problems for some time, while, on the other hand, states particularly needed massive credit money creation for their war-financing and were ready to take more risks than normal (rather than running out of bombs). Thereafter, the post Great Depression and post World War II regulatory situation did not significantly change before globalization and neoliberalism swept through Western banking laws in the nineties; accordingly, the *Glass-Steagall Act* was revoked in 1999.

19   It can be argued that allowing the Lehmann Brothers to go bankrupt, which is believed to have greatly deepened the financial crisis of 2008, was either the result of misguided intent or of reasonable "brinkmanship". It may not be in the interest of states and central banks to let the public become too convinced that similar non-intervention-policies will not be repeated.

rates. The world saw the absolute high of the US Fed Fund Rate of around 20 % under Fed chairman Paul Volcker in 1980. Since then, over forty years, it has witnessed an almost uninterrupted fall down to zero or below zero almost everywhere, which of course favored a parallel and general worldwide build-up of sovereign and private debt. In the US, this build-up was backed by several waves of central bank easy money-policies under Fed chairmen Alan Greenspan, Ben Bernanke, Janet Yellen, and Jerome Powell. In all smaller or larger crises, such as the dot.com-bubble, the financial crisis of 2008, and the Corona-shock, the Fed always applied the same recipe: easy money for more debt build-up.[20] In each of these crises it transgressed new borderlines, which had appeared to be sacrosanct and inviolable in the wave before. The following graph shows the Fed Funds Rate since the sixties of last century until 2020.

Figure 19: Fed Funds Rate from before 1960 until 2020

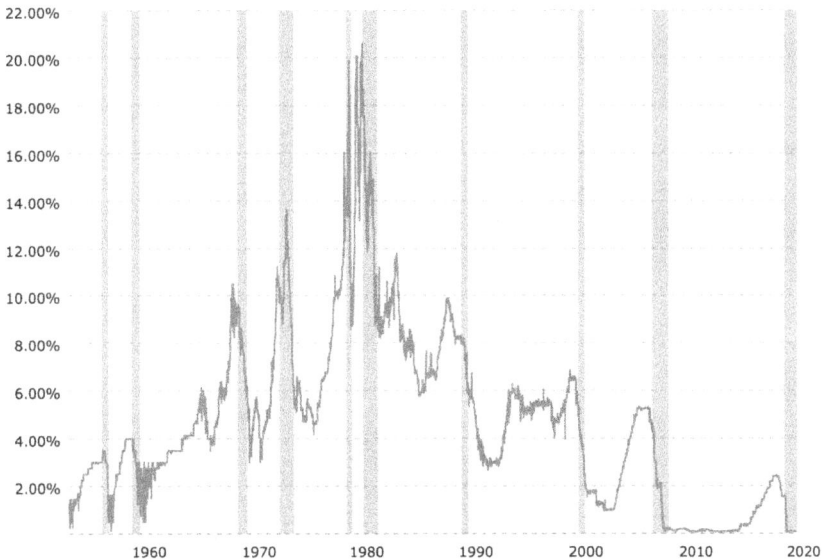

Source: http://www.macrotrends.net

The interest rates in *China* used to be higher and did not drop so much as in other countries. Still, they followed the general downwards trend, particularly when China used its maneuvering space to, as many Western commentators said, "save the world economy" after 2008. Since the bursting of the Japanese asset bubble in

---

20   This at first meant only pushing interest rates down. Massive asset purchases became an additional "more of the same"- tool of central banks after 2008.

1990, the Bank of *Japan* massively lowered interest rates and has kept them ultra-low, as one "arrow" of "Abenomics", for three decades. *Germany* saw rising interest rates in the early nineties connected with the debt build-up in the German reunification and Germany's traditional "austerity"-politics. As German reunification's main task was completed, and as the ECB took over monetary politics from the Bundesbank, the German rates, though, adjusted to the general trend and fell. Countries in which yields on sovereign debt had traditionally been higher – Italy, Spain, Portugal and Greece – used the introduction of the Euro, which boosted their creditworthiness, to lower their interest rates on sovereign debt and to build up further sovereign debt. Just as the former East-Germans received some "Begrüßungsgeld" (welcome-money) after the German reunification, peripheral European countries were flooded with loans at lower-than ever interest after joining the Eurozone. *France* also built up more sovereign debt following the "unification" into one currency. Although the UK remained outside of the Eurozone, rates fell there no less than elsewhere. The rates in the US, China, Japan, the UK, Germany, France, Italy, Spain, Portugal, and Greece, as they developed from 1980 (Japan) or 1995 (all other countries) via 2007 to 2020 are shown on the following table.

Figure 20: Interest rates of major economies 1995 – 2007 –2020[21]

Interest rates	December. 1995 (Japan 1980)	December 2007	December 2020
US[i]	5,78 %	4,28 %	0,09 %
China[ii]	12,60 %	7,40 %	3,85 %
Japan[iii] June 1980	9,00 %	0,50 %	-0,10 %
UK[iv]	7,59 %	4,70 %	0,26 %
Germany[v]	6,07 %	4,21 %	-0,62 %
France	6,75 %	4,35 %	-0,34 %
Italy	13,50 %	4,00 %	0,50 %
Spain	12,35 %	4,35 %	0,14 %
Portugal	10,43 %	4,47 %	0,02 %
Greece	15,35 %	4,53 %	0,63 %

Since 2020 the rates slowly began to rise but nevertheless debt-mountains continued to grow.

Low rates enable massive build-up of sovereign debt

The overall low rates of the past enabled a massive debt build-up between the nineties of last century and today, thereby financing prosthetics at large scale, in the form of public debt. New Eurozone-members, e.g., Greece, Portugal, and Spain, give an example how productive investment, and increases of employment, arose out of debt build-up. The mentioned countries and others rewarded themselves with thousands of miles of new highways, often consisting of hundreds of bridges and tunnels through hilly beautiful landscapes along coastlines, which would never have been built under normal capitalist profit criteria and/or if they had been

---

21   [i] Fed Funds Rate. Source http://www.macrotrends.net.

[ii] PBC base interest rate. Sources: www/tradingeconomics.com (1995, 2007); http://www.gl obal-rates.com (2020).

[iii] Bank of Japan interest rate. Source: www/tradingeconomics.com/japan/interest-rate

iv Long-term interest rate for convergence purposes – 10 years maturity, denominated in UK pound sterling – United Kingdom

[v] Long-term interest rate for convergence purposes – 10 years maturity, denominated in Euro: Source ECB. The data for France, Italy, Spain, Portugal, and Greece are the same data from the same source

financed by taxation.[22] These investments, if megalomaniac and dubitable as far as their values-in-use are regarded, were still employment-generating and served the interest of local firms and of local workers (and of state bureaucrats) very well for some time. Indeed, most of the spending of sovereign debt in Eurozone countries, which led to the Eurozone debt crisis in 2009, went predominantly into productive investments.

In addition, of course, as always, a large chunk of the new debt throughout the world, in particular in the US, went into the military, be it via research and development (think of all the technological miracles, which are no paraded in the Ukraine war), arms production or payments to soldiers and veterans.

Figure 21: Military spending in major economies from 2006 to 2023

Military Spending in Billions US$							
Year	US	UK	Germany	France	Japan	Russia	PRC
2023	↑	↑	↑	↑	↑	↑	↑
2022	↑	↑	↑	↑	↑	↑	↑
2021	800,67	68,37	56	56,65	54,12	65,91	293,35
2020	778,23	59,24	52,76	52,75	49,15	61,71	257,97
2019	734,34	56,86	49,01	50,12	47,61	65,2	240,33
2018	682,49	55,68	46,42	51,41	46,62	61,61	232,53
2017	646,75	51,63	42,21	49,2	45,39	66,91	210,44
2016	639,86	53,33	39,86	47,37	46,47	69,25	198,54
2015	633,83	59,99	38,17	45,65	42,11	66,42	196,54
2014	647,79	67	44,66	53,13	46,9	84,7	182,11
2013	679,23	63,84	44,24	52	49,02	88,35	164,07
2012	725,21	65,45	43,8	50,22	60,01	81,47	145,12
2011	752,29	66,57	45,16	54,12	60,76	70,24	125,29
2010	738,01	63,98	43,03	52,04	54,66	58,72	105,52
2009	705,92	64,01	44,53	56,44	51,47	51,53	96,6
2008	656,76	72,92	45,1	55,37	46,36	56,18	78,84
2007	589,59	73,45	40,11	50,68	40,53	43,53	62,14
2006	558,34	64,22	35,88	45,79	41,55	34,53	51,45
Sources: www. Macrotrends.net and de.statista.com							

The ratios of state debt, private debt, and aggregate debt to GDP in 1995 (1980 for Japan), 2007, and 2020, which does not include the massive public spending in the Corona crisis and the huge increases of military spending since the Ukraine war yet, are shown in the following table.

---

22   Greece, where most vacationers go by plane, is today a wonderful country for an automobile vacation with a most generous network of new, empty highways or new countryside roads, e.g., from Thebes (ancient Thiva) to Delphi. The hilly Portuguese Island of Madeira, where the vacationers mostly use rental cars, is another example.

Figure 22: Development of sovereign and private debt in leading capitalist countries 1995–2020[23]

In %	1995 (unless otherwise indicated)			2007 (unless otherwise indicated)			2020 (unless otherwise indicated)[i]		
	State debt/ GDP	private debt[ii]/ GDP	total debt/ GDP	State debt/ GDP	private debt/ GDP	total debt/ GDP	State debt/ GDP	private debt/ GDP	total debt/ GDP
US[iii]	64.2	162.9	227.1	62.8	223.7	285.5	132.5	218.0	350.5
China[iv]	21.4	78.0	99.4	29.0	105.8	135.6	45.8	188.9 (2018)	233.7
Japan[v]	50,0 (1980)	291.9	341.9	175.4	227.3	402.7	224.8	223.8 (2018)	448.6
UK[vi]	44.5	160.0	204.5	41.5	231.7	272.2	84.6 (Q3)	190.3 (2019)	274.9
Germany[vii]	54.9	149.4	204.3	64.0	162.6	226.6	70.0	159.9	229.9
France[viii]	60.0	163.6	223.6	64.5	202.5	267.0	118.7	264.8	383.5
Italy[ix]	116.9	119.8	236.7	99.8	168.0	267.8	155.6	161.5	317.1
Spain[x]	61.5	129.9	191.4	35.8	276.1	311.9	117.8	190.4	308.2
Portugal[xi]	58.3	163.1	221.4	68.4	278.4	346.8	137.2	236.0	373.2
Greece[xii]	99.5	50.7	150.2	101.3	114.6	215.9	205.2	123.1	328.3

23   [i] State debt 2020, Private debt 2019 (unless stated otherwise indicated). Total debt includes state debt of 2020 and private debt of 2019 or of indicated date.

[ii] Debt of non-financial corporations, households and non-profit institutions serving household. Resource: stats.oecd.org (2007 and 2018, 2019).

[iii] US. Government-debt-to-gdp: Sources http://www.fred.stlouisfed.org (1995, 2007), http://www.ceicdata.com (2020). Private debt: http://www.tradingeconomics.com.

[iv] China. Government debt/gdp: Sources: www/tradingeconomics.com (1995, 2007), http://www.caixinglobal.com (2020). Private debt/gdp: Total stock of loans and debt securities issued by households and non-financial corporations as a share of gdp. Source: http://www.imf.org.

[v] Japan. Government debt/gdp: Sources: www/tradingeconomics.com (1995, 2007); http://www.ceicdata.com (2020). Private debt/gdp: http://www.tradingeconomics.com.

[vi] Government debt/gdp UK. Sources: http://www.eurostat.com (1995, 2007); http://www.ons.gov.uk. Private debt/gdp. Private debt/gdp: http://www.tradingeconomics.com.

[vii] Germany. Government debt/gdp Sources: http://www.tradingeconomics.com (1995, 2007). http://www.ceicdata.com (2020). Private debt/gdp: www.tradingeconomics.com.

[viii] France. Government debt/gdp: Source: http://www.tradingeconomics.com. (1995, 2007) http://www.statista.com (2020). Private debt/gdp: http://www.tradingeconomics.com.

[ix] Italy. Government debt/gdp Source: http://www.tradingeconomics.com. Private debt/gdp: http://www.tradingeconomics.com.

[x] Spain. Government debt/gdp Source: http://www.countryeconomy.com. Private debt/gdp: http://www.tradingeconomics.com.

[xi] Portugal. Government debt/gdp Sources: http://www.tradingeconomics.com (1995, 2007), http://www.statista.com (2020). Private debt/gdp: http://www.tradingeconomics.com.

[xii] Greece. Government debt/gdp Sources: http://www.tradingeconomics.com (1995, 2007), http://www.statista.com (2020). Private debt/gdp: http://www.tradingeconomics.com.

As the table shows, private debt experienced a particular jump between 1995 and 2007, which contributed a lot to the period's increased prosthetic employment-generating spending. One might expect that *corporate debt* would have massively financed firms' productive investments, which was the main argument officially justifying low interest rate-policies. Yet, this was not necessarily so. Low interest rates did not induce as much productive investment as was hoped but rather financed many sterile investments, e.g., stock repurchase programs.

Low rates enable massive build-up of workers' debt

A more substantial support for employment-generating spending arose from the already touched upon growing private indebtedness, in particular from *an increase of workers indebtedness in the period*. As we have set out, debt build-up requires a coming-together of money, creditors, and debtors.[24] Workers (in the wide meaning of non-owners), with a little help from the aforementioned favorable institutional and legal framework and falling and low interest rates, significantly increased their presence in debt markets in this period. They were now, contrary to the 19th and early 20th century, heartily welcomed by creditors (banks, wealth owners) hunting sterile investments. The increased workers' debt can be split up into three sub-categories: real estate debt, educational debt, and general consumption debt. Workers, and even jobless people, were enabled to debt-finance houses, at a scale, which had been unimaginable before. This was largely employment-generating if the houses were newly built. Workers were now also more welcome by banks if they wanted to finance general consumptive purposes, such as the education of their kids, automobiles, motorcycles, sports equipment, long-lasting household goods, electronics, or even their daily subsistence by leasing-arrangements, consumer loans, overdraft facilities, or credit card or other forms of private debt. This debt, except for rolling over prior debt and interest payments, financed employment-generating spending almost exclusively. Rather than the state issuing sovereign debt and making transfer payments to workers, workers would take care of the necessary money creation and debt build-up themselves (obviously in conjunction with banks). This may also partially have been a reaction of workers to stagnant or falling real salaries in the period and to reduced social transfers in many countries.

The US subprime housing loans, which triggered the 2008 financial crisis, are an important example: Sterile wealth owners speculated in subprime loan markets (and may also have taken up non-subprime-loans themselves in this context to leverage their sterile investments there) and subprime loans were handed to workers and financed the construction of, to a significant extent, new working-class dwellings in the US (and very often of new cars etc. on top). *Without* subprime loans, thus, the US would have seen *much less construction and industrial activity*, have been

---

24   See page 399 et seq.

much less prosperous, and there would have been much more unemployment in the period. All this was only enabled by working class debt build-up in conjunction with sterile investments by wealth owners. Similar jumps in private debt occurred in Greece, Portugal, Spain, and in other European countries; here, the debt build-up was largely enabled by falling interest rates connected to the Euro-introduction in peripheral Eurozone countries. Once more, spending financed by private debt build-up boosted economic activity and employment. Alternatively, when looked at it from the other side, had workers not loaded up significant debt on their shoulders, the worker-borrowers themselves, like their colleagues in the firms in which the borrowers spend the money, would not have gotten close to the living standards they actually had. Unfortunately, though, this jump in workers' indebtedness, which elevated employment-generating spending and workers' quality of life beyond the "natural" economic level, was a one-time event, which cannot be repeated after the level of workers' indebtedness has reached the limits of its sustainability. The crisis of 2008 arrived when sterile wealth owners got aware that they were financing houses and other expenditures that the purchasers could, ultimately, not afford.

They, too, contributed to prosperity in the period in the respective countries. In other words, without the falling, low, and ultra-low interest rates that we have witnessed since the nineties, there would only have been a significantly lower volume of employment-generating spending across all major developed countries of the world; hence, a significant outfall of circuit closure, a material additional depressive force on the economies, and much more unemployment, and human suffering over decades.[25]

The dilemma of private bank credit money creation in state fiat money regimes

There is a major structural dilemma of money creation by private banks in a state fiat money regime: Even if, in conjunction with rising private and public debt and before the background of state fiat money creation with its extended bail-out-possibilities, the volumes of prosthetics financed by private wealth owners, and thus the debt held by them, skyrocket at first, there comes a moment where private debt holders get irritated, feel uncomfortable and do not want to hold so much debt anymore. The more massive the debt build-up enabled by low interest rates is, the more certain, there will be a *deficiency of possible debt-holders* at some juncture. No optimization of debt and bond markets, of inter-bank and of repo-markets, and no market-making (including "dealer-of-last-resort-ship") by central banks and no regulatory improvements can maintain the willingness of creditors to absorb increasingly more junior,

---

25   Obviously, the debt to GDP-ratios also mirrors voluminous central bank debt purchases and asset holdings in the period between 2008 and 2020.

more subprime, riskier and low interest public and private debt on the creditors' side. This will unload not so much in a falling readiness to absorb new debt issues (which will be connected to higher rates), but in a collapse of a reliable "shiftability" of old debt instruments between debt-holders, which would, though, be required to meet the ever-growing hunger for new debt on the debtors' side.

At some stage, the high risk, resulting from the high levels of worker debt, and the low rewards, resulting from the low interest rates, which enabled the high debt-levels, will dry out unloading-possibilities for creditors and, accordingly, dry out debt-sourcing for debtors. Euphemizing (or even deceptive or criminal) "restructuring", "repackaging", etc. of debt may also help for some time (in essence by reducing transparency of risk), as may debt insurance by credit-default-swaps (CDS, or other credit derivatives) – until doubts arise in the insurers' solvency –, but not forever. The process of loss of trust in the debt can, thus, only be slowed down and delayed, but cannot ultimately be dismissed. It will bring the rolling over existing debt, to a grinding halt. As processes of insight proliferation and opinion changes travel very fast, it will strike suddenly and everywhere.

This is what happened in the US subprime crisis: A huge private debt market had evolved for a certain type of private debt, housing, and ancillary debt of workers and the jobless, and not enough private wealth owners wanted to hold onto it any longer. Worse still, nobody either wanted to longer hold debt of units who were known to insure such debt or to hold much of this debt on their asset side. Basically, the same happened in 2009/2010 to sovereign debt for Greece, Italy, Spain, and Portugal. In the financial crisis of 2008 and the Eurozone sovereign debt crisis of 2009, in other words, the point was touched where the limits of the readiness of private wealth owners to absorb the (available) debt, which had been created by private banks' fractional reserves credit money creation, were hit. This appears to have spelled the end of continued debt build-up based on low interest rates and predominant fractional reserves credit money creation without significant central bank debt holding and without significant state fiat money creation.[26]

---

26 Sometimes it is believed that states could only afford massive indebtedness as long as interest rates are low or moderate. This view is certainly true in commodity money regimes where the means to repay the debt must mainly be procured by redistributive means (e.g., taxation, expropriation or protectionism) with their palpable limits. Yet, in state fiat money regimes, even if interest rates rise significantly, central banks can simply print even more money to either pay the higher interest rates to privates or to purchase more of the outstanding debt and thereby neutralize it. Central banks will return the interest payments, which they receive from states at the front door, at the back door – as profits distributable to the state as their shareholder. Who sits on an unlimited money creation gland is less afraid of rising interest rates than privates (without money creation gland) or even states (as long as they did not control the fiat money creation gland).

Central banking and debt purchases by central banks

Buying up of sovereign debt by central banks was, at first, an exceptional means of state financing, e.g., in wars. After not long, sovereign debt holding by central banks became a macroeconomic means to steer business cycles. Central banks should buy and hold significant debt in a depression to stimulate activity and to overcome deflation. Conversely, central banks were said to sell the debt in a boom to calm down excessive activity and to avoid inflation. That remained the general official theory on central banks' debt holding during most of the 20th century.

It is worthwhile to look at this theory in greater depth: How, specifically, should debt purchases by the central bank help economic activity and employment? There was a sober and rather crude and a more "sophisticated" and ambitious explanation. The more crude and sober explanation, which probably ruled in the brains of politicians, the military, and in trade unions and continues to rule there until today, was quite simply that if the central bank bought sovereign debt from private entities, then private entities might consequentially recuperate this money to hand out new loans to the state or to privates who would spend more, and that this would have either a prosthetic macroeconomic or a welcome value-in-use effect. It did not matter in this context whether the central bank debt purchases were regarded as having motived privates to give loans already in the past, as they had been foreseen, or whether their execution re-equipped privates with the cash needed for future debt issues as a surprise. The relevant transmission mechanism was thus: Purchases of existing debt by the central bank enabled consecutive debt-build up, which enabled additional prosthetic employment-generating spending. The official, more "sophisticated" explanation, which labeled central bank debt holdings "open market policies", though, built upon Keynes' "inducement to invest". It turned away from the added masses of available credit and spending to a single peculiar effect of the debt purchases, which allegedly resulted from higher volumes of money being shed into the markets. This effect was *lower interest rates*, which were expected to influence the investment *calculus* of firms towards more investment. A twofold mechanism was believed to operate into this direction: First, lower costs of present investments (because of lower interest rates) would open up spaces to profitably more sell produce. Second, higher asset valuations were expected to be forthcoming, also because of lowered interest rates (by lesser discounts on future surpluses), which would also render setting up new businesses more rewarding.

As central banks bought debt, additional employment-generating spending actually did take place, but neither of the two theories was thereby vindicated. Was the additional spending because the lower interest rates had improved the calculus of firms or simply only because additional money had been made available to spenders with a high propensity to spend, i.e., to the state and non-owners, which afterwards added to higher debt mountains? For skeptics, the latter was always more convincing. In the meantime, the question has become almost obsolete. At first, it is impossible to reconcile the "open market"-theorem used in by the more sophisticated interpretation with the *consistent fall of interest rates* and the *consistent growth of central banks' balance sheets* over the last almost four decades.[27] "Open market policies" have too obviously changed into a one-way-thing, a permanent flow in the same direction, which has also led to the talk about "quantitative easing" displacing the talk about "open market policies". Second, it has even become more dubitable than before whether lower interest rates really induce firms to invest more. We have had falling and radically low, ultra-low rates interest rates, even zero or below, for around two decades – but we experience "secular stagnation" instead of a boom in the productive economy, which would need to be tamed down.[28] The crucial thing that bothers firms in their investment decisions is not interest rates, but *too few investment opportunities*, i.e., to limited employment-generating spending or too limited demand. Additional investment will only be rewarded if the aggregate volume of employment-generating spending is increased. If new products can only succeed by *displacing existing products* and drawing away employment-generating spending from them, e.g., following technological or institutional innovations (mobile phones, internet purchases, changes in consumer preferences like electrical cars or biological food), even if the investment in these novelties were helped by low interest rates, it will be at the cost of reduced investment of the displaced firms.

Accordingly *Richard Koo*, when he studied the "lost decades" of Japan since 1990, found that the overwhelming part of massive and cheap credit facilities offered by the Japanese government and banks *were not used by firms as they did not expect sufficient demand*.[29] Rather, highly indebted firms only reduced old debt, in particular debt resulting from earlier speculation in the sterile economy, such as real estate and stock speculation, before they considered new ventures in the productive economy.[30] Even authors who believe that "quantitative easing" works, see the main effective "transmission channel" in manipulations of foreign exchange rate, which is ultimately a protectionist thing.[31] Similar findings appear frequently in the Annual Reports of

---

27 The composition of assets, of course, changed with roll-overs – old bonds becoming due and new bonds becoming purchased – and with central bank trading, but the volume only grew.

28 If there were booms in the last decades, then in BRICS-countries, especially the once-in-human-history growth period in China.

29 *Koo* (2009) page 43, 47.

30 *Koo* (2009) page 39 et seq.

31 "Lesson one is that monetary policy works. The initial 'bazooka' of massive debt purchases by the bank of Japan in 2013 was highly effective. Bond yields fell; stock markets boomed; and most important, the yen fell below ¥100 to the dollar, a boon to Japanese industry." (*Harding*, Abenomics and the fight against 'Japanification', in: *Financial Times* of 7 September 2020). *Münchau*, The success of eurozone QE relies on a confidence trick, in: *Financial Times*

the Bank for International Settlements (BIS) in Basle or in macroeconomic writing.[32] Sometimes it is also argued that Quantitative Easing could work via "what is known as the 'portfolio rebalancing' channel – the idea that people who sell bonds to the ECB will need to put their money elsewhere, such as in the real economy".[33] But this would require that there are attractive alternative investment opportunities, which do not exist.

Carl Christian von Weizsäcker and *Hagen Krämer* took Keynes' identity of saving and investment and showed that, if it ever had existed, at least a notable divergence has arisen between saving and investment today. They found a lot of saving, but little investment[34] – notwithstanding the ultralow rates of the time. It was also observable in recent years that top-level-firms, who have proven to be able to make substantial successful investments as leaders of innovation, preferred to carry significant cash reserves over long periods or sought to shift them into the wealth economy, e.g., by re-purchasing their own stock, rather than making new investments in the productive economy. If *Apple* and *Microsoft* held reserves approaching $1 tn. or above $1 tn., their not-investing these amounts in the productive economy was certainly not due to the existing interest rate having been too high! Mainstreams economist too, today often admit that investment does not normally react much to a drop in interest rates.

Thus, a lot seems to speak for the "crude" theory! If there is a transmission belt between central bank debt purchases and increasing employment in the productive economy, it seems to be the spending of the net debt build-up (if the debt purchases are followed by a new debt-build up). Enable a raise of aggregate debt by central bank debt purchases and what you get is a raise in employment-generating spending by roughly the same amount after the state has channeled the money into transfer payments, military, or infrastructure spending. The simplest and most mechanic transmission belt of central banks debt purchases, which is openly unsustainable, appears to be the only reliable one.[35]

---

of 21 March 2015, is more skeptical, even with regard to effects on the exchange rate. He only agrees that QE has certain "effects on the "exchange rate", but, adds "it is not clear that this effect will be permanent".

32   E.g., International Bank for Settlement (BIS) at Basle (2016) page 13 .

33   See also *Münchau*, The success of eurozone QE relies on a confidence trick, in: *Financial Times* of 21 March 2015.

34   *Weizsäcker/Krämer* (2021).

35   It fits together with this suspicion that in the Corona crises, central banks announced *in advance* that they would buy ("back") the sovereign debt, which states or the European Union was issuing to fight the crisis. See page 485 and footnote 2 there.

Section 4. Expansive prosthetics funded with state fiat money creation

"Overt" and "Covert" Monetary Financing

There are two different ways to fund prosthetics with state fiat money creation. The first one operates without public debt and without central bank debt holdings. Its proponents call it *"overt monetary financing"* ("OMF".) The second way is the presently dominating practice of funding prosthetics by states issuing public debt and central banks purchasing this debt with newly created fiat money and holding it on their balance sheets. The latter, more conventional way is known as "Quantitative Easing", "QE" or "central banks' asset purchases". The purchased assets are predominantly sovereign debt. But central banks also purchase educational debt, credit card debt, housing debt, corporate debt or other private debt. "Overt monetary financing" presents itself as the more honest and more rational form to do what is being done anyhow and what is believed to have to be done, without alternative: money creation. This self-baptizing implies that the alternative, the conventional practice, should, consequentially, be called *"Covert Monetary Financing"* (CMF), which the adherents of the conventional practice will obviously not like. Ultimately, the naming-issue is irrelevant, but only the two options of funding prosthetics through state fiat money creation, either in conjunction with debt and central bank debt holdings or without debt and without central bank debt holdings – seem to exist.

The legality and legitimacy of both, "covert" and "overt", monetary financing is disputed. Fundamental, classic-liberal or libertarian opponents of state fiat money creation for monetary state financing reject it as morally, politically, and/or economically illegitimate. Their main argument is that if the substitution of commodity money (with remaining value-in-exchange if demonetarized) by state fiat money (without remaining value-in-exchange if demonetarized) is at all acceptable (because of its practical advantages), it would be a corrupt abuse of state fiat money to create it to selectively redistribute wealth.[36] The Germans, in particular, were horrified by the experience of German and Austrian inflation in 1923, which came very close to a general "euthanasia of the creditors". This inflation and the consecutive currency reform, in fact, economically annihilated the greatest part of the traditional German or Austrian political elites, which had been the backbone of the

---

36   In Germany, this is called "Ordnungspolitik", literally "order policies". The idea concerns the maintenance of abstract rules or of an order that enables a proper and "pure" operation of capitalism in a liberal, non-interventionist sense. It does not exclude social policies in general, but sets limits to them and, in particular, disallows infringement of a holy inner space of such structures. I do not know of a similar term in other languages. The trick of the term "Ordnungspolitik" is to coin as an active state policy that which, in fact, consists in a declaration of some sort of Wu Wei, i.e., of no-go-zones for the state.

"Kaiserreich" – and this annihilation surely contributed to paving the way for the Nazis.[37] In the forty years that followed World War II, the German "Bundesbank" was extremely conscient of this lesson and consistently supported a strong German currency, the Deutsche Mark; probably for this reason, the German Bundesbank had better approval rates than all German governments. Furthermore, the main German political parties only (ultimately univocally) convinced the Germans to acquiesce to the Euro-introduction with the (as we can now see: false) promise that the new European central bank would be as independent, unpolitical and supportive of a strong Euro as the German Bundesbank had. After that expectation was visibly disappointed, no surprise, conservative Germans brought numerous lawsuits to the German Constitutional Court to declare the European Central Bank's debt buying programs unconstitutional. The German Constitutional Court, indeed, expressed significant concerns about this matter several times and even called for a conditional halt to the European Central Bank's bond buying programs in a ruling of 5 May 2020.[38]

It was also widely held in economic theory that central banks' purchases, at least in "primary markets", hence central banks directly making loans to states, is dangerous and should be omitted. Still many economists today consider it as inadvisable for central banks to transfer *newly* created state fiat money as "overt monetary financing" to states and jurists argue that central banks' purchases in "primary markets" and "overt monetary financing" would be illegal in the Eurozone under Article 123 TFEU (which restates the consensus prior to the Euro-introduction).[39] Others argue that Article 123 TFEU at least does not prohibit asset purchases in "secondary

---

37   Polanyi (1944) page 24: "...the expropriation of the *rentier class*, which followed in its wake [of the German inflation, G.W.] laid the foundation for the Nazi revolution... the intellectual middle class was literally pauperized" (page 24, 25). As *Niall Ferguson* writes: "The hyperinflation could not wipe out Germany's external debt, which had been fixed in pre-war currency. But it could and did wipe out all the internal debt that had been accumulated during and after the war, levelling the debt mountain like some devastating earthquake...This amounted to a great levelling since it affected primarily the upper middle classes, *rentiers*, senior civil servants, professionals." (*Ferguson* (2008) page 106 et seq.)

38   2 BvR 859/15, 2 BvR 980/16, 2 BvR 2006/15, 2 BvR 1651/15. That decision was quickly sidestepped by the German government and the large majority of the German Bundestag by simply declaring that the requirements of the constitutional court had now been fulfilled by the European central bank, clearly showing the court the limits of its power.

39   Article 123 TFEU Sec. 1:"Overdraft facilities or any other type of credit facility with the European Central Bank or with the central banks of the Member States ... in favour of Union institutions, bodies, offices or agencies, central governments, regional, local or other public authorities, other bodies governed by public law, or public undertakings of Member States shall be prohibited, *as shall the purchase directly from them by the European Central Bank or national central banks of debt instruments.*" (italics added).

markets", in particular, if they are made with the declared intent of an exit there-after, hence, along the lines of the former "open market policies". We will leave the constitutional and political battles as they stand, yet having to note that from a sober perspective there is no real macroeconomic difference between central banks' asset purchases in "secondary markets", purchases in "primary markets" or "overt monetary financing" without involving debt.[40]

"Overt monetary financing", State fiat money creation without debt and without central bank debt holdings

Of the two options, funding prosthetics without public debt and central bank debt holdings, "overt monetary financing", is the purest, most naked, most radical, most utopian, and most technocrat version of funding prosthetics with state fiat money creation. We shall first look at it in more detail for this reason.

The view that debt is equal with money or is always connected to money and money creation has become the favorite view of many non-mainstreams-economists. Yet, this view is flawed: Assume that a Spanish convoy of ships returns from Potosi, via Havana, to Sevilla or Cadiz, in the 17th century. The ship is filled with silver. The Spanish king will be at the port, might say a few words, praise God, the seamen, and himself, make a sweeping gesture and have his share of the loot carried to his vaults. He will get some coins embossed (some were already embossed in Potosi), will begin spending the new commodity money – and will wait for the next convoy. *There is no debt involved*. If he at all book the occurrence, he will book the silver as a new asset on the assets side and will raise his equity as a counter entry (debit: silver stock, credit: equity or earnings).

Centuries later, if in a fiat money regime, a state treasury has received a truck load of new monnaie papier from its printing-press, how will it book this? Not much speaks against applying the same procedure of the Spanish king. As the new *monnaie papier* has value-in-exchange – the state can pay suppliers and state functionaries

---

40 *Martin Wolf* also writes in the Financial Times of 7 April 2020: "Central banks must do what it takes. This means monetary financing of governments. Central banks pretend that what they are doing is reversible and so is not monetary financing. If that helps them act, that is fine, even if it is probably untrue". The substantial identity of "outright monetary financing" and central banks purchasing sovereign debt in secondary markets is also quite clear in *Adair Turner*'s discussion of the case of Japan. "That debt [of Japan to the Bank of Japan, G.W.] could be written off and replaced on the asset side of the bank of Japan's balance sheet with an accounting entry – a perpetual non-interest-bearing owed from the government to the bank". "The immediate impact of this [of a write-off of government debt of Japan to the Bank of Japan, G.W.] would be nil, since the interest, which the government currently receives from the bank is currently returned as a dividend by the bank to the government as the bank's owner." (*Turner* (2016) page 229).

with it, who, in turn, can pay taxes and their creditors with it – and as the monnaie papier is certainly owned by the state, it can be shown as an asset on the assets side of the balance sheet. If we abstract from the costs of paper, printing, and transport, as little is debt creation involved as when the Spanish king received his gold or silver delivery. Nothing would change if the money were to arrive as an entry on credit accounts, be it with a central bank or with private banks, [41] or as digital money. The proper counter entry would be "capital", or "revenues from fiat money creation" in a profit and loss statement. In summary, whether a miner has found gold, an alchemist has produced gold, a robber has robbed gold, or a financial alchemist has created fiat money, this will increase the recipient's wealth or equity, but will normally *not* involve debt.

If the state uses the arriving money, then this will lead to an expense. If the state has helicopters drop *monnaie papier* over football stadiums, if it stuffs bills into cash machines where withdrawals can be made for free, or makes transfers to bank accounts of citizens, e.g., as a monthly basic salary, [42] then this is an expense to the state, which reduces its capital. In profit and loss statements, it may, e.g., be booked as "expenses for social transfers".

There is no technical or mechanical economic reason why states should not orient their fiat money creation system in this direction. As we said, states could even compete with their central bank in fiat money creation or revoke the fiat money creation power, which they delegated to the central bank, and reassign it to sub-departments of their finance ministry. Many different combinations are possible depending on political circumstances. One path to general "overt monetary financing" could be for central banks, upon request of the state, to create fiat money and to purchase the existing sovereign debt from private bond holders and to waive the payment claims against the state, which it conveys. States would, thus, enjoy a grand ultimate debt-forgiveness and could, from there on, procure the money, which they

---

41   The account holder, of course, has a claim to the bank that he has his account with, but that is only a transitory technical debt resulting from the fact that money is held as book money, not the type of debt meant by the adherents of a money-debt-connection. This can be seen if the account holder has his credit paid out to him. He has the cash and nowhere is there any debt left.

42   The state can also annihilate existing debt in favor of private parties. It can, for instance, go through a list of debtors of educational debt, credit card debt or housing debt and selectively annihilate this debt by paying state fiat money some of the respective creditors. This can be done following the social impulse, e.g., to release those debtors of US-educational debt who did not make partner in a Wall Street investment bank or following the macroeconomic impulse to generate new producive spending (instead of sterile debt service), first by freeing existing income for the purpose, second by enabling new debt build-up.

need in excess of their income from taxes etc., by "overt monetary financing" alone – without new debt issues.

There is a notable backside to this. The burial of sovereign debt would also bury the sovereign debt market for the respective currency – image it would happen to US-treasuries – and be like an earthquake in sterile wealth markets in general. With the lack of tradable objects, Sovereign debt markets would cease to exist. As a result, the private money creation gland, private bank credit money creation, would shrink drastically, as private banks would lose a main debt customer. High income-accustomed traders in sovereign debt markets, the sovereign debt sub-departments in the fixed income departments of investment firms, and sovereign debt investment advisers would lose their jobs. For the lowered relevance of private bank credit money creation, the staff in private bank watchdogs could be significantly reduced. Moreover, 90 percent of the employees in central banks and in finance ministries, which had been were involved in sovereign debt issues and the administration of interest and debt payments or in sovereign debt purchases and collections of debt service, could be dismissed.[43] If finance ministers, thereafter, find out as part of their budget and tax planning that they need additional money, as they are sure to, they will simply determine the amount and make a proposal to the cabinet. The cabinet will pass a resolution that may be published in the Federal Gazette or some such, and the central bank (if it at all still exists and has not been swallowed by the state) will transfer the amount of money required to an account of the state. From there on out, it will be business as usual, money may flow opulently, without debt creation.

Some authors, e.g., *Adair Turner*, who have critically and sensibly analyzed the macroeconomic and monetary situation of the leading capitalist states, in fact, stress advantages, which "overt monetary financing" is supposed to have over essentially the same thing being done "covertly".[44] First, they ask – with reference to rationalist tradition – is it not always more rational and intelligent to deal openly with a problem than concealing what is being done, in particular as this tends to also conceal the dangers and risks involved? Did speaking openly about sex not help to prevent the spread of AIDS? Second, if monetary financing is rightly judged

---

43   The question obviously arises concerning where the billions of money that used to populate the markets for sovereign debt of the respective state would go. We pursue the new practice of money creation further before we go to this important point.

44   The selection of the term "overt monetary financing" was a smart tactical move by its proponents. It implies that monetary financing takes place anyhow (which is correct) and, thus, already by its name belies the official view that there is presently *no* monetary state financing. This forces opponents of overt monetary finance to either also object to the long-established conventional practices (of "quantitative easing" etc.) or to explain where the differences are supposed to be (which is very difficult). It also reframes the debate into: "What we already do (and have to do!), given ideals of honesty and transparency, should it not be done in an open and better way?"

to be dangerous but if there is still consensus that it has to happen, then should it not better be taken away from private banks, who have a financial interest in overusing it to make profits, and be entrusted to the state? Do we not generally take dangerous activities, such as running armies, the police, the certification of drugs and atomic plants etc. away from private entities and assign them to the state? Third, "nationalizing" dangerous money creation via state fiat money (while scaling down private fractional bank money creation) would allow states to better steer the direction and volume of money creation. The collateral damage of private money creation, e.g., in the busts after artificial booms in sterile wealth markets, could be neutralized.[45] Fourth, could not "overt monetary financing" be an exceptional tool to annihilate excessive old sovereign debt, e.g., following a pandemic or war etc., and thereby support future traditional "covert monetary financing", i.e., new traditional debt issues, after a clean-up of states' balance sheets? The deletion of sovereign debt from states' balance sheets would make states more eligible to take on new debt in the future again, would it not? "Overt monetary financing" and "covert monetary financing" could, thus, instead of being mutually exclusive, become a complementary system. For instance, "overt monetary financing" might require a constitutional political majority etc. – politicians will probably like this idea. Fifth, we have already touched upon the fact that covert monetary financing by central bank debt purchases requires many transactions between huge bureaucracies with significant costs, which can be spared. Moreover, states could spare the revenues that private banks and their consultants draw from the issuance of bonds and, possibly again, when the bonds are purchased by the central banks. One can see this as a foregone opportunity to keep that money in the public sector.[46] Finally, states and central banks could get rid of the intellectual embarrassment of pretending that what is obviously essentially the same – "covert" and "overt monetary financing" – is not the same. OMF could make states and politics honest again.

The arguments for "overt monetary financing" are, thus, quite plausible as such. If this is so, why did states and central banks not embrace them long ago? A pragmatic answer might be: The present covert practice still functions well, and there is no strong case why "overt monetary financing" should function so much better.[47] There is, hence, no need to rush into a switch, which remains available in the future

---

45   See *Turner* (2016) page 3, 218, 232, 239, 250. The line of argument resembles the Chicago Plan.

46   The pro-OMF argument puts emphasis on this. But it is also possible that states see the flow to private banks and consultants (who are often banks as well) as an advantage. By enriching banks, states stabilize the central bank-private banks-tandem-relationship.

47   In particular, as, by announcing that they *will* purchase new issues of bonds, they can already today initiate new private fractional reserve credit money creation if they feel that new prosthetics need to be funded. Why alter anything as long as it works?

anyhow. For the time being, states and central banks may also consider it as favorable to stay in the "cover" of a Byzantine hullabaloo, which plays to the illusion that they are still operating in the framework of conventional "open market operations". This can de-thematize the movement of central banks into unchartered and novel terrains and maintain trust. Yet, as we shall see when we consider the dilemmas of funding prosthetics with state fiat money creation, states may have even stronger reasons to remain skeptical about "overt monetary financing".

"Covert monetary financing", State fiat money creation with debt and central bank debt holdings

As we have seen, "open market operations" had never really functioned in the way they were officially explained to function. They did not stimulate firms significantly to invest more in the productive economy through lower interest rates. The alleged sophisticated transmission belts – lower rates were supposed to bring about increased profitability of investments and higher business values – did not work. Yet, the mistaken sophisticated explanation hid simpler, more banal and crude mechanics that did:[48] Debt purchases returned cash for new debt issues to investors and liquid debt market raised their willingness to hold more debt. Furthermore, falling interest rates facilitated taking out loans by private borrowers as they became more

---

48   It is not all that uncommon for social institutions' official legitimation to be "half wrong". I found the same result in my dissertation on criminal law. The "true" social function of criminal law is to sharpen and to strengthen social values and ideologies by re-expressing them and by re-elevating them through a monopoly to scandalously inflict violent damage to he who disrespected them. A fitting official legitimation of punishment – since the ascent of the state – was thus to measure punishment by the evil will which was expressed in the committed deed; a sort of an educated and emotion-free revenge by the state, which was targeted at the general values, which the state wanted society to hold, substituted the prior emotional and hateful revenge of the family of the victim, which targeted family values or an archaic order of custom. That justifying ideology ran into problems in the Enlightenment as an admittedly backwards-oriented practice (*Malum passionis propter malum actionis*) did not fit in a world of future-oriented social engineering. The enlightened punishment, thus, had to be based on its (alleged) future effects on the individual or on society. The modern, rational purposes of punishment, which are deterrence, incapacitation or betterment of the "patient criminal" arose from here. However, nowhere were they, in fact, allowed to fully displace the punishment of the evil will – as that would have threatened what society truly continuously wants punishment to achieve. As a result, social institutions or practices that "get the job done" (in the view of the ruling powers) tend to survive, even if ruptures in the official legitimizing facade become visible. In that sense, "open market operations" and talk about lowering interest rates and rising asset prices may remain the official story, while in truth the really workable effect is procuring money to productive spenders. On criminal law see *Wächter* (1987).

affordable and supported private bank credit money creation.[49] This way, open markets operations helped to further prosthetic employment-generating spending and to mitigate the modern master drama – even under conditions of primary fractional reserves bank credit money creation. Banks and wealth owners were ready to give more loans as they could rely on getting rid of them quickly and at decent terms.[50]

While states could live well with this situation, a problem arose at the other side of the market. As the crisis of 2008 taught, wealth owners' willingness to absorb certain private debts, which were a large component of aggregate private debt, – "US-subprime private debt" – had been overstretched at some point. Similarly, as the European sovereign debt crisis of 2010 taught that wealth owners' willingness to absorb a certain type of sovereign debt – "European subprime sovereign debt" so to speak – had also been overstretched, at least at given interest rates or yields.

When the crisis hit – long before the head of the ECB *Mario Draghi*, in masculine warrior-tones, committed to "do what it takes" to save the Euro, the governments, not the central banks, had to act. States actually *love* emergencies and to unleash drastic political and legal measures. Within days they promised to provide loans to "system-critical" banks and other, mainly financial, firms and institutions, and soon actually provided government money in the form of loans as first emergency measure. This was necessary to save them from illiquidity as some of them could no longer finance their daily payment obligations. Such rapid loans would, though, only solve liquidity concerns, but could not, ultimately, improve the balance sheets and solvency of the banks and financial institutions. Equity-injections were required too. Yet, as there were limits to the readiness of states to make presents to private firms and as, according to – unfortunately still liberal – corporate laws, shareholders have to decide themselves whether they accept equity contributions and in exchange against how many shares, "shareholders democracy" came obstructively into play here. Yet, there was no time for observing the petty procedures of corporate laws or for a long-winded negotiation of deals. (Typically, an agreement would have been necessary by how much the stated capital of the affected corporations had to be reduced, and then increased again, and under what conditions, which mostly requires

---

49 Lower rates helped states, too, to build up debt. Yet, the obligation to pay interest only seriously burdens state budgets if the debt is still mostly privately held. As seen, the higher the percentage of sovereign debt, which is held by central banks, which return their profits to states, the less the nominal amount of interest rates matters.

50 Polanyi already wrote: "The integrating power of monetary policies surpassed by far that of the other kinds of protectionism...What the businessman, the organized worker, the housewife pondered, what the farmer who was planning his crop, the parents who were weighing their children's chances, the lovers who were waiting to get married, revolved in their minds when considering the favor of the times, was more directly determined by the monetary policy of the central bank than by any other single factor" (*Polanyi* (1944) page 214).

the consent of 75 percent of the shareholders.) Thus, the legislative dashed in in executive style and laws, which were made in a great hurry, allowed government buy-ins into "system critical" corporations *outside of normal corporate and capital market laws* and *even against the will of the majority of existing shareholders*. The emergency laws were arch-capitalist in their purposes, but commando-socialist, if not bolshevist, in their methods. They disregarded not only shareholder democracy but also the holy idea of property behind it (shareholder democracy is ultimately only *how* the owners manage their joint ownership). The emergency-commando-politics also – surprisingly? – disclosed consensus among the political elites of the leading capitalist countries, from the left to the right, that they did not at all trust the self-regulation of markets, which most of them normally so much praise. In a crisis, it appeared, that everybody was ready to give his Sunday-speeches and to interfere into capitalism as if liberalism and neo-liberalism had never existed.

After the first emergency phase of the mission was completed, time was gained to now grant loans to further increase the liquidity of the endangered businesses, in particular if new bad assets were discovered or if claims against insurers, which had insured bad assets, were raised. State guarantees also greatly helped to calm the nerves of creditors This re-infused trust into the system.

Only now, after important battles were won, central banks joined the scene. They essentially repeated what the Bank of Japan had already done for almost two decades and which had become known as "quantitative easing". As in innocent times of open market policies, they bought debt, but *much more than before* and they now did it utterly *unconcerned about selling it back* to private wealth owners any time soon. Economic, political, and cultural practices and institutions possess a remarkable flexibility to adjust to changes. At first, it appears that they are only used as they were used before; then it appears that they are adjusted to specific circumstances, later that they are being used a bit more often and at larger volumes than before.... However, the "filling of new content" into them, in fact, transforms "old tubes" – and soon they are something quite different.[51] Such was the destiny of central banks' previous "open market policies". Even if they were never really working well as two-way open market policies, oscillating between "easy" and "tight"-money periods, now even the official explanation of the central banks' doing in these terms could no longer be upheld. Too much debt was attracted in only one direction without any relevant effect on interest rates, which were already at zero or below, and it was held for too long. The times of "open market operations" were over and the times "non-conventional monetary policies", i.e. debt accumulation by the central banks, had arrived.

---

51   In a similar sense, *Polanyi* (1944) page 192 writes "...it would be truer to say that no institution ever survives its function – when it seems to do so it is because it serves in some other function or functions, *which need not include the original*" (italics by Polanyi).

To be clear: All debt that is held by central banks normally only gets into their balance sheets because they *pay for it with newly created state fiat money*. Thus, central bank debt holdings as such normally indicate state money creation or monetary financing. Still, as long the purpose of these debt holdings remains within the framework of traditional "open market policies" – to officially work as a vaccine to lower interest rates and to stabilize private debt markets – and as the volumes and the time of central banks' debt holding are limited, that is one thing. Yet, this changes when central banks debt holding becomes a *substitute* for private creditors. *Perry Mehrling* has attempted to describe this change as central banks transforming from "lenders of last resort" to "market makers" or "dealers of last resort",[52] with the purpose of still securing the "shiftability" of debt.[53] Mehrling sees the trend, but he only describes what central banks, in fact, already did with their open market policies. His conceptualization also overemphasizes the formal side – whether loans are given or assets are bought –, yet he underrates the essence of the change. We have to go a step further in order to grasp the "qualitative jump", which is happening. The central banks post 2008 became more than just dealers (which buy *and* sell). They instead became *net debt accumulators* or *debt absorbers of last resort*. They consciously ignited a massive uninterrupted flow of debt into their balance sheets, more voluminous and more quickly than ever before, and this debt was meant to stay.[54] The idea of a cyclical change between central bank asset purchases and asset sales had become obsolete.[55]

Emergencies are times, at which pragmatists with lots of the "have-to-do-what-it-takes"-hormone offer themselves to step in. They know that somebody has to show confidence and they feel selected to be that person. This may explain why the helm of central banks were, since, more often taken by personalities who thought and acted like politicians, or had been politicians, and less often by typical scientific economists.[56]

---

52   *Mehrling* (2011).

53   See *Mehrling* (2011), in particular page 132 et seq.

54   "It is the Fed's acceptance of its role as dealer of last resort that finally put a floor under the crisis..." writes Perry Mehrling (*Mehrling* (2011) page 115). Yet, it may rather have been the Fed's acceptance, to buy and hold the purchased assets, irrespective of any realistic expectation to shift them back to private debt holders, which brought about the healing effect.

55   If matured debt was repaid by the sovereign or private debtors, i.e., "rolled over", then central banks would also buy the new, rolled over debt.

56   E.g., *Christine Lagarde* started off as a business lawyer (by chance in the Paris office of the international law firm, in whose Frankfurt office the present author began his career), then became French Finance Minister (amongst other government posts), followed her compatriot Strauss-Kahn after his unfortunate New York hotel-room-incident as managing director of the International Monetary Fund in 2011, and, although she was found guilty of abuse of office as finance minister (by accepting, as the French court found, an excessive

Occasionally, hope arose amongst the conservatives that there might be a way back to the status *quo ante*, that debt could be unloaded again to privates, interest rates would rise, and that "normal" "open market policies" could be resumed. The often-used terms "tapering" and "exit" pointed to this at the time. However, until after the Corona-crisis, the worlds' central banks only bought more and more debt (and sometimes other assets) through "central bank asset purchase programs" etc., losing their "natural" inhibitions more and more. The volumes of intended new debt purchases were now even more generally openly announced before the fact – with the obvious purpose to let the subscribers know that they would not have to worry about opportunities unload the new debt quickly, reliably and profitably.[57] The Corona crisis, the Ukraine war, the coming armament build-up across the world in a now generally more bellicose geopolitical atmosphere (or even in extended wars), this all led or will lead to additional sovereign debt build-up. Therefore, it is hard to see that any significant unloading is coming soon, rises of interest rates and some inflation in the productive economy following 2022 (with the inflation appearing to partially result from the loss of output and interruptions of the cheapest supply chains in the Corona crisis and from increased energy costs following the Ukraine war) notwithstanding.

Overall, the combined effect of the state and central bank actions following the crisis of 2008, was to, in one blow, *retroactively refinance a huge part of the privately held outstanding debt,* which the central bank itself had indirectly enabled by its easy-money-policies, *by direct state fiat money creation.* From that point forward, a large chunk of all newly issued sovereign and working-class debt was picked up by central banks as well. This is what happened in numbers:

---

settlement payment made by France to Bernard Tapie) in 2016, became President of the European Central Bank in 2019. *Mario Draghi* was still an economics professor, but turned politician and became prime minster of Italy. *Janet Yellen*, too, was still an economics professor before she became President of the Fed and, then, US Finance Minister. It was also seen as a recommendation for a second term of *Jay Powell* as President of the Fed that he had "shown himself to be a nimble central banker and not tied unduly to dogma or ideology." *Colby Smith* and *James Politi* quote this statement by *Peter Conti-Brown*, a Fed historian, in the Financial Times of 23 November 2021 page 3. Powell was also praised for having had his "Draghi moment and [to have] met it in any way" (loc. cit.)

57   This situation between states, sovereign debt creditors, and central banks compares to the situation that existed during the build-up of subprime debt: US saving banks would give out subprime (ninja etc.) real estate loans knowing that they could quickly resell them to other banks who bought them to structure, repackage, insure and resell them. Debt generation is encouraged if you can recoup the principal at a profit and soon hand over the risk to somebody else.

Figure 23: Total assets of Fed, ECB, BoJ and PBoC (individually)

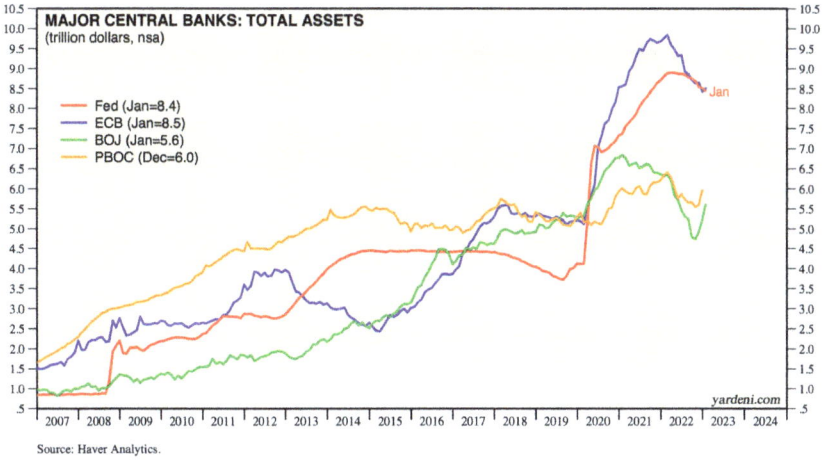

MAJOR CENTRAL BANKS: TOTAL ASSETS
(trillion dollars, nsa)

Fed (Jan=8.4)
ECB (Jan=8.5)
BOJ (Jan=5.6)
PBOC (Dec=6.0)

yardeni.com

Source: Haver Analytics.

Figure 24: Total assets of Fed, ECB, BoJ and PBoC (aggregated)

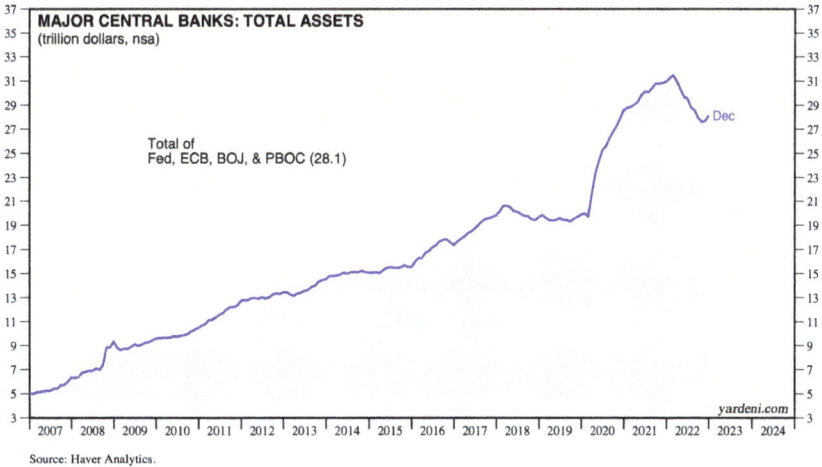

MAJOR CENTRAL BANKS: TOTAL ASSETS
(trillion dollars, nsa)

Total of
Fed, ECB, BOJ, & PBOC (28.1)

yardeni.com

Source: Haver Analytics.

Since 2007, the central banks of the most important capitalist economies (the Fed, the ECB, the Bank of Japan, and the People's Bank of China) have collectively increased their asset holding from roughly US$ 5 tn. to just short of US$ 30 tn. in December 2022.[58] Sovereigns, firms and workers issue debt to banks or wealth owners who sell this debt to central banks without much delay. Loans, which are ini-

---

58   https://www.yardeni.com/pub/peacockfedecbassets.pdf.

tially funded by old pre-existing wealth or by private bank credit money creation, are thereby re-financed by state fiat money creation. Existing wealth and fractional reserves bank credit money creation kickstart prosthetics funding, but the original financiers are bailed out after a short time. Of course, central banks will pay a premium to the investors who play by these rules. While there is not much money to make with the low interest, there may at least be some capital gains from selling the bonds to central banks. Some of it is an "anti-embarrassment-fee", saving central banks face. Profits are no longer made by holding debt and collecting the interest based on the coupons, neither by reselling the debt at a capital gain to other privates, but by exiting from the debt to central banks, which investors have already in mind when they purchase the freshly issued debt.

Considering that in 2021/2022 the US had a GDP of approx. 26 trn., China of 19 trn., Japan of 4.3 trn., [59] and the Eurozone of 14,5 trn.,[60] each in US\$, (together 63.8 trn. US\$, of a world GDP of approx. 104 trn. US\$[61]), as of this writing, these largest capitalist states have supported their economies with prosthetics financed with state fiat money creation through assets held by their central banks in a total amount of around 47 % of their GDP.[62]

**

These 47 %, however, only express the volume of debt that could *no longer be absorbed by private creditors* or that central banks would rather not risk to sell to private wealth owners. *Privately held debt must be added* in order to appreciate debt's full prosthetic contribution to the output and employment of the respective economies in the past. In the aggregate, the amounts shown in the table "Development of sovereign and private debt in leading capitalist countries 1995–2020" on page 447 – between approx. 225 % (China, Germany) and 450 % (Japan) – were debt financed and pumped into the economies of leading capitalist states already until 2020. Sovereign debt can be expected to have largely, except to the extent it financed interest to private creditors, flown into the productive economy, either directly as social transfers or as spending on infrastructure or the military, which is, largely employment-generating.[63] The largest chunk of automobile debt, educational debt, and of other non-

---

59   https://www.populationu.com/gen/countries-by-gdp. (each 2022)
60   https://tradingeconomics.com/euro-area/gdp (2021)
61   https://www.populationu.com/gen/countries-by-gdp.
62   We abstract from objections that might be raised against methods of GDP-calculations; the statistical evidence is so strong that such details do not matter. We assume that most of the enabled spending was productive spending. The spending certainly did not always remain in the domestic economy, but there was crosswise spill over into other countries.
63   States seldom purchase wealth assets, particularly, they did not in the recent neo-liberal decades. State money, which is lost for producive spending, mostly goes into interest pay-

real estate consumer debt, such as credit card debt, can also be expected to have gone into employment-generating spending; the slippage, again, mainly consists of most interest payments.[64] Whether real estate debt is used productively largely depends on whether old or new buildings are financed and on the size of the share, which finances transactional costs. Corporate debt partially finances employment-generating spending, such as new factories, but also sterile asset purchases, e.g., of land, in M&A, by stock repurchase program, or short-term sterile portfolio or treasury investments in stock or bond markets. Corporate debt, which finances interest payments or sterile rent etc., is also lost as employment-generating spending.

After all, it is safe to say that the leading capitalist countries, as of today, have boosted their Output and employment by between 150 % and 300 % of the GDP,[65] only via debt financing in the past. Hence, they have used *prosthetic employment-generating spending in a volume of between one and a half and three years of their output*. Prosthetics financed in other ways, e.g., employment-generating spending drawn away from other countries via protectionism or procured by taxation, is not included. We are not talking about sub-Saharan Africa or other poor or undeveloped regions of the world; this is about what politicians of the far better-off capitalist countries, such as the US, China, Japan, the UK, and the Eurozone felt necessary to mitigate the modern master drama in *their privileged* home countries!

The dilemmas of funding prosthetics with state fiat money creation

Central bank purchases of old and new debt

The main story of the political economy since 2008 consisted in the re-financing of massive amounts of already existing debt, which had originally been privately financed and which had enabled prosthetic spending in the past, by the creation of new state fiat money. It was combined with, from thereon, financing larger parts of new employment-generating spending with state fiat money creation, only after a short interim-stop with private debt-holders. This combination, which also opened up new reservoirs for private loans, led to the historic peak of debt and prosthetic spending, which we witness in the early 21th century. Whether this practice will continue in the old merry-go-round-like style of "covert monetary financing" or whether it will wholly or partially be switched into "overt monetary financing" would not change the substance. Both forms lead into dilemmas.

---

ments. However, interest is presently low and has been for a long time and interest on sovereign debt held by central banks is recycled to states as central banks dividends.

64   Interest rates in this sector are obviously higher than for sovereign debt, particularly on sub-prime debt or if repayments are overdue. They were still generally rather low.

65   As the data are from 2020, they do not yet reflect spending due to the Corona-crises and worldwide increases of military budgets.

No low-rates-private debt holders available

Central banks' attempts to resell a significant part of the debt presently accumulated in their balance sheets to private wealth owners runs into difficulties.[66] The first difficulty lies in the limited will of private wealth owners to absorb risky low-rates debt. This limitation already caused the shocks of the US subprime crisis of 2008 and of the European debt crisis in 2010. These limits, while they are not fix and may move to some degree, have not gone away. The issued debt has even significantly grown since 2008, which raised the risks involved in holding it; this will hardly increase the hunger of private wealth owners to buy large chunks of it. On the other hand, true, interest rates have risen since the Corona-crisis. Yet, they have only risen from zero to the levels of around 2007 and the fact that private wealth owners were trying to unload their subprime debt in a hurry then, does not render it very likely that they may now massively buy debt at similar rates – even if the debt offered today is somewhat better than the historic subprime-debt. There is, thus, insufficient demand of wealth owners for low-rates-private debt.

States feel comfortable if sovereign debt is held by central banks

While it is difficult to unload debt held by central banks, already for the preceding reason, it is less difficult to keep debt on central banks' balance sheets. In the case of *sovereign debt*, this is, if old biases are stripped-off, even particularly simple, as interest paid by the state to the central bank is automatically cycled back to the state who owns the central bank as dividends. How much interest states have to pay to the central bank on central bank held sovereign debt is, thus, – it the matter is considered with radical sobriety – ultimately *no relevant factor* at all. The money leaves through the front door as interest and comes back in through the back door as dividends, and the amount, which is being re-cycled does not matter.[67]

States could also live well with sovereign debt being held by private wealth owners

If sovereign debt is re-privatized, the interest on the re-privatized sovereign debt would flow into the private sector and stay there. States could still live with that.

---

66   Except for if OMF or a yet unknown fake maneuver is used to equip the private wealth owners with the needed money and/or to relief them of risks.

67   Of course, there are some politicians, economists, bankers, and central bankers out there, who, notwithstanding their radical doing, still think in old-fashioned terms and will, thus, suffer. They will suffer even more if the higher interest rates for new debt since the Corona crisis apply *generally to all sovereign debt*. This, yet, takes time until *the whole sovereign debt has been rolled over* and all low interest coupons have been replaced by the new higher coupons. As long as the outstanding sovereign debt still largely consist of old cheap debt, the average interest rate remains moderate. The good news is that the compensating effect of "dividends" from the central bank to the state will also apply to high interest invoices.

As states or their central banks sit on the state fiat money gland, they could simply have their central banks *also create the fiat money additionally needed* to cover the additional, even rising, interest-costs, which will not be recycled from the private sector (or only partially via taxes) – and have this money forward to them via "covert" or "overt" monetary financing. In times of "whatever it takes" the public will quickly get accustomed to this.

Sales of central bank-held debt at discount-prices lead into dilemmas

Central banks might consider to offload debt, which they hold, at attractive discount-prices. This would, yet, lead to higher yields on the old debt and, thus, raise interest rates for new loans, in particular to workers and firms. Such higher rates would, of course, also apply to roll-overs of old debt of workers and firms. This way, the re-selling of old debt at discount-prices would, via higher rates, infringe upon the possibility of maintaining and continuing the build-up of workers-debt, e.g., of housing, educational, automobile, consumer and credit card debt, which funds prosthetic employment-generating spending. The higher interest rates connected to cheap sell-offs of debt would also lead to collateral damage by giving *coups de grace* to "zombie-new-economy-firms" as well as "zombie-old-economy-firms". High rates just do not go together with ongoing build-up of workers-debt and the survival of dubitable firms.

If states and central banks were to allow significant raises of interest rates, they would, accordingly, have to compensate for them by additional transfer payments to workers and firms. This would, though, require them to issue even more sovereign debt in the aggregate, which could raise interest rates further, the more so the higher the part of the debt, which is privately held. (Of course, if to avoid rising rates, central banks buy this new debt, they would again upload debt on the one side whilst they are trying to offload debt on the other). There is no way out. A return to normalcy regarding rates is paid for with less non-normalcy regarding central banks' debt holdings. Both goals, more normal, i.e., higher than near zero percent interest rates, and more normal, i.e., lower, at before 2008 levels, central bank debt holdings, are incompatible with growing sovereign and other debt, which are though needed to fund prosthetics.

Central banks feel as comfortable holding high mountains of dubitable debt as states feel being indebted

If clearing central bank asset sheets of the debt mountains by reprivatizing debt to private wealth owners turns out problematic, why, then, not keep the debt on central banks' balance sheets and allow a further build-up of debt there?

There is, in fact, no fundamental problem with that: As soon as debt arrives on a balance sheet of a central bank, it enters a better world. Central banks are not greedy and not obsessed with hunting profit; moreover, they are free of liquidity pressures, survival constraints or other necessities, which may force them into reckless acts. They can be generous as they are blessed with the power to create as much money as they desire.[68] *They do not need it, but they can have as much of it as they could wish!*

Of course, as far as states are concerned, central banks are friends with their states. They are like wealthy fathers having purchased their lavish sons' notes; the sons can hope that the father may not claim the money. In fact, this comparison even misrepresents a crucial moment: The state is the *sovereign*, it can politically decide to dissolve the central bank, can create a new central bank or recall the fiat money creation power that it has conveyed to it; lavish sons normally have not so much power over their fathers. Apart from these political powers, central banks are also – in different constructions – legally owned by their states. Therefore, as we have mentioned, they have to return the profits from interest paid by their states to them as dividends to states as their owners. Central banks are not only very relaxed, but *subservient creditors* to their sovereign debtors (compare that to the obstinate private bankers of the states since the Middle Ages, e.g., the Jewish, Lombards, and Cahorsians!).[69]

In the aggregate, the classic economic dilemma for states in commodity money regimes – issuing too much debt would bring them to the brink of illiquidity, insolvency, and bankruptcy, which exerted an unforgiving discipline over them – is no longer, at least not for the privileged group of leading states that can issue debt in their own currency, i.e., most major developed capitalist countries such as the US, China, Japan, the UK, the Eurozone-countries (to a lesser degree as they only have a "collective" central bank) etc.

Increase of the money volume and means to handle the additional money

However, even the privileged states that can indebt themselves in their own currency, and who can fund the prosthetics, which can no longer be lastingly financed out of existing private money or private bank credit money creation, by state fiat

---

68   Until, of course, some day when people no longer want fresh money as no more value-in-exchange is attributed to it.

69   As the public debt mountains on the shelves of the central bank grow higher, it is easily possible to conceal what is going on by all kinds of cosmetic moves. We may see transfers of debt to subsidiaries of central banks or subsidiaries of the state, even to apparently private units, which either do not have to pay a purchase price or ultimately receive finance from the state or from the central bank. We may also see debt contracts to be amended in different directions: interest lowered, delays granted, overdue payments waived, the debt mutated into some a conditional, mezzanine-like form of debt, etc. A lot is imaginable here for economists and lawyers to confuse others and themselves about the underlying realities. Ultimately, it is in the central banks' power to do what final disposal facilities for nuclear or chemical toxic waste can never achieve: Central banks can wholly do away with the debt by simply forgiving it.

money creation, and maneuver their central bank to take this debt on its balance sheet, cannot avoid that thereby the *money volume is greatly increased*. We may hold for a moment and ascertain where we are with our argument: Capitalism is structurally stricken with deficient employment-generating spending. Capitalist states apply a number of prosthetics, of which expansive prosthetics, by debt-build-up funded by state fiat money creation ("covert monetary financing"), has presently become the main method. It allows to handle the debt, which originated in the process, by simply accumulating it on central banks' balance sheets. But what about the simultaneously also increased money volumes? Are *they* leading to dilemmas? What can be done, if anything, about such dilemmas?

We now see that the problem of deficient employment-generating spending is substituted by the *problem of having to handle the increased money volume*. There are two obvious means to do this. Both work via containment of this money and both were already practiced after central banks massive money creation following the financial crisis of 2008 and are still being practiced.

One option is simply to allow the additional money to be invested in such *assets markets, which are not simultaneously product markets*, hence in debt and stock markets. As long as sovereign debt markets exist, they offer themselves particularly well for this purpose, as money going there is, by the same token, refunding prosthetics. Already Marx, although he did not make a systematic contribution to state and prosthetics financing, observed, they are great money absorbers.[70] In fact, the usefulness of debt markets as playground for money may be a strong reason in favor of maintaining the conventional way of prosthetics financing, hence "covert monetary financing". As long as with newly created money also new debt, in particular sovereign debt, is created on the flipside as an asset, it can at least still be offered to private wealth owners, and they may hold a portion of it. The two sides, which originate with "covert monetary financing" can pair and keep busy with each other. "Overt monetary financing", which does not involve debt, forecloses this option.

The second option consist in channeling back the newly created money to their creators, the central banks. The storyline of this practice is: Central banks create money to buy existing debt-instruments. The wealth owners who receive this money deposit it on bank accounts or buy assets in asset markets from other wealth owners with it, who in turn deposit the received money on bank accounts... Ultimately, central banks absorb this money by offering to private banks to *redeposit it with central banks for some interest*. Central banks, observed *Benjamin Friedmann*, "have made it advantageous for banks to redeposit the additional reserves instead of lending against them."[71] Like central banks pick up the new debt by money creation, they also pick up

---

70   See e.g., *Marx* (1976) chapter 31.

71   *Friedmann*, The perils of returning a central bank balance sheet to 'normal', in *Financial Times* of 20 June 2014. The *Neue Züricher Zeitung* of 22 February 2010, page 9, makes the same

the newly created money – by also creating new money to pay interest on this money if it is shuffled over to them. What happens if these – or other methods– fail?

Inflation, employment-generating spending and prosthetics

Increases in the money volume lead to inflation where the money goes – if there is sufficient effectual demand. [72] If the "money-containment" or other methods do not suffice, therefore, the newly created money will appear *on product markets* or on markets, which are *both product and asset markets*, and raise price there. Massive amounts of money have already taken this route after central banks' increases of the money volume following the financial crisis and have brough about the effect, e.g., on real estate and commodity markets. More recently, the interruption of certain production activities of supply chains in the Corona-crisis and a further partial deglobal-

---

point: "Die Geschäftsbanken haben nämlich damals einen beachtlichen Teil der Notenbankgeldmenge aus dem Wirtschaftskreislauf genommen, indem sie den Notenbaken das Geld gleich wieder zurückgaben."

72   If new state fiat money (or even private bank credit money) is continuously created and sovereign debt markets as classical money absorbers shrink, then a lot of the newly created and of pre-existing money, which is no longer absorbed by the debt markets, must go into other asset markets, e.g., real estate markets. Price rises in housing markets of major capitalist countries are already well underway since decades. The money goes into expensive areas and low-income districts (where the trend is called "gentrification") and it has two-fold consequences. First, it has become increasingly difficult for average or low-income earners to find dwellings in attractive places. To some extent this raises salaries and to some extent states compensate the back-door effects of their own front-door prosthetics with secondary prosthetics, e.g., rent subsidies, state finance the construction of low budget housing, or support private financing working-class house-building through different schemes (which contributed to the US savings and loan or subprime crisis). States also make rental laws protecting tenants and restricting the freedom of contracts for landlords. The general result is still increased inequality and more acute social conflict. Conversely, asset inflation or bubbles in real estate markets are a serious opportunity for heirs of formerly less valuable real estate or for high earning workers to increase their individual wealth or to recoup some wealth for the social middle-classes. If they are lucky to have owned or acquired real estate, which is sucked into real estate bubbles, then they may – like fishermen in sea villages, which become fancy sea baths, or mountain peasants in areas, which become exclusive ski resorts – sell their property and make a killing. This will significantly increase their future consumptive productive spending. Such capital gains in favor of *nouveaux riches* contribute materially to the present consumptive spending, e.g., in luxury cars, luxury vacations, luxury housing, including producive spending in newly built houses, luxury watches, luxury clothes, luxury furniture, etc. – although the occurrence is essentially a one-time-event and will mostly be a goodbye-present. At least, the heirs of these lucky ones will likely leave the middle class again after having eaten up their capital gains. Afterwards, the properties will only be sold forward and backwards between sterile wealth owners without stimulating producive spending and only a sharpened class difference between owners and non-owners will be left over.

ization in favor of intensified trade in political blocks, e.g., the reduction of energy supplies of the West by Russia, significantly risen military employment spending, prices are now also almost generally rising in the productive economy, have further contributed to inflation.

If globalization was, as it was in many regards, a means of costs reduction – hunting low labor costs, low regulatory costs, low commodity costs and saving due to economies of scale – then deglobalization will by necessity mean *cost increases*, which firms will try to recoup with price raises. A decade ago, I visited Morocco on a business delegation. We were brought to a light Aluminum hall (with the main purpose to allow an air-condition to do its job inside), in which at seven or eight small kidney-shaped "islands", tables at bar-level with bar-like stools, young men and women were sewing fine black ladders around what would become steering wheels for luxury limousines. The metallic wheel inside came from China. Afterwards, the wheels would travel to Poland to build in the electronics from Vietnam; only then would they go to final assembly into Germany and France. About the same time, I was told by an official of the German Traffic Ministry that the costs of transport for a large TV-screen from Shanghai to Hamburg (harbor to harbor) were 9 Cent per piece (at the time). Quite obviously, many such delicate supply lines will collapse if put in disuse for some time (as the Corona-crisis did) or hit by differently rising energy, labor or commodity costs or by expectation of political cuts. Prices will then rise a lot and even if new "nearly as cheap" configurations can be put together again, firms will nevertheless seek to maintain the higher prices, now for higher profits. Let us also not be naïve: Even firms, which suffer from no or little price increases, will take the news of generally rising prices as an invitation to raise their prices as well, almost as if they had formed a cartel. There is no shortage of agents that feel they are underpaid!

In what was called a deflationary period between 2008 and 2020 many mainstreams economist almost identified deflation and depression and central banks targeted an inflation rate of 2 % as if this would generate higher employment and growth. Even if this approach was dominating the talk of politicians talk and of the business media, it was never sound. Investment too obviously depends on the differences between M and M' or between c + v and M' or on s etc., i.e., the gap between input-costs and the price for the output realizable in the market, but *not on the absolute level of prices*. Even if price rise at different speeds in different sectors, that will not always favor investment: E.g., if input-prices (labor, commodities, interest) rise before output-prices, it will work against more investment. In fact, in the most advantageous constellation, if output-prices, e.g., prices for consumption goods, luckily, rise first, this rise will almost necessarily be followed by rising input-prices, labor-costs in particular. And if not, nobody would be there to buy the additional goods...

Following these considerations, we must disparage, first, the idea that the inflation enabled by the increase of the money volume could possibly do away with the deficiency of producive spending. Inflation will not generate full employment. Secondly, on the other side, inflation will also not render prosthetics unfeasible. The main effect of inflation will remain that he who has the option should better be holding assets than money during inflation and he who does not have the option will lose if the price rises overwhelmingly occur in what he has to buy, e.g., consumption goods, rather than in what he has to offer, e.g., labor.

The international monetary system and the perils of divergent inflation for the money creation glands of imperial powers

Yet, inflation is, nevertheless, not neutral, and it may be very consequential. The world is not one single economy but there are rivaling imperial powers, which are each predominantly concerned with their own economy and their own prosthetics, e.g., the US, China, the Eurozone, Japan, the UK, the BRICS-states. The currencies and the activities of these states and their central banks and of international institutions have integrated into an international monetary system, in which currencies, factually, and based on conventions of different origins, have assumed unequal roles. These roles can be more favorable or disfavorable. The worst position for states is not even to have a fiat money currency of their own, which they can issue. They can, thus, not even draw a seignorage from their own population and others on their territory at the initial issuance of state fiat money. States that do have a state fiat money gland of their own are better off; yet, will they also be able to take out loans, i.e., sell their debt, in this currency? This depends on their solvency and on whether their central bank, if needed, would print new money to buy the debt from the creditors, and whether creditors would want to hold this money; the latter, of course, depends on whether the currency will be foreseeably affected by inflation. If the before is not practically possibly, the reach of their monetary sovereignty of states is very limited. States are far better off if they have a fiat money currency of their own and can indebt themselves in this currency as they are considered solvent, have a central bank who can buy the sovereign debt and if their currency is not expected to lose a lot of its value.[73] Such states mainly differ in the sizes of their economy and population, the ongoing evolutions, their political power, international alliances and military might as well as from different effects of existing institutional arrangements. Presently only the US and the Dollar assume an outstanding role here. This position is often described as the respective currency having a "reserve currency func-

---

73   In this sense argues *Wolfgang Münchau* that sovereign bonds from eurozone countries are actually structurally "risky assets because eurozone countries issue sovereign debt but no longer have their own autonomous central bank as a buyer of last resort. This is why the eurozone debt markets are inherently more crisis-prone than those of countries with an independent monetary policy." (*Münchau*, Eurozone reformers act as if the crisis never happened, in: *Financial Times* of 18 February 2018).

tion". It means that private wealth owners and other states have a preference to hold significant parts of their wealth either in this currency in cash or in debt denominated in that currency, of debtors, which are considered solvent, before anything the sovereign debt of this state of course. This made the market for US-treasuries the most important asset of the planet (except for, may be, the planet's land) and the US-treasury-market "the biggest, deepest and most essential bond market" in the world.[74] It goes without saying that sitting on the gland, which can exclusively produce the commodity traded on this market, at very little costs, is in incredible advantage.

It is here, where inflation may become a crucial factor. It does not matter how much a unit of a leading currencies can buy compared to other currencies, e.g., whether one Dollar can buy more than one Renminbi; it does also not matter if general inflation reduces the purchasing power of all currencies by the same percentage and an elusive position of a currency is even often not endangered by the currency losing more purchase power than its competitors for some time... Still, *expected significantly higher inflation*, compared to other currencies in connection with an *expected worsening of the exchange rate* of the currency, will do great damage to a currency. It will disincentivize creditors to buy and hold debt in it and to even use it for transactions. This reduces the possibilities of the state, which issues the currency, to fund its prosthetics with money from private creditors. It may try to correct the situation by raising interest rates to improve the post-inflation-losses and post-exchange-rate-losses of investors, but that may not work. It can, then, only resort to finance more prosthetics with domestic money creation, which will expand the money volume once again and will worsen the situation even more. There is no difference in this regard about whether states go on with conventional monetary financing (accumulating debt on central banks' balance sheets) or switch to "overt monetary financing" (by central banks "printing" new money without new debt or waiving their debt repayment claims against states).

Ultimately, thus, expected future inflation in relation to other currencies determines how powerful a state's fiat money creation gland is. Foreign exchange rates and their trend make the relative power of the fiat money creation glands of different states most comparable. Wealth owners will prefer debt issues in currencies with no or little inflation and stable or improving exchange rates, so that states with such currencies have the best odds to attract private investors in the whole world as co-financiers of their prosthetics. Such favored states will, by the same token, be able to use their currency best to purchase goods abroad at advantageous prices.

States, accordingly, cannot help but *look out for means to strengthen their money creation gland*. This is, of, course, presently particularly a concern for the US with

---

74   Financial Times of 29 July 2021, page 1. At the time the market's size was $22trn.

its enormous amount of outstanding sovereign debt of US\$ 31,5 trn[75] and with its geopolitical ambitions, as the geopolitical defender, and for China, as the geopolitical challenger, but, to a lesser degree, for the Eurozone, the UK, Japan and Russia, too. It appears the expanding BRICS-states are about to form an alliance to support the Renminbi. Unfortunately, as inflation of a currency and its foreign exchange rate greatly depend on the issuing country's *geopolitical might in other regards, and on its military might* in particular, which feedback on the economy and vice versa, this may render the future funding of home-prosthetics dependent on a defiant, adamant, assertive or aggressive or expansive geopolitical and military stance in the world.

Already the elementary (pre-prosthetic) economics of profit economies taught us that capitalism as such may be *pacegenetic*, i.e., operate via free exchange, as well as *bellogenetic*, i.e., operate via goods procurement by violence, and, thus, sometimes go to war, depending on the circumstances.[76] At a second level of observation we noted that as capitalism needs to fund prosthetics, and the funding of prosthetics can work via goods procurement by violence and protectionism, it may be induced to take aggressive stances as well. We now have to acknowledge a third-level, a more advanced dynamic, which yet again pushes towards confrontation and war: Even if states almost seem to abjure violent wealth procurement and protectionism in favor of financing prosthetics by domestic money creation, which appears utterly peaceful at first, we have to acknowledge now that they may be thrown back – by objective necessities – into a geopolitically and militarily unyielding and expansive position to only protect the power of their existing state fiat money creation gland. Deficient employment-generating spending necessitates prosthetics, prosthetics rely increasingly on state fiat money creation, the power of a state's fiat money depends on its relative political and military power... This politicizes the situation and forces states to strengthen their geopolitical might and military to strengthen their currency. Additional bellogenetic dynamics arise from here. The political economy and prosthetics ultimately glide into the purest geopolitical stuff.

A political-ideological dilemma

Prosthetics by state fiat money creation, finally, give rise to a political-ideological dilemma: States that open the floodgates of state fiat money creation, to mitigate the modern master drama, may, by the same token endanger capitalism's political-ideological bases. Capitalism is an owner society built upon respect for private property, which decides on the exclusive access to goods. These characteristics apply to money, too. The money code organizes and legitimizes the social distribution

---

75   https://tradingeconomics.com/united-states/government-debt (as of the end of 2022)
76   See on page 56 et seq.

of scarce goods through their exchange against scarce money.[77] The money code is, of course, still observed by making loans; the owner gives away the money in view of the future repayment of the principal with interest. The money code is also observed if somebody pays alms or charity, given that the money given away reduces the money held by the charitable person and that the transfer as a gift is based on a free decision of its owner. If states levy taxes, this constitutes an exception in so far as money wanders from one person to the state involuntarily; yet the existing volume of wealth is only redistributed, it is like a forced gift. If, now, though, money is visibly created anew but still exerts its usual grip on scarce goods, then the money code and, thus, the property-code, are partially lifted. Money is no longer stubbornly exclusive and scarce (like the property of something) but has visibly become a *mere technical method of goods re-distribution*. Money mutates from a neutral scarcity-mechanism into an administered political technique to distribute goods by state decision (like ration cards). Where this happens, "not having money" ceases to be a conclusive justification for why access is denied to goods, e.g., to dwelling, health care, children's education, or the conveniences of life. If it becomes common practice that money is created ex nihilo to finance social transfers by political decision, the Pandora's box is open and hedonistic, mass-democratic politics will likely want to make a lot more out of this possibility than the conservative central bankers who still sit on the money creation gland (and are torn back and forth between their neoliberal or even "Ordnungspolitik"-education and the pressure of politicians for prosthetics) dare to think of. General demands to increase sovereign indebtedness are already being made publicly today. They are *not* only raised by so-called "populist" parties but widely practiced by classical conservative, social-democrat, liberal parties and certainly by "green" parties, whose ideology is largely free of structured non-moral content. For the moment, central banks are still protected by a veil of misconceptions. Amongst them are a traditional respect vis-à-vis money, an unjustified memory of the times of commodity money, and a trust in a scientific and super-technocratic character of the doing of their managers. People are also impressed by the Byzantine cult of fiat money creation. However, that is already changing and it will not hold. A new brand of "unbiased" career-politicians is arriving at the helms of governments who are accustomed to cutting of old braise. Changes also arise out of the ideological sphere of economics. Conservative and liberal economics is under attack worldwide since the financial crisis of 2008, rightly so of course. So-called "Modern Monetary Theory" formulates a credo, which, even if it is too simplistic to become the official doctrine of monetary politics in the near term, may well function as *hidden mental door opener* to massive state fiat money creation; it is so simple that even politicians can understand it. The Institute for New Economic Thinking (INET), which had organized very stimulating economic discussions in its founding

---

77   See on page 53 an 78 et seq.

years, has now transformed into a platform, which promotes ant-traditional economic contents of a wide spectrum, many of a lesser quality, but which willingly offer themselves for use by taboo-breaking politicians. Digitalization, as everywhere, will allow to create further confusion, e.g., by involving some kind of digital money in the mix.

Already the dot.com-bubble, the financial crisis and the Eurozone debt crisis, which resulted from debt build-up and money creation, lead only to more debt-build-up and more money creation. Arrived the Corona pandemic, as a real bad surprise, leading to, once more, debt build-up and money creation. With the demise of the virus, the most "classical" reason for debt-build-up and money creation raised its head: war. And there is unfortunately probably more war to come at the main geopolitical fault lines between the West (plus Japan, Korea, Australia etc.) and Russia and China (plus some other BRICS- countries). The leading capitalist states stumble and the world stumbles from one exceptional state into the next one, each getting worse and more dangerous, letting, in hindsight, the merely *financial* crisis of 2008 appear as quite innocent. For the moment, fear of war and preparation for war, alone, suffice to justify further debt build-up and money creation at large scale and silence even the most hard-core austerity advocates.

Two main future developments appear possible from here: If a grand war can be avoided, politicians and the people of developed capitalist states will nevertheless get more accustomed to the benevolent effects of prosthetics and we could enter into a situation, where the democratic discourse – with arguments from morals, religion, beauty, truth, universal love, or political ideologies, etc. – may demand permanent "super-prosthetics", including a social redistribution of wealth with the help of the money printing press. While previous discourses in favor of a more egalitarian wealth redistribution, e.g., the socialist-communist discourse, were so *honest* as to acknowledge that their realization would require *taking away* wealth from others, which necessitated a moral or historical *justification*, this may now be considered as superfluous, to some extent. If the state can create value-in-exchange with an alchemistic money creation gland, apparently, without taking anything away from somebody else, then much of what may have been in the way of generating more equality in the past may disappear. Proponents of greater equality or "super-prosthetics" may now believe to be able to doing good to everybody without doing bad to anybody. The state may, e.g., be expected to build decent dwellings for low-income strata, pay for their better medical treatment and education or, to even buy them Janis Joplin's proverbial "Mercedes Benz" – all this funded by monetary financing. The illusionary moment that *is already* (!) intrinsic to fiat money – the distinction between *valeurs* and *non-valeurs* becomes fluid – could replicate itself in the realm of political ideology as the illusion that a more just world can peacefully be achieved through the money printing press. What may result from this is unclear.

With a view to the Ukraine war, the military build-up throughout the world, and the increasing bellicosity between the West, Russia and China, the even greater problem, and the second possible development, may be that we will not even learn how specifically the extensive debt build-up and money creation would have exploded, imploded or not. Rather we may witness, as times before, a reset of the economic and political systems on the graves of millions of dead, the ruins of hundreds of cities and of thousands of factories, and, possibly, on ten thousand or more square kilometers of radiated land.

Chapter XIII. The dilemmas of the prosthetics of modern capitalism

In the beginning, capitalism was a superior hunter in a paradise of abundant prey of producive, employment-generating spending. This enabled huge profits for a great number of firms in the productive economy. But not before long, it began to suffer under the barrier of deficient producive spending. The limitation of ongoing prey reproduction – employment-generating spending being the prey –, like in any predator-prey-system became a disturbing feature of the *conditio capitalistica*. Violent wealth procurement, protectionism, expropriations, taxes, and redistributive debt were used to prosthetically bring up "prey". Goods procurement by external violence and protectionism became the preferred prosthetic means of a privileged group of the fastest developing and strongest capitalist countries with an edge over peripheral regions. Domestic taxation and expropriations were of additional, albeit limited, effect.

However, prosthetic spending funded by violence and protectionism depends upon hinterlands that remain subservient, but still possess enough funds to sufficiently function in a complementary way. This condition faded away as times went by. Hinterlands' absorption potential shrank relative to the hunger of the metropoles, and, equally importantly, the hinterlands no longer wanted to remain subservient and complementary hinterlands. They rebelled against the metropoles and liberated themselves. In fact, formerly important hinterlands (e.g., Brazil, Argentina, Japan, Korea, China, Vietnam, etc.) became symmetric competitive capitalist predators and also went out to worldwide hunt for the same prey – employment-generating spending – abroad that the metropoles were after.[1]

Redistributive spending via taxation and expropriations had always only worked where the recipient of the appropriated money had a higher propensity for producive spending than the money-dispatcher. Debt-based redistributive prosthetic employment-generating spending, even largely lost its over-all effect if the debt was

---

[1] "Countries, willing and able to run offsetting external deficits do not exist" (*Wolf,* China's tough fight to escape its debt trap, in: *Financial Times* of 12 April 2017.

repaid with interest, which it normally had to. Then only a small net gain for employment-generating spending remained. Structurally, debt, too, was an apt means to generate aggregated additional prosthetic employment-generating spending over time only, if, while the individual debt might be repaid, there was a continuous aggregate net debt build-up, a growing debt mountain. Continuous debt build-up, though, also requires plentiful or inexhaustible funds of money and lenders willing to hand out loans and holding the resulting debt-claims in the long term. This condition did not sufficiently exist as long as commodity money, gold and silver, was the base money as the mining of precious metals did not provide sufficient relief; physical alchemy failed constantly. Thus, when capitalism was being re-activated and European powers began to fight out their rivalry since around 1500, it was most welcomed by them that a kind of financial alchemy was discovered by private banks in the form of fractional reserves credit money creation, be it as bank notes, token coins or credit entries on bank accounts. Already this first artificial gland added a thick layer of credit money to the commodity money base, enabled a more voluminous debt build-up and extended prosthetic options. How private bank credit money creation could be managed to best fit to the needs of states was the subject matter of the two famous monetary debates in Great Britain between the Bullionists and the Anti-bullionists and the Currency school and the Banking school. If the states welcomed private bank credit money creation to enable the debt-financing of capitalist growth and of their colonial or imperial wars, they were still fearsomely aware that the greed of private banks might yet ruin the precious money creation gland. So, states had to defend this gland against their inventors through fractional reserves requirements, policing banks, selecting one bank as their central bank and allying with it in particular. They adjusted their stand to changing situations. In the frequent times of war, they preferred the risks involved in overstretching bank credit money creation to the risk of losing the war and mostly recklessly encouraged banks to create more credit money. They would then even oftentimes issue state credit money or, sometimes, state fiat money in addition. When peace was restored, states would, though, at first go back to convertible credit money, i.e., to commodity money as the base money again. This was repeated after World War I and even until World War II.

But in 1971, the US undid its return to commodity money of after World War II, and generally switched into a state fiat money regime. State fiat money, thus, became the new base money. Other states followed suit and established their monetary sovereignty. Noteworthily, this change left private bank credit money creation unaffected – only the underlying base money was changed to state fiat money. Hence, the tandem in money creation of private banks and the central bank could remain in place; it became only more powerful than before. The state established a fiat money currency and provided a basic money volume of it. In times of normalcy, private banks would create further money by fractional reserve bank credit money creation above this base. As, theoretically, any amount of the new base money could now be procured at discretion by the state, the bail-out of private banks, if they should get into trouble, had become much easier, too. Accordingly, more liberal reserve fractions could be allowed and a more generous spirit imbued the tandem system. In addition, of course, states retained the option to make further use of their own fiat state money creation gland as an *ultima ratio* reserve money creation facility if private bank credit money creation was insufficient.

At some point, a crucial *novel use* of the state fiat money creation gland in this tandem was discovered. The output of private bank money creation had always been, first, money on the one side, and, second, debt on the other side, which was tradable. The state and the central bank now found out that the central bank could purchase this tradable debt with newly created state fiat money. The baby was initially baptized "open market policies". At first, it only appeared to be a tool of influencing interest rates and to steer the economy through a corridor between inflation and deflation. That implied that central banks would buy and sell debt according to economic cycles. The idea was that their debt holdings would somewhat grow in deflations and drop back to near zero in inflations (which was mostly conceptually identified with depressions and booms). But babies grow up and the adolescence of the baby "open market policies" consisted in central banks beginning to use debt purchases to stabilize the continuous prosthetic debt build-up by providing market liquidity and "shiftability" (de-investment in loans by individual investors without the loan having to be repaid as such) as "market-maker" or "dealer of last resort". The ascent of this second reason to hold debt raised the volumes on central banks' balance sheets visibly. But the evolution of the baby did not stop here. It reached adulthood with the rather recent discovery that the debt, which had arrived at central banks, could stay there for a very long time or for good, and that central banks could be "debt holders" and "debt financers of the last resort". Thereby a method had been contrived, by which significant volumes of money could be created *independent of private creditors' appetite to hold debt lastingly*. After this upgrading of the monetary arsenal, in fact, theoretically nothing was in the way to autonomously procure the needed continuous flows of prosthetic employment-generating spending.

At this juncture, one might say that the state had, in fact, acquired the means to assume the role of wealth owners in Quesnay's tableau and to purchase the parts of the annual produce, which would otherwise go unsold. Thereby, all capitalist circuits could be closed and the wheels of the machinery could be kept turning, independently of the old-fashioned means of goods procurement by violence, protectionism, domestic taxation and expropriations. States had availed themselves with a new means, which consisted of a novel type of financial transactions. The main form of ancient prosthetics had consisted in the subjugation of foreign tribes and countries and had necessitated ugly "hinterlands". Modern protectionism, colonialism and imperialism, too, could not operate without creating ugly losing "hinterlands", with, in fact, even a certain remaining risk of things being turned upside down – in antiquity as well as in modernity. State fiat money creation, e.g., by central banks buying up sovereign debt from privates with newly created money, at first, rendered the funding of prosthetics independent of foreign countries; violent victimization disappeared and the funding of prosthetics became, like taxation and debt build-up, a purely national and peaceful nice and clean affair. The following tableau shows the economy with this triangle, which makes "milk and honey" flow. It builds upon the original "naked" tableau of "original" capitalism (on page 122) and superimposes prosthetic layers, including the debt build-up, which is enabled by central bank debt purchases and funded by state fiat money creation. *First*, it shows redistributive prosthetic debt (out of existing money, i.e., without money creation) and expansive prosthetic debt financed by private bank credit money creation; this money flows from wealth owners and banks to firms, workers and the state in the form of loans. Due to its combined redistributive and expansive character these loans are shown in thin parallel lines. If central banks purchase existing loans made to states (sovereign debt), or to wealth owners or workers (private debt), then they refinance these loans by state fiat money creation. When they resell the debt to private wealth owners, the newly created state fiat money is abolished once again. Yet, as central banks transform from being "market makers" or "dealers of last resort" to becoming "debt holders" and "debt financers of the last resort" by holding debt lastingly (even if the individual debt is rolled over occasionally), state fiat money creation becomes permanent. The time comes at which wealth owners and banks, when they initially grant loans to states, firms, or workers already expect to soon sell this debt to the central bank. From that point forward, the new debt is in fact funded by state fiat money creation. The evolving cycle between wealth owners and banks, making loans to the state (or privates) and the central bank buying these loans is, *second*, shown in two arrows with *thick dotted lines*. In the *third* place, the tableau shows the state forwarding prosthetics (funded in any forms) to employment-generating wealth owners (firms) and workers in a triple grey line. Prosthetics resulting from protectionism and coming from abroad are, *forth*, shown in the lower left-hand corner. Purchases of firms' and workers' debt by the central bank are not shown.

Figure 25: Tableau of capitalism including redistributive and expansive prosthetic spending

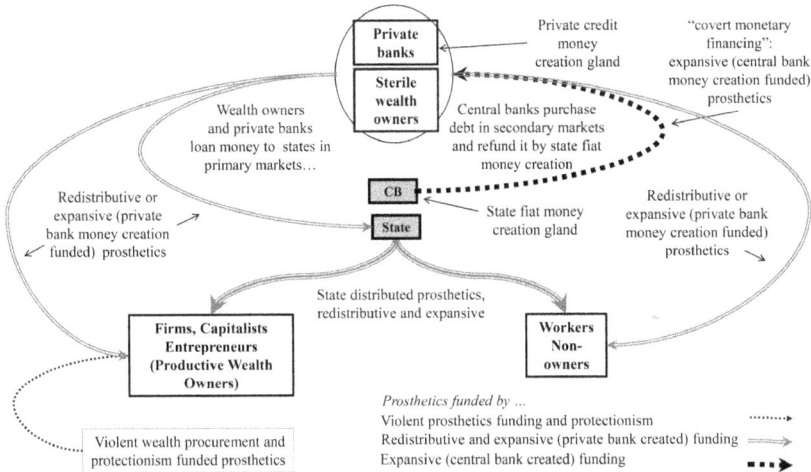

The break-through for massive, continued debt holding by central banks took place after the financial crisis of 2008. Since then, they buy great volumes of debt knowing (or they should at least know!) that it will stay on their balance sheets for a long time or forever, or, at least, not leave again in a normal way (i.e., other than by a debt jubilee or a currency reform or substitutes). They, thereby, refinance debt issues to private wealth owners and banks and refund the liquidity to them, which they may possibly use to finance the next round of debt issues. As private wealth owners and banks make their outlays first, and central banks restitute them only thereafter, central banks now use "guidance" and publicly announce their intent to buy certain volumes of newly issued debt to induce privates to sign the debt in the first place. The expected later central bank debt purchases, by which they keep their commitments (the dotted black line on the right-hand side), thus, are the real causes for the previous loans by wealth owners and private banks (the dotted arrow on the left-hand side).[2] As is common in economics, the chronologically second step – debt purchases by the central bank in secondary markets – is causally and logically the first step. The expectation of the later debt purchases by the central bank induce wealth owners and banks to make the initial loans, for which state fiat money creation will provide the lasting financing.

---

2   The relationship between bond purchases by central banks and sovereign debt issues is highly transparent. E.g., writes the *Financial Times* of 5 June 2020 on the ECB's €1.35 trn. pandemic emergency purchase program on its front page: "Some investors had been concerned that the ECB's initial bond-buying plan would be insufficient to soak up the €1tn–€1.5tn of extra debt that eurozone governments are expected to issue this year…".

The more voluminous and the more lastingly central banks hold debt, the more they transmute to financiers of last resort. As they have no M–C–M'-desires and are not subjected to a financial survival constraint, they are free of concerns that the assembled loan claims (workers debt, firms' debt, sovereign debt, or sterile wealth owners' debt) might not be honored. Capitalism creates a general and strict discipline of rationality through M–C–M' in one sector, but it also needs a complementary sector *without this M–C–M'-rationality* to allow the operation of the first sector. The debt on central banks' balance sheets falls out of the profit logic and transforms into a peculiar existence; we enter a kingdom of undead or unborn. While a legal debt claim is still there, the usual distinctions of a M–C–M'-world apply as little as Euclidian geometry to a non-Euclidian world. In the case of sovereign debt, there is formal, nominal debt, but nobody cares how much it is. Interest has to be paid, and, in fact, is normally paid, but – at least in the case of sovereign debt – the payor and the payee do not care. The receiving central bank, the payee, does not care as it will return the receipts to the state as quasi-dividends; the payor, the state, does not care either as the paid interest will be returned to it as quasi-dividends.[3] The capitalist logic is outsmarted. Therefore, central banks may allow the purchased debt to rest on their shelves for a very long time and these shelves to, ultimately, become places for debt restructurings, debt forgiveness, hence, crematories for debt or places for the euthanasia of debt, where the already hybridized debt makes the step from the semi-dead to the wholly dead, e.g., after a debt jubilee or a currency reform.[4]

---

3   It is, thus, quite logical if *Harding*, Fears about Japan's debt are overblown, in: *Financial Times* of 6 September 2017, after a study of four other options, recommends: "That leaves a more plausible fifth option. Do not resolve the public debt. Live with it. This is surprisingly do-able". On the other hand, as this debt does not really matter, another option for public debt is also feasible. As *Dowding*, We need to think about debt cancellation, in: *Financial Times* of 5 December 2021, reports "senior Italian officials (asked) the European Central Bank to ease debt burdens [following the Corona crisis, G.W.] by forgiving sovereign bonds it owns." Dowding criticizes Christine Lagarde for dismissing the idea too rapidly: "In a world, where a lot of sovereign debt is being bought by central banks, intrinsically, all we are doing is allowing the left hand of government to owe the right hand of the government a lot of money. At some point, they should just shake hands and throw the debt away". Dowding is fully aware that debt cancellation would amount to "helicopter money". "Consider what would happen if governments issued 10,000-year bonds at a zero interest rate and central banks bought them up. That is in effect the same thing as cancelling the debt."

4   Private debtors, whose debt is bought by central banks, of course, continue to care about having to serve their loan debt, even if it is to the central bank. Central banks could also help them, though, by debt restructurings or waiver, or states might compensate the debtors for the debt service or make payments to the central bank on their behalf (for instance US-President Biden's mentioned program of waiving educational loans).

The second tableau shows only the next possible, but not necessary, step, the radicalization and simplification of what exists already today to "overt monetary financing" (OMF). States say Adieu to the Byzantine hullabaloo. Private banks and wealth owners are completely side-stepped; the "tandem-agreement" between the central bank and private banks is now, indeed, cancelled: "The moor (of fractional bank credit money creation) has done his duty; the moor can go". Prosthetics are, thence, funded without states issuing debt and without central banks purchasing and holding onto it. Central banks simply distribute money to the firms, workers, or the state, where it is needed, who will use it for prosthetics.[5]

Figure 26: Tableau showing prosthetics by "Overt monetary financing"

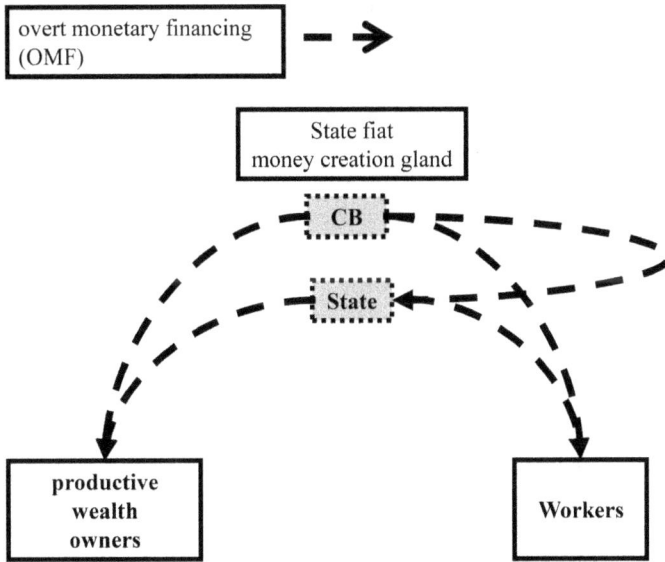

Now, only the central bank and the state form the prosthetic apparatus that, when reduced to its elementary function, handles deficient employment-generating spending, almost like a heart-lung-machine. The apparatus could even be further simplified by the state revoking its delegation of the fiat money creation to the

5   Central banks can also "buy" debt at the debt issuance from states, i.e., from what are called primary markets, by making the original loans to states. This creates the debt as an asset. Or the can even "buy" debt at the debt issuance from privates (mainly workers or firms) by also directly making loans to them. In this case, the recipients immediately receive newly created state fiat money and never even touch existing money or newly created bank credit money. Legal debt relations are, of course, still formally involved.

central bank, dissolving the central bank, and assigning this power to a department of the finance ministry.

Ultimately, there would not even be a significant difference between the present practice and these variations of "overt monetary financing". The old way or another, all prosthetics financing by state fiat money creation is caught in dilemmas and is, therefore, approaching exhaustion. Whether new money is created with debt ending on central banks' balance sheets or without such bookkeeping entries, nobody has control over the masses of newly created money, which is floating around. They cannot but ultimately do what money causes wherever it goes: It will bet up prices and, thereby, domestically, cause inflation, in markets for sterile investments and in markets for productive investment and consumption, if the money goes there. This will worsen the foreign exchange rate of the most inflationary economies. States are crippling their own state-fiat-money-creation glans by its reckless use; the more they use it, the more the consequential inflation falls upon them. What to do? How to defend an auto-destructive state-fiat-money-creation-gland, which has become a primary means of state policies, if you cannot quit what damages it most? First, if you remain addicted to state fiat money creation, try everything else possible to keep inflation under control; for example, keep sovereign debt markets in existence for as long as possible to channel the masses of floating money to places where they do the least inflationary damage – this, in fact, speaks strongly against a switch towards "Open Monetary Financing". Second, provide incentives for the newly created money to return to the central bank, rather than doing more damage elsewhere, particularly in product markets – this speaks in favor of maintaining the central bank as a separate institution aside the state. If you, nevertheless, witness an erosion of the power of your state-fiat-money-creations-gland, third, you may try to use your geopolitical and military might (and wars) to strengthen your state-fiat-money-creation-gland, at least relative to the ones of other states, meaning that in the 21th century it is the dilemmas of state-fiat-money-creation – not primarily the hunt for territories, populations, resources and markets– , which drive the world into new imperialist contests. Today's mass democracies can hardly be expected to oppose this. The more they become accustomed to the benefits from money creation, the more they are likely to support imperial policies – like the Greek in their people's assemblies and the Roman legionaries roaring in support of their emperors. Moderation is not their thing; they "want the world" and they "want it now."

Afterword: An outlook in questions and answers

A few questions and answers regarding the future of capitalism and its prosthetics, say in the next fifty years, may be appropriate at the end of this book:

Questions on capitalism

Question I: Will deficient employment-generating spending go away, even while M–C–M' remains in place?

No. Human existence is stricken with illness and death and the capitalist economic system is stricken with the deficient-producive-spending-syndrome, which expresses the essence of the modern social master drama. The paradise, which Ricardo's Law of Say promises – the closure of any and all circuits – is only possible if all expected productive economy profits are used to buy the productive economy's products, but this is not happening. Rather, wealth needed for circuit closure in the productive economy is perpetually absorbed into a wuthering sterile economy, which implies unemployment in the productive economy. The practice of mankind, to superimpose motives for production of values-in-use with motives of profit-making, while it works powerfully on the one side, unavoidably carries this shadow side.

Question II: Can the dilemmas of funding prosthetics through domestic taxation, domestic expropriation or through redistributive debt be solved?

No. As long as the M–C–M'-world continues, money or other value-in-exchange will be needed to fill the gaps of employment-generating spending or to feed those who remain unemployed. Domestic financing of prosthetic, which consist in claiming existing wealth without repayment (expropriation, taxation) and redistributing it to firms that invest it in the productive economy or to non-owners that spend it consumptively there, are insufficient in terms of achievable volumes and they have strict political limits. At some point they will become socialist expropriations of the present wealth owners, which they will eventually oppose by civil war. Redistributive debt, i.e., debt in a monetary regime without significant money creation, cannot solve the problem either. As money is scarce, there are no creditors who will enable the needed continuous build-up of debt.

Question III: Can the dilemmas of funding prosthetics by means of violent wealth procurement abroad, protectionism, and war be solved?

No. Concerning violent wealth procurement abroad and protectionism: As already stated in the main part of this book, a regression to violent wealth procurement or to protectionism (i.e., colonialist, imperialist, etc.) is no longer promising for the lack of a sufficient number of sufficiently attractive and easy-to-hunt prey in relation to the number and the hunger of predators. The easy prey-regions are only the poorer regions of the world – but meager nutrition will not feed the hungry predators around. This is worsened by the fact that many former prey-countries have become predators or prospective predators themselves, not only the BRICS-states, but many smaller states as well, – and they do not want to regress into "hinterlands" again. If however, developed capitalist countries were to become so desperate to try to turn each other into hinterlands and to directly violently or via protectionism procure wealth from each other, in particular energy and other natural resources, this will very likely result in a large war. Accordingly, violent wealth generation or protectionism, who promise proper booty, would first have to go through a phase of serious war.

War itself, is, now, were things get a little bit more complicated and ambiguous. This is so because wars are not only a means of *funding prosthetics* (enabling violent wealth appropriation or protectionism after they have been won) or to *otherwise ease the implementation of prosthetic policies* but they also change the conditions under which M–C–M' and the economic system will *"naturally"* or *"capitalistically" operate afterwards. First*, already if wars are only planned and long before they may possibly be won, the inputs that must go into their preparation and the warfare for reasons of sheer military necessity are *mega-prosthetics* themselves. If countries with significant armament production enter wars, the warfare will, e.g., greatly stimulate employment-generating spending to the *armament industries*, which spending will be further dispersed to supplier-firms. While this does, obviously, not solve the funding of these efforts yet, already the decision of going to war by itself will greatly ease this funding: The *exceptionalism of war* as such will politically allow to raise taxes, sovereign and other indebtedness, and money creation, far beyond the "normal". *Second*, if major states unleash wars, they will typically *draw along alliance-partners* that will want to or have to follow them. Even larger such follower-states will, then, have to purchase at least some weaponry and equipment from the armament industries of the lead-states; smaller follower-states will practically have to buy the whole of their armament from them. This, too, will channel additional employment-generating spending into the lead-states, which is funded by the follower-states – through their increased taxation, indebtedness and money creation or even through their wealth appropriation in other countries. The lead-states are thereby enabled to *externalize* the funding of some of their new prosthetics. *Third*, even alliance partners of lead-states, who may be able to avoid being drawn in the war themselves, will often have to make silent or open "solidarity" payments to the lead-states, which will equally allow the lead-states to externalize parts of their prosthetics funding. *Fourth*, wars mean destruction and this destruction has become much more effective with modern war technology. This destruction that war delivers goes deeper than just facilitating the funding of prosthetics or politically easing it. Like a natural catastrophe, it rather interferes into *how the post-war economy will "tick" according to its own natural logic*. Wars, thus, change the factors that influence producive spending in their aftermath; they are much like bottles with bank-notes being buried to dig them up later again in Keynes' illustration of prosthetics. War destruction, in particular, significantly raises the attractivity of the productive economy for employment-generating investment in the post-war period by improving the profitability of investment in the productive economy compared to investment in the sterile economy at such later time. Therefore, post-war-periods are often earmarked by a transitory increase in employment and a transitory significant diminishment of the deficient-producive-spending-syndrome; wars not only facilitate solutions – They partially make the problem smaller! *Fifth*, as war destruction also involves the killing of men – may be of more women in the future, too – wars reduce the number of the non-owners depending on employment as salaried workers. They, thereby, also interfere in the modern social master drama via a second path – on the side of the victims of the master drama – by reducing their number, and, eventually, the costs of future prosthetics to maintain them.

We are not saying that politicians consciously run such a cynical calculus if they decide on war. The algorithms they actually use may, in fact, be less rational. Many of them may simply not know what they are doing and later regret what resulted from their decisions. Often, politicians will tend to be overoptimistic in believing that their side will likely win the war – and that the war will be short – and primarily act on the basis of such deceptions. Politicians may also fall victim to their own moralizing speeches, or, more general, their moralistic attitudes. Or they will make their war-related decisions in the same way they decide on everything else – by looking at the anticipated reaction of their party superiors, of the press or of polls. As modern democracy forces career politicians to invent and to parade themselves like products with trademarks and unique sales positions etc., some will also speak up for adamant and aggressive policies because they expect to improve their visibility and achieve career success. If a serious war is waged, its outcome will mostly be more important than all other present issues or the warring parties. For this property wars become a great means to buy time and to hide that politicians (on both sides) are unable to solve other urgent domestic issues. It is great to be relieved of the many burdensome, boring, practical, technocratic but unsolvable tasks and to heroically and "idealistically" rush oneself (and one's fellow countrymen, particularly the soldiers) into the exceptionalism of war. The answer to the question remains that war can neither lastingly solve the deficient-producive-spending-syndrome of the *conditio capitalistica* nor the dilemmas of prosthetics. This, though, may not keep war from becoming more prominent (again) in the 21th century.

Question IV: Can the dilemmas of funding prosthetics through money creation be solved?

No. Money-creation already greatly helped capitalism's evolution when it operated mainly with private bank credit money creation. At the time, state fiat money creation was only a complementary tool, e.g., in wartime or other distress, or a stabilizer and amplifier to private bank credit money creation. The state fiat money gland and state fiat money creation only became the financier of prosthetics of the last resort after 2008. However, it is struck with dilemmas, whether it operates by covert monetary financing (with sovereign debt and central bank debt purchases and holdings) or "overt monetary financing" (without sovereign debt and central bank debt holdings). In both cases it can only solve the problem of procuring the money needed for the prosthetics by creating new money, but this expands the volume of money (as no existing money is taken away from somewhere else). This will be inflationary and will worsen the respective country's exchange rate, which will damage the power of money creation gland of the respective state itself. An economic system, which is built on the fundamental distinction between value (in-exchange) and non-value (in-exchange) may continue to function for some time even if non-values-in-exchange are permanently and massively elevated to values-in-exchange in the form of money. However, the system will never forget about its fundamental distinction. It may be surprised by such in-flows and it may need time to conceive of a reaction; it may also be able to digest significant injections of artificial or even false value before it reacts, *but react it will, at some time or another*. It may stutter, and seek to discriminate "artificial" non-value from "better" value, and to repulse non-value. If that is not possible, as there is only one undistinguishable money, and this money has turned into state managed ration cards or entitlement cards, wealth owners will transition from holding wealth in money or in forms based on money, such as debt, into other assets. This flight will substantially weaken the state fiat money creation gland and reduce it to generate token money for immediate needs, such as paying ongoing social security, even if it is only reluctantly accepted in shops. States must seek to keep their inflation relatively lower and the yield of their bonds relatively higher than in other states, which is in full contradiction to their need of ongoing money creation to fund their prosthetics. Unless states allow their modern master drama to drastically sharpen, they must increase the might of their money creation and of their currency in the international arena. The dilemmas of money creation may, thus, induce states to regress to war and old-fashioned violent wealth procurement and protectionism.

Questions on social alternatives to capitalism

Question VI: Will M–C–M' be displaced by some kind of a revival of the Middle Ages?

While this question is less weird than it appears to be, the answer is still no – at least for the leading capitalist countries. Nevertheless, we ought not to forget that roughly a thousand years after M–C–M' had come into being, mankind made a serious effort to materially limit its dynamics and to regress to C–M–C', which led to roughly another thousand years of the Middle Ages throughout most of the world. There existed no modern state, no political parties, and no enlightenment at that time. Another credence – religion such as Catholicism, Buddhism, Hinduism, and Islam – provided the ideological stronghold for strangling M–C–M'. It materialized in religious institutions, such as the catholic church, but was also diffusedly imbued in the whole fabric of social relations, e.g., between peasants, lords and overlords. All this proved to be a noticeable check to M–C–M' for the time being and probably in fact resulted in betterment of the lives of the masses of the population compared to antiquity (at least in the heydays of feudalism). As a result, the technological and economic development was, of course, seriously retarded. Whoever, as a state, after M–C–M' rebounded strong in Venice, the other City states of Northern Italy, in Spain, or the Netherlands, continued to opt for an anti-M–C–M'-regime always lost (in wars and competition) – think of Pre-Meiji-Japan, and of how the formerly technologically and economically superior China lost its position after the 18th century. Yet, he who threw themselves into capitalist evolution, Northern Italy, Spain, the Netherlands, the UK, later France, still later Germany, Japan, and, of course, the US, succeeded.

However, this failure of medieval anti-M–C–M'-policies is no guarantee against political forces considering a regression towards it. Catholicism could have appeared to be the most promising bridge back to the Middle Ages in the West, but following the religious wars in 16th and 17th centuries and after the Peace of Westphalia of 1648, if found itself, along with its former protestant enemy, demoted. Religious tolerance, as it was then established, meant that religions fell underneath the state, and religions, consequently were reduced moralizing narration-tellers, philanthropic organizations, or places for spiritual or mystical retreats, but they lost the power to, founded in the unconditional, the all-encompassing and the ultimate, demand radical political and social consequences. Catholicism, in addition, had the bad luck of having its center in regions, in which the economic winners were sitting. Catholicism, or Protestantism alike, can, thus, not become leaders of a regression to new Middle Ages or to any new anti M–C–M'-regime the West.[1]

This remains somewhat different with Islam. Islam, which was dominant between Southern Spain and India in the Middle Ages, although it also knew a schism and fights between the Sunni and Shia since long ago, so far has not had something comparable to the European "Peace of Westphalia-experience". Islam could, thus, not only retain more of its original grip on the unconditional and the supreme level of human existence, but can still more convincingly claim that human existence and society ought to follow its God-pleasing rules. Family, loyalty, honor, trust, smaller and more locally integrated communities, it could argue, instead of exposure to the murderous globalist greed of M–C–M', offer a decent live for every human being. This even, if this life is not necessarily (why should it be?!) symmetrical and equal, but knows different ranks, roles, sexes, etc. Globalization and financialization have revigorated Islam in poorer regions, amongst the local rebellious youth in particular. Without the prospect of becoming a winner under M–C–M'-rules, they embrace Islam as a source of meaning and legitimacy, including as a model for anti-M–C–M' regimes, which are sometimes regionally erected. This even remains true, if such movements rise to organizations or states, which throw terrorist attacks, or cruel and weird regimes. E.g., Afghanistan, which went through a conventional communist-party-led socialist antifeudal and anti-monarchist revolution in the late seventies, after forty years of civil and external war, swung over to a Middle-Ages-and Islam-oriented anti-M–C–M'-regime. The so-called "Islamic State", which ruled in

---

1   There are, of course, philosophical reactionaries in the West. Like revolutionaries, they are dreamers, but they dream not of a to-be-construed future, but instead of an idealized and euphemized past. Presently, the reactionary version of Anti-M–C–M' is very dispersed in the West. It appears as a contemplative "Kultur-Kritik" of intellectual elites following thinkers like Edmund Burke, Friedrich Nietzsche, José Ortega y Gasset, Nicolás Gómez Dávila, or others. It goes without saying that we should not expect the erection of a new Middle Ages through them in the next fifty years. Fascist parties differed in essence from them as they differed from monarchist reactionaries. Although fascists featured traces of the Middle Ages (with their emphasis on family and local communities, leadership, and allegiance), fascism, ultimately, was a modern mass democratic and, some say, even "socialist" offer (therefore, NSDAP, "Nationalsozialistische deutsche Arbeiterpartei" etc.) with the intent to fund prosthetics, as in ancient Greece and Rome, mainly through violent wealth procurement abroad. There exist, today, in the West reactionary Anti M–C–M' dreamers in new right-wing parties, movements and politicians ("Front Nationale/Rassemblement Nationale" in France, "Alternative für Deutschland" in Germany, partially former US-President Donald Trump etc.) but these are not positioned to lead a serious Middle-Ages-oriented regression against M–C–M' for a number of other reasons too.

parts of Syria and Iraq for some months, pointed in this direction too. There are similar movements throughout the Arab world, which, though, have not yet reached state power.

Perspectives for Islamic-anti-M–C–M'-regimes to rise to power exist probably only in poor, undeveloped, and less important areas of the world and such regimes will, very likely, not last. Richer Islamic countries, like in the Gulf region, have long made peace with M–C–M' and have silently re-enacted the "Peace-of-Westphalia-experience" of the West for themselves. In these countries, probably Islam may, ultimately, follow Catholicism suit on its way into social irrelevance. The winners of M–C–M' have taken control and they will certainly not switch to anti-M–C–M'-politics, which they rightly see as a losing-strategy in international geopolitical rivalry. In fact, the smaller, but oil-rich or gas-rich Islamic countries have presently several huge advantages: They do not need a money-press for prosthetics, they only pump oil or gas out of the desert to finance their prosthetics. Furthermore, Islam is still strong enough as a religion to provide social and ideological cohesion, which lacks in most highly developed Western capitalist countries. After all, nevertheless, and most importantly, a rebirth of medieval anti-M–C–M'-regimes is no realistic option for the world.

Question VII: Will M–C–M' be displaced by new socialist endeavors?

No, not in the next fifty years, except for from the ruins of World War III. In the West, the first part of the answer will be willingly accepted. The qualification "not in the next fifty years" may raise some eyebrows as it implies that "socialism" (in a sense that retains resemblance with former socialist projects of the 19th and 20th centuries) may not be a dead dog forever. This is true and there are three main reasons for it: *First*, if the practiced socialist attempts have been unconvincing since the Russian Revolution, the problems that led to "socialism" in general, deficient employment-generating spending and the master drama of modernity, will neither go away nor are prosthetics capable of overcoming them. It, thus, remains plausible for mankind to continue or to recommence to think about a modification or cancellation of the (fictious) social contract that introduced capitalism.[2] Already therefore, it is likely that new generations of thinkers and dreamers may like to conceive of a world again, in which humanity might organize its goods procurement without M–C–M', whether or not it seeks parallels with predecessors in the past, be it Keynes' "cooperative economy",[3] Marxian socialism, or whatever.

---

2   See on page 132 et seq.
3   See *Keynes*, Collected Writing, volume XXIX, page 67 et seq. He also called it "real exchange economy" (*Keynes*, Collected Writing, volume XIII, page 408 et seq.)

Second, it cannot be denied that *even* soviet-style socialism had somewhat improved the condition of the working classes compared to the profit economies of antiquity or of modern capitalism. It increased employment security – one might say that employment itself became prosthetic as it was wholly detached from the necessity to generate profits – and the access of workers to education, culture, and medical treatment, etc. was palpably improved, including compared to highly developed capitalist countries, e.g., the US. Furthermore, what rendered the Soviet Union's socialist model unattractive for Western workers after World War II – the higher living standards of the elite of employed workers in the rich capitalist countries of the West – may not apply indefinitely. It is also obvious that the Soviet Union started from a less developed scientific, technological, and economic base than the capitalist countries in the West and that Western attacks on the Soviet Union further pushed its economic performance below what would have been possible otherwise.[4] Proponents of future new socialist projects may argue that these impediments would not burden a new socialist endeavor. For this the argument could be made that a novel socialist effort would start from a much higher technological and economic base, which has been created by capitalism in the meantime, and that this base would allow a new socialism to – if more slowly than capitalism – further develop from thereon, in particular if it was a *joint world-wide effort* (all countries being socialist and, hence, without imperial rivalry, military and war) and if reasonable population policies were practiced.

Third, the imprisonments and killings in the Soviet Union, mainly under Stalin, and other longer-lasting restrictions of liberties of speech, press, and culture became convincing arguments against soviet-stye socialism in the West, including for Western workers – especially after the Western culture revolution of 1968. Yet, these bad historic facts, too, may be unable to keep new traditionally socialist projects from the table indefinitely. Closer analysis may show that there were several layers of "repression" in soviet style socialism, which will not all have to re-appear in a future socialist endeavor. Layer 1, though, will definitely have to re-appear: As M–C–M' grows naturally and spontaneously out of exchange by itself, all anti-M–C–M'-regimes, socialism or the Middle Ages, *must always be repressive insofar as they have to repress M–C–M'*. That is not greatly different from Western capitalist countries repressing the application of M–C–M' in particular trades or policing it, e.g., trading in humans (since the end of slavery, not before), trading of human organs, the trading of humans for prostitution, armament trade, the drug trade, etc.

---

4   Russia, as a largely underdeveloped country, had to go through civil war in 1917, supported by intervention of the West, and subsequently World War II. After World War II, during the cold war, the Soviet Union had to deflect massive resources for armament build up once again.

or from the Middle Ages repressing money lending. Overall, this layer 1 of repression may be seen as no big deal. Layer 2: Anti-M–C–M'-regimes of the socialist type presuppose expropriation of the greatest part of the wealth from the wealth owners. Undoubtedly, the act of expropriation is an exercise of repressive state power, which wealth owners, as we stated repeatedly, will resent. Yet, such acts of repression are not even uncommon in capitalist countries (as nationalizations or taxation witness) and they can take different shapes, even include compensation. Layer 3 is where it gets uglier: Wealth owners will, quite simply, if they can (and they normally can) try to violently oppose their expropriation. This will lead to civil war, political oppression, imprisonment and killings. That type of killing and repression also existed in non-socialist revolutions; in the US civil war anti-slaveholders killed pro-slaveholders, in the French revolution anti-aristocrats killed aristocrats, etc. As bad as it is, such killing is normally accepted by history – and proponents of socialism will argue it is better to go through it once more than to continuously suffer from capitalism, its wars included. Layer 4 of repression in the Soviet Union came into play in connection with counter-revolutionary efforts, which were supported from the outside, such as the intervention of the Entente or the attack by Nazi Germany in World War II. Partisans of a new socialist venture will argue that this layer was not socialism's fault. Layer 5 involves internal repression during the cold war, such as restrictions of freedom of speech, of political organization, of press and culture, including imprisonments, and even killings. That was a kind of worsened and permanent McCarthyism, by which the Soviet Union reacted to its disadvantages in the ongoing financial, economic and ideological competition. Proponents of a new socialist attempt will argue that this situation may not arise again, in particular if the world marches into socialism as a joint project. Layer 6: Ultimately, Stalin killed oppositional fellow countrymen and even his own communist comrades[5] in great numbers. We may also add another layer, Layer 7, in which we might assemble brutalities that either appear irrational as such or follow a particularly reckless military or economic logic, such as famines, the Katyn massacre, etc. [6]

In fact, there is one tradition even in orthodox socialism, which appears to be well-positioned sidestep the criticism of soviet-type socialism altogether: *Trotskyism*. Trotskyism brings two strong elements to the table. Trotsky had essentially taught that socialism "in one country" is impossible and, thus, already 100 years

---

5   Quite interestingly, a very strong point used to blame communists is to blame them for killing other communists.

6   Many readers may feel uncomfortable with even listing up these points, which must read like excuses. The issue here is not, though, whether they are ultimately convincing and legitimate or not, but whether they are so strong as to lastingly foreclose a political rebirth of socialist projects given that the master drama of capitalism continues to exist and that prosthetic means may dry out.

ago, proffered an explanation not only for why the revolution in the USSR was destined to fail, but also why it would likely revert to repression (which could be unneeded if a socialist society was erected more or less simultaneously in many countries). Second, no other Russian revolutionary has a more pronounced and credible history of being anti-Stalin than Trotsky (killed by Stalin in Mexico-City).

If still no new socialist venture is likely to become a major political proposition in the next fifty years, except for the terribly case of a new World War, this is so for the following reasons: The world, in which a "workers and farmer's paradise" was attractive for workers, is no more. Today's "working class", notwithstanding its continued existence as a social economic class of non-owners, does not feel like a social class any more. Workers do not aspire to socialism any more, if they ever did in their majority. Some, who are rather well of, feel superior to others who receive transfer payments or live a precariat life. Others, worse, are marginalized and move in the shadow, become alcoholics, addicts to opiates, get sick, and die early. There was a great decay of working-class identity, working class culture, and working-class organizations for decades. E.g., trade-unions, social democracy, socialist and communist parties, if they still exist at all, are often irrelevant and their remnants have changed their profile towards general human rights policies, ecology, gender, anti-racism, etc., and are hard to distinguish from other present parties. Large working-class areas in big capitalist cities near huge factories or mines no longer exist and nobody is there to eventually lead workers to a serious socialist effort. Occasionally erupting revolts, such as of the "Gilets Jaunes" in France, "Podemos" in Spain, or SYRIZA in Greece are no substitute – and they do not last. Finally, of course, wealth owners, to whose disadvantage any socialist project would be, are as powerful as ever. They would, once more, fight fiercely against their expropriation and against anti-M–C–M'-policies. But all that does not exclude that a new socialist project may remerge, say after fifty years, if in completely new forms and shapes, because the social master drama of modern capitalism still continue to exist.

Question VIII: What about China?

China is run by a communist party, yet as there is significant factual private property in means of production and M–C–M', its economy is capitalist. China's historically singular growth over the last decades has been enabled by an especially powerful capitalist dynamic under a very successful planning catch-up leadership of its communist government. The Chinese people's rich intellectual and culture heritage and their ambition to, after being demoted and insulted by colonial powers in the 19th century, return to the technological and economic top of the world, it had held between 200 BC to 1800 AD, certainly contributed to this performance.

The catch-up dynamics of original capitalism were complemented by protectionist policies, taxation and, other prosthetics, yet initially only moderate debt build-up. Since the aftermath of the financial crisis of 2008, China is now catching up in indebtedness, too, and using prosthetics funded by money creation. So far, the modern master drama has not yet posed a particular challenge. Rather, Chinese workers have experienced a significant improvement of their income and living conditions, including former rural laborers that migrated to more industrialized regions or to big cities. Whether China's efforts to switch from an investment-driven to a consumption-driven economy, as the communist party announces since some time, will succeed and allow to uphold this situation, is uncertain. It would basically mean to substitute investive employment-generating spending, which was prosthetic in part, by consumptive employment-generating spending, which would also have to be prosthetic in part. We remember that since the early 20th century many economists, e.g., Tugan-Baranovsky and Keynes, saw a necessity to substitute deficient consumptive spending by investive spending; China appears to now consider just the opposite direction. The feasibility of this transition will depend on whether higher producive consumption spending of lower income strata can be funded without simultaneously canceling out the profitability of firms. Under the rule of the deficient-producive-spending-syndrome this appears straightforwardly impossible. The only alternative remains to fund the higher consumption through prosthetics. Yet, increased confrontation with the West and between Russia and the West will likely loosen the connections between China's economy and the West and reduce China's chances to sell its output in the West. By the same token, China may lift new synergies from cooperation with non-Western countries and find new markets there, yet that may not suffice to compensate for the loss of Western markets. In the aggregate, we shall likely see a world economy more broken up into blocks with generally less access to producive spending from outside of the own block. Someday, China too, will, thus, much more than today, have to face the deficient-producive-spending-syndrome and resort to prosthetics to deal with the modern master drama. Its main options, as everywhere in today's world, shall be the build-up of debt and money creation, with a significant part of the prosthetic spending increasing its military spending. The funding of the prosthetic spending will lead into the known dilemmas of these prosthetics.

The widespread feeling of a rebirth of a grand nation, socialist tenets, and communist party rule, which greatly simplified the making and execution of decisions, jointly facilitated the capitalist catch-up of China over the last thirty years.[7] It is rather likely that these will continue to be helpful and to maintain social cohesion if the modern master drama becomes more poisonous. China should, in particular,

---

7   Note by comparison that when the UK, France, Germany or Japan experienced their original capitalist growth period they were *no* democracies as well, certainly not in the present sense of the word in the West.

remain better positioned to demand sacrifices from wealth owners *and* from work-ers than, e.g., in the US or West Europe.

The lack of significant private bank fractional reserve credit money creation, the lack of a functioning banking system steered by a central bank and the lack of func-tioning state fiat money creation had materially contributed to China's decay in the 18th and 19th century. Undoubtedly, similar deficits had expedited the collapse of the Warsaw Pact states in the 90ties of last century, China and the Warsaw Pact states then suffered especially badly under the impossibility to pay international liabili-ties out of money created in their own currencies. China appears to be on track to now overcome this restriction, which would greatly enhance its power of funding its prosthetic spending.

We should also expect that China's communist party will run the Chinese econ-omy and state less ideologically and more pragmatically than the Russian Commu-nist party did in the last century and that China will not sacrifice economic and po-litical effectivity on an altar of socialist anti-M–C–M'-credence. This does not yet answer the question whether the Communist Party of China still seriously pursues the erection of a Marxian style socialist society (like the former communist party of Russia or the communist party of Cuba etc.), or whether "communism" has become just a label for a party dynasty that primarily pursues nation rebirthing, economic development and dynastic and national self-assertation. This question may remain undecided for some time ahead.

Questions on future options and the role of politics

Question IX: Where will deficient employment-generating spending and the dilemmas of prosthetics drive the world in the next fifty years?

If several possibilities exist, it is a legitimate guess that history may try them all out, it not neatly separated, one after the other, but, erring back and forth and interrupt-ing its attempts into one direction with new attempts into another. This may not be different if *no* real way out exists. We may then see an oscillation between these non-possibilities. This is particularly so, as all of these non-solutions will, if they remain caught in dilemmas, continue to contain at least some trace of prosthetic poten-tial. In fact, through destructions that they cause, if pushed to extremes, they may even temporarily improve the conditions for circuit closure, e.g., in restart-booms after wars or currency reforms. The unending erring may thus even partially miti-gate the original deficient employment-generating spending and re-create an illu-sion of manageability of circuit closure.

We have gotten to know three main directions that prosthetics can take, first, vi-olent wealth procurement and protectionism, second, taxation and expropriations, which in the extreme, leads to socialism, and, third, expansive debt financing and money creation.[8] If we consider them in a row, we get:

Assume, first, an attempt to fund prosthetics through violent wealth procurement and protectionism. The preparatory armament build-up, e.g., funded by higher taxation, greater debt build-up or more money creation, will already improve circuit closure of the respective country. The more attractive the intended prey, the more likely it is that a serious war breaks out. If this occurs, the consecutive warfare will necessitate further massive employment-generating spending, which is financed by, once again, higher taxation, greater debt build-up, and more money creation. If the war is over, the reconstruction of infrastructure and houses will bring about greater production for fewer employment seeking workers (because of war killings), which will, once more, lead to increased employment-generating spending and even, likely, to post-war booms. There may be debt jubilees and currency reforms during or after the war, which will greatly facilitate the situation. War and after war booms will be based on original employment-generating spending and on additional state-financed prosthetic spending funded by taxation, new debt build-up and money creation. If the war has a winner, he will thence also use violent wealth procurement and protectionism.

Assume, second, high taxation and expropriations of wealth owners and anti-M–C–M'-reforms are implemented and glide into some neo-socialist drive. That will initially also allow the additionally collected taxes and the proceeds from the expropriations to be spent prosthetically. There may also be some additional redistributive debt or money-creation that finances prosthetics. During the time of the anti-M–C–M'-expedition, though, firms will most likely omit or postpone investments altogether, which they would have carried out otherwise. After the anti-M–C–M'-reforms have failed and a pro-M–C–M'-government is re-established, firms will catch up on the omitted or postponed investments and this will increase original employment-generating spending again. It is obvious that the first development's prosthetic effects – centered around violent wealth procurement, protectionism, and possibly war – will be much stronger than those connected to an (unlikely) renewed socialist effort.

Assume, third, expansive debt financing, hence by money creation, is pushed to excesses. Then, sooner or later, the currency will dwindle into inflation and its exchange rate will degenerate compared to other currencies. This will lead to a currency reform, which will be connected to a debt jubilee. All this will, indeed, lay foundations and reserves for new rounds of expansive prosthetics through private bank and central bank money creation, but the leading capitalist states will certainly want to avoid to go through all this as it will imply a material loss of their power and reputation. Unfortunately, as seen in the book and touched upon in connection with the

---

8   We skip prosthetics by redistributive debt as they are far less effective.

option to fund prosthetics through violent wealth procurement and protectionism, in order to preserve and strengthen the power of their fiat money creation gland, states may be driven into imperial and war policies.

Question X: What may influence democratic and authoritarian politics as they err back and forth between non-solutions in the next fifty years?

Since democracy came into being as the concept of the people's rule, there was a contradiction between it and the existing social and economic order. Democracy meant equality and people's rule; the social order consisted of inequality and the rule of wealth owners. That contradiction is well-known since ancient Greece, where Aristotle defined democracy as "the rule of the poor". In the motto of the French revolution, the aspect of democracy, which was directed against social inequality appeared twice, in "fraternité" and in "égalité". Nevertheless, after two hundred years of modern democracy, the wealth and income distribution in capitalist societies stays as unequal as ever.

There are several reasons for this. First, political attempts of social democracy, socialism, and communism, to seriously change the situation, simply failed. Social democracy and socialism become currents within the party systems, which only leaned more towards prosthetics than others, soviet style communism collapsed in the nineties of last century. Second, it may be that there are intrinsic reasons why a workable alternative that can economically, socially, and militarily compete with rivaling and hostile capitalist states, which use the fiercer dynamics of inequality, does not exist. Third, the arena, in which democracy and social inequality met, appears to have been structured in a way, which favors wealth owners' efforts to preserve social inequality, even under conditions of democracy. These structures can be regarded as a series of open or closed gates or *filters*, which shape the outcomes of the democratic process; they are ideological, social, and institutional (constitutional, legal, economic).

In the next fifty years, democratic politics, may be influenced by the fact that many of the old shaping structures are about to be swept away or have been swept away recently. With reference to a Marxian-Gramscian idiom, one might speak of "changes of structures or the superstructure" in Western capitalist democracies. Before this change, the vast majority of the masses and of the elites in Western democratic countries essentially adhered to pre-democratic conservative values, such as religion, family, traditional morals, patriotism, and nationalism. These values were attacked in the Western cultural revolution of 1968, with centers in France, West-Germany, and the US. The revolution successively conquered strongholds in education, the universities, and the media and, following movements against nuclear energy and armament build-up, new "green parties" arose out therefrom and helped to spread it. A second "great jump forward" in this cultural revolution in the West was ignited by the collapse of soviet style communism. That, now, opened the door to a rather *general historic political and cultural compromise*. A significant share of political leaders, including leaders representing wealth owners' interests, became or outed themselves as "green", "pro-ecology", "pro-gender", and "anti-discrimination", including "anti-racist" and, more explicitly than ever before, "anti-antisemite". The part that had preferred to maintain previous attitudes (cigar smoking, churchgoing, law and order-oriented, heterosexual, rank-conscious, ecologically unconscious, limousine-driven, old white men, etc.) was overwhelmed by this wave. Yet, there was a trade-off. The novel-style representatives of wealth owners remained in favor of wealth owners and claimed and were conceded *a global neoliberal capitalist ecstasy, including in finance*. Ex-68ers, green and social democrat parties, accordingly, dropped much of their anti-capitalist and egalitarian ambitions in *social* and *property* matters. Businesses, provided that they were "politically correct" or "woke", used proper language and introduced symbolic reforms (which could be low-cost and lip-service) to bow before the new golden cows, were set free to exploit the opportunities of the new globalized and financialized world. The European Union whose role grew significantly after the German reunification and the Euro-introduction, became the European propagator and bureaucratic implementer of the new, beautiful world. The internet brought global communication and young, unconventional entrepreneurs who drive bicycles or electro vehicles, communicate on a first-name-basis mostly and smoke pot instead of cigars occasionally, took over.

The compromise was economically supported by a series of (very favorable) economic macro-moments. China and other BRICS-states rose economically, and the countries of soviet style communisms collapsed. Both events triggered huge investive and consumptive producive spending, which generated employment and relative wellbeing. In addition, a massive worldwide prosthetic spending, whose volume had been hitherto unimaginable, was unleashed: After Volcker's anti-inflation and austerity-policies in the 1980s, the US pursued a prosthetic debt-build-up course, which persists even today, with material beneficial effects on employment. In connection with the European integration and the Euro-introduction, a significant rise of sovereign and private debt build-up in Europe sent waves of prosthetics throughout Europe, too, particularly through peripheral Europe. When the time of punishment arrived, with the European national debt crisis in 2010, European politicians added more debt, now directly at the level of the European Community. In fact, the European Union was (re)born as a new "super-debtor" in these days. The European Central Bank began to subsidize debt-issues of the member states by asset purchases and took a great share of them on its balance sheet. As mentioned elsewhere, China, too, after three decades of growth with little public debt, changed course after the financial crisis and nearly caught-up with the West's debt levels, thereby greatly helping Western economies. Most recently, the Corona-crisis kicked expansive prosthetic spending to higher levels. The Ukraine war is already providing new reasons to continue to create further state fiat money. If it escalates into a lastingly bellicose international situation or a larger war, much more will follow. All of these movements, taken together, raised employment and working-class well-being in highly developed Western capitalist countries in the last thirty years *enormously*, *much beyond what would have been possible without them.*

In turning away from the difference between owners and non-owners and from the modern social master drama, and, in fact, from the issue of war and peace and violent goods procurement, too, the compromise has elevated the ideological debates into a realm of fuzziness and of simulation. Due to the economic wellbeing of the last decades in most relevant regions, it has so far remained untested how the compromise may influence the future narrative of the social master drama, which cannot but err back and forth, as we said, between non-solutions regarding deficient employment-generating spending and the between different prosthetics with their dilemmas, if it is put under stress. With the compromise, the militants on both sides, of the working class and wealth owners, have, at first, abandoned the old trenches of traditional ideological warfare. E.g., it used to be a holy credence for wealth owners, over which they would go to civil war, that the freedom of economic behavior and private property are premier, natural human rights. Yet, quite paradoxically, very shortly after the demise of socialism-communism, in the crisis after 2008, all capitalist countries massively intervened in the economy with instruments from the horror-kit of their very same late socialist and communist arch-enemies, e.g., large sale nationalizations of banking. The visible and massive role played by state fiat money creation, too, is even more incompatible with traditional pro-capitalist world views (as only a few Austrian economists seem to remember). The question is, whether, if need should arise, pro-capitalist militants can re-occupy their former ideological warfare trenches? Or, if they have to invent and build new trenches – what will they be? Working class-ideologues, too, have cleared their old positions, and may not be able to recuperate them easily. In fact, the tectonic shift of the last thirty years goes even deeper, down to the very intellectual foundations of all debates between conservatism, liberalism and socialism since the 18th century. ... *All* these historic parties justified their proposals as *intellectually rational*, hence derivable from and in accordance with the best available notional and logical thinking and with experience. This fundament is shaking. The compromise has not only disparaged "grand narratives" but undermined the very basis for such narratives by de-intellectualizing and de-rationalizing the political discourse and reducing it either to a small coins' affaire or overwhelming it with ecological, gender or anti-discrimination moral discourses in great fervor. If the *ideal of truth*, formerly shared by the parties, loses ground, emotions and interests of swarm-like moving social groups must become dominant and children expressing innocent feelings must appear as the most legitimate and trustworthy voices in politics. The growing role of women in the media, education, politics, law etc. has not helped to halt this trend. If fits together with this that the compromise particularly features a worldview arranged around so-called human rights. Anything can be easily declared as a "human right" and such "rights" (which are, of course no "rights" in any reasonable sense) cannot be but limitless and fuzzy on the one side and moralistic and aggressive on the other. They, thus, always offer more than what is needed for a specific political purpose and require permanent fine-tuning, which, for the lack of rational derivability, is only possible through further compromises. Such further, secondary compromises that set out how to implement a premier fuzzy and simulative compromise, will, therefore, be an almost daily challenge if the modern master drama seriously raises its head again. We live in a highly irritable, and instable ideological and political situation, in which unprepared and inexperienced actors will move in little rational, but very moralistic, often aggressive and possibly hysterical, ways. It is, thus, very unpredictable, in which direction the players will to move and how they will battle it out.

Of course, the compromise has left behind non-adherents to it, bearers of more conservative values, for instance, whether rural or urban, and whether wealth owners or non-owners. They felt already irritated when the compromise was entered into and the vigorous re-education attempts and the canceling out of these non-adherents by the missionaries of the compromise has further alienated them. Rural non-owners are particularly offended; they do not profit from the globalized economy and very little, if at all, from feminism, gay culture, transsexuality, or legalized pot, etc. Parts of well-educated and wealthy urban elites, too, feel repulsed by seeing conservative tenets, which once made their country great, "canceled out" (as if it were fascist). Even remaining left-wing working-class traditionalists feel disrespected. Whether this reservoir of homeless leftovers, stays marginalized or it somehow recuperates influence upon political processes in Western democracies, particularly under great economic and social stress or following wars, is, aside the unforeseeable inside-dynamics of the proponents of the compromise, a further open question. As moderating filters have been removed from political processes, and as political winners will have more immediate and direct access to state power to execute new policies, we shall likely see several sharp ruptures.

More authoritarian systems, e.g., in China and Russia, as we have said, are also committed to delivering well-being for the people and their legitimacy; social peace there depends on meeting basically similar benchmarks as those in the West. However, these countries have not experienced the historic compromise encountered in the West and the ideas of the Western cultural revolution of 1968 have not nearly achieved a similar hegemonic position as in the West.[9] More authoritarian regimes,

---

9   Quite interestingly, even though Russia and China have driven their populations through
     decades of cultural revolutions!

quite obviously, possess more means by which to steer, influence, and control public opinion and the political process and their populations, especially in Russia and China, may be ready to accept a lower level of wellbeing and to endure greater suffering. Therefore, it may appear that, as long as these countries maintain their internal unity and do not collapse, they may possess a higher capacity to implement somewhat calmer long-term policies. If they collapse, they will simply westernize – all this in a world with only non-solutions.

Appendix

Conventions

Certain notional conventions are used throughout this book. For ease of reference, they are listed below:

C–C': means the exchange of a commodity against another commodity without the use of money, hence barter.

C–M–C': means the exchange of a commodity against money as a medium of exchange with the intent to exchange the money into another commodity. The notation, as well as M–C–M', dates back to Marx. There are two legs before the purpose is reached. In the first leg, it exchanges a commodity against money; in the second leg, the money procured against another – the desired – commodity. The purpose of the exchange is value-in-use (see page 84 et seq.). C–M–C' also expresses the ability to give away labor, hence working, for money to then exchange the money into another commodity, mostly for consumption, e.g., for food. See also M–C–M' or M–C...C'–M'.

Circuit ("Umschlag"): The term "circuit", which is widely used throughout this book, describes a completed M–C–M'-drive (see M–C–M'), for which Marx also used the German word "Umschlag" or "Kapitalumschlag". The term circuit is in this sense is not to be confused with the idea of circles of exchanges between units or classes. Therefore, Quesnay's tableau on page 206 and the graphics on pages 119, 121, 122, 485 and 487 of this book do not represent "circuits".

Commodities: Goods (including services) looked at from a combined values-in-exchange and values-in-use perspective.

Commodity money: Commodity-money is a term used by Ludwig von Mises. It describes when gold or silver, or other commodities, to whom markets attribute value-in-exchange outside of its monetary use, are used as money. Hence, they maintain a value-in-exchange even if they are demonetized (no longer used as money). E.g., if a coin of gold or silver-money is demonetized, e.g., melted, and the state's embossing is removed, it retains its value-in-exchange in the amount of the value-in-exchange attributed to the precious metallic material. If the value-in-exchange of a metal used for money is negligible, as in the case of aluminium or iron, this is no commodity money. In this book we identify commodity money mainly with gold or silver money. Theoretically, commodity money could also consist of platinum or jewels etc.

Consumption: We normally use "consumption" as opposed to investment. Thus, we only call such customers **of** firms' "consumers" that purchase goods not to make profits but to fulfill human physical or narrative needs or desires. Some authors use the distinction of "consumptive consumption" (eating bread) and "investive consumption" (feeding bread to chickens in a chicken meat factory). "Investive consumption" is investment.

Coupon: The fixed, mostly annual, amount that a sovereign bond or other debt pays. If the bond/ the debt is traded at a higher or lower level than at par value, the coupon, does not change, but the yield (coupon/market price of bond) does change.

Covert monetary financing (CMF): See "Overt Monetary Financing" (OMF).

Customers: They are the addressees of firms. They purchase for consumptive or investive reasons.

Economy, economic system, **exchange economy, money economy, profit economy, and even capitalism** have all basically the same meaning. The words only emphasize different aspects (economy and economic system are like manhood and human biological system) or relate to one another (i.e., exchange economy, money economy, profit economy and capitalism relate to each other roughly like fertilization, pregnancy, and baby). A money economy (already C–M–C') grows out of exchange (C–C') almost instantly and a profit economy or capitalism (i.e., M–C–M') quickly grow out of a money economy following an unavoidable role differentiation between C–M–C'-players and M–C–M'-players. This role differentiation superimposes an order of two classes over the original equality. The economic system is *one* way through which to procure goods and services for humans. Other ways, which we do not count as "economic" but as "praeter-economic") would be direct autarchic self-supply by families, groups or tribes of humans or "violent wealth procurement" as part of the economy. , Marxian socialism or Keynes' "cooperative society" could use money or not use it.

Effective demand: What the community is *expected* to consume and to invest. Effective demand has its *effects on entrepreneurs* who derive business plans and production plans from these expectations when they make investments and create employment on this basis. Expected demand has direct effects on the investing firms' M-outlays for the employment of their workers and on the sales of their supplier firms and indirect effects on the employment of workers of their supplier firms through and so on. Effective demand leads to *money leaving the pockets of entrepreneurs* and flowing into the pockets of either workers or of other firms. Some money then always also, unavoidably flows to sterile wealth owners as "tributes" to the sterile economy.

Effectual Demand: is what firms or consumers *actually spend later* in the M–C'-leg of their circuits, and which vindicates (or not) firms' previous investment. Effectual demand has no more effects on *past* employment; it only shows the extent to which the effective demand (or purchase power) expected by entrepreneurs, when they made their investment or M–outlays earlier, really exists. The "effectual effects" is *cash flowing into the entrepreneurs' pockets* as M' at the end of the circuit.

Employment: The term "employment" gains its relevance from the master drama of modernity and means primarily the employment of labor or of workers who are propertyless non-owners and can only subsist (apart from state transfer payments, family support and alms) from being employed. The employment of workers is, though, always connected to purchases for equipment and inventories, which indirectly lead to more employment of equipment and inventories of other firms. Employment is only created in the productive economy by employment-generating or producive spending. There is no employment at all in the sterile economy; productive splitters or components, which are connected to sterile activities, e.g., the employment of bankers, real estate agents, bond traders, etc., have been "carved-out" before. See productive and sterile economy.

Equipment and inventories: Equipment has so-called fixed capital in mind (land, buildings, machines, tools...), inventories circulating capital (raw materials, energy, ancillary materials, intermediate produce...). But inventories also include services, such as architectural or engineer services, transportation, consulting, lawyering, advertising, accounting, etc. Firms, in order to produce, only need the inputs of labor, equipment and inventories. Money enables them to buy them.

Esoteric demand: Physical and narrative needs and desires to possess or to use goods for consumptive purpose or reasons to acquire goods for investive reasons. Esoteric demand stands behind expected "effective demand" and later actual "effectual demand" (see effective and effectual demand), but in order for it to be reasonbly considered as "effective demand", and to later become actual "effectual demand", money must be available and the readiness to sacrifice it must be present, too, in those who have "esoteric demand".

Fiat money: This is money from material or are objects, which do not carry value-in-exchange (at least not nearly in the amount of its prior nominal value) outside of its monetary use, in particular if demonetized. The typical examples include paper money or token coins without content of precious metals. Commodity money or "Kurantgeld" (cows, corn, skins, copper, silver, or gold; in this book, we always primarily think of gold and silver), on the contrary, even if demonetized, retains the value-in-exchange of its precious material.

Firms, entrepreneurs or capitalists are only alternative names for the same thing, which arise out of different theoretical traditions and carry different connotations. They assume the role of an M–C–M'-player in the *productive* economy (we use them in the productive economy only!). The expression "firm" is neutral, the expression "entrepreneur" emphasizes the daring, creative, and admirable aspect of their doing (which is often, but not always, crucial for being able to generate a positive M'-M), the expression "capitalist" emphasizes the availability of a capital M at the beginning of a M–C–M'-circuit and the motive to increase it. In the individual case, we mostly select the term by the theoretical – general, Keynesian, Schumpeterian, Marxian – context. Productive wealth owners are wealth owners who, themselves, use their wealth in the productive economy, whereby they always also become firms, entrepreneurs or capitalists or they finance them in one or the other way. Therefore, they receive revenue-payments M' only through wealth owners' producive, employment-generating arrival ports. If we want to refer to sterile wealth owners specifically, we speak of sterile wealth owners. Sterile wealth owners receive payments through their sterile arrival port; they do not invest in the productive economy and do not create employment. Sterile wealth owners initiate M–C–M'-circuits in the wealth economy by drawing revenues from debt (interest), real estate (rent), business profits from existing businesses (e.g., as dividends), or capital gains by selling wealth assets.

Goods: Goods encompass goods and services, e.g., advice, treatment, and transportation. The term "goods" primarily emphasizes the values-in-use. The expression "commodities" also include goods and services, but equally emphasizes value-in-exchange.

Gold or silver-money: See commodity money.

M–C–M' (M–C...C'–M'): A notation developed by Marx to describe major economic processes that include system-building combinations of more elementary economic events. The idea behind M–C–M' was implicit in economic thought, social critique, and the self-understanding of merchants long before Marx, but they became clearer and precise ("pregnant", as Keynes said) thanks to Marx's notation. It includes investing money to buy and resell a pre-existing commodity, e.g., only after storing, transporting, re-bundling, or marketing it in a new market, as well as after processing it, i.e., after producing something new out of equipment, inventories, and labor. Both cases are jointly abbreviated by M–C–M' (money–commodity–more money). If Marx wanted to emphasize that inputs of equipment and inventories were physically processed by labor, then he used M–C...C'–M'. The intermediate "C...C'" can be seen to expresses the physical change, first, but also, second, the increase in value that the commodities experience during the process (C'>C!). M–C–M' involves an initial (investive) leg, when money is given up in order to acquire commodity inputs (M–C); this money goes to workers as salaries (v) or to other firms (c) for equipment and inventories. The c-outlays unavoidably contain sterile components that flow into the wealth economy as "tributes". (Marx coined v for "variable capital" and c for "constant capital" in connection with his labor value and exploitation theory which we reject, but we still use c and v as many readers will be familiar with these abbreviations.) For a further explanation of M–C–M', see page 86 et seq. The C–M'-leg or, in the extended notation for processed commodities, the C'–M'-leg, is the sale of the commodity to realize a profit. M' is the sales price or revenue and M'-M the profit. In Marx, M'-M also corresponds to s ("surplus value"). (This term is also connected to Marx's false labor value and exploitation theory, but we still occasionally use it all the same).

Market economy: Markets result from there being owners of things with owner power and fields of human existence, even if they are limited, in which they are allowed to enter into exchanges at their own free will, i.e., without the conclusion and contents of transactions being prescribed by a superior instance, e.g., by the order of custom, tradition, individual violence, or by legal rules. If there is more than one owner who offers a commodity for exchange, this implies competition and there may be winners and losers amongst the offerors. Overall, markets are important, but only as the spaces in which exchanges take place and the capitalist M–C–M'-logic can unfold, which is the game being played. The term "market economy" not only ignores or belittles the many non-market-style activities of the state in capitalism, including fiat money creation,[1] but also often claims an explanatory

---

1   Accordingly, quite interestingly, *Myers/Wang*, in their study of economic evolution in Qu'ing China, use the opposition between "market economy" and "command economy" not as mutually exclusive but as necessarily complementary. While in the customary or market economy, which *Myers/Wang* treat as closely connected, "people bartered goods and exchanges labor services", in the "command economy, the military and bureaucracy mobilized resources through direct taxation and corvée labor." (*Myers/Wang*, Economic developments, 1644–1900, page 563).

power for it, which it does not possess. Accordingly, we prefer the terms "profit economy" or "capitalism".

"Narrative needs and desires": Humans have physical and narrative needs and desires. Physical ones relate to food, clothing, housing, heating, medical services etc. Narrative ones cover everything, which is often referred to as "symbolic", "semantic" "psychological", "social", "cultural" or "communicative", including, if economists speak of "positional goods". Physical and narrative needs and desires, thus, encompass all possible human motives to purchase goods outside of sheer physical needs. The emphasis on "narration" is derived from the idea that humans almost permanently narrate their life to themselves and to other humans and that they make great efforts to get their practical lives to conform to their narratives.

Overt Monetary Financing (OMF): (also called "outright monetary financing") consists in state fiat money creation without sovereign debt being issued by the state and without debt held by central banks, which has been purchased by newly created money. As there is no longer any sovereign debt, it will be impossible to hold sovereign debt for private wealth owners and sovereign debt markets (bond markets) must cease to exist. Either central banks or the state will issue the state fiat money – in whatever form: notes: token coins, credit entries on accounts, digital money – and the state will directly use it for prosthetic employment-generating spending, e.g., to pay the state's own costs (state employees, rent, etc.) or for transfers to workers or firms. Conventional monetary financing consists in states issuing sovereign debt and central bank purchasing the debt with newly created state fiat money, in so-called secondary markets, and holding it (commonly referred to as "quantitative easing" or "central bank asset purchase programs"). In opposition to "overt monetary financing" (OMF), the conventional practices of state fiat money creation, which use debt, could also be called "covert monetary financing" (CMF) but its proponents do not use this expression.

"Ports", employment-generating and sterile port of wealth owners: We figuratively equip the wealth owners' class with *four "ports"*. It has *two "arrival ports"* through which it *receives* incoming revenues, a sterile arrival port for sterile revenues, i.e., for sterile spending of others, and a producive, employment-generating arrival port for producive, employment-generating revenues or spending of others. Wealth owners also have two *"departure ports"*, a *consumptive* and an *investive departure port*. If they consume, then they emit payments via their consumptive port; if they invest, then they dispatch them via their investive departure port. Flows leaving from there will be partly sterile and partly productive; accordingly, they will in part arrive at other wealth owners' sterile or producive, employment-generating ports. Workers need *only one in-and-out-port*; their departing spending are only consumptive (sometimes sterile and sometimes employment-generating)[2] and their arriving revenues are only producive, employment-generating (as firms made them to induce them to work). Wealth owners make salary payments to workers from either the consumptive or investive departure port.

Producive spending and productive economy: This book applies the distinction between *producive*, employment-generating spending and *sterile spending* across the (more commonly encountered) distinction between *investment* and *consumption*, thereby leading to Matrixes I and IV (see Figures 1 and 13). The intersection part of employment-generating spending with investment or consumption is the sole driver of employment. Consumptive producive, employment-generating spending is caused by human physical or narrative needs of desires, and requires, in order to become effective, a sufficient budget and a will to sacrifice the needed money as a purchase price. Its place is mostly in the second leg of C–M–C-circuits. Investive employment-generating spending is driven by the search of the money-sacrificing unit, which is then the payor, for profit; its place is the first leg of M–C–M'-circuits. Decisions about investment in the productive economy, what we call producive or employment-generating spending, are the most crucial moments in the recursive circuits of economic events. The realm of producive or employment-generating spending, which flows to wealth owners' employment-generating arrival ports (i.e., to firms, capitalists, or entrepreneurs), constitute the productive economy. The opposite of producive or employment-generating spending, which flows to wealth owners' sterile arrival port, is the realm of the sterile economy or wealth economy. The productive and the sterile economy is to be understood *already after* "carve-outs" (see page 123). Producive spending is only beneficial in a strictly macroeconomic sense of contributing to mitigating the modern master drama by employment. It may otherwise be detrimental, even highly detrimental, e.g., military or warfare spending, drug production, reckless production of dangerous equipment, murderous mines with deficient workers' safety measures, maltreatment of the ecology, or employment in "bullshit jobs" (such as in call centers) [3] . Keynes' term "aggregate demand" is only mere nuances away from producive or employment-generating spending.

---

2   If workers make investive spending, then they do not do so as workers but as wealth owners, see page 120. Workers, contrary to what may appear as implied in Marx's reproductions schemes, cannot use their full salaries for consumptive producive spending, i.e., consumption to Marx's II.b.-department; they may also have to make sterile spending in the form of rent and debt services.

3   See *Graeber* (2018).

Profit economy is used as a notion that stresses the importance of the search for profit by M–C–M'-players. Almost all systems of goods procurement after the Neolithic revolution became profit economies rather quickly. While the period of pre-economic goods procurement in primitive or tribal society lasted several ten thousand years and covered the greatest part of human existence, profit economies, so far, last only around three thousand years; capitalism is the most modern version of profit economies.

Prosthetics: Prosthetics means "artificial" mobilization (outside of the "natural" C–M–C'-logic or M–C–M'-logic) of pre-existing or newly created wealth to – directly or indirectly – support deficient "natural" circuit closure or the subsistence of non-owners in other ways. Prosthetic techniques range from violent wealth procurement, war, and protectionism (e.g., mercantilism, colonialism, imperialism) to taxation, sovereign and private debt, and, increasingly, value-in-exchange-creation by money creation. They include redistributive prosthetics, which do not necessitate money creation, and expansive prosthetics, which employs money creation. The word "prosthetics" was chosen to avoid moral and political valuations of the denoted measures. The word is equally unpartisan on whether prosthetics are seen as a means to "appease the working classes" to save an existing profit economy in the interest of its wealth owners or as a means of social progress towards a more just income and wealth redistribution. Readers who do not embrace this ambiguity, may not come to appreciate the full importance of prosthetics throughout history.

Sterile spending and sterile economy: The parts of the economy in which M–C–M' is realized without producing new tangible or intangible goods, including services, and, hence, without generating employment. The term is understood in a "purified" meaning, i.e., after "carve-outs" of all employment-generating spending components, such as e.g., the original physical production of buildings and factories, ongoing maintenance, repair, remodeling, and activities by banks, stockbrokers, traders, real estate agents, lawyers, tax advisers, secretaries, drivers, and other service suppliers, in connection with the sale of assets.[4]

"Tributes" to the wealth economy: Producive, employment generating spending, e.g., by productive investments, or consumption, including by workers, is mostly not possible without also making some sterile "tribute"-payments to the wealth economy, such as interest or rent payments or payments for the purchase of land (see page 354 and seq.).

---

4   See on page 123.

Violent wealth procurement: is the procurement of goods not by free exchange, such as by barter or through money, but by violence, i.e., directly robbing existing goods or threatening to take them away by violence, or by subjugating tribes and countries and forcing their people to work (enslavement) or to deliver produce as tribute. It is not, strictly speaking, a part of the economic system, which is defined by free exchange. Therefore, If an economic system exists, we often speak of "sliding off in goods procurement by violence" as into a praeter-economic method. Domestic taxation and domestic expropriations are, indeed, also forms of violent wealth procurement. Modern slavery of European countries and the US involved violent wealth procurement. Protectionism, colonialism, imperialism, and fascism tend to combine violent wealth procurement with protectionism and free exchange. As the disadvantaged side in violent wealth procurement receives nothing in exchange (or less than the value-in-exchange given away), it normally *requires ideology* to legitimate violent wealth procurement (e.g., religion, racism, etc.). Violent wealth procurement as such was no evolutionary stage of economic history. While pre-economic procurement of goods in primitive and tribal society, which was a stage in economic history, contained moments of violence, it was not primarily built on violence but on family and tribe-centered traditions.

Wealth owners: The aggregate social class of owners of wealth, in particular of land and of other means of production, which arose as the winners from the ancient master drama or later otherwise appropriated their wealth. Wealth owners cannot be by-standers, they must hold positions in asset classes; they can only choose where, whether, and by how much they want to be long or short, and even that only within limits. They will, thus, always shift around wealth between asset classes in an activity called *portfolio management* as time passes by and as insights change. This also includes switching their wealth back and forth between sterile and productive investments. Wealth owners may also partly be workers, given that we allow individual humans to belong to several classes.

Workers, non-owners constitute the social class that came out as losers from the ancient master drama or subsequently lost its wealth. The crucial criterion is, due to the lack of wealth, to have to sell one's labor for salaries to be able to subsist (and for some enjoyments). They could also be classically called "proletariat". They are a "flow-through"-class, which normally roughly receives just enough salaries to reproduce itself, but has to fully spend what it earns. (If individual workers don't receive enough income for that, they get sick and die away; sometimes they become rebellious or revolutionaries before that). As we have allowed for individual human beings to belong to several classes, if they earn more (e.g., some employed managers, state functionaries, employed lawyers, employed physicians etc.), they then become wealth owners *with that portion*. Often, that portion is quickly used-up and they fall back to being workers solely. Their economic existence is just too marginal to self-insure; if anything goes wrong, this will often force them to liquidate their wealth to consume it. However, they also sometimes lastingly move up into the wealth owners-class.

List of Figures

References[1]

Werner Abelshauser (2011), Wirtschaftsgeschichte der Bundesrepublik Deutschland 1945–1900, Frankfurt a. M., Suhrkamp

Aristotle, Politics, approx. 350 BC

Aristotle, The State of the Athenians, approx. 328–323 BC

William Atwell, Ming China and the emerging world economy c. 1470–1650, in: The Cambridge History of China, volume 8, part 2, page 376 et seqs

Dirk Baecker (1988), Information und Risiko in der Marktwirtschaft, Frankfurt a. M., Suhrkamp

Dirk Baecker (ed.) (2005), Schlüsselwerke der Systemtheorie, Wiesbaden, VS Verlag für Sozialwissenschaften

Dirk Baecker (2006), Wirtschaftssoziologie, Bielefeld, transcript

Dirk Baecker (2008), Womit handeln Banken? Frankfurt a. M., Suhrkamp

Hanno Beck, Urban Bacher, Marco Hermann (2017), Inflation – die ersten zweitausend Jahre, Frankfurt a. M., Frankfurter Allgemeine Verlag

Eric D. Beinhocker (2007), The origins of wealth. Evolution, complexity and the radical remaking of economics, London, Random House

Hans Bielenstein, Wang Mang, The restoration of the Han dynasty, and later Han, in: The Cambridge History of China, volume 1, page 223 et seqs.

John *Boardman, Jasper Griffin, Oswyn Murray* (ed. 1986), The Oxford History of Greece and the Hellenistic World, Oxford, Oxford University Press

Derk Bodde, The state and empire of Ch'in, in: The Cambridge History of China, volume 1, page 20 et seqs.

Moritz Julius Bonn (1896), Spaniens Niedergang während der Preisrevolution des 16. Jahrhunderts. Ein induktiver Versuch zur Geschichte der Quantitätstheorie, Stuttgart, Verlag der j.G. Cotta'schen Buhhandlung

Sergej Nikolajewitsch Bulgakov (1897), Über die Absatzmärkte der kapitalistischen Produktion. Eine theoretische Studie, Moskau, zitiert nach Luxemburg (1966)

---

1   Contributions in compilations are only shown underneath the author's name (not under the editor's name). Books and Articles with several authors are only shown underneath the first author's name.

Andrew Robert Burn (1990), The Penguin History of Greece, London, Penguin Books

Jean Cartelier (2008), Introduction, in *Cartelier* (2008)

Jean Cartelier (ed.) (2008), Physiocratie, Paris, Flammarion

Paul Cartledge (ed.) (1998), The Cambridge Illustrated History of Ancient Greece, Cambridge, Cambridge University Press

Paul Cartledge (1998, 1), Historical Outline C. 1500 – 146 BCE, in: *Cartledge* (1998)

Paul Cartledge (1998, 2), Power and State, in: Cartledge (1998)

Central Committee of the Sozialistische Einheitspartei Deutschlands (ed.), Marx Engels Werke, 39 main volumes, edited between 1955 und 1966, abbreviated "MEW", Berlin, Dietz Verlag

Carl von Clausewitz (1980), Vom Kriege, first ed. 1832–1834, Berlin, Ullstein

Manfred Clauss (1993), Einführung in die Alte Geschichte, München, C.H. Beck

Liu Chungqiang/Dai Nierui (2014), A general history of China, Beijing, volume VI

Martin van Creveld (2001), Men, woman & war, London, Cassell&Co.

Richard L. Davis, The reign of Li-Tsung (1224–1264), in: The Cambridge History of China, volume 5, part 1, page 839 et seqs.

Deutsche Bundesbank (2017), Anmerkungen zu einer 100-prozentigen Deckung von Sichteinlagen durch Zentralbankgeld, Anhang zum Monatsbericht vom April 2017, Die Rolle von Banken, Nichtbanken und Zentralbank im Geldschöpfungsprozess, Basel

Taisen Deshimaru-Roshi (1994), Zen in den Kampfkünsten Japan, 3rd ed., Heidelberg, Werner Kristkeitz Verlag

Stanley Diamond (1971), The rule of law versus the Order of Custom, Social Research, Vol. 38, No. 1 (Spring 1971), pp. 42–72

Mark Dowding, We need to think about debt cancellation, in: *Financial Times* of 5 December 2021

Patricia Ebrey, The economic and social history of the later Han, in: The Cambridge History of China 1, page 608 et seqs.

Elizabeth Endicott-West, The Yüan government and society, in: The Cambridge History of China, volume 6, page 587 et seqs.

Friedrich Engels (1885), Vorwort zu Das Kapital. Der Zirkulationsprozess des Kapitals, MEW volume 24

Gilbert Faccarello/ Heinz D. Kurz (2016), History of Economic Analysis, volume I, Cheltenham, Edward Elgar

Gilbert Faccarello (2016, 1), Anne-Robert-Jacques Turgot Cantillon (1727–1781) in: *Faccarello/Kurz* (2016), page 19 et seqs.

Gilbert Faccarello (2016, 2), Pierre le Pesant de Boisguilbert (1646–1714) in: *Faccarello/ Kurz* (2016), page 9 et seqs.

Bernhard Felderer, Stephan Homburg (2003), Makroökonomik und neue Makroökonomik, 8th ed. Berlin, Springer

Niall Ferguson (2008), The Ascent of Money, London, Penguin

Irving Fisher (1933), The Debt Deflation Theory of Big Depression, Econometrica, volume 1, 337 et seqs.

Nick Fisher (1998), Rich and Poor, in *Cartledge* (1998)

Duncan Foley (1986), Understanding capital, Cambridge (Mass), Harvard University Press

Georg Forest (1986), The History of the Archaic Period, in (Boardman et al. 1986)

Benjamin Friedmann, The perils of returning a central bank balance sheet to 'normal', in: *Financial Times* of 20 June 2014

Peter Furth (2015), Massendemokratie. Über den historischen Kompromiss zwischen Liberalismus und Sozialismus als Herrschaftsform, Berlin, Landtverlag

Peter Furth (2008), Rückblick auf den Marxismus, in: Troja hört nicht auf zu brennen. Aufsätze aus den Jahren 1981 bis 2007, (edited by Olaf Weißbach, 2. ed., Berlin, Landtverlag

Jacques Gernet (1972), Le monde chinois, tomes I, II, III, Paris, Armand Colin

A. Gerschenkron (1962), Economic Backwardness in Historical Perspective: A Book of Essays, Cambridge (Mass), Harvard University Press

Silvio Gesell (1916), Die natürliche Wirtschaftsordnung durch Freiland und Freigeld, pdf

Hans-Jörg Gilomen (2014), Wirtschaftsgeschichte des Mittelalters, München, C. H. Beck

Johann Wolfgang Goethe (1832), Faust. Der Tragödie Zweiter Teil

Peter J. Golas, The Sung fiscal administration, in: The Cambridge History of China, volume 5 part 2, page 139 et seqs.

David Graeber (2011), Debt. The first 5000 years, New York, Melville House

David Graeber (2018), Bullshit Jobs: A Theory, New York, Simon & Schuster

Michael Grant (1992), A Social History of Greece and Rome, New York, Maxwell Macmillan

Benjamin Graham, David Dodd (1934), Security analysis, 5th ed., photographic reproduction of 1st ed. New York, Wittlesey House

Linda-Marie Günther (2011), Griechische Antike, 2. ed., Tübingen, UTB

Robin Harding, Fears about Japan's debt are overblown, in: *Financial Times* of 6 September 2017

Roy Harrod (1982), The life of John Maynard Keynes, New York, W. W. Norton and Company

Douglas Hay (1975), Property, Authority and the Criminal Law, in: *Douglas Hay, Peter Linebaugh, John G. Ruie, E.P. Thompson and Cal Winslow*, Albion's Fatal Tree, New York 1975, page 17 et seqs.

Friedrich von Hayek (1944), The Road to Serfdom

Henry Hazlitt (1959), The Failure of the 'new economics'. An Analysis of the Keynesian Fallacies, D. van Nostrand Company, Princeton

Eli F. Heckscher (1932), Merkantilismus, Jena, Verlag Gustav Fischer in Jena

Georg Wilhelm Hegel (1986), Vorlesungen über die Geschichte der Philosophie, Werke, Frankfurt a. M., Suhrkamp, volume 12

Georg Wilhelm Hegel, Lectures on the History of Philosophy, translated from the German by E. S. Haldane, volume One, Greek Philosophy (Project Gutenberg)

Georg Friedrich Wilhelm Hegel (1983), Philosophie des Rechts. Eine Vorlesung von 1819/20 in einer Nachschrift. Ed. Dieter Henrich, Frankfurt a. M., Suhrkamp

Gunnar Heinsohn/Otto Steiger (2009), Eigentum, Zins und Geld, Marburg, Metropolis, 7. ed.

Martin Heijdra, The socio-economic development of rural China during the Ming, in: The Cambridge History of China, volume 8 part 2, page 417 et seqs.

Rudolf Hickel (1979), Konjunktur und Krise, neu betrachtet, in: K. Diehl/P. Mombert [ed.], Wirtschaftskrisen, 1979, page XXXVII – LV, Berlin, Ullstein

John R. Hicks (1937), Mr. Keynes and the "Classics"; A Suggested Interpretation, Econometrica, Vol. 5, No. 2 (Apr., 1937), page 147 et seqs.

John. R. Hicks (1976), Some questions of time in economics, in: Evolution, welfare and time: Essays in honor of Nicholas Georgesca-Roegen, pages 135–151

John. R. Hicks (1980) IS-LM: An explanation, Journal of Post-Keynesian Economics, 1980, 3(2), page 139 et seqs.

Rudolf Hilferding (1910), Das Finanzkapital, Wien, Verlag der Wiener Volksbuchhandlung

Douglas R. Hofstadter (1985), Gödel, Escher, Bach – An Eternal Golden Braid, New York, Basic Books

Werner Hoffmann (1971), Theorie der Wirtschaftsentwicklung. Vom Merkantilismus bis zur Gegenwart, Berlin, Duncker&Humblot

Werner Hoffmann (1964), Wert- Preislehre, Berlin, Duncker&Humblot

Ray Huang, The Ming fiscal administration, in: The Cambridge History of China, volume 8 Part 2, book 2, page 106 et seqs.

Chen Huan-Chang (2015), The economic principles of Confucius and his School, Beijing, The Commercial Press

Alexander von Humboldt (1811), Essai politique sur la Nouvelle Espagne

International Bank for Settlement (BIS) (2016), 86th Annual Report, 2016 (German Version)

Michael Ignatieff (1978), A just Measure of Pain. The Penintentiary in the Industrial Revolution, 1750 – 1850, New York, Pantheon Books

Karl Jaspers (1949), Vom Ursprung und Ziel der Geschichte, Frankfurt a. M., Fischer Verlag

Klaus-Peter Johne (1994), Von der Kolonenwirtschaft zum Kolonat. Ein römisches Abhängigkeitsverhältnis im Spiegel der Forschung, Antrittsvorlesung am 20. Oktober 1992 an der Humboldt-Universität zu Berlin, Fachbereich Philosophie und Geschichtswissenschaften, Institut für Geschichtswissenschaften, Berlin, pdf

Michal Kalecki (1971), Selected Essays on the Dynamics of the Capitalist Economy, London Cambridge University Press

Michal Kalecki (1937), A Theory of Commodity, Income and Capital Taxation, in: *Kalecki* (1971) page 35 et seqs.

Michal Kalecki (1943, 1954), Determinants of Investment, in: *Kalecki* (1971) page 110 et seqs.

Michal Kalecki (1935), The Mechanism of the Business Upswing, in: *Kalecki* (1971) page 26 et seqs.

Michal Kalecki (1934), On Foreign Trade and "Domestic Exports", in: *Kalecki* (1971) page 15 et seqs.

Michal Kalecki, Outline of a Theory of the Business Cycle (1933), in: *Kalecki* (1971) page 1 et seqs.

Michal Kalecki (1943, 1954), The Business Cycle, in *Kalecki:* (1971) page 124 et seqs.

Michal Kalecki (1933, 1954), The Determinants of Profits, in: *Kalecki* (1971) page 78 et seqs.

Michal Kalecki (1967), The Problem of effective demand with Tugan-Baranovsky and Rosa Luxemburg, in: *Kalecki* (1971) page 146 et seqs.

Michal Kalecki (1968), Trend and the Business Cycle, in: *Kalecki* (1971) page 165 et seqs.

Louis H. Kaufmann (2005), Das Prinzip der Unterscheidung, in: *Baecker* (ed.), (2005), page 173 et seq.

Steve Keen (2011), Debunking Economics, 2nd ed., London, Zed Books

Paul Kennedy (1987), The rise and fall of the great powers, quoted from the German translation of Aufstieg und Fall der großen Mächte. Ökonomischer Wandel und militärischer Konflikt von 1500 bis 2000, translated by Catharina Jurisch, Frankfurt am Main, Fischer, 2000

John Maynard Keynes (1936), General theory of employment, interest and money, London, Macmillan, Reprint of first edition

John Maynard Keynes (1937), The General Theory of Employment, in: The Quarterly Journal of Economics, February 1937

John Maynard Keynes, Collected Writings, editors Austin Ronaldson and Donald Moggridge, volumes XII, XIV, XVIII, XIX, XXII, XXIX, Cambridge, Cambridge University Press

Hartmut Kiehling (1991), Kursstürze am Aktienmarkt, München, DTV

Charles P. Kindleberger (1978), Manias, panic and crises. A history of financial crises, New York, Basic Books

John Edward King (2015), Advanced introduction to Post Keynesian Economics, Cheltenham, Edgar Elgar

Georg Friedrich Knapp (1905), Staatliche Theorie des Geldes, Leipzig, Verlag von Dunkler & Humblot

Panajotis Kondylis (1991), Der Niedergang der bürgerlichen Denk- und Lebensform. Die liberale Moderne und die massendemokratische Postmoderne, Weinheim, VCH Verlagsgesellschaft

Richard Koo (2009), The holy grail of macroeconomics. Lessons from Japan's great recession, Singapore, John Wiley & Sons

Janós Kornai (1992), The socialist system. The political economy of communism, Clarendon Press, Oxford

Jürgen Kuczynski (1951), Allgemeine Wirtschaftsgeschichte. Von der Urzeit bis zur sozialistischen Gesellschaft, Berlin, Dietz Verlag

Philip A. Kuhn, The Taiping rebellion, in: The Cambridge History of China, volume 10, page 264 et seqs.

Lohn Lea (1979), Discipline and Capitalist Development, in: *Bob Fine et al.*, Capitalism and the Rule of Law, 1979, page 76 et seqs.

Wladimir Ilic Lenin (1917), Imperialism, the highest Stage of Capitalism

Steven D. Levitt, Stephen J. Dubner (2005), Freakonomics, London, Penguin Books

Peter Linebaugh (1976), Karl Marx, The Theft of Wood, and Working-Class Composition, in: *Crime and Social justice*, Fall/Winter 1976, page 5 et seqs.

Michael Loewe, The former Han dynasty, in: The Cambridge History of China, volume 1, page 103 et seqs.

Michael Loewe, The structure and practice of government, in: The Cambridge History of China, volume 1, page 463 et seqs.

Julio G. López/Michaël Assous (2010), Michal Kalecki, London, Palgrave Macmillan

Niklas Luhmann (1988), Die Wirtschaft der Gesellschaft, Frankfurt a. M., Suhrkamp

Niklas Luhmann (2011), Einführung in die Systemtheorie. Transcript of lectures of Niklas Luhmann at Bielefeld University in the winter semester 1991/1992, editor *Dirk Baecker*, 6th ed., Heidelberg Carl Auer Verlags GmbH

Niklas Luhmann (1974), Reflexive Mechanismen, in: Niklas Luhmann, Soziologische Aufklärung, volume I, 4th. ed., Köln/Opladen, Westdeutscher Verlag

Niklas Luhmann (1984), Soziale Systeme, Frankfurt a. M., Suhrkamp

Niklas Luhmann (1991), Wie lassen sich latente Strukturen beobachten? in: *Paul Watzlawick/Peter Krieg*, Das Auge des Betrachters. Beiträge zum Konstruktivismus. Festschrift für Heinz von Foerster, page 61 et seqs., München/Zürich, Piper

Rosa Luxemburg (1966), Die Akkumulation des Kapitals, reprint of the original of 1913, Frankfurt a. Main, Verlag neue Kritik

Charles Mackay (1841), Extraordinary popular delusions and the madness of crowds, New York, John Wiley & Sons

Thomas Robert Malthus (1798), An essay on the principle of population, London Penguin Books

Thomas Robert Malthus (1836), Principles of Political Economy, Variorum edition, Cambridge, Cambridge University Press

Charles Mackay (1841), Extraordinary popular delusions and the madness of crowds, London, George Routledge and Sons

Crawford Brough Macpherson (1962), The Political Theory of Possessive Individualism: From Hobbes to Locke, Oxford, Clarendon

Ernest Mandel (1972), Der Spätkapitalismus, Frankfurt a. M., Suhrkamp

Ernest Mandel (2007), Marxistische Wirtschaftstheorie, Köln/Karlsruhe, Neuer ISP Verlag

Francesco de Martino (1991) Wirtschaftsgeschichte des alten Rom, München C. H. Beck

Karl Marx, Das Kapital, volume I, MEW 23

Karl Marx, Das Kapital, volume II, MEW 24

Karl Marx, Das Kapital, volume III, MEW 25

Karl Marx (1976) Capital, volume I, translation by Ben Fowkes

Karl Marx, (2008) Debatten um das Holzdiebstahlsgesetz, MEW 1, page 109 et seq.

Karl Marx, (1983) Grundrisse der Kritik der politischen Ökonomie, MEW 42

Karl Marx, (1973) Grundrisse. Foundations of the Critique of Political Economy (Rough Draft), translated by Martin Nicolaus

Karl Marx, Theorien über den Mehrwert, MEW 26. 1, 26.2 and 26.3 (English translation taken from http://www.marxists.org/archive/marx/works/1863/theories-s urplus-value)

Joseph P. McDermott/ Shiba Yoshinobu, Economic change in China, 960–1279, in: The Cambridge History of China, volume 5, part 1, page 321 et seqs.

Michael McGrath, The reigns of Jen-Tsung (1022–1063) and Ying-Tsung (1063–1067), in: The Cambridge History of China, volume 5, part 1, page 279 et seqs.

Perry Mehrling (2011), The New Lombard Street. How the Fed became the Dealer of last Resort, Princeton & Oxford, Princeton University Press

John Stuart Mill (1848), Principles of Political Economy, Project Gutenberg

Hyman P. Minsky (1966), Financial instability revisited: The economics of disaster, in: Minsky (1982) page 90 et seqs.

Hyman P. Minsky (1972), An exposition of a Keynesian theory of investment, in: *Minsky* (1982) page 203 et seqs.

Hyman P. Minsky (1975), John Maynard Keynes, New York, Columbia Unievrsity Press

Hyman P. Minsky (1977), The financial instability hypothesis: An interpretation of Keynes and an alternative to "standard" theory, in *Minsky* (1982), page 59 et seqs.

Hyman P. Minsky (1978), Capitalist financial processes and the instability of capitalism, in: *Minsky* (1982) p. 71 et seqs.

Hyman P. Minsky (1980), The financial instability hypothesis: A restatement, in: *Minsky* (1982) page 90 et seqs.

Hyman P. Minsky (1980/2), Finance and profits: The changing nature of American business cycles, in: *Minsky* (1982) page 14 et seqs.

Hyman P. Minsky (1982), Can "it" happen again? Essays on Instability and Finance, Armonk, M.E. Sharpe. Inc.

Hyman P. Minsky (1986), Stabilizing an unstable economy, New York, McGraw Hill, reprint of 2006

Hyman P. Minsky (1993), The Financial Instability Hypothesis, in: *Philip Arestis, Malcolm Sawyer* (ed.), Handbook of Radical Political Economy

Ludwig von Mises (1949), Human Action, Indianapolis, Liberty Fund

Ludwig von Mises (2013), The Theory of Money and Credit (first German edition 1912), New York, Skyhorse Publishing

Theodor Mommsen (1976), Römische Geschichte, volumes 1–8, 1976, (first edition 1854), München, Deutscher Taschenbuch Verlag

Frederik W. Mote, The rise of the Ming dynasty, in: The Cambridge History of China, volume 7 part 1, page 11 et seqs.

Wolfgang Münchau, Eurozone reformers act as if the crisis never happened, in: *Financial Times* of 18 February 2018

Herfried Münkler (2017), Der Dreißigjährige Krieg: Europäische Katastrophe, deutsches Trauma 1618–1648, Berlin, Rowohlt

Antoin E. Murphy, John Law (1671–1729) in: *Faccarello/ Kurz* (2016), page 16 et seqs.

Antoin E. Murphy (2016), Richard Cantillon (1689/90-1734) in: *Faccarello/ Kurz*, (2016), page 19 et seqs.

Ramon H. Myers/Yeh-chien Wang, Economic developments, 1644–1900, in: The Cambridge History of China, volume 9 part 1, page 563 et seqs.

Emil Nack/ Wilhelm Wägner (1975), Hellas. Land und Volk der alten Griechen (as revised by Herbert Ossowski), München, Verlag Carl Ueberreuter

Josiah Ober (2016), Das antike Griechenland, Stuttgart, Klett-Cotta (German translation of "The Rise and Fall of Classical Greece", 2015)

Thomas Piketty (2013), Le capital aux XXIe siècle, Paris, Éditions du Seuil

Thomas Piketty, Capital et idéologie, 2019, Éditions du Seuil.

Karl Polanyi (1944), The Great Transformation, Boston, Beacon Press

Plato, Phaidon, ca. 380 BC

François Quesnay, Analyse de la formule arithmétique due tableau économique. De la distribution des dépenses annuelles d'une nation agricole, in: *Cartelier* (2008), page 207 et seqs.

François Quesnay, Du commerce. Premier Dialogue entre H.M. et M.N..., in: *Cartelier* (2008) page 299 et seqs.

François Quesnay, Les rapport des dépenses entre elles, in: *Cartelier* (2008) page 154 et seqs.

François Quesnay, Maximes générales du gouvernement économique d'un royaume agricole, in: *Cartelier* (2008) page 235 et seqs.

François Quesnay, Sur les travaux des artisans. Second dialogue, in: *Cartelier* (2008) page 357 et seqs.

François Quesnay, Tableau économique, deuxième édition, in: *Cartelier* (2008) page 137

François Quesnay, Tableau économique, in: *Cartelier* (2008) page 87 et seqs.

David Ricardo (1961), On the principles of political economy and taxation, volume 1 of the works and correspondence of David Ricardo, edited by Piero Sraffa with the collaboration of M. H. Dobb, Cambridge, Cambridge University Press

David Ricardo (1991), Notes on Malthus's 'Measure of Value', Sraffa edition, Cambridge, Cambridge University Press

Joan Robinson (1966) "Kalecki and Keynes". Problems of Economic Dynamics and Planning: Essays in Honour of Michal Kalecki, page 337, quoted from Wikipedia

Joan Robinson (1977), Michal Kalecki on the economics of capitalism, Oxford Bulletin of Economics and Statistics, 39, 1, page 8, 9

Joachim Rohlfes/Horst Rumpf (1970), Die griechische Polis. Der römische Staat, Stuttgart, Ernst Klett Verlag

W. W. Rostow (1990), The stages of economic growth. A non-communist manifesto, 3rd. ed., Cambridge, Cambridge University Press

Morris Rossabi, The reign of Khubilai khan, in: The Cam-bridge History of China, volume 6, page 414 et seqs

Georg Rusche/Otto Kirchheimer (1974), Sozialstruktur und Strafvollzug, (translation of "Punishment and social structure", 1939), Frankfurt a. M., Europäische Verlagsanstalt

Nishijima Sadao, The economic and social history of former Han, in: The Cam-bridge History of China, volume 1, page 545 et seqs.

Friedrich Carl von Savigny (1822), Über den römischen Colonat, Abhandlungen der Königlich Preußischen Akademie der Wissenschaften, Philosophisch-historische Klasse, Berlin

Jean-Baptiste Say (1803), Traité d'économie politique ou Simple exposition de la manière dont se forment, se distribuent et se consomment les richesses, http://www.institutcoppet.org/wp-content/uploads/2011/12/Traite-deconomie-politique-Jean-Baptiste-Say.pdf.

Jean Baptiste Say (1996), Lettres à M. Malthus, Lettre première, in: Philippe Steiner (ed.), Say, Cours d'économie politique, page 223 et seqs., Paris, GF Flammarion

Tatjana Schönwälder-Kuntze, Katrin Wille, Thomas Hölscher (2009), George Spencer Brown, 2. ed., München, Verlag für Sozialwissenschaften

Josef A. Schumpeter (1912), Theorie der wirtschaftlichen Entwicklung, Berlin, Dunker & Humblot

Josef A. Schumpeter (1954), History of Economic Analysis, New York, Oxford University Press

Harm G. Schröter (2005), Von der Teilung zur Wiedervereinigung, in: Michael North (ed.), Deutsche Wirtschaftsgeschichte, München C.H. Beck

Tao Jing Shen, The move to the south and the reign of Kao-Tsung (1127–1162), in: The Cambridge History of China, volume 5, part 1, page 644 st seqs.

Bai Shouyi (2010), An outline history of China, Foreign Languages Press, Beijing

Jean Charles L. Simonde de Sismondi (1827), Nouveaux Principes d'Économie politique ou de la richesse dans ses Rapports avec la Population, tome II, 2nd ed., Paris, Delaunay Libraire (reprint) ARY

Adam Smith (1776), The wealth pf nations, London, Everyman's library

Paul Jakov Smith, Introduction: The Sung dynasty and its precursors, 907–1279, in: The Cambridge History of China, volume 5 part 1, page 1 et seqs.

Paul Jakov Smith, Sheng Tsung's reign and the new policies of Wang An-shih, 1067–1085, in: The Cambridge History of China, volume 5 part 1, page 347 et seqs.

Peter Slotederdijk (2005), Im Weltinnenraum des Kapitals, Frankfurt a.M. Suhrkamp

Werner Sombart (1902), Der moderne Kapitalismus, Die Genesis des Kapitalismus (volume 1); Die Theorie der kapitalistischen Entwicklung (volume 2), Leipzig, Verlag von Dunkler& Humblot

Robert M. Somers, The end of the T'ang, in: The Cambridge History of China, volume 3, part 1, page 682 et seqs.

Steven Spitzer/Andrew Scull (1977), Social Control in Historical Perspective: From Private to Public Responses to Crime, in: David F. Greenberg (ed.), Corrections and Punishment, London, Beverly Hills 1977, page 276 et seqs.

George Soros (2003), The Alchemy of Finance, 1987, 2003-edition, Hoboken, John Wiley & Sons

George Soros (2010), The Soros Lectures, New York, Public Affairs

Georg Soros (1995), Soros on Soros. Staying ahead of the curve, Hoboken, John Wiley & Sons

George Spencer Brown (1999), Laws of Form, Leipzig, Bohmeier Verlag

Arvind Subramanian, Secular stagnation's era may be drawing to close, in: Financial Times of 1 July 2021

Nassim Nicolas Taleb (2012), Antifragile. Things that gain from disorder, London, Penguin Books

Gemma Tetlow, Theories behind productivity woes range from tech troubles to zombies, in: *Financial Times* of 23 October 2016

Lukas Thommen (2019), Archaisches und klassisches Griechenland, Stuttgart, W. Kohlhammer

J. J. Tobias (1979), Crime and Police in England 1700 – 1900, New York, St. Martin's Press

Hubert Treiber/Heinz Steinert (1980), Die Fabrikation des zuverlässigen Menschen, München, Heinz Moos Verlag

Adair Turner (2016), Between Debt and the Devil, Princeton University Press, Princeton and Oxford

E. P. Thompson (1975), Whigs and Hunters. The Origin of the Black Act, New York, Pantheon Books

Thucydides, The history of the Peloponnesian war, ca. 410 BC

Michail Tugan-Baranovsky (1901), Studien zur Theorie und Geschichte der Handelskrisen in England, Jena

Denis Twitchett/Michael Loewe (ed.) (1986), The Cambridge History of China, New York, Cambridge University Press

Denis Twitchett, Introduction to volume 3, in: The Cambridge History of China, volume 3, part 1, page 1 et seq.

Joseph de la Vega (1688), Confusion de confusiones, Boston, Baker Library

Jacob Viner (1936), Mr. Keynes on the causes of unemployment, Quarterly Journal of Economics, November 1936, reprinted in: John Maynard Keynes Collected Writings, editors Austin Ronaldson and Donald Moggridge, volume XIV page 109 et seqs.

Kai Vogelsang (2013), Geschichte Chinas, 4th ed., Stuttgart, Reclam

Jacob Viner (1936), Mr. Keynes on the causes of unemployment, Quarterly Journal of Economics, November 1936, reprinted in: Collected Writings XIV page 109 et seq.

Gerhard H. Wächter (1983), Der doppelte Charakter des Strafrechts, Kritische Justiz 1983, page 161 et seqs.

Gerhard H. Wächter (1987), Strafrechtliche Aufklärung, Strafrecht und soziale Hegemonie im 18. Jahrhundert, (doctoral thesis)

Gerhard H. Wächter, Zweifelsfragen beim Erwerb von Risikopositionen nach dem Finanzmarktstabilisierungsgesetz, ZIP 2008, 2301 (together with Frank Roitzsch)

Gerhard H. Wächter, Gesellschaftsrechtliche Probleme des Finanzmarktstabilisierungsgesetzes, DZWIR 2009, 1 (together with Frank Roitzsch)

Gerhard H. Wächter (2022), M&A Litigation, 4th ed., Köln, RWS Kommunikationsforum

Gerhard H. Wächter/Christoph Wollny (2018), A Proposal for the Calculation of Damages in Post-M&A Disputes over Deceptions and Breaches of Guarantees, in: SchiedsVZ 2018, page 80 et seqs.

Leon Walras (1874), Éléments d'économie pure: Ou, theorie de la richesse sociale, Lausanne, L- Corbaz & Cie

Robin Waterfield (2018), Creators, Conquerors, & Citizens. A History of Ancient Greece, Oxford, Oxford University Press

Max Weber (1980), Wirtschaft und Gesellschaft, 5. edition, Tübingen, J.C.B. Mohr

Carl Christian von Weizsäcker/Hagen Krämer (2021), Saving and Investment in the Twenty-First Century. The Great Divergence, Chambridge (CH), Springer

Martin Wolf, Fear of hyperinflation is a delusion of the ignorant, in: *Financial Times* of 11 April 2014

Martin Wolf, Reform alone is no solution for the eurozone, in: *Financial Times* of 22 October 2014

Martin Wolf, The curse of weak global demand, in: *Financial Times* of 19 November 2014

Martin Wolf, Radical cures for unusual ills, in: *Financial Times* of 26 November 2014

Martin Wolf, Germany is the eurozone's biggest problem, in: *Financial Times* of 11 May 2015

Martin Wolf, The corporate contribution to the savings glut, in: *Financial Times* of 18 November 2015

Martin Wolf, The welfare state is a piggy bank for life, in: *Financial Times* of 1 April 2016

Martin Wolf, Negative rates are a symptom of our ills, in: *Financial Times* of 15 April 2016

Martin Wolf, How to defeat rightwing populism, in: *Financial Times* of 25 May 2016

Martin Wolf, Trump's false promises to his supporters, in: *Financial Times* of 16 November 2016

Martin Wolf, China's tough fight to escape its debt trap, in: *Financial Times* of 12 April 2017

Martin Wolf, Challenges of a disembodied economy, in: *Financial Times* of 29 November 2017

Martin Wolf, Monetary policy has run its course, in *Financial Times* of 13 March 2019

Martin Wolf, Monetary policy in a low rate world, in *Financial Times* of 14 September 2019

Martin Wolf, The threat and the promise of digital money, in: *Financial Times* of 23 October 2019

Martin Wolf, We must focus attention on our next steps, in:*Financial Times* of 7 April 2020

Martin Wolf, What central banks ought to target, in: *Financial Times* of 3 March 2021

Martin Wolf, Inequality is behind central bank dilemma, in: *Financial Times* of 22 September 2021

Arthur F. Wright, The Sui dynasty (581–617), in: The Cambridge History of China, volume 3, part 1, page 48 et seqs.

GPSR Authorized Representative: Easy Access System Europe, Mustamäe tee 50, 10621 Tallinn, Estonia, gpsr.requests@easproject.com